African Islands

Rochester Studies in
African History and the Diaspora

Toyin Falola, Series Editor
The Jacob and Frances Sanger Mossiker Chair in the Humanities
and University Distinguished Teaching Professor
University of Texas at Austin

Recent Titles

Cotton and Race across the Atlantic: Britain, Africa, and America, 1900–1920
Jonathan E. Robins

*Islam, Power, and Dependency in the Gambia River Basin:
The Politics of Land Control, 1790–1940*
Assan Sarr

Living Salvation in the East African Revival in Uganda
Jason Bruner

On Durban's Docks: Zulu Workers, Rural Households, Global Labor
Ralph Callebert

*Mediators, Contract Men, and Colonial Capital:
Mechanized Gold Mining in the Gold Coast Colony, 1879–1909*
Cassandra Mark-Thiesen

Muslim Fula Business Elites and Politics in Sierra Leone
Alusine Jalloh

Race, Decolonization, and Global Citizenship in South Africa
Chielozona Eze

Plantation Slavery in the Sokoto Caliphate: A Historical and Comparative Study
Mohammed Bashir Salau

African Migration Narratives: Politics, Race, and Space
Edited by Cajetan Iheka and Jack Taylor

Ethics and Society in Nigeria: Identity, History, Political Theory
Nimi Wariboko

A complete list of titles in the Rochester Studies in African History and the
Diaspora series may be found on our website, www.urpress.com.

African Islands

Leading Edges of Empire and Globalization

Edited by
Toyin Falola, R. Joseph Parrott,
and Danielle Porter Sanchez

R UNIVERSITY OF ROCHESTER PRESS

First published 2019

University of Rochester Press
668 Mt. Hope Avenue, Rochester, NY 14620, USA
www.urpress.com
and Boydell & Brewer Limited
PO Box 9, Woodbridge, Suffolk IP12 3DF, UK
www.boydellandbrewer.com

ISBN-13: 978-1-58046-954-8
ISSN: 1092-5228

Library of Congress Cataloging-in-Publication Data

Names: Falola, Toyin, editor. | Parrott, R. Joseph, 1985– editor. | Sanchez, Danielle Porter, 1986– editor.
Title: African islands : leading edges of empire and globalization / edited by Toyin Falola, R. Joseph Parrott, and Danielle Porter Sanchez.
Other titles: Rochester studies in African history and the diaspora ; v. 83
Description: Rochester, NY : University of Rochester Press, 2019. | Series: Rochester studies in African history and the diaspora | Includes bibliographical references and index.
Identifiers: LCCN 2019013735 | ISBN 9781580469548 (hardcover : alk. paper)
Subjects: LCSH: Islands—Africa. | Africa—Politics and government—1960– | Africa—Economic conditions—1960– | Africa—Colonial influence. | Islands of the Atlantic. | Islands of the Indian Ocean. | States, Small.
Classification: LCC DT30.5 .A3645 2019 | DDC 960.32—dc23 LC record available at https://lccn.loc.gov/2019013735

This publication is printed on acid-free paper.

For those who lost their lives crossing the seas and those forced to forge new lives on distant shores

Contents

Introduction: Arbiters and Witnesses of Change
Contextualizing Conversations on African Islands   1
    Toyin Falola, R. Joseph Parrott, and Danielle Porter Sanchez

Part 1: Atlantic Ocean Islands

1   The Canaries to Africa: The Atlantic Strategy of "To Be or
    Not to Be"   39
    Germán Santana Pérez

2   Sugar, Cocoa, and Oil: Economic Success and Failure in
    São Tomé and Príncipe from the Sixteenth to the
    Twenty-First Centuries   68
    Gerhard Seibert

3   The Bijagos of Canhabac Island (Guinea-Bissau)   96
    Joshua Bernard Forrest

4   An Island in the Middle of Everywhere: Bioko under Colonial
    Domination   125
    Enrique N. Okenve

5   Cursing in Bioko and Annobón: Repeating Islands that Don't
    Repeat   157
    Michael Ugarte

6   African Ports and Islands during the Second World War   170
    Ashley Jackson

7   "Nos lingua, nos kultura, nos identidadi": Postcolonial
    Language Planning and Promotion in Cabo Verde and the
    Cape Verdean Diaspora   208
    Carla D. Martin

Part 2: Indian Ocean Islands

8   Africa's Indian Ocean Islands, Near and Distant   245
    Edward A. Alpers

9   Monsoon Metropolis: Migration, Mobility, and Mediation
    in the Western Indian Ocean   267
    William Bissell

10 The Mascarenes, Indian Ocean Africa, and Global Labor
    Migration during the Eighteenth and Nineteenth Centuries   294
    Richard B. Allen

11 The Island as Nexus: Zanzibar in the Nineteenth Century   317
    Jeremy Prestholdt

12 Slavery and Postslavery in Madagascar: An Overview   345
    Denis Regnier and Dominique Somda

13 The Comoros: Strategies of Islandness in the Indian Ocean   370
    Iain Walker

14 Gendered Pioneers from Mayotte: An Ethnographic
    Perspective on Travel and Transformation in the Western
    Indian Ocean   397
    Michael Lambek

Notes on Contributors   417

Index   423

Introduction: Arbiters and Witnesses of Change

Contextualizing Conversations on African Islands

Toyin Falola, R. Joseph Parrott, and Danielle Porter Sanchez

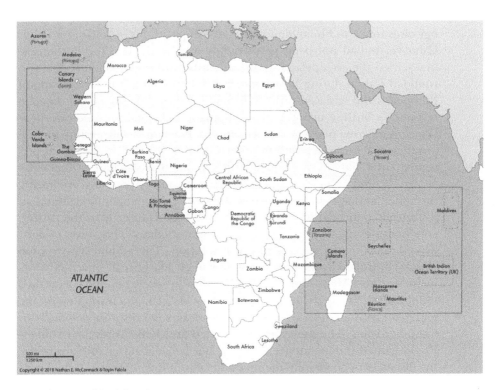

I.1: Africa and its islands

Amílcar Cabral is the founding father of two countries: the island nation of Cabo Verde and the mainland state of Guinea-Bissau. As the first and most influential leader of the Partido Africano da Independência da Guiné e Cabo Verde (African Party for the Independence of Guinea and Cabo Verde, or PAIGC), Cabral spent much of his life trying to achieve independence for two places that he considered home. While they are two separate countries today, the revolutionary Cabral envisioned a single post-colonial nation that would unite the former Portuguese possessions. The metropole had for centuries viewed the colonies as uniquely interrelated, using the more assimilated and racially mixed populations of the islands of Cabo Verde to help administer the mainland in Guinea, where relatively few Europeans had settled. Cabral was born in Portuguese Guinea to Cabo Verdean parents filling such intermediary roles, and it therefore seemed natural for him to envision a united struggle. Cabral fought to bring independence to two colonies connected—not separated—by water and shared history.[1]

Cabral's biography is important here because his revolutionary ideology owes much to his ambiguous relationship with his own island identity. Cabo Verde had not been permanently inhabited when the Portuguese first settled the archipelago in the fifteenth century. The culture that surrounded Cabral during his formative years grew from the intermixing of Europeans and enslaved Africans brought from the mainland. By the time of Cabral's birth, a majority of its population claimed a mixed-race heritage and received privileges associated with Portuguese citizenship, though insufficient education and dire poverty on the drought-prone islands prevented any claims to true equality with the metropolis. Rather, the archipelago existed somewhere between Europe and Africa. By embracing this latter heritage, Cabral rejected Portuguese domination, claiming an historically informed identity that tied the islands directly to the African continent despite centuries acting as an intermediary. This vision of unity proved vital for the success of the revolution. The archipelago was too closely controlled by the Portuguese to launch a large-scale guerrilla movement, so the PAIGC looked to Guinea-Bissau when planning its armed independence struggle. In 1963, the PAIGC launched a revolution on the mainland with an army of mostly local soldiers led disproportionately by Cabo Verdeans. The movement succeeded and Cabo Verde and Guinea-Bissau gained independence in 1974, but it could never fully overcome the distances of geography, identity, and culture that separated Cabo Verde from the mainland. By 1980, internal tensions—formed, in part, along island-mainland antagonisms—split the PAIGC and led to the two-state system.

During the revolutionary struggle, Cabral could not overcome the ambiguous relationship that existed not just between Cabo Verdeans and Bissau-Guineans, but also between islanders and African continentals more generally. For Cabral, the embrace of African identity meant a rejection of Portugal, the privileged position of his island within the empire, and the adoption of a wholly continental perspective that neither he nor his family had ever truly known. This was in many ways the origin of his famous call to "return to the source."[2] This source was the African heritage and culture that he believed served as the hidden center of Cabo Verde's cosmopolitan identity, lost from view by distance, time, and the long process of transculturation that resulted from the islands' role as a point of articulation in Portugal's global empire. Cabral was able to bridge this gap and lead the binational revolution due to his personal charisma and the sincerity with which he embraced a self-consciously African identity.

Yet what Cabral struggled to understand was that these differing identities and histories ran deep. The educated, globally conscious Cabo Verdeans who made the PAIGC an internationally recognized revolutionary party continued to view themselves as the natural and necessary leaders of both the islands and Guinea-Bissau. At the same time, some mainland soldiers continued to resent the predominantly island-born leadership as they had when earlier generations acted as Portuguese middlemen. The result was a tenuous unity dependent almost entirely on Cabral and the common struggle for liberation. His assassination in 1973—perpetrated by disaffected Bissau-Guinean party members who referenced the mainland-island divide—robbed the PAIGC of the glue keeping the binational experiment intact.[3] Unable to replicate his brother's unifying personality, Luís Cabral presided over an increasingly divided transoceanic country before suffering a coup in 1980 that split the PAIGC and resulted in the formation of independent archipelago and mainland states.[4] The histories of these once-linked nations have since diverged. Cabo Verde reinvented itself as one of Africa's most stable and democratic countries with the assistance of international aid and a growing tourist sector, while Guinea-Bissau has suffered from repeated military coups and a depressed economy.

The case of Amílcar Cabral and the Cabo Verde-Guinea-Bissau divide captures many of the historic themes of life on African islands. From Cabo Verde in the Atlantic to Zanzibar and Mauritius in the Indian Ocean, geography and contingency made islands avenues for integrating Africa into wider networks of trade, migration, and empire—sometimes against the will of local populations. As centers for exchange and expansion, these islands historically occupied positions of importance far out of scale to their meager sizes. But so too did their inhabitants become part of a series of complex regional and international relationships that have had lasting repercussions on island societies. Often, itinerant travelers and settlers from mainland Africa, Europe, East Asia, and the Middle East first interacted on these global nodes, which acted as liminal spaces to blur the borders between continents.[5] As a result, these islands became uniquely amalgamated spaces, creating distinct cultures and social relations that both reflected and continuously grappled with these intersecting forces. This volume seeks to explore these insular themes at a continental level, placing individual histories of all of Africa's major islands—and some of its minor ones—into conversation with each other across regional and chronological delineations.

Outposts in Ocean Worlds: The Historiography of African Islands

This volume pushes away from narrowly defined nationalist histories and encourages larger conversations on the transnational as unique spaces of analysis for understanding the history and cultures of the African continent. Though there are few studies that consider Africa's islands in a broad comparative perspective, many scholars recognize the important role these lands have played in African and global histories. There is excellent scholarship on individual islands and archipelagos, including a number of works that expertly fit African examples into broad transnational networks.[6] Yet the volume of such studies remains relatively small since the national histories popular after independence, as well as the more detailed studies produced after the cultural turn, have understandably prioritized mainland states. The complex domestic interactions of more populous and politically powerful nation-states such as Nigeria or South Africa receive the lion's share of scholarly attention, marginalizing less populated and geographically isolated islands to the periphery. The key port-island of Zanzibar and the massive Madagascar are perhaps the most prominent exceptions to this rule, but even here the Arab-influenced cosmopolitanism of the former and the Austronesian-derived Malagasy culture of the latter often mark them as exceptional cases in African history.[7]

In overlooking these islands, scholars have missed an opportunity. Focusing narrowly on national and subnational histories has reified tendencies in postcolonial historiography to promote African history by downplaying connections to wider global trends and placing African developments in opposition to foreign imperial projects. While regional historiographies of Asia and Latin America have begun systematically exploring international connections, Africanist scholars are only beginning to rediscover the role that African peoples played in shaping and adapting wider global forces. The continent's islands have the potential to be key components of such avenues of study. They were pivotal in forming the regional and global networks that linked the continent to the world before the age of steam, capturing an outward-looking African history that predates European exploration and continues to influence the evolution of contemporary societies.

The embrace of oceanic histories has led this redirection of scholarship, but even here a tendency to emphasize geographic distinctions obscures the extent to which the active participation of Africans in global systems of exchange produced common trends across time and space. Therefore, a primary goal of this volume is to understand the role islands played in Indian and Atlantic Ocean worlds, and to put these distinct areas of study into conversation with each other. Oceanic scholars have recognized the roles of islands as nodes in intercontinental networks, blurring the lines of center and periphery that long typified global history.[8] These growing fields have taken seriously pioneering Mediterranean scholar Fernand Braudel's challenge to move away from the national histories that dominate traditional historiographies and toward a scholarly center on what were literally seas of exchange between continents, revealing worlds populated by actors with outsized influence that often operated on or from coastal and island nodes.[9] The most prominent and well developed of these areas of study has focused on the Atlantic, but in the last thirty years an arguably more dynamic field has developed around the more ancient Indian Ocean.[10]

While this volume seeks to blur the regional and chronological limitations of oceanic world systems by placing Africa at their center, an overview of the extant historiography on the Atlantic and Indian oceans will contextualize the specific histories and terminologies of the continent's islands. Beginning with the more developed Atlantic World, we see that Africa's Western islands first gained prominence during Europe's Age of Discovery. Most West African peoples had limited their operations to the shorelines, primarily inhabiting islands accessible from the coast such as the Bijagos in modern Guinea-Bissau and Bioko in Equatorial Guinea. As a result, more distant archipelagoes provided fertile ground for European expansion as maritime empires searched for routes around Africa to gain access to Indian trade. The Canaries were among the first European conquests in the fourteenth century—populated by people likely descended from North African Berbers—and provided an important launching point for continental commerce and expansion to uninhabited islands.

Soon, the Portuguese and Spanish began the settlement of Madeira, the Cabo Verde archipelago, the Azores in the mid-Atlantic, and the islands of the Gulf of Guinea: São Tomé and Príncipe, then Bioko and Annabón.

These bases of operation—usually unencumbered by hostile populations and often possessing fertile volcanic soil—provided agricultural products and enabled exploration further south and west across the Atlantic.[11] John Thornton, among others, argues that Europe's use of islands proved especially vital for expansionist ambitions in and beyond Africa as they provided safe havens during early periods when Europeans struggled to establish preponderance on the continent's coastline.[12] Historians—most prominently Alfred Crosby in his seminal work on the Atlantic Exchange—note that the introduction of cash crops such as sugar to settlements in Madeira, São Tomé, and elsewhere demanded greater labor than the Iberian nations could supply, leading to the importation of mainland Africans and the emergence of a prototypical plantation slave agriculture that would reach its maturity in the New World.[13] Africa's islands served in many ways as the first stages in the creation of an Atlantic World, proving the value of both colonization and staple agriculture, as well as pioneering models of (forced) labor and commerce that would motivate European imperialism.

Even as European attention shifted toward the newly discovered Americas, continental islands grew in importance as nodes in the transatlantic trade networks of Europe's empires. After 1492, the islands held value for the material they produced and as points of transition between the Old World and the New World. The Canaries, Azores, and Cabo Verde islands, along with São Tomé further south, became final victualing stations as ships set sail across the Atlantic. Cabo Verde, the Gulf of Guinea archipelago, and offshore islands along the Western coasts became way stations for slaves waiting to be transported to labor in American plantations. As eminent historians Philip D. Morgan and Jack P. Greene have argued, Africa's islands became "leading edges" of the Atlantic World and "stepping stones from one hemisphere to the next":

> The archipelagos of the Azores, Madeira, the Canaries, Cape Verde, and the islands of São Tomé, Fernando Pó, Príncipe, and Annabón in the Gulf of Guinea assumed special importance in the Atlantic World. These islands were hubs for a series of complex commercial networks; they were points of articulation between North and South Atlantic, North and South America and the Caribbean, Africa and the New World, Africa and Europe, and Europe and America. (Philip D. Morgan and Jack P. Greene, "The Present State of Atlantic History," in *Atlantic History: A Critical Appraisal*, ed. Jack P. Greene and Philip D. Morgan [New York: Oxford University Press, 2009], 12–13.)

Africa's islands acted as bridges to link continents through global exchange of goods, peoples, and ideas, giving rise to unique sets of social and economic cultures that helped facilitate the growth of these networks. Yet for millions, they also acted as liminal spaces between independence and bondage, symbolized famously by Gorée's House of Slaves and its "Door of No Return" off the Senegalese coast.

These small islands, then as now, deserve attention for the pivotal roles they have played in an Atlantic World. As global historian Alison Games argues, Atlantic history "is a way of looking at global *and* regional processes within a contained unit, although that region was not, of course, hermetically sealed off from the rest of the world . . . the Atlantic can offer a useful laboratory within which to examine regional and global transformations."[14] Scholars have embraced this concept as a way of emphasizing the role Africans played in the development of commerce and relationships with Europe and the Americas, recentering the historiography away from imperial histories of oceanic expansion or national histories of resistance to one of oceanic exchange.[15] Major contributions by James Sweet, Kristin Mann, Robin Law, and Rebecca Shumway have revealed the ways that slavery, governance, and commerce all evolved within broad transnational contexts, while pushing new theses about the Atlantic's relationship with African practices of urbanism, medicine, and intellectual history.[16]

As geographically bounded intersections of oceanic networks, Africa's islands hold a special position in this search to identify and articulate the specific processes and legacies of interaction. They are individual experiments in Games's historical laboratory. Trends and themes, oceanic historian Michael Pearson argues, "are exaggerated and magnified when we look at them in an island context."[17] In these settings, historians can explore in great detail the various strands of commerce, political expansion, and migrations that influenced Africa, and the way these processes changed over time. Such trends can be obscured in mainland societies, where exchanges operating mainly at coasts and frontiers are overwhelmed or subsumed within dominant national trends. On Africa's islands, the ways in which African peoples built upon transnational interactions to forge new realities take center stage, rather than existing at the margins.

In highlighting processes of adaptation that occurred across time and space, this volume offers the opportunity to understand how the famed triangular trade that dominates Atlantic studies represented just one component of a long history of African engagement with foreigners. This is apparent in the burgeoning field of Indian Ocean studies, which like its historiographical predecessor is coming to appreciate the roles that islands played in facilitating patterns of economic, political, and cultural exchange. Monsoon winds powered a regional cycle of migration and trade long before Europeans crossed the Atlantic, but serious study of this ancient Eastern exchange was slower to take hold in academia. Much of the scholarship originally pivoted around the projecting point of India and a perceived cultural dominance in the region.[18] Such continent-centered scholarship continued as emphasis shifted toward Arabia and, increasingly, East Africa, and the littoral societies that developed on the Swahili coast from the interaction between a core of Bantu-speaking peoples with Arab and Asian traders. While studies have focused heavily on mainland centers of foreign trade and offshore port cities, the importance of Zanzibar, Mauritius, and Madagascar is helping to push scholars toward a greater appreciation of the role that islands played in this network.[19]

As Edward Alpers has argued in his call to move away from strictly continental perspectives, insular societies were wholly created by an extended Indian Ocean exchange.[20] In contrast to Africa's Atlantic islands—which were largely unpopulated and therefore most noteworthy for the European conquests that helped open the Atlantic World—those of the Indian Ocean were part of a longer and more complex history. As a result, they offer important avenues for studying shifting trade and social networks in the region over thousands of years. At an indeterminate point during the first millennium CE, Austronesian sailors established permanent settlements on Madagascar long after Africans had begun to establish fishing camps on coastal islands such as Zanzibar. Long, thin-hulled dhows used monsoon winds to carry Indonesian, Indian, and (especially) Arab traders across the ocean, where they exchanged ivory, gold, and timber from the East African hinterland for cloth, glass beads, and other trade goods produced in India and the Mediterranean. A slave trade also developed along the coastline that Arab traders knew as the Zanj, with the Comoros archipelago possibly being used as a depot for Africans destined for locations further afield, including Madagascar, the Arabian Peninsula, and China.

These sustained interactions between Bantu-speaking Africans and foreign traders laid the foundation for Swahili culture and, after roughly the tenth century, enabled Islam to flourish along the coast as well as in the Comoros archipelago.[21] Both Arab seafarers and local Swahili established trading centers on offshore islands that were accessible by boats, but offered a defense against the mainland—including Lamu and Mombasa in modern Kenya, Zanzibar and Kilwa Kisiwani in Tanzania, and Mozambique Island—and this logic carried over to settlement in the Comoros and northern Madagascar. These islands became important for the diffusion of foreign ideas into the interior; increasing demand for ivory and gold encouraged local Swahili traders to press their networks further inland,

and Sufi orders established headquarters in places such as Zanzibar Town in the sixteenth century.[22] The Swahili coast, which stretched from modern Somalia south to Mozambique, became the first example of a truly Oceanic world in Sub-Saharan Africa, nourishing an extended interaction between African, Muslim Arab, and Indian migrants in particular.[23] As Indian Ocean studies have become increasingly decentralized, this reality has motivated scholars to propose alternatives to Indian Ocean naming conventions that better capture the region's complexity, most notably Michael Pearson's argument for the "Afrasian sea."[24]

Only in the sixteenth century did Europeans become active in the region, hundreds of years after Afro-Islamic societies established their own hybrid cultures. What these earliest explorers found when they rounded the Cape of Good Hope was a complex commercial society, with a handful of urban centers in major trading ports such as Mombasa. Yet this did not stop them from asserting themselves, adding yet more layers to the socioeconomic tapestry that found its clearest manifestations on a series of islands. As in the Atlantic, the Portuguese forcibly occupied mostly island ports such as Mozambique Island, Mombasa, and Zanzibar in order to benefit from trade with the interior, but faced opposition in the latter locations from Arab sultans, particularly the Omani, who took both Mombasa and Zanzibar in 1698. Other European powers focused on India and minimized conflicts with local peoples by establishing victualing stations on the uninhabited Seychelles and Mascarenes between the sixteenth and eighteenth centuries, with the Dutch, French, and British all competing for these strategic outposts. The importation of labor to work the agricultural land on these victualing stations—first in the form of primarily African slaves, later indentured Indians—helped create Creole societies around European foundations similar to those in the Atlantic World, though distinct in their integration of strong Arabic and Asian influences. The cosmopolitanism of this region and its legacies for contemporary nations have become central themes for Indian Ocean historians.[25]

The longer history of the Indian Ocean World and the greater complexity of both its cultural and economic evolution have marked it as distinct from the Atlantic World, which developed after the fifteenth century, but these facts should only reinforce the value of approaching these islands as laboratories. While part of the same Indian Ocean World and at the center of similar patterns of migration, the positioning of these archipelagoes in relation to the monsoon cycle, as well as the timing and character of migrations, has done much to define starkly different identities for islands such as the Islamic-dominated Comoros and more culturally European Mascarenes, which otherwise share similar characteristics. They capture shifts in the dominant cultures, trading systems, ideas of political control, and transportation that operated in the region. These islands—as in the Atlantic—were spaces for imperial barter with Africa. They played important roles facilitating great power interaction with the continent, creating composite societies that continue to adapt to changing conditions and global networks.

Patterns of Islandness Across Oceanic Divides

The rise of Atlantic Ocean and Indian Ocean historiography has greatly enriched African studies and justified attention to the continent's small islands, but it too has its limitations. With the exceptions again of the well-studied Zanzibar and Madagascar, the oceanic approach can reduce islands to mere nodes of larger Atlantic and Indian worlds, bounding these histories both geographically and temporally in ways that fail to capture their vitality and the commonalities of their experience. The result is a sometimes one-dimensional portrayal of islands that emphasizes individual aspects of their history, such as commodities trading or plantation agriculture, as mere illustrations of wider phenomenon. Underappreciated is the way individual islands reacted to external impositions, and how these sustained interactions across time and place illustrate Africa's fluid position in global networks.

Such utilitarian approaches to islands also tend to minimize the important effects that changing forms of transportation, agriculture, and governance had on islands themselves. Once excluded from the prime pathways of oceanic exchange—noteworthy in both the Atlantic Ocean and Indian Ocean with the opening of the Suez Canal, the coming of steam-powered sailing, and later the development of air travel—islands stagnate in terms of their global historiography. Historians have been too quick to accept such pithy chronologies as J. R. McNeill's contention that "The Portuguese caravel opened the Atlantic World, and the railroad closed it," failing to pay serious attention to most of Africa's islands after their periods of prime importance passed.[26] Far from stagnating as once prominent avenues of exchange withered, Africa's islands and their societies continued to adapt and innovate. These responses often reflected and depended upon broader continental trends, but they also pioneered paths of their own.

At the same time, placing islands into neatly defined ocean worlds has limited the understanding of them as distinct spaces in the African context, overlooking what their comparative histories might reveal about ocean-centered processes in relation to broader continental histories. Linking the experience of Africa's islands can help reveal two key insights. First, ocean winds and currents defined specific cultural and commercial worlds, but borders between these worlds were fluid. Indian Ocean historians have noted that American bullion was critical to European entrance into the spice trade, and Nigel Worden has explored the ways in which Cape Town acted as a hinge point between oceans.[27] As similar maritime centers and victualing stations, Africa's islands became, in the words of historian Reed Ueda, "interoceanic crossroads" where worlds often overlapped and avenues opened for African and foreign agents alike.[28] This is especially true in the case of Africa, where the continent's integration into the Atlantic World was itself a product of the European ambitions to access the Far East trade, and which stood at the center of a truly global system of enslavement and migration.

Second, linking the histories of Africa's islands can reveal broader trends in African history. The laboratory quality of insular settings helps distill how processes of empire, enslavement, migration, and integration transformed the cultures, economies, and politics of the continent from precolonial times to the present. The patterns through which trade acted as a centripetal force pulling disparate peoples together becomes more apparent, as does the tendency for these islands to encourage the penetration and, at times, colonization of mainland areas. Islands also prominently capture in a condensed setting the complex social and cultural exchanges that have occurred as local African peoples have expanded and made contact with subsequent waves of foreigners, producing a cultural and social layering that has taken different forms based most clearly on those contacted, the timing of this interaction, and the transformation of ideological and political systems. And while these factors differed between the Atlantic and Indian oceans, they nonetheless produced some surprisingly similar products, especially when historical relationships with the mainland are taken into account.

This volume explores these commonalities by putting scholarship centered in these two oceanic worlds into communication with each other. Borrowing from the emerging field of nissology—or the study of the history and sociology of islands as spaces with shared characteristics—we propose a few theoretical concepts that help illuminate these overlapping histories and their larger meaning for African studies. Though the nascent field continues to debate the full meaning of islandness, there is agreement that it applies most clearly to small landmasses that are isolated and bounded by water. Their small size generally limits their resources, making them dependent on the sea and often stronger powers, creating tendencies toward migration and the cultural mixing that accompanies conquests and constant flows of people.[29] Oceanic littorals endow islands with distinct and immediately understandable borders, while making them vulnerable to penetration, effectively making each island a potential "frontier zone" defined, according to J. C. Heesterman, by their permeability.[30] The result, as anthropologist William Bissell notes in this volume, is that shores, and in particular island shores, have "long served as a shifting space for cultural exchanges and encounters that could not occur in the more settled spheres of *terra firma.*"[31]

While such instability and porousness might make islands seem less than desirable possessions, the history of Africa's islands show that from small traders to great powers, these landmasses have consistently proved invaluable. The compact size, relative isolation, and historically small or absent populations have often allowed more powerful newcomers to reshape the islands to fit their specific needs, even as most extant cultures proved surprisingly resilient in their ability to absorb and adapt to new influences. As Rod Edmond and Vanessa Smith have argued, "Boundedness makes islands graspable, able to be held in the mind's eye and imagined as places of possibility and promise."[32] It is exactly this faith in the ability of islands to be reshaped and reordered that has encouraged foreigners to use them to establish footholds in alien and enigmatic lands. In these interactions, scholars can follow the construction and replication of spaces, peoples, and practices that historian-anthropologist Greg Denning has characterized as "in-between" worlds, capturing the role of islands as not just political or economic intermediaries, but also sociocultural ones as well.[33] Importantly, it was through these islands' networks and interoceanic exchange that new ideas of imperial governance, economic organization, and culture traveled from one region to another, helping to reshape African history in the process.

Themes in the History of Africa's Islands

The chapters presented here contend that despite individual oceanic histories, Africa's islands share common characteristics.[34] Yet in identifying these commonalities, it is worth keeping in mind that oceanic histories influenced by geographic position and contingency mark categories of islands as distinct. In this volume, Edward Alpers argues for experiences specific to offshore, foreland, and "distant-water" categories in understanding the Indian Ocean, the first two of which are defined by stronger identification with Africa.[35] Offshore islands such as Mombasa and Zanzibar, easily accessible from the continent, provided a setting where

Africans mixed with foreign seafarers to create cultures and institutions closely linked to the continent, though heavily influenced by such outside forces as Islam. Foreland islands refer to those such as the Comoros, Madagascar, Mauritius, and the Seychelles, which reflect linguistic and cultural traditions related to but identifiably distinct from the Swahili coast. While we can usefully extend Alper's approach to the Atlantic—Bioko and the Bijagos being offshore islands, Cabo Verde a foreland, and the Caribbean islands fulfilling the distant water variety—an additional factor will aid in comparing Atlantic Ocean and Indian Ocean experiences.

In adopting a continental approach to Africa's islands, a further distinction is apparent in processes of creolization. By this we do not mean an Indian Ocean versus Atlantic Ocean paradigm, but rather a juxtaposition between the extended interactions that informed the Swahili coast, complex social relationships of Madagascar, and the more historically recent plantation islands such as São Tomé or Mauritius.[36] When Europeans entered the Indian Ocean, they found dynamic hybrid cultures in Zanzibar, the Comoros, and Madagascar born of the fluid economic and political relationships carried by the monsoon winds. The cosmopolitan identities of these islands had formed over hundreds, even thousands of years by a mixture of wayward seamen, merchants, religious leaders, and empire-builders. Europeans contributed new elements to this ongoing process of exchange and creolization via imposed trade structures and imported labor, but historic traditions proved resilient in the face of these new forms of direct control, economic organization, and social engineering. Europeans were just a few of the many influences that mixed together to shape these societies, and were relative latecomers at that.

The experiences of these established cultures contrast with processes of creolization that occurred on the mostly uninhabited plantation islands whose modern histories began at the intersection of European colonization, slavery, and forced resettlement.[37] In such places as Cabo Verde, São Tomé, Príncipe, Mauritius, and the Seychelles, the importation at their founding of slaves and forced laborers—both from Africa and elsewhere—led to the purposeful creation of Euro-African societies to further the exploitation and conquest of the continent. Carefully defined power relationships shaped these island societies with the specific goal of enriching metropolitan empires. Individual identities took shape in relation to centers of power and culture on these island chains, which were themselves deeply influenced by their structural proximity to the metropolis and maritime lifelines. In comparing Zanzibar with Mauritius, or Guinea-Bissau's Canhabac Island with those of Cabo Verde, differences depend not only on geographic proximity to Africa, but the reality that foreign—specifically

European—control of the sociopolitical structures in which creolization occurred in the formerly uninhabited islands was more constant, lengthy, direct, organized, and globally integrated.

Importantly, the preponderance of power wielded by any one group or actor does not necessarily imply a uniform Creole identity across archipelagos or even within islands. As in the mainland, identities formed in relation to centers of local power and the extent to which they effectively adapted or promoted foreign influences. The chapters in this volume show that various factors guided—and continue to guide—the heterogeneous formation of Creole societies, including class, ethnicity, gender, geography, and many other contingent decisions. In Cabo Verde, for instance, people in the interior of Santiago have created a Creole cultural character more closely tied to African traditions than that long practiced by elite citizens of the capital of Praia, while the small island of Brava boasts extensive ties to the United States due to migration begun after decades of American whaling. Keeping such complexity in mind, there is little doubt that decisions and relationships on such plantation islands operated within the limits set by European powers who largely managed, if never fully controlled, the genesis of these island populations. These histories contrast with those of Zanzibar and Madagascar, where chronologies of colonization and processes of exchange were more comparable to the continent, though adaptation sometimes occurred more rapidly than on the mainland due to historic cosmopolitanism and their unique roles as depots of international economic exchange.

With these caveats about geography and historical circumstances in mind, the comparison between islands is nonetheless quite fruitful. Each of the authors in this volume presents a specific examination of an island or islands. They generally consider the complex internal and transnational dynamics that saw indigenous peoples resist and adapt to outside forces at the expense of deeper explorations of the commonalities that link each of these landmasses together. Therefore, this section of the introduction will attempt to highlight the linkages present and implied in these individual chapters and the wider literature, identifying some broad themes and the historical context that link the experiences of these islands.

Bases for Intervention and Expansion

Africa's islands have historically operated as bases for penetration of the continent. They offered readily available outposts for foreign traders and their local collaborators that were both easily accessible by sea and relatively defensible from the mainland. This allowed them to act as both administrative centers and entrepôts, where goods could be assembled and protected while waiting for shipment abroad or into the interior. In the Indian Ocean, this process operated more indirectly before the coming of Europeans. Regional centers such as Mombasa and, later, Zanzibar prospered by creating conditions conducive for attracting traders, which promoted the expansion of commercial networks deeper into the hinterland as demand for gold and ivory grew. The precolonial slave trade operated similarly, creating networks whereby people from the interior were exported via coastal settlements to Madagascar, the Comoros, Arabia, and locations more distant. Islam and goods from the Indian Ocean trade accompanied these caravans. For much of this pre-European period, the primarily Arab traders operated almost exclusively at the margins—on islands and littoral settlements—with acculturated Swahili middlemen controlling access to the African hinterland.

In the Atlantic, too, islands offered possibilities for entrance into the continent, but Europeans brought with them new ideas of governance and control of sea-lanes that slowly made their way into the Indian Ocean. Germán Santana Pérez notes in this volume that the Canaries operated initially as a base for Spanish ambitions in Morocco, though they later became more important for providing a launching port for exploration and colonization of the Western Hemisphere, as did Portugal's Atlantic islands. They also served as important waypoints on the way to India and the Far East. Yet Africa's islands quickly found similar uses to their better-established Indian counterparts, opening avenues for metropolitan expansion into Sub-Saharan Africa, even when imperial priorities sometimes dissuaded such behavior. Islands thus facilitated the commercial penetration of the African continent by providing safe harbors for foreigners, which traders and empires alike reshaped to meet their needs.

The Portuguese islands provide an example. Cabo Verde served as an administrative and ecclesiastical center safe from potentially hostile Africans that could deploy supplies and reinforcements to the small, widely scattered Portuguese trading posts stretched along the 2,000 miles of the Guinean coast. Gradually, both whites and Creole Cabo Verdeans became prominent among the intermediaries who facilitated European trade in continental Africa, adopting positions akin to the Swahili in the east. The islands also produced the textiles that dressed the upper class of Guinea and became a focus for the collection and distribution of goods that kept the hinterland open to Portuguese commerce, even as locals sometimes skirted metropolitan monopolies on such exchange. Creoles in São Tomé opened some of the first commercial contacts with Angolan chiefs to acquire slaves in exchange for European goods, despite Lisbon's restrictions.

These exchanges—and inter-European competition—were promoted and protected by the might of Europe's naval arms, which introduced a maritime militarism largely unknown to Sub-Saharan Africa. Control of these islands meant control of trade routes, fueling competition from and invasions by European powers. Europeans gradually exported this ideology of oceanic sovereignty into the Indian Ocean, beginning again with islands. The Portuguese unsuccessfully (and somewhat inconsistently) tried to use early possession of Mozambique and Mombasa to forcibly direct regional trade through their ports, abandoning such strategies when local agents found that competing within the traditional monsoon trade proved more profitable. Yet Europeans remained committed to establishing clear, proprietary economic routes and blocks, which would eventually fuel colonization as ambitions to control trade expanded to include production as well. In the Indian Ocean, Mauritius and Réunion helped European states project their naval power in the region, with the former being a key component in Britain's naval dominance of the region into the twentieth century. The islands thus became centers for the application and enforcement of new rules of commerce, even as they continued to accommodate older economic patterns.

This island role of intermediary in the exploitation and integration of the African continent within shifting economic networks is perhaps most apparent in the slave trade beginning with the Swahili coast and extending to the modern transatlantic trade. Indian Ocean islands, including Zanzibar and possibly the Comoros, had long been way stations for the inland trade, operating as points of embarkation for Arabia, India, and even China. Europeans discovered a similar value in their Atlantic possessions, first in the reexport to the New World of slaves seasoned on African island plantations, and later as entrepôts where traders could acquire their human merchandise. Deep-water islands such as Cabo Verde and São Tomé became preferred ports because their established colonial administrations, milder oceanic climates, and lack of disease were more welcoming to slavers willing to pay extra to avoid the hostile and unhealthy mainland and foreland areas. Between 1809 and 1815 alone more than 33,000 slaves were shipped to São Tomé, most bound for destinations such as Brazil and Cuba.[38] Islands thus acted as important components in the process of slave export, helping to acclimatize, subjugate, catalog, and sell enslaved Africans destined for distant destinations.

As these islands prospered, they became models of a new kind of expansion. They legitimized the concept of extra-European political enlargement and became centers through which European governments could manage trade, promote religious conversions, and ultimately extend their direct sovereignty over nearby regions. This emphasis on centralized political control differentiated these modern empires from earlier Arabic and Asian influences on East African culture and commerce. This began among Iberia's Atlantic islands, where the occupation and transformation of Madeira and the Canaries into plantation agricultures under direct European management established a prototype, which was replicated first in Portugal's African possessions, then in the Americas, and later in the Franco-British islands of the Indian Ocean. The application of this successful model of political and economic governance to the mainland would increasingly become a goal of most European empires, though one that proceeded slowly. Europeans faced strong opposition from mainland Africans and established island populations in Madagascar and the Bijagos, and for centuries settlement in the New World proved more attractive. Nonetheless, as historian T. Bentley Duncan argues regarding Madeira and Cabo Verde, it was on islands that "the Portuguese developed colonial structures—with economic, social, political and ecclesiastical features—that were applied on a much wider basis in Brazil, Angola, Mozambique, and elsewhere."[39]

As Europeans shifted their goals in Africa from establishing commercial arrangements to modern imperial domination, the plantation islands continued to operate as facilitators—and even advocates—of empire on both sides of the continent. The highly Europeanized Creole populations that emerged in the wealthiest islands of the Mascarenes became especially vocal in support of expansion. Mauritius helped settle and administer the Seychelles and provided expertise to develop sugar cultivation in South African Natal, helping to push the European plantation system inland. Creole elites in neighboring Réunion had long urged France to colonize nearby islands in order to open up new economic opportunities in the region, establishing early and influential settlements in Mayotte after 1841 and in Madagascar after a fourth military expedition finally led to its annexation in 1896. In the Atlantic, Cabo Verde, São Tomé, and Spanish Bioko all served as bases for Portugal and Spain to press into the African interior, then later as colonial administrative centers. Cabo Verde, of course, became noteworthy for providing middle administrators for Portuguese colonialism, with a large number of islanders working in Guinea-Bissau.

The small populations, sympathetic leadership, and clear borders of the foreland plantation islands provided Europeans with a sense of security. This was rare in settled mainland areas, where indigenous kingdoms resisted annexation, revolts were common into the twentieth century, and interventions by Arab and Malagasy polities repelled European impositions on the Swahili coast. The trend of plantation island refuges would largely continue through the period of decolonization, when empires found their authority challenged across the continent. European control of the islands and their relatively privileged places in the colonial system constrained nationalist agitation, as did heavy economic dependence on metropolitan patronage. These realities forced some nationalist parties to operate in exile, as Cabral's example and the Tanzanian founding of the Mouvement de la Libération Nationale des Comores (National Liberation Movement of the Comoros) illustrate. It was in part for these reasons that Africa's islands—with the exception of Madagascar and Zanzibar, which more closely followed mainland time lines—experienced some of the latest dates for formal independence, and account for the only remaining European outposts south of the Sahara: Mayotte, Réunion, and the Chagos archipelago. As a result, islands continued to project foreign power into recent times. As late as the 1960s, colonial São Tomé became a base for foreign intervention in Nigeria's Biafran War, and the British forcibly depopulated the Chagos islands over local protests in order to facilitate the establishment of an American military base on Diego Garcia.

Plantation Agriculture and the Reinvention of Island Economies

Africa's islands shared the experience of plantation agriculture with other areas of the continent, but this activity operated for a more extended period than on the mainland and witnessed numerous shifts in production as the islands adjusted to meet the demands of global markets. Indeed, the plantation system had its origins in islands and proved replicable as new territories came under European domination. Sugar was the first major product, helping colonizers to wring a profit from island possessions they occupied primarily as nautical waypoints. On Madeira, the Portuguese outlined what would become an exportable system: large plantations raised a labor-intensive cash crop worked by slaves imported from the African continent. The embrace of a fashionable monoculture reduced self-sufficiency on many islands, but it also led to short-term riches through exports, both of which were encouraged and made sustainable by the islands' positions as nodes of commerce. This model spread quickly throughout the island possessions of the Iberian world, with São Tomé becoming the world's largest producer of sugar by the sixteenth century.

This plantation system and the technology it used would become the foundations for the even more successful operations begun in the

Caribbean and Brazil. Sugar production, as well as that of coffee and other products that Europeans would soon introduce, benefited greatly from characteristics shared by many of Africa's islands. Settlers found virgin agricultural land and climates suitable for the crop, and an export-focused economic infrastructure was developed to service ports. Africa's islands also featured a readily available source of cheap labor in the form of continental slaves. Combined with the political stability that generally accompanied tight European control of clearly defined island borders, here was a clear economic formula. But islands were soon to find that mainland areas in the Americas and, later, Africa shared many if not all of these characteristics, and made up for shortcomings in security or location with the ability to expand production freely while being more self-sufficient due to a greater variety of resources. By 1600, for example, many of São Tomé's successful planters had left for Brazil in search of the greater profits possible in the New World. As much as islands offered opportunities to test and innovate systems of empire, most occupied precarious positions in this increasingly global system of trade and migration.

The evolution of this plantation model in the Indian Ocean reveals the extent to which the Eurocentric imperial economic system gradually integrated much of Africa, passing through island territories that so often represented the first sites of European control and transformation. As in the Atlantic, the future plantation isles were initially most important for their strategic value, offering first Dutch and then French navies the opportunity to press claims in Asia while harassing competitors, most notably the British. In these early decades, the islands were primarily places of resupply, valuable for water, foodstuffs (including turtle and the ill-fated dodo), and forests for shipbuilding. Yet as British domination of the region replaced great power competition, profit motives encouraged the embrace of staple monocultures alongside ongoing maritime activities in an attempt to replicate, and even replace, the wealthy Caribbean. In the early nineteenth century, the British allowed sugar production in Mauritius despite West Indian objections. France encouraged Réunion to shift from coffee production to sugar, hoping to replace the production lost from the Caribbean after the successful slave rebellion in Haiti (though Parisian authorities legislated the island simultaneously to maintain its ability to resupply ships). Even the small Seychelles found success growing cotton for a short period. The journey of the plantation labor model from Africa's Atlantic coast to the New World and back again to the Indian Ocean reveals the expanding global logic of empire, and how models of African labor exploitation came full circle as Africa was incorporated into an international system of production and trade.

Plantation agriculture also became prominent in Indian Ocean areas that remained independent of European rule into the nineteenth century, with islands once more playing a key role in the continental adoption of European economic models. The rise of Zanzibar's clove economy offers an example. While the origins of the plant's introduction remain open for debate, it likely came via the Mascarenes, testifying to the role these islands had in promoting the diffusion of European ideas. Prominent Omani merchants who governed Zanzibar at the time sought to replicate the success of the well-known sugar islands, using slaves who were more difficult to export as the British attempted to suppress the trade in the first half of the nineteenth century. The resulting clove mania greatly enriched Zanzibari elites and led to new plantings in the neighboring island of Pemba, but the market collapsed within a few decades. That Arab and other regional rulers adopted the plantation system not because of European imperialism but in order to compete with it demonstrates the power of the plantation system, as well as Europe's successful integration of the Indian Ocean World into a global economy.

Yet as these illustrations show, the dependence of islands on global market trends has created a tendency toward boom, bust, and reinvention. This predated the rise of plantation agriculture since oceanic trading outposts have, according to K. N. Chaudhuri, "prospered and declined in a pendulum motion of long-term cycles."[40] But the plantation agriculture reified this trend by discouraging self-sufficiency, making diversification yet more difficult, and inspiring local elites and imperial agents to envision the wholesale economic reorientation of islands as inherently possible. This approach has produced great wealth for landowners when islands have successfully anticipated or created global trends, but it has largely ignored the needs of local peoples and puts these same places at a disadvantage when patterns of travel shift or larger states begin to compete. Gerhard Seibert's chapter on São Tomé and Príncipe provides one example, tracking the islands' repeated reinvention of their economy around sugar, coffee, cocoa, and, finally, an oil boom that has never arrived. Islands like these have been, in Braudel's pithy phrasing, caught between the "poles of archaism and innovation," constantly reinventing themselves in order to prosper in changing continental and global contexts.[41]

As islands have once more sought to reinvent themselves in the contemporary age of long-distance shipping and mass agriculture, many have found a solution in tourism. As ports declined, the opening of new international airports allowed countries to attract foreigners, using the same pleasant climate and natural fecundity that once drove plantation agriculture for new ends. Over the past twenty years, tourism has become a prominent part of the economy in the Canaries, Mauritius, the Seychelles, Réunion, and Zanzibar, and it is growing steadily in value for Cabo Verde and Madagascar. This industry has adapted or reinvented much of the traditional work that went into servicing maritime travelers but, now with a greater emphasis on luxuries, benefiting from cosmopolitan traditions long central to island identities. Yet so too has this shift toward tourism reified past inequalities. Though Mauritius, the Seychelles, and Cabo Verde rank highly in terms of both human development and gross domestic product per capita in Africa, these benefits have not been distributed evenly. Reinvention has not overcome traditional social, economic, or geographic divisions, merely reorienting the benefits bestowed by international exchange and travel to a new set of actors.

Acculturation and Creolization

Given the place of Africa's islands as waypoints and end points in an increasingly globalized political economy, it is not surprising that they stand out most clearly from their continental neighbors in the unique social dynamics of their societies. From their earliest points, both plantation and the older island cultures of the Indian Ocean saw a diverse array of settlers due to their positions as oceanic crossroads, leading to polyglot demography that encouraged Creole societies. The Swahili coast provides an early and informative example. The monsoon trade linked African and Asian peoples into a regional network, creating conditions where cultural and linguistic elements interacted. As Islam spread through the Arabian Peninsula, it traveled with the ubiquitous Arab traders to Africa, where it gradually became essential to the emergence of a unique Swahili identity on the edges of the continent. While the process of conversion remains debated, adoption likely occurred in order to cement African links with these predominantly Muslim traders, providing a set of transnational incentives that encouraged assimilation and adaptation. Importantly, this form of coastal Islam—grafted as it was onto an already heterogeneous network of trade—proved tolerant of diverse traditions, allowing the Swahili culture to incorporate elements that not only distinguished it from nearby Africans but also from Arab or South Asian coreligionists. The result was the creation of "in-between" identities that were identifiably African but nonetheless looked outward from the coasts. As Ross Dunn has argued, "in the Indian Ocean lands where Islam was a minority faith, all Muslims shared acutely this feeling of participation. Simply to be a Muslim in East Africa . . . was to have a cosmopolitan frame of mind."[42]

These interconnected ideas of international exchange and cosmopolitanism are central to understanding the unique characteristics of most African islands. Swahili ports such as Kilwa, Mombasa, Zanzibar, and later the Comoros operated at the center of this maritime network, meaning new cultural and economic inputs continued to shape this sense of openness. These cosmopolitan centers generally lacked the suspicions and wonderment that could greet outsiders in interior societies, allowing islanders to adopt and adapt more readily practices that benefited their societies. This ranged from the plantation agriculture described above to language, clothing, and styles of governance. Importantly, islanders felt motivated to adopt foreign characteristics because they simultaneously operated within regional and global spheres, as Jeremy Prestholdt argues in chapter 10. In essence, they measured themselves both by African and broader standards of wealth, privilege, and power. The creation of dominant cultures as a result of this diversity of inputs and as a way to manage participation in this interconnected world marked Africa's islands as distinctive in the larger continental experience.

Given the debate that continues to surround the origins of Swahili culture, the plantation islands provide an even clearer historical narrative of cosmopolitanism, capturing Alison Games's idea of the oceanic laboratory. From their origins in the Atlantic to their later settlement in the Indian, these islands featured the demographic hallmarks of the plantation system: a small group of European settlers imported an increasing number of mostly African slaves (and later indentured or impressed labor from India or nearby colonies in Africa) to raise crops and service ships. By the time Europeans began to populate the uninhabited islands of the Indian Ocean, this model was clear. The first settlers of the Seychelles, for example, included fifteen whites, eight slaves, five South Asians, and an African woman drawn from the plantations of Mauritius and Réunion.[43] Whites on these islands did not dominate by demographics, but rather through the political and economic institutions that controlled migration, labor, and international exchange. In São Tomé, for example, the white population never numbered more than a few hundred for much of the island's history, only breaking 1,000 during the coffee boom of the late nineteenth century, when the number of new laborers drawn mostly from Angola was more than ten times as much.[44]

The plantation islands thus evolved in a way not wholly unique to Africa, where a dominant African culture existed alongside a minority European population that controlled much of the official institutions. The need to communicate across these boundaries gave rise to a linguistic and cultural synchronicity, whereby local Creole languages and cultures displayed strong European foundations but with varying degrees of influences from

African, Asian, and even American sources. Since few European settlers to the islands brought families—and many settlements featured exiled convicts and itinerant seamen—sexual relations across racial and ethnic boundaries were common on all but a few islands, which further opened the door for cultural exchange. As a result, Africa's plantation islands came to resemble Caribbean societies, featuring large mixed-race populations speaking a Creole patois borrowed from the language of the metropolis, and practicing a culture that linked European aspirations with African custom.

Yet in contrast to the Caribbean, Africa's islands were unique in that the primary purpose of all but a few remained in the maritime realm well into the twentieth century, even on successful plantation islands like Mauritius and Réunion. Sailors from across the globe regularly passed through the victualing and later coaling stations established in the widely scattered archipelagoes, settling or leaving traces of their cultures, foreign goods, and—not uncommonly—children.[45] Locales at the center of global trade like Zanzibar featured "all the known races of the world," as Bissell quotes an Anglican missionary in this volume, with smaller ports hosting populations bounded in their diversity by the specific routes that passed through them.[46] Locals fleeing poverty or seeking opportunity beyond the limited confines of the island often sailed with visiting ships as hired hands, only to return home later or send back remittances and letters. Such interconnections gave many islands an outward-looking, cosmopolitan identity that proved receptive and adaptive in the face of new socioeconomic exigencies. Cabo Verde, for example, established an especially influential diaspora in New England, which has continued to shape the language and culture of their home islands, as shown in this volume by Carla Martin.

This more fluid maritime identity combined with innovative attempts to replace slave labor with indenture from other parts of the various empires to reveal the complexity of island identities. São Tomé continued to import Angolan labor after slavery was officially abandoned and used short indentures to lure Cabo Verdeans fleeing famines, while Richard Allen notes in this volume that British Mauritius imported over 450,000 laborers primarily from India, but also from China, Madagascar, Southeast Asia, and Yemen.[47] The influx of indentured laborers added a further level of complexity to many islands, especially on Mauritius, where Hindu has become the dominant religion—the only such country in Africa. Generally, though, these new arrivals adopted the language and practices of the existing community, at least in the public sphere, most clearly evidenced in the continued usage of historically inflected Creoles as the lingua francas of most islands. This process helps explain the situation in Mauritius, for example, where many in the Hindu-majority former British colony rely on a French-based Creole for regular communication. Well before most European empires began to divide the continent in the late nineteenth century, Creole societies had begun to take shape on the continent's islands from the intersection of diverse cultural traditions, which incorporated additional elements as sociopolitical developments demanded.

Importantly given this continuous influx of peoples, it appears that this process of acculturation on Africa's islands may follow a surprisingly common pattern. Early mass settlements created foundational cultures that modified the linguistic, political, and cultural aspects of subsequent waves of immigrants. The examples above—and in this volume—draw heavily from the plantation isles, whose more recent origins allow a greater sense of specificity for these historic interactions. But this process of adaptation rather than adoption has parallels with the Swahili coast and, notably, in the somewhat exceptional Malagasy example. In Madagascar, the interaction of early Austronesian immigrants with Africans and Muslims gradually defined social hierarchies related to slavery, geography, dialect, and political alliances. But even here, as Solofo Randrianja and Stephen Ellis lyrically note, "The initial patterns of Madagascar's cultures have been robust enough to become a fugue, a musical form in which distinct lines combine to form a harmonious whole."[48] Austronesian characteristics remain at the core of the mutually intelligible Malagasy dialects, reverence for ancestors, and Hindu-derived ideas of status or value, despite centuries of interaction with outsiders that added vocabulary, religious beliefs, and economic structures. While the specific methods through which extant cultures absorbed new influences remain topics of debate, it might owe a debt to patterns of cultural interaction promoted by maritime societies. Predominantly male newcomers must adapt to local traditions, not only to function within the established economic system but to find partners among island women. This constant layering of diverse cultures has contributed to the creation of uniquely complex island identities linked to economic, cultural, and social dynamics.

African Island Identity in Continental Context

These maritime and Creole identities have meant that islanders often have a complicated relationship with Africa, especially beyond the immediate offshore areas. The mediating positions these more distant islands occupied both culturally and commercially have historically allowed their

citizens to at least imagine themselves as both part of Africa and somewhere else entirely. How this has affected specific cultural articulations of
identity has varied across place and time, from the Malagasy's mythic origins on their island to Cabo Verdean claims to a strictly Portuguese identity. What is common is that a fluidity born of their complex cosmopolitan
cultures has allowed islanders to adjust their self-identifications to pursue
goals by staking claim to various spaces in the global social order.

The fluidity of these island identities can be traced back largely to the
processes of ethnic interaction and acculturation described above. Though
there were exceptions, the centrality of racial and ethnic identity on many
of Africa's islands became less important, particularly after slavery was
abolished. As the decades progressed and the number of self-consciously
foreign settlers remained small, wealth and connections eclipsed ethnicity or race as the primary indicators of social status on many islands. The
persistence of such identity politics in Mauritius and Madagascar owed
much to their specific historical circumstances, namely the major influx of
Indian laborers to an already stratified Creole society and the intersection
of slavery with the Malagasy status system, respectively. Such processes preserved and racialized distinctions, as Denis Regnier and Dominique Somda
note in chapter 11. Yet even in these divided societies, language and certain cultural aspects provide the basis for pan-islandic identities. Distinctions remain and occasionally create conflict, but most islands have moved
toward a certain level of collective identity, especially over the past twenty
years. This unity in diversity has been achieved based on a public culture
that emerged from common—if not necessarily shared—histories, defined
by clear borders and reinforced by the tendency of these maritime centers
to absorb newcomers. The traditional de-emphasis, though not erasure,
of ethnic or racial identity contrasted sharply with the increasing institu-
tionalization of racial differences imposed by European colonialism on the
continent, and would prove shocking to islanders who found equally strict
delineations were made in most metropoles.

Gradual changes in self-perception were reinforced by the fact that, in
many cases, islands were by far the most acculturated of African territories.
Zanzibar and the Comoros reflected strong Arabic and Islamic influences,
and plantation societies generally became the most Europeanized of the
African colonies. This owed much to time and extent that extra-African
influences wielded preponderant power on these islands. As Tony Hodges
and Malyn Newitt have said of São Tomé, "no other area was so early and
for so long exposed to European settlement and plantation capitalism," but
much the same could be said of the majority of Africa's plantation islands,
or even of Arabian trade and religious traditions in Zanzibar.[49] So too did

the self-consciously European plantation culture take root so firmly during the colonial period in the Mascarenes that August Toussaint has argued that foreign attitudes, manners, and even architecture had fully taken hold of society by 1789, at least at the elite level: "Few other trading posts in the Indian Ocean were as completely European as [St. Denis in Réunion and Port Louis in Mauritius]."[50] As a result, outside influence became particularly ingrained in many of these islands, fueling foreign attachments and providing justifications for empires. As a result, Réunion and even the Muslim-majority island of Mayotte, for example, continue to envision themselves as extensions of France, maintaining ties to a distant metropolis that reflect their self-perceptions vis-à-vis the continent and their ambitions for future socioeconomic development.

While these final two examples are perhaps extreme, this blurring of racial and cultural distinctions has allowed islanders to lay claim not simply to a geographical and cultural identity as Africans, but also to assert membership in broader and more powerful political constellations. In the Creole islands this took the form most commonly of claims to European identity. In Cabo Verde, for instance, both light- and dark-skinned citizens have claimed Portuguese identity in specific contexts, a habit that continued to be noteworthy among island immigrants to New England, considered black by American custom. They did this not only because of the widespread racial mixing that occurred on the islands, but because many islanders received special privileges of empire, thereby defining themselves in opposition to continental Africans who were not Portuguese with varying levels of ease or comfort. And this phenomenon is not limited to the European Creole context, with both Indian and Arab groups attempting to parlay once-privileged Indian Ocean positions into continued advantage. Ian Walker argues in this volume that despite affection for France, the Comoros have increasingly benefited from membership in the Arab League, along with participation in the international Organization of Islamic Cooperation.[51] Semiautonomous Zanzibar also joined the latter organization in 1993, but protests from the majority Christian population of Tanzania forced an end to this brief association, revealing the extent to which cultivating such foreign ties can place islands at odds with mainland Africans.

Islanders have thus positioned themselves between worlds. This extra-African identity has provided benefits, but it has also fueled a complex relationship with the continent, which was placed under a stark light by decolonization. As nations abandoned colonialism and embraced African nationalist ideologies, islanders had to grapple with their historic roles as intermediaries and possessors of "in-between" cultures. A sense of alienation fueled Cabral's revolutionary ideology, but so too did it produce the eventual collapse of his binational vision for Cabo Verde. As with political leaders, cultural producers have also grappled with this reality of being both of and distinct from Africa, including the Cabo Verdean Cesária Évora, Francisco Tenreiro of São Tomé, and Bi Kidude in Tanzania. Yet for every Kidude who finds her voice in the intersection of African and Arab tradition, there are others like Cabral whose ultimate goal of reconciling island cosmopolitanism with African nationalism has been frustrated. The inward-looking ideology of the nation-state has clashed with the outward gaze of island societies and led to the targeting of their polyglot societies as vestiges of imperialism, especially in offshore areas. This has manifested not only in Guinea-Bissau's split from Cabo Verde, but also in the anti-Indian and anti-Arab violence that has occurred on Zanzibar and the subjugation of Bubi of Bioko by Fang mainlanders. These tensions between traditions of cosmopolitanism and African nationalism have provided unique pressures that have simultaneously pulled islands toward the continent while reinforcing a sense of distinction from it.

The ambiguous positions of contemporary islands are especially apparent in issues of migration. Islands have, like their mainland counterparts, experienced growing populations in the last thirty years, but limited opportunities for social advancement born from their small, often precarious economies have encouraged emigrations. Flows have often followed historic pathways, using diasporas produced by maritime and imperial traditions to facilitate a consistent exchange of peoples primarily with non-African states. As Michael Lambek notes in his chapter on Mayotte, financial remittances from emigrants to Europe and other more economically successful states, along with the related ideas of exodus and return, have become central to island identities. While these ideas have historic precedents, it is worth noting that decolonization and the shift from sea to air travel has affected historic patterns of migration. Immigration in the Indian Ocean region has especially pushed the limits of insular traditions of incorporating new peoples, notably in the hostile treatment of Comorians in Madagascar and Mayotte. While past and current ties to international networks have continued to offer islanders successful avenues for migration, there is no doubt that the shift from empire to nation-states has challenged the traditions of cosmopolitanism central to Africa's insular histories.

Yet it is worth noting that, despite the occasional tensions that have been created by these political shifts, Africa's independent islands have largely defined their national identities in ways that contrast with their continental neighbors. Much of African history and historiography over the past five decades has been dedicated to engineering national unity based in large part on the creation of a mythic—and sometimes contested—origin identity, often defined as predating or opposing colonialism. To be sure, these social constructs operate with varying levels of importance on African islands, including the central role of a common Malagasy ancestry in Madagascan nationalism, mythic Comorian references to Arabic and Portuguese origins, and the popularity of Rei Amador's slave revolt in São Tomé. Yet many islands have chosen a different path, especially those Creole cultures whose history began with foreign colonization and has since reflected a regular influx of new peoples. They have found greater success engineering unity through appeals to widely cosmopolitan identities. In this process, most island states have embraced a complex nationalism. A unity in diversity has arisen based on shared cultural elements and goals, with common language offering a key component in the creation of a pan-islandic identity. This cosmopolitan nationalism, combined with the profitable historical and ethnic ties to wealthy nations, has helped Africa's island states claim disproportionately stable political and social relationships despite common problems of ecological limitations, economic frailty, and population pressure.

Structure of the Volume

While it is impossible to assemble in one volume a comprehensive overview of Africa's islands, we have made an attempt to reflect both the diversity of island experiences and the common themes that bind them together. We have done so by replicating the oceanic approaches that have so far best integrated these islands into African history, ordering the chapters so that they build on each other while highlighting parallels that exist across the continental divide. Part 1: Atlantic Ocean Islands offers a multidisciplinary exploration of African islands. The first three chapters in this section focus on the intersection of economics and identity in the long history of Africa's islands. Germán Santana Pérez focuses on the Canaries, a Spanish territory that played a key role in opening the African continent to Europeans, but has since continued to seek economic relevance by linking the two continents through tourism and the distribution of aid. This history, which stretches from the fifteenth century to today, challenges the chronological boundaries of the dominant Atlantic World scholarship, while highlighting how Canarians have juggled contested European and African identities as a way of staying afloat in an economically turbulent world. In contrast, Gerhard Seibert focuses on São Tomé and Príncipe's struggle to move beyond its colonial commodity economy. At the leading edge of sugar and cocoa production during the colonial period, attempts to exploit its offshore oil resources have demonstrated the limitations of relying on the expertise and cooperation of nearby states competing in the same global markets. In this way, it pushes African scholars to consider how the economics of minor states have been influenced not just by foreign empires, but by more powerful neighbors that have adopted the mantles of regional hegemon. Joshua Forrest moves closer inland to examine the social-military history of Guinea-Bissau's Canhabac Island, which demonstrates that even successful resistance to conquest has not prevented islands from integrating into wider international networks.

The next set of chapters in this section looks closer at the way the complicated legacies of imperialism have influenced the political cultures of African islands. Enrique Okenve's chapter on the Equatorial Guinean island of Bioko asserts that the Bubi people, who built their autonomous society at the peripheries of the continent, found themselves increasingly marginalized as their island became important for foreigners, first as an imperial administrative center and more recently in the twentieth and twenty-first centuries as the seat for a postcolonial government dominated by mainland interests. In so doing, he provides a stark example of how postcolonial states often inverted the ethnic politics of the colonial period, unleashing the animosity of peoples considered by imperial powers as more "African" and less acculturated. For Michael Ugarte, Equatorial Guinea—and indeed similar mainland states—are examples of the literary concept of the "repeating island." International and domestic structures maintain experiences of subjugation, isolation, and penetration despite the political transformations launched by decolonization and globalization, simply gaining a new master equally focused on retaining power through domestic division. Ashley Jackson's chapter evaluates the role of Africa's coastal waters, ports, and islands during the Second World War and describes the military activity that took place there. In doing so, it offers a unique account of the continent's strategic importance in a global conflict. Linguist Carla D. Martin concludes the section by arguing that a unique Cabo Verdean identity depends greatly on its Creole language, which has been formalized not in an African context but through connection with schools for expatriates in the United States. As in Equatorial Guinea, the experience of Cabo Verde demonstrates that, for many African states, the adoption of a singular identity remains deeply intertwined with international trends that go beyond historical colonialism.

Part 2: Indian Ocean Islands moves to the other side of the continent to consider the diversity of experiences on Africa's eastern coast. Edward

Alpers begins the section by considering a general classification of Indian Ocean islands discussed above. He finds that the strong, constantly changing ties of the Indian world operated with increasing strength as one approaches shore, while the neat segregation of oceanic spheres breaks down as one considers the African influence on more distantly related islands facilitated primarily by global European empires. In contrast with this metanarrative, William Bissell considers Indian Ocean connections in his case study of songstress Bi Kidude and the changing economics of Zanzibar. He finds that Kidude's famed interpretations of *taarab* and *unyago* music emerged from the cosmopolitan space of the monsoon-driven dock life that has increasingly evolved into a tourist destination, revealing in concrete terms the tendency toward transculturation and adaptation in littoral societies spread along the Swahili coast.

Next, Richard Allen considers how multidirectional labor migrations tied the Mascarene islands of Mauritius and Réunion to Africa and the wider Indian Ocean World. In so doing, he reveals in microcosm how the massive movement of peoples reshaped and expanded the diversity of the continent's ocean-looking population. Jeremy Prestholdt's chapter finds that nineteenth-century Zanzibar became an economic and social nexus that linked East Africa to global consumer trends that stretched beyond the Indian Ocean to Europe and the Americas, inspiring Zanzibaris to use the display of imported goods to both define and challenge local hierarchies. The legacy of slavery in Madagascar provides the subject for the contribution from Denis Regnier and Dominique Somda, who explore the contested meanings of this sometimes stigma in local societies. Iain Walker provides an engaging study of the Comoros from the dawn of European exploration to the present. He finds the archipelago experienced four distinct eras defined by shifting foreign alignments over the last 500 years, offering conclusions about the bounded agency of islanders. Finally, Michael Lambek considers France's Indian Ocean outpost of Mayotte. He finds that the full integration of the island into the metropolitan state has promoted noticeable social change and "intranational" migration, as evidenced by a number of women who used travel to advance their autonomy.

Ultimately, one of the key goals of this volume is to move African islands away from the margins. We hope the volume navigates the intricacies of these insular histories and cultures to create a compelling case for understanding these maritime spaces on their own terms. Yet, we must also reiterate the fact that one cannot disconnect African islands from the larger field of African studies. The histories of the continent's islands emphasize the profound significance of the movement of ideas, people, and commodities over space and time. Thus, scholars of continental Africa would do well to recognize the importance of these small landmasses as both arbiters and witnesses of change, and dynamic spaces worthy of comparative study in a meaningful way.

Notes

1. For biographies of Amílcar Cabral, see Patrick Chabal, *Amilcar Cabral: Revolutionary Leadership and People's War* (Cambridge: Cambridge University Press, 1983); Gérard Chaliand and Michel Vale, "Amilcar Cabral," *International Journal of Politics* 7, no. 4 (Winter 1977–78): 3–17; Julião Soares Sousa, *Amílcar Cabral: Vida e Morte de um Revolucionário Africano*, 2nd ed. (Lisbon: Vega, 2012), 41–118.

2. Amílcar Cabral, "Identity and Dignity in the Context of the National Liberation Struggle," in *Return to the Source: Selected Speeches of Amilcar Cabral*, ed. African Information Service (New York: Monthly Review Press, 1973), 63.

3. For more on the event and the reasons for the assassination (which remain hotly debated), see António Tomás, *O Fazedor de Utopias: Uma Biografia de Amílcar Cabral*, 2nd ed. (Lisbon: Tinta da China, 2007), 265–75; Sousa, *Amílcar Cabral*, 430–34, 505–20.

4. Joshua Forrest, "Guinea-Bissau," in *A History of Postcolonial Lusophone Africa*, ed. Patrick Chabal (Bloomington: Indiana University Press, 2002), 250–51; Rosemary E. Galli and Jocelyn Jones, *Guinea-Bissau: Politics, Economics, and Society* (London: Frances Pinter, 1987), 31–32, 92–99.

5. Many of Africa's islands have been known by various names, some of which are discussed in individual chapters. For the sake of simplicity, we try to refer to islands and archipelagos in this introduction by their current preferred names.

6. See, for instance, Richard B. Allen, *Slaves, Freedman and Indentured Laborers in Colonial Mauritius* (New York: Cambridge University Press, 2006); Ashley Jackson, *War and Empire in Mauritius and the Indian Ocean* (New York: Palgrave, 2001); Catherine Higgs, *Chocolate Islands: Cocoa, Slavery, and Colonial Africa* (Athens: Ohio University Press, 2013); Tony Hodges and Malyn Newitt, *São Tomé and Príncipe: From Plantation Colony to Microstate* (Boulder, CO: Westview Press, 1988).

7. See Gwyn Campbell, *An Economic History of Imperial Madagascar, 1750–1895: The Rise and Fall of an Island Empire* (New York: Cambridge University Press, 2008); Solofo Randrianja and Stephen Ellis, *Madagascar: A Short History* (Chicago: University of Chicago Press, 2009); Jane Hooper, *Feeding Globalization: Madagascar and the Provision Trade, 1600–1800* (Athens: Ohio University Press, 2017); Erik Gilbert, *Dhows and the Colonial Economy in Zanzibar: 1860–1970* (Athens: Ohio University Press, 2005); Laura Fair, *Pastimes and Politics: Culture, Community, and Identity in Post-Abolition Urban Zanzibar, 1890–1945* (Athens: Ohio University Press, 2001). Both islands, particularly Madagascar, have also attracted the attention of anthropologists.

8. For example, see Filipa Ribeiro da Silva, "African Islands and the Formation of the Dutch Atlantic Economy: Arguin, Gorée, Cape Verde and São Tomé, 1590–1670," *International Journal of Maritime History* 26, no. 3 (2014):

549–67; Martin Lynn, "Commerce, Christianity, and the Origins of the 'Creoles' of Fernando Po," *Journal of African History* 25, no. 4 (1984): 257–78; John R. Gillis, "Islands in the Making of an Atlantic Oceania, 1500–1800," in *Seascapes: Maritime Histories, Littoral Cultures, and Transoceanic Exchanges*, ed. Kerry Bentley, Renate Bridenthal, and Karen Wigen (Honolulu: University of Hawai'i Press, 2007), 21–37; Christopher Eberg, "European Competition and Cooperation in Pre-Modern Globalization: 'Portuguese' West and Central Africa, 1500–1600," *African Economic History* 36 (2008): 53–78.

9. In reference to islands, Braudel—with his characteristic tendency to think in timeless and often literary terms—spoke of the "one physical law . . . that the life of the sea, a vital force, would first of all have taken control of the smallest and least weighty fragments of land, the islands and coastal margins." Fernand Braudel, *The Mediterranean and the Mediterranean World in the Age of Philip II*, vol. I, trans. Sian Reynolds (New York: Harper Colophon Books, 1976), 166.

10. For example, see Edward A. Alpers, "Recollecting Africa: Diasporic Memory in the Indian Ocean World," *African Studies Review* 43, no. 1 (2000): 83–99; Gwyn Campbell, "Madagascar and Mozambique in the Slave Trade of the Western Indian Ocean, 1800–1861," in *The Economics of the Indian Ocean Slave Trade in the Nineteenth Century*, ed. Gervase Clarence Smith (London: Frank Cass, 1989), 166–93; Nicole Boivin, Alison Crowther, Richard Helm, and Dorian Q. Fuller, "East Africa and Madagascar in the Indian Ocean World," *Journal of World Prehistory* 26, no. 3 (2013): 213–81; R. Harms, B. Freamon, and D. Blight, eds., *Indian Ocean Slavery in the Age of Abolition* (New Haven, CT: Yale University Press, 2013); Edward A. Alpers, *East Africa and the Indian Ocean* (Princeton, NJ: Markus Wiener, 2009); Gaurav Desai, "Oceans Connect: The Indian Ocean and African Identities," *PMLA* 125, no. 3 (2010): 713–20; Gwyn Campbell, ed., *The Structure of Slavery in Indian Ocean Africa and Asia* (London: Cass, 2004).

11. For a good overview of this period, see Kenneth J. Andrien, "The Spanish Atlantic System," and A. J. R. Russell-Wood, "The Portuguese Atlantic, 1415–1808," in *Atlantic History: A Critical Appraisal*, ed. Jack P. Greene and Philip D. Morgan (New York: Oxford University Press, 2009), 81–109.

12. John Thornton, *Africa and Africans in the Making of the Atlantic World, 1400–1800*, 2nd ed. (New York: Cambridge University Press, 2008), chap. 1.

13. See Alfred Crosby, *Ecological Imperialism: The Biological Expansion of Europe, 900–1900*, 2nd ed. (New York: Cambridge University Press, 2004), chap. 4, particularly 78–79; J. H. Galloway, *The Sugar Cane Industry: An Historical Geography from Its Origins to 1914* (New York: Cambridge University Press, 1989), 50–61, 70–78; and articles by Germán Santana Pérez and Gerhard Siebert in this volume.

14. Alison Games, "Atlantic History: Definitions, Challenges, and Opportunities," *The American Historical Review* 111, no. 3 (2006): 741–57.

15. Thornton, *Africa and Africans in the Making of the Atlantic World, 1400–1800*; David Northrup, *Trade Without Rulers: Pre-Colonial Economic Development in South-Eastern Nigeria* (Oxford: Clarendon, 1978); Ivor Wilks, *Asante in the Nineteenth Century: The Structure and Evolution of a Political Order* (Cambridge: Cambridge University Press, 1989); Robin Law, *The Slave Coast of West Africa*

1550–1750: The Impact of the Atlantic Slave Trade on an African Society (Oxford: Clarendon, 1991).

16. James Sweet, *Domingos Álvares, African Healing, and the Intellectual History of the Atlantic World* (Chapel Hill: University of North Carolina Press, 2011); Kristin Mann, *Slavery and the Birth of an African City: Lagos, 1760–1900* (Bloomington: Indiana University Press, 2007); Robin Law, *Ouidah: The Social History of a West African Slaving "Port," 1727–1892* (Athens: Ohio University Press, 2004); Rebecca Shumway, *The Fante and the Transatlantic Slave Trade* (Rochester, NY: University of Rochester Press, 2014).

17. Michael Pearson, *The Indian Ocean* (New York: Routledge, 2003), 258.

18. As recent as 2006, the American Historical Review Forum on "Oceans in History" excluded the Indian Ocean World as a topic of conversation, focusing exclusively on the more developed historiography of the Mediterranean, Atlantic, and Pacific. See *American Historical Review* 111, no. 3 (2006). Early Indian Ocean studies emphasized the subcontinent since in many ways it was the pivot around which other regions interacted in a much different way than in the Atlantic. For the origins of Indian Ocean historiography, see S. Arasaratnam, "Recent Trends in the Historiography of the Indian Ocean, 1500 to 1800," *Journal of World History* 1, no. 2 (Fall 1990): 225–48; Sebastian R. Prange, "Scholars and the Sea: A Historiography of the Indian Ocean," *History Compass* 6, no. 5 (2008): 1382–93.

19. See, for example, K. N. Chaudhuri, *Trade and Civilisation in the Indian Ocean: An Economic History from the Rise of Islam to 1750* (Cambridge: Cambridge University Press, 1985); Kenneth McPherson, *The Indian Ocean: A History of the People and the Sea* (New York: Oxford University Press, 1993); There were some early exceptions pushed mostly by nationalist historians from Indian Ocean islands. See, for instance, Auguste Toussaint, *History of the Indian Ocean*, trans. June Guicharnaud (London: Routledge & Kegan Paul, 1966).

20. Edward A. Alpers, "The Islands of Indian Ocean Africa," in *The Western Indian Ocean: Essay on Islands and Islanders*, ed. Shawkat M. Toorawa (Port Louis, Mauritius: The Hassam Tarawa Trust, 2007).

21. For John Middleton, the adoption of Islamic practice is the essential characteristic of Swahili identity, differentiating them from neighbors and linking them to Arab traders. John Middleton, *The World of the Swahili: An African Mercantile Civilization* (New Haven, CT: Yale University Press, 1994), 36–37.

22. See Tor Sellström, *Africa in the Indian Ocean: Islands in the Ebb and Flow* (Boston: Brill, 2015), 1–16; David C. Sperling, "The Coastal Hinterland and Interior of East Africa," in *History of Islam in Africa*, ed. Nehemia Levtzion and Randall L. Pouwels (Athens: Ohio University Press, 2000), 273–302; Alpers, "The Islands of Indian Ocean Africa."

23. See Alpers, *East Africa and the Indian Ocean*; Abdul Sherrif, *Dhow Cultures and the Indian Ocean: Cosmopolitanism, Commerce, and Islam* (New York: Oxford University Press, 2010).

24. M. N. Pearson, *Port Cities and Intruders: The Swahili Coast, India, and Portugal in the Early Modern Era* (Baltimore: Johns Hopkins University Press, 1998), chap. 2.

25. See Megan Vaughan, *Creating the Creole Island: Slavery in Eighteenth-Century Mauritius* (Durham, NC: Duke University Press, 2005); Jonathon Glassman, *War of Words, War of Stones: Racial Thought and Violence in Colonial Zanzibar* (Bloomington: University of Indiana Press, 2011); Ned Bertz, *Diaspora and Nation in the Indian Ocean: Transnational Histories of Race and Urban Space in Tanzania* (Honolulu: University of Hawai'i Press, 2015); Edward Simpson and Kai Kress, eds., *Struggling with History: Islam and Cosmopolitanism in the Western Indian Ocean* (New York: Columbia University Press, 2008); Abdul Sheriff et al., *Transition from Slavery in Zanzibar and Mauritius* (Dakar: CODESRIA, 2016).

26. J. R. McNeill, "The End of the Old Atlantic World: America, Africa, Europe, 1770–1888," in *Atlantic American Societies: From Columbus through Abolition, 1492–1888*, ed. Alan L. Karras and J. R. McNeill (London: Routledge, 1992), 246.

27. See, for example, Pearson, *The Indian Ocean*, chap. 5; Nigel Worden, "VOC Cape Town as an Indian Ocean Port," in *Cross Currents and Community Networks: The History of the Indian Ocean World*, ed. Himanshu Ray and Edward A. Alpers (Delhi: Oxford University Press, 2007), 142–62; Nigel Worden, ed., *Cape Town between East and West: Social Identities in a Dutch Colonial Town* (Johannesburg: Jacana, 2012).

28. Reed Ueda, "Pushing the Atlantic Envelope: Interoceanic Perspectives on Atlantic History," in *The Atlantic in Global History, 1500–2000*, ed. Jorge Cañizares-Esguerra and Erik R. Seeman (Upper Saddle River, NJ: Pearson-Prentice Hall, 2007), 163–74.

29. Grant McCall, "Nissology: A Proposal for Consideration," *Journal of The Pacific Society* 17, no. 2–3 (1994): 1–14; see also R. Gerard Ward, "South Pacific Island Futures: Paradise, Prosperity, or Pauperism," *The Contemporary Pacific* 5, no. 1 (1993): 20; Pete Hay, "A Phenomenology of Islands," *Island Studies Journal* 1, no. 1 (2006): 19–42. For some competing considerations on the common experiences of islands, see S. A. Royle, "A Human Geography of Islands," *Geography* 74, no. 2 (April 1989): 106–16; Philip Conkling "On Islanders and Islandness," *Geographical Review* 97, no. 2 (April 2007): 191–201; Godfrey Baldacchino, "The Coming of Age of Island Studies," *Tijdschrift voor economische en sociale geografie* 95, no. 3 (July 2004): 272–83; Godfrey Baldacchino, "Islands, Island Studies, Island Studies Journal," *Island Studies Journal* 1, no. 1 (2006): 3–18.

30. J. C. Heesterman. "Littoral et intérieur de l'Inde,"in *History and Underdevelopment: Essays on Underdevelopment and European Expansion in Asia and Africa*, ed. Rudolf von Albertini et al. (Leiden, Netherlands: Leiden Centre for the History of European Expansion, 1980), 87. See also Greg Dening, *Beach Crossings: Voyaging Across Times, Cultures, and Self* (Philadelphia: University of Pennsylvania Press, 2004), 16.

31. William Bissell, "Monsoon Metropolis: Migration, Mobility, and Mediation in the Western Indian Ocean," chap. 9 in this volume.

32. Rod Edmond and Vanessa Smith, eds., "Editors' Introduction," *Islands in History and Representation* (New York: Routledge, 2003), 2.

33. Dening, *Beach Crossings*, 16.

34. The following section attempts to draw transcontinental connections from the chapters in this volume, as well as historical works cited above. Except where specific quotes or numbers are cited, we have limited the use of notes to minimize clutter.

35. Edward A. Alpers, "Africa's Indian Ocean Islands, Near and Distant," chap. 8 in this volume.

36. Pearson makes the distinction in the Indian Ocean between settler regions (Australia, South Africa) where Europeans displaced indigenous inhabitants; plantation societies (Mauritius, Réunion) created by the importation of labor; and mixed areas (Zanzibar, the Comoros, Madagascar) where Europeans imported labor and ideas into areas where they largely ruled indigenous peoples. The idea of the plantation society is useful even in the context of islands like Cabo Verde, where the climate and environment hindered the growth of a true plantation system because there existed similar power relationships even if imported slaves eventually worked in ports or service industries as much as in agriculture. Pearson, *The Indian Ocean*, 223.

37. As anthropologist Derek Pardue notes, rather than becoming Creole, uninhabited islands like Cabo Verde and Mauritius were "were born as creole." Derek Pardue, "The Role of Creole History and Space in Cape Verdean Migration to Lisbon, Portugal," *Urban Anthropology and Studies of Cultural Systems and World Economic Development*, 42, no. 1/2 (2013): 98.

38. Hodges and Newitt, *São Tomé and Príncipe*, 26.

39. T. Bently Duncan, *Atlantic Islands: Madeira, the Azores, and the Cape Verdes in Seventeenth-Century Commerce and Navigation* (Chicago: University of Chicago Press, 1972), 23.

40. Chaudhuri, *Trade and Civilisation in the Indian Ocean*, 99.

41. Braudel, *The Mediterranean and the Mediterranean World*, 150.

42. Ross Dunn, *The Adventures of Ibn Battuta: A Muslim Traveler of the Fourteenth Century* (Berkeley: University of California Press, 2012), 116.

43. Marcus Franda, *The Seychelles: Unquiet Islands* (Boulder, CO: Westview Press, 1982), 7.

44. Hodges and Newitt, *São Tomé and Príncipe*, 49.

45. Even nominally European ships featured international crews, adding to the cosmopolitanism of Africa's islands.

46. See chap. 9.

47. See chap. 10.

48. Randrianja and Ellis, *Madagascar*, 6.

49. Hodges and Newitt, *São Tomé and Príncipe*, 17.

50. Auguste Toussaint, *History of Mauritius*, trans. W. E. F. Ward (London: Macmillan Education, 1977), 41.

51. Illustrating just how fluid identities can be, the island of Anjouan seceded from the Comoros in 1997 as part of an unsuccessful attempt to rejoin France alongside Mayotte, though it has since returned to the Comoros.

Part 1

Atlantic Ocean Islands

1

The Canaries to Africa

The Atlantic Strategy of "To Be or Not to Be"

Germán Santana Pérez

While the Canaries undoubtedly belong geographically to the African continent, and although their first settlers came from Africa, inhabitants have not always accepted this connection. From the Castilian conquest onward, the islands formed an eminently Atlantic territory that served as a bridge between Europe, America, and Africa. The intensity and consistency of relations with the latter continent were quite strong throughout the centuries. However, as a colonized territory, its capacity for decisions was limited and depended on the choices made outside of the archipelago, including conversations about relations with Africa.

The Canaries was always a territory that stood out in its relation with Africa and Africans, both north and south of the Sahara.[1] In comparison with the rest of Spain, its linkages with the continent of Africa have been undoubtedly the most regular. Various causes explain this fact. First, it is necessary to highlight the geographical position of the Canaries. The archipelago is situated on the African tectonic plate, only about sixty miles from the continent, while it is 680 miles from the closest point of Europe. Due to its political allegiance, the Canaries forms part of the European Union, which recognizes its ultraperipheral character; that is to say, it lies beyond the traditional frontiers of Europe itself.

In contrast, throughout its history, Canarian culture has reflected its tricontinental nature, mixing African, European, and American influences in different proportions depending on the historical moment under consideration. Because of its role as an intersection of routes, the Canaries developed as a crossing place obligatory for Spanish interests in Africa in addition to those of other European authorities and, more recently since the beginning of the twentieth century, world powers. The Canaries works as a gateway that opens in various directions, one that is permeable for comings and goings. Moreover, due to its special historical development, the regularity of contacts has been constant to the point where the development of life on the islands cannot be understood without this bond.

Along with the geographical position, there are other conditioning factors that limited the connections with the African continent. One of these is the development of the Canarian productive forces themselves and the productive model developed at each historic economic cycle. The islands based their productive model on the export of different raw materials concerning food (sugar, wine, bananas, tomatoes, etc.) or related with different industries situated off the islands (orchilla, saltwort, cochineal) along with the import of manufactured goods and other raw materials that met the demands of the Canarian people. This model conditioned the strength of the Canarian bourgeoisie and, of course, the development of its industry, making it clearly dependent on imports. Thus, this model created a situation in which the islands were not even able to cover the needs for employment of all the population, and people had to emigrate. This was a common factor until the Spanish Transition in the twentieth century. This reality, in addition to the weakness of the Canarian economy, conditioned relations with the rest of Africa, which did not prevent merchants from reaching any geographical location on the continent and making an effort to consolidate their position and compete at an advantage with other foreign powers.

The Castilian Crown accepted the existence in the islands of a tax regime that was relatively light with the object of favoring the repopulation of the islands. Its most characteristic feature was the absence of the *alcabala*, a tax imposed on sales. Islanders were liable to pay the *almojarifazgo* tax on exports and imports in the *realengo*, or royally controlled, islands.[2] In fact, Tenerife and La Palma enjoyed complete exemption from this tax until 1522. This same tax was initially paid at 3 percent until its value increased to 6 percent in 1528 and continued at this level until the Cádiz Courts.[3] Departures to America were also taxed, although at only 2.5 percent, and obviously only from those ports where permission was granted. The percentage was less than those of the *almojarifazgo* taxes, as in the origins of its implementation the idea was to stimulate commerce with the Indies. This level of 2.5 percent was raised to 3.5 percent in 1659 when a 1 percent tax was established. Similarly, arrivals were taxed at 5 percent.[4]

Furthermore, the survival for many years of a subject society after the conquest established a clear hierarchy that benefited the conquerors and new colonizers who arrived with capital. This was a very particular characteristic that became central to the economy and regulation of the colony. The colonial Canaries was a society in transition between Europe and America. In the words of Wallerstein, it would form part of the semi-periphery[5] and this position would condition its links with the rest of the continent of Africa. Thus, we must take into account that although the islands maintained regular and important connections with Africa, these were at the expense of the political decisions made outside the archipelago in order to develop them. Thus, a great part of the profits derived from these exchanges were used to cover deficits with Europe.

The Nearby North African Coast: A Reality Impossible to Hide

The first inhabitants of the islands came from the north of Africa. The Guanches, ancient Canarians, were of African origin. Although we do not know exactly when the first ones arrived, it is probable that it was around the sixth century BC.[6] After this, other population groups continued to arrive in a series of waves, which continued until the first century of the modern era. The islands developed a particular culture that survived in isolation for centuries. After the Castilian conquest in the fifteenth century, an important part of the indigenous population survived, around at least 40 percent, who mixed with the colonizers who settled on the islands (as one study of mitochondrial DNA has shown), whether these settlers were European, especially Spanish, or African.[7] Many in the local population were also sold as slaves in markets on the Spanish mainland.

The European discovery of the islands in the fourteenth century and subsequent conquest between 1402 and 1496 was part of the exploration and conquest of the African coasts, especially by the Portuguese and Castilians. At this time, the race for the domination of the Canaries was also the race for control of the route to Africa.[8] This struggle, concentrated between Castile and Portugal during the fifteenth century, effectively ended with the signing of the Treaty of Alcaçobas-Toledo from 1479 to 1480, in which the former renounced its leading position in the exploration of Sub-Saharan Africa. The discovery of America and the real possibilities of Iberian unity at the end of the fifteenth century reinforced this tendency.

Even though the conquest of the Canaries had not yet ended, the Castilians insisted on the occupation of territories between Cape Aguer and Cape Bojador, installing the factory tower of Santa Cruz de la Mar Pequeña in 1496. The governors of Gran Canaria, as direct representatives of the Crown, controlled commerce.[9] The islands already conquered by that point served as a base to continue with the conquest of the continent. It is important to note that by the end of the fifteenth century and the beginning of the sixteenth, the Canaries played the role of a platform for a possible Castilian conquest in the north of Africa as a way to continue the Reconquista, after the fall of Granada in 1492. Even at the end of the sixteenth century some people, such as the governor of Tenerife, Juan Álvarez de Fonseca, continued with the aim of occupying territories south of Morocco. He proposed in 1575 before the council of war to take the base of Cape Aguer, because it was a flourishing business in the distribution of Moroccan sugar. The city was "the key to these islands," according to Fonseca himself.[10] But other events demanded Castilian attention, including the discovery of America, the urgent needs of Carlos I in Europe, and conditions in North Africa—with the birth of the Saidí dynasty and where Castile had to respect the limits of Portuguese influence (the Kingdom of Fez for Portugal, the Kingdom of Tremecén for Castile). They would combine to destroy the dream of a Christian Mahgreb.

At the same time, a range of individuals organized incursions, known as *cavalcades*, to capture slaves and other merchandise. The conquerors of the islands formed these expeditions beginning in the fifteenth century, but so too did other Europeans who arrived after the conquest and even some of the conquered, such as the indigenous leader Maninidra, who would lose his life fighting alongside the Castilians in North Africa.[11] Although Felipe II prohibited *cavalcades* in 1572, the practice continued until the beginning of the seventeenth century.

Another function that the Canaries fulfilled historically, due to its close proximity and strategic position, was observing and informing the Crown of what was happening in Africa. In the north of the continent, the Inquisition of the islands acted as receiver of information on possible Berber attacks, military forces, internal political weaknesses, and the moral and religious behavior of the Canary slaves captured in this territory.[12] This function increased in the eighteenth century with the arrival of Muslims, who formally renounced their faith voluntarily and adopted Catholicism.[13] With respect to the Sub-Saharan region, the Canaries provided information about movements of arms, corsairs, and ships of potential enemies and competitors.[14] At the end of the fifteenth century and the beginning of the sixteenth, the African orientation of the Canaries was a reality.

Parallel to the *cavalcades*, another activity flourished in the islands throughout the centuries: fishing in the Canary and Saharan waters. Although it is true that Andalusians participated in this even before the time of the conquest of the island, it was the Canarians who in the end would achieve greater prominence. Although officially fishing was carried out between the limits of Cape Aguer and Cape Bojador, the reality adapted to the natural frontiers of the bank, that is to say from Cape Aguer to Cape Blanco.[15] Dozens of boats and hundreds of families based their livelihoods on fishing.

During the sixteenth century, the Canaries maintained regular commercial contacts with Moroccan ports, especially that of Santa Cruz de Berbería (Agadir) but also with Safi and Fedala. Canarian experts in sugar traveled to this area from the mid-sixteenth century, sharing their knowledge, collaborating in the production of Moroccan sugar, and establishing themselves in the area.[16] However, with the end of the *cavalcades*, commerce halted. Consequently, contacts remained, although primarily through European ships, which stopped over in Morocco where they loaded some of the merchandise and then went on to the Canaries. Nevertheless, a regular form of illegal traffic occurred in search of cereals, leather, wax, feathers, amber, dates, and cattle in exchange for wood and articles that originated in America.

Starting with its foundation in 1483, contacts began with the factory and the coast of Arguín. During the sixteenth century, encounters on the Mauritanian coast were regular and occurred mainly to obtain slaves, although they were not exempt from some episodes of piracy, which endangered agreements with Portugal "as they had no one to control them they could do what they wanted."[17] Beginning in the mid-sixteenth century, commerce, instead of piracy, began to take over, such as the interest in taking advantage of salt, supplying the base, and making the most of fishing resources. The subsequent Dutch, Brandenburg, and French occupations during the seventeenth and eighteenth centuries did not interrupt these contacts.[18] The Imraguens, who lived in the Bank of Arguín, developed fishing activity using boats and fishing techniques that were used by the Canarians in the seventeenth and eighteenth centuries and continued until the first decades of the twentieth century.[19] The influence of these contacts was so strong that the boats they used were called *canarias*, launches with lateen sails without a motor, which were ideal for shallow depths.

Pirate attacks on the islands and the assaults on merchants and fishermen in the Canaries were more frequent from the second half of the sixteenth century and continued until the first half of the nineteenth century. There was practically no year in which there was not some incident by the Berbers in Canarian waters in the sixteenth and seventeenth centuries, the time of greatest activity. Lanzarote and Fuerteventura, which were closest to the Saharan coast, were most affected by the "invasions," but in general the losses caused to Canarian boats were far higher than those of land attacks. Sale and Algiers stood out as the main centers from which these expeditions originated. Thousands of Canarians were captured and taken to North Africa, where they were sold as slaves or, in many cases, returned to the archipelago after paying a ransom.[20] These attacks were so important that they came to condition the mentality of the islanders, the military organization, and the defense of the archipelago.

Sub-Saharan Africa and Indispensable Economic and Social Support

At the end of the fifteenth century, the first Sub-Saharan slaves began to arrive through Portuguese traders and through the captures undertaken by the *cavalcades*. The islands needed forced repopulation due to the loss of people caused by the conquest and the fact that European contingents did not replace those lost in the same way. Moreover, the conquerors were not prepared to undertake work of such intensity. At the same time, from 1483, cultivation of sugar cane was introduced from Madeira, which dominated production in the sixteenth century. Sugar, although it was cultivated on smaller properties and demanded a more diverse manpower than in America, also needed a lot of slave labor. The proportion of slaves never came to be dominant in the Canaries, but the islands held the highest percentages of slaves in all of Spain. In the main ports of the islands, the number of slaves reached around 15 percent, and in islands like Lanzarote this threshold even went beyond 20 percent.[21] Although scholars estimate that 10,000 slaves came to Gran Canaria alone in the sixteenth century,[22] I believe that this figure is very high for the island and that it is possible that this is the number of slaves that arrived in the whole archipelago in the sixteenth century. Similarly, I believe that until the middle of the seventeenth century another 5,000 slaves may have been brought over. Historians Torres Santana and Santana Perez have investigated the reigns of Philip III and Philip IV to demonstrate that in the eastern Canary Islands alone, more than 3,000 slaves were sold in the first fifty years of the seventeenth century.[23] We must add slaves sold on islands such as La Palma and Tenerife, where most of the slave population resided, to that number.

At the end of the fifteenth century, the islands acted as a jumping-off point for various events in Sub-Saharan Africa. Juan and Pedro de Lugo, from Seville, began the exploitation of orchilla in the islands of Cabo Verde, using the experience they had previously utilized in the Canaries.[24] In 1466, the inhabitants of the island of Santiago, among other places, were excused payment of the tithe in exchanges with the Canaries, which spoke of the interest in encouraging relations between the two archipelagos. At the beginning of the reign of the Catholic kings, various expeditions set out from the Canaries to Guinea. Similarly, on the coast of the islands, shells existed in relative abundance, and Castilian merchants took advantage of this and sold the shells to the Portuguese, who then sent them south, from Guinea to Elmina. The merchants, in turn, paid a portion of the proceeds as "standing rent" to the feudal owner of the islands. Finally, the monarchy established a monopoly on the sale of shells in 1497.[25]

The strategic role of the Canaries was a key part of securing the supply of slaves for transport to America. The islands formed part of the base ports (along with Lisbon, Seville, Sanlúcar and Cádiz) from which ships could set off to buy slaves in Africa and then head for Spanish America. Ships that sailed from other ports were only allowed to stop off in the islands before continuing for African factories.[26] A smaller number of slaves also left for the Indies as contraband. The islands, moreover, proved an exception in the monopoly of Seville and Cádiz to trade with America and enjoyed permission for a limited number of tons (between 300 and 1,000, as long as they were Canarian articles). Moreover, from 1659, registered ships could make the return journey directly to the archipelago. Many individuals took advantage of the connection between the Canaries, Africa, and America to travel to the Indies and at the same time carry contraband goods.[27] Authorities installed officials of the Casa de Contratación in the islands in an attempt to control all of this traffic. Furthermore, slavery allowed municipal governments to finance (or attempt to finance) many expensive works, including the walls of the city of Las Palmas, port buildings in Santa Cruz de La Palma, and fortifications in La Gomera.

The need for slaves made trade with Sub-Saharan Africa increasingly profitable. The colony of Portuguese based in the islands, in particular those from Madeira, opened the doors to African markets. The Treaty of Alcaçobas-Toledo prohibited the access of Castilians to areas south of Cape Bojador unless permission was requested from the Portuguese king. Cabo Verde enjoyed an exemption and the monarchy did not require special dispensation to trade with the Canary Islands. Also, merchants from other places such as England considered the islands a convenient place to stop over and set off for the African coast.[28] Canarian ships arrived fairly regularly in the first three-quarters of the sixteenth century, both legally and illegally, and became much more frequent after the Iberian union. For example, the greater portion of the ships that arrived at the island of Santiago in the first decades of the seventeenth century came from the Canaries.[29] Canarian ships regularly visited places like Cabo Verde, Ríos de Guinea, Sierra Leona, Magarobomba (Liberia), Elmina, São Tomé, and Angola.[30] Angola, despite its distance, played a growing role in Canarian slave interests to the point that it became the main destination of Canarian ships in the decades prior to Portuguese independence. In a letter to the Council of the Tax Office in January 1630, Fernando de Sousa maintained that many ships from Seville and the Canaries habitually came to the port of Luanda carrying wine and other products, "on which depended the support of this kingdom, so that if we had to prohibit the entrance of ships from Seville and from the Canaries this land would suffer a great lack of necessities to the extent that it could probably not be maintained."[31]

The Canary Islands exported primarily wine, vinegar, liquor, tar, preserves, dried fruits, stones for purified water, textile manufacturers, iron, and glass. However, wine dominated as the main export. Between 1610 and 1620, scholars calculate that the islands exported an annual average of 20,000 casks, or 2,641,720 gallons of wine, carried by Portuguese traders from the Canaries to Brazil and Angola, although such a high number is unlikely.[32] Even if only 1 percent of this wine had remained in Luanda, which is an extremely conservative estimate, it would mean that at least 26,417 gallons arrived annually at this single port.[33] In exchange they primarily received slaves, but also other products, including sugar, ivory, leathers, wax, salt, and cattle from Cabo Verde.

Like elsewhere, animal and botanical exchanges were constant throughout the history of this region.[34] Cultivations as significant as the banana or the yam had arrived on the islands by the end of the fifteenth century.[35] Camels were introduced to the Canary Islands from the Iberian peninsula, but also from the south of Morocco and from the Spanish Sahara by Castilian conquerors and those who carried out assaults on the neighboring African coast. At the end of the eighteenth century, the Botanical Garden of Acclimatisation of La Orotava in Tenerife was established and became the second botanical garden in Spain. Similar to its namesake in Madrid, it included primarily American plants, but also provided a small space for the sowing of seeds and plants from Africa. The Portuguese government was very active in the first half of the nineteenth century through its consulate in the Canaries by transporting plants to the islands of Cabo Verde. Similarly, the Portuguese also took camels to Angola in the same period.[36] Carlos Gallardo points out how Guinea Conakry imported a variety of banana initially called *Musa sinensis* and later called *Cavendish enano* in 1899 from the Canaries, and that in the middle of the twentieth century he himself sent 50,000 pineapple plants of the Cayenne variety through the Society Intercasa to his brother José Luis, through the port of Conakry, destined for greenhouses in the south of Gran Canaria.[37]

Both before and after Portuguese independence, the rupture of the monopoly of exclusivity of the Spanish Crown in Africa challenged the

Canarian presence in the continent and in the long term necessitated a restructuring of Canarian interests in the region. These events, along with the prohibition of continued trading with the Berbers in the seventeenth century, clearly conditioned the African orientation of the Canaries. The occupation of settlements mainly by the Dutch, English, and French, and their growing pirate activity against Spanish ships, increased the risk of the commerce of slaves. The 1640s and 1650s were very unstable as the Portuguese colonies in Africa accepted the fidelity of the House of Braganza. The Portuguese confiscated various ships sailing from the Canaries. Despite this, ships continued to set sail from the Canaries during this tumultuous period. Canarian ships took advantage of Ríos de Guinea[38] as a space of special activity, as Portuguese control was fairly limited and it was relatively close to the islands. Moreover, the Dutch stood out in the supply of slaves to the archipelago in the decades of the 1640s and 1650s.[39] Contraband merchandise also reached the islands of Cabo Verde. Thus, for example, in 1661 the ship *San Juan Bautista* from La Palma reached the island of Santiago. The ship carried wine, iron, tar, some money, and many silks, which found markets with people eager to supply slaves, who were then transported to the Indies. To solve the problem of the prohibition, the ship stopped at Praia instead of Ribeira Grande (with the connivance of the authorities), where the ship and its captain, Joao Salazar, brought and sold the merchandise without difficulty. Similarly, this allowed the ship to avoid the port customs controller and correspondent taxes.[40]

The mid-seventeenth century featured major changes that drastically altered the role of the Canaries in the Atlantic World, largely due to the peace treaty between Holland, England, and France and the recognition of Portuguese independence. Ships continued to set off for African destinations, but the role of the Canaries as a stopping-over port for European ships became increasingly important on their way to their settlements and factories, many of them taking on board provisions of Canarian products like wine. From at least 1685, various French ships participated in this practice in exchange for black slaves, wax, and other articles from the African coast. A report by Michel J. La Courbe for the Compagnie Royale du Sénégal et Coste d'Afrique, discussed these commercial activities in 1685.[41] The French traveler Bory de Saint-Vincent viewed this business as highly positive because "whatever the colonial system that is adopted, it would be easy to look for manpower for cultivation, without a long journey which causes sickness and loss of Negroes."[42]

While this trend in trade sacrificed the export of island products to Africa to a great extent, the Canaries consolidated its role in international commerce in the following centuries—at least until the establishment of new Spanish colonies in Africa—with the exception of certain nearby and relatively marginal territories where the Canarians continued to participate. Cabo Verde was one of the aforementioned exceptions,[43] but, nevertheless, the Canarian presence was increasingly weakened both there and especially in the rest of the continent. While commerce varied significantly over space and time, it is evident that trade relied less on the traffic of slaves and more on other articles, such as cattle, leather, and cereals. The problems in the supply of slaves in Cabo Verde in favor of Ríos de Guinea and the reduction of the slave demand in the Canaries provide an explanation for this change of direction. These commercial contacts reduced profits in contrast to the sixteenth and early seventeenth centuries, but they continued to be regular with direct Canarian participation. In a royal seal from May 1690, Portuguese authorities still commanded that no ship from Castile or the Canary Islands could negotiate directly with Ríos de Guinea, on pain of losing the load.[44]

Another complementary market—South Africa and the Indian Ocean islands of Réunion and Mauritius—opened in the mid-seventeenth century. This provided the French and the Dutch with the opportunity to take advantage of stopovers in the Canaries to procure certain merchandise. Although it was a smaller market than others, this newer European demand from southern Africa and the Indian Ocean World represented how far Canarian trading had come from the second half of the seventeenth century until the beginning of the nineteenth century.

The Dilemma of "Africanness" in the Eighteenth Century

Canarian interests in the eighteenth century reflected the dominant commercial trends of the era, including the reduction of African markets (except Cabo Verde), the increased role of stopover ports, and reduced participation in the slave trade. We must remember that French and British companies handled the transport of slaves to Spanish America until 1750, which limited any other Spanish interest. Despite its proximity to Africa, Canarian interests in the continent were reduced to a minimum. On the one hand, Spain continued to ban trade with Morocco. On the other hand, the Spanish Crown mortgaged almost all its hopes on monopolizing the supply of slaves to America and establishing its own colonies in Africa, only to relinquish that monopoly to the British in the Utrecht Treaty. Furthermore, the demand for slaves decreased drastically in the Canarian archipelago during this period. Nevertheless, the supply of foreign ships traveling through the islands maintained commercial exchanges.

Commercial activity entailed the export of a small number of tons, commerce with limited profits with Cabo Verde, occasional exchanges with Saharan and Mauritanian coasts, fishing on the Berber coast and in the Canarian-Saharan fishing banks, and pirate activity by the Spanish in Africa in periods of wartime conflicts.[45]

However, the crisis in the export of wine in the Canaries, the main production of the archipelago in the eighteenth century, gave the weak Canarian bourgeoisie hope of recovering former splendors and supported any initiative that attempted to encourage commerce with Africa, from both within the Canaries and from Spain. It is noticeable how, precisely at this moment, part of the controlling class reclaimed the "Africanness" of the islands so that the possibility of exporting wine freely to England could potentially open up again after it was largely closed as a result of the Navigation Acts instituted in 1651. Thus, the Spanish ambassador in London received many requests that he should gain a declaration of the British government to this end.[46] In 1720, Antonio de la Rosa, consul in London, in a letter to the Marquis of Grimaldo, affirmed still that the British Crown had no right to confiscate the fruits of the Canaries in its colonies since this act only extended to fruit and wine from Europe, while the Canaries was on the African coast. According to de la Rosa, British merchants who traded with the island supported this measure.[47] In 1721, D. Jacinto de Pozobueno insisted in his correspondence in improving the possibility with the British court of the trading of wine and dessert wine from the Canaries in English colonies and plantations without having to pay more taxes than those applicable in the islands of the Azores or Madeira.[48]

After the signing of the Treaty of Aachen (1748), relations with Great Britain were reestablished and the subject returned to the agenda of Canarian hopes and Spanish diplomacy. The jurisdiction of the Canaries became a critical point of contention as individuals debated whether the Canary Islands were an African or American territory. In June 1749, Ricardo Wal proposed that the Canaries should be considered part of Africa. However, in December 1749, D. José de Carvajal y Lancaster, in a letter to Ricardo Wal, indicated that it would be suitable for the islands to be declared part of America and not of Europe so that their wines could be transported directly to English colonies without passing through English ports.[49]

After the signing of the commercial treaty between Spain and Morocco in 1766, trade began to flow again with the Canaries too, both controlled by the Spanish and other Europeans. Although the Canaries maintained contacts with various ports, trade relations with Mogador (Essaouira) had the greatest intensity. The main imports were cereals in grain and flour, in an attempt to cover the structural deficit of food that the Canaries suffered at the end of the eighteenth century.[50] In exchange, the islands could offer little to the Alawite Kingdom so American silver largely covered the sales. Trade developed so far during the reign of Muhammad III that Mogador became one of the main foreign imports for the Canaries in the final decades of the eighteenth century. The death of the monarch, Moroccan political instability, territorial disputes with Spain, and competition from American cereals destroyed the positive trading relationship by the end of the eighteenth and the beginning of the nineteenth century.

During the eighteenth century, fishing continued along with regular dealings with people on the Saharan coast. George Glas, a British agent, commented that, despite the prohibitions, Canarian fishermen carried out small exchanges with the "Moors" on the coast, giving "to the inhabitants of the desert old leathers, which the latter unraveled and then made into threads or bramantes to make fishing nets; they also gave them bread, onions, potatoes and different kinds of fruits in exchange for which the Moors let them collect water and wood on their coast whenever they needed these essential products and gave them presents of ostrich eggs and feathers."[51] In a similar vein, Álvarez Rixo indicated that at the end of the eighteenth and the beginning of the nineteenth centuries, "sailors came ashore at a place they called 'los Garitos' which were south of Guader(a) [*sic*] Santa Cruz de Mar Pequeña, to Cabo Blanco, and gave the Berbers hooks, thread, *gofio* (Canarian flour), tobacco, old shirts, receiving in exchange wax, honey, tallow, skins, animals, wool and Orchilla."[52]

On the other hand, Spain—mainly due to the pressure of the Cuban demand for slaves—decided finally to establish itself in Sub-Saharan Africa in a permanent way. In 1778, Spain signed the Treaty of San Ildefonso-El Pardo with Portugal, for which it obtained the territories of Fernando Pó, Annobón, and the adjacent continental coast. Although the first expedition, led by the count of Argelejo, set off from Montevideo to take possession of the territory, subsequent ships and expeditions set off from the Canaries under the supervision of Bartolomé Casabuena y Guerra, the Indies judge in Tenerife.[53] The Spanish abandoned the first occupation of Equatorial Guinea after a few years, but it relaunched the role of the Canaries for other Spanish attempts at occupation of territories both in the North and in Sub-Saharan Africa. At the end of the eighteenth century, Spanish slave traders began to replace the British, French, and Dutch gradually in supplying Atlantic slaves, particularly to Cuba, and especially after 1789, with the declaration of the freedom of trade in the supply of slaves with Spanish America. Canarians also participated in the slave trade at the end of the eighteenth century and during the nineteenth century.

The Canary Islands played a role for most of the eighteenth century as Bourbon projects to encourage commerce with Africa or to establish new factories in the area grew. An example was that which Floridablanca gave to the Marqués de Branciforte, general captain of the Canaries, who was told to provide information about the possibility of slave trading with the West African coast. The Spanish government weighed various advantages, such as the argument that the islands were sufficiently populated and loyal to Spain, which would provide infrastructure for the undertaking. Similarly, the Spanish authorities argued that they did not need large movements because of the geographical situation, and the possibilities of Canarian meteorology for the acclimatization both of Europeans and enslaved Africans before being moved to a much further destination, which would reduce the number of deaths caused by sickness and increase profits.[54]

The Spanish Crown's growing interest in the East increased prominence and scale of the islands in the Atlantic World. The ships of the Philippines Company, which sometimes called at African territories, could also use the ports of the Canary Islands to take refuge in them. This happened in the attack on Horatio Nelson in Tenerife in July 1797, in which one of the partial objectives was to capture the riches held by ships that came from Asia or Africa and found refuge in this port in the face of the unstable situation caused by the British blockade of Cádiz. The year of 1797 saw the arrival of the frigate *Príncipe Fernando*, whose captain was Juan Ignacio de Odria, and the frigate *Princesa*, whose captain was Fernando Méndez de Miranda, the former of which came from the island of Mauritius and the latter from the Philippines. In fact, an intrepid assault by the English on March 18, 1797, captured the *Príncipe Fernando* in the port of Santa Cruz de Tenerife itself, and its cargo was worth 400,000 pesos.[55]

The Canaries and the New Process of Imperialism

The nineteenth century began with the struggle for the abolition of slavery and the objections of Portugal, Brazil, and Spain to carrying out the prohibition at the same speed, especially when their capitalist strengths were so much weaker than the rest of western Europe or the United States of America. In 1817, Great Britain pressured Spain to sign a treaty for the abolition of slaves, in which England would control the fulfillment of the pact. The agreement was to create two mixed commissions to decide on the cases that arose. One was established in Sierra Leone, although world powers seriously considered holding it in the Canaries,[56] while Havana became the base for the second commission. Despite all this, the slave trade continued both legally and illegally. The archipelago played its role. In the mid-nineteenth century, a Spanish slave trader called Don Crespo gained a certain notoriety when, although expelled from Gallinas in 1849, he returned in 1852 to continue with the trade under the protection of Harry Tucker in Shebar. Nevertheless, antislavery pressures caught up with him in Gran Canaria.[57] Both the American and British authorities repeatedly denounced continued arrivals of slave ships in the archipelago in the first half of the century.[58]

Neighbors from the north continued arriving at the islands too, heading onto their African colonies established initially on the coast, trading for palm oil to use in soaps and for lubrication. Once more, there were missions and exploration travels, encouraged now by geographical societies. This first phase of imperialism offered sufficient previous knowledge so that occupation of the continent became possible. At this time, the Canaries became important for an aspect that was known in previous periods, but now became clearer: the acclimatization of people, plants, and animals. It was understood that the climate of the islands, with temperatures that were more tropical, was close to what would be found in the continent, and therefore the risk of contracting disease was less. Some of the most famous explorers of Africa spent long periods on the islands to prepare for their future journeys, including Guillemard de Aragón in 1845, the expedition of Carlos Chacón in 1858, José Muñoz Gaviria in 1860, Manuel Iradier in 1874–75, and Richard F. Burton.[59] This custom was not new, for at least since the seventeenth century, Capuchin missionaries took advantage of their stopovers in the island to stay for longer or shorter periods before setting off to the African continent.[60]

During the nineteenth century, the Canaries benefited economically from the extension of European colonialism in Africa. Mainly the British, but also the French and the Germans, invested in the main productive sectors of the islands: in the port, in agriculture for export, and in tourism. They first participated in the production and commercialization of cochineal, and then bananas, tomatoes, and potatoes. In the main cities of the islands, foreign houses were established along with coal warehouses to supply steamships that headed south. The declaration of free ports in 1852 and the construction of the ports of La Luz, Las Palmas, and Santa Cruz de Tenerife strengthened the role of the Canaries as an African stopover point. Moreover, on the return journey European ships also landed to take on board agricultural products that were later sold in the ships' countries of origin. If this were not enough, at this time, the second half of the nineteenth century coincided with Spain's definitive occupation of Equatorial Guinea and the recognition of a possible settlement in the Sahara and the south of Morocco. Spain recognized Guinea as a territory of expansion for Canarian colonial interests, but the Sahara represented above all a hinterland that provided security to the islands and Canarian fishermen, keeping it apart from foreign interests.

In April 1860, thanks to the agreements of Tetuan, Spain received sufficient territory near Santa Cruz de la Mar Pequeña for the establishment of a fishing industry. Spain recognized that Spanish Sahara was desolate; however, it was an essential territory to support Canarian fisheries, and also to increase the security of the archipelago and as prestige territory within the process of imperialism, which Spain was also involved in, although only in marginal regions. Between 1860 and 1874, Canarians launched the first of the efforts to open up commerce in the area between Cape Nun and Cape Blanco.[61] In 1881, the Society of Canarian African Fishing encouraged the purchase of the peninsula of Río del Oro, where a factory opened with the support of the Africanist Society, in addition to Cape Blanco and the Bay of Cintra at the same time as expeditions traveled to explore the interior.[62] It was Canarian Fernando León y Castillo, of the Liberal Party and main representative of the dominant Canarian groups, who negotiated with France the limits of Spanish colonies in Africa, receiving in recompense the title of the Marquis of Muni. Although the coast of Sahara was obtained through the agreements of Paris in 1900, the territories in the south and north of Morocco and the small space of Equatorial Guinea—areas of great economic importance—were excluded. Spanish control passed to France, and there was a notable reduction in Spanish interest in Equatorial Guinea. The Spanish-French treaty of 1912 reduced the dimensions of Spanish territory in the north of Africa even further.

The occupation of the Saharan enclaves was very slow and it was not until the 1920s that Spain occupied Cape Juby, La Güera, and Ifni. With the beginning of the military coup of 1936, Villa Cisneros and to a lesser extent La Güera were turned into prisons for Canarians loyal to the Republic. In 1937, these deportees, with the connivance of the soldiers who were guarding them, managed to escape in the *Viera y Clavijo* mailboat to Dakar, and similar actions began among soldiers of La Güera. Immediately, new Canarian detachments arrived to control the security of the area and prevent future escapes.[63]

Under the protection of the second colonization of Equatorial Guinea, coinciding with the widespread adoption of quinine as the drug of choice for preventing malaria and a new phase of European imperialism, some Canarians began to colonize this space.[64] In 1856, Casimiro Rufino Ruiz, a member of the Matritense Economic Society, presented a project to the Constitutional Courts, which, among other ideas, presented the case for the transfer of orphans and sentenced criminals from fourteen to forty years of age from the Canaries to Corisco.[65] After the failure of population growth in Fernando Pó using Cuban deportees, future deportees were ordered to be sent to the Canaries.[66] Both Spanish and foreign transports heading to Fernando Pó stopped off in the Canary Islands. Barcelona Transatlantic Company's 1887 inauguration of the line that united Barcelona with Guinea by way of the Canaries consolidated the role of the archipelago as a major transit point. The Canarian ports supplied merchandise for Guinean territories through both Canarian products and reexported goods. The colonial apparatus guaranteed that the islands would play an essential role in the supply of the colonial administration. The archipelago sent food, medicine, equipment, and materials to the colonial administration. By the royal order of July 26, 1884, the administration ordered that payments for services provided should be sent directly from the Canarian marine commander to the governor general of Fernando Pó, who was then responsible for payments.[67] Various Canarians presented projects for the economic exploitation of Guinea at the end of the nineteenth century.[68] Moreover, in 1902 the law courts of Santa Isabel, with jurisdiction over all Spanish territories from the Gulf of Guinea, became dependent on the Law Court of Las Palmas. At the beginning of the twentieth century, the Great Regional Lodge of the Canaries included in its Masonic jurisdiction the Canarian Archipelago, the west coast of Africa, and the Spanish possessions in the Gulf of Guinea.[69]

Canarians emigrated primarily to Equatorial Guinea and the Sahara, but also to other territories in West Africa, including Senegal, Guinea Conakry, Sierra Leone, and Liberia. Although most of them went in search of better economic conditions, a small group emigrated for political motives, especially after the military coup of 1936 and the subsequent repression. It is important to emphasize the high proportion of women who chose to emigrate, although they were still a minority. In general, the people who migrated were largely unskilled, many coming from the Canarian countryside. These immigrants dedicated themselves to various tasks in new lands, both in rural and urban areas, and worked in settings that they would not have likely experienced previously, such as cocoa or coffee plantations.[70] Moreover, they contributed with their labor and with the acceptance of the system of economic and social exploitation to support the colonial apparatus both of Spain and of other European powers. Texts by Agustín Miranda, a Canarian who traveled to Equatorial Guinea between 1937 and 1939, exemplify the colonial mentality of the period: "to civilise the Negro is, then, in the most literal meaning of the word, to free him. To free him from the world in which he lives to transport him to a world of light and hope, and ordered and stable world, ruled by reason."[71] When independence came to these countries, most of these colonists left hurriedly and returned to the Canary Islands. Despite a good quality of life in Africa, only a few managed to accumulate considerable wealth and invest in the productive sectors of the island that were growing in the 1960s and 1970s.

The Canaries experienced growth in economic relations with Spanish colonies in addition to the rest of Africa in the second half of the nineteenth century. Canarian exports to Africa, especially West Africa, increased considerably as the Canaries exported wine, rum, aniseed, cork, filter stones, oil, paper, rice, salt fish, almonds, market products, tobacco, paving stones, potatoes, onions, and other fruits and vegetables.[72] English, French, and German shipping lines often stopped in the Canaries in their travels between the metropole and their respective colonies.[73]

The value of import trade from Fernando Pó to Las Palmas de Gran Canaria in 1893 was 1,100 pesetas, which represented less than 0.1 percent of all trade. Similarly, trade between the Canaries and the west coast of Africa, which included the fishing industry, accounted for 106,488 pesetas, corresponding to 1.1 percent of the total value of trade. With respect to exports, they reached a value of 323,327 pesetas for the west coast, which represented 3.8 percent. Most export transactions consisted of petrol, potatoes, and strong liquor, stones for construction, fish, cereals, flour, vegetables, onions, tomatoes, nuts, bananas, other fruits, wine, tobacco, and other articles. The value of exports to Fernando Pó was 56,374 pesetas, or 0.7 percent of the total.[74]

As the twentieth century advanced, some African agrarian producers began to compete with their Canarian counterparts. The export of African bananas from British and French colonies, in addition to Equatorial Guinea itself, created fear among local island producers in the Canaries. Alarm triggered action by the Regional Confederation of the Banana (CREP) and the civil governor of Las Palmas, who requested by telegraph the banning of the cultivation of the banana in Guinea in 1957 due to the arrival in Barcelona of bananas from Equatorial Guinea. As a consequence, the civil governor of Fernando Pó defended the interests of the Equatorial Guineans and wrote: "Like the Canarian region, not half of the bananas that will be consumed in the Spanish mainland at the remunerative price, if there was organization, there is sufficient room in the capitals for the four ananas of Guinea; and any complaint about this is unfounded and baseless."[75] A February 1957 issue of the Barcelona newspaper *Avanzada* contained a criticism of the competition of bananas from Equatorial Guinea for the unfair conditions of labor: "While the workers in the Canaries are in practice associated with the Company in a social regime which is very advanced and in accordance with the Christian principles of the Movement, the workers in Guinea do not receive a single advantage of our social provision."[76] The press also noted the fact that Canarians could send bananas to South Africa in periods of low production in that country, and for this reason the commission of the Banana Control Board went to Gran Canaria and Tenerife in the company of Don Esteban Arriaga, director of Incoinsa, and Don Jorge Coll, director of the General Society of Industry and Markets. The commission visited companies that used modern packing machinery and maintained conversations with the presidents of the CREP.[77]

During the first quarter of the twentieth century, Canarian ports also had to compete with other African ports as stopovers for supplying fuel. Some foreign shipping companies even moved from the Canaries to other ports, including Mindelo, Dakar, and Funchal to carry out their activities. Nevertheless, strong competition between the ports of La Luz (Gran Canaria) and of Santa Cruz (Tenerife) continued.

The fishing industry continued to be an important part of the basic sectors of the island economy during the twentieth century. The Canaries consistently exported fish to Africa throughout the century. A 1930 Chamber of Commerce record from Las Palmas stated that a majority of dried and conserved fish exported through the ports of La Luz and Las Palmas was channeled through African territories. More specifically, 1,454,226 pounds, or 29.6 percent of the total exports of this sector, went to Spanish possessions in Africa, while 3,009,574 pounds (61.4 percent of sector exports) went to English colonies, and 33,069 pounds (0.7 percent of sector exports) went to French colonies.[78]

Since the 1920s, the Canaries also served as an aeronautical stopover for communications with the rest of Africa. In 1922, the Fairey XV *Lusitania* hydroplane landed in the port of La Luz on the way to Cabo Verde. The stopover was the first transoceanic link with the islands.

The *Plus Ultra* arrived in Gando from Palos de Moguer on the way to Praia in 1926. Similarly, the Canaries served as one of the first air connections with Senegal. The commission of the Lignes Aeriennes Latecoére visited Gando in 1923 to study the opening of the section between Las Palmas and Cape Juby on the route from Toulouse to Dakar. One of the first planes on this route landed in Gran Canaria and Tenerife in 1924. Furthermore, the Breguet XIX of Commander Barnard landed in Gando on the Paris-Madagascar route in 1926. The role of the Canaries as an aeronautical stopover increased beginning in the 1930s with the construction of permanent airports in Tenerife and Gran Canaria. Beginning in 1930, Germans began the Seville-Bathurst, Gambia route, with stops in Gandi, Villa Cisneros, Fort Etienne, Saint Louis and Dakar for JU-52 planes.[79] The Canaries was also an obligatory stopover when the connection between Equatorial Guinea and Iberia began in the 1940s. During the same time period, there were regular flights from Luanda to London with South African Airways (SAA), Madrid to Monrovia with KLM, and Bordeaux to Dakar with Air France. Similarly, chartered flight companies operated in the region, including Spantax, which served routes from London to Bata and Santa Isabel to London. SAA also operated with connections in South Africa. Despite many possibilities of air links with these territories,[80] large-scale connections never materialized in the Canaries largely because decisions about connections favored centralization in Madrid.

The 1960s was an exciting era as the moment of independence arrived in many places throughout Africa. Equatorial Guinea gained independence in 1968, and Spain turned over Spanish Sahara to Morocco and Mauritania in 1975. The end of the Spanish dictatorship and the withdrawal of Spain from Sahara in 1975 meant the end of an era and the birth of new relations with Africa in the following decades. Canarians, in addition to Saharawis and Equatorial Guineans, went to the archipelago from Guinea and Spanish Sahara after Spain ceded control over these spaces. After the return, many of these former colonists continued to maintain friendship networks created through periodic meetings. Above all, they missed the land where they had lived, which some would never see again. Some of these people went on to publish their memories and experiences.[81]

The Canarian independence movement is clearly associated with African independence processes, especially Algeria, or the yet to be concluded process in Western Sahara. Antonio Cubillo, the leader of the Movement for the Independence and Self-Determination of the Canaries Archipelago (MPAIAC), advocated for recognition from the Organization of African Unity (OAU). The Canary Islands Independence Movement received recognition in a solemn declaration by the OAU during its sixth meeting of the heads of state on July 20, 1968. A decade later, the OAU agreed that the General Assembly of the United Nations should discuss the colonial problem of the Canaries. Following celebrations of independence sweeping throughout Africa, traditional links to imperialism collapsed and the relationship between the Canaries and Spain desperately needed to change. Transitions began as African emigration to Europe, possibilities of increased investment, and cooperation and the development of business with Africa became major concerns for Canarians and Spain.

From Oblivion to the Reclaiming of "Africanness"

The Canaries suffered after the 1960s, partially because of a constant loss of power in relation to Africa. The withdrawal from Equatorial Guinea and Western Sahara created lethargy in Canarian relations with these territories. Various agreements between Spain and the European Union and Morocco imposed restrictions on fishing on the Saharan bank from the 1970s to the 1990s, which made it practically impossible for Canarians to fish in waters in which they had previously fished for more than five centuries. Furthermore, Spain joining the European Economic Community and the reactivation of the tourist sector, along with an improvement in the standard of living and the arrival of democracy, drastically influenced politics and society in the Canaries. At this time, with the regime of ultraperipheral region within the European Community and later the European Union, the islands became unequivocally European, and this sentiment became instilled in the population and its institutions. The Spanish nature of the islands was reaffirmed along with its European nature, which Spanish colonization through a growing number of settlers from the mainland ultimately supported. It was, and still is to some extent, the southern frontier of Europe. At the same time, small boats from economically disadvantaged areas of the continent began arriving in the archipelago. Many in the Canaries perceived Africa as impoverished, while they saw the Canaries as exempt from such a standing as they were on the road to riches of the Europeans.

In the last decade of the twentieth century, interest in Africa gradually increased. One must contextualize this within the economic landscape of the Canaries as the Canarian economy continued to show little diversification, with levels of unemployment, inequality, and poverty that were the highest in the entire country. Moreover, from the early 2000s, the Canaries exhibited symptoms of stagnation in the tourist industry, which added to the general economic crisis that began in 2008. The government of the Canaries (which has a general director of relations with Africa) and the Chambers of Commerce in the Canaries currently understand the promise of strengthened economic relations with Africa, especially geographically close countries like Morocco, Mauritania, Senegal, the Gambia, and Cabo Verde. Ideally, small dimensions of Canarian companies could be competitive, and little by little exports have displayed continued growth. Similarly, China and US interests in the archipelago reflect the potential of the Canaries serving as a platform for their business on the African continent. The International Red Cross and the United Nations (World Food Programme) use the port of La Luz and Las Palmas as a huge warehouse and logistic base for redistribution in Africa. Similarly, Canarian nationalism highlights the role of the Republic of Cabo Verde as something that could be imitated in a hypothetical independence in which the dominant island class controls internal resources to a greater extent against decisions from Madrid. Canarian companies, both air- and sea-based, became international in the immediate African hinterland, apparently improving communications. Canarian companies began following the same trajectory, almost always within the food sector.

The problem of migration and the growing Western fear of an expansion of radical Islam reinforced the role of the Canaries as controller and observer of what is happening on the continent. Frontex, the European agency for the control of external borders, received notable investments in personnel and detection apparatus. In fact, the strategic importance of the islands from a military point of view or in terms of control of possible epidemics increased in the last decade. The founding of Casa África in 2006 was a notable event in African relations as the institution, based in Las Palmas de Gran Canaria, reflects the growing interest in everything African and seeks to encourage relations between Africa, Europe, and Spain. The possible discovery of oil in Canarian waters represents another challenge to the Canaries' capability of making its own decisions about its resources and also its relationship with Africa. In fact, those supporting drilling for oil argue that it should be done in waters off the Canaries because it is already being done on the Moroccan side. The reclaiming of this part of the African identity grows every day, according to Canarian interests, and we see once more the Atlantic strategy of "to be or not to be."

Concluding Thoughts on the Making of the Canaries

The history of the Canaries provides an important dialogue about the connections between global processes and the movement of peoples, commodities, and ideas. Furthermore, political and economic changes challenged the role of the Canary Islands locally and globally, while the territory also struggled to define itself in conversation with both the West and Africa. From the arrival of the first settlers to the present, the Canaries represent an important space of opportunity, both from those within and outside. Yet, opportunity also came with the task of defining this space, often as either African or European. As time progressed, conceptualizations of the islands shifted internally and externally, often according to prevalent political and political trends. Yet, what is clear is that the Canaries, like many other African islands, exist in a space that is not quite African or European.

Thus, we must recognize the importance of global, regional, and local factors in not only the making of the Canaries, but also the making of the modern world.

Canary relations were conditioned by internal and external factors. The limitations of its own production, the organization of trade, the weakness of its own bourgeoisie, the need for labor in the early centuries of the early modern history and its strategic position, determined its relationship to Africa. But so did the proximity to the Sahara desert and, above all, the big decisions that had to do with this relationship were made in Madrid, London, or New York. In this sense, the archipelago eventually became the border of Europe and in the territory of the European Union, despite belonging to Africa. This land was used for the benefit of the West as a control platform, trade and military observatory to Africa. The Canaries worked as a gateway that opens or closes in various directions.

Notes

1. Germán Santana Pérez and Juan Manuel Santana Pérez, *La puerta afortunada. El papel de Canarias en las relaciones hispano-africanas* (Madrid: Los Libros de La Catarata, Cabildo de Gran Canaria, Cabildo de Lanzarote, 2002).

2. The islands of *señorío* pay the *quintos* tax to the seigneurs. Señorío is a feudal territory with manorial features and quintos is an obligatory contribution, consisting of one-fifth of exports and imports.

3. Eduardo Aznar Vallejo, *La integración de las Islas Canarias en la Corona de Castilla (1478–1526)* (Las Palmas: Cabildo Insular de Gran Canaria, 1992), 139–40.

4. Francisco Morales Padrón, *El comercio canario americano (siglos XVI, XVII y XVIII)* (Las Palmas de Gran Canaria: Cabildo de Gran Canaria, 2011), 158.

5. See Immanuel Wallerstein, *El moderno sistema mundial: la agricultura capitalista y los orígenes de la economía mundo europea en el siglo XVI* (Mexico City: Siglo XXI, 2011).

6. A. José Farrujia de la Rosa, *An Archeology of the Margins: Colonialism, Amazighity and Heritage Management in the Canary Islands* (New York: Springer, 2014), 9.

7. Nicole Maca Mayer, "ADN antiguo y el origen de la población canaria," *El Indiferente* 19 (May 2007): 43–51.

8. See Florentino Pérez Embid, *Los descubrimientos en el Atlántico y la rivalidad castellano-portuguesa hasta el Tratado de Tordesillas* (Seville: Escuela de Estudios Hispano Americanos de Sevilla, 1948); Antonio Rumeu de Armas, *Piraterías y ataques navales contra las Islas Canarias* (Madrid: Consejo Superior de Investigaciones Científicas, 1947); Paulina Rufo Ysern, "La expansión peninsular por la costa africana. El enfrentamiento entre Portugal y Castilla (1475–1480)," in

Congresso Internacional Bartolomeu Dias e a sua época, vol. III (Porto, Portugal: Universidade do Porto, Comissao Nacional para as Comemoraçoes dos Descobrimentos Portugueses, 1989): 59–79; Ana María Carabias Torres, coord., *Las relaciones entre Portugal y Castilla en la época de los descubrimientos y la expansión colonial* (Salamanca, Spain: Universidad de Salamanca, Sociedad Quinto Centenario del Tratado de Tordesillas, 1996).

9. Rumeu de Armas, "La torre africana de Santa Cruz de la Mar Pequeña," *Anuario de Estudios Atlánticos* 1 (1955): 377–97.

10. Archivo General de Indias (AGI), Guerra y Marina, leg. 80, 4.

11. Roberto Hernández Bautista, *Los Semidanes en Canarias. Anotaciones a la cultura y el linaje de los Semidanes en los siglos XV y XVI* (Madrid: Anroart Ediciones, 2012), 118–22.

12. Bartolomé Bennassar, "El Santo Oficio de Canarias observatorio de la política africana: el caso de las guerras civiles marroquíes (1603–1610)," in *VIII Coloquio de Historia Canario-Americana (1988)*, Tomo I, 5–16 (Las Palmas: Cabildo de Gran Canaria, 1991), 16.

13. Archivo de Acialcázar, Berbería, s./fol. In 1713, Juan Arguello, a native of Marseille, said he had been captured at age eight and led to Fez, where he lived a long time until his escape through the port of Agadir and his arrival in Tenerife after taking an English ship. In addition to Fez, where he had been in the king's house, he had resided in Torudan and Meknes, serving the son of the viceroy.

14. AGI, Indiferente General, leg. 3.094, nº 3. In La Palma, on May 20, 1572, Mr. Daça Maldonado, official judge of record on that island, said on the information requested by the court about a Portuguese privateer named Bartholomew Bayon, that he was taken and sent prisoner to Castile. He had only been able to find out what the official judge of Gran Canaria wrote, that is to say, that he was sailing around the island, but had not dared to go to its home port with two British ships, and since then had set sail, thinking they were going to Guinea.

15. See Santana Pérez and Santana Pérez, *La pesca en el Banco Sahariano: Siglos XVII y XVIII* (Madrid: Los Libros de La Catarata, 2014).

16. Benedicta Rivero Suárez, *El azúcar en Tenerife 1496–1550* (San Cristóbal La Laguna, Spain: Instituto de Estudios Canarios, 1991), 168.

17. Avelino Teixeira da Mota, "Viagens españolas das Canarias à Guiné no século XVI. Segundo documentos dos arquivos portugueses," in *III Coloquio de Historia Canario-Americana (1978)*, Tomo II, 220–50 (Salamanca: Cabildo Insular de Gran Canaria, 1980), 224.

18. See Germán Santana Pérez, "Arguín y Canarias durante la Etapa Moderna (ss. XV–XVIII)," in *Culturas del Litoral*, coordinated by Alberto López Bargados (Barcelona: Ediciones Bellaterra, 2010): 45–66.

19. See Juan Manuel Santana Pérez, "Relaciones entre la pesca preindustrial canaria con la actividad del Banc d'Arguin," in *Encrucijadas de la historia: Experiencia, Memoria, Oralidad*, vol. 2 (Istanbul, 2000): 871–74.

20. On this topic, see Antonio Rumeu de Armas, *Piraterías y ataques navales contra las Islas Canarias* (Madrid: Consejo Superior de Investigaciones

Científicas, 1948); Luis Alberto Anaya Hernández, *Moros en la costa. Dos siglos de corsarismo berberisco en las Islas Canarias (1569–1749)* (Las Palmas de Gran Canaria: Gobierno de Canarias, Fundación de Enseñanza Superior a Distancia de Las Palmas de Gran Canaria, UNED, 2006); Luis Alberto Anaya Hernández, "Consecuencias materiales y espirituales," *Boletín Millares Carlo* 23 (2004): 11–35; G. Santana Pérez, "Actuación de los corsarios berberiscos sobre el comercio canario durante el siglo XVII," in *II Congreso Internacional D'Estudis Històrics*, 213–20 (Santa Pola [Alicante]: Ajuntament de Santa Pola y Caja de Ahorros del Mediterráneo, 2000), 213–20; Manuel de Paz Sánchez, *La piratería en Canarias: ensayo de historia cultural* (La Laguna: Centro de la Cultura Popular Canaria, 2009).

21. Fernando Bruquetas de Castro, *La esclavitud en Lanzarote* (Cabildo de Lanzarote, Madrid, 1995), 139–40.

22. Manuel Lobo Cabrera, *La esclavitud en las Canarias Orientales en el siglo XVI (negros, moros y moriscos)* (Santa Cruz de Tenerife: Cabildo Insular de Gran Canaria, 1982), 144.

23. See Elisa Torres Santana, *El comercio de las Canarias Orientales en tiempos de Felipe III* (Las Palmas: Cabildo Insular de Gran Canaria, 1991); G. Santana Pérez, *Mercado local en las Canarias Orientales durante el reinado de Felipe IV* (Las Palmas de Gran Canaria: Cabildo de Gran Canaria, Cabildo de Fuerteventura y Cabildo de Lanzarote, 2000); Santans, *El comercio de las Canarias Orientales en tiempos de Felipe III.*

24. Antonio Carreira, *Estudos de Economía Caboverdiana. Estudos de Historia de Portugal e dos Portugueses* (Lisbon: Impresa Nacional/Casa da Moeda, 1982), 10, 17.

25. Rumeu de Armas, *España en el África Atlántica*, Tomo I (Las Palmas de Gran Canaria: Cabildo Insular de Gran Canaria, 1996), 493–94.

26. AGI, Indiferente General, 3096, n° 26. In August 1587 the ship *San Antonio*, accompanied by the ship *Nuestra Señora del Buen Viaje*, were in the port of Garachico on Tenerife. Manuel Antonio, fifty-eight, was first master and pilot, and Esteban Francisco was the second. They had left Lisbon and were loading to go to Cape Verde and Guinea rivers, calling at Garachico after deciding to take on some wine. The ultimate goal was New Spain, for which His Majesty had given permission. The ship's goods were worth over 3,000 ducats.

27. AGI, Indiferente General, 3096, n° 5. An example is Friar John Wood, a native of the Canary Islands, who was arrested in 1602 (along with a large load of smuggled goods) while trying to move to the Indies because he said he was aware that people could reach America by way of Guinea.

28. Kenneth R. Andrews, *Trade, Plunder and Settlement: Maritime Enterprise and the Genesis of the British Empire, 1480–1630* (Cambridge: Cambridge University Press, 1984), 104, 107.

29. M. E. Madeira Santos, coord., *Historia Geral de Cabo Verde*, vol. 2 (Lisbon: Centro de Estudos de História e Cartografia Antiga, Instituto de Investigaçao

Científica Tropical e Instituto Nacional de Investigaçao Cultural Cabo Verde, 1995), 37.

30. Teixeira da Mota, "Viagens españolas das Canarias," 219–50.

31. Beatrix Heintze and Maria Adélia de Carvalho Mendes, eds., *Fontes para a História de Angola do século XVII. II Cartas e documentos oficiais da Colectánea documental de Fernao de Souza (1624–1635)* (Stuttgart: Franz Steiner Verlag Wiesbaden GmbH, 1985), 251–52.

32. We must bear in mind that the production of Tenerife (the island with the highest wine production) was about 20,000 tons annually, heading mainly to England and Hispanic America, so it is almost impossible that exports to Africa and Brazil exceeded those that were intended for major markets.

33. José C. Curto, *Enslaving Spirits: The Portuguese-Brazilia Alcohol Trade at Luanda and Its Hinterland, c. 1550–1830* (Leiden, Netherlands: Brill, 2004), 56–58.

34. Germán Santana Pérez, Marcos Salas Pascual, and M. Teresa Cáceres Lorenzo, "Historia de la incorporación de los cultivos vegetales africanos en Canarias durante los siglos XV al XVIII," *Revista Historia Canaria* 20 (2004): 219–34.

35. J. Pérez Vidal, *Aportación de Canarias a la población de América* (Las Palmas de Gran Canaria: Excmo. Cabildo Insular de Gran Canaria, 1991), 13.

36. Arquivo Torre do Tombo, Ministerio Negocios Etrangeros, caixa 322.

37. Carlos Gallardo Navarro, *Guinea: Diario de un emigrante canario* (Gran Canaria: C. Gallardo, 2007), 75, 276.

38. Arquivo Histórico Ultramarino, Cabo Verde, caixa 3, doc. N° 59 A and 75. Also in Guiné, caixa 1, doc. 47.

39. Archivo Histórico Provincial de Las Palmas (AHPLP), ÁLVAREZ DE SILVA, Diego, leg. 1.270, año 1652, Gran Canaria, fol. 367 r. In November 1652, Capt. Lucas Perez de Guadalupe sold a black slave named John, who had bought a Dutch ship that arrived at the port of La Luz in 1648, with a number of slaves sold in Gran Canaria; ÁLVAREZ DE SILVA, Diego, leg. 1.268, año 1650, fol. 210 r. In April of that year a black slave named Isabel, who had arrived with a Dutch ship at the port of La Luz, was sold; Also MOYA, Francisco de, leg. 1.203, año 1652, fol. 554 v. The Dutchman Cornelis Lonch, hispanicized Pedro Lunque, sold a slave for twenty-two pesos of eight reales, goods of blacks that in 1652 had been brought to Gran Canaria. In 1651 he had sold slaves who had arrived on the ship of the Dutch Cornelius Grenengil, at VERGARA RENDA, Juan de, leg. 1.302, año 1655, fol. 332 r. There are other references at BANDAMA, Juan, leg. 1.315, fols. 301 v.–302 r.; ALGIROFO, Juan Bautista, leg. 1.220, año 1652, fol. 385 r.; GONZÁLEZ PERERA, Baltasar, leg. 1.230, año 1652, fol. 483 r.v.; ACANIO, Luis, leg. 1.264, año 1653, fols. 124 v.–125 r., fol. 239 r.; ÁLVAREZ DE SILVA, Diego, leg. 1.271, año 1653, fol. 10 r.; ASCANIO, Luis, leg. 1.265, año 1654, fols. 110 v.–111 r. y 150 v.–151 r.; ÁLVAREZ DE SILVA, Diego, leg. 1.273, año 1655, fol. 181 r. y fol. 640 r.

40. Daniel A. Pereira, *Estudos da História de Cabo Verde* (Praia, Cape Verde: Alfa-Comunicaçoes, 2005), 69–70.

41. Berta Pico and Dolores Corbella, dir., *Viajeros franceses a las Islas Canarias. Repertorio bio-bibliográfico y selección de textos* (Santa Cruz de Tenerife: Instituto de Estudios Canarios, 2000), 64.

42. J. B. G. M. Bory de Saint-Vincent, *Ensayos sobre las Islas Afortunadas y la antigua Atlántida o compendio de la Historia General del Archipiélago Canario* (La Orotava, Spain: JADL, 1988), 116, 117.

43. In 1668 a ship from Cape Verde reached the port of Santa Cruz de Tenerife loaded with leathers and slaves, in Morales Padrón, *El comercio canario-americano* (Seville: Escuela de Estudos Hispano-Americanos), 46. Other news on the same year is AHPLP, ÁLVAREZ DE SILVA, Diego, leg, 1.285, año 1669, Gran Canaria, fols. 43 v.–44 r. In January 1669, Doña Beatriz de Herrera, a novice nun in the convent of San Bernardo de Las Palmas, sold to Don Miguel Machado, a resident of Las Palmas, a black slave named Catherine for 2,100 reales. She was a Cape Verdean Creole, who had been bought from a group of slaves who came from a Portuguese archipelago in the ship that had come to Gran Canaria six months previously. Also in AHPLP, ÁLVAREZ DE SILVA, Diego, leg. 1.286, año 1671, Gran Canaria, fol. 167 r. In June 1671 the field master Olivares Alonso del Castillo, a resident of Las Palmas, sold to Capt. Don Bartolome Muxica Lezcano, a resident of Havana, a thirty-year-old slave who had come in a Portuguese ship that sailed from Cape Verde to Tenerife. She sold her for 1,600 reales.

44. Archivo Histórico Nacional de Cabo Verde, Comunicaçoes Gerais, Sec A1, SR: 1, A1/A1.1/Cx.1, fol. 7 r.

45. Archivo Histórico Nacional (AHN), Estado, leg. 550. In 1741 the substitute in Tenerife Canary commanding general, José de Andonaegui, reported how the corsair Antonio Miguel had arrived in Tenerife with a British corvette that had been seized on the banks of the Gambia and the coast of Goré.

46. Antonio Béthencourt Massieu, *Canarias e Inglaterra: el comercio de vinos (1650–1800)* (Las Palmas: Cabildo Insular de Gran Canaria, 1991), 114–17.

47. Archivo General de Simancas (AGS), Estado, leg. 6849.

48. AGS, Estado, leg. 6849.

49. AGS, Estado, leg. 6914.

50. Mariano Arribas Palau, "Notas sobre el abastecimiento de granos a Canarias desde Marruecos (1769–1789)," *Anuario de Estudios Atlánticos* 25 (1979): 359–410; Ramón Lourido Díaz, *Marruecos y el mundo exterior en la segunda mitad del siglo XVIII. Relaciones político-comerciales del sultán Sidi Muhammad B.'Allah (1757–1790) con el exterior* (Madrid: M. A. E. Agencia Española de Cooperación Internacional. Instituto de Cooperación con el Mundo Árabe, 1989); G. Santana Pérez, "Navegación de Santa Cruz de Tenerife con África a finales del siglo XVIII," in *XIV Coloquio de Historia Canario-Americana (2000)* (Las Palmas de Gran Canaria: Cabildo de Gran Canaria, 2002): 623–39.

51. George Glas, *Descripción de las Islas Canarias 1764* (Tenerife: Instituto de Estudios Canarios, 1999), 143–44.

52. José Agustín Álvarez Rixo, *Historia del puerto de Arrecife. En la isla de Lanzarote, una de las Canarias* (Santa Cruz de Tenerife: Cabildo Insular de Tenerife, 1982), 146.

53. See Mariano L. Castro, and Mª Luisa de la Calle, *Origen de la colonización española en Guinea Ecuatorial (1777–1860)* (Salamanca, Spain: Universidad de Valladolid y Caja Salamanca y Soria, 1992); Justo Bolekia Boleká, *Aproximación a la historia de Guinea Ecuatorial* (Salamanca, Spain: Amarú Ediciones, 2003); M. Dolores García Cantús, *Fernando Poo: Una aventura colonial española. I: Las Islas en litigio: entre la esclavitud y el abolicionismo, 1777–1846* (Barcelona: Ceiba Ediciones, Centros Culturales Españoles de Guinea Ecuatorial, 2006).

54. Encarnación Rodríguez Vicente, "Un proyecto de participación canaria en el comercio de negros con América española, 1785," in *V Coloquio de Historia Canario-Americana (1982) Coloquio Internacional de Historia Marítima*, Tomo IV (Madrid: Mancomunidad de Cabildos, 1985): 390–91.

55. Armas, *Piraterías y ataques navales*, 802–5.

56. AHN, leg. 8015, nº 4.

57. Christopher Fyfe, *A History of Sierra Leona* (New York: Oxford University Press, 1962), 273–74.

58. At the end of the 1830s, the US representative in Madrid, Mr. Eaton, communicated that the brig *Dos Amigos*, which had left New Orleans with an American flag to engage in the slave trade, had arrived at Puerto de La Cruz in Tenerife. He asked for it to be delivered to the United States for breaking the law and its captain and crew tried. Some of these subjects had invoked the jurisdiction of the navy and others called for relief under pardon. Moreover, the Spanish authorities did their best to delay the resolution and opposed his return to the US government. The minister of England in Madrid, Mr. Arthur Aston, claimed that several ships in the Canaries were prepared to engage in the slave trade, including the brig *Constancia*, formerly called *Two Friends*, whose Petty officer, José Miguel Jotasan, resided in Gallinas as agent to handle the shipment of slaves. This was in breach of the 1835 treaty with Great Britain.

59. See Carlos González Echegaray, "Las Islas Canarias vistas por los viajeros al Golfo de Guinea (1832–1956)," in *II Aula Canarias y el Noroeste de África (1986)* (Madrid: Cabildo Insular de Gran Canaria, 1988), 311–38.

60. One example is the various groups of Capuchin friars in 1645, 1647, 1657, and 1678, who were to stay in the Canary Islands before continuing their journey to the missions in Congo, Sierra Leone, and Guinea rivers. P. Mateo de Anguiano, *Misiones capuchinas en África II. Misiones al reino de la Zinga, Benín, Arda, Guinea y Sierra Leona* (Madrid: Consejo Superior de Investigaciones Científicas, Instituto Santo Toribio de Mogrovejo, 1957), xxx–xxxii; B.N., Ms. 3818, fol. 318 r.v.; *Monumenta Missionaria Africana*, 274–76; *Monumenta Missionaria Africana*, 108–10.

61. Víctor Morales Lezcano, "Canarias y el noroeste de África: Panorámica general," in *Canarias y África (Altibajos de una gravitación)* (Las Palmas de Gran Canaria: Mancomunidad de Cabildos, 1985), 34.

62. José Ignacio Algueró Cuervo, *El conflicto del Sáhara Occidental, desde una perspectiva canaria* (Santa Cruz de Tenerife: Gobierno de Canarias, 2003), 42–44.

63. Jesús Mª. Martínez Milán, *España en el Sáhara Occidental y en la zona sur del protectorado en Marruecos 1885–1945* (Madrid: Universidad Nacional de Educación a Distancia, 2003), 139–61.

64. Mariano L. Castro, and Mª Luisa de la Calle, *La colonización española en Guinea Ecuatorial (1858–1900)* (Barcelona: Ceiba Ediciones, 2007), 12, 49–50.

65. Juan José Díaz Matarranz, *De la trata de negros al cultivo del cacao. Evolución del modelo colonial español en Guinea Ecuatorial de 1778 a 1914* (Barcelona: Ceiba Ediciones, Centros Culturales Españoles de Guinea Ecuatorial, 2005), 46.

66. Candelaria González Rodríguez, "Insurrectos Cubanos deportados hacia Canarias y Fernando Poo (1869): Un ejemplo de deportación política," in *Actas III Coloquio Internacional de História da Madeira* (Madeira: Secretaría Regional do Turismo e Cultura, Centro de Estudos de História do Atântico, 1993): 703–19.

67. T. Pereira Rodríguez, "Apuntes para un esquema de las relaciones marítimo comerciales entre Canarias y los territorios del Golfo de Guinea (1858–1900)," in *VI Coloquio de Historia Canario Americana (Aula Canarias-Noroeste de África) (1984)*, Tomo III (Santa Cruz de Tenerife: Gobierno de Canarias, Cabildo Insular de Gran Canaria. Santa Cruz de Tenerife, 1987): 417–52.

68. See G. Santana Pérez, "Colonos canarios en Guinea Ecuatorial," *Canarii, Revista mensual de Historia del Archipiélago* 12 (2008): 6–7.

69. Manuel de Paz Sánchez, "Hipótesis en torno a un desarrollo paralelo de la masonería canaria y cubana durante el primer tercio del presente siglo. Acotaciones para un estudio," in *IV Coloquio de Historia Canario-Americana (1980)*, Tomo II (Las Palmas de Gran Canaria: Cabildo Insular de Gran Canaria, 1982), 575.

70. See G. Santana Pérez, *Canarios con salacot: África subsahariana como lugar de emigración (1936–1975)* (Tenerife: Fundación Mapfre Guanarteme, 2008).

71. Agustín Miranda, *Cartas de la Guinea* (Madrid: Espasa-Calpe, 1940), 57, 90.

72. Francisco Quintana Navarro, *Informes consulares británicos sobre Canarias (1856–1914)*, Tomo I (Madrid: Seminario de Estudios Canarios del Centro Asociado de la UNED de Las Palmas, Universidad de Las Palmas de Gran Canaria, Centro de Investigación económica y social de La Caja de Canarias, 1992), 9, 263, 129, 270, 288–89, 302, 323.

73. Ulises Martín Hernández, *Tenerife y el expansionismo europeo (1880–1919)* (Santa Cruz de Tenerife: Aula de Cultura de Tenerife, 1988), 228.

74. Quintana Navarro, *Informes consulares británicos*, 447–52.

75. Archivo General de la Administración, Caja G-1948, Exp. 2.

76. Archivo General de la Administración, Caja G-1948, Exp. 2.

77. *La Provincia*, October 6, 1968, 7.

78. Leoncio Afonso, *Geografía de Canarias. III. La pesca* (Santa Cruz de Tenerife, Editorial Interinsular Canaria, 1984), 221.

79. Luis Beizus de los Ríos, "Las Islas Canarias en las comunicaciones aéreas euroafricanas (1910–1958)," in *II Aula Canarias y el Noroeste de África (1986)* (Madrid: Cabildo Insular de Gran Canaria, La Caja de Canarias, 1988), 33–40.

80. While large-scale connections were elusive, the Canaries did service these specific territories.

81. Elsa López López, *El corazón de los pájaros* (Barcelona: Planeta, 2001); Carlos Fleitas Alonso, *Guinea: Episodios de la vida colonial* (Madrid: Agencia Española de Cooperación Internacional, 1989); María del Carmen Lorenzo Delgado, *Guinea en mi corazón* (Las Palmas de Gran Canaria: M. C. Lorenzo, 2002).

2

Sugar, Cocoa, and Oil

Economic Success and Failure in São Tomé and Príncipe from the Sixteenth to the Twenty-First Centuries

Gerhard Seibert

Boom, Decline, and Frustrated Hopes

São Tomé and Príncipe played a pioneering role in the economic history of sugar and cocoa in the sixteenth and nineteenth centuries, respectively, while in the late twentieth century the small country was a latecomer in the development of oil. In the sixteenth century the Portuguese established on the hitherto uninhabited islands the first plantation economy in the tropics, based on sugar monoculture and slave labor. The sugar industry boomed for almost a century. However, at the end of the sixteenth century sugar production began gradually to decrease due to a variety of factors, predominantly the emergence of Brazilian sugar, forcing the island to adapt to changing global exchange patterns. In the course of the seventeenth century, the plantation economy virtually disappeared, reducing the island to subsistence agriculture and the provisioning of slave ships. The introduction of coffee in 1787 and cocoa from Brazil around 1820 enabled the reestablishment of the plantation economy in the nineteenth century. At the end of this century cocoa production surpassed that of coffee and became by far the most important export crop. In the early twentieth century the archipelago was even for a couple of years the world's largest cocoa producer, although after the First World War, cocoa production began progressively to decrease due to various socioeconomic and ecological factors, including pest infestation of crops and the competition of smallholders in the neighboring continent.

After independence from Portugal in 1975 the downfall of cocoa accelerated due to mismanagement by the ruling regime. Finally, in the 1990s the plantation economy ceased to exist when plantation lands were divided and distributed to small farmers. Despite a currently low output, cocoa remains the principal export product since several attempts of economic diversification have failed. The country's oil hopes began in 1997 when the government signed the first oil exploration agreement with foreign investors, but initial optimism has been replaced by increasing doubts as various offshore exploration drillings have failed to discover commercially viable oil. The chapter analyzes the successes and failures of the country's economy since the archipelago's settlement in the late fifteenth century and puts them in a wider historical and sociopolitical context. While sugar in the sixteenth century and cocoa in the nineteenth and twentieth centuries put São Tomé and Príncipe on the map as an economic success story, the failure of oil production in the twenty-first century has reinforced the economic dependency of the country on foreign aid, at least as long as alternative sources of income have not been developed. However, one should not ignore that the success of sugar and cocoa were largely based on slavery and the harsh conditions of contract labor respectively.

Settlement and Colonization

When the tropical islands of São Tomé (332 square miles) and Príncipe (55 square miles) were discovered by the Portuguese around 1471, they were uninhabited. From the beginning the Portuguese expected São Tomé to become a sugar producer. However, the archipelago's colonization proved to be difficult due to the insalubrious tropical climate and a lack of both food crops and domestic animals. The first Portuguese settlement attempt made in the northwest of São Tomé between 1486 and 1490 failed due to tropical diseases and a lack of food. Finally, in early 1493, the island's third captain, Álvaro de Caminha (1493–99), succeeded in creating the first settlement in the northeast of the island, which formally became São Tomé town in 1535. Deported convicts constituted a significant proportion of the Portuguese settlers, as did dozens of Jewish children who had been separated from their parents by force.

The early years of colonization were difficult. Food had to be imported along with the slaves from the neighboring Niger delta.[1] The Portuguese introduced domestic animals, sugarcane, and food crops from the Americas and the African continent in the archipelago. Nevertheless, food shortages continued until at least 1499, when starving settlers were sent to

Príncipe.[2] Regardless of the availability of food, the mortality rate among whites due to tropical diseases always remained high, and whites were always a small minority in São Tomé. Probably even during the boom of the sugar industry the entire white population did not exceed 500 inhabitants. The mortality rate among slaves was also high, but it was easier to replace them than the white settlers.[3]

The power vacuum created by the high mortality rate among Portuguese officeholders caused considerable political instability in São Tomé. After the establishment of a Catholic diocese on the island in 1534, the bishop, the Crown-appointed governor, and the wealthy planter-dominated town council clashed often. From 1548 to 1770 the city council ruled in the event of the governor's absence or death. From 1586 to 1613 alone, São Tomé was ruled by eighteen governors, including both those appointed by the Crown and interim rulers elected by the town council.[4] Other Europeans added to the instability, as both the French and Dutch repeatedly raided and occupied the two islands during its first period of relative prosperity between the mid-seventeenth and early eighteenth centuries, with the Dutch holding power in São Tomé from 1641 to 1649.[5]

The most successful early commercial activity of São Tomé's settlers was the slave trade, which was also necessary to obtain labor for the local economy. The first slaves were traded in the Slave Coast, the Niger Delta, and the island of Fernão Pó. In the early sixteenth century the slave trade began with the kingdom of Kongo and subsequently with Angola. The transatlantic slave trade from São Tomé to the Americas began around 1525.[6]

The Portuguese Crown stimulated mixed-race unions between white settlers and African slaves in an attempt to ensure the colonization of the archipelago. In 1515 a royal decree granted manumission to the African wives of white settlers and their mixed-race offspring. Two years later, the king freed the male slaves who had arrived with the first colonists. These decrees marked the birth of São Tomé's free African population known as Forros.[7] This free black population would assimilate slaves liberated in subsequent periods. In 1520 a royal charter allowed free mulattoes to hold public offices in the local council.[8] A quarter century later, another royal decree equated them with white settlers, granting them suffrage and the right to hold office on the city council.[9] Free mulattoes and blacks participated actively in local religious, political, and economic affairs, playing a substantial part in shaping São Tomé's emerging Creole society.

In addition to the free black community, there also developed an extralegal population of runaway slaves in the island's inaccessible mountainous interior. The first forms of runaway slave organizations appeared in the 1530s, when they formed gangs and assaulted settlers and raided plantations. In 1533 the local authorities created a local militia to fight these maroons, known as Angolares since the early nineteenth century.[10] In 1693, the last large military action against the maroons was carried out, after which confrontations with settlers occurred only sporadically. Maroon communities enjoyed political autonomy until 1878, when their territory in the south of São Tomé was occupied by the colonial authorities. Subsequently they were increasingly assimilated into the larger Creole society, though they have preserved their distinct cultural identity to some extent.

At the beginning of the seventeenth century, São Tomé ceased to be an important slave trade entrepôt. In 1614 the São Tomé settlers lost access to the slave markets in Kongo because they had become a threat to other Portuguese commercial interests and their operations remained restricted to the Gulf of Guinea. Furthermore, from the mid-seventeenth century Angolan slaves were shipped directly to Brazil and the Spanish Americas and São Tomé's access to the market in Luanda was disrupted.[11] The re-export of slaves continued, but on a much smaller scale than in the sixteenth century. The end of São Tomé's key role in the slave trade contributed considerably to its economic decline in the seventeenth and eighteenth centuries.

The Rise and Fall of Sugar[12]

Beginning in the early sixteenth century, sugar export had become as lucrative as the slave trade. Sugarcane and the people skilled in its cultivation and processing came to São Tomé from Madeira. The cultivation of sugarcane concentrated in the island's northern flatlands started soon after Caminha's arrival. The forest was gradually chopped down for the expanding plantations in the island's northern third, while the other two-thirds remained covered by tropical forest largely inaccessible to the settlers. Sugarcane in São Tomé proved successful thanks to fertile volcanic soils, the tropical climate, sufficient rainfall, and, most important, the availability of cheap African slave labor.

Most plantations were privately owned by royal officials and settlers, though several belonged to the Crown and the Catholic Church. The first mulatto plantation owners born on the island are recorded as early as 1521. On the plantations, the owners, who maintained private armies of armed slaves, exercised great power, while the local authorities were unable to enforce their authority there.[13] Power struggles between rival plantation owners occurred frequently, contributing to political instability.[14] Thanks to their wealth, they constituted the most important socioeconomic group in the islands.

Table 2.1. Operating sugar mills on São Tomé

Year	1517	c.1550	1595	c.1600	1610	1645	c.1672	c.1710	1736
Number	2[a]	ca. 60[b]	ca. 85[c]	ca. 120	45	54	31	18–19	7[d]

Source: Cristina Maria Seuanes Serafim, *As Ilhas de São Tomé no século XVII* (Lisbon: Centro de História de Além-Mar [CHAM], 2000), 258.

[a] Hélder Lains e Silva, *São Tomé e Príncipe e a Cultura do Café* (Lisbon: Junta de Investigação do Ultramar, 1958), 83.
[b] Arlindo Manuel Caldeira, *Mulheres, Sexualidade e Casamento no Arquipélago de S. Tomé e Príncipe (Séculos XV a XVII)* (Lisbon: Grupo de Trabalho do Ministério da Educação para as Comemorações dos Descobrimentos Portugueses, 1997), 17.
[c] "'Relatione uenuta dall' Isola di S. Tomé,'" in *Monumenta Missionária Africana: África Ocidental (1570–1599)*, ed. António Brásio, vol. 3(Lisbon: Agência Geral do Ultramar, 1953), 523.
[d] Cristina Maria Seuanes Serafim and Lúcia M. L. Tomás, "Os séculos XVII–XVIII. O lento declinar da economia. A economia: a produção açucareira, o comércio e o regate. A fiscalidade e as finanças. O Arquipélago do Golfo da Guiné: Fernando Pó, São Tomé, Príncipe e Ano Bom," in *A Colonização Atlântica*, vol. 2, ed. Artur Teodoro de Matos (Lisbon: Editorial Estampa, 2005), 358.

Sugar production in São Tomé started around 1517 and grew rapidly.[15] Pablo Eyzaguirre believes that during the height of the sugar boom the number of mills possibly reached 200, while he estimates the average number of slaves per sugar mill at fifty.[16] Robert Garfield claims that each mill had an annual production capacity of up to 5,000 arrobas of sugar[17]—roughly equivalent to 73.5 tons—which is considerably higher than the approximately 15–25 tons per mill given by Stuart Schwartz.[18] In the mid-sixteenth century, planters owned 150, 200, and up to 300 slaves.[19] During the height of the sugar industry in the sixteenth century São Tomé's plantations accommodated a total of about 9,000 to 12,000 captives.[20] Due to the extension of sugar cultivation, less land was dedicated to food crops, which in turn resulted in a shortage of food and caused famine among the slaves.

During the production process the sugar juice was boiled three to four times to dry it, then put into semiconical containers while still semimoist to further dry and become firm, earning the sobriquet sugar loaves (*pães de açúcar*). However, due to the high humidity, the sugar did not dry sufficiently and quality was low, which drove down prices. From 1578 to 1582 when São Tomé's annual sugar production reached its peak, prices ranged between 630 and 950 reis per arroba in Lisbon, while Madeira's sugar was traded for 2,500–3,000 reis per arroba.[21] Brazil, which had begun large-scale production around 1533, also achieved higher prices, with 1,400–1,850 reis per arroba.

Regardless, by the 1510s São Tomé produced an estimated 100,000 arrobas a year, replacing Madeira as the primary producer of sugar.[22] In the mid-sixteenth century thirty to forty Portuguese ships arrived every year at the port of São Tomé, where they remained for six or seven months to load sugar, predominately destined for Antwerp.[23] The demand for São Tomé's sugar was due to its abundance and cheapness rather than quality since it was rather dark and not very solid as a result of the humid climate. In Antwerp, São Tomé's sugar was considered the "worst in the world" since the loaves were moist and full of tiny black ants.[24] Whatever the quality, the Portuguese Crown profited from the sugar, with the king receiving one-tenth of the sales as taxes.[25]

Estimates of sugar production differ by author and some are inconsistent with each other since they are based on tax revenue, ship loads, or the number of sugar mills. The highest figure is 800,000 arrobas for the years before 1578, based on an estimate of forty shiploads a year of 20,000 arrobas each, which seems rather unlikely.[26] However, there is no doubt that sugar production reached its height in the third quarter of the sixteenth century and a gradual decline began after that due to various internal and external causes.

The gradual decline of São Tomé's economy started in the last quarter of the sixteenth century when Brazil emerged as a large, fast-growing sugar producer. After 1579, sugar production in São Tomé dropped by 35 percent due to both drought and infestation of the plants by worms attacking the roots. This decline in production was not offset by higher prices as Brazil was already producing considerable quantities of sugar for the European markets at three to four times higher productivity.[27] Equally important was the higher quality of Brazilian sugar, which was white, dry, and achieved better prices on the world market. Brazil also provided planters with a more stable political environment and a healthier climate. While competition from Brazil was the most important reason for the gradual collapse of São Tomé's sugar industry, other external and internal causes contributed to the course of events.

The constant political instability caused by frequent conflicts between the political and religious authorities was exacerbated by the assaults of the Angolares maroons, who constituted a permanent threat to the sugar estates. A serious blow for the local sugar industry was Rei Amador's great slave uprising in 1595, in which roughly 5,000 slaves raided plantations and burned settler homes for nearly three weeks. The rebels destroyed at

Table 2.2. São Tomé's sugar production estimates

Year	1517	1529	1531	1554	c.1570	1578	1579	1580	1584
Arrobas	100,000	123,170	135,860	150,000[a]	800,000[b]	120,000[c]–175,000	200,000[d]	20,000–24,000	250,000[e]

Year	1588	1590	1591	1602	1610	c.1624	1645	1651	c.1672	1684
Arrobas	60,000	64,000[f]	10,000–12,000	40,000	60,000	89–100,000	100,000	40,000	ca. 27,000	2,000

Sources: Isabel Castro Henriques, *São Tomé e Príncipe: a Invenção de uma Sociedade* (Lisbon: Vega, 2000), 92 (for the period 1517–91); Serafim and Tomás, Os séculos XVII–XVIII, 355 (1602–84).

[a] Lains e Silva, *São Tomé e Príncipe*, 84.
[b] Lains e Silva, *São Tomé e Príncipe*, 84.
[c] Lains e Silva, *São Tomé e Príncipe*, 84.
[d] Lains e Silva, *São Tomé e Príncipe*, 85.
[e] Eyzaguirre, "Small Farmers and Estates," 60.
[f] Eyzaguirre, "Small Farmers and Estates," 60.

least sixty sugar mills—more than 70 percent of production capacity. The slave revolt occurred at a time when the economic decline had already begun accelerating the exodus of São Tomé's planters to Brazil, where they encountered better conditions for sugar production.

Externally, from the late sixteenth century the archipelago was increasingly threatened by the appearance of other European powers in the Atlantic. The local economy suffered severe damages as a result of the consecutive foreign attacks. The sugar industry never recovered entirely from the destruction suffered during the slave revolt and by the Dutch raid in 1599. However, to some extent the sugar economy recovered, as the statistics for mills and sugar production in the seventeenth century show. The scarcity of available ships also affected sugar exports to Portugal. The increasing activity of pirates and corsairs had resulted in the loss of Portuguese ships, while others were used to protect merchant ships in other territories like Brazil, which were given priority.[28]

The decline gradually continued until sugar production ceased almost completely in the early eighteenth century. In the seventeenth century most of the remaining planters had left for Brazil in search of new opportunities. Sugar production expanded to the Caribbean but never returned to São Tomé since the island could not compete in any way with the new producers in the Americas. As a consequence of the settler exodus from São Tomé, the local white population almost disappeared and the mulatto population gradually became more African in appearance. At the same time, the island's total population also decreased as a result of the overall economic decline. Caldeira estimates that the number of blacks dropped from 6,000–10,000 at the end of the sixteenth century to 4,000–5,000 in the seventeenth century, while that of whites decreased from 200 in the beginning of the seventeenth century to less than 100 by 1700.[29]

The plantation economy virtually disappeared, while the tropical forest covered many of the former sugar estates. In 1736 the seven sugar mills still in existence in São Tomé produced mainly gin, which was consumed locally and bartered in the coastal slave trade. The sugar monoculture was gradually replaced by diversified subsistence agriculture, whose surplus was sold to passing slave ships. This smallholder agriculture was complemented by the breeding of pigs and chickens. Slavery continued without the plantations, though it was predominantly of the household variety. Meanwhile, most slave owners were also African, which enabled slaves to become incorporated into the free Forro category through intermarriage and assimilation.[30] Largely abandoned by the Portuguese and virtually controlled by the local Creole elite, São Tomé and Príncipe became predominantly a food supplier for slave ships in the Gulf of Guinea, which took on water and provisions before sailing to the Americas.

The Cocoa Boom and Decline

In the mid-nineteenth century the plantation economy reemerged when, following the introduction of coffee (1787) and cocoa (c. 1820) from Brazil, the Portuguese recolonized São Tomé and Príncipe by setting up large plantations to produce the new cash crops.[31] São Tomé and Príncipe was the first African territory where cocoa was cultivated. From São Tomé, cocoa was taken to Fernando Pó and from there it reached the Gold Coast (Ghana) in 1879. Before the archipelago's recolonization, most of the land belonged to the Forros, either by title or customary usufruct.[32] During the expansion of the coffee and cocoa plantations in the latter half of the nineteenth century, the Portuguese gradually dispossessed the landholding Forros through land purchases, fraud, and force.[33] European planters also benefited from faulty land titles, chaotic registration practices, and conflicting boundary claims. Creole landowners also showed a penchant for lavish consumption rather than reinvesting their profits.[34]

The resulting debts often compelled the Creole planters to sell their lands to the Portuguese colonists. As a result, the Forro landowners were gradually marginalized, both politically and economically.

The first large plantations—Monte Café (1858), Bela Vista (1863), Rio do Ouro (1865), Boa Entrada (1870), and Uba Budo (1875)—were all founded on former lands of Creole planters.[35] In 1872 96 landowners were local Creoles out of a total of 153.[36] However, by 1898 Portuguese planters owned 90 percent of the land.[37] By that time, the Portuguese had established the financial system, administrative and social infrastructures, as well as the communications necessary for an effective colonization. At the beginning of the twentieth century, only a few Creole planters remained successfully engaged in cocoa production. In the interwar period, most of these remaining plantations gradually disappeared due to their division through inheritance and to bankruptcies frequently caused by the wastefulness of their owners. Consequently, the colonial administration became the principal avenue of upward social mobility for educated Forros.

In the nineteenth century, the production of cash crops started with coffee, but cocoa was more suited to cultivation by unskilled labor and its growth was favored by booming world market prices. By 1890 cocoa had surpassed coffee both in terms of volume and value, and since then has dominated the local cash crop production, despite several attempts of export crop diversification in the colonial and postcolonial period. The expansion of cocoa included large areas that had never been cultivated before. In contrast to the sugar plantations in the sixteenth century, the plantations, locally known as *roças*, now covered much larger areas in the archipelago. By 1913, cocoa was cultivated on 154,440 acres in São Tomé and approximately another 24,710 acres in Príncipe, almost three-quarters of the archipelago's total area.[38]

In 1905, 1906, 1907, 1909, and 1912, São Tomé and Príncipe became the largest cocoa producer, surpassing Trinidad, Ecuador, and Venezuela in terms of quantity. In 1912–13, São Tomé's cocoa production reached its peak of 36,500 tons, the highest output ever.[39] In 1918 the cocoa crops were severely hit by a pest of cacao thrips (*Heliothrips rubrocintus*).[40] International cocoa prices also dropped sharply resulting in a drastic decline of cocoa production and a contraction of the planted area. São Tomé's cocoa exports decreased from 26,283 tons in 1921 to 12,471 tons in 1926, and dropped further to only 6,972 tons in 1940. From 1954 to 1957 cocoa exports recovered from 7,416 tons to 10,562 tons. By 1968 cocoa exports amounted to 11,086 tons, less than a third of the quantity achieved in 1913.

Initially, the production of coffee and cocoa was based on slave labor from the African continent, but this changed when the Portuguese abolished slavery in São Tomé and Príncipe in 1875. The roughly 7,500 freed slaves refused to return to the plantations as wage laborers. The consequent labor crisis was resolved by the introduction of contract labor, predominantly from Angola at first, to satisfy the increasing labor demand from the newly established coffee and cocoa plantations. The contract workers, known as *serviçais*, were recruited by a labor bureau called Curadória Geral dos Indígenas (Plantation Labor Inspectorate). From the early twentieth century, contract workers were also recruited in the other Portuguese colonies of Cabo Verde and Mozambique, where regular recruitment started in 1903 and 1908 respectively. The *serviçais* constituted a new sociocultural category within the local population situated at the bottom of the colonial hierarchy. The children of the contract workers born in the islands were called *tongas*. The *serviçais* lived within the plantations, thus spatially separated from the local Creoles, who lived in the dispersed settlements known as *luchans* and small towns. Due to their history as free blacks, the Forros were the only Africans on the island who owned small private plots of land, the *glebas*. The Angolares were predominately fishermen and lived in their nucleated settlements in the south and northwest of the island.

São Tomé was a plural society in which the different groups were strictly stratified and divided according to sociocultural characteristics and their time of arrival on the archipelago. The local Creoles maintained an attitude of superiority toward the Angolan and Mozambican plantation workers. Afraid of becoming associated with the plantations, the Forros excluded the *serviçais* from participation in their religious and cultural institutions, such as the Catholic brotherhoods and their annual parish festivals, along with community-based theater groups and dance troupes. The social and cultural life of the contract workers was restricted to the plantation communities. Unlike the Cabo Verdeans, whom the Portuguese considered more civilized, Angolans and Mozambicans were classified inferiorly as indigenous (*indígenas*), according to a colonial legislation formally introduced in 1926. In 1947, Portugal classified the Cabo Verdeans as citizens, while the discriminatory indígenas status was abolished only in 1961, the year when the armed liberation struggle began in Angola. The local Creoles in São Tomé and Príncipe were not categorized as indígenas either but formally received citizenship only in 1953.

The massive recruitment of African contract workers soon changed the demographic balance in the archipelago to the detriment of the native Creole population. From 1900 until the 1940s the contract workers outnumbered the native islanders. Frequently the living and working conditions of the African contract workers on the estates were similar to those of the slaves before. Generally, the local Creole population, Forros and Angolares alike, refused to do contract labor as they considered it beneath their status as free Africans. However, the Forros accepted wage work in the repair shops, offices, and hospitals on the *roças*, while others occupied the lower functions in the colonial bureaucracy. The Angolares carried out odd jobs as woodcutters on the plantations and as boatmen in the coastal shipping of cash crops from the plantations to the harbor. Forros who did not work for the colonists were able to subsist on the produce of their small *glebas*, the sale of palm wine and locally produced gin to the plantation workers, and the sale of cocoa stolen from the *roças*.[41] The coexistence of the subsistence of the *glebas* and the cash crop production of the plantations corresponded to two lifestyles, described as "two mentalities that react in a different way in the presence of a common nature."[42]

Having been descendants of manumitted slaves, the harsh labor regime on plantations reinforced the Forros' negative view toward manual field labor. Due to their aversion to plantation labor, the Forros had a bad reputation among the white colonists. The whites considered them lazy, arrogant, and a threat to the labor discipline of the *serviçais*, but also recognized that this attitude was possibly a legacy of slavery. The tension between a white-dominated labor system and the local Creoles' persistent refusal to work on the plantations contributed to racial divisions. The colonial government's attempt to break the Forro resistance resulted in the bloody events of February 1953, known as the Batepá War. At the time, persistent rumors that Gov. Carlos Gorgulho (1945–53) wanted to force the Forros to work on the *roças* to solve the labor shortage provoked a spontaneous protest of Forros, to which the governor responded with a wave of excessive violence that killed hundreds of unarmed and innocent Creoles over several days.[43] In the 1960s, the bloody events proved the violent character of Portuguese colonialism and justified demands for the archipelago's independence.

Since the 1930 the *roças* had been inefficient and unprofitable due to the imbalance between their costs of production and the international cocoa prices.[44] Increasing competition by more efficient West African smallholders contributed to the decline of São Tomé's cocoa plantations. For example, in 1955 the labor costs in São Tomé, including salary, food, medical assistance, recruitment, and repatriation, absorbed 70 percent of the gross value of exports, whereas on the Gold Coast and Fernando Pó at the same time the production costs were only 33 percent and 38 percent, respectively.[45] While the wages of the plantation workers were very low, the total costs of contract labor were comparatively high due to high

Table 2.3. São Tomé's cocoa exports in tons and share of total exports in terms of value

Year	1900	1907	1910	1920	1930	1940	1950	1960	1968
Quantity	11,429	22,861	36,148	19,019	9,646	6,972	8,003	10,169	11,086
Percentage	91.4	97.0	96.8	95.1	74.1	76.2	67.1	73.9	80.7

Source: F. M. Carvalho Rodrigues, *S. Tomé e Príncipe sob o ponto de vista agrícola* (Lisbon: Junta de Investigações Científicas do Ultramar, 1974), 70.

recruitment costs, an expensive supervisory labor force, and the low productivity of poorly motivated and unskilled workers.[46] The inefficiency of the allocation of labor further increased the total labor costs. Due to the resulting decline, by independence in 1975 the total area planted with cocoa had dwindled to less than 61,776 acres.[47]

Until independence the majority of the plantations were owned by private limited companies based in Portugal and mostly controlled by a single family.[48] The absentee owners, who often possessed several *roças*, were represented by administrators who managed the plantations. The estates varied considerably in size, ranging from some twenty-five acres to about 24,710 acres. The larger estates featured all the characteristics of a total institution, as described by the sociologist Ervin Goffman. They were not exclusively agricultural enterprises but self-contained communities with their own chapel, school, kindergarten, and health services. The labor decree of 1903 fixed the daily working hours at nine hours a day, except on Sundays, when the workers were supposed to work five hours. From 9 p.m. to 5.30 a.m. the plantation workers were locked up in the quarters. Until the 1950s workers could not leave the *roças* freely outside working hours. They were not allowed either to till provision grounds or to gain any additional income from other activity outside the estate because the planters monopolized the use of both land and labor. Half of a worker's salary was deposited in a Repatriation Fund and paid only when the contract worker returned home.[49] Every June and December the plantations distributed clothes to the workers, and once in May a cotton blanket.

Until 1909 the legally obligated repatriation of the contract workers at the end of their contract was rarely honored.[50] Frequently the planters extended the contracts without consent of the workers. Many African workers did not survive the hard life in the archipelago. Between 1911 and 1928 a total of 23,866 plantation workers died.[51] Mortality rates among the African workers varied considerably from 22 percent in Príncipe in

1902, due to the outbreak of sleeping sickness, to 2.5 percent in Príncipe in 1917, three years after the Portuguese had successfully eradicated the disease on the small island.[52] Although legally prohibited, corporal punishments were frequently applied on many estates. Reports by British missionaries and journalists of the brutal practices of the recruitment agents in Angola, the miserable living and working conditions on the estates, and the fact that they were rarely repatriated prompted a campaign by British antislavery circles that culminated in 1909 in a boycott of São Tomé cocoa by William Cadbury of Birmingham and other British and German chocolate manufacturers. The Portuguese, however, suggested that the true reasons for the boycott were not humanistic concerns but rather the competition of the Gold Coast cocoa.[53]

In response to the cocoa boycott, the Portuguese Republican government that came to power in 1910 introduced some measures aimed at improving the living conditions of the contract workers. The enforcement of regular repatriation resulted in the departure of 40,880 *serviçais* between 1908 and 1928. From 1928 to 1958, another 92,277 workers returned to their home countries.[54] A second reform of the contract labor regime occurred after the Second World War as a response to labor shortages in the archipelago. The plantations were obliged to provide school education for the children and medical assistance according to the number of the workers employed on the estate. The estates had to provide food and housing with a minimum of 43 square feet per worker.[55] The third reform of the system was the abolition of the discriminatory indígenas status in 1961, which at least formally abolished the legal distinction between Angolans and Mozambicans and the native and Cabo Verdean Creoles.

Interestingly, in contrast to the plantation slaves in earlier periods, and despite their significantly larger communities, the contract workers did not organize any collective resistance action. Due to the repressive structures of the modern plantation system, the *serviçais* were subject to more strict control, impeding them from organizing. Unlike during the sugar era, almost the entire archipelago was covered by plantations, depriving rebellious contract workers of potential refuge. Furthermore, while revolting slaves in earlier times were confronted with only the planters and settlers, the *serviçais* had to deal with white colonists, who controlled and oppressed them, and the native islanders who excluded and disdained them. Finally, they could preserve a glimmer of hope since they stayed only temporarily and at least theoretically could leave the islands freely after the end of their contracts. Since independence in 1975, the former contract workers have been gradually assimilated into the Forro society through migration, acculturation, and unions, which has blurred the former sociocultural differences between the different groups.

Conditioned by the political context of the decolonization process in Portuguese Africa, São Tomé and Príncipe became a socialist one-party state ruled by the Movimento de Libertação de São Tomé e Príncipe (MLSTP), or the Liberation Movement of São Tomé and Príncipe, after independence in 1975. Consequently, the country maintained preferential relations with Angola, Cuba, China, the former Soviet Union, and other former socialist countries. However, Western states remained the most important trading partners. By independence, most of the roughly 2,000 Portuguese colonial officials and plantation managers had already departed, depriving the newly independent country of trained and experienced personnel to run the public administration and the plantations. Due to a lack of adequate training, most Sãotomeans who took over the public administration and the plantations were largely ill prepared.

While most Angolan and Mozambican contract workers returned to their home countries, some 9,000 Cabo Verdeans remained in São Tomé.[56] Their poor, drought-stricken country was not prepared to receive so many returnees, while the Sãotomean government was aware of their importance for the plantation economy. Due to the local Creoles' traditional disdain for plantation work, not even poorly educated Forros were ready to replace the repatriated contract workers on the plantations.

As already pointed out, by independence about 61,776 acres were still cultivated in cocoa. On September 30, 1975, the MLSTP regime decreed the nationalization of the plantations. Twenty-three Portuguese-owned medium to large-scale *roças* over 494 acres were nationalized without compensation.[57] In 1978 another 27 privately owned estates were confiscated by the government.[58] In 1979 the nationalized estates were regrouped into 15 so-called Empresas Estatais Agro-pecuárias (State Agriculture and Livestock Enterprises), which were managed by the ministry of agriculture.[59] The areas of these large-scale plantations ranged from about 5,856 acres to 42,141 acres. Under state ownership, the Portuguese were replaced by local Creoles, but the physical layout and the whole internal structure of the estates remained virtually unchanged. The state now possessed about 92 percent of the total land, whereas only the *glebas*, totaling 12,108 acres remained privately owned by Forro smallholders. The ministry of agriculture, which was formally in charge of the *empresas*, also appointed the directors of the plantations, who were exclusively prominent Forros. The new managers of the plantations lacked adequate experience and were unfit to run the enterprises efficiently.

Due to the departure of the Portuguese and the transition to a state-run economy, in 1975 cocoa production declined by some 50 percent to 5,000 tons. The independent state failed to replace the colonial regime of forced labor by a productive work ethic and incentives for plantation workers. Nevertheless in 1979–80, the *empresas* partially recovered, reaching an annual cocoa output of 7,000 tons, thanks to a three-year rehabilitation program of $18.4 million financed by international donors. Since 1976, the country benefited from the sudden rise in world cocoa prices, which lasted until 1980, when prices slumped drastically. However, the higher output and the temporary price boom helped to disguise the true deficiencies of the country's plantation economy.

In fact, the state had invested little in the *empresas* to purchase new machinery, plant young cocoa trees, or improve the management. Although the national economy was based entirely on agriculture, only 22 percent of total investment from 1975 to 1987 supported this sector. Consequently, cocoa output began gradually to decrease when the existing infrastructures of the nationalized plantations had been depleted. Except for a few estates, almost all the others fell into decay and some secondary plantations were abandoned completely due to mismanagement and other shortcomings. As a result, not even half of the available land was cultivated. Estates with an annual production capacity of 2,000 tons of cocoa produced only between 300 and 400 tons. The productivity of the plantations dropped from 882–992 pounds per 2.5 acres of cocoa before independence to only 507 pounds per 2.5 acres in 1981 and continued trending down.[60] After 1980, total annual cacao production declined gradually to the low point of 3,400 tons in 1984. The government also failed to achieve its target to diversify agricultural exports. At independence in 1975, cocoa accounted for 90 percent of all exports, while in 1987 the crop represented 94 percent of total export income.[61]

The economic failure prompted the MLSTP regime to abandon its socialist policies and approach the West for development assistance. At the same time, the government initiated a gradual liberalization of the domestic economy. In 1984, the MLSTP-regime signed an agreement with the World Bank and the International Monetary Fund on the rehabilitation of the cacao plantations through private foreign management contracts financed by multilateral creditors. Three years later, both sides agreed that the cocoa rehabilitation project would be carried out under a Structural Adjustment Program (PAE). The World Bank attributed São Tomé's failure under the one-party regime to pervasive government control of economic activity and to externally financed investments that did not build on the local economy's comparative advantage. These investments did not lead to

Table 2.4. Cocoa, annual production in tons 1988–2003

Year	1988	1990	1992	1994	1996	1998	2000	2002	2003
Quantity	4,560	3,640	3,688	3,392	3,500	3,928	2,883	3,462	3,820

Source: Gerhard Seibert, *Comrades, Clients and Comrades* (Leiden, Netherlands: Brill, 2006), 601.

economic growth or new sources of export income but deprived the traditional cash crop sector of necessary inputs and resulted in an unsustainable foreign debt—$144.1 million (322 percent of GDP) at the end of 1990.[62]

Between 1986 and 1990, the management of five state-owned estates was transferred to various European companies under renewable contracts with a fixed term of between ten and fifteen years. The remaining ten estates failed to attract foreign investors. The management contracts, agricultural inputs and machinery, civil works, and equipment for the five enterprises under rehabilitation were financed by bilateral and multilateral institutions with funds of some $40 million. The principal objective of the rehabilitation project was to increase cocoa output in order to assist the country to achieve quick economic recovery.

In the years 1988 and 1989, the five enterprises with foreign management succeeded in increasing cocoa output by 17.5 and 7.9 percent, respectively. Their average annual yield was 520 pounds per 2.5 acres by 1991, while that of the other estates continued to decline.[63] However, given the falling international cocoa price, the five estates produced at the margins of or beyond profitability. Although the overall cacao production increased to 4,800 tons in 1988, it again declined to 2,799 tons in 1990. Due to decreasing cocoa prices on the world market, the initially increased annual production did not result in higher export incomes. The calculations of the Bretton Wood institutions were based on a cocoa price of $1,526 per ton, whereas in October 1990 this rate was less than $1,000. Consequently, instead of the targeted export income of $8.4 million in 1989, exports were worth only $5.9 million.

In view of the failure of the cocoa rehabilitation project with private management, the World Bank recommended that São Tomé dismantle the estates. Soon after the country's transition to multiparty democracy in 1991, the first democratically elected government announced a land reform intended to transform the plantation economy into a new agrarian structure dominated by small and medium-sized farmers. The latter were mostly local merchants and politicians. The project, financed by the World Bank, aimed at diversifying and increasing food and cash crop production to considerably reduce food imports and increase agricultural exports.[64] In 1990 the proportion between plantation lands and smallholder plots (*glebas*) had remained virtually unchanged since 1926. About 86 percent of the agricultural area of 188,328 acres was in the possession of the large plantations, which were nationalized in 1975. Only 83,575 acres (52 percent) of the plantation lands were under cultivation, of which 54,963 acres were in cocoa, 17,915 acres in coconuts, 6,758 acres in oil palms, and 2,426 acres in coffee.[65]

In 1993 the government initiated the distribution of former estate lands on a usufruct base as it was not willing to grant full possession rights. By 1997, 112 medium-sized enterprises had received a total of 12,775 acres.[66] From 1993 to 2003, 107,545 acres were distributed to a total of 8,735 small farmers. The average size of their plots was eight acres.[67] The small farmers were constrained by several shortcomings, including a lack of training, a shortage of tools and credit, and poor access to markets due to deficient transport.

One objective of the privatization of agriculture had been to increase the output of cocoa from 8,000 to 10,000 tons, the production level prior to independence. In fact, however, cocoa exports dropped from 4,800 tons in 1991 to 3,200 tons in 1996, even less than the low 1984 output of 3,400 tons that prompted the cocoa rehabilitation program. Despite the declining production, in 1996 cocoa accounted for 96.6 percent of export of goods.[68] In the last fifteen years the highest cocoa output was 3,820 tons in 2003, while the lowest production was 2,208 in 2011. In 2013 cacao exports still represented 92.4 percent of agricultural exports.[69] From 2016 to 2017, cocoa exports increased from 3,000 tons to 3,500 tons and represented 93.5 percent and 92.9 percent of the export of goods in terms of value, respectively.[70] The various figures indicate the complete failure of the land distribution program to boost cocoa production and diversify agricultural exports.

The Oil Boom That Never Was[71]

While the dismantling of the plantation economy was still under way, the country began to place great hopes in the development of an oil industry. Experts considered the terms of São Tomé and Príncipe's first oil agreements as unfavorable for the country. The one-sided agreements were due to the inexperience of São Tomé negotiators and bribery. In 1997 São Tomé signed its first oil production agreement with the little-known Environmental Remediation Holding Company (ERHC), at the time owned by American businessmen. The following year, São Tomé signed an agreement on seismic surveys with Mobil (presently ExxonMobil). In 1999 São Tomé's government unilaterally rescinded the agreement with ERHC, arguing that the company had failed to meet is contractual obligations. In response, ERHC lodged a request for arbitration at the International Chamber of Commerce in Paris. Meanwhile, following bilateral negotiations, São Tomé reached maritime border agreements with Gabon and Equatorial Guinea. After maritime border talks with Nigeria failed, the two countries achieved an agreement on the establishment of a 10,811 square-mile large Joint Development Zone (JDZ) in the disputed waters, which was formally signed in February 2001. Under the agreement, the JDZ was to be managed by a Joint Development Authority (JDA) based in Abuja, while costs and profits were divided in the ratio 60:40 between Nigeria and São Tomé and Príncipe.

Shortly before the treaty with Nigeria was signed, São Tomé concluded an agreement with the Norwegian oil service company Petroleum Geo-Services (PGS) on the execution of additional seismic studies. In May 2001, São Tomé settled the conflict with ERHC that meanwhile had been taken over by the Houston-based company Chrome Energy Corporation, owned by the Nigerian businessman Sir Emeka Offor. In the settlement São Tomé allowed the company, now renamed ERHC Energy, far-reaching financial advantages within the JDZ in return for the company's support in the development of the country's oil sector. Consequently, the IMF blamed the São Tomé government for a lack of transparency in its oil dealings and considered the agreement with ERHC Energy as prejudicial for the country's national interests. In April 2002 American legal experts considered the agreements with ERHC Energy and PGS as extremely one-sided in favor of the two foreign companies that had received preferential rights in various oil blocks. They only assessed the agreement with Mobil as in line with similar contracts in the international oil industry.

Finally, the three agreements with ExxonMobil, PGS, and ERHC Energy were all renegotiated with slightly improved terms in early 2003. In April that year the licensing round for the first nine blocks in the JDZ was officially launched in Abuja. Optimistic estimates of oil reserves in the nine blocks ranged from six to eleven billion barrels of crude oil. At the time, the JDA fixed the minimum bid per block at $30 million.

In October 2003, twenty oil companies submitted thirty-three bids for eight of the nine oil blocks in the JDZ that had been offered for public tender. Block 7 did not receive a valid bid and Block 8 failed to attract any bid at all. Chevron submitted the highest bid of $125 million for Block 1, then the most promising block. Altogether a total of about $500 million in signature bonuses was offered for the seven blocks. However, except Chevron and Anadarko, most of the bidders were unknown small companies without proven technical and financial capacities. Nevertheless, the result of the licensing round provoked a wave of enthusiasm in São Tomé since the amount was equivalent to about eight times the country's annual GDP at the time. People expected oil production to start within a few years. However, the start of oil production was postponed again and again since no company has discovered commercially viable quantities of oil in the country's territorial waters. Curiously, despite the absence of any production, São Tomé and Príncipe has had fourteen different oil ministers since 1999.

In 2004, São Tomé and Príncipe set up a National Oil Agency (ANP), whose staff was subsequently trained by foreign oil experts financed by the World Bank and the Norwegian Agency for Development Aid (Norad). In April of the same year, the JDA awarded the exploration rights for Block 1 jointly to ChevronTexaco (51 percent), ExxonMobil (40 percent), and Dangote Equity Energy Resources (DEER, 9 percent), a company owned by Nigerian business tycoon Aliko Dangote. Block 1 entitled São Tomé and Príncipe to a signature bonus share of $49 million. Simultaneously, the JDA decided to withdraw blocks 7–9 from the auction and organized a new bidding round for blocks 2–6 since the JDA wanted to avoid awarding the blocks to companies with dubious financial and technical capacities. The outcome of the second licensing round revealed in December 2004 was disappointing since no major oil company participated and only the highest bid of $175 million for Block 4 was considerably higher than the previous offer of $100 million.

Attracted by São Tomé's anticipated oil wealth, a self-proclaimed STP country advisory group, headed by the development economist Jeffrey Sachs of the Earth Institute at Columbia University in New York, arrived in São Tomé in November 2003 and offered the local authorities free assistance to elaborate São Tomé's oil revenue management law, demanded by the IMF. Sachs seemed determined to make São Tomé and Príncipe a showcase, where oil wealth would become a blessing, not a curse, as had happened in so many other oil-producing countries. The Sachs team prepared the text of the Abuja Joint Declaration, a nine-point agreement on transparency in payments, expenditure, and other dealings in the transactions in the JDZ, signed by Nigerian President Obasanjo and President Menezes in June 2004. The guidelines for reporting of this document were those adopted by the Extractive Industries Transparency Initiative (EITI). All information to be made public according to the declaration would appear on the Web site of the JDA. However, the Abuja Joint Declaration was a mere declaration of intention without any legally binding force. Not surprisingly, from the beginning the guidelines of the Abuja Joint Declaration have been widely ignored.

Initially São Tomé welcomed the engagement of Columbia University since it could improve the negative associations of the local authorities with corruption and mismanagement. Besides, the country lacked the legal expertise to elaborate its oil legislation. In addition to the Sachs advisory team, the government asked the World Bank for assistance in drafting the oil legislation. Subsequently, the World Bank paid another expert team headed by former Alaska governor Steve Cowper to draft a legal proposal. The oil revenue management law approved by the National Assembly in November 2004 was largely based on the draft of the Columbia University expert team. The bill provides for the creation of a National Oil Account, the establishment of a Permanent Reserve Fund for future generations, annual audits of the oil accounts, and transparency principles.

Besides the law, the Sachs team elaborated an integrated development plan for the country called "Towards a Consensus Plan of Action for São Tomé and Príncipe" and carried out consultancies in several socioeconomic areas. The various consultancy reports were published in English and Portuguese on the Earth Institute's Web site. President Menezes's relationship with the advisory team soon deteriorated since he viewed their engagement increasingly as interference in his country's internal affairs, while the government largely ignored the reports and recommendations produced by the US experts. In turn, the Sachs team was disappointed by Menezes, who turned out to be less responsible than the experts had anticipated. Largely ignored by the local authorities and frustrated by the absence of oil, the Sachs team left São Tomé unheralded in 2007. The Earth Institute's only legacy in the archipelago has been the oil revenue management law. However, this legislation, internationally praised as exemplary, has never actually been fully applied for the simple reason that the country has not produced a single drop of oil yet.

In April 2005 in Abuja, the JDA approved the awards of the five JDZ blocks. The announcement, however, was delayed by fierce accusations of irregularities in São Tomé. In a report, the country's ANP blamed the JDA of having done insufficient due diligence of bidders' backgrounds and expressed fears that awards given to inexperienced Nigerian companies might frustrate seasoned operators. São Tomé's parliamentary Committee for Oil Affairs concluded that the decision of the awards had violated the established rules and asked the Public Ministry to investigate the case. Pressured by his Nigerian counterpart, in May 2005 Menezes approved the original award recommendations. Nigerian officials had allegedly threatened to withhold São Tomé's share of the signature bonus for Block 1 unless Mene-zes ratified the awards.

The five blocks were awarded to different consortiums that all included ERHC Energy. Following the request of the parliamentarian oil commit-tee, São Tomé's attorney general began an investigation into the five block awards. In October, the attorney general declared that the investigations in São Tomé had revealed serious irregularities in the process of the second licensing round, including a lack of due diligence about the Nigerian bid-ders' financial and technical capabilities.

Soon after the end of the second licensing round, the ownership of the licences in four blocks changed considerably through consecutive acquisi-tions by the Swiss company Addax Petroleum and the Chinese Sinopec, which became the majority stakeholders.

Still in January 2006, ChevronTexaco started drilling the first explora-tion well in Block 1 of the JDZ. The well was finished at the cost of $37 million in March, but no commercially exploitable oil was discovered. In the same month, the JDA signed production sharing contracts (PSC) for blocks 2, 3, and 4, for which signature bonuses of $71 million, $40 million, and $90 million were paid respectively. The signature of PSC's for blocks 5 and 6 was postponed.[72] Due to ERHC's bonus-free options, São Tomé was entitled to receive only $28.6 million of the total amount. From this amount the country had to settle a debt of $15 million with Nigeria.

With the support of the World Bank in early 2008, São Tomé and Prín-cipe applied for candidate status of EITI, a global standard to improve transparency in natural resources. In April 2010, the EITI board rejected the government's request for voluntary suspension and excluded the country from the application process because it had not implemented the established minimum requirements for candidate countries. In a letter to President Menezes, EITI chairman Peter Eigen informed that "In taking its decision, the Board concluded that implementation had been stalled mainly due to circumstances related to the joint management with Nigeria of the Joint Development Zone, and that São Tomé and Príncipe should re-apply when the circumstances for rapid implementation were more favourable."[73] Finally, in May 2012 São Tomé's government reapplied for the candidate status. In October of that year the EITI board approved the application and asked the country to publish its first EITI report by Octo-ber 2014. The report covering the period from 2003 to 2013 was pub-lished in December that year and a second and third EITI report on the years 2014 and 2015 followed in September 2015 and December 2017, respectively.[74]

In late 2009 Sinopec and Addax Petroleum, which had been taken over by Sinopec in October that year, started exploration drillings in JDZ blocks 2, 3, and 4. The results revealed in 2012 were disappointing since no commercially viable oil was discovered. Consequently, in that year Sinopec, its subsidiary Addax, and other companies abandoned the three oil blocks, leaving ERHC Energy as the only stakeholder. Following the debacle with the three blocks, São Tomé put all remaining hopes on JDZ Block 1, whose ownership had also changed in 2007 and 2010 respectively when Addax acquired ExxonMobil's 40 percent working interests, while the French Total took over Chevron's majority stake. In December 2011, Total announced it would invest $200 million in the drilling of two wells in Block 1. Despite the negative results of Chevron's earlier exploration drillings in Block 1, Total's takeover heightened renewed expectations since the block is located adjacent to OML 130 in Nigerian waters, where the French company successfully extracts oil.

In 2012, Total drilled the two announced exploration wells. Eventually, in September 2013, Total announced it would abandon Block 1, arguing that the hydrocarbon reserves discovered were too limited to justify further investments. Addax followed suit, leaving DEER as the only remaining stakeholder in the acreage. Despite the enormous setback, the JDA in Abuja showed confidence to attract other smaller oil companies willing to invest in the four JDZ blocks abandoned since 2012. In June 2015 the JDA signed a new production-sharing contract for Block 1 with two Nigerian companies. One month later, DEER exited the block. In September 2016, the ownership of Block 1 was restructured, the operatorship changed, and another two Nigerian shareholders were included.

JDZ blocks 5 and 6, awarded in 2005, have not been developed at all. Since 2004, the JDA has not organized any other licensing round for the JDZ. Meanwhile, the office in Abuja, staffed by fifty-nine employees, has become a financial burden with an annual budget of about $13 million, 40 percent of which has to be financed by São Tomé, a poor country with an annual budget of about $150 million. From 2001 to 2014, the JDZ has generated revenue of about $303 million, of which $272 million were signature bonuses. However, in the same period, the operation costs of the JDA accounted to $129 million (43 percent of total revenue). São Tomé's 40 percent share of this amount was $41.9 million. Until 2007, São Tomé paid its share of $15.2 million. Since 2008, however, São Tomé has not paid its 40 percent share of the JDA's expensive operation costs, resulting in a $26.7 million bilateral debt with Nigeria until 2014.[75]

In March 2014, during a hearing at the Nigerian parliamentary Committee on Co-operation and Integration in Africa in the National Assembly,

Foreign Minister Nuruddeen Mohamed described the JDZ as a loss-making venture and the chairman of the committee, Abukar Momoh, declared that Nigeria could not continue to fund a joint venture that was of no economic benefit and, consequently, could revoke the treaty with São Tomé. Evidently prompted by the Nigerian threats, one week later, the executive directors of the JDA in Abuja, Luís dos Prazeres and Kashim Tumsah, publicly claimed that thanks to the application of new drilling techniques, oil production in JDZ Block 1 could start within eighteen months. By the end of 2018, however, oil production in Block 1 had not started, while blocks 2, 3, and 4 had failed to attract new investors.

After initial setbacks, the developments in São Tomé's own EEZ have been somewhat more promising since 2016. In March 2010, the ANP launched the first licensing round for seven oil blocks in the EEZ. Shortly before, blocks 4 and 11 had been allocated to ERHC Energy and blocks 5 and 12 were awarded to Equator Exploration (the company had acquired PGS rights in these blocks in 2004) under preferential agreements. Only six companies submitted bids for the EEZ blocks. Again, the oil majors did not show up. In May 2011 the government awarded the exploration license for Block 3 of the EEZ to the Nigerian company Oranto Petroleum, while the other six blocks were not attributed to any of the other five third-tier oil companies. In October the same year, the government signed a PSC with Oranto that paid a signature bonus of $2 million.

Until March 2018, PSC have been signed for another seven EEZ blocks with Equator Exploration, Sinoangol, Kosmos Energy, Galp Energia, British Petroleum. and ERHC Energy, respectively. Altogether the government received signature bonuses of $23.5 million for the eight blocks. Since 2016, Kosmos Energy has become the largest investor in the EEZ with stakes in six of the eight blocks with a PSC. In 2017, 3D seismic surveys were carried out in four blocks jointly owned by Kosmos and Galp. However, exploration drillings have not yet taken place in any of the EEZ blocks. Despite the block awards from 2015 to 2018, there is little doubt that until exploration drillings have definitively proved the existence of commercially viable oil, the prospects of the EEZ will remain uncertain.

The excitement and high hopes of rapid oil wealth in São Tomé and Príncipe, first sparked by the first licensing round of the JDZ in 2003, have long faded away. However, despite the poor prospects, international organizations like the IMF and the African Development Bank have maintained optimistic economic growth forecasts for the impoverished twin-island republic, based largely on erroneous oil production forecasts.[76] Based on the archipelago's anticipated oil revenue, still in October 2012 the US online business news site *Business Insider* even forecast São Tomé and Príncipe as the world's fastest-growing economy from 2013 to 2017. Yet, the consecutive exit of ExxonMobil, Chevron, Sinopec, and Total from the JDZ has exposed such optimistic economic growth forecasts as wishful thinking, if not sheer fantasy. The truth is that currently there is no guarantee that São Tomé and Príncipe will become an oil producer, at least not in the near future. Only in January 2014 did the IMF admit that "Total's withdrawal has diminished oil prospects for the foreseeable future."[77]

A History of Economic Success and Failure

Since the inexorable decline of its plantation economy after independence, São Tomé and Príncipe has become largely dependent on international development aid. Long ago the small archipelago in the Gulf of Guinea has played an important role in economic history. In the sixteenth century, São Tomé became the first plantation economy in the tropics and an important producer of sugar. It was also the origin of one of the first Creole societies in Atlantic history. The islands had ideal conditions for sugar cultivation, but not for its production since the tropical humidity lessened the quality of São Tomé's sugar. Consequently, when Brazil emerged as a large sugar producer in the late sixteenth century, the sugar industry in São Tomé and Príncipe gradually disappeared. The local plantation economy only reemerged in the second half of the nineteenth century when the Portuguese established large coffee and cocoa plantations. The archipelago was the first place in Africa where cocoa was cultivated. By 1890, cocoa became São Tomé's most important export crop, both in terms of volume and value. During a few years at the beginning of the twentieth century, the small archipelago even was the world's largest cocoa producer. After the Second World War, cocoa production began gradually to decline due to pest infestation and the competition by small farmers in West Africa, whose productivity was higher than the plantation economy based on contract labor in São Tomé. Both in the sixteenth century and in the nineteenth and twentieth centuries, the boom of the plantation economy was based on forced labor.

Despite the downfall of cocoa after independence, it has remained the most important agricultural export crop since consecutive attempts of diversification of cash crops have failed. Both the cocoa rehabilitation with private management in the 1980s and the subsequent distribution of former plantation lands to small farmers in the 1990s have failed to increase cocoa production. In the early 2000s, São Tomé was expected to quickly become a wealthy oil producer, but the beginning of production has been postponed again and again since no oil in commercially viable quantities has been discovered yet. In contrast to sugar and cocoa, the oil boom never was. Consequently, more than forty years after independence, the country remains largely dependent on foreign aid, at least as long as other sources of income have not been developed.

Notes

1 Catarina Madeira Santos, "A formação das estruturas fundiárias e a territorialização das tensões sociais: São Tomé, primeira metade do século XVI," *Studia* 54–55 (1996): 56.

2. Pedro José Paiva da Cunha, "A Organização Económica em São Tomé (de início do povoamento a meados do século XVII)" (MA diss., Coimbra University, Faculdade de Letras, 2001), 27.

3. Cunha, "A Organização Económica," 47.

4. Cunha, "A Organização Económica," 33.

5. Gerhard Seibert, *Comrades, Clients and Cousins: Colonialism, Socialism and Democratization in São Tomé and Príncipe*, 2nd ed. (Leiden, Netherlands: Brill, 2006), 29.

6. John L. Vogt, "The Early São Tomé-Príncipe Slave Trade with Mina, 1500–1540," *International Journal of African Historical Studies* 6, no. 3 (1973): 466.

7. The term is derived from the Portuguese *carta de alforria*, meaning letter of manumission.

8. Rui Ramos, "Rebelião e sociedade colonial: 'alvoroços' e 'levantamentos' em São Tomé (1545–1555)," *Revista Internacional de Estudos Africanos* 4/5 (1986): 24; Izequiel Batista de Sousa, *São Tomé et Príncipe de 1485 à 1755: Une Société Coloniale du Blanc au Noir* (Paris: L'Harmattan, 2008), 41.

9. Cunha, "A Organização Económica," 52.

10. Arlindo Manuel Caldeira, "Rebelião e outras Formas de Resistência à Escravatura na Ilha São Tomé (Séculos XVI a XVIII)," *Africana Studia* 7 (2004): 110.

11. Caldeira, "Rebelião e outras Formas de Resistência," 104.

12. See also Gerhard Seibert, "São Tomé and Príncipe: The First Plantation Economy in the Tropics," in *Commercial Agriculture, the Slave Trade and Slavery in Atlantic Africa*, ed. Robin Law, Suzanne Schwarz, and Silke Strickrodt (Oxford: James Currey, 2013), 54–78.

13. Ramos, "Rebelião," 33.

14. Luís da Cunha Pinheiro, "A conflitualidade social e institucional em S. Tomé ao longo do século XVI" (paper presented at the International Congress Espaço Atlântico de Antigo Regime: poderes e sociedades, Universidade de Lisboa, Portugal, November 1–5, 2005).

15. Hélder Lains e Silva, *São Tomé e Príncipe e a Cultura do Café* (Lisbon: Junta de Investigação do Ultramar, 1958), 83.

16. Pablo B. Eyzaguirre, "Small Farmers and Estates in São Tomé, West Africa" (PhD diss., Yale University, 1986), 60.

17. Robert Garfield, *A History of São Tomé Island 1470–1655: The Key to Guinea* (San Francisco: Mellen Research University Press, 1992), 73.

18. Stuart B. Schwartz, "Introduction," in *Tropical Babylons: Sugar and the Making of the Atlantic World, 1450–1680*, ed. Stuart B. Schwartz (Chapel Hill: University of North Carolina Press, 2004), 18.

19. Cunha, "A Organização Económica," 46.

20. Garfield, *A History of São Tomé Island*, 80.

21. João Lúcio de Azevedo, *Épocas de Portugal Económico*, 2nd ed. (Lisbon: Livraria Clássica, 1947) quoted in Francisco José Tenreiro, "Descrição da ilha de S. Tomé no século XVI,'" *Garcia de Orta* 1, no. 2 (1953): 227.

22. Virginia Rau, "O açúcar de S.Tomé no segundo quartel do século XVII," in *Elementos de História da Ilha de S. Tomé*, ed. Centro de Estudos de Marinha (Lisbon: Centro de Estudos de Marinha, 1971), 8–9; Garfield, *A History of São Tomé Island*, 64.

23. Cunha, "A Organização Económica," 117.

24. Garfield, *A History of São Tomé Island*, 72.

25. Rau, "O açúcar de S. Tomé no segundo quartel do século XVII," 8–9.

26. Lains e Silva, *São Tomé e Príncipe*, 84.

27. Schwartz, "Introduction," 18.

28. Cristina Maria Seuanes Serafim, *As Ilhas de São Tomé no século XVII* (Lisbon: Centro de História de Além-Mar [CHAM], 2000), 210.

29. Arlindo Manuel Caldeira, *Mulheres, Sexualidade e Casamento em São Tomé e Príncipe* (Lisbon: Edições Cosmos: Grupo de Trabalho do Ministério da Educação para as Comemorações dos Descobrimentos Portugueses, 1999), 38.

30. Eyzaguirre, "Small Farmers and Estates," 98.

31. Portuguese colonial literature affirms that cocoa was initially introduced in Príncipe in 1822 as an ornamental plant. However, according to a letter dated November 30, 1821, kept in the Arquivo Histórico Ultramarino (AHU) in Lisbon, at that time cocoa was already introduced from Bahia explicitly as a cash crop in response to a request of King João VI (1816–26), dated October 30, 1819.

32. Eyzaguirre, "Small Farmers and Estates," 161.

33. Francisco José Tenreiro, *A Ilha de São Tomé* (Lisbon: Junta de Investigação do Ultramar, 1961), 81.

34. Orest V. Martyushin, ed., "História da República Democrática de S. Tomé e Príncipe: Esboço Histórico, Económico, Social e Político, 1985," unpublished manuscript, Moscow, 129.

35. Eyzaguirre, "Small Farmers and Estates," 196.

36. Tony Hodges and Malyn Newitt, *São Tomé and Príncipe: From Plantation Colony to Microstate* (Boulder, CO: Westview Press, 1988), 30.

37. Pablo B. Eyzaguirre, "The Independence of São Tomé e Príncipe and Agrarian Reform," *The Journal of Modern African Studies* 27, no. 4 (1989): 672.

38. Robert Nii Nartey, "From Slave to Serviçal: Labor in the Plantation Economy of São Tomé and Príncipe" (PhD diss. University of Illinois at Chicago, 1986), 88.

39. Lains e Silva, *São Tomé e Príncipe*, 106.

40. Josef Matznetter, "Das Problem der Arbeitskraft in Afrika am Beispiel der Kontraktarbeiter der Plantagen von São Tomé und der Minen des Witwaterrandes," *Mitteilungen der Österreichischen Geographischen Gesellschaft* 104, nos. 1–2 (1962): 91.

41. Eyzaguirre, "Small Farmers and Estates," 116.

42. Tenreiro, *A Ilha de São Tomé*, 113.

43. For an account of the events, see Gerhard Seibert, "The February 1953 Massacre in São Tomé: Crack in the Salazarist Image of Multiracial Harmony and Impetus for Nationalist Demands for Independence," *Portuguese Studies Review* 10, no. 2 (2002): 52–77.

44. Eyzaguirre, "Small Farmers and Estates," 289.

45. Ricardo Vaz Monteiro, "A Província de São Tomé e Príncipe na Colonização Portuguesa," in *Conferência Internacional dos Africanistas Ocidentais, 6ª Sessão, 5º Volume* (São Tomé: N.p., 1956), 310.

46. William Gervase Clarence-Smith, "The Hidden Costs of Labour on the Cocoa Plantations of São Tomé and Príncipe, 1875–1914," *Portuguese Studies* 6 (1990): 152.

47. Eyzaguirre, "Small Farmers and Estates," 302.

48. Josef Matznetter, "Die Guineainseln São Tomé und Príncipe und ihre Plantagen," *Geographische Zeitschrift* 4 (1963): 285.

49. Jorge Eduardo da Costa Oliveira, *A Economia de S. Tomé e Príncipe* (Lisbon: Instituto para a Cooperação Económica: Instituto de Investigação Científica e Tropical, 1993), 130.

50. Nartey, "From Slave to Serviçal," 77.

51. Oliveira, *A Economia de S. Tomé*, 244.

52. Clarence-Smith, "The Hidden Costs of Labour," 157.

53. Tenreiro, *A Ilha de São Tomé*, 231.

54. Oliveira, *A Economia de S. Tomé*, 246.

55. Adelino Macedo, "Aspectos Sociais do Trabalho na Província de São Tomé e Príncipe," in *Conferência Internacional dos Africanistas Ocidentais, 6ª Sessão, 5º Volume* (São Tomé: N.p., 1956), 276.

56. Eyzaguirre, "Small Farmers and Estates," 350.

57. Law decree no. 24 (October 31, 1975).

58. Law decree no. 32 (October 24, 1978).

59. Law decree no. 14 (March 20, 1980).

60. International Monetary Fund, *São Tomé and Príncipe: Recent Economic Developments* (Washington, DC: International Monetary Fund, 1988), 2.

61. Martin Schümer, "Demokratisierung in São Tomé und Príncipe," in *Demokratie und Strukturreformen im portugiesisch-sprachigen Afrika*, ed. Peter Meyns (Freiburg i. Br.: Arnold Bergstraesser Institut, 1992), 209.

62. The World Bank, *São Tomé and Príncipe, Country Economic Memorandum* (Washington, DC: World Bank, June 1993).

63. Direcção de Estudo e Planeamento do Ministério de Agricultura, São Tomé, 1991.

64. The World Bank, "Projecto de Privatização da Agricultura e de Desenvolvimento da Pequena Propriedade," Report no. 9963-STP (November 1991).

65. Recenseamento Agrícola, 1990.

66. The World Bank, "São Tomé and Príncipe," *Public Finance Review* (September 1997): 12.

67. Gerhard Seibert, "São Tomé and Principe," in *Africa South of the Sahara 2015* (London: Routledge 2014), 1014.

68. The World Bank, "São Tomé and Príncipe," 11.

69. Seibert, "São Tomé and Principe."

70. Instituto Nacional de Estatística, Estatísticas do Comércio Externo. Ano 2017, São Tomé, 2018, 15.

71. For a more detailed account of the period 1997–2007, see Gerhard Seibert, "São Tomé and Príncipe: The Troubles of Oil in an Aid-Dependent Micro-State," in *Extractive Economies and Conflicts in the Global South: Multi-regional Perspectives on Rentier Politics*, ed. Kenneth Omeje (Aldershot, UK: Ashgate Publishing, 2008), 119–34.

72. In 2012 a PSC was signed for Block 5.

73. Letter from Dr. Peter Eigen to HE President Fradique de Menezes, Democratic Republic of São Tomé and Príncipe (April 29, 2010).

74. Available at http://www.eiti.st.

75. São Tomé and Príncipe, Second EITI Report 2014, São Tomé, 2015.

76. A. Segura, "Management of Oil Wealth under the Permanent Income Hypothesis: The Case of São Tomé and Príncipe," IMF Working Paper (Washington, DC: International Monetary Fund, 2006), 20.

77. International Monetary Fund, "Democratic Republic of São Tomé and Príncipe," Country Report no. 14/2 (Washington, DC: International Monetary Fund, December 30, 2014), 24, http://www.imf.org/external/pubs/ft/scr/2014/cr1402.pdf.

3

The Bijagos of Canhabac Island (Guinea-Bissau)

Joshua Bernard Forrest

It is difficult to imagine a more defiantly quixotic and historically bellicose people than those who inhabit Canhabac Island in the Bijagos Archipelago, just off the southerly coast of Guinea-Bissau. Since the settlement of the archipelago in the thirteenth to the fourteenth centuries, the indigenous people of Canhabac, called Canhabacers or the Bijagos of Canhabac, have proven their skill not only as fishermen, builders of seafaring canoes, agriculturalists, barter merchants, artisanal craftsmen, and spiritualists, but also as coastal slave raiders, slave traders, international commercialists, and capable of a fierce and effective defense of their islands against a lengthy historical train of would-be invaders. The Portuguese waged repeated wars against Canhabacers, usually to be repeatedly turned back or worn down; French and British warships had several military encounters with Canhabac war canoes on the high seas, mostly ending badly for the Europeans. Enthusiastic to develop economic exchange relations with coastal peoples—and with European settlers—and happy to join a network of global trade relations throughout their storied history, Canhabac islanders also have made clear, over the centuries, their determination to retain political autonomy over their habitat.

In this study, these themes are pursued in order to make clear the unusual ways in which the Bijagos of Canhabac have asserted themselves in the past several centuries both defensively as well as in pursuing offensive military operations; actively engaging in global commercial relations while at the same time painstakingly recreating a self-sustaining economic neoautarchy. Social relations were characterized by an enduring village-centered authority system in which decision-making roles were remarkably

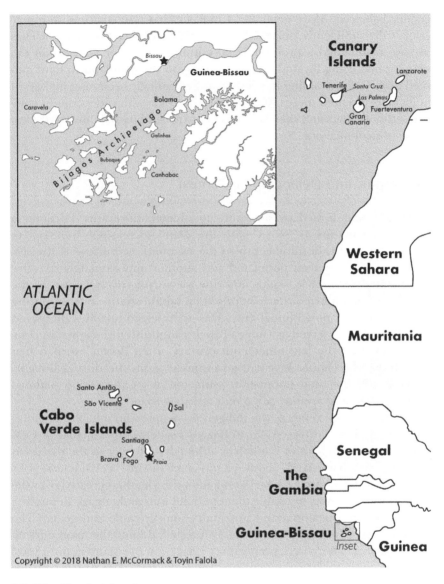

3.1: The North Atlantic

gender balanced. More generally, I indicate that Canhabacers were geographically sufficiently isolated from mainland Guinea-Bissauan societies to have maintained a profoundly decentralized form of self-rule on the island, while being located sufficiently close to the mainland to have pursued massive slave raiding in prior centuries, initially becoming immersed in globally oriented mercantile relations via trade with independent colonial settler-farmers and then via "development" and partial monetarization in the postcolonial era.

Geographic and Demographic Context

Canhabac—mentioned in sixteenth- to nineteenth-century Portuguese archival documents as "Roxa" with the island increasingly referred to as "Canhabac" in the nineteenth to the twentieth centuries—is the second largest of nineteen populated and another approximately sixty-five uninhabited very small islands and tiny islets, collectively known as the Bijagos, an archipelago that comprised an administrative district during the colonial and postcolonial eras. This archipelago includes the island of Bolama, which served as Guinea-Bissau's administrative capital in colonial times until the late nineteenth century, when Bissau usurped that role. Today the Guinea-Bissauan government terms the district Bolama-Bijagos, with the total population estimated at 34,563 (2009 national census), including around 7,650 on Canhabac Island.[1]

The Bijagos also refers to the indigenous people who inhabit the entire archipelago. For clarity we refer to Bijagos residents of Canhabac as Canhabacers or the Bijagos of Canhabac, although they refer to themselves as Anhaki. Canhabac Island, about 33,359 acres in size, is characterized by heavily forested, densely packed woodland, with clearings created over the centuries by islanders to enable them to build huts and engage in farming (mostly rice and peanuts) and husbandry (mostly cattle and goats). The island still remains remarkably densely forested, despite the many agricultural clearings. There were twenty-three villages on the island in the 1800s; contemporarily there are nineteen villages, the largest of which contains 300–400 inhabitants.[2] (Population figures are approximate at best, due to temporary out-migration flows for purposes of education or job seeking.)

As the island is located about twelve miles from the Guinea-Bissau mainland,[3] Canhabacers were able to row their seagoing canoes into the rivers of Guinea-Bissau (four principal rivers extend considerably far inland),[4] which they have been doing since at least the sixteenth century and, in all likelihood, for centuries prior to that.

Origins

Until the 1990s, most historians specializing in Guinea-Bissau concurred that the people now known as the Bijagos settled Canhabac and nearby islands in the thirteenth century, having first been expelled from what is today mainland Guinea-Bissau by the Biaffada, who had themselves fled from the expanding Mali Empire.[5] However, based on a linguistic analysis, an alternative origin is suggested by the fact that the Bijagos language has a word base that is closer to Bantu speakers in southern Africa than to the indigenous languages spoken along the Guinean coast.[6] As much as 40 percent of the Bijagos language base as spoken on Canhabac is very similar to Bantu words, whereas only approximately 10 percent of their word base can be linked to Atlantic coastal languages.[7] Based on this morphological analysis, it appears likely that Canhabac was settled earlier than the thirteenth century, that is, before the expansion of the Mali Empire, prior to when they might otherwise have been integrated with Atlantic coast populations enough to absorb more Atlantic language influences. This raises the possibility that they arrived on Canhabac directly from southern Africa in perhaps the eleventh or twelfth century and without yet mixing extensively with local coastal Guinean populations.[8] This might account for the relative uniqueness of their language and could help to explain that they were already well entrenched long before they were confronted by European sailors, initially briefly in the mid- to late fifteenth century and then more consistently as of the end of the sixteenth century.

War Making, Slave Raiding, and the Slave Trade

From the written record we know that Canhabacers were producing palm oil; raising small and large livestock; growing rice, corn, and beans; and doing deep-sea fishing by the 1590s (and in all likelihood well before then), enabling them to be largely self-sufficient in terms of food consumption when they needed to be, according to the first "thick description" of them by a Lusophone observer.[9] But they were also already heavily engaged in external trade, exchanging agronomic products with Europeans and other outsiders for cattle, cloths, brass and copper basins, and iron. Canhabacers were constructing large, deep canoes that could hold "many people" as they sailed the deep seas.[10] They were also producing weapons that proved quite effective in battle: large, curved swords, long spears made of braided reeds and topped with a bar of iron, and arrows tipped with poisonous fish spines.[11]

In 1594, the Portuguese observer André Alvares d'Almada described the Bijagos of Canhabac as "very warlike," sending their "armored canoes" to the shores of Guinea-Bissau to attack the "Burames" and the "Beafadas" so frequently that those peoples felt it necessary to maintain patrol watches not only throughout the day but also at night.[12] The key goal of such attacks was to capture young people to sell to foreign vessels that arrived at Canhabac specifically to purchase slaves[13] or to sell them to international slave merchants in Bissau and other entrepôts in Guinea-Bissau.

Indeed, from the sixteenth until the mid-nineteenth century, Canhabac war parties continued to plunder the Guinea-Bissauan mainland for slave-trading purposes, attacking most of the societies located alongside the Geba and Grande rivers.[14] These included Pepel, Manjaco, Beafades, and Brames—essentially the major groups living near the rivers—and many other smaller groups. The war-making and military-raiding abilities of Canhabacers were so effective that mainland villagers were virtually unable to defend themselves against these Bijagos slave raiders.[15]

In the 1700s to the early 1800s, as many as several thousand mainland Africans per year may have been captured for this purpose.[16] Another goal was to obtain slaves to forcibly integrate them into Canhabac war parties as canoe rowers and fighters, or in the case of captured girls or young women for them to become wives of Canhabacer young men.[17] The Bijagos had distinguished themselves as the most militarily feared people in the Guinea-Bissau region.[18] Typically, certain Bijagos village chiefs from Canhabac would be responsible for designing and overseeing the attack plans, and they would accompany the war parties on a slave raid, giving instructions and making strategic decisions as they went.[19]

On occasion, they were brazen enough to raid the mainland Portuguese town of Cacheu,[20] which in the seventeenth to eighteenth centuries was typically defended by a Portuguese army regiment. However, over time, the Bijagos developed increasingly friendly commercial relations with Portuguese-speaking settlers, merchants, and military officials, many of whom were themselves key players in the international slave trade. By the late 1700s to the early 1800s most slaves captured by Bijagos fighters were exchanged at Portuguese forts for cash or finished goods. Once a group of young people had been captured, the war party would often travel to Portuguese fort-towns to make deals with slave traders.[21] There, Canhabac chiefs would negotiate deals to exchange their would-be slaves for finished products, such as weapons, cloths, steel, cattle, pots and pans, bronze bells, horsetails, tobacco, and alcohol.[22]

Usually, on the purchasing end, Kristões—Christianized, "free" Africans (*tungumá* in local crioulo) living in the Portuguese fort-towns would do the actual negotiating with the Canhabac village chiefs. The Kristões some-times obtained slaves for themselves through such deals, but they primarily represented the interests of Portuguese administrators, military officials, and merchants.[23] These negotiations produced such large profits for the Portuguese that Portuguese settlers and military commanders would often compete with each other for access to the Canhabac chiefs in charge of slave-raiding parties, to the considerable benefit of those chiefs as well.[24]

The Bijagos of Canhabac, Kristões, and Portuguese traders would nego-tiate slave prices up and down the Guinean coastline and alongside the settlements of the Geba and Grande rivers of the mainland. The ruling elites of both Portuguese Guinea and Canhabac Island (that is, village chiefs) made mutually profitable deals in the course of this slave trading up through the mid-1800s, when slave-trading bans became enforced internationally. Indeed, these extensive trade relations with the Portuguese combined with the high regard that the Portuguese had for the military skills of the Bijagos of Canhabac led the Portuguese military authorities to sign a friendship treaty with them in 1844 such that Canhabac fighters would provide protection for the fort of Bissau in exchange for easy access by Bijagos traders to Bissau's markets.[25]

Interestingly, the end of the international slave trade led to an initial rise in hostility between the Bijagos of Canhabac and the Portuguese on the Guinea-Bissau mainland because the Bijagos blamed the Portuguese for the loss of this profit-making pipeline.[26] But the colonial economy soon provided economic opportunities for farmers on Canhabac, who in the late 1800s began growing peanuts and brought them to Portuguese settlements on the Grande River, such as Bissau, and to newly established European and mixed-race-run farms on other islands in the Bijagos Archi-pelago, especially Bolama.[27] The extensive agricultural trade that ensued facilitated the eventual spread of Lusophone settlements alongside the riv-ers of mainland Guinea-Bissau precisely because Canhabacers were able to help assure the economic vitality of those settlements via their frequent canoe-based travels.

Canoes and War

The Bijagos of Canhabac had become well respected by Europeans for their fighting skills by the late 1500s,[28] and, as indicated earlier, they repeatedly defeated British and French warships at sea from the sixteenth through the eighteenth centuries and in land battles with European sail-ors who had been shipwrecked. In 1792, shipwrecked British sailors were captured and apparently enslaved by the islanders.[29] The British had also tried to establish a settlement on the Bijagos island of Bolama, near Canhabac, in the late 1700s, but attacks by Canhabacers eventually led those British sailors to abandon that idea.[30]

It is difficult to adequately explain why the Bijagos of Canhabac were so effective in their armed confrontations with other peoples, both those who were indigenous to the Guinea-Bissau mainland, and with European colonial armed forces. After all, the political system on Canhabac was decentralized (as I discuss later), without a standing army per se. Furthermore, many of the Guinea-Bissauan peoples they attacked—the Beafada, the Manjaco, the Brames, and to some extent the Pepel—had more or less centralized political systems and could mobilize for war relatively quickly, and they would pose all kinds of military problems for would-be African conquerors from Mali and later for the Portuguese. Moreover, these Guinea-Bissauan mainland peoples were being attacked on their own territories, which they had often successfully defended against previous external assaults.

Here I may stress a number of factors that provided the Bijagos of Canhabac with certain advantages. Firstly, as we now know from testimonials and eyewitness accounts as early as 1457 up through the 1800s and as late as the 1920s, Bijagos war canoes were unusually large—forty feet long, five feet wide, more than three feet deep—and contained as many as forty to fifty rowers and fighters, although some had fewer so as to be able to ferry captured villagers to be sold as slaves. Rowers were muscular, skilled, and fast—they rowed in a highly coordinated manner and propelled each vessel at an unusually high speed. Eight rowers were in the back, with the strength of their strokes often propelling the front of the canoe high out of the water.[31]

Secondly and crucially, when Bijagos war canoes departed Canhabac, they did so en masse with some forty canoes or more (containing a total of 1,000 to 1,600 fighters) coursing through the waters in sync and closely together.[32] It was, to say the least, intimidating for any witnesses to observe their arrival near a settlement in such numbers and at high speeds, and villagers simply did not have time to organize an appropriate defense. Thirdly, they often attacked at night, apparently guided by moonlight, or before dawn, increasing the element of surprise.[33] Fourthly, they did not typically stay long enough for villagers to contact other settlements to obtain help—the Bijagos attackers would focus on capturing several dozen or more villagers and then they would depart quickly. Fifthly, they were known to be very capable and determined fighters; their reputation alone was intimidating.[34]

The first two factors proved key to understanding their relative success in attacking European vessels, which they did when they perceived them to be hostile. Being quickly surrounded by forty or more war canoes carrying over 1,000 armed Bijagos fighters made for an effective attack strategy, with the canoers often able to overcome cannon and rifle fire from the ship by quickly mounting the vessel and overwhelming the crew. Also, the Bijagos of Canhabac were, since the sixteenth century, actively engaged in international trade, and regularly insisted on being provided with rifles and ammunition in exchange for slaves and, later, other products. Thus, Canhabacers had a robust supply of modern guns, and they could often match or nearly match the level of war technology of European sailors.

By the end of the nineteenth century, however, the ability of Canhabac war canoes to sail the rivers of Guinea-Bissau or to attack passing European vessels was sharply reduced because European warships had by then become more effective with much larger and faster warships and machine guns mounted on deck. At the same time, as noted earlier, international commerce had left the slave trade in its wake and Canhabacers had, in consequence, shifted their attention to agricultural, livestock, and handicrafts-based exchanges. For these reasons, by the turn of the twentieth century, Canhabacers were no longer building and maintaining war canoes, and by the 1920s, there were no longer any that were seaworthy.[35] As the decades of the mid- to late twentieth century ensued, Canhabac deep-sea fishermen, who had for centuries carved out a reputation in Guinea-Bissau for their canoe-rowing ability and their ocean-going, fish-catching skills, began to abandon their craft, as modern fishing trawlers scoured the seas while Canhabac men increasingly turned their attention to agronomic concerns. In the 1980s, in the course of a development project aimed at assisting Canhabac fishermen in reviving their craft, it became clear, ironically, that there were no longer any specialized fishermen left among the Bijagos of Canhabac, and since there were no longer any seaworthy canoes available, young Canhabacers interested in relearning how to ocean-fish had to purchase small canoes built elsewhere, often in Senegal (this is further discussed later).[36]

Canhabac Political Structure: Decentralized

If the observations and analysis of Portuguese naval Capt. André Alvares d'Almada, writing in the late sixteenth century, are accurate, Canhabac was characterized by an acephalous political system in which each local community was led by an elder to whom local villagers were loyal.[37] As we make clear in this section, anthropological observation and historical research from that time forward suggest that that was indeed the case: there was no political hierarchy per se on Canhabac in the 1600s through the twentieth century.[38] Some chiefs may have had greater influence than others due to their advanced age or lengthy number of years serving as chief, but even so, such chiefs did not have the power to issue directives regarding other villages.[39] There was no single leader or island-wide ruling council that held authority over other chiefs or villages;[40] this remained the case through the 1900s,[41] with a "spirit of independence" for which the Bijagos of Canhabac had become renown.[42]

In the late 1850s, on a visit to Canhabac, Portuguese Guinea Gov. Honorio Barreto observed that the Bijagos "kings" are "simply heads of their deliberative assemblies, in which take place negotiations of issues of general concern."[43] Barreto was underlining both the collective structure of the principal Canhabac political institution—the deliberative assembly—and the fact that their leaders were village chiefs who did not hold special powers apart from running these collective meetings ("kings" was a poor choice of words in this respect). But it should be added that these "deliberative assemblies" took place at the village level and were not island-wide.

A dramatic indicator of this commitment to decentralized governance was an incident that took place in 1853 involving a trade misunderstanding with a French merchant that led the governor of Senegal to punish the Bijagos with a military expedition. French warships attacked Canhabac Island and the resulting battle produced a number of French casualties and led to a treaty agreeing to a cessation of hostilities. However, this treaty was made with a villager who apparently was not a village leader of any kind and held no special status. Later that same year (1853), of the twenty-three chiefs who did hold the status of chief on Canhabac Island, eighteen declared that that treaty had no validity, and they remained distrustful of the French.[44] What we can derive from this account is the fact that the twenty-three chiefs on Canhabac (in the 1850s) did not have a single leader or ruling body; each chief independently decided on the quality of his village's relations with the French. This confirms the profoundly decentralized character of political rule on the island.

Fast-forward to the mid-twentieth century: in the mid-1930s, former governor of Guinea(-Bissau) Carvalho Viégas wrote that on Canhabac, "there are no kings"[45] and that each village is typically governed "by its own chief" but that it is also common to find villages "without any chief."[46] This phenomenon appeared to baffle colonial administrators as they could not generally conceive of villages essentially governed collectively and lacking adherence to a higher, centralized authority. A different colonial-era observer, Santos Lima, writing in about that same time period (1930s–1940s), emphasized that Canhabac villages were indeed self-run, each being led by a council composed of elders who made the key decisions regarding land-use practices and other crucial economic activities.[47] Each Canhabac community reflected lineage ties to a community founder and to a specific land area presumed to have originally been demarcated by that founding ancestor. Canhabac villagers self-identified as members of a territorial community that was distinct from and independent of the others on that island. This assertive autonomy was clearly a defining characteristic of Canhabac society.[48]

The reality of decentralized governance by no means precluded intensive horizontal interactions and mobilizations. On the contrary, in the mid-1930s, Canhabacers were observed traveling "constantly" between villages and often stayed away from their home village for weeks at time, during which it was taken for granted that they would be provided with food and shelter by the host village.[49] Their ability to communicate rapidly between villages was repeatedly made clear by that fact that on many occasions (see below, "Anticolonial Resistance") they coordinated an intervillage military defense of the island that involved fighters from villages throughout the island. Canhabac village communications took various forms, including wrapping rope around tree branches and rubbing them together to indicate to community members that a seafaring vessel with likely hostile intentions was rapidly approaching.[50]

It is also clear that in previous centuries when they made frequent trips to the mainland in pursuit of slaves, hundreds of fighters were mobilized (these attacks are discussed later), which means that they were recruited from most of the villages, implying well-coordinated intervillage cooperation. But intervillage mobilization did not, for them, necessitate a formal hierarchy. Island-wide initiatives such as waging war or defending the island against an external attack were made on the basis of informal discussions, understandings, and cooperation by the twenty-three island communities.[51]

Canhabac Intravillage Leadership and Gender Roles

The intravillage Canhabac authority system in the sixteenth to nineteenth centuries was characterized by male-female divisions and separate political responsibilities, although there were occasions, including agricultural prayer recitals and planting and harvest activities, when the two genders performed their economic activities conjointly. Exclusively male "political spaces" on Canhabac included collecting arboreal products such as palm nuts; clearing trees from land designated for farming; and manning ocean-going canoes for purposes of war, or capturing slaves, or for fishing.[52] The tropical forest itself was considered, in the Bijagos spiritual belief system, to represent a special territorial preserve in which different male age groups assumed various responsibilities regarding the economic exploitation of palm trees and other forest products.[53]

The position of village chief—*olonho* (or *oronho*) in the Bijagos language—was reserved for elderly male descendants of the founder lineage of a particular village, although he ruled in concert with a council of village elders, who selected him in the first place, and of which he was the chairman.[54] The potential to attain the position of chief accrued to those who had distinguished themselves in battle (battles were commonly fought in the sixteenth to the nineteenth centuries to capture slaves, livestock, or harvested grains on the mainland, or to fend off attacks by Europeans).[55] Once chosen to lead the village, the olonho was responsible for denoting the borders of the village, for interacting with spiritual forces to assure that the village remained protected from outsiders, for organizing a defense of the village if necessary, and for serving as interlocutor with any non-Canhabacers.[56]

If a war party carried out a raid on a mainland Guinea-Bissauan community, the olonho would receive one-third to one-half of the war booty, and would then be responsible for determining how the captured goods would be distributed.[57] It was generally expected that a portion would be accorded to the key builder of the war canoes and to the "war captain," who was responsible for the key decisions in battle.[58] This reflected the high social status of these male villagers.

A further crucial role of the olonho was that of the spiritual "keeper of the land," meaning that it was his responsibility to keep the land deities satisfied so that the village lands would prove productive, and to decide on the timing for sowing, planting, harvesting, and other agricultural tasks.[59] It is interesting to note that a certain modesty of power was suggested by the fact that this village chief personally participated in all of the agricultural work, showing that he was one of their own and unpretentious in his status.[60] The agricultural responsibilities of the olonho have become even more enhanced in the twentieth to the twenty-first centuries with the demise of coastal raiding and the cessation of any war making.

Historically, the role of the olonho was counterbalanced by an unusually significant role accorded to the most powerful woman in each Canhabac village, known as the *oquinca*, who was appointed by the olonha in consultation with the male council of elders. Like the olonha, she had to be a descendant of the village's founding clan. The oquinca assisted the olonho in all significant rituals, including those regarding agronomy and war making, and she had the power to make decisions regarding the other women in the village.[61] In the twentieth century (and probably prior to that as well), each oquinca was assisted by a female council of elders. The colonial Portuguese administrator Augusto J. Santos Lima, writing in the 1930s and 1940s, emphasized that the oquinca relied heavily on her female advisers in decision making.[62]

A crucial power wielded by the oquinca was her role and responsibility in spiritual affairs, as she held a key position in allowing entrance (or not) to the spirit world, in particular of young men who had died prior to undergoing the rites allowing them to be considered adults.[63] The oquinca worked to appease the spiritual gods in order to keep the arable lands "healthy," assuring bounteous harvests.[64] She coordinated this function with the olonho; they worked cooperatively, sitting together while performing their spiritual blessings of the fields, and if the olonho died without a successor already selected, the oquinca would carry out these spiritual blessings until a new olonho was appointed.[65]

In the era of slave trading by the Bijagos from the sixteenth to the nineteenth centuries, the oquinca played important spiritual roles in blessing warriors prior to their departure from Canhabac. In addition, the oquinca, in consultation with her advisers, had decision-making power over captured young male slaves.[66] After that time period, the oquinca continued to act as a diviner and as an intermediary between the spiritual and material worlds, with the ability to inflict spirit-based curses on malevolent village members.[67] These oquincas offered advice to individual villagers regarding the consequences of their life choices as well as helping to determine their fate in the afterworld.[68]

As for a more microlevel understanding of gender relations, in the past as well as contemporarily, the sociological management of the bread-and-butter aspects of local society has been the responsibility of women, both within the household and village-wide. Canhabac women were observed in the sixteenth century fully engaged in farm labor, building houses, fishing, gathering shellfish, and in general "doing all that men do elsewhere."[69] Female "space" since that time has included crucial agronomic activities such as producing rice, marketing food, selling food products at local markets, producing palm oil, extracting coconut milk, and removing rice husks, as well as fishing and collecting shellfish.[70] In the 1930s to the 1940s, the colonial-era observer Lima described women as having considerable social power and influence from the family to social decision making at the village level. They could divorce their husbands without seeking approval from anyone else, and the children took their mother's surname. Inheritance was treated matrilineally, so that property was bequeathed only to a woman's descendants.[71] That remains the case today.

Nineteenth-Century Canhabac External Relations within Guinea-Bissau

It cannot be sufficiently emphasized how skilled the Bijagos of Canhabac were at balancing the relative autarchy of their island society on the one hand with their immersion in trade, politics, and social relations on the mainland on the other. To be sure, Canhabacers were familiar with mainland communities from the slave-raiding days of yesteryear, but in the early to mid-1800s, some Canhabacers stayed long enough on the mainland to mingle with Portuguese-speaking inhabitants of coastal enclaves, including colonial settlements—Bissau, Cacheu, Bolama—where some of them intermarried with and/or developed extended family ties with colonial society mixed-race individuals and with some white Portuguese military officials (originally from Lisbon) holding significant political power or influence.[72] In addition, building on the Canhabac-Portuguese trust developed during the long decades of slave trading (discussed earlier), some of the sons of several Canhabac Island olonho were sent to Bissau to become formally educated and Christianized, deepening the social inroads into Lusophone colonial society.[73]

Moreover, some Canhabac olonho cut deals with mixed-race planters, farmers, and traders on neighboring islands, especially Bolama but also Galinhas, and on the mainland through which extensive land tracts for farming were ceded with the understanding that Canhabacers would benefit economically as their trading partners. It should be noted that colonialists in the nineteenth century still had enormous respect for the fighting ability of Canhabacers; these planters established themselves on the Bijagos islands of Bolama and Galinhas and later on the mainland coast only because they came to an understanding with the olonho of Canhabac. That understanding was facilitated by the fact that some of the planters enjoyed direct or indirect family linkages with people on Canhabac Island.[74]

Here is where we see the emergence of what came to be called *pontas*, or trading farms, which tended to be located near the geographic starting points (estuaries) of the major rivers of the Guinea-Bissauan mainland. Pontas alongside the relatively accessible banks of the Grande River served to jump-start an extensive barter-trade network within which Canhabac traders were active participants.[75] Such products as Canhabac-produced rice, fruit, palm oil, beeswax, sweet potatoes, peanuts, cattle, and chickens would be exchanged for cotton cloth, rum, tobacco, guns, and gunpowder.[76] In this way, Canhabacers were intricately engaged in trade relations with Portuguese, other Europeans, and mixed-race settlers on the Guinea-Bissau mainland for many decades, and while they were self-sufficient in terms of their own food production, it would be an error to perceive them as economically insular.

On the contrary, the mercantile aggression of Canhabacers in earlier decades (here referring to slave capturing) would now shift into an intensification of barter-based exchanges and increasingly peaceful relations with Lusophone settlers. This would also be represented by the eventual agreement through which olonho chiefs ceded Bolama Island—part of the Bijagos Archipelago to which the Canhabac chiefs had historic claims— to the Portuguese with certain stipulations (see below).[77] This concession did not hinder Canhabacers from continuing to trade on Bolama. On the contrary, Canhabacers traded extensively with the mixed-race plantation owners on Bolama.

In the mid-1800s, slave trading came to an end in Portuguese-speaking colonies but slavery itself often continued, albeit clandestinely to avoid punishment by British war vessels seeking to assure the end of slavery worldwide. Thus, in the 1840s to the 1860s, Bolama's plantation owners became enormously wealthy by using hundreds of previously purchased slaves to cultivate peanuts, rice, and coffee, which they often exchanged for a variety of food products with Canhabacers,[78] who, in turn, resold those food products for profit in Bolama or Bissau. In addition, Canhabacers provided shoreline security to Bolama plantation owners, warning them of approaching British vessels, for example, while actively trading with them throughout the nineteenth century.[79]

The case of an indigenous Canhabacer living in Bissau in the early 1800s, Júlia da Silva Cardoso, known as Mãe Júlia, is particularly intriguing, as revealed in Philip Havik's path-breaking study of the history of women entrepreneurs in Guinea-Bissau. Mãe Júlia made the most of the fact that she was a cousin of a Canhabac olonho by the name of Damião, the head of Inorei village, which historically had asserted authority over the neighboring islands of Bolama and Galinhas. Mãe Júlia was able to secure land concessions for the governor of Guinea-Bissau, Joaquim António de Mattos, and other Portuguese and Europeans on Bolama and Galinhas islands precisely because of her Canhabac lineage and connection to Chief Damião. For example, as part of the concessions treaty, Canhabacers would still be able to cultivate rice on Bolama island on plots located apart from

the conceded land areas used for plantations. Prior to that, she had cultivated strong social and economic ties with key Portuguese officials in Bissau, including Mattos, governor of Guinea-Bissau from 1805 through the
1830s, and during those decades she succeeded in negotiating and consolidating many slave-based exchanges between the Bijagos of Canhabac
on the one hand, and Mattos and other Portuguese investors or planters
on the other.[80] (It may also be noted that Mãe Júlia herself owned sev-
enteen slaves, and she would eventually become involved with and would
have four children with Governor Mattos; he was her next-door neighbor
in Bissau.)[81]

Mãe Júlia's contributions to Canhabac-Lusophone trade relations
helped set the stage for the spread of European trading farms from the
1840s through the rest of the nineteenth century, not only on Bolama
and Galinhas islands but also throughout the riverine shorelines of
Guinea-Bissau.[82] A number of other indigenous women from Canhabac
and from other Bijagos islands (Orango in particular) would prove to
play similarly crucial intermediary roles in promoting Bijagos-Portuguese
negotiations and mutually beneficial trade relations as the slave trade
ended and peanut and rice farms, owned by Europeans and mixed-race
Guinea-Bissauans, expanded along the rivers and in some of the Bijagos
islands.[83]

The blood ties of prominent Bijagos-originated women with influential lineages on Canhabac Island was clearly the essential factor in their
ability to influence Canhabac fighters *not* to launch violent raids on those
European farms and trade centers and instead to negotiate deals to the
mutual economic advantage of both the Canhabac olonho and the colonialist European and mixed-race planters.[84] These peaceful relations also
helped to produce a formal treaty of friendship in 1856, signed by Portuguese Guinea Gov. Honorio Barreto, who had personally conducted
what he referred to as successful negotiations with Canhabac Island village
chiefs.[85] For the remainder of the nineteenth century, Canhabacers traded
ever more frequently with settlers on farms sitting alongside Guinea-Bissau's rivers.

Thus, the external relations of Canhabacers and their interactions with
colonial society actors represented a form of social and commercial bar-
gaining through which they preserved the territorial autonomy of their
island even as they perceived ways of economically profiting from their
ties to high society colonialists, such as commercial planters on Bolama
as well as mixed-race communities along the rivers of the Guinea-Bissau
mainland.

Anticolonial Resistance

Despite the intricate social and economic ties developed between Canhabac chiefs and Lusophone planters, in the 1890s to the 1910s, political pressure built up in Lisbon for the Portuguese colonial authorities to press forward with a full-scale assertion of political authority throughout the mainland countryside of Guinea-Bissau, as well as in the offshore Bijagos Archipelago. This coincided with Lisbon's increasing interest in colonialist political and military penetration of the colony, provoked by the 1884–85 Berlin Conference and spurred on in part through concern over francophone interest in Guinea-Bissau, especially if Lisbon should fail to demonstrate sufficient penetrative military potency in its claimed colonial jurisdictions. All of this would generate the infamous "wars of pacification" launched in fits and starts in rural Guinea-Bissau in the 1890s to the early 1900s, then all-out beginning in 1910 on the mainland, and then finally on Canhabac Island, starting in 1916.

> *1916 Resistance War:* According to the French consul to Portuguese Guinea, based on "the documents available in our consular office archives," a military operation carried out by the Portuguese in 1916 intended to compel Canhabacers to pay a colonial tax—the not-so-symbolic acceptance of Portuguese overrule—was marked by the following course of events. In the absence of agreement to pay this tax, Canhabacers relocated with all their families, farm animals, and possessions to neighboring islands. A cadre of Canhabac fighting men remained on the island, hidden in thickly forested areas alongside forest paths. When a battalion of 1,000 Portuguese soldiers arrived on the island and made their way along those paths, the fighters fired their weapons at the invading battalion until their ammunition ran out and they then fled deeper into the island. Approximately twenty-five Portuguese were killed, with about eighty wounded. The Portuguese would proceed to burn down all the huts they could find, and then leave the island, after which Canhabac families returned to rebuild their huts and reclaimed their control over the island.[86] In essence, the Portuguese "pacification" campaign had been in vain.

> *1925 Resistance War:* A virtual repeat of the 1916 invasion took place nine years later, in April 1925, when Portuguese Guinean Gov. Jorge F. Velez Caroço insisted that Canhabacers pay a colonial tax; they refused. The subsequent invasion force of colonialists succeeded in burning down many unoccupied huts on Canhabac, after which the Canhabacers returned from their hideouts in the woods and on neighboring islands to their villages and continued to refuse to pay taxes.[87]

1936 Resistance War: By 1935 the Portuguese had become determined to finally assert sovereignty over Canhabac and in early January 1936 sent waves of Portuguese troop battalions and African auxiliary soldiers to the island, with total attack forces numbering around 1,300–1,500 per mission. Before the first mission, most Canhabaque villages had already been depopulated, as per the 1916 and 1925 events, with the men bringing their wives and children to neighboring islands.[88] In January 1936, during the first attack, it was reported that the Portuguese and their African auxiliaries suffered "dozens" killed and wounded, and retreated from the island.[89] Later that same month, the Portuguese brought a larger force of several hundred Portuguese soldiers and some 2,000 auxiliaries to Canhabac and proceeded to rout the Canhabac defenders. Still, the resistance of the islanders was such that 35 of the invaders were killed and 171 were wounded.[90]

Here we may note that the principal firearm used by the Bijagos defenders of Canhabac was the "long gun," which was very slow to reload, in contrast to more quickly reloading rifles and some submachine guns the Portuguese brought to the island.[91] This suggests how skilled the Canhabacers were in using inferior firearms. During the 1936 resistance, many Canhabac fighters were so well hidden that Portuguese auxiliaries commonly were felled without having a clear idea where exactly the rifle fire came from. In such cases, the Canhabacers dragged some of them away before fresh Portuguese troops were able to arrive on the scene.[92] Portuguese soldiers later testified that even with all their hundreds of colonial fighters, they were still unable to defeat the Canhabacers in "regular" combat and that they were able to secure an advantage only because of their extensive reliance on submachine guns (semiautomatics).[93]

After the final battle and the Portuguese could claim victory in mid-February 1936, full territorial control was hardly enforced; groups of Portuguese soldiers limited themselves to only occasional forays outside their barracks. Indeed, despite the colonial conquest, Canhabacers would find multiple means of what the Guinea-Bissauan historian Peter Karibe Mendy refers to as "passive resistence"—relocating to neighboring islands instead of paying a tax, relocating to the mainland for months at a time, repeatedly submitting formal protests to local Portuguese officials instead of agreeing to work on proposed projects, and simply failing to adhere to colonial dictates. This is why Mendy concludes that the Bijagos were never fully subdued.[94] We concur, in the sense that they were not subjugated to direct colonial oversight or policy enforcement. The Portuguese authorities lacked the finances, soldiers, and political will to carry out regular, annual attacks on Canhabac, enabling the Bijagos of that island to largely avoid paying taxes or abiding by other official colonial government policies.[95]

Recent History I: The Dialectics of Monetarization and Development

After the conclusion of these wars, the Bijagos of Canhabac reengaged in active trade with the aforementioned *ponteiros* along mainland rivers and with traders in neighboring islands. Barter exchanges represented the key method of economic transaction as it had for at least five centuries. In the 1930s to the 1940s, the chicken was used as the standard of value; in that time period, one cow was worth approximately between forty-five and a hundred chickens (depending on the size of the cattle); a pig was valued at forty to sixty chickens; and a goat at two to four chickens.[96] Using this exchange value, Canhabacers exported rice, vegetables, cattle, pigs, chickens, coconuts, oranges, and palm oil. They imported rice, salt, clay pots, empty cans, cotton panels, and nails.[97]

In subsequent decades, and especially as the postcolonial period (1974 to the present) progressed, Canhabac was marked by a gradual rise in economic monetarization and the influence of "development" ideas and projects from the mainland.[98] Barter trade is still heavily practiced on Canhabac, but some Canhabac youth were attracted to the consumption economy and the use of cash gradually increased on the island. By the 1990s to the 2000s (the first decade), companies sought to obtain access to swampland traditionally used for mangrove harvesting, and by that point less agricultural land on the island was being devoted to rice cultivation and other foods than in previous decades, but rice was still grown on a considerable number of land tracts and remained the central grain in their diet.[99] Some members of the younger generation began to seek jobs outside Canhabac to obtain cash for consumer spending.

Despite these changes, many Canhabacers remained committed to preserving the sanctity of their lands and their intraisland economic practices, including agronomy, herding, mangrove growing, shoreline fishing, as well as their political and social traditions, including village-based decentralized governance and particular spiritual practices. Canhabacers in the 1990s to the 2000s still allowed portions of rice-devoted lands to lie fallow for a decade at a time so that the soil could naturally replenish.[100] If more farming lands were needed, Canhabac farmers temporarily moved to other less populated Bijagos islands (as they had done in the past) such as Galinhas, Bissâssema, or Rubane for the specific purpose of cultivating rice there (after having concluded negotiations with indigenous Bijagos residents of those islands in previous decades)[101] as well as carrying out spiritual ceremonies associated with those rice harvests.[102] On Canhabac as on other Bijagos islands, well-organized teams of young men and women of various age groups, including many elderly, planted and then collected rice at harvest time, which was then shared, as in the past, among those who assisted with one or more stages of the rice production process.[103]

The Bijagos of Canhabac also actively protected mangrove swamps to assure the production of edible mangroves and other useful plants (many of which can be ground into spices and other products), and because the mangroves harbor large quantities of oysters and edible small fish. These aquatic spaces are especially valuable to Canhabacers during the several months preceding rice harvests, when village food supplies often may be running low.[104] In the 1990s some of those mangrove swamps were purchased by—or were subject to attempted purchase by—external developers seeking to build a commercial oyster business or other businesses based on mangrove products, but most Canhabac mangrove areas remained intact and were being actively used by local villagers in the historical manner just described. In fact, it is noteworthy not only that most villagers rejected the purchase offers by outsiders, but also that educated youth were front and center of such resistance to external pressure: It was the educated youth who made certain that their elders were not duped into signing over their lands to businessmen or to government organizations.[105]

This point bears further and more specific explication. In 2006–8, some Canhabac high school students perceived that a growing number of business investors were seeking to open tourist sites along various parts of the shoreline on Canhabac island. These students organized into activist groups with the specific purpose of assuring that traditional agricultural and mangrove areas historically used by Canhabac villages not be threatened by any new coastal developments. The students insisted not only that they be allowed to carefully consider new investment project proposals, but also that they be allowed the time to discuss the details of any such proposals with olonho, oquinca, other respected elders, and traditional councils in affected villages. As a result, the external businesses agreed to give the students an entire year—2009—to discuss it with village authorities and elders throughout the island. This was done, and the elders agreed to sign a document effectively allocating responsibility to the students for assuring that any new agreements with investors do not threaten existing arable and mangrove areas. The end result was that businesses sought to purchase user rights on small nearby islands, but not on Canhabac itself.[106]

Still, new complications emerged. Firstly, there were apparent misunderstandings over whether Canhabacers would have continuing access to engage in rice farming in parts of a tiny nearby island that had been contracted to a French-Guinean company for tourist activities. Secondly, aggressive, unfriendly commercial fishermen from various parts of the Guinea-Bissau mainland were illegally fishing the coastal waters of Canhabac in quick raids to scoop up shellfish and other fish variants with commercial value. To prevent this, Canhabac youth tried to raise money to pay watchmen and guards, but to little effect; as a result, there was rising concern on Canhabac regarding the security of local marine resources.[107]

Thirdly, in certain Canhabac villages, tension rose because *some* of the educated younger generation, who graduated from high school and had "development" ambitions for the Bijagos islands, wanted to see more contracts signed with tourist businesses while many other educated youth were determined to limit such contracts because they perceived them as potential threats to land rights and shoreline shellfish habitats.[108]

The cumulative effect of these three economic, security-related, legal, and sociopolitical complexities was a general determination by Canhabacers, in effect, to step back and reunify, to overcome internal tensions, and to present a collective island-wide defense of the island's territories.[109] As the first decade of the twenty-first century concluded, there was a sense that internal differences had to be resolved so that outsiders could not take advantage of them or harm Canhabac's natural resources.

Recent History II: Fishing, External Investment, and Change

The postcolonial dynamics regarding a fishing development project can be better appreciated in view of the dilemmas depicted in the previous section regarding the impacts of modernization. As indicated in the section "Canoes and War," there were no large-scale traditional Bijagos war canoes left, nor had there been for many decades, but only very small ones used with a hand-crafted net or a line close to shore.[110] Fishing had become a subsistence activity intended for consumption (raw, grilled, or smoked).[111] Bijagos fishermen on Canhabac and the other islands were no longer full-time fishermen; they were full-time agriculturalists, principally engaged in farming activities in or near their home villages, and fished as a supplementary activity when time permitted.[112]

From 1978 through the 1980s, a government-initiated, Swedish NGO-facilitated fishing project aimed to retrain Bijagos youth in the art of deep-sea commercial fishing, hoping to revive this long-lost practice for their income and food sources and to augment fish consumption on those islands and more generally in Guinea-Bissau via offshore fish selling. But young men who wanted to participate would have to apply formally to this program in order to obtain the necessary tools, such as specialized fishing gear and small freezers in which to store their fish catches, as well as to obtain low-interest lines of credit, which were needed to obtain canoes, motors, and gasoline. Ironically, considering their impressive seagoing past, most of the young Bijagos men who wanted to participate in this program did not even know enough about the basics of deep-sea fishing to be accepted into this program. As a result, many of the successful participants ended up being from Senegal and, to a lesser extent, from the Guinea-Bissau mainland. But since the aim in part was to increase the volume of fish catches by restoring deep-sea fishing among the Bijagos, young men from Canhabac and other Bijagos islands ended up being selected anyway. To increase their likelihood of success, they were paired with the more experienced Senegalese fishermen.[113]

The participants from Senegal already possessed the materials—long boats, netting, large motors, etc.—associated with commercial fishing and helped their Bijagos partners learn how to better equip their own boats and how to use the more complex large-scale fishing materials.[114] However, an unanticipated complication ensued. The Bijagos participants' devotion to their farms—recall that they were primarily agriculturalists—became relevant because even after the project was begun, the Canhabacers returned home to take part in the hard-core tasks associated with rice farming for three to six months of each year.[115] Some Canhabac participants did obtain new skills and acquired some cash, which helped to pay for school fees, clothing, taxes, and materials for important ritualistic festivities. However, they were not prepared to forsake their intraisland social and economic obligations for the sake of the fishing development project.[116]

In this respect, this project was symbolic of the previously mentioned modernization dialectic. Some of the project participants, due to their earnings, became more integrated into the cash economy without, however, forsaking their agronomic and village society obligations.[117] For most project participants, farming remained the number one priority, but some began increasingly using cash earnings to purchase consumption goods. As a result, the long predominance of intravillage cooperative ethics was not displaced but was increasingly subject to an alternative, more competitive mode of socioeconomic relations. Monetarization further encouraged external migration among youth to pursue cash-paying jobs elsewhere, which was another challenge to the heretofore internal coherence of local Canhabac society.[118] It also generated a modicum of social anomie as some islanders became more competitive with one another.[119] This is to a large extent what provoked anthropologist Christine Henry, writing in the 1990s, to exclaim that more external penetration of Bijagos society on Canhabac took place in the previous few decades than in the first several hundred years of warfare with Europeans, slave trading, and colonialism.[120]

On the other hand, however, those steps toward commercialization have been by no means unilinear or unchallenged; on the contrary, most Canhabacers, including many educated youth, remained intensively enmeshed in locally determined lifeways and village-based sociohistorically crafted commitments.[121] This was dramatized in 1988 in the holding of a traditional ceremony, generally held annually, organized by Canhabac youth who managed to secure, over the course of months, enormous quantities of rice, palm products, shellfish, pork, and other products to be consumed during this gathering. Young people generally put together this ceremony, which rotates from one village to another year to year, in order to impress their elders in the hope of hastening the process of initiation into adulthood.[122]

In this and other respects, despite the increasing influence of monetarization, the indigenous Bijagos of Canhabac still place enormous value in determining the structure and orientation of their own society. Indeed, as Henry emphatically and descriptively makes clear, despite undisputed social and economic changes on Canhabac, the Bijagos of that island remain the most autarchic of any group of Guinea-Bissauans and have preserved to a larger degree than others their historical values, modes of in-village social interaction, initiation rites, spiritual practices, social functions of age-group classifications, as well as their ancient architectural styles of houses, village designs, and methods of granary storage.[123] And despite the aforementioned introduction of partially monetarized economic relations, the people of Canhabac remain actively engaged in such self-sustaining, locally and historically valued economic activities as rice-based agriculture, small livestock raising, palm tree extraction, and shellfish collection.

Continual Adaptation to Preserve Self-Direction

Throughout its history, Canhabac Island has been simultaneously self-sufficient and autarchic, aggressively engaged in social and economic networks extending onto the Guinea-Bissau mainland, and well integrated into global commercial circles. Canhabacers' determined and uncompromising assertion of local autonomy—demonstrated in numerous and often-changing manifestations of their particularistic intraisland territorial, economic, social, and spiritual lifeways—has been perpetually counterbalanced by their ambitious immersion in armed confrontations on the mainland as on the high seas, and by their enthusiastic participation in a variety of regional and international markets, commercial investments, and social and interpersonal networks.

On Canhabac, the Bijagos developed a social and political system marked by gender balance in decision making at all levels of society and governance, including rule making and enforcement, crucial spiritual leadership roles, and important agricultural and farming responsibilities. Women and men tend to work together in many hard-labor tasks and serve cooperatively in key economic activities, even as they also have historically and contemporarily developed defined gender spaces, such as seafaring, war making, and forestry resources collection for men, and certain agronomic and spiritual roles for women.

Awe-inspiring in their war canoes from the sixteenth through the mid-nineteenth century, and fearsome as slave capturers on the Guinea-Bissau mainland, the energies of Canhabac men on the high seas and among riverine communities would gradually become transformed into engagement in more peaceable commercial exchanges and via investments in ponta-based trade along Guinea-Bissau's rivers from the mid-nineteenth through the early twentieth centuries. Another dramatization of the insular-leaning cum exogenous-oriented dichotomy now becomes manifest as some ambitious Canhabac women had intermarried with high-level military and political figures in Bissau and Bolama, and they eventually became remarkably successful, highly respected, independent commercial plantation owners. Meanwhile, on the island itself, Canhabacers adamantly resisted colonialist incursions of any kind, fending off two (almost three) major Portuguese armed invasions, and they never consistently paid colonial taxes.

During the last three decades of the twentieth century, the assertion of territorial autonomy on Canhabac combined with active engagement in external commercial markets assumed a very different format, being manifested by the gradual monetarization of the economy and the incorporation of a segment of Canhabac youth into a consumptionist, globally integrationist mentality and mode of economic behavior, while at the same time many other Canhabac youth actively resisted such pressures. Those resisters used their high educational levels to carefully parse through various proposed "development" plans, sharing the details of those plans with traditional elders to assure a society-wide strategy to defend the territorial integrity of Canhabac's farmland and to protect its valuable mangrove swamplands.

In these and other ways, Canhabac's classic embrace of global commercialism while simultaneously reinforcing the island's relative insularity and social autonomy reflected the inhabitants' remarkable adaptability as has been the case since its recorded history, beginning in the late sixteenth century. Nor is such a versatile duality limited to the Bijagos of Canhabac or, for that matter, to African islands. Indeed, an intriguing comparison can be made between the history and people of the Bijagos on Canhabac Island and the English of Great Britain. Both are islanders who, for various reasons in the early modern period, improved their seagoing technologies and became capable of attacking and conquering lands near and relatively far. Both peoples spent centuries aggressively conquering offshore peoples, selling some of them into slavery, while also effectively defending their respective islands against persistent attacks by outsiders. Both would subsequently abandon their involvement in slave trading, albeit for different reasons. Both proved unable to maintain their martial dominance on the high seas by the late nineteenth century. Both, however, remained determined to defend at all costs their respective island territories, and indeed to this day, neither England nor Canhabac has been territorially occupied by would-be conquerors during the past half-millennium, despite having been invaded multiple times. Finally, both Canhabacers and the English would transfer their much-vaunted vigor and energy in offshore war making to an intensification of intraisland and externally oriented economic activities as the twentieth century unfolded.

In retrospect, Canhabacers, like other island peoples but in their own distinct manner, have displayed a remarkable capacity for international exploration on the open seas, engagement in the globalized world economically and militarily, while above all remaining determined to defend the territorial autonomy of their particular island. Canhabacers were, and remain, enthusiastically enmeshed in offshore markets while simultaneously preserving, to the extent possible, the sanctity of their own island habitat. The relative insularity of their society enabled the Bijagos of Canhabac to embrace aspects of modernity and global mercantilism without risking their impressively equitable gender relations or other aspects of their carefully crafted and socially embedded intraisland lifeways.

Notes

1. Rui Rebelo and Paulo Catry, "O Arquipelago Bíjagos (Guiné-Bissau): valores de biodiversidade," *Ecologi* 2 (May 2011): 8–15; "National Census of Guinea-Bissau 2009," Ministry of Economics, Planning and Regional Integration, Guinea-Bissau, http://www.stat-guinebissau.com/.

2. Christine Henry, *Les îles où dansent les enfants défunts. Âge, sexe et pouvoir chez les Bijogo de Guinée-Bissau* (Paris: CNRS Éditions, 1994), 73.

3. Rebelo and Catry, "O Arquipelago Bíjagos," 9.

4. The four rivers are the Grande (the closest to Canhabac), the Geba (which leads to Bissau and hundreds of other smaller communities), the Mansoa, and the Cacheu rivers.

5. Guillaume Ségérer, "L'Origine des Bijago," in *Migrations anciennes et peuplement actuel des Côtes guinéennes*, ed. Gérald Gaillard (Paris: L'Harmattan, 2000): 183–91; see 185; also see Henry, *Les îles*, 11, 37.

6. Ségérer, "L'Origine des Bijago," 183–89.

7. Ségérer, "L'Origine des Bijago," 188–89.

8. Ségérer, "L'Origine des Bijago," 188–89.

9. André Alvares d'Almada, *Tratado Breve dos Rios de Guiné do Cabo Verde*, document written in 1594; published book: Porto, Lisbon: The Polytechnic Institute, 1841; "Brief Treatise on the Rivers of Guinea," trans. P. E. H. Hair, Dept. of History, University of Liverpool (typescript, 1984), 99.

10. Alvares d'Almada, *Tratado Breve dos Rios de Guiné*, 97.

11. Alvares d'Almada, *Tratado Breve dos Rios de Guiné*, 97.

12. Alvares d'Almada, *Tratado Breve dos Rios de Guiné*, 96–97.

13. Alvares d'Almada, *Tratado Breve dos Rios de Guiné*, 98.

14. George E. Brooks, *Western Africa and Cabo Verde 1790s–1830s* (AuthorHouse, 2010), 66; Philip J. Havik, *Silences and Soundbytes: The Gendered Dynamics of Trade and Brokerage in the Pre-colonial Guinea-Bissau Region* (Munich: Lit Verlag Publishers, 2004), 115.

15. Augusto J. Santos Lima, *Organização Económica e Social dos Bijagós* (Lisbon: Imprensa Nacional de Portugal, 1947), 15; see also Carlos Lopes, "A Transição Histórica na Guiné-Bissau," mémoire (master's thesis, Institut Universitaire d'Etudes du Développement, Geneva, 1982), 24, 31.

16. Henry, *Les îles*, 46–47.

17. Lima, *Organização Económica e Social dos Bijagós*, 50.

18. Lopes, "A Transição Histórica na Guiné-Bissau," 32.

19. Christine Henry, "Marinheiros Bijogós: Passado e Presente," in *Revista de estudos guineenses* [Bissau] 8 (July 1989): 25–46; see 29.

20. Lima, *Organização Económica e Social dos Bijagós*, 15.

21. Havik, *Silences and Soundbytes*, 257.

22. Havik, *Silences and Soundbytes*, 301; Henry, "Marinheiros Bijogós," 25–46; see 29.

23. Havik, *Silences and Soundbytes*, 257.

24. Havik, *Silences and Soundbytes*, 115.

25. Havik, *Silences and Soundbytes*, 280.
26. Havik, *Silences and Soundbytes*, 115–16.
27. Havik, *Silences and Soundbytes*, 117.
28. Alvares d'Almada, *Tratado Breve dos Rios de Guine do Cabo Verde*, 100.
29. Lopes, "A Transição Histórica na Guiné-Bissau," 65.
30. Lima, *Organização Económica e Social dos Bijagós*, 23.
31. Henry, "Marinheiros Bijogós," 30–31.
32. Henry, "Marinheiros Bijogós," 26.
33. Henry, "Marinheiros Bijogós," 27.
34. Henry, "Marinheiros Bijogós," 27.
35. Henry, *Les îles*, 64; Henry, "Marinheiros Bijogós," 27.
36. Henry, "Marinheiros Bijogós," 27. For the pertinent discussion below, see "Recent History II: Fishing, External Investment, and Change."
37. Alvares d'Almada, *Tratado Breve dos Rios de Guiné*, 97.
38. Nor is there any suggestion or evidence of hierarchical leadership on Canhabac Island prior to the 1600s or since the nineteenth century.
39. Henry, *Les îles*, 39.
40. This differed from other islands in the Bijagos archipelago, most notably Orango, where there was a political hierarchy marked by clan leaders, a ruling council, and a matrilineal island-wide leadership.
41. Henry, *Les îles*, 39, 49.
42. Luigi Scantamburlo, *Etnologia dos Bijagós* (Bissau: INEP, 1991), 48.
43. João Barreto, *História da Guiné 1418–1918* (Lisbon: J. Barreto, 1938), 236.
44. Henry, *Les îles*, 52.
45. Luis António de Carvalho Viégas, *Iha de Canhabaque: Relatório das operações militares em 1935–1936* (Bolama, Guinea-Bissau: Imprensa Nacional, 1937), 9, 20.
46. Viégas, *Iha de Canhabaque*, 9.
47. Lima, *Organização Económica e Social dos Bijagós*, 54–55, 60–61.
48. Lima, *Organização Económica e Social dos Bijagós*, 111; Henry, *Les îles*, 15.
49. Viégas, *Iha de Canhabaque*, 20.
50. Canhabac elder interviewed by Joshua Bernard Forrest, Bissau, February 1, 1984.
51. Havik, *Silences and Soundbytes*, 114.
52. Raúl Mendes Fernandes, "O Espaço e o Tempo no Sistema Político Bidjogó," in *Revista de Estudos Guineenses* [Bissau] no. 8 (July 1989): 6.
53. Henry, *Les îles*, 181; Fernandes, "O Espaço e o Tempo no Sistema Político Bidjogó," 16.
54. Scantamburlo, *Etnologia dos Bijagós*, 48; Fernandes, "O Espaço e o Tempo no Sistema Político Bidjogó," 6.
55. Henry, *Les îles*, 39–40, 53.
56. Henry, *Les îles*, 183, 188.
57. Henry, *Les îles*, 39.
58. Henry, *Les îles*, 39.

59. Henry, *Les îles*, 170, 181; Scantamburlo, *Etnologia dos Bijagós*, 51.

60. Henry, *Les îles*, 181.

61. Henry, *Les îles*, 15, 183, 185, 187; Fernandes, "O Espaço e o Tempo no Sistema Político Bidjogó," 7–9.

62. Lima, *Organização Económica e Social dos Bijagós*, 75, 114.

63. Henry, *Les îles*, 15, 183, 185, 187; Fernandes, "O Espaço e o Tempo no Sistema Político Bidjogó," 8–9.

64. Lima, *Organização Económica e Social dos Bijagós*, 75, 114.

65. Henry, *Les îles*, 184.

66. Henry, *Les îles*, 39.

67. Havik, *Silences and Soundbytes*, 114.

68. Havik, *Silences and Soundbytes*, 114.

69. Alvares d'Almada, *Tratado Breve dos Rios de Guiné*, 97.

70. Fernandes, "O Espaço e o Tempo no Sistema Político Bidjogó," 7–8.

71. Lima, *Organização Económica e Social dos Bijagós*, 101.

72. Havik, *Silences and Soundbytes*, 114; Henry, *Les îles*, 62.

73. Havik, *Silences and Soundbytes*, 257.

74. Henry, *Les îles*, 62.

75. Lima, *Organização Económica e Social dos Bijagós*, 116.

76. Havik, *Silences and Soundbytes*, 117.

77. Henry *Les îles*, 63, and Havik, *Silences and Soundbytes*, 276.

78. Havik, *Silences and Soundbytes*, 276–77.

79. Havik, *Silences and Soundbytes*, 277, 310.

80. Havik, *Silences and Soundbytes*, 258–63.

81. Havik, *Silences and Soundbytes*, 266.

82. Havik, *Silences and Soundbytes*, 265.

83. Havik, *Silences and Soundbytes*, 278–310.

84. Havik, *Silences and Soundbytes*, 277, 283.

85. Barreto, *História da Guiné*, 235–37.

86. Letter from Hostains, the French consul to Portuguese Guinea, to the governor-general of French West Africa, titled "Troubles dans les Bissagos," written in Bissau, May 28, 1925, French Colonial Archives, Dakar, Senegal: Répertoire des Archives, Série F, Guinée Portugaise, Sous-Séries 2F 7, Versement 14, "Iles Bissagos."

87. Peter Karibe Mendy, "A Conquista Militar da Guiné: da Resistência à Pacificação do Arquipelago dos Bijagos 1917–1936," in *Soronda* 13 (January 1992): 41–57, see esp. 49.

88. Viégas, *Ilha de Canhabaque*, 79.

89. Letter from Hostains, the French consul to Portuguese Guinea, to the governor-general of French West Africa, titled "Troubles dans les Bissagos," written in Bissau, January 17, 1936, French Colonial Archives, Dakar, Senegal: Répertoire des Archives, Série F, Guinée Portugaise, Sous-Séries 2F 7, Versement 14, "Iles Bissagos."

90. Letter from Hostains to the governor-general of French West Africa, January 17, 1936.

91. Mendy, "A Conquista Militar," 47, 53.

92. Viégas, *Iha de Canhabaque*, 102.

93. Viégas, *Iha de Canhabaque*, 134, 138.

94. Peter Karibe Mendy, *Portuguese Colonialism in Africa: The Tradition of Resistance in Guinea-Bissau 1879–1959* (Birmingham: University of Birmingham Centre for West African Studies, 1987); see also Mendy, "A Conquista Militar," 54.

95. Joshua B. Forrest, *Lineages of State Fragility: Rural Civil Society in Guinea-Bissau* (Athens: Ohio University Press, 2003), 135.

96. Lima, *Organização Económica e Social dos Bijagós*, 135–36.

97. Lima, *Organização Económica e Social dos Bijagós*, 57, 136.

98. Philip J. Havik, "As sociedades agrárias e a intervenção rural na Guiné-Bissau," in *Revista Internacional de Estudos Africanos* no. 14/15 (1991): 279–310; see 294; Mette Baekgaard and Henrik Overballe, "When Is a Fishing Man a Fisherman? Artisanal Fishery Development in Guinea-Bissau," in *Fishing for Development: Small Scale Fisheries in Africa*, ed. Inge Tvedten and Bjorn Hersoug (Uppsala: Nordiska Afrikainstitut, 1992), 173–90; see 180.

99. Havik, "As sociedades agrárias," 279–310; Raúl Mendes Fernandes, "Dilemmes et conflits aux îles Bijagós," in *The Problem of Violence: Local Conflict Settlement in Contemporary Africa*, ed. Georg Klute and Birgit Embaló (Cologne: Rudiger Koppe Verlag, 2011), 377–403; see 385; Baekgaard and Overballe, "When Is a Fishing Man a Fisherman?," 178–80.

100. Fernandes, "Dilemmes et conflits aux îles Bijagós," 385.

101. Fernandes, "O Espaço e o Tempo no Sistema Político Bidjogó," 5–23; see esp. 17–18.

102. Fernandes, "Dilemmes et conflits aux îles Bijagós," 386–87.

103. Fernandes, "Dilemmes et conflits aux îles Bijagós," 384; Baekgaard and Overballe, "When Is a Fishing Man a Fisherman?," 180.

104. Fernandes, "Dilemmes et conflits aux îles Bijagós," 386.

105. Fernandes, "Dilemmes et conflits aux îles Bijagós," 387–88.

106. Fernandes, "Dilemmes et conflits aux îles Bijagós," 393.

107. Fernandes, "Dilemmes et conflits aux îles Bijagós," 393–95.

108. Fernandes, "Dilemmes et conflits aux îles Bijagós," 395.

109. Fernandes, "Dilemmes et conflits aux îles Bijagós," 395.

110. Baekgaard and Overballe, "When Is a Fishing Man a Fisherman?," 182; Raúl Mendes Fernandes, "Nhomingas e Bidjogos—da Pesca de 'Subsistência' à Pesca 'Comercial,'" *Revista de estudos guineenses* 4 (July 1987): 58–94, 59.

111. Henry, "Marinheiros Bijogós: Passado e Presente," 40–41; Fernandes, "Nhomingas e Bidjogos—da Pesca de 'Subsistência' à Pesca 'Comercial,'" 59.

112. Baekgaard and Overballe, "When Is a Fishing Man a Fisherman?," 179, 186; Fernandes, "Nhomingas e Bidjogos—da Pesca de 'Subsistência' à Pesca 'Comercial,'" 61, 67.

113. Baekgaard and Overballe, "When Is a Fishing Man a Fisherman?," 185–86; Henry, "Marinheiros Bijogós: Passado e Presente," 41, 43; Havik, "As sociedades agrárias e a intervenção rural na Guiné-Bissau," 294.

114. Fernandes, "Nhomingas e Bidjogos—da Pesca de 'Subsistência' à Pesca 'Comercial,'" 59, 64, 67.

115. Fernandes, "Nhomingas e Bidjogos—da Pesca de 'Subsistência' à Pesca 'Comercial,'" 73.

116. Fernandes, "Nhomingas e Bidjogos—da Pesca de 'Subsistência' à Pesca 'Comercial,'" 91.

117. Baekgaard and Overballe, "When Is a Fishing Man a Fisherman?," 187.

118. Havik, "As sociedades agrárias e a intervenção rural na Guiné-Bissau," 294.

119. Havik, "As sociedades agrárias e a intervenção rural na Guiné-Bissau," 294.

120. Henry, *Les îles*, 68.

121. Baekgaard and Overballe, "When Is a Fishing Man a Fisherman?," 188–89.

122. Fernandes, "O Espaço e o Tempo no Sistema Político Bidjogó," 21.

123. Henry, *Les îles*, 68–150.

4

An Island in the Middle of Everywhere

Bioko under Colonial Domination

Enrique N. Okenve

Before 1967 it is difficult to tell how the Bubi felt about the ties that linked their native island of Bioko—Fernando Po at the time—to continental Equatorial Guinea, Rio Muni.[1] For most of the Spanish colonial era (1858–1968), the inhabitants of Bioko had lived with their backs to Rio Muni. Even though the Spanish claimed historical rights over nearly 77,220 square miles of the mainland territory on the basis of the 1777 Treaty of San Ildefonso-El Pardo between Portugal and Spain, European colonial powers refused to acknowledge such rights.[2] Not until 1883 did Spain timidly begin to make effective its presence on a very small portion of the mainland—the Muni Estuary area—and, especially the nearby small islands of Corisco and Elobey Chico. In 1900, after the signing of the Franco-Spanish Treaty of Paris, Spanish rights over what became known as Rio Muni were eventually recognized and integrated into a single colony with the rest of Spanish possessions in the Spanish Territories of the Gulf of Guinea.[3] The treaty, however, dampened Spanish colonial ambitions south of the Sahara, for Spain was awarded only 10,038 square miles of a territory relatively distant from Bioko.[4] Following such a disappointment, Bioko remained the center of political authority during the entire period of Spanish colonial domination as well as the main focus of economic investment and development. Rio Muni was, to a large extent, an appendage, especially after the late 1920s, when it became clear that it could not provide the much-needed labor force for the thriving cocoa plantations of Bioko. In many ways, Bioko had been both island and mainland with Rio Muni largely depending on the political decisions and economic handouts delivered from Bioko. By the

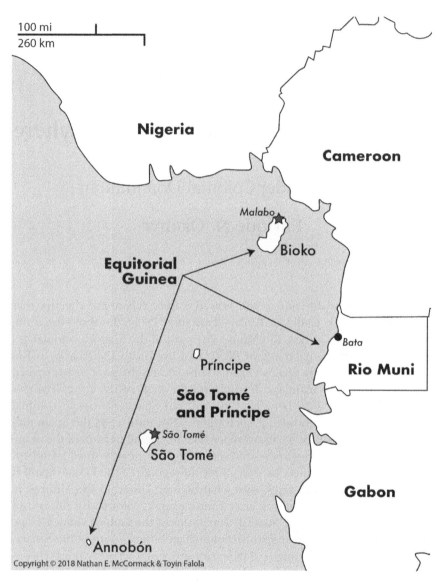

4.1: The Gulf of Guinea

mid-1960s, however, the situation was about to change. Negotiations leading to independence designed a future in which the two territories, Bioko
and Rio Muni, would become part of a single sovereign nation, Equatorial
Guinea. The reaction from segments of the Bubi population was quick and,
with the help of Spanish settlers, they founded Unión Bubi (UB), the political organization that would represent the interests of Bioko's indigenous
people and which was granted a seat at the Constitutional Conference
(1967–68). During the acrimonious discussions that sought to establish the
legal and political framework for the new country, it became apparent that
the self-proclaimed representatives of the Bubi people were not in favor of
the political union between the island of Bioko and the much more populous Rio Muni. They opposed an independence model in which Spanish
colonizers would be replaced by the much less trusted Fang mainlanders.

The fears of some of the Bubi were somewhat unfounded. Fang presence on the island had remained relatively small throughout most of the
period of Spanish domination and, therefore, interaction between Bubi
and Fang peoples had been rather limited.[5] Much of Bubi antagonistic sentiments toward Riomunians, especially the Fang, seemed to have
been heightened by Spanish colonizers.[6] During most of the colonial era
Spanish rhetoric had depicted the Fang as the archetypical African savage—uncivilized and, for the most part, violent. As the reality of unified
independence approached, anti-Fang stereotypes became useful to Spanish settlers on Bioko who, along with their commercial partners in Spain,
feared their economic interests would be undermined by the seemingly
radical Riomunian nationalists. Although not for the same reasons that
originally informed Bubi opposition to the union between Bioko and Rio
Muni, the series of political developments that followed independence on
October 12, 1968, soon confirmed the worst fears of much of the Bubi
population. They also crashed the hopes of the rest of Equatoguineans.
Five months within independence, the democratically elected president,
Francisco Macías Nguema (1968–79), took an autocratic turn and began
the brutal repression that would put him on par with the likes of Idi Amin
Dada in Uganda and Jean-Bédel Bokasa in the Central African Republic.

Like the rest of the population of Equatorial Guinea, the Bubi suffered
greatly under the new regime. Yet many Bubi interpreted that the government led by Francisco Macías Nguema targeted them in particular. In a
letter sent to the Spanish government in 1972, the situation in Equatorial
Guinea was described in the following terms:

Cities like Santa Isabel [modern-day Malabo] and Bata resemble dead
towns, after totally losing their [daily] activities because of a primitive
madman who does not know anything about the juridical and political

significance of [signed] agreements. He has surrounded himself by a clique of cannibal sheikhs of his tribe. They are no less cruel than the President who, holding power firmly in his hand, has established a despotic regime in [Equatorial] Guinea based on violence and oppression thanks to the majority granted by his N'tumu tribe . . . (Memorándum presentado al Generalísimo FRANCO por el Grupo BUBI y Tribus playeras sobre la situación en la República de Guinea Ecuatorial, May 1972?, 81/11524, exp. 1, AGA.)

The letter addressed to Gen. Francisco Franco was signed by the "Bubi Group and *Playero* [coastal] Tribes" in an attempt to obtain support from Spain against the so-called Ntumu. The use of this term—a subdivision of the Fang ethnic group—suggests the presence of coastal Fang among the signatories, as only they would disdainfully refer to all Fang people from the interior of Rio Muni as Ntumu. More importantly, the spirit of the letter reflects the identification of the Fang people with political oppression by the Bubi and other signatories in the aftermath of independence. More than forty years later, this trend is still evident as reflected by the rhetoric employed by UB's political successor, Movimiento para la Autodeterminación de la Isla de Bioko (Movement for the Self-Determination of Bioko Island, MAIB).

The development of Bubi nationalism since the mid-1960s is an example of similar separatist trends across postcolonial Africa, but it is also an exception. Although Christopher Young points out that, by and large, "ethnicity does not mutate into ethno-nationalism," everything seems to suggest that right from the beginning, Bubi nationalism was separatist.[7] To be fair, we still know very little about the development of Bubi ethnicity and nationalism prior to the mid-1960s. Unlike the Fang, who notoriously developed a strong cohesive ethnic identity that transcended colonial territorial borders and was able to shape anticolonial nationalism in the region, there are no indications that similar developments took place among the Bubi.[8] While unified independence was widely rejected in Bioko, this cannot be simply attributed to the existence of deep-seated nationalist sentiments among the majority of the Bubi population at the time. Instead, it is necessary to examine the impact of their historical experience since the 1820s.

Looking at political developments in Africa since the wave of democratization of the 1990s, political scientists have explored the connection between political exclusion and marginalization and the challenges that this posed to the integrity of the postcolonial state.[9] Although such works have provided valuable insight on the subject, historians are well aware that political exclusion and the challenges derived from it are not recent phenomena.

The aftermath of independence was also characterized by the political exclusion of segments of the African population combined with the fragility of democratic regimes established at the advent of independence. Jonathon Glassman broadly explores this situation in the case of Zanzibar, where political competition was framed around notions of racial and ethnic identities. Here the adversary of the native Zanzibari was not the mainlander but the Arab whose presence on these Indian Ocean islands dates back to nearly 2,000 years ago.[10] In Bioko, it was not the presence of some 35,000 Nigerian workers, by far the largest population group on the island at the time of independence, who posed a significant threat to Bubi interests. Their lack of Equatoguinean citizenship excluded them from political competition, but this was not the case of the looming mainlander, particularly the Fang.

Certainly the Bubi have not been the only marginalized group in Equatorial Guinea since 1968. The vast majority of the country's population, including the Fang, have suffered from political and economic exclusion. Nowhere was this more evident than in Annobón. The population of this island has also suffered from marginalization and neglect but perhaps for the opposite reasons as the Bubi. Annobón is much smaller—almost seven square miles as opposed to the 779 square miles of Bioko; it has much fewer inhabitants; and it is located more than 340 miles away from mainland Equatorial Guinea. In the 1970s, the regime led by Francisco Macías Nguema completely neglected the island while much of its population perished as a result of a cholera epidemic.[11] The people of Annobón have been historically neglected because of the peripheral and marginal importance of their island to the Spanish colonizers first and the Equatoguinean government since 1968. In contrast, Bioko, for the past two centuries, has been at the center of major social, political, and economic developments in what today is Equatorial Guinea. Indeed, it is the centrality of Bioko that has largely contributed to the marginalization and exclusion of the Bubi as they were pushed aside in favor of late-comer groups with interests on the island. First, the British naval officers established a station in Clarence (Malabo) in 1827 to enforce the ban on the trade in enslaved Africans. Simultaneously, freed Africans—Krio or Fernandinos—were resettled on Bioko. There, they underwent a process of creolization as they remained largely independent after the British withdrew from the mid-1830s. From 1858, Spain began to concretize its claim over Bioko and by the end of the century, their position was strong enough to make it possible for Krio and Spanish settlers to take large portions of Bioko's land for the expansion of cocoa agriculture while facilitating the relentless work of the Catholic Claretian Mission. Since the country gained independence in 1968, scores of Fang civil servants and farmers have moved to Bioko to take jobs in the administration or work on the properties abandoned by Spanish plantation owners. By taking a quick glimpse at three episodes in the history of Bioko—the settlement of freed Africans, the development of cocoa plantation agricultures, and the transition to independence—it will become evident that the centrality of Bioko has worked to the detriment of Bubi interests and has contributed to their marginalization for the past two centuries.

Strangers on the Island

Very little is known about the circumstances that led to the settlement of Bioko by groups of African migrants arriving from the neighboring mainland. While we need to be cautious regarding our understanding of the early history of this African island, the consensus is that migrant groups arrived in Bioko in at least four separate waves.[12] This was facilitated by its proximity to the continental shores, over 18 miles from the mouth of the Wouri River in Cameroon. Thus, unlike the near islands of São Tomé and Príncipe and the somewhat more distant Annobón, Bioko has remained inhabited for over 1,500 years. During this period, successive groups of settlers contributed to the development of a distinctive Bantu culture, which, until the nineteenth century, was characterized by its remarkable heterogeneity. Within its limited 772 square miles, it was possible to find several subcultural groups that spoke dialectal variations of what today is known as the Bubi language. Cultural differences were especially acute between peoples living on the south and north of the island to the point that their dialects were not mutually understandable.[13]

From the moment that Portuguese explorers first set foot on Bioko in 1472, European accounts stressed the unfriendly and bellicose character of its inhabitants, who first resisted Portuguese efforts to establish plantation agriculture and subsequently European attempts to create permanent commercial stations.[14] In addition, endemic malaria contributed to keeping European settlers and traders off the island until the nineteenth century. A different look at the migration patterns that shaped Bioko's composite culture can perhaps provide a better understanding of the reasons that led both to its colonization by Bantu groups and their resistance against European presence. The settlement by succeeding groups of Bantu migrants indicates that early inhabitants did not necessarily resist the arrival of foreigners to the shores of Bioko. In fact, "outsiders" did contribute to the development of Bubi culture. Although the military superiority of mainland migrants is sometimes cited in explaining this phenomenon, this alone cannot account for this outcome, otherwise Europeans would have also been able to occupy Bioko before 1827. There are indications that early Bubi communities were somewhat receptive to the arrival of foreign groups and individuals who were willing to merge with them. Rather than conquering, immigrants blended in with the existing society, making their arrival less of a threat. The island appeared to serve as shelter for displaced populations from the neighboring mainland and, later on, for runaway slaves from São Tomé and Príncipe.[15] Somehow, the sanctuary character of Bioko was accentuated by the expansion of the transatlantic slave trade.

Bubi reluctance to allow the establishment of permanent European settlement on Bioko triggered the contempt of early European explorers. At the beginning of the eighteenth century, a Dutch trader described the inhabitants of Bioko as "a savage and cruel sort of people" who should not be trusted.[16] No doubt disdain for the Bubi was motivated by what European observers perceived as the reclusive nature of this African people. Considering the circumstances that characterized the Gulf of Guinea in the eighteenth century, it should not come as a surprise that Bioko islanders chose to minimize their contact with European traders. This was still the situation in 1778 when the first Spanish expedition arrived to take possession of the island, which had been formally handed over by Portugal a year earlier. The Spanish report made reference to the lack of native settlements in and around the "bay of San Carlos" (Luba) as well as the difficulty of "subduing and civilizing those islanders as they are used to live on the hills."[17] Their wariness continued to be used against them even after the British settled on the island in the late 1820s. Then, the Bubi were said to be "different in their manners and appearance from their neighbours on the coast" and this was seen as "proof of the little interaction they have had with the [outside] world" and hence their backwardness.[18]

Notwithstanding European accounts, one should not overstate the so-called isolation of Bioko and its inhabitants. The island was not cut off from the mainland as indicated by the arrival of successive waves of migrants until at least the fifteenth century. Furthermore, there are indications that traders from Calabar and Doula used to exchange unspecified goods for yams grown on the island.[19] The 1778 Spanish expedition also mentioned that British slave traders used to visit the north of Bioko, where they obtained "supplies for their slaves" in exchange for "iron bars, bells, knives, fish hooks and other trinkets."[20] The foundation of Clarence by the British in 1827 and especially the rise in palm oil trade provided some of the Bubi with a much safer opportunity to participate in commercial exchanges on a regular basis. Although British observers still lamented that the island

could provide more than the "300 tons of palm oil in the year" that it produced, Bubi participation in this thriving trade clearly indicates their dis-
position for trade and contact with outsiders if deemed beneficial.[21]

The establishment of Clarence and the subsequent development of a
creolized community have been sufficiently documented in the historiography. In their effort to stop the illegal shipment of enslaved Africans, the
British decided to create a naval base in Bioko to patrol the heavily traf-
ficked waters of the Gulf of Guinea. Soon after the foundation of Clarence, it was decided that recaptured Africans could be disembarked there
instead of subjecting them to the long journey to Freetown, which was the
main British center for the resettlement of Africans rescued on board slave
ships. Ibrahim Sundiata provides perhaps the best account of the development of the Krio community of Bioko, from their initial settlement and
acculturation to their material rise, initially, as middlemen in the palm oil
trade and, from the late nineteenth century, as successful cocoa plantation owners.[22] Indeed, Bioko's Krio, like other Krio communities across
West Africa, were a rather heterogeneous group, made up of individuals
of diverse geographical origins. Among them, one could distinguish Krio
traders from Freetown, workers from the Gold Coast or Igboland, and, of
course, liberated enslaved Africans. The historiography of Clarence reveals
a common denominator regarding the relationship between the native
Bubi and the groups of Africans who arrived on the island from the late
1820s. Thus, this relationship was characterized by deep-seated antagonism, distrust, and at times violence between the indigenous Bubi and the
African groups of latecomers.

From the beginning of the foundation of Clarence it became clear that
newly arrived Africans refused to integrate into the indigenous Bubi society. This was particularly reflected in a number of petty and not so petty
crimes against Bubi communities, especially those closer to Clarence. As
early as 1827, Governor Nicolls wrote about this problem, expressing that
"the Liberated Africans having behaved so ill in robbing the yam stores of
the inhabitants are not to be trusted."[23] Nicholls failed to explain, however,
that the lack of British prevision and support for Clarence made the survival of African settlers rather precarious during the early years of the settlement. Indeed, food supply became one of the main concerns of the British
authorities who had expected the Bubi to be more enthusiastic about trading their foodstuff for British goods. It is likely that Bubi reluctance had
to do with the lack of a sizable food surplus as, until then, they had mainly
produced only enough food to supply their needs. Nonetheless, it did not
help that, right from the start, newly arrived Africans tended to victimize
Bubi communities. Dishonesty and deception came to characterize most

commercial exchanges between these two groups. Ultimately, this posed the most serious obstacle for the development of more solid commercial relations. Thus, soon after being appointed by the Spanish in 1843, Gov. John Beecroft, passed a series of regulations that directly addressed this matter: "All persons accused of unfairly trading with the island's natives; or of obtaining an improper or wrongful profit from the exchange of yams, [palm] oil or any other item; or of taking from them, without their permit or authority, fish catch, palm wine . . . will be found guilty . . . and subject to be punished as judged and ruled by the Governor and Council."[24] Deceptive commercial dealings and robbery were not the only grievances experienced by Bubi communities during much of the nineteenth century. The abduction of children for domestic service and especially women became the main cause of Bubi resentment against African settlers. Accordingly, the same regulations established that the "taking of indecent liberties with . . . [Bubi] wives and girls" by African settlers as well as their attempt to "persuade such women and girls to run away and live with them" would be deemed sufficient grounds for conviction.[25]

In addition to the quarrels between the two communities, the process of creolization that African settlers experienced during the early stages of Clarence is crucial in understanding the shared history of Bubi and Krio communities, for it shaped their relationship for decades to come. After the settlement was officially abandoned by the British government in the mid-1830s, the Baptist Missionary Society took over the task of "civilizing" freed Africans from Clarence.[26] Similarly to other creolized communities across West Africa, Bioko's Krio sought to distance themselves from the "primitive" Bubi. Ultimately, they aspired to assimilate themselves with their British "liberators." Not surprisingly, Bubi society identified creolized settlers, including migrant laborers, with the Europeans established on Bioko from early on. Writing in the late 1850s, Thomas Hutchinson explained that "'Apoto' is the title which the Fernandians [Bubi] give to the Europeans and colonisers of Clarence, and which in their language signifies a stranger, or one speaking a foreign tongue."[27] By then, creolization was well under way as reflected in Hutchinson's account: "negro residents, save the Krumen, nearly all dress in European style, and are very courteous in their bearing when met in the streets."[28] Western-style dress was highly valued by the Krio community, being the most evident marker of their degree of civilization and distance from the "ostentatiously unclothed" Bubi.[29] Furthermore, sources indicate that the Krio developed a special relationship with the British, which was reflected in frequent displays of gratitude as well as loyalty.[30] Indeed, this became one of the main concerns for the Spanish authorities after taking full control of the island in 1858.[31] This was still evident at the beginning of the twentieth century when the Spanish governor-general denounced "the evident English spirit that transpires among a great deal of the population." According to him, "the main reason for this is the extent to which, from early on, protestant practices became rooted on the island."[32]

No doubt, Krio's acculturation and close relationship with the British contributed to their material success. In turn, they became the most influential group on the island until the 1920s, when they were eventually displaced by Spanish plantation owners and traders. The Krio, however, never were the largest group of Africans to arrive in Bioko during this period. From the time of British settlement to the early twentieth century, the so-called Krumen became the main source of labor on the island. This is partly explained by British reluctance to employ freed Africans in any capacity that could resemble slave labor, but also by the widespread refusal of Bubi men and women to sell their services for the construction of Clarence, first, or any strenuous task its inhabitants required. Some seventy years after the foundation of Clarence—by then renamed Santa Isabel—Bubi attitudes toward paid labor had barely changed. Mary Kingsley explained how "Now and again a [Bubi] man or woman will come voluntarily and take service in Clarence . . . And just when their owner thinks . . . he knows how to manage them better than other men . . . [t]he Bubi has . . . softly and silently vanished away."[33] Imported labor, therefore, became crucial for the survival of this settlement from its inception and, later on, for the development of the plantation economy for which Bioko became renowned. The massive influx of Kru laborers created problems for all of the island's inhabitants, particularly for the Bubi. If local authorities tried to prevent—at least on paper—abuses against the indigenous population, there is little indication that they had much success. The continuous inflow of single male workers posed a serious challenge for the maintenance of social order in Clarence and Bioko at large. Indeed, this was a price worth paying. From the late nineteenth century, the beginning of cocoa plantation made it necessary to increase the arrival of recruited workers. In light of the accelerated growth of the non-indigenous population and their territorial expansion across the island, Bubi communities were forced to retreat further inland.[34] Whether they initially found shelter in Bioko against threats that they faced on the mainland and, later on, against menace that arrived from the sea, by the late nineteenth century the Bubi were on their way to becoming "prisoners" on their island. Aware of some of the challenges faced by the indigenous population, the Spanish authorities tried to convince the scattered Bubi communities to resettle in larger villages so as to facilitate their protection "against violent acts committed against them by runaway Krumen from the plantations."[35]

Bubi retreat from areas now occupied by African and Spanish settlers was not only motivated by criminal actions against them. Perhaps the most dangerous challenge that the arrival of these latecomers posed for Bioko's indigenous population was the spread of epidemic outbreaks. Yellow fever in particular had a terrible impact on the Bubi as well as the settler population throughout most of the nineteenth century. The first epidemic outbreak on record took place as early as 1829 after the arrival of two British Navy ships from Sierra Leone.[36] Similarly, epidemic outbreaks of smallpox and yellow fever also wreaked havoc among the island population in the 1860s, coinciding with the arrival of emancipated workers from Cuba.[37] Official accounts mentioned the virulent effects of this epidemic outbreak in Santa Isabel, but little or nothing is said about the effects on Bubi communities.[38] From the late nineteenth century and especially during the first two decades of the twentieth, the Spanish believed that there was a serious chance that the Bubi might disappear as a people. Missionaries in particular began a campaign for their protection. But the biggest threat against Bioko's Bubi communities was yet to materialize. Writing at the end of the 1890s, Mary Kingsley insightfully pointed out that "if the coffee and cacao thrive on Fernando Po to the same extent that they have already thriven on San Thomé there is but little doubt that the Bubis will become extinct."[39]

Cocoa Takes over the Soil

Claims about the imminent disappearance of the Bubi were certainly exaggerated. In fact, all across Africa one can find similar examples of European reports warning about high mortality rates among recently colonized African peoples. Such was the case in Rio Muni, especially after some of its population were hit by severe famine and a subsequent epidemic outbreak in the late 1910s and early 1920s. Perhaps what made European perceptions on the state of Bioko's indigenous people so alarming was the small size of the island's population along with the continuous arrival of African workers from the continent. Sundiata takes as valid reports that estimated Bioko's indigenous population around 30,000 people during the nineteenth century. This figure is likely to have been taken from Spanish missionaries' calculations at the end of the century.[40] Yet, as Hutchinson warned almost thirty years earlier, it is very difficult to gather an accurate sense of the size of the Bubi population at the time because of the scattered nature of their settlements as well as their wish to limit interaction with outsiders as much as possible.[41] There is little question that European concerns about the future of Bioko's indigenous population were shaped by the state of malaise that they appeared to undergo at the turn of the twentieth century. In addition to the number of epidemics that affected the inhabitants of Bioko since 1827, the Spanish were particularly preoccupied about the effects that alcohol was having on the African population. In 1902 the governor-general shared this concern with the metropolitan authorities in his annual report, as he explained that during that year: "900 barrels of alcohol and 10,000 boxes of the worst quality gin have entered this island . . . this is not only prompting the evident degeneration of the Bubi race . . . but it is also affecting migrant workers from the continent . . . this causes a considerable amount of deaths among the negro race to the extent that this island . . . can be considered to be Africa's sanatorium."[42] While Spanish accounts on the extent of alcohol abuse by African individuals might be somewhat exaggerated, there are indications that a significant number of the Bubi were indeed demoralized at the turn of the twentieth century.[43] No doubt, the same could be said about many recently colonized African peoples at the time, but we have yet to determine if insularity played any role in exacerbating the effects of colonial conquest for peoples like the Bubi. Whether geographical retreat became the main strategy to deal with the arrival of African and European settlers, the island's relatively small size did not allow much room for this, especially once cocoa plantations began to expand.[44]

The development of cocoa agriculture provided the necessary sense of purpose for Spanish colonialism in the Gulf of Guinea. Until then, Spain had shown very little interest in the colonization of Africa even in the midst of the European scramble. Immersed in a profound political and economic crisis, Spain's loss of what remained of its traditional overseas empire in the 1890s intensified the isolationist tendency that came to characterize its foreign policy for much of the twentieth century. It is symptomatic that the initial expansion of cocoa agriculture in Bioko had little to do with Spain. Instead it was the Krio who were responsible for the development of cocoa plantation agriculture on the island after this crop was introduced from São Tomé in the 1860s.[45] The sharp decline in palm oil prices from the late 1880s accelerated the shift to cocoa farming as the Krio's main economic activity, though trading was never completely abandoned.[46] This change was crucial for the economic and social transformation of the island in the decades to come. Krio settlers led the way for the economic colonization of Bioko and, by 1893, the governor-general acknowledged that "the creation of cocoa and coffee farms was the future of the island."[47]

Right from the start both Krio planters and the Spanish authorities realized that the steady supply of labor was crucial for the consolidation of labor-intensive cocoa agriculture in Bioko. In many respects, it was the need for labor that led the Spanish authorities to pursue their so-called historical rights on the mainland. Until 1900, Spain's presence in Rio Muni was limited to a short coastal strip north of the Muni estuary and the nearby islands of Elobey Chico, Elobey Grande, and Corisco. The strong opposition from the French and, especially, German governments rendered useless Spain's claims over almost 77,220 square miles in the area of the Gulf of Guinea. Eventually, Spain had to do with barely 10,038 square miles, which were granted by France after the signature of the Treaty of Paris in 1900. As such, Bioko remained the central piece of Spanish colonialism in the region and, despite the great disappointment the signature of this treaty posed to Spain's late colonial aspirations in Africa, the colonial authorities still hoped that this would "open up the path to solve the labor shortage problem that we were to face in Fernando Po."[48] Indeed, this was not the case. As Sundiata and Gervase Clarence-Smith have shown for the early period of cocoa agriculture, the so-called labor question remained the principal threat for the expansion of the main economic activity on the island.

The small size of the Bubi population contributed to the search for labor outside Bioko, but, above all, it was their opposition to working on the existing cocoa plantations that became problematic for both settlers and Spanish authorities during the early stages of cocoa agriculture.[49] In line with European rhetoric elsewhere in the colonized world, Bubi refusal to sell their labor was portrayed as a sign of their lack of material ambition, unprogressive spirit, and, ultimately, laziness—stereotypes that survived beyond the colonial era. Spanish and Krio settlers' views hid that, in fact, Bubi individuals did become cocoa farmers and, by 1910, they produced as much as one-third of Bioko's total cocoa output on their small farms.[50] This went against the grain of an agricultural model that favored large estates over small-scale production. In essence, Spanish colonial authorities prioritized the interests of European and wealthy Krio planters for whom small producers—Bubi and non-Bubi—represented some sort of "unfair competition" due their lower production costs. Furthermore, small farms used labor that plantation owners badly needed. As a result, cocoa planters intensified their pressure on Bubi farmers, as Governor Barrera acknowledged to the government in Madrid.[51] Colonial authorities' position on this issue was paradoxical, to say the least. Barrera himself believed that Bubi smallholdings mainly served a spurious purpose: "Little by little, the Bubi, who have become half-civilized, have been made owners of two-and-a-half or five-acre smallholdings that have been dedicated to cocoa farming. Since the necessary work to maintain such small farms is insignificant, once the land is cleared, they rely on their smallholdings and the pompous property title that is issued to them to live idly . . ."[52] Implicitly, Barrera was accusing the Claretians of being responsible for the implementation of a strategy that, according to him, sought to excuse Bubi farmers from participating in the so-called *prestación personal* or corvée.[53]

Attempts to either convince or force the Bubi to provide labor for Bioko's plantations repeatedly failed throughout the 1910s and 1920s. This was partly because of missionary opposition to it, but it was also a consequence of the lasting memories of the so-called Belebú-Balachá uprising of 1910. The unrest was triggered by Bubi opposition to labor conscription in the village of Belebú-Balachá, southern Bioko. Colonial authorities reacted by sending a five-man-strong military expedition, but this met firm opposition from Bubi villagers, resulting in the death of three privates.[54] The reaction of the colonial government was both swift and brutal. Spanish and Krio settlers joined a larger expedition force that killed an undetermined number of Bubi individuals in and around the area of Luba.[55] The Belebú-Balachá uprising left a number of important consequences for the future relations between the island's main social groups—the Bubi, Krio, and Spanish. The active participation of Krio settlers in the repression reinforced Bubi mistrust toward them.[56] Following the armed clash, the Spanish authorities became much more reluctant to use force in dealing with Bioko's indigenous people. In addition, Bubi communities, especially from northern Bioko, strengthened their opposition to labor conscription and colonization believing that the "island's soil belonged to them."[57]

A year after the uprising, Governor Barrera intensified his efforts to recruit Riomunian laborers in the hope that the Fang would become the labor force the island's plantations needed. But given Spain's precarious position on the mainland and, above all, Fang widespread reluctance to sign up for work in Bioko, the authorities in Santa Isabel had no choice but to rely on migrant workers from across West Africa. By 1914, Spain believed they had found the solution to their labor problem after signing a treaty with the government of Liberia for recruiting workers from the independent West African nation. The successive renewal of the agreement alleviated the situation on the island and made possible the boom of cocoa agriculture. However, cooperation between the two governments came to a halt in 1930 after quasi-slavery working conditions on the island were denounced in the international arena.[58] Given the historical background behind the foundation of Liberia, it is not surprising that the government in Monrovia was quick to dissociate themselves from anything that suggested their complicity in the enslavement of their citizens. International pressure and embarrassment was certainly more effective than Spain's attempts to minimize the effects of what they regarded as a British-led campaign to favor their cocoa production in West Africa; similar complaints were made against labor conditions in neighboring São Tomé and Príncipe.[59] It is likely that the British made use of labor conditions in Bioko to their benefit, but there is little doubt that damning reports about the island's plantations were a rather accurate representation of the reality on the ground. In fact, those conditions explain, to a significant extent, why Fang men were so reluctant to work on the island's plantations.[60] Violence and abuse, however, were not limited to the treatment that African workers received on the plantations. As Enrique Martino shows, brutality and deception also became the norm in the recruitment of Fang workers, especially in the late 1920s. The situation became so outrageous that it prompted a number of Spanish colonials to compare government recruitment of workers in Rio Muni to a "black man hunting" for its use of methods of the "slave trade" era.[61] Eventually these atrocities were leaked to the Spanish press, contributing to the downfall of Gov. Miguel Núñez de Prado in 1931.[62] Since then, mass recruitment of Fang workers for Bioko's cocoa plantations was discontinued, a measure that had the support of the Chamber of Commerce of Bata because of the lack of economic development in Rio Muni.

The chronic lack of labor during the early stages of cocoa agriculture did not discourage Spanish and Krio planters, who were aware that the island's rich volcanic soils created almost perfect conditions for cocoa farming. As mentioned earlier, Bubi communities had been forced to retreat further inland throughout the nineteenth century, which, combined with the expansion of plantation agriculture, posed a serious challenge to Bubi access to land. In light of this, in 1904 colonial authorities passed a royal decree that legally protected African land rights by banning the transfer of native-owned land without court authorization. However, at the same time that the authorities claimed to guarantee Africans' access to land, the same decree implicitly protected the interests of the island's plantation owners. By law, indígenas—"uncivilized" Africans—could own a maximum of about ten acres, which prevented potential successful Bubi farmers from expanding their farms if they wished to.[63] Not surprisingly, legislation failed to guarantee Bubi access to land. In fact, the situation worsened in the years that followed the enactment of the decree to the point that colonial authorities expressed concern about what appeared to be an ever greater possibility that the Bubi would become landless. On too many occasions, Bubi individuals were forced to transfer their small farms because of debts. Thus, in 1911, Governor Barrera timidly wrote in favor of protecting "natives' property" to guarantee "the future of this race, because they must be the ones in charge of exploiting the land and exchanging what they produce for our manufactures."[64] Barrera's policies leave little doubt that the main goal was to boost the expansion of plantation agriculture and facilitate overall exploitation of the colony's resources. To him, the prosperity of cocoa planters represented the best way to protect Spain's interests in the Gulf of Guinea.

Parallel to the growing marginalization of the Bubi, they became the main "beneficiaries" of Spanish colonial paternalism, especially under the umbrella of the Claretian missionaries. Although it is not clear what motivated this policy, it is likely that the marginalization and displacement of Bioko's indigenous people created a guilty conscience among some of the Spanish colonists. Signs of paternalism were evident as early as the first decade of the twentieth century. Thus, a colonial official justified the difference in treatment of African peoples as follows: "The fearful Bubi of Fernando Po [is] so different from the arrogant *Pamue* [Fang] from the continent . . . [they] demand a different treatment. . . . Regarding the Bubi . . . I believe the so-called 'attraction policy' should be transformed into 'protection policy' . . . thus he should be compelled to work but without using excessively violent methods."[65] Indeed, the issue of labor became the central piece of Spanish paternalism toward the Bubi. After the signing of the labor treaty between Spain and Liberia in 1914, no further serious efforts were made to conscript Bubi workers for the island's plantations. Furthermore, the Bubi became exempt from the prestación personal, unlike Riomunians, who were all compelled to work for the state for up to forty days a year unless they could demonstrate they were wage earners. In many respects, this indicates the influence and power the Claretian Mission had. While their relationship with some of the colony's governors was not always smooth before the late 1930s, the Claretians were still able to shape colonial polices through their influence over other colonial administrators and, in particular, thanks to their connections in Spain. The Claretian Mission became the main advocate for the victimized Bubi as part of their renewed proselytizing strategy. Although Claretian attempts to gain the trust of Bubi communities failed during the late nineteenth and early twentieth centuries, from the mid-1910s they were able to make rapid progress. The Mission's protective role proved to be rather effective, so much so that by the 1940s, a Spanish observer argued that "none of the African natives can show such a rapid and complete transformation of its culture like the Bubi do."[66] This was indeed the price for becoming recipients of paternalist "protection" from the Claretian Mission and ultimately the Spanish colonial state.

The Threat from the Mainland

There is little doubt that throughout the entire colonial period, there were significant differences between Bioko and Rio Muni. One such difference was the "privileges" that Spanish colonizers bestowed on the Bubi compared to the rest of Africans in the colony. Writing at the end of the 1940s, Gov. Bonelli Rubio expressed his perplexity about this situation when he pointed out that the *"Curaduría Indígena* [native labor department] . . . inexplicably [used to] defend the theory that the native of Fernando Po should not work, as a means to protect this race . . . but, at the same time, [the Curaduría] used to allow and even encourage the recruitment of workers in our continental region. This resulted in a difference in treatment between the Bubi and Pamue which, in no way, can be satisfactorily explained."[67]

But differences between Bioko and the rest of the Spanish colony went much further than the treatment Africans received. These were visible at all sorts of levels, from economic development to administrative presence on the ground, basic infrastructure, educational opportunities, and so forth. Rio Muni had remained virtually untouched by Spanish colonial policies, especially before 1939. To a large extent, Spanish administrators had lost all interest in the mainland once labor recruitment schemes failed at the end of the 1920s. Its size, however small, became too much to handle for the limited material resources of an impoverished nation that, to make matters worse, underwent a civil conflict between 1936 and 1939.[68]

For the most part, Spain focused their colonial efforts on Bioko, where most of their economic interests were located. The relatively sizable presence of Spanish settlers as well as the small size of the island made it easier for the colonizers to extend the "benefits of civilization" to the island's inhabitants, especially after 1939, when the so-called civilizing mission became a central element of the rhetoric of General Franco's fascist regime.[69] As such, the Patronato de Indígenas (Native Affairs Department) became the principal tool of Spanish native policy in the Gulf of Guinea. The Patronato was given the responsibility of looking after African indígenas since they were considered legal minors under colonial legislation. Although the Patronato was officially established in 1904, it was not until its statutes were approved in 1928 that its activity became more forceful.

Quite significantly, the Claretian Mission was given a central role in running the Patronato, being represented at its board by the vicar general.[70] The institution, therefore, was largely in charge of designing and implementing native policy in the colony. Perhaps one of the most salient tasks of the Patronato in Bioko was the development of agricultural cooperatives that allowed Bubi farmers to benefit from the thriving cocoa sector.[71] Under the leadership and protection of this institution, from the mid-1940s cooperatives were set up on the island through the provision of technical assistance and funding. The latter was crucial to protect islanders from burdensome debts that had been used to take over their land plots in the past. While the vast majority of these cooperatives remained financially dependent on the Patronato, they continued to expand throughout the 1950s. Thus, by the next decade, there were a total of thirty agricultural cooperatives in Bioko. In contrast, in the much more populous Rio Muni there were only four cooperatives in the early 1960s.[72]

The lack of development of the agricultural cooperative movement on the mainland is clearly indicative of the marginal position this region occupied in Spanish colonialism in the Gulf of Guinea. In fact, until 1938, Rio Muni did not have its own branch of the Patronato, and it was not until 1945 that it was granted greater autonomy from the Bioko branch.[73] Indeed, part of the problem was that the Patronato was funded by the fees that employers had to pay for every worker they hired. Since most employment was located on the island, the Bioko branch of the Patronato had more resources at its disposal. As mentioned earlier, this was reflected in differences in public investment between the two regions. Not only did Bioko have better infrastructure from which both Europeans and Africans were able to benefit, but there were also more educational opportunities on the island. In 1943 a colonial report highlighted the existence of educational disparities between Bioko and the rest of the colony in terms of both the number of schools and the qualifications of teachers. According to the same report, in Bioko the colonial state ran twenty schools, whereas in Rio Muni, including the smaller islands, there was a total of twenty-five public schools. Meanwhile, the Catholic Mission had seven schools in Bioko and nine on the mainland.[74] The disparity in public investment in education between the two regions becomes particularly evident when we consider that Rio Muni is thirteen times the size of Bioko and, at the time, it ought to have had ten times the population of the island if we exclude the African migrant labor force and European settlers.

As in much of colonial Africa, education became the main avenue for Africans' social and material advancement. This was especially so in regions where economic development was sluggish, like Rio Muni. As a result, differences in educational opportunities between Bioko and Rio Muni led to the development of grievances and resentment among segments of the mainland population.[75] To a large extent, Riomunians misread Spanish paternalism as privilege, being unaware of the trauma that Bubi communities endured as a result of their closer interaction with colonizers. After all, they had been territorially displaced—when not dispossessed—and ultimately they were materially and politically marginalized. Not even the establishment of agricultural cooperatives allowed them to regain their economic autonomy because limited access to land prevented these cooperatives from becoming self-sufficient.[76] Thus, it can well be argued that the Patronato, through the agricultural cooperatives, solidified Bubi dependence on the Spanish. Native policy in Bioko sought, above all, to appease the consciences of Spanish colonizers while legitimating the state of affairs.

Until the last few years of colonial domination, there were many settlers who believed that Spain would never leave the island. To be sure, the existence of an indigenous Bubi population was an impediment to this project, especially in light of changing international attitudes to colonialism since the end of the Second World War. This is precisely why the Spanish tried so hard to "Hispanize" both the island and Bubi people. To this effect, the role of Spanish missionaries as agents of Hispanization was crucial for it was believed that they could ultimately secure Spanish settlers' interests in Bioko. By the mid-1950s, it became clear that the main objective of the colonial authorities was to strengthen the ties between the colony—namely Bioko—and Spain, and hence create the illusion that the island was an integral part of this southern European nation. An article banned by the Spanish government illustrates what the position of Spanish settlers was in the late 1950s: "The continental part . . . is slipping through our fingers. It is a matter of time. There is nothing else we can do about it. I wish we knew how to retreat to Fernando Po wisely. . . . Even a primary school student can see that our new province [Fernando Po and Rio Muni] is actually divided in two . . . [which are] completely different . . . in their past, their present, and, fatally, their future."[77]

Oblivious to the sign of the times, Spanish colonial officials and settlers believed that they could maintain control over the island if they were able to gain the support of Bioko's indigenous people. To this end, aggressive acculturation and paternalism sought, somehow, to eliminate Bubi cultural identity.

Overall, it can be argued that the comparative neglect between the two territories partly explains why anticolonial nationalism was much more vigorous in Rio Muni than in Bioko. Whether deep underground nationalist

sentiments developed on the island, we do not know. Admittedly, throughout the twentieth century the Bubi appeared to develop a strong sense
of autochthony in reaction to the continuous arrival and establishment
of "outsiders" on "their" island since the late 1820s. However, there are
no indications that such sentiments led to the development of some sort
of Bubi anticolonial nationalism before the mid- to late 1960s. Colonial
records of the early 1960s show that as far as Spain's positon in Bioko was
concerned, their main preoccupation was potential Nigerian expansionist
aspirations, given the sizable presence of Nigerian workers in Bioko, by far
the largest demographic group.[78] Indeed, poor labor conditions and the
ill treatment Nigerian workers often received provided fertile ground for
generalized unrest, but this never happened.[79]

Despite the apparent lack of anticolonial sentiments in Bioko before
the 1960s, we know that a number of Bubi and Krio individuals were dis-
satisfied with the state of affairs. This was reflected through their active
participation in the development of Equatoguinean anticolonial nationalism. Such was the case of two Bubi notables, Luis Maho and Pastor Torao
Sikara, leading figures of the incipient nationalist movement.[80] However
rarefied Equatoguinean nationalism was on the island prior to 1964, there
is evidence of close cooperation between nationalists from Bioko and Rio
Muni in pushing for political reforms. Nationalist activism as well as international pressure forced Spain to initiate timid reforms from 1956. That
year Spain changed the status of Equatorial Guinea from colony to province. Reforms became more effective in 1959, when the recently created
province was divided in two—Fernando Po and Rio Muni—and, more significantly, legal differences between so-called "uncivilized" and "civilized"
Africans were abolished. As a result, all Equatoguineans became Spanish
citizens. These reforms, however, did not satisfy Equatoguinean nationalists, forcing Spain to grant Equatorial Guinea autonomous status in 1964
after the reform was approved in a referendum in December 1963.

Certainly, the autonomy referendum signified a rare occasion, as
Equatoguineans were able to express their will in a free and democratic
manner at a time when Spaniards could not do so at home. In addition to
commencing the political process that led to the independence of Equatorial Guinea in 1968, the results and outcome of this referendum are significant on two levels. On the one hand, they revealed clear differences
regarding political independence between Bioko and Rio Muni. On the
other, they accelerated and deepened sociopolitical tensions between the
two territories. In Bioko the majority of the population voted against the
proposed autonomous status, which, in essence, reflected the will of many
Bubi people to maintain close ties with Spain.[81] The reform, however, was

approved thanks to the greater demographic weight of Rio Muni. The importance of this cannot be overstated enough, for it is crucial to our understanding of the relationship between Bioko and the mainland since the mid-1960s. For the first time, political participation made Rio Muni relevant. Despite the role Bioko had played as the administrative and economic center of Spanish colonialism in the Gulf of Guinea, the developments leading to independence showed that while Bioko would continue to be the formal seat of government, the people of Rio Muni were about to become the real source of power. The Spanish authorities were aware of the implications of this shift. Hence in developing the political structure of the autonomous government, Bioko was given disproportionate representation in relation to the size of its population. Accordingly, the Government Council, which mostly took over the functions of the governor-general, was formed by four Equatoguinean members from each of the two provinces. Only the fact that the president of the council was a Riomunian—Bonifacio Ondo Edu—tilted the balance in favor of the mainland. In light of this reality, a Spanish official expressed his doubts about the new political arrangement: "since there is certain antagonism between both [provinces], I wonder if this will cause any trouble among them." To his mind there was a risk that Rio Muni's one vote advantage in the council could be used to "focus on [Rio Muni] all the government protection, because they already say that they had been ignored until now."[82] While progress had been made to address underdevelopment in Rio Muni from the late 1950s, this could not hide that mainland Equatorial Guinea had been "neither economically nor politically important to Spain," as the US ambassador to Gabon acknowledged after a visit to Rio Muni in 1962.[83]

The short-lived self-government experience made it patent what most people had known for a long time; the two territories and their inhabitants shared a common colonizer but no significant ties or affinity. Though formally Bioko and Rio Muni had been a single colony, in reality, they were de facto two colonies that were administered very differently.[84] Having such distinct experiences under colonialism, people's views on independence differed across the two territorial divisions. Samuel Decalo argues that most Bubi people saw Spain as some sort of protector.[85] However, it is difficult to argue whether at the time this protective role was wanted as a result of Spain's policy toward the Bubi since the mid-1910s or, rather, due to the fear of being dominated by the Fang mainlander. Whatever the case, it is clear that political developments during the autonomous period exacerbated Bubi mistrust and fear of political union between Bioko and Rio Muni in a future independent country. Right from the start, political bickering and confrontation dominated the agenda of the autonomous

Government Council. This was especially palpable in Bioko, where politicians from all over Equatorial Guinea now competed for power and supporters. Less than nine months after the establishment of the Government Council, Ondo Edu had to appeal to civil servants and the population at large for calm because, according to him, their constant demands were affecting the normal running of the Council. As Ondo Edu admitted, at this point competition and instability were not directly motivated by so-called tribalism.[86] Among the Fang, internal divisions were—and continue to be—obvious at the time. Perhaps the only area where Fang and Riomunian politicians at large agreed on was their aspiration for full political independence.[87]

In January 1966, two Fang members of the Government Council filed a motion to initiate negotiations on independence from Spain.[88] The process officially began in October 1967 with the opening of the Constitutional Conference. It soon became clear that discussions would not be smooth, as the recently created Unión Bubi party was committed to impede the unified political independence of Bioko and Rio Muni. Most observers agree that the foundation of this party responded to the machinations of the Dirección General de Plazas y Provincias Africanas—the branch of government responsible for Spanish territories in Africa—and Spanish settlers. Once the cocoa and commercial lobbies on the island realized independence was inevitable, they saw no choice but to press for the separate independence of the two territories. In the process, they fueled Bubi fears about the consequences of being dominated by the mainland Fang. Given the history of Bioko for the past century and a half, it did not take much for those fears to take root among most of the Bubi population. Nonetheless, neither UB demands nor the pressure from the Spanish lobby were able to derail negotiations leading to unified independence. Their combined strategy proved to be an uphill battle against Riomunian nationalist organizations, the Spanish the Ministry of Foreign Affairs, and the United Nations, which were all determined to maintain the existing administrative ties between the two territories, however artificial they might be. Eventually negotiators agreed on a draft constitution that, in addition to granting regional autonomy for both territories, gave Bioko disproportionate representation in the future national assembly. Once again, Rio Muni's demographic weight was crucial for the outcome of the process. The constitution was approved in referendum in August 1968, despite the opposition of most voters in Bioko.[89] Political developments since 1963 led French historian, René Pélissier, to argue that the country was "less prepared for unified independence . . . than they were when autonomy was granted."[90] Equatorial Guinea gained independence on October 12, 1968, and within five months it became all too clear that the country was not ready to face the enormous challenge of independence, whether unified or not. By March 1969, the constitution that had been so arduously drafted was de facto defunct. A new phase of oppression and domination opened up for all Equatoguineans, particularly for the Bubi, who had to coexist with a new set of oppressors on "their" island.

Two Centuries of Resistance Against Marginalization from Within

For much of its history, Bioko became shelter and home for groups of African migrants arriving from the neighboring mainland. There, they were able to enjoy a great degree of political autonomy and benefit from the island's fertile soils. Over the centuries, these groups of migrants developed a unique culture as well as an acute sense of belonging. The Bubi were, in fact, "the people of the island." Even after the Atlantic coast of Africa became of interest to European nations' expansionist and commercial aspirations, Bioko remained marginal to outsiders. In turn, this allowed the Bubi to retain their central role on the island, where they reigned supreme until the late 1820s. Yet as Bioko became increasingly relevant to peoples beyond its shores, the Bubi came to be rapidly marginalized. Indeed, one cannot deny the correlation between the opposite fates of the island and its inhabitants. This trend has been further accentuated by the discovery of rich oil deposits off the coast of Bioko since the mid-1990s. It was irrelevant to those in power as to whether or not this island was inhabited as they successively imposed their social, political, and economic structures on Bioko and its people. The Bubi simply became collateral damage in the name of a self-proclaimed greater good. At a time when the vast African continent still remained unknown and seemingly untamable to the Europeans, islands like Bioko became experimental enclaves where Europeans could incorporate African spaces and peoples into an increasingly globalized economy. The success of such experiments, no doubt, showed the way for the European colonial expansion of the late nineteenth century. The historical experience of the Bubi since then is a clear example of the extent to which globalization did contribute to disempower indigenous communities in the absence of the necessary mechanisms to guarantee their political inclusion and participation. Equally, it shows the enduring nature of a people who, after being dominated for nearly two centuries, still refuse to accept the loss of ownership over "their" island.

Perhaps the most outstanding feature of Bubi modern identity is their acute sense of belonging in relation to their homeland. It is unclear the extent to which this can be attributed to their historical experience prior to 1827, but there is little doubt that historical developments since then have deeply shaped an identity that can hardly be detached from the dichotomy between autochthons and allochthons. The case of Bioko and the Bubi suggests that geographical conditions are likely to make insider-outsider tensions more acute on island spaces. It also shows how modern notions of belonging, characterized by their expansive and inclusive character, can at times exacerbate social tensions and even infringe on the interests of indigenous peoples, especially when they become a minority, as in the case of the Bubi. The conspicuity of these notions in Bubi identity and national-ism are clearly an invitation to ponder upon the extent to which notions of "belonging" and "first-comer" can be more meaningful within the ter-ritorial confines of islands. In Bioko, evidence indicates that these notions became particularly powerful within a context characterized by the rela-tively small size of this island, the continuous arrival of outsiders, and the subsequent pressure on Bubi people's access to land.

Far from simply considering Bioko's indigenous people as victims, the development of their identity is another example of how marginalized peo-ples can effectively take ownership over their condition and turn it into a potent conceptual tool for the construction and strengthening of their identity. Whether autochthony has too often been used to exclude and marginalize minorities in Africa since independence, the case of Bioko exemplifies that minorities can also use the experience of exclusion as a tool to minimize and, hopefully, reverse domination by so-called outsid-ers. Interestingly, Bubi agency over the exclusion and marginalization they have undergone predated Equatorial Guinea's independence from Spain. Separatist nationalism became rapidly visible on the eve of independence not because of a long history of shared antagonism with Riomunians, but because of their accumulated, antagonistic interactions with outsid-ers since 1827. In other words, both the nature of Bubi modern identity and nationalism cannot be simply understood as a result of the animosity between Bubi islanders and Fang mainlanders for the past five decades. Undoubtedly, this is just a brief episode in the much longer history of exclusion and marginalization of the Bubi since Bioko became a central location in the abolition of the trade in enslaved Africans, the expansion of cocoa agriculture, and the late development of Spanish colonialism in the Gulf of Guinea.

The modern history of the Bubi can also help us to reconsider center-periphery notions in explaining power relations. Historical developments since the late 1820s placed Bioko at a geographical center of international and regional transformations. Hence, this island became both economically and politically meaningful. However, it can easily be argued that parallel to these developments, Bioko's indigenous people remained on the periphery. That is to say, as the island became increasingly important to hegemonic "outsiders," the policies and decisions that so greatly transformed Bioko had little or nothing to do with the needs and concerns of Bubi society. The island's experience of the past 200 years exemplifies the extent to which center-periphery notions must consider not only the analysis of the uneven relationship between geographic spaces but also the unequal social spaces created by this relationship. As some Bubi nationalists understood by the mid-1960s, independence would do nothing but reinforce their exclusion. Within unified Equatorial Guinea, Bioko would continue to be the geographical center of the new country, while the Bubi would remain on the social periphery. Meanwhile, Rio Muni, geographically displaced during Spanish colonialism, was en route to becoming Equatorial Guinea's social center thanks to its demographic hegemony. Despite two successive dictatorial regimes led by Fang men that have equally subjugated islanders and mainlanders since 1968, the existence of shared sociocultural networks has allowed sections of Fang society to somehow alleviate their exclusion and marginalization. Nearly five decades since independence, perhaps the only consolation that the geographical centrality of Bioko affords the Bubi is the capability of voicing their grievances more loudly and further than other marginalized peoples in Equatorial Guinea.

Notes

1. Bioko's indigenous population used several terms to refer to themselves in different parts of the island, none of which was Bubi. It is the local term *boobé* (man) that caused the British to believe that *Boobi* (Bubi) was the name Bioko's islanders gave themselves.

2. While Spain was granted the territories of the Gulf of Guinea in 1777 after the signing of the Treaty of San Ildefonso-El Pardo between Spain and Portugal, it did not make effective its rights till much later. After several failed attempts, in 1858 Spain was finally able to establish possession over the islands of Fernando Po, Annobón, and the smaller islands off the southern coast of Rio Muni: mainly Corisco, Elobey Chico, and Elobey Grande.

3. Spain, however, did not begin to effectively occupy Rio Muni till 1915.

4. Enrique N. Okenve, "They Were There to Rule: Culture, Race, and Domination in Spanish Equatorial Guinea, 1898–1963," *Afro-Hispanic Review* 35, no. 1 (2016): 44.

5. The change in status of Equatorial Guinea from colonies to Spanish provinces in 1959 and especially the granting of an autonomous status from 1964 facilitated the arrival of Fang people to the island where there were more job opportunities, especially within the administration. According to the 1966 census, the Fang population on Fernando Po was some 5,000 whereas the Bubi population was over 15,000 and migrant Nigerian population amounted to more than 35,000 people. Nota adjunta a una información sobre el plan de desarrollo, October 18, 1967, caja 81/11528, expediente 1, Archivo General de la Administración, Alcalá de Henares (Madrid) [hereafter 81/11528, exp. 1, AGA].

6. Although the Spanish sought to create the impression that the Fang inhabited only the interior of Rio Muni, in reality there were Fang villages on the coast by the turn of the twentieth century. The 1966 census identified as Fang nearly 96 percent of the native population of Equatorial Guinea's mainland region. Only on the coast can one find a number of small, unrelated ethnic groups such as Benga, Kombe, Bisio, Balengue, etc. The Spanish artificially labeled all these groups as *playeros* (literally beach people). In recent times, some have adopted the name *ndowé* to refer to themselves. Censo de población de Guinea Ecuatorial año 1966, 81/11531, exp. 1, AGA.

7. Christopher Young, "Nation, Ethnicity, and Citizenship: Dilemmas of Democracy and Civil Order in Africa," in *Making Nations, Creating Strangers: States and Citizenship in Africa*, ed. S. Dorman, D. Hammett, and P. Nugent (Leiden, Netherlands: Brill, 2007), 252.

8. Enrique N. Okenve, "They Never Finished Their Journey: The Territorial Limits of Fang Ethnicity in Equatorial Guinea, 1930–1963," *International Journal of African Historical Studies* 47, no. 2 (2014): 259–85.

9. See an interesting discussion on the subject in W. Alade Fawole and Charles Ukeje, eds., *The Crisis of the State and Regionalism in West Africa: Identity, Citizenship and Conflict* (Dakar: CODESRIA, 2005); Dorman, Hammett, and Nugent, *Making Nations*.

10. Jonathon Glassman, *War of Words, War of Stones: Racial Thought and Violence in Colonial Zanzibar* (Bloomington: Indiana University Press, 2011).

11. Samuel Decalo, *Psychoses of Power: African Personal Dictatorships* (Boulder, CO: Westview Press, 1989), 33.

12. Archaeological evidence suggests that the island was inhabited from about the first century CE. Between this period and the fourteenth century, there were at least three more migration waves. It appears that after the fourteenth century, the sociocultural features of the population remained relatively stable, with no large group of migrants settling on the island until the nineteenth century. A. Martín del Molino, *Los bubis: Ritos y creencias* (Madrid: Centro Cultural Hispano-Guineano, 1989), 19–20; Jan Vansina, *Paths in the Rainforests: Towards a History of Political Tradition in Equatorial Africa* (Madison: University of Wisconsin, 1990), 139.

13. For more details on the early colonization of Bioko and the development of Bubi culture, see Vansina, *Paths*, 137–46.

14. Ibrahim K. Sundiata, *From Slaving to Neoslavery: The Bight of Biafra and Fernando Po in the Era of Abolition, 1827–1930* (Madison: University of Wisconsin Press, 1996), 14, 18–19.

15. As late as the 1860s, Spanish sources make reference to the arrival of runaway slaves from São Tomé. Carta remitida al Sr Encargado de los Emancipados, May 1, 1864, 81/7956, exp. 2, AGA.

16. Willem Bosman, *A New and Accurate Description of the Coast of Guinea, Divided into the Gold, the Slave, and the Ivory Coasts* (London: J. Knapton, 1705), 399.

17. In 1777 Spain and Portugal signed the Treaty of San Ildefonso-El Pardo, which granted Spain rights over Bioko and Annobón. Only a year later did Spain realize that "the Portuguese have never established themselves on that island [Bioko] or carried out any trade with its inhabitants." Expediente sobre el proyecto de colonización de las islas de Fernando Poo y Annobón, 1778 (copy 1843), 81/7051, exp. 3, AGA.

18. Richard Lander and J. Lander, *Journal of an Expedition to Explore the Course and Termination of the Niger* (London: John Murray, 1832), 296–97.

19. Antonio Aymemí, *Los bubis en Fernando Poo: Colección de artículos publicados en la revista colonial la Guinea Española* (Madrid: Dirección General de Marruecos y Colonias, 1942), 114.

20. Expediente sobre el proyecto de colonización de las islas de Fernando Poo y Annobón, 1778 (copy 1843), 81/7051, exp. 3, AGA.

21. Thomas J. Hutchinson, *Impressions of Western Africa* (London: Longman, Brown, Green, Longmans, & Roberts, 1858), 192.

22. Ibrahim K. Sundiata, "The Fernandinos: Labor and Community in Santa Isabel de Fernando Poo, 1827–1931" (PhD diss., Northwestern University, 1972).

23. Quoted in Sundiata, "The Fernandinos," 63.

24. Joaquín J. Navarro, *Apuntes sobre el estado de la costa Occidental de África y principalmente de las posesiones españolas en el Golfo de Guinea* (Madrid: Imprenta Nacional, 1859), 145.

25. Navarro, *Apuntes*, 147.

26. From the late nineteenth century, the Primitive Methodist Society came to replace the Baptist as the main English missionary presence on Bioko.

27. Hutchinson, *Impressions*, 201.

28. During much of the nineteenth century, the Krumen, or Kru people from coastal Liberia, were the main labor force employed by both Europeans and Krio people on Fernando Po. Along the West African coast, Europeans' recruitment of migrant Kru laborers was a common practice prior to the establishment of the British in Fernando Po. The first group of Kru laborers arrived in the island in 1827, when the British hired some 130 Kru workers to assist with the construction of what became Clarence. While the Kru became an important part of the island's social landscape during much of this period, they rarely integrated with either Krio or Bubi groups. For the most part, they kept a separate existence and their relationship with the other social groups

on the island remained strained. A. Martín del Molino, *La ciudad de Clarence: Primeros años de la actual ciudad de Malabo, capital de Guinea Ecuatorial, 1827– 1859* (Madrid: Centro Cultural Hispano-Guineano, 1993), 15–16; Hutchinson, *Impressions*, 181; Sundiata, "The Fernandinos," 91.

29. Mary H. Kingsley, *Travels in West Africa: Congo Français, Corisco and Cameroons* (London: Macmillan and Co. Limited, 1897), 57.

30. Henry Roe, *West African Scenes: Being Descriptions of Fernando Po, Its Climate, etc* (London: Elliot Stock, 1874), 19, 39; Jerónimo M. Usera y Alarcón, *Memoria de la isla de Fernando Poo* (Madrid: Imprenta de Tomás Aguado, 1848), 27.

31. In 1893 the governor-general expressed his concern that most of the non-Bubi population on the island had been registered in the British consulate as British citizens. Comunicación del Gobernador de Fernando Poo al Ministro de Ultramar, February 17, 1893; Comunicación del Gobernador de Fernando Poo al Ministro de Ultramar, June 17 1893, 81/7066, exp. 2, AGA.

32. Memorias del Gobernador General de Fernando Poo y sus dependencias: Marqués de Montefuerte para el año 1902, January 30, 1903, 81/7075, exp. 1, AGA.

33. Kingsley, *Travels*, 62.

34. Report addressed to the General Missionary Committee about school closure and labor shortage, July 1892, Box 1155, Microfiche 225, Methodist Missionary Society Archives, School of Oriental and African Studies, London [hereafter Box 1155, mf 225, MMSA, SOAS].

35. Informe del Gobernador General al Ministro de Estado, Santa Isabel, December 14, 1910, 81/7061, exp. 10, AGA.

36. Hutchinson, *Impressions*, 154, 158–59.

37. Informe emitido por el Gobierno General de Fernando Poo al Ministerio de Ultramar, October 28, 1864, 81/7958, exp. 9, AGA; Kingsley, *Travels*, 53.

38. Informe emitido por el Gobierno General de Fernando Poo al Ministerio de Ultramar, October 28, 1864, 81/7958, exp. 9, AGA.

39. Kingsley, *Travels*, 71.

40. In 1889, Father Vall-Llovera estimated the Bubi population to be around 35,000 people. Quoted in Cristobal Fernández, *Misiones y misioneros en la Guinea Española: Historia documentada de sus primeros azarosos días (1883–1912)* (Madrid: Coculsa, 1962), 270.

41. Hutchinson provided a much more conservative figure regarding the size of the Bubi population—between 7,000 and 10,000 people. Hutchinson, *Impressions*, 136.

42. Memorias del Gobernador General de Fernando Poo y sus dependencias: Marqués de Montefuerte para el año 1902, January 30, 1903, 81/7075, exp. 1, AGA.

43. British missionaries also voiced their concern about the extent to which "intoxicants could be regularly obtained" in Bioko and even indicated that "in the future all Bubis . . . who desire to become members of the church shall be

required to become total abstainers." Special Report on San Carlos Mission as for request of Missionary executive (late 1890s?); Minutes of Court of Missionaries, Santa Isabel, February 8, 1899, Box 1155, mf 223 and 238, MMSA, SOAS.

44. On the mainland, it is well known that village communities often crossed colonial borders and settled in neighboring territories to avoid particularly taxing colonial demands. Rio Muni, for example, was the recipient of migrants from German Cameroon and French Gabon, where obligations were more onerous than in the Spanish colony. This was partly because European domination was more consolidated in these colonies. Spanish administrators were particularly careful not to use excessive violence in enforcing the prestación personal in border districts as there was a greater risk that colonial subjects would escape to the neighboring colony. Nsork, April 25, 1931, 81/8145, exp. 1, AGA.

45. Ibrahim K. Sundiata, "Prelude to Scandal: Liberia and Fernando Po, 1880–1930," *The Journal of African History* 15, no. 1 (1974): 98.

46. W. G. Clarence-Smith, "African and European Cocoa Producers on Fernando Póo, 1880s to 1910s," *The Journal of African History* 35, no. 2 (1994): 180.

47. Informe del Gobernador, Dionisio Shelly al Ministro de Ultramar, July 16, 1893, 81/7051, exp. 5, AGA.

48. Memoria mercantil y agrícola de las posesiones españolas en el África Occidental, F. Vázquez Zafra. Madrid, December 12, 1901, 81/6435, AGA.

49. Data point out that in 1902, out of 2,256 new workers employed in Bioko, only 74 were Bubi. Memoria del Secretario del Gobierno General J. Álvaro de Zulueta para el año 1902, December 31, 1902, 81/7075, exp. 1, AGA.

50. Informe del Gobernador General al Ministro de Estado, Santa Isabel, December 14, 1910, 81/7061, exp. 10, AGA.

51. Informe del Gobernador General al Ministro de Estado, Santa Isabel, December 14, 1910, 81/7061, exp. 10, AGA.

52. Informe del Gobernador General al Ministro de Estado, Santa Isabel, May 29, 1911, 81/7061, exp. 10, AGA.

53. The prestación personal was, in fact, a form of taxation that all natives of the Spanish colony were subject to. This served two main purposes. On the one hand, it built and maintained colonial infrastructure. On the other, it encouraged colonized Africans to get employment, since all African employees were excused from the obligation to provide the state with temporary labor. Gobernador General Ángel Barrera al Ministro de Estado, Santa Isabel, October 13, 1911, 81/6271, exp. 1, AGA.

54. C. Crespo Gil-Delgado, *Notas para un estudio antropológico del bubi de Fernando Poo* (Madrid: Instituto de Estudios Africanos, 1949), 183.

55. See Crespo Gil-Delgado, *Notas*, 182–84; Mariano de Castro and D. Ndongo-Bidyogo, *España en Guinea: Construcción del desencuentro 1778–1968* (Madrid: Sequitur, 1998), 148.

56. For the most part of the nineteenth century, the Krio had resisted Spanish administration, but by the early twentieth century, they became extremely concerned about labor shortages. Thus, they chose to become closer to the Spanish colonial authorities in order to deal with the problem. In this respect,

both Krio and Spanish colonizers considered their interests to be similar. Sundiata shows how Maximiliano Jones, one of the wealthiest Krio planters at the time, fully supported the Spanish intervention against the Bubi villagers. Sundiata, "The Fernandinos," 272–73.

57. Gobernador General Ángel Barrera al Ministro de Estado, Santa Isabel, October 13, 1911, 81/6271, AGA.

58. Sundiata, *From Slaving*, chap. 7.

59. For more details on the case of São Tomé and Príncipe, see Catherine Higgs, *Chocolate Islands: Cocoa, Slavery, and Colonial Africa* (Athens: Ohio University Press, 2012).

60. In 1911, for instance, Gov. Ángel Barrera informed the authorities in Madrid that members of a Fang clan threatened to kill the Spanish Africanist and explorer, Enrique D'Almonte, after thirty workers of their clan died in Bioko. The report makes no reference to the circumstances leading to the death of these thirty Fang workers. Gobernador General al Ministro de Estado, July 2, 1911, 81/6437, AGA.

61. Comisión de agricultores de Fernando Poo al presidente del Consejo de Ministros, June 23, 1930; Biblioteca Catón al presidente de la Liga Catalana de Defensa de los Derechos del Hombre y del Ciudadano, December 21, 1931, 81/11531, exp. 2 and 11, AGA.

62. Enrique Okenve, "Equatorial Guinea 1927–79: A New African Tradition" (PhD diss., University of London, School of Oriental and African Studies, 2007), 150–51.

63. While this measure applied to the entire colony, in reality it was mostly implemented in Bioko. In Rio Muni, where land availability was greater and there was a much smaller number of white settlers, Africans were able to own larger farms than what was prescribed by law.

64. Memoria del Gobernador General Ángel Barrera, May 14, 1911, p. 266, 81/6436, AGA.

65. Memoria Comisaría Regia en las posesiones españolas del Golfo de Guinea, 1906–7, 81/6435, AGA.

66. Crespo Gil-Delgado, *Notas*, 191.

67. José María Bonelli Rubio, Concepto del indígena en nuestra colonización de Guinea: Conferencia pronunciada el 17 de diciembre de 1946 (Madrid: Dirección General de Marruecos y Colonias, 1947), 13.

68. In an effort to address the difficulties colonial officials had in administering "too large" districts, the Spanish authorities reconfigured the existing territorial divisions in 1938. They divided existing districts into smaller ones. Curiously, Annobón, along with the smaller islands off the coast of Rio Muni, was administratively assigned to the continental region. Subgobernador al Gobernador General, March 6, 1936; Proyecto de Decreto sobre provisión y funcionamiento Administraciones Territoriales del Gobierno General al Jefe del Servicio Nacional de Marruecos y Colonias, November 18, 1938, 81/8015, exp. 2, AGA.

69. Okenve, "They Were There to Rule," 46.

70. For more details, see Hermenegildo Altozano, "El Patronato de Indígenas de Guinea. Institución Ejemplar," *Archivos del Instituto de Estudios Africanos* 10, no. 40 (1957): 49–63.

71. The Spanish government gave a further boost to this sector when they introduce a subsidy for the colony's cocoa production in 1948.

72. R. Cosio y de Cosio, "Problemas que afectan a la estructura económica de la Guinea Ecuatorial," *África* 271 (1964): 10.

73. Gobernador General Juan Bonelli al Subgobernador accidental de la Guinea continental, September 12, 1945, 81/8195, exp. 1, AGA; Memoria de la filial de Bata del patronato de indígenas, December 31, 1946, 81/8176, exp. 4, AGA.

74. Breve resumen del estado actual del servicio de enseñanza y labor realizada por el mismo en el año y curso escolar 1942, July 7, 1943, 81/8183, exp. 1, AGA.

75. Whether or not grievances were legitimate, there is no doubt that the perception existed. Following the complaints of a group of youngsters from Rio Muni, including the future president of Equatorial Guinea Francisco Macias Nguema, the subgovernor in Bata tried to address the so-called advantages that students from the island had regarding access to the Escuela Superior Indígena. This was the higher educational institution for natives at the time, providing training in different auxiliary capacities. The governor, however, dismissed any suggestion of impartiality. Subgobernador Pérez Barrueco al Gobernador Alonso, January 27, 1943; Gobernador General al Subgobernador, February 8, 1943, 81/8195, exp. 2, AGA.

76. Cosio y de Cosio, "Problemas," 10.

77. The article was written by a Spanish Jesuit and should have appeared in the weekly magazine *Blanco y Negro*. Director General de Plazas y Provincias Africanas al Gobernador General de la Provincia del Golfo de Guinea, Madrid, December 7, 1957, 81/8221, exp. 1, AGA.

78. Telegrama cifrado de Dirección General de Plazas y Provincias Africanas al Gobierno General Madrid, March 10, 1962, 81/11846, AGA.

79. While labor conditions in Bioko before 1930 have been widely studied, not much work has been done on this subject for the latter period. This gap is addressed by Enrique Martino in his recently completed PhD dissertation. Enrique Martino, "Touts and Despots: Recruiting Assemblages of Contract Labour in Fernando Pó and the Gulf of Guinea, 1858–1979" (PhD diss., Humboldt-Universität zu Berlin, 2016).

80. Decalo, *Psychoses*, 43.

81. Decalo points out that non-Bubi minorities in Bioko voted in favor of the autonomous status as they sought to benefit from "greater local autonomy from Spain." Decalo, *Psychoses*, 45.

82. Pedro la Torre al Director General de Plazas y Provincias Africanas, J. Díaz de Villegas, Santa Isabel, May 20, 1964, 81/11846, AGA.

83. Traducción del informe realizado por el embajador USA en su visita particular a Río Muni, August 15, 1962, 81/11531, exp. 1, AGA.

84. José María Bonelli Rubio, "Diferencia del concepto económico en la colonización de Fernando Poo y Guinea Continental," *Archivos del Instituto de Estudios Africanos* 3, no. 7 (1949): 71–79.

85. Decalo, *Psychoses*, 45.

86. Discurso del Presidente del Consejo de Gobierno Autónomo, copiado del semanario de Río Muni, *Potopoto*, Bata, August 24, 1964, 81/11528, AGA.

87. Fang internal divisions became clearer during the 1968 presidential campaign. The three main contenders—Macias Nguema, Ondo Edu, and Ndong Miyone—mainly represented the division of Fang interest along territorial lines.

88. Copia del punto decimotercero del acta del Consejo de Gobierno Autónomo, January 13, 1966, 81/11528, AGA.

89. Decalo, *Psychoses*, 45–46.

90. René Pélissier, "Uncertainties in Spanish Guinea," *Africa Report* 13 (1968): 16.

5

Cursing in Bioko and Annobón

Repeating Islands That Don't Repeat

Michael Ugarte

All the infections that the sun sucks up
From bogs, fens, flats, on Prosper fall, and make him
By inchmeal a disease! His spirits hear me,
And yet I needs must curse.

—William Shakespeare, *The Tempest*

Shakespeare's *The Tempest* is about the relations between two cultures: one imperial, the other a dependent island. There are many possible allegorical allusions to the area out of which Prospero and company are sailing, and one of them is the Spanish Empire. But the allegorical significance of Caliban (the island dweller) has much to do with the precivilized island where he resides. His relationship with Prospero is not a binary opposition, as both Shakespeare and certain proponents of postcolonial studies want to imply (in the former case unwittingly): to simply describe it as a relation of oppressor to oppressed, colonizer to colonized, civilized to uncivilized, dominator to dominated, speaker to voiceless would be to deny that complexity and the multifariousness of their interactions and symbolic importance.

In an oft-cited essay "Learning to Curse," Stephen Greenblatt goes beyond the obvious social and historical relations between the two pivotal characters by centering his discussion of *The Tempest* on the act of cursing.[1] Caliban rejects Prospero's gift of language as an act of defiance, and, as Shakespeare implies to us, his defiance is to speak on his own terms as he says to Prospero in one of his first speeches: "This island's mine . . . which thou tak'st from me."[2] And later on,

But they'll nor pinch,
Fright me with urchin-shows, pitch me I'th'mire;
Nor lead me, like a firebrand, in the dark
Out of my way.
(Shakespeare, *The Tempest*, act 2, scene 2, p. 65.)

The alliteration of the *p* sound—the *P* of Prospero ("on Prosper fall") as well as "pinch" and "pitch"—is Shakespeare's way of allowing his islander to curse, as he asserts that no one can lead him, that he shall go his own way.

Addressing myself to the theme of African islands, I want to emphasize (as does Greenblatt) the discursive aspect of the Caliban-Prospero relationship in terms of the island, its idea, both real and imaginary, by focusing on two islands, equally real and imaginary, in the Gulf of Guinea: Annobón and Bioko. But Greenblatt's penetrating analysis of the native Caliban's use of language and Shakespeare's implicit commentary on it does not include a discussion of the place in which we hear that language: the island. The play begins in the middle of a storm that takes the crew to a faraway place, as Prospero utters, "Now I arise. . . . Here in this island we arrived."[3] Indeed the excerpt that begins this chapter is a description of an island: Caliban is cursing Prospero by wishing that all the island's maladies will fall on him. I sense it is crucial that the give-and-take between Prospero and Caliban takes place in a distant land mass surrounded by water with no trace of what the people of Prospero's ilk call "civilization."

Famously, Roberto Fernández Retamar, in what today might sound like an apology or fundamental explanation of the importance of Latin American culture in the eyes of the "West," begins his lengthy essay "Caliban" with an anecdote in which his leftist friend asks him, "Does Latin American culture exist?"[4] He follows with an analysis of the question itself, an analysis that includes one of the first attempts to connect Shakespeare's play with the reality and perception of Latin American literature with special emphasis on the island of Cuba. Yet here again, what Retamar does not analyze in detail is the aspect of Caliban's language that has to do with the discourse of the island. "To question our culture is to question our very existence," he says, "since it suggests that we would be but a distorted echo of what occurs elsewhere."[5] It is precisely the "elsewhere" dimension of the discourse that I want to emphasize. Elsewhere here refers to the place of civilization, a place far removed from the island surrounded by water, isolated, a place that lays bare the issue of nonexistence, and nonexistence is something with which the people from Annobón are directly familiar, as we shall see.

Also pertinent in what I shall call island discourse is the notion of the island that repeats itself. In Antonio Benítez Rojo's *The Repeating Island*, his penetrating discussion of Cuba and the Antilles, the social system that existed and persists in a different way today in the Antillean Archipelago is what he calls a "machine," following Gilles Delueze and Félix Guiattari's designation of specific organisms within a larger context of related organisms.[6] Benítez Rojo, in his determination to go beyond the conventional wisdom about the place of the history of Cuba and the Antilles within world history, emphasizes that every one of the Antillean islands has its specificity, its circumstances, its context, but at the same time all the islands relate to one another within a larger system of organisms. He refers to the science of Chaos Theory as an explanation of the occurrence of natural phenomena and as a way to understand these "repeating islands," one of which may very well be the place where Prospero has haphazardly landed:

> Unstable condensations, whirlpools, turbulences, clumps of bubbles, frayed seaweed, . . . in tune with the objectives of Chaos. . . . Within the (dis)order that swarms around what we already know as Nature, it is possible to observe dynamic states or regularities that repeat themselves globally. . . . Chaos looks at everything that repeats, reproduces, grows, decays, unfolds, flows, spins, vibrates, seethes; . . . Thus Chaos provides a space in which the pure sciences connect with the social sciences, and both of them connect with art and cultural tradition. (Antonio Benítez Rojo, *The Repeating Island: The Caribbean and the Postmodern Perspective*, trans. James Maraniss [Durham, NC: Duke University Press, 1996], 2–3.)

All those "condensations" harken back to the island that shapes the dramatic structure of *The Tempest*. And within that cultural tradition I would add the particularity of discourse, the discourse of island chaos.

Indeed *The Tempest* has a great deal to do with an attempt to turn the "Chaos" into order. Moreover, Prospero's multifaceted relationship with Caliban is also about the issue of speech. Does Caliban speak? If so, what does he say? How do we interpret his "articulations" within the context of an overpowering, conquering, usurping political social system that shapes the relation between the European rulers and those who inhabit these islands? "Can the subaltern speak," as Gayatri Spivak famously asked, and what does that question have to do with the speech uttered (or not uttered) in the repeating islands?[7] Can the subaltern speak amidst the island chaos?

I ask these questions within the context of another group of (repeating) islands far removed from the Antilles yet perhaps within the same system of machines in Chaos: Bioko and Annobón, both of which are areas under the sovereignty of Equatorial Guinea. And I want to explore these issues through the fiction of an author—Juan Tomás Ávila Laurel—whose subject position encompasses both islands.

But context is necessary, particularly when trying to make sense of the "Chaos" of Equatorial Guinea, a nation that comprises both island and mainland cultures. The archipelago of the Gulf of Guinea contains many islands, not all of which came under the same colonial domination, much like the Antilles. It has been subject to colonialist exploitation of its natural resources; its islands were visited, discovered, explored, investigated by powers from elsewhere, in this case Portugal and Spain (later by England). In Benítez Rojo's terms, referring to the Caribbean islands, "the colonies began to exploit the land with total abandon according to the model of the slave plantation."[8] But of course while this is the overall model, each island is different—each island represents its own form of Chaos.

Also, Equatorial Guinea comprises other islands in addition to Bioko and Annobón: Corisco and Elobey off the southwestern coast of mainland Africa. Looking at the map of the area, the "repeating islands" that appear vertically on the map from north to south of the Gulf of Guinea are: Malabo, Príncipe, Elobey, Corisco, San Tomé, and Annobón. These islands were not all colonized by the same powers, thus they follow different patterns according to the European power that colonized them; and at the same time, they fall within a general system ("machine"). To the immediate east of these islands lies the African continental area of Equatorial Guinea, Rio Muni. What makes my specific subject areas, Bioko and Annobón, different is that they are today dominated by that continental area, which has itself been the victim of colonialist domination. Rio Muni is located between Cameroon and Gabon in Central West Africa. Almost as a mocking imitation of the European imperial power's domination of islands throughout the Black Atlantic, the controlling oligarchs of Rio Muni, made up largely of an ethnic group, the Fang—known for their conquering and dominating energy throughout their history—have to this day exercised their own form of colonialism in these islands. Today, the fear of the Fang in the noncontinental areas is palpable. President-dictator Teodoro Obiang is seen as the ruling chief of an invading tribe, just as his predecessor Francisco Macías was. While Macías and Obiang are not like Prospero in the latter's benign attempt to tame through the act of civilizing, the African dictators are themselves forms of Caliban who have seized the reins formally held by a Prospero whom they are (badly) imitating.

These fears and resentments of an invading force complicated by the postcolonial indigenous power structures are reflected in much of the cultural production of Equatorial Guinea. As one who has studied this cultural production, I sense that the writer who best reflects these patterns due not only to the subject of his writing but also to his subject position is Juan Tomás Ávila Laurel (although there are other writers who do so, including some of the Fang ethnicity).9 Reading and rereading Ávila Laurel's work in the light of postcolonial studies, and within the context out of which it emerges, I suggest he writes and speaks as Caliban. Yet he does so in his own way. That is, while he rejects the colonizer's language as a means of domination, he also appropriates it, employs it as an act of self-definition. He curses elegantly, with both rage and well-placed rhetorical figures. He tells his readers his island is overpowered by unfamiliar forces, forces that later become all too familiar. Yet the language he uses is a subtle, seemingly and deceptively benign way of cursing them.

In one of his early works, *Áwala cu sangui* (Awala with Blood), he describes what by all accounts is an invasion, even though he does not use the word. The following is from the prologue to the short novel.

> And when all the natives thought that everything was over, that Macías's representative had bid farewell, since the gangplank had been pulled back and the ship had blown three whistles signaling its departure by fir- ing up the engines, they saw that it turned back aiming the bow menac- ingly at the island and making its way back over waters already navigated. All the islanders brought their hands to their chests, without knowing the cause of the strange return. What could Macías's representative have forgotten? . . . They approached the land. For what? Everyone was afraid. Maybe it was because of my age back then, but the reason for their sur- prise return was not communicated to me. I don't know. (Juan Tomás Ávila Laurel, *Awala cu sangui* [Malabo, Equatorial Guinea: Ediciones Pán- gola, 2000], iii.) [10]

Like much of Ávila Laurel's writing, these words have an allegorical tone. He tells us he does not understand, perhaps due to his "age back then." Like Caliban when he first encountered Prospero, he is uncouth, inno- cent, unaware or unsure of the invaders' motivations. But at the same time while he did not know what was happening "back then," he does now. He suggests that the turnaround of the boat he describes is the reinvasion of the island by Macías's nephew, Teodoro Obiang. In his words, the bow of the ship was "aimed menacingly at the island." Indeed, these are repeating islands, repeating patterns, repeating dictatorships, all the same and all dif- ferent, all a perfect and symmetrical reflection of Chaos. It is Ávila Laurel's form of elegant cursing.

Today we have the luxury of being able to talk to Caliban. In the age of globalization and hypertechnology some of us are able to take the form of a Prospero who has learned a lesson in Caliban's language. When I spoke with Avila Laurel in Barcelona, I asked him if he considered going back to his native Annobón (four miles long and two miles wide with a population of some 5,000), an island *literally* not on many maps.[11] He replied that he has no intention of going back as long as the Fang are in control of his island. The thought of getting off the boat from Malabo and having his documentation checked by Fang authorities representing Obiang made his stomach turn. In fact, I heard him curse those in power in the old-fashioned way. Indeed, like a typical exile, he has vowed not to return until the government changes. What I find interesting and pertinent in all this is that he is referring to an inner domination, the invading force not of neo-colonialism, neoliberalism, or multinational oil corporations (although all that is part of it); he is referring to the invasion of his island by an ethnicity from the African continent, an ethnicity itself the object of colonization.

Ávila Laurel continues his irreverent critique of the Fang in a collection of short satirical-political pieces compiled in a book titled, *Diccionario básico y aleatorio de la dictadura guineana* (Basic and Random Dictionary of the Guinean Dictatorship, 2011):

> The Fang: Natives of the interior region of Equatorial Guinea, they are a Bantu people who believe they come from Sudan or Egypt when the most powerful pharaoh became weak and allowed some of his slaves to leave. They headed south pushing other peoples and tribes out of their way; this was land they thought was theirs. Then they rested for a while to recover energy until destiny brought them to Equatorial Guinea . . . The most powerful members of this community [tribe] are clustered together in neighborhoods of Malabo [Bioko] and Bata [Rio Muni], trying to survive and looking for work in the ports, which is too bad because in the continental area there is no lack of land, and that land is fertile. The rumor that the Fang are spendthrifts is widespread. Even their own people believe it. Among those who say so are the few who have had the luck to latch on to a woman living in Obiang's palace. And that's where it gets all fucked up. (Juan Tomás Ávila Laurel, *Diccionario básico, y aleatorio de la dictadura guineana* [Basic and Random Dictionary of the Guinean Dictatorship] [Barcelona: Ceiba, 2011], 75.)

The sardonic tone is typical of Ávila Laurel, and in this case the last uncouth sentence lays bare what Greenblatt (and Ugarte) are saying about cursing. But I think it is also representative of what I am calling island discourse: the discourse of a dominated island, an urge to debunk and thus resist the power of the continent over an area less powerful: a type of cursing that uses the colonizer's language against the colonizer. I suggest that a case might be made that island discourse consists of ironic debunking of power, a subtle form of cursing, much like the discourse of power recreated in Shakespeare's *The Tempest.*

But the writing of Ávila Laurel is even more complicated. The author considers himself a native son of Annobón, even though he was born in Malabo, the main city of the island of Bioko and the capital of Equatorial Guinea. When he was at an early age his family went back to Annobón, where he attended elementary school. At the age of two Ávila Laurel witnessed the independence of Equatorial Guinea in 1968 and shortly thereafter the invasion of Macías and the subsequent holocaust. He completed his studies in Malabo and remained there throughout much of the turbulent history of his country. Thus, the subject position of Juan Tomás Ávila Laurel is that of an insider and an outsider, the dweller of two islands drastically different in many ways: one island is his home, his *patria chica*, his land of formation, where he grew up (the land that tends to remain most solidly in our imaginaries), and the other is the island of power and politics; it is the area from where he can bear witness to what he has lived, as something of an outsider.[12]

What also interests me in this island discourse is its authenticity, or lack thereof, that is, the problems it poses in terms of what Gayatri Spivak calls subaltern speech. Gayatri Spivak, the famous Indian critical theorist, feminist, deconstructionist, advocate for the subaltern, wrote a seminal essay in 1988, "Can the Subaltern Speak?" questioning the assumptions of subaltern studies, represented by, among others, Ranajit Guha, who called for the rethinking and rewriting of world culture from a "nonelitist" or noncolonialist point of view. Guha and others wished to recover, discover, and expose the voices of the receiving end of colonialism by establishing something he and others called "Subaltern Studies."[13] Due to the essay's impact among critical thinkers, Spivak wrote another version in 1999, elaborating and clarifying her ideas, which were seen by some as overly pessimistic and fatalistic.[14] In both versions for Spivak, subaltern studies wanted to allow the subaltern to speak in its own voice, "the empire writing back." She questioned the very attempt to do so in her essay and directed herself to Guha, pointing out that to speak from the subject position of a colonized and/or subaltern entity is itself a questionable enterprise, if it is at all even possible. Quoting Spivak from both the 1988 and 1999 versions:

A curious methodological imperative is at work [in subaltern studies] . . . a postrepresentationalist vocabulary hides an essentialist agenda. In subaltern studies, because of the violence of imperialist epistemic, social and disciplinary inscription, a project understood in essentialist terms must traffic in a radical textual practice of differences. The object of the group's investigation, in the case not even of the people as such

but of the floating buffer zone of the regional elite subaltern, is a devia-
tion of an idea—the people or subaltern—which is itself described as a
difference from the elite. . . . Guha sees his definition of "the people"
within the master-slave dialectic—their text articulates the difficult task
of rewriting its own conditions of impossibility as the condition of its possibility. (Rosalind Morris, ed., *Can the Subaltern Speak: Reflections on the History of an Idea* [New York: Columbia University Press, 2010], 39, 254.)

As I read Spivak (not only in this passage, but in virtually all of her writings on the subaltern), I sense that her main objection to Guha and the
proponents of subaltern studies is that their assumptions about the relations between colonialist and colonized, those with power and those without, and beyond that the speech of the powerless assumes un unmediated
understanding of the latter, and in this assumption (or presumption) to
speak for the subaltern from the position of power is always questionable,
if not even an act in the exercise of power. Also missing in subaltern studies is an acknowledgment of the grades of (sub)alterity, for indeed there
are subaltern elites who are subaltern only in terms of the colonizers but
clearly not in terms of those who are further under those in power.

Looking at this issue from the point of view of these two Equatorial
Guinean islands and the discourse that comes out of them, interesting to
me is the "master-slave dialectic" that subaltern studies emphasizes. While
Juan Tomás is aware of the history of the master-slave relationship in his
islands, he does not speak as a slave but as one who suffers the domination of a group that has itself been dominated. He writes of the history of
his island, an island whose problems have more to do with oblivion and
neglect than with the consequences of slavery. Annobón's repeating chaos,
unique among islands, is that no one seems to care about it; it is an island
whose few resources are no longer of value. After the Portuguese and
Spanish colonizers deforested the island for lumber, it was abandoned. In
the 1980s and 1990s, the government of Equatorial Guinea sold permits to
multinational companies in the United States and the United Kingdom to
accept and hide 10 million metric tons of toxic waste and 7 million metric
tons radioactive waste.[15] And today there is more interest in Annobón and
its surrounding waters because of oil reserves, although drilling has not yet
begun. Clearly the relation between the subaltern residents of the island
and those interested in its resources is one of dependence. But do those
island residents have a voice?

In an essay of 2005 *Cómo convertir este país en un paraíso*, in his typically
sardonic tone Ávila Laurel offers his reading of the history of Annobón. In
all my readings about Equatorial Guinea and Annobón in particular, this
short text is among the most incisive, precisely because it seems conscious

of its own marginality and subaltern condition. He begins by describing Annobón's insularity, unlike the other islands of Equatorial Guinea, particularly Bioko, an island connected to power, and it is precisely this insularity, its abandoned island condition, that defines it: "isolated, unconnected, too far from everything."[16] It is the only island of Equatorial Guinea geographically located in the Southern Hemisphere. In a way he is cursing the world's inattention to his island as he asserts that Annobón incarnates the poverty of the Global South: "It was a place forgotten by the whole world. The whole world. It was a distant place, without a past, whose inhabitants have remained in abject poverty. And to top it all off, at one point in its history an outbreak of cholera was on the verge of doing away with all the natives of this island."[17] Ávila Laurel continues in this vein when he talks about the ephemeral contacts the island has had with other countries and other peoples, mostly from the Global North: "As we lived in this kind of misery, as we breathed this desperation, one afternoon, one morning, and another morning, we saw boats approaching our island, and we saw how they cast out their nets. Our strong men then grabbed their canoes and oars and tried to approach these boats, but their crew preferred not to be a witness of anything, so they fled the island coast further out to sea."[18]

In the above passage, Ávila Laurel feigns a certain civilized objectivity as he recounts a history not related in the historical record compiled by the librarians of Prospero's world. But at the same time clearly the oblivion he describes is an object of reproach; it is his way of cursing with Prospero's language. Indeed, feigned objectivity is part of the structure of one of Ávila Laurel's most penetrating novels dealing with an island. In this novel, *Arde el monte de noche*,[19] he calls this island "Atlante," and its resemblance to Annobón is palpable. In my reading of Juan Tomás Ávila Laurel's extensive corpus of literature, this one is the literary text that stands out in terms of his interrogation (witting or unwitting) of the concept of the subaltern. It is a text written with a deep understanding (witting and unwitting) of the issues surrounding the authenticity of narratives coming from islands inhabited by Caliban; it is as if Caliban were writing his own testimony, cursing the entire way. *Arde el monte* is at once an apt manifestation of island discourse as well as the issues surrounding subaltern speech. As in virtually all of his narratives, and very much unlike his political writings, the reader is never absolutely sure where everything is taking place or what exactly is happening. This novel seems to manifest itself from the voice of a child, that is, the voice of someone unsure how to assimilate all the strange happenings in his life, thereby echoing the tone of his previous work, *Áwala cu sangui*. *Arde el monte* is the story of the narrator's childhood on this strange island in the Atlantic, "Atlante." He talks about his mysterious grandfather, who constantly stares at a mountain, of several mothers whose husbands are God knows where because it seems (that is, we surmise) that someone or something took them away in a boat. There are descriptions of calamities, hardships, violence (indeed chaos), and not much explanation of them, that is, the easy theory that this is all part of the postcolonial condition is by no means obvious, if it is even present at all. *Arde el monte* is a memoir, and like many memoirs, it flaunts objectivity while it tells a story of difficult happenings. It may even be considered literature of testimony, but not really because the author, like any decent fiction writer, is representing (alluding to), not simply telling. So my point is that this novel, for me, does not necessarily offer a real subaltern voice; rather, it raises questions about that very voice.

The novel is typical of Ávila Laurel's elegant cursing, but here he adds self-consciously a commentary on the very voice he is using that has to do, perhaps unwittingly, with the issue of subaltern speech. In a crucial passage toward the end of the novel, the narrator talks about those who one day might tell his story or stories. One of them is about a woman who disappears after falling in a rut in the sand and is found on the beach between two canoes with her dead child at her side. This is one of many stories of occurrences in the narrator's coastal village, but this one occurs toward the very end of the novel. The curious aspect of this one is the narrator's interruption:

> I'm not a writer, or a teacher, or a priest. I don't know anyone on the island who could be described as a writer. . . . The only people who ever knew how to write on the island were, the teacher, the priest and the functionaries. . . . What I have spoken of is what I experienced, heard, and saw when I was a child. It has never been put down in writing before because, as I said, I'm not a writer; nobody on the island is. If this story becomes known it will be because of some white people. They came to our island and wanted to know our folk tales, the stories we tell at night before going to sleep. . . . The white people said they had come to recover our oral storytelling tradition, and their leader, a man named Manuel, said I could tell him whatever story I liked, because childhood memories would likely hold some significance too. . . . I know you can't cover everything in a story told over just a few hours. But I thank Manuel for allowing my story, which is also the story of many people on the island, to take the place of the folk tales he wanted for his work. (Juan Tomás Ávila Laurel, *By Night the Island Burns*, trans. Jethro Soutar [London: And Other Stories, 2014], 270–71.)

What I have quoted has something of an ironic, even picaresque tone, but I think there is something more to it. The narrator goes on to say that he wishes he were a writer so that he could tell the story himself, but stresses he is thankful to Manuel "for allowing my story," a collective story that Manuel will record, transcribe, and disseminate. So the question becomes: who is speaking in the telling of the story? The narrator, Manuel, or both? My sense is that Juan Tomás Ávila Laurel is asking the very same question.

Here the relationship between Caliban and Prospero has made a 360-degree turn. It is almost as if Manuel, alias Prospero, is learning the language of the narrator-protagonist, alias Caliban. Despite Spivak's well-advised warning about the authenticity of the speech transcribed, copied, modified, mediated, exploited, and published by the proponents of subaltern studies (the new benign Prosperos), it seems, at least in this passage, that those transcriptions, those attempts to understand, are worth listening to. Moreover, implies the protagonist, Manuel has made a journey to a neglected island whose only worth comes from the possible discovery of oil or its willingness to accept toxic waste dumps, but he arrives, it seems, with a serious urge to make contact and to learn. The protagonist describes this urge in a positive way.

Returning to the concept of the repeating island in systematic chaos, as well as to the Prospero-Caliban relationship, Benítez Rojo suggests Cuba was a "Great Zoo," "with its North American and South American rivers, its Indians and Negroes, its forests and islands, its poetic children and its White Fathers. America is, above all, a book of impossible poems for impossible readers: it is the Great Zoo speaking of itself and of the Other."[20] Indeed, this could be a description of the writing of Ávila Laurel, "a book of impossible poems for impossible readers." And I would add that this "book" *is* a case of the subaltern islander speaking, or trying to speak, or interrogating the authenticity of this type of speech.

"Can the island subaltern speak?" My answer is yes, but we have to listen, interpret, mediate, question that speech. In the last analysis, what makes Avila Laurel's subaltern speech worth our trouble, more so than that of someone who clearly is in the business of making themselves palatable—no cursing allowed—to publishing industries is that he is keenly conscious of the ambivalences, complexities, and questions that arise when a subaltern like him dares to speak.

Notes

1. Stephen Greenblatt, *Learning to Curse: Essays in Early Modern Culture* (New York: Routledge, 1990). See the first essay, "Learning to Curse: Aspects of Colonialism in the Sixteenth Century," 16–39.

2. Shakespeare, *The Tempest*, act 1 scene 2, p. 45.

3. Shakespeare, *The Tempest*, act 1, scene 2, p. 38.

4. Roberto Fernández Retamar, "Caliban: Notes Toward a Discussion of Culture in Our America," *The Massachusetts Review* 15, no. 1/2 (1974): 7. See also Roberto Fernández Retamar, *Caliban and Other Essays*, trans. Edward Baker (Minneapolis: University of Minnesota Press, 1989).

5. Retamar, "Caliban," 7.

6. Antonio Benítez Rojo, *The Repeating Island: The Caribbean and the Postmodern Perspective*, trans. James Maraniss (Durham, NC: Duke University Press, 1996), 6.

7. Gayatri Spivak, "Can the Subaltern Speak," in *Can the Subaltern Speak: Reflections on the History of an Idea*, ed. Rosalind Morris (New York: Columbia University Press, 2010), 21–78.

8. Benítez Rojo, *The Repeating Island*, 61.

9. For information and analysis of the Literature of Equatorial Guinea, see Marvin Lewis, *An Introduction to the Literature of Equatorial Guinea: Between Colonialism and Dictatorship* (Columbia: University of Missouri Press, 2007); Michael Ugarte, *Africans in Europe: The Culture of Exile and Emigration from Equatorial Guinea to Spain* (Urbana: University of Illinois Press, 2010); Donato Ndongo and Mbaré Ngom, *Literatura de Guinea Ecuatorial (Antología)* (Madrid: Sial, 1999).

10. All translations are mine unless otherwise specified.

11. Juan Tomás Ávila Laurel interviewed by Michael Ugarte, Barcelona, September 15, 2014.

12. For a penetrating and informative overview of Ávila Laurel's writing, see Elisa Rizo and David Shook, "A Conversation with Juan Tomás Ávila Laurel," *World Literature Today* 86, no. 5 (2012): 41–44.

13. For an overview and discussion of specific issues related to subaltern studies, see Ranajit Guha, ed., *The Subaltern Studies Reader 1986–1995* (Minneapolis: University of Minnesota Press, 1997).

14. Spivak's original essay appeared in 1988. Later in her book, *A Critique of Postcolonial Reason: Toward a History of the Vanishing Present* (Cambridge: Cambridge University Press, 1999), she revised some of her ideas. Morris's edition contains both versions, 21–79 and 273–91.

15. Those figures are from Alexander Smoltxzyk, "Torture and Poverty in Equatorial Guinea," Der Spiegel, August 28, 2006. While the veracity of these reports is disputed, the point I am making is that the perception of Annobón in the international community is of an island barely visible with no interest to anyone outside of the island. The suggestion that its commercial use is to serve as a place for toxic waste is itself an indication of the abandonment it has suffered from the time the Portuguese first set foot on the island.

16. Juan Tomás Ávila Laurel, *Cómo convertir este país en un paraíso: Otras reflexiones sobre Guinea Ecuatorial* (Malabo, Equatorial Guinea: Pángola, 2003), 11.

17. Ávila Laurel, *Cómo convertir*, 12.

18. Ávila Laurel, *Cómo convertir*, 13.

19. Juan Tomás Ávila Laurel, *Arde el monte de noche* (Madrid: Calumbar, 2009). An excellent English translation has appeared recently: Juan Tomás Ávila Laurel, *By Night the Island Burns*, trans. Jethro Soutar (London: And Other Stories, 2014).

20. Rojo, *The Repeating Island*, 138.

6

African Ports and Islands during the Second World War

Ashley Jackson

This chapter evaluates the role of Africa's coastal waters, ports, and islands during the Second World War and describes the military activity that took place there. In doing so, it offers a unique account of the continent's strategic importance in a global conflict. The generosity of the editors in permitting a substantial word tally enables the chapter to address macrostrategic themes while also detailing their macrolevel permutations. What this means is that the chapter is able to demonstrate connections between strategically important shipping lanes around Africa and the military goods that traversed them, with the airstrips, wharves, jetties, cookhouses, and ammunition storage facilities maintained on African soil that enabled them to function. By looking at African ports and islands as a whole while simultaneously detailing the military infrastructure they contained and the military roles they performed, the whole appears greater than the sum of its parts. This is important because apparently peripheral military activity on, say, an African lagoon or coastal airstrip was always part of a chain of military provision and was directly linked to global logistics and military operations. For example, air cover mounted from bases in the Gambia provided protection for Allied convoys traveling between the Eastern and Western hemispheres, handing over to escort and patrol aircraft bases in places such as Sierra Leone and South Africa as those convoys moved around Africa's coastline. In such complex global military systems as that developed by Britain and its allies in the Second World War, small cogs are just as important as big wheels in enabling the system to operate. The extensive archives charting the development of places such as Bathurst, Massawa, and Port Sudan, some of which are used to provide an original archival contribution in this chapter, offer a vivid impression of the complexity, scale, and significance of the infrastructure offered by African ports, vital yet rarely acknowledged in general war literature and even specialist works on topics such as logistics and military operations. The chapter is divided into five sections. An introduction is followed by an explanation of the importance of ports and islands in times of war and the reasons for Africa's strategic consequence during the Second World War. The chapter then turns to West Africa, detailing the military infrastructure within and the military operations conducted from Bathurst, Freetown, Takoradi, and Fernando Pó. The next section turns to East Africa and three strategically important ports: Kilindini, Massawa, and Port Sudan. The final section assesses the role of the islands of the Comoros, Madagascar, Mauritius, the Seychelles, and Zanzibar.

The African continent's strategic significance during the Second World War and the military activity that occurred on African soil revolved around *ports*. Some of them were located on islands, but the majority were on the mainland. Between 1939 and 1945 numerous African ports and islands acquired military and strategic prominence, particularly because of their proximity to key sea lines of communication and the access that they gave to overland (that is, air, road, and rail) routes that were logistically essential for the movement of military goods and for delivering military effects to the battlefield. The research questions posed in this chapter, therefore, are: (1) what was the strategic significance of Africa's ports, islands, and coastal waters during the war? and (2) how was this manifest in terms of military activity? To adumbrate the answers, Africa was strategically important because of its resources, which needed to be utilized by belligerents while at the same time denied to enemies, continuing the colonial practice of resource extraction. It was also strategically important because some of the major belligerents possessed African colonies that were a source of military competition—Italy attacking British colonies, for example, which eventually sucked in American and German forces, and the British attacking French and Italian colonies. Africa was also strategically important because of the valuable ports and sea routes that enveloped its coastline, many of which were vital for belligerents transporting military personnel and equipment from one part of the world to another, and vital for the maintenance of the global trading activity of the Allied powers.

These strategic factors meant that Africa was subject to significant military action. Heavy fighting took place in North Africa and East Africa, and smaller military operations occurred in West Africa, Madagascar, and islands such as Fernando Pó and Réunion. There were also extensive military operations in Africa's coastal waters. Its ports and islands, such as the Comoros, Mauritius, and the Seychelles, were used as military bases and for a range of other war-related tasks such as intelligence gathering, surveillance, cable and wireless communication, and radar direction finding. African ports were the must-have military shunting yards of the imperial and Allied war effort.

The enormous range of wartime military activity in and around Africa requires more thorough integration into our understanding of the Second World War and Africa's pivotal role in it. This chapter contributes to the slowly emerging body of work that records Africa's involvement in the war.[1] Despite this corpus, the military and strategic approach taken in this chapter remains unusual in the work of Africanists, and so the chapter hopes to introduce more Africanists to the military and strategic history of the war and its significance for the African continent. The chapter advances the scholarship relating to Africa and the war in two main ways. Firstly, by providing a unique overview of the extraordinary extent of military activity in Africa's ports, islands, and coastal waters and offering an explanation of the strategic value of these locations. Secondly, in order to offer an original archival contribution to the field, the chapter focuses on a number of particular ports and islands using material drawn from over fifty files stored at the British national archives. The records were produced by the British Admiralty, Air Ministry, Colonial Office, Foreign Office, Government Code and Cipher School, and War Office. The selected locations are Bathurst (Gambia), Pamanzi (Comoros), Tuléar (Madagascar), Massawa (Eritrea), Fernando Pó (Gulf of Guinea), and Port Sudan (Sudan). The rationale behind the selection of these examples is that other locations considered in the chapter, such as Cape Town, Freetown, Madagascar, Mauritius, and the Seychelles, have relatively well-developed published histories relating to their wartime experience. Conversely, those chosen as examples have very little (if any) published record of their wartime experiences and the manner in which they were utilized, and allow valuable insight into just how important African ports and islands were during the war.

The Importance of Ports and Islands in Times of War and Africa's Strategic Position

Ports and islands have always been important in times of war, particularly in conflicts fought at distance and across oceans.[2] Belligerents have sought to have and to hold major ports so as to be able to continue to import and export the foodstuffs and other goods upon which lives and livelihoods depend, in war as in peace, and to supply their war-making capacity. Likewise, they have sought to have and to hold islands in order to protect the sea-lanes connecting the ports, and to employ them as bases for military operations in surrounding areas. Historically, ports and islands have been conquered and colonized for their strategic location and the facilities they offered, especially their harbors. In the British case, Ceylon, Heligoland, Malta, Mauritius, Minorca, the Seychelles, Singapore, and a host of other islands around the world were contested during times of war as great powers sought advantage in attack or defense, and strove to defend sea routes and prevent enemies from utilizing key harbors. Likewise, ports, on the coastlines of larger land masses, were fortified, blockaded, and attacked because of their strategic importance.

To appreciate the significance of Africa's ports and islands during the Second World War, it is useful to recount some basic tenets of sea power (defined as naval strength, especially as a weapon of war), and some abiding verities regarding world trade and the logistics involved in sustaining complex military operations overseas. Throughout history, projecting military power beyond a nation's own shores has depended upon capable maritime forces and their ability to use sea lines of communication to deliver troops and all of their equipment to combat zones, and to ensure that merchant vessels and troopships are able to continue to use those sea-lanes even as enemy forces attempted to interdict them. What connects the beginning and end points of those sea lines of communication are *ports* and the facilities they provide. In turn, what protects those sea lines of communication are *islands*, defensive and offensive way stations strung out along them. Islands variously performed the role of mid-ocean sally points as well as recuperation, repair, victualing, fueling, and ammunitioning bases for merchantmen and warships. They also provided wireless and cable facilities, acting as links in a global communications chain. Islands were also employed as forward supply bases and jumping-off points for land, air, and maritime forces assaulting major land masses, and for forces conducting operations in the surrounding area.

Africa is surrounded by important sea lines of communication and maritime choke points such as the Cape and the Suez Canal.[3] During the Second World War it was a continent that needed to be worked around by shipping between the Eastern and Western hemispheres and was itself utilized for its resources, both human and material, the extraction of which buttressed the Allied war effort. Africa's eastern seaboard and its offshore islands were part of an extensive network of sea-lanes, port facilities, and military bases stretching across the Indian Ocean to the Persian Gulf, the Bay of Bengal, and the East Indies. The Cape and the Red Sea were key waterways upon which the British and Allied war effort in the Middle East and beyond depended. West Africa, meanwhile, was a crucial variable in the security matrix of the Atlantic and in the all-important battle to protect the convoys sailing between Britain and the Americas, and those sailing toward or returning from destinations east of Suez. Control of the waters of the Mediterranean, the Gulf of Guinea, the Mozambique Channel, Cape Agulhas, the Cape of Good Hope, and the Red Sea was ultimately indispensable to a British and Allied war effort dependent upon the movement of military goods by sea.

In order to conduct operations in the Second World War, powers such as the United States, Britain, Germany, Italy, and Japan required overseas ports at which to unload men and materiel transported across the oceans from home ports of embarkation. Strategically placed islands were required to protect the ships in which they sailed, and, crucially, so that they could be denied to the enemy. African ports and islands were valued and utilized for these reasons during the Second World War. Andrew Stewart describes the scale and significance of Africa's coastline and the harbors that it contains:

> The African coastline covers in excess of 16,000 miles and at the start of the Second World War there were eighty-eight harbours that were protected from wind and sea on all sides and were spacious enough and had sufficient depth to accommodate a considerable number of large, ocean-going vessels simultaneously. At this stage British control extended to thirty-seven percent of the total African coastline and within this there were a total of 32 of these "first-class" maritime ports, a combination of undeveloped and developed natural facilities—most notably Freetown in Sierra Leone and Port Sudan in Anglo-Egyptian Sudan—and a number that had been artificially developed such as at Simon's Town in the Union of South Africa and Takoradi on the Gold Coast. Along the whole of the Indian Ocean coast from central Mozambique northward along Tanganyika and Kenya to the boundary of Italian Somaliland there were a total of 14 of these most highly sought after harbors. Not including East London and Durban, once again in the Union, there were seven others either under direct British control or within the territory of one of its Dominion partners that faced towards the Indian Ocean. Only two of these were developed and the depth of the natural harbor in Mombasa was significantly greater than that of Dar es Salaam. (Andrew Stewart, "'This Temporary Strategic Withdrawal': The Eastern Fleet's Wartime African Sojourn," in *New Interpretations in Naval History: Selected Papers for the Sixteenth Naval History Symposium Held at the United States Naval*

Academy, September 10–11, 2009, ed. Craig C. Felker and Marcus O. Jones [Newport: Naval War College Press, 2012], 87–98.)

Demonstrating the continent's often overlooked strategic importance, Africa was home to major British and Allied military command structures, often headquartered in port cities. Middle East Command, Britain's most important overseas command, was headquartered in Egypt. As the war spread across the Maghreb, Allied Force Headquarters North Africa was established in Algiers.[4] West Africa Command was established in Accra in 1940, recruiting 200,000 soldiers and supervising the transformation of the region into one capable of supporting frontline theaters further east while defending itself against potential Vichy aggression. East Africa Command covered East Africa, the Horn of Africa, and British Central Africa. It was created in 1941 to relieve pressure on the overstretched Middle East Command. Headquartered in Nairobi, it in turn spawned a subsidiary command, designated Islands Area Command with headquarters in Diego Suarez in Madagascar, which became responsible for Madagascar, Mauritius, Réunion, Rodrigues, and the Seychelles.[5] Military minutiae, one might think. But this was a global war, one in which such military microsystems were connected to bigger systems of trade, logistics, and offensive and defensive military operations. They demonstrate how global war was conducted at the grassroots level.

As well as such strategic-level command organizations, Africa also hosted important military command structures. After the Japanese raids on Ceylon in April 1942, the headquarters of the Royal Navy's Eastern Fleet, responsible for guarding the sea-lanes of the Indian Ocean and the eastern shores of Africa, was transferred to Kilindini Island in the port of Mombasa in Kenya. The Royal Navy's Mediterranean Fleet was based on Alexandria. The navy's South Atlantic Command was based in Freetown in Sierra Leone. Extensive use was also made of South African bases such as Simon's Town, Cape Town, and Durban by both the Royal Navy and the South African Naval Force. Royal Air Force (RAF) Coastal Command maintained a presence in West Africa for Atlantic operations, and squadrons of Catalina flying-boats were stationed in South Africa to extend the range of searches for enemy vessels. East Africa was home to an RAF group dedicated to Indian Ocean patrols and searches in conjunction with the ships of the Eastern Fleet. The RAF's 246 Wing comprised three Catalina flying-boat squadrons (209, 259, and 265), which patrolled the Indian Ocean from March 1942 until the end of the war. There was a major base at Kipevu in Mombasa and detached bases in Aden, Diego Suarez, Kurasini Creek (Dar-es-Salaam), Masirah, Mauritius, Oman, the Seychelles, and

Tuléar (Madagascar). These flying-boats also used bases in South Africa at Congella in Durban harbor, Langebaan in the Western Cape, Lake St. Lucia in Natal, and Lake Umsingazi at Richards Bay, also in Natal.[6] Not only were Africa's ports, islands, and coastal waters important during the war, but also its lakes and lagoons.

During the war, ports were prized assets to be utilized, denied to the enemy, and, if possessed by the enemy, attacked. In September 1940 the British raided Dakar in a failed attempt to acquire the important colony of Senegal for the Free French and Allied cause, and to secure a better located and better equipped port than Freetown for the task of Atlantic convoy protection.[7] Cape Town and the naval base at Simon's Town were both used as staging posts for warships, troopships, and merchantmen traveling between east and west, and Simon's Town also acted as a base for submarines and warships operating in the South Atlantic, Indian Ocean, and Southern Ocean as Axis raiders and submarines were hunted and convoys protected.[8] The Allied war effort depended upon the movement by sea of large numbers of service personnel and military equipment, and the Cape route attained a status unknown since the opening of the Suez Canal because, for long periods of the war, the Mediterranean was closed to shipping and the canal itself threatened by Axis bombs and sea mines. The entire British and Allied military position depended upon this sea route, and it was heavily used; for example, the fifty-two separate "Winston Special" convoys that sailed between Britain and the east via the Cape and South Africa's ports comprised a total of 458 troopships carrying 1,173,010 British and Allied military personnel.[9]

On North African shores, Alexandria was the major naval base for the Royal Navy's Mediterranean Fleet. It was the scene of a costly Italian attack in December 1941, when three human torpedoes and a submarine seriously damaged two British battleships, a destroyer, and a tanker, swinging the naval balance in the Mediterranean in favor of the Axis. The port of Mers El Kébir in Algeria was the site of a grisly episode in which the Royal Navy attacked a heavy concentration of the French fleet in order to prevent it from falling into German hands and to demonstrate Britain's resolve to fight on against the dictators to the Americans, killing over 1,200 French sailors in the process. Tobruk in Libya was a pivotal port in the fighting between British and Axis forces that extended back and forth from Egypt to Tunisia, because it allowed armies to be supplied as they fought along the coastal strip. Benghazi, another strategically important Libyan port, changed hands no fewer than five times between British and Axis forces during the seesaw fighting across the coastline of the Maghreb. The Anglo-American invasion of Algeria and Morocco in November 1942 witnessed the landing of over 100,000 Allied troops at Algiers, Casablanca, Oran, and Safi. This invasion initiated the final phase of the fighting in Africa, eventually overwhelming the Axis forces, which surrendered in May 1943 following the capture of the port cities of Bizerte and Tunis. In the Horn of Africa, the British blockaded and from late 1942 occupied the French port of Djibouti, from where Vichy sympathizers had been providing information on Allied convoys crossing the Red Sea. Having analyzed the overall importance of African ports and waters, the chapter now turns to examine some of West Africa's ports and islands, and the region's strategic significance.

West Africa: Bathurst, Freetown, Takoradi, and Fernando Pó

A wartime report compiled by American naval intelligence summed up the problem the Allies faced in the West African region: "The West Coast of AFRICA is handicapped by a lack of harbour and port facilities. With the exception of the natural harbors of FREETOWN, SIERRA LEONE, LAGOS and PORT HARCOURT, NIGERIA, and the artificial harbor at TAKORADI, GOLD COAST, there are practically no facilities for unloading cargoes."[10] Freetown, therefore, became a vital port, especially when the Mediterranean sea route was closed by enemy activity.[11] The origin or destination port for no fewer than thirty-two convoy routes, it was a peacetime backwater transformed by war into a major hub.[12] As the American report explained: "FREETOWN in normal times is no more than a small trading post and fuelling station. However, it is now very active as all convoys going around AFRICA stop here for fuel. There are several convoys in port at one time. The harbor is used for assembling convoys for north and south routing. . . . Approximately seventy-five to 150 freighters and several tankers are standing in the harbour at all times."[13]

Capable of accommodating up to 250 ocean-going vessels, Freetown came into its own. The British, of course, had been aware of its importance for some time. A report of June 1940 considered the German threat to the region and the ramifications of French collapse in Europe. "In the last event it is essential that the port of Freetown should be secured at all costs as a naval fuelling base," stated the directive given to Lt.-Gen. G. J. Giffard when he became commander-in-chief West Africa.[14] Two years later, the importance of West Africa was still growing, with the region described in a Dominions Office telegram as a "vital link in communications and as a source of essential supplies."[15]

A wartime map of Freetown supplied to the American military illustrates the scale of port facilities required for the operation of peacetime and wartime maritime activity.[16] World war meant the maintenance of a vast number of overseas bases, and this meant infrastructure and the forces with which to utilize it and defend it. The map labeled key geographical features in and around Freetown, betraying the British colonization of this particular space: Cape Sierra Leone, Cockerill Bay, Bunce River, Bullom Shore, Destruction Bay, White Man's Bay, Pirate Bay, Aberdeen, and Kru Bay. The map detailed the port's extensive facilities: the government headquarters, port war signal station, cable and wireless office, wireless telegraphy mast, boom defense jetty, man-of-war hulk, quarantine anchorage, and emergency landing ground.[17] Torpedo nets guarded the entrance to Freetown and a channel running twenty miles out to sea was regularly swept by minesweepers.

The American intelligence report documented the location and capacity of all of Freetown's wharves and jetties. It noted, for example, that at the boom defense jetty at King Tom peninsula a new steel jetty was being constructed that would extend about 100 feet from the shore then 300 feet in a northeasterly direction. Here it would be possible to berth a minelaying ship. The three jetties extending from the government wharf were handling about 600 tons of supplies daily. There was a radar station at Cape Sierra Leone, a runway under construction at Makeni, and a landing field under construction at Port Loko, defended by an infantry battalion. Waterloo aerodrome, fifteen miles north of Freetown, was defended by two Vickers machine guns, two eighteen pounders, two 3.7 antiaircraft guns, four Bofors, and an infantry company. There were other landing fields at Bo, Daru, Hastings, and Wellington, and a seaplane base in Freetown harbor. Stocks of fuel in Freetown were replenished from Lagos, where Shell held 3,000–4,000 tons of each grade of fuel. Ships in harbor were supplied with water from Charlotte Falls and, to a limited extent, from the City of Freetown's water supply. HMS *Invella* was a stationary Royal Navy water supply ship with a capacity of 2,200 tons. At Kissy East there were two 1,000-ton oil tanks used for water from Charlotte Falls and at Kissy Oil Jetty there were two 500-ton open-water tanks. The Sierra Leone Coaling Company operated two water boats, which supplied water to ships in harbor. Bunker oil and diesel oil were available in large quantities, brought in by tankers from Venezuela and the West Indies. There were always several oil tankers in port, and when the American intelligence report was compiled in November 1942, there were 80,000 tons of oil ashore in tanks.[18] Extensive infrastructure and concentration of supplies, it can be seen, was crucial to using such bases during the war, and in turn this usage had implications for social and economic relations.

Sustaining forces overseas required food, often in competition with local consumers. A summary of the supply situation concluded that bananas, papayas, pineapples, limes, oranges, and sweet potatoes were available locally in fair quantity, though Irish potatoes were unobtainable and meat was scarce. In terms of human resources, the picture painted by the American observer was not encouraging: "The natives are reported to be the least honest and reliable of all the tribes of WEST AFRICA. They are inclined to be insolent and troublesome." Later on, the report returned to this subject: "For the most part, labourers for unloading cargoes are inexperienced, uneducated, South African 'Blacks' who are slow and inefficient. However, some stevedores are 'Kru' men mostly from LIBERIA—tall, husky natives— who have spent most of their lives on the ocean and are efficient."[19] These unfair, poorly informed, and biased opinions were based on ignorance and racial prejudice, and colored by exceptional wartime conditions, which squeezed African communities while simultaneously allowing in-demand African labor to flex its muscle. The British also expressed concerns about the slow speed of dock work, which was understandable given the rapid growth of the traffic in and around Freetown. The "appalling congestion" afflicting Government Quay, for instance, was noted.[20] Plenty of ostensible "solutions" were proffered by British service personnel; an officer from HMS *Vindictive* reported that there was "insufficient white supervision" of African labor: if "the coloured labour were forced to work there would be a subsequent speed-up of 100%," he opined.[21]

British military authorities cataloged perceived problems too, relating especially to African labor, crime, and general challenges faced as the traffic through the port and the numbers it accommodated expanded rapidly. The commander-in-chief of the Royal Navy's South Atlantic Station described Freetown and environs as "a foul place for sailors," lacking in amenities.[22] Nevertheless, this was being addressed; the Fourth Sea Lord was sending out seven buses to ferry sailors on leave to Lumley Beach, and two Seaman's Institutes had opened. There were other problems, too, such as those documented in a file entitled "Question of gangsterism and lawlessness in Freetown."[23] The file contains reports such as "Molestation and robbery of service personnel by Africans" (May 1943). This comprised a collection of reported incidents of people being robbed, on the streets or in their homes. At pains to emphasize that all servicemen understood how imperative it was not to strike a "native," thereby augmenting the desired impression of restraint on the part of military personnel, it was suggested that off-duty servicemen should be armed, and accused the local colonial police force of inefficiency. Some officers advocated flogging to discourage robbery. There were certain thieving hotspots, such as around the Lion and Palm Tree Club and on Lumley Beach, from where the clothes of bathers were regularly stolen. There were incidents of gang fights between Africans and British servicemen, and organized street robbery was common. The commander, Sierra Leone Area, wrote to the governor in July 1943, stating that there had been 133 reported cases of larceny from British military personnel in the three months since April. There was also thieving in billets, camps, and residences. "Burglary," it was reported, was "a flourishing industry in Freetown and takes bungalows and messes of Service people in its unhampered stride." As well as crime targeted at individuals and their homes and property, there was a problem with theft from government and military stores, including "wholesale robberies" from Government Wharf and "pilferage of Army and other service stores in transit" on a "huge scale."[24]

American servicemen also served in West Africa, not least through wartime expansion in Liberia. A new American footprint appeared at Takoradi in the Gold Coast, an important link in an Allied supply chain connecting North and South America, Britain and the Middle East and South Asia via a South Atlantic stop-off on Ascension Island.[25] This enormous supply network funneled thousands of military aircraft from Britain to Takoradi, and from America via Brazil and Ascension to Takoradi, for onward travel across the belt of Africa to the Sudan and Egypt, for use by either Allied forces fighting in North Africa and the Middle East, or by Allied forces fighting in the China-Burma-India theater. These aircraft, which numbered nearly 10,000 in total, arrived at Takoradi by ship, packed in crates. They were then assembled at the airbase, a facility run by the RAF but heavily used by the US Army Air Force, before beginning their journey along the Trans-African ferry route. The Takoradi airbase was also home to 26 Squadron South African Air Force and its Wellington bombers, deployed on antisubmarine patrol and convoy protection duties off the West African coast.

Bathurst, the capital of the Gambia located on St. Mary's Island, housed a subsidiary fueling base used by forces policing the Central Atlantic sea routes. It was also a key point on the medium bomber air route to the Middle East and India from Europe and the Americas. Aircraft were stationed at Bathurst for antisubmarine patrols and convoy protection off the West African coast, including the eight Sunderland flying-boats of RAF Coastal Command's 204 Squadron based there from July 1941 until the end of the war. The archives show plans of the RAF landing strip on the mainland opposite St. Mary's Island at Jeswang.[26] This new airbase became home to

200 Squadron RAF from 1943. Flying Hudsons and then Liberators, this squadron was responsible for antisubmarine patrols and convoy escort off the West African coast. The station at Bathurst had opened in December 1940 with the arrival of a flying-boat control unit. It became an advanced operational base for Sunderlands of 95 Squadron based at Freetown, 400 miles south, and was used by British Overseas Airways Corporation flying-boats between Britain and Lagos. The 204 Squadron's flying-boats moved in, and up to 100 American aircraft a month were handled here as they flew from America to the Middle East via Brazil and Bathurst. There was a similar base at Yundum and a flying-boat base at Half Die Marine.[27]

In summer 1941 the Americans examined the possibility of opening a defended airbase in the Gambia as a staging post on the air route to the Middle East. The fact that the survey was conducted by President Franklin Roosevelt's son set British officialdom atwitter. London was keen to ensure that colonial and military authorities were as accommodating as possible, the lead set by Prime Minister Winston Churchill, who welcomed the prospect of an American base as it would be yet another tie binding the United States to the British war effort.[28] In a telegram to Roosevelt, Churchill said that he welcomed the proposal and envisaged extending the same kind of arrangement as that which had seen the lease of bases in the British West Indies as part of the destroyers-for-bases agreement.[29] But there was also concern lest the unfavorable impressions of British Africa gained by Captain Roosevelt during his visit should unduly influence the thinking of the president and his administration. Officials in Whitehall lamented the condition of the "old and somewhat squalid coast settlements" that Captain Roosevelt had visited. As a Colonial Office minute put it: "It is a serious misfortune to us that the development of the air route to the East since the fall of France has brought into the limelight three of our most unattractive colonial towns. Lagos, Freetown, and Bathurst were never designed for the shop window: and the war has not improved their appearance. Accra, which relatively is a model of amenity and enlightenment, is unfortunately off the air route."[30]

This sparked familiar alarms and exasperations at the Colonial Office. Officials worried about the probable "political motive behind American criticism." They fortified themselves with calls to "advance to the attack" in the light of such criticism and devise propaganda to counter common American "misperceptions" about British colonialism, echoing wider themes in British policy to deal with incipient American anticolonialism through argument and propaganda.[31]

One of the major consequences of the great increase in traffic and facilities at these key ports was that Africans had to leave requisitioned or compulsorily purchased land. In negotiations between the Colonial Office and the Air Ministry regarding the RAF's acquisition of land plots in and around Bathurst, consideration had to be taken of the cost of "evacuating the people and clearing the site."[32] The Air Ministry agreed "to accept the capital cost of the re-settlement of persons evicted form the land required for the flying-boat base." While these official correspondences give no insight into what this meant for Africans, it was clearly a significant issue, compounded by population increases and overcrowding caused by wartime employment opportunities and the rising cost of living. The governor of the Gambia wrote of the "imperative need for alleviating the over-crowding in and around Bathurst by the resettlement of persons evicted from land required for the Flying-Boat Base in a model village to be situated in the Province of Kombo St Mary."[33] Accommodation was needed in the Gambia for a flying-boat squadron and two squadrons of general reconnaissance aircraft and the hundreds of RAF personnel that this entailed, as well as 10,000 tons of aviation fuel to be housed in both the Gambia and Sierra Leone.

Other parts of West Africa were also subjected to the strategic gaze of war leaders and the military operations that tended to follow. Spanish-controlled Fernando Pó (Bioko) was of interest to British intelligence because of its location and proximity to key Atlantic shipping lanes. Considerable effort was invested in establishing a network of spies and intelligence gatherers, revolving around a pair of British agents. The lead in this region was taken by the Ministry of Economic Warfare and its Special Operations Executive (SOE) organization. SOE monitored Spanish, Portuguese, and Vichy territories in this region "in order to detect and disrupt any activity threatening British possessions and in preventing the smuggling of diamonds from West Africa to the Axis powers (Operation Malpas)."[34] A covert inspection of the island was conducted in order to infiltrate British agents and to increase knowledge of it, especially the east coast and Concepcion, which were areas "completely unknown to us." A network of "carefully chosen and specially trained natives" were "to be infiltered and contracted on to those plantations in areas of military and strategical interest." In pursuit of this and to provide a cover for an extra British agent, a labor treaty was concluded between the Nigerian government and the Spanish territories of the Gulf of Guinea. A detailed report of the island contained geographical and topographical information and comprehensive Photostat plans of the north coast defences.

The Germans understood just how important West Africa's shipping routes were for the British war effort, and so deployed submarines there. This led to worrying losses of merchant vessels, and plans were therefore developed to counter the threat. The Admiralty believed that the enemy submarines were refueling at Equatorial African bases, a region largely under the control of pliable Vichy administrations. SOE, therefore, was ordered to gather intelligence, and in August 1941 the *Maid Honor*, a Brixham trawler crewed by commando-trained SOE personnel, set sail for Sierra Leone. Here it spent a few months combing the mangrove swamps of the French West African coast. Then the SOE station in Nigeria identified a new target: the island of Fernando Pó, lying twenty miles out in the Gulf of Guinea. The Spanish colonial government had provided a neutral haven for three Axis ships anchored there for more than a year. They were the 8,000-ton Italian merchantman *Duchessa d'Aosta* with a cargo valued at £355,000, and the German tug *Likomba* and barge *Bibundi*. Mindful of the delicacy of the situation and the need to avoid an obvious breach of Spanish neutrality, the Foreign Office reluctantly agreed that SOE should try to hijack the vessels. The British vice-consul at Santa Isabel, working for SOE, facilitated reconnaissance visits and blackmailed the governor.[35]

The assault party assembled at Lagos. The plan was to enter the port on a moonless night, disable the wireless, blow the mooring chains, and tow the vessels out to sea. Loaded with ammunition and weapons, the Nigerian government tugs *Nuneaton* and *Vulcan* left Lagos in the dead of night on January 11. Just before midnight on January 14, they were 200 yards off the harbor of Santa Isabel. At midnight, on cue, the lights of Fernando Pó vanished; SOE had bribed the wife of the power station's chief electrician with a diamond bracelet. To further aid the raiders in their task, the crew of the three Axis ships had been invited to an event at the casino organized by the British consul. The scene was set for the raiders to go about the business of planting explosive charges on the vessels' cables. *Duchessa* was detached from her moorings and towed off by *Vulcan*, while *Nuneaton* towed *Bibundi* and *Likomba* away from the port. All three vessels were successfully returned to Lagos, where the raiders were welcomed by the governor himself on the landing stage, whiskey and soda in hand. Congratulatory cables from Foreign Secretary Anthony Eden and Prime Minister Churchill followed, and the SOE agent on Fernando Pó escaped to the Cameroons by canoe.

Further off the West African coastline, Churchill planned to occupy the Canary Islands should the Germans take Gibraltar. Madeira, ruled by neutral Portugal, received 2,000 Gibraltarian evacuees when the British removed Gibraltar's civilian population in order to fully militarize the territory and because of the threat of Axis occupation. The Allies also prevailed on the Portuguese to allow them to develop military facilities in the Azores. Having offered insights into some key West African examples of wartime activity and the manner in which infrastructure and activities in the region were linked to broader wartime initiatives, the chapter now turns to some of East Africa's most important ports.

East Africa: Kilindini, Massawa, and Port Sudan

This section moves to East Africa and focuses upon the military and strategic role played by three important, though rarely heard of, ports. Kilindini harbor, located between the East African mainland and the west coast of Mombasa Island where the harbor facilities are centered, gained new strategic significance when the Royal Navy's Eastern Fleet was forced to leave Ceylon following the Japanese raids on the island in April 1942. Retreating to the Swahili coast, the fleet was to remain stationed at Kilindini until autumn 1944. Before war broke out, Kilindini had been developed to such a point that it could provide a measure of protection for convoys and escorts along with the maintenance of an examination service to provide a security inspection of visiting ships before they entered harbor, a port war signal station, and a small number of minesweeping and other patrol vessels. Six-inch coastal guns had been installed and trenches dug in case of Italian air raids, and in some parts of the town bomb and splinter barricades had been constructed. An air-raid precaution system had been organized and a partial blackout was in force.[36]

With Japan's rude arrival in the Indian Ocean, Kilindini's strategic importance escalated, and it needed to be transformed into a major fleet base capable of accommodating a large fleet comprising all classes of warships. This meant speedy infrastructural development; the construction of new defences, berths, and accommodation; and an influx of people, centered on the 15,000 men of the Eastern Fleet. All of this took place in an already crowded environment, bringing attendant cultural, social, and economic changes. All ports along the coast were to be defended because even if one was captured, Japanese forces could potentially land and then attempt to capture the larger ports from the landward side. The British envisaged an estimated scale of Japanese attack involving 150–200 aircraft operating from three or four aircraft carriers supported by a bombardment by fourteen-inch gun battleships, along with attacks by torpedo and minelaying craft. Accompanying this, the British estimated, would be a land force of approximately one brigade equipped to seize and hold a base or to "smash and burn facilities."[37]

Detailed notes were therefore prepared on all of East Africa's strategic coastal points, but with the prevailing scarcity of resources, it was recognized that it would not be possible to defend all 600 miles of British-held East African coast. As a result, it was decided that coastal and antiaircraft guns would be sent to Zanzibar and Berbera, some equipment would go to the port of Tanga, but Mogadishu and Kismayu would have to be left undefended. In all of the planning, Kilindini was held to be "undoubtedly the primary port" for it would not be possible without it "to maintain a force of any size" nor conduct "a defensive campaign of any magnitude."[38] Hence it was agreed that it would receive the greatest resource and become a base for the Eastern Fleet with the neighboring island of Zanzibar earmarked as an overflow. Kilindini was not just a potential dockyard and repair facility but also a convoy assembly and commercial port. There was also an oil fuel depot, ammunition storage facilities, a cable and wireless station, and an aerodrome at Port Reitz.

Contemporary aerial photographs give an excellent sense of Kilindini's facilities and layout, and the island's relationship to the mainland.[39] They show Port Mombasa, Old Town, Port Tudor, and the causeway to the mainland on the far side of the island. On the southern side of the island, defensive batteries guard the channel leading to the "entrance to deep-water ports." On Kilindini Island can be seen the "European residential area," the lighthouse, and Mombasa Golf Course along the shoreline. The naval base is marked, along with oil storage areas, the British Overseas Airways Corporation's shore station and depot, antiaircraft gun emplacements, the wireless station, oil jetty, docks, deep-water wharves, and another golf course. Behind the naval base lie the Kenya and Uganda Railways' yard and track leading over the causeway to the mainland. Pictured opposite the Kilindini naval base is Port Reitz and a spit of land where the RAF had a base and a slipway for flying-boats.[40]

The war, specifically the Eastern Fleet's arrival in Africa, brought extensive military development to Kilindini Island and its environs, including new forts, bunkers, gun emplacements, tunnels, and command towers, representing a very large investment in new infrastructure.[41] By 1943 there was 130,000 square feet of workshop space, and facilities approximating to one-and-a-half times those that had been available at Simon's Town, one of Africa's most significant naval bases, on the outbreak of war. In 1943, quarters for 500 female naval personnel were prepared at Kilindini, women who would primarily be employed in handling signals communications, and at English Point a "Naval Pool Camp" capable of accommodating 1,500 service personnel under canvas was readied.[42] Far East Combined Bureau, the main Bletchley Park code-breaking facility for the east of Suez region, also moved to Mombasa for over a year in 1942–43, evacuated from Ceylon because of the Japanese threat. The code breakers took over Allidina Visram High School in the Mzizima district of Kilindini Island.[43]

Elsewhere on Africa's eastern seaboard, the garrison defending British Somaliland was evacuated by sea from the port of Berbera in August 1940, along with civilians of the colonial administration. All together, the Royal Navy took 7,000 people from the port as the Italians closed in. As the East Africa campaign swung in Britain's favor, Massawa (Eritrea) and Mogadishu (Italian Somaliland) became prime targets because their possession would better secure the sea route to the Middle East and neuter Italian maritime activity in the western Indian Ocean. At a meeting of the British War Cabinet on March 31, 1941, Churchill decreed that steps should be taken to ensure that the Italians did not scuttle the twenty-five merchant ships reported to be in Massawa harbor. As a result, the Duke of Aosta, commanding Italian forces in East Africa, was told that if the Italians did so, the British would "consider ourselves free of any obligation to feed the Italians in Eritrea or Abyssinia or to remove them from those countries."[44] Plans were made to counter the Italian threat in the Red Sea and to protect Port Sudan, aimed particularly at destroying the Italian warships based in Massawa. The commander-in-chief of the Eastern Fleet maintained a "Red Sea Force" for this purpose. The senior naval officer Red Sea had at his disposal a striking force based at Port Sudan, another at Suez, and ships patrolling the Bab el Mandeb.[45]

The secret combined outline plan for Operation Abaft, the capture of Massawa, offers an appreciation of why the port was so valued. The port's capture "would have very considerable results." It might well "break the enemy's will to resist in ITALIAN EAST AFRICA."[46] From the naval point of view, it would free warships of the Eastern Fleet for other duties, "dispose of remaining Italian warships in the RED SEA," "considerably reduce time of passage of shipping from UK and elsewhere," and "avoid present necessity in certain cases for transshipment at Bombay and Aden."[47] It would release army units for operations elsewhere, and remove the need for RAF Red Sea patrols from Port Sudan and fighter protection for convoys from Aden.

Massawa, the headquarters of the Italian East Africa Command, was naturally well defended because of the many islands and shoals to the east of the harbor. Not only did these islands and shoals form natural obstacles that any seaborne invaders would have to negotiate, they also contained military and surveillance equipment. Islands such as Taclai, Difnein, Mersa Deresa, Harat, Dohul, Isratu, and Hamil contained listening posts and coastal defense and antiaircraft guns. During the East Africa campaign, the British assailed Massawa by air, land, and sea. Naval attacks were aimed at demoralizing the enemy, destroying enemy units and installations, and preventing Italian forces on land from being resupplied, especially with petrol. Operation Composition on February 13, 1941, for example, saw fourteen Fairey Albacores from HMS *Formidable* attack Massawa, sinking SS *Monacalieri*. A week later *Formidable* passed Perim en route to Suez and seven of its aircraft launched a dawn dive-bomb attack on Massawa.[48] As the senior officer Kilindini signaled to the director of naval intelligence on February 22, 1941, "Kismayu evacuated in 2 panic repeat panic stages. . . . Inevitable conclusion enemy terrified of sea and air bombardment especially of aircraft carriers. Considered that similar display of naval force prior to military investment of Massawa and Mogadiscio may accomplish same results."[49] Operation Canvas on February 14 had seen the coastal batteries of Kismayu and Muanga bombarded by warships at a range of 2,300 yards. Supporting troops advanced on land, while British warships were called upon to bombard the coast road north of the Juba River, the offshore islands and mainland batteries, and Massawa town itself.

Victory for the British in East Africa brought control of Africa's coastal waters, meaning that Italian forces in East Africa were starved of supplies, choked by Britain's maritime stranglehold as surely as they were defeated by the activities of imperial troops on land. Clearing the Italians out of East Africa secured the entirety of the East African coast for Britain and its allies. Strategically, this was very important. Not only did it bring greater security for convoys and merchantmen using the busy sea-lanes along the African coast and across the Indian Ocean, it also meant that American merchant vessels were able to help supply British imperial forces fighting out of Egypt. This was because the Red Sea route, in terms of the American Neutrality Act, could now be classified as a neutral zone, and therefore a permissible one for American merchant vessels to traverse. The port of Massawa became a joint Anglo-American concern following its capture. Soldiers of the US Army's Corps of Engineers arrived to clear sunken floating docks and the merchant vessels that the Italians, despite Churchill's admonition, had scuttled. As the American naval commander in charge of operations, Capt. Edward Ellsberg, put it, the port contained "the greatest mass of wrecks in the world (not excluding Pearl Harbor)."[50] In a well-planned and systematic scorched-earth operation, the Italians had blown up the floating docks, sunk a string of large ships across the harbor entrance, and smashed up the naval installations ashore. Much of the salvage and repair work was undertaken by American personnel working under the President's Scheme of Technical Assistance to British Forces, and the regional umbrella of Gen. Russell Maxwell's US Military North African Mission. The important work of salvaging the ships sunk in harbor and generally making the harbor operational was conducted by Ellsberg and his men. So impressed were the British by his labors that Ellsberg was recommended for a decoration. He raised numerous ships, two floating docks, and a ninety-ton crane. Among the salvaged ships was the German freighter *Frauenfels*, which was raised along with its valuable cargo of 1,400 tons of ore. Massawa's harbors and naval repair base was fully restored by the time he left. Three cruisers had "docked and repaired there under his direction at a time when it was impossible to deal with them elsewhere in the Near East owing to enemy activity."[51] It is worth dwelling on the significance of this because it perfectly demonstrates the value of African (and other colonial bases) and the infrastructure that they contained: if warships could not have been repaired in Massawa or Colombo, or Durban, then they would have had to have been returned to Britain's oversubscribed, bomb-threatened shipyards. Simply put, fighting a global war *depended* upon these colonial facilities.

As well as Americans, British units were also involved in Massawa's operations, and their activity provides further evidence of how the logistical sinews of a global conflict were configured. August 1941 found No. 4 Detachment Docks Group Royal Engineers laboring in stifling heat and sandstorms loading and unloading ships. On August 7, a "huge fire" developed at the ordnance sheds at Campe di Marti, spreading to and destroying the "native quarters." Ammunition stores went up "in great profusion" throughout the day, the conflagration subsiding only five days later.[52] Military administrators from another department based in Massawa, the Port Transit Depot, organized stores and provisioned service personnel passing through the port. On December 14, 1941, for example, it dispensed rations to Movement Control to provide 500 British soldiers with rations for a four-day sea voyage and ten days on land, and 600 tons of flour destined for Aden arrived from Middle East Command, Massawa functioning as a regional transit hub. The military establishment in port housed facilities such as bakeries and butcheries in order to feed thousands of service personnel and laborers, as well as a military hospital.[53] A Field Supply Depot unit was responsible for unloading and loading ships in port and repairing them.[54] Up to 1,000 tons a day of coal, supplies, and ammunition were being discharged, much of it American.[55] Massawa's storehouses extended to 30,000 square feet, and 1,500 workmen were employed there. To enhance the port's capacity, a 6,000-ton floating dock was brought from Bandar Shapur in Iran, capable of accommodating light cruisers.[56] The new base established at Massawa had advantages over Port Sudan in terms of its existing facilities and because of its immunity from air raids.

As well as being highly valued for its location, Massawa was required by the Admiralty as a repair and maintenance base for light cruisers, destroyers, and small craft, an assembly depot for RAF and Fleet Air Arm aircraft, and as an armament storage depot.[57] This was particularly important in the year after its capture. The commanders-in-chief of both the Royal Navy's Mediterranean and Eastern fleets wanted it developed as a central ammunition reserve for their ships, and lobbied for its current facilities to be extended to a capacity of 20,000 tons. Massawa was considered "most desirable" because it was far removed from areas exposed to enemy attack, beyond the reach of Gen. Erwin Rommel's Afrika Korps in the Western Desert, and too far away from the focal point of Japanese activity on the other side of the Indian Ocean.[58] It was far away from places such as Alexandria and Lake Timsah, where the Mediterranean Fleet's main ammunition stores were located, and from the Eastern Fleet's exposed ammunition dumps in Ceylon. Responding to this demand, the Americans operating the port developed semiunderground magazines at Embatcalla, and ammunition trains began to run between Massawa's docks and this central magazine facility. About 2,000 feet below Embatcalla, a new depot storing 5,000 tons was built at Ghinda.[59]

The Eastern Fleet was particularly keen on the ammunition storage facility at Massawa and its expansion. The Italian depot at Embatcalla was capable of holding 4,600 tons, and the hulk *Danubian* arrived and could hold 2,000 more.[60] The Eastern Fleet came increasingly to depend on its African facilities as those in South and Southeast Asia were either lost to the enemy or put at serious risk from enemy attack. The hulk *Corsica* was sent to Durban and could hold 1,000 tons of shells and cartridges, and Durban's facilities were extended to handle and store armaments to the tune of 10,000 tons, as was Port Elizabeth. Temporary storage for 5,000 tons was also arranged in a disused magazine at Umbogintwini (eZimbokodweni), located on the coast about twelve miles south of Durban.[61] The extent of African facilities employed by the Allies in the Second World War was staggering.

Further north along the vital East African sea line of communication, Port Sudan was a notable strategic point, linked by rail to Khartoum. When Italy entered the war, the captain of the merchant ship *Umbria* scuttled his vessel off the port in order to prevent its cargo of 360,000 aircraft bombs falling into British hands. In May 1940 a section from 112 Squadron RAF was ordered to Summit Airfield south of Port Sudan to form "K" Flight, tasked with the defense of Port Sudan and the conduct of operations in the Red Sea. Flying Gloster Gladiators, it also helped defend Egypt from Italian aircraft. The 114 Squadron was also based at Port Sudan, and with

Italy's declaration of war, its Wellesley bombers launched attacks on Italian fuel storage and other facilities at Massawa. Significant work was undertaken to improve Port Sudan's coastal defenses, install antiaircraft guns, and augment its capacity to examine ships entering the harbor for security reasons. Boom defenses were installed and mine-swept entrance and exit channels instituted.[62]

Port Sudan was an important hub for military operations during the East Africa campaign. 114 Squadron, now equipped with Blenheim bombers, attacked Keren in Ethiopia in support of advancing ground forces, and in March 1941 the aircraft carrier HMS *Eagle* disembarked two squadrons of Fleet Air Arm Swordfish torpedo bombers—813 and 824 squadrons, both of which had taken part in the famous raid on the Italian naval base at Taranto the previous November. While based in Port Sudan, these aircraft were used for convoy escort and reconnaissance of the Suez Canal and the Red Sea. In anticipation of their arrival, the RAF assembled drums of fuel and stacks of 200-pound bombs. These aircraft also attacked Italian destroyers in Massawa, sinking two of them. The extensive archives on the development of places such as Massawa and Port Sudan offer a vivid impression of the complexity, scale, and significance of the infrastructure offered by African ports and their wartime expansion. One War Office file contains twenty plans of Port Sudan, showing its extensive facilities.[63] Surveyed by the Royal Navy in 1904 and further developed by the Sudan government and the navy in the 1920s, the map "Port Sudan" and "Approaches to Port Sudan" depicts the port and town and the location of a twelve-pounder battery installed in 1940.[64] It shows a shaded arc indicating the radial reach of the port's Defence Electric Lights (manned by the Royal Engineers), and the radial reach of the nearby guns, extending out to sea for 16,500 yards. The map also shows the examination anchorage just inside Wingate Reefs where vessels visiting the port could be inspected before being allowed to enter. Another plan, dating from December 1939, shows the port's coast defences, which included antiaircraft gun installations. A series of detailed plans illustrate the scale of construction required to install a magazine for the storage of 550 shells and cartridges for the two six-inch coastal defence gun emplacements, range finder, and engine room, testifying to the extensive and intricate construction and engineering work required in order to secure and utilize such facilities.

The war diary of the Movement Control section at Port Sudan details the comings and goings of this extremely busy and strategically located port. It captures the logistical complexity of military operations as troops and supplies were shunted hither and thither as the pulse of war dictated.[65] Numerous ships arrived each day from ports such as Aden, Berbera, Bombay, and Massawa. Movement Control had to arrange for the arrival and unloading of these ships and the disembarkation of troops and their onward passage. The port was serviced by Indian soldiers and workers (coolies) of the Indian Army Service Corps, used for unloading and stevedoring, and by local hired labor. After military units had been disembarked, Movement Control then had to cater for their temporary accommodation, rationing, water, latrine and ablution facilities, medical inspections, and air raid shelter arrangements.

Movement Control was also responsible for the onward movement of the military units that disembarked at Port Sudan, and this meant troop trains. The war diaries for 1941 detail the large numbers of troops and tons of supplies being dealt with by this Base Transit Supply Depot. British and Indian Army formations were arriving in large numbers, as well as the less frequent transit of Free French forces and bodies such as the Sudan Defence Force's band and the 883 African and 21 British officers and non-commissioned officers of the 3rd Ethiopian Battalion. With the East Africa campaign in full spate, there were also large numbers of Italian prisoners of war being handled by the port as they were shipped off to internment in South Africa and elsewhere within the Empire. The thousands of troops transiting through Port Sudan were moved on along the railroad lines to places such as Atbara, Derudeb, Haiya, Kassala, Khartoum, and Suez. This was all part of a complex system of moving military resources over vast distances; the railhead at Haiya, for instance, was the point at which the roads and railroads from Atbara and Kassala met, and continued toward Suakin.[66] The distances involved were great: the running time from Port Sudan to Haiya was seven hours, Atbara by rail was fourteen-and-a-half hours, and Kassala was twenty-one hours. From Kassala some of the troops went on for another two hours to Tessenei (Teseney) in Eritrea during the campaign against the Italians.

Large amounts of rolling stock were required for military purposes: to transport a company of 365 men, 9 fourth-class carriages were required, along with an antiaircraft truck, a brake van, and a driver's coach. As well as moving troops, it was all about moving military supplies. Port Sudan, clearly a very important military junction, was capable of handling (in 1941) up to 3,000 tons of supplies per day. In May 1941 alone, the Movement Control authorities handled 1,500 wagons of military stores. In the same month the shipment of cased vehicles from America and Canada to the Middle East increased greatly, arrivals at Port Sudan and Port Suez expected to be as high as 9,000 by July.[67] Space in the port area was at a premium; when storage was required for the surplus baggage of the 5th Division, a warehouse belonging to Barclays Bank was earmarked for the purpose.

It was not only the great ports of the East African coast that were employed by the Allies in this strategically important region. The utterly obscure RAF Bendar Alula was located on the northern shores of Italian Somaliland, a simple runway strip on the edge of the Red Sea. The operations record book of the RAF unit based here reveals a busy transit point connecting African destinations and linking across the Red Sea to Aden. The unit comprised about 100 RAF personnel and employed local labor.[68] Having examined the significance and the work of three important East African ports, the chapter moves to consider the strategic role of the islands off the East African coast, and the military activity that took place there.

African Islands in the Indian Ocean: Comoros, Madagascar, Mauritius, the Seychelles, and Zanzibar

Axis forces sought to interdict Allied vessels sailing between Europe and the East by way of Indian Ocean shipping routes. Especially important and vulnerable was the vital route that ran all along the coast of East Africa as ships sailed around the Cape, passed Durban, and proceeded through the Mozambique Channel and the Red Sea and on to the battlefronts of the Western Desert and the wider Middle East via places such as Port Sudan and the Suez Canal. Japanese submarines reconnoitered African islands and operated off the East African coast, as did surface raiders and submarines of all three major Axis powers. The British, meanwhile, launched operations against the Comoro Islands, Réunion, and Madagascar in order to prevent Vichy authorities granting bases to the Axis, and to help secure the sea lines of communication along the African coast and also across the Indian Ocean toward the Persian Gulf, India, and the Far East. Further off Africa's shores, the British used the Mauritius and Seychelles island groups for a range of military purposes.

A small defense force was raised in the Seychelles and placed under War Office control. Two companies of military pioneers and artisans, totaling nearly 1,000 men, were sent to the Middle East, where they and other soldiers from Mauritius and Rodrigues joined tens of thousands of other colonial recruits forming a rear echelon military labor force to support the fighting formations of the 8th Army.[69] All together, over 1,500 Seychellois served in the forces, representing 4 percent of the population. The scattered Seychelles were difficult to supply, given their remoteness, and in anticipation of war the colonial government advanced money at low interest to traders in order that they might build food reserves. In a bid to develop local production and relieve unemployment arising from the depression in the copra and guano markets caused by wartime shipping shortages, the government arranged to employ 500 workers on Crown Land to produce food. In line with people across the British Empire, Seychellois contributed to war charities and funds such as the Win the War fund and the Red Cross.

The Seychelles were strategically located on important trade routes and acted as a depot for refueling ships, a staging post for aircraft traveling to the Far East, and an operational base for squadrons under Air Headquarters East Africa, RAF Seychelles being officially formed in June 1943. It was also part of a chain of flying-boat bases stretching from East Africa to Ceylon known as Allied Surveillance Net East. Flying below Japanese radar cover, for two years the RAF flying-boats involved provided the only available intelligence regarding Japanese movements in the Indian Ocean. Given the strategic significance of the Seychelles, garrison forces were brought to the island, commanded by HQ Troops Seychelles, which by December 1942 was responsible for the 27th Coast Battery Hong Kong and Singapore Royal Artillery (manning a brace of ex-naval six-inch guns at Port Victoria), the 3rd Indian Garrison Company, and the Diego Garcia Garrison Company. It also commanded the Seychelles Defence Force, which consisted of a transport unit, a Royal Engineers unit, a rifle and machine-gun unit, and a coast-watching unit. The Seychelles' value increased when the cable line through the Mediterranean was cut, meaning that the Seychelles was the only British territory with a cable station available to contact South Africa and thence India and Australasia. The cable and wireless station was located on Mahé Island, camouflaged and protected by splinter-proof barricades and a company of imperial troops.

From July 1940 all Vichy territories were subjected to a blockade by the British. The blockade was "imposed above all upon French North Africa and the Indian Ocean territories of Madagascar, Réunion, and French Somaliland."[70] From 1941, Madagascar depended on American trade to provide essential imports, though this trade diminished as President Roosevelt was wary of breaching the British blockade. According to Martin Thomas, the blockade of Madagascar was the most effective of any Vichy colony: "By 1942 the economic hardships it produced were biting hard among the French planter community and Madagascar's town populations. By the time of the invasion, Madagascar's export trade was only 22 per cent of its pre-war level."[71]

Madagascar was a source of anxiety for members of the British War Cabinet because of the threat of enemy occupation and the use of the island as a base at the invitation of the Vichy government. The British feared a repeat of what had happened in Southeast Asia. Here, the Vichy administration granted Japan bases in Indo-China, which were then used to attack Malaya and sink HMS *Prince of Wales* and HMS *Repulse*, a disaster for British power in the region. Madagascar possessed a fine natural harbor ideally suited as a major naval base large enough to accommodate the entire Japanese fleet. This was Diego Suarez, located at the northern tip of the island. Japanese submarine and surface raider offensives in the Mozambique Channel, the stretch of water separating Madagascar from the African mainland and a major shipping route, were common from the summer of 1942.

On March 14, 1942, Grand-Admiral Raeder told Hitler that the Japanese were eyeing Madagascar for bases after their intended occupation of Ceylon. On April 24, 1942, plans for a British assault on the island were reviewed. While these discussions were in motion, the SOE was busy in Madagascar, running agents from its regional headquarters in neighboring Mauritius. A Franco-Mauritian agent, Percy Meyer, and his wife regularly relayed intelligence by wireless, and in February 1942 made an attempt to bribe the French naval commander to give up his post and allow British forces to occupy Diego Suarez unopposed. Despite these attempts to sway the French authorities toward the Free French and Allied cause, they remained stubbornly loyal to the Vichy government in France. Indeed, Léon Cayla, governor of Madagascar, attempted to ingratiate himself with his superiors in Paris by applying Vichy edicts with particular vigor. He identified and incarcerated those among the colonial administration in Tananarive likely to support Gen. Charles de Gaulle and the Free French cause, and took measures to crush Free French support in the colony.[72]

The South African prime minister, Jan Smuts, was particularly concerned by the possibility of a Japanese strike at Africa, which would threaten African territories, disrupt sea routes around Africa to the Middle East and Far East, and present the prospect of the Japanese linking hands with Axis forces in North Africa. A friend and confidant of Churchill, Smuts urged a preemptive strike, telling him that Madagascar was "the key to the safety of the Indian Ocean."[73] For obvious reasons, Smuts appreciated the island's strategic value, and realized that nearby Durban might become a principal fleet base for the Royal Navy should Japan come to dominate the Bay of Bengal.

The fall of Singapore made a preemptive British strike against Madagascar worthwhile, and the passage of a troop convoy destined for Ceylon provided the opportunity. Paul Annet, governor at the time of the invasion, was instructed to resist, though the British took Diego Suarez with relative ease. As soon as Diego Suarez had been secured, the British troops originally bound for Ceylon were required to continue their journey east.

The Vichy administration of Madagascar, however, refused to capitulate. From May to September 1942, forces on the ground in Madagascar conducted informal discussions with Annet's government while also preparing to march south from Diego Suarez to conquer the rest of the island. This was because other ports, especially Majunga and Tamatave, might still be used by Japanese submarines. So the plan was adopted at a conference in Pretoria in June to attack them and then move inland against Tananarive once the rainy season lifted in the autumn. The French governor and his garrison finally surrendered in September 1943. Most of the island, after a period under British military administration, was handed over to a Free French administration early in 1943, though Britain retained control of "Fortress Diego" in the north. Madagascar soon began to contribute to the Allied cause through the export of strategic raw materials, which meant the continuation of forced labor exactions for the Malagasy, and the requisitioning of foodstuffs. This fueled the growing appeal of Malagasy nationalism.

The invasion and occupation of Madagascar has been relatively well covered in the literature, though here we outline the little-known occupation of Tuléar (Toliara) and its subsequent military utility. Capt. A. G. S. Forrest, part of the Royal Marine detachment aboard the cruiser HMS *Birmingham*, wrote a narrative of the operation to take Tuléar, sited on Madagascar's southwest coast on the Mozambique Channel. The assault took place between September 26 and 29, 1942, a military operation "designed to secure the peaceful capitulation of the town by an ostentatious display of overwhelming force," which it succeeded in doing with no significant casualties. The operation was mounted by *Birmingham*'s complement of eighty-four marines together with two companies of the Pretoria Rifles, covered by *Birmingham*'s twelve six-inch guns. The cruiser's Walrus seaplane and the transport vessel *Empire Pride* were in support. The operation began with a wireless signal demanding the town's surrender. Soon after, a white flag was visible, the Vichy governor wisely deciding to avoid unnecessary bloodshed. The troops went ashore as the seaplane circled the town dropping leaflets. The marines were met by "local Malagache," who were described as "deferential" and "conspicuous by their ragged attire and somewhat dejected demeanour." The marines were greeted by a "little white man," who proclaimed himself British and offered to act as a translator. His sole request, "pathetically enough, was for a loaf of bread which he said he had not seen since Christmas last." Free French flags appeared in the streets, and the police force was drawn up ready to surrender. "Greetings and gratitude unfortunately took the shape of bottles of a particularly noxious and potent rum, of which there seemed an unending supply. Eventually quite large patrols had to be maintained to check this form of generosity." All key points were soon occupied without incident. The "appalling lack of everyday necessities was very noticeable." Before departing the following day, HMS *Birmingham*'s band gave a concert in the square, concluding the performance with "La Marseillaise."[74]

The war diary of the Tuléar Garrison, the military force that was stationed in and around the town for the rest of the war following its capture, offers an insight into the activity of this little-known military outpost.[75] In 1944 the garrison comprised two companies of African troops (the King's African Rifles, replaced by the Northern Rhodesia Regiment), RAF personnel servicing the airbase and flying-boat anchorage, and an East African coastal battery unit manning the guns protecting the garrison from seaborne attack. Stationed nearby was a battalion of French African pioneer laborers and prisoners of war who were used as laborers too, working on the petrol dump or quarrying. This meant that even in this military outpost in a strategic backwater, around 2,000 military personnel were required in order to make it fulfil its operational role. There was a jetty and a petrol dump, a detention center, and an airstrip. Catalinas, Hudsons, and Lysanders called at the airbase or were based there for operational purposes, particularly maritime patrol, and RAF Hurricanes conducted meteorological flights from Tuléar. The port was visited by destroyers and motor torpedo boats. Frigates and minelayers arrived to refuel on their way from Durban to Majunga, and a regular air service linked Tuléar to Diego Suarez.[76]

Life in an outpost away from the front line presented challenges for the troops and the officers responsible for them. There was a great deal of cricket and football, units taking on other units, the army taking on the air force, or "British" Africans playing "French" Africans. A tour of duty in Tuléar presented the opportunity for sustained troop training, and routinely one of the garrison's African companies would be devoted to training while the other performed garrison duties. Entertainments were periodically provided by the French community, local festivals, and the occasional visit by entertainers such as the Royal Artillery concert party and the "Hullo Africa" Entertainments National Service Association concert party, which arrived by flying boat from Pamanzi in July 1945. There were other recreational pursuits available, too, and successive garrison commanders lamented the high incidence of venereal disease—the "prevalent crime of breaking barracks," as it was put, "caused by prostitutes living within a few yards of the Camp."[77]

Other French islands in the region were also attacked and occupied by the British for maritime security. In June 1942 the British decided to occupy the Comoro islands of Mayotte (Maore) and Pamanzi (Petite Terre). The airfields at Mayotte were considered a threat to Allied shipping in the Mozambique Channel, and facilities here made a useful addition to the British network of flying-boat bases in the region. It was duly taken by a raiding party from Eastern Fleet destroyers sent from Mombasa (Operation Throat). In June 1942, 209 Squadron's Catalina flying-boats arrived in East Africa tasked with making antisubmarine sweeps from Mombasa. In need of a stepping stone between East Africa and Madagascar, Pamanzi was chosen and duly taken by naval forces. An expedition was dispatched to occupy the airfield and wireless station at Pamanzi, at the request of Jan Smuts, who viewed it as a useful antisubmarine base and staging post for fighters traveling from Tanganyika to Madagascar. A cruiser and destroyer were sent along with King's African Rifles troops, a company of which were to remain as an occupying force. The occupation was a straightforward affair, "[l]ocal government officials and approximately 60 police captured in bed in barracks," as the official report put it.[78]

The severing of commercial links with countries that became enemy territory, coupled with the dearth of merchant shipping, created serious food shortages in Zanzibar. It was dependent on food imports, and was one of the many territories in the region that had depended on rice from Burma.[79] The need to bring more land under cultivation in order to produce more food locally contributed to soil erosion, which in turn contributed to the silting up of the Chake Chake creek on Pemba and the encroachment of mangroves into the creek's channel, making it impassable. The colonial government and the Zanzibar Naval Volunteer Force made plans for the defense of the wireless station at Chake Chake, and carefully monitored the arrival of immigrants. Wartime conditions led to a renaissance of the dhow trade: for decades the colonial government had tried to replace dhows with modern steamers, though the chronic lack of such vessels in wartime allowed the dhows to claw back some of the lost ground. Before the war, dhows had dominated private shipping between Pemba and Zanzibar, but the transport of the valuable clove exports had been reserved for steamers, as was the transport of government supplies. But with the general wartime shortage of shipping and as more steamers were requisitioned for war service (for example, the Royal Navy requisitioning a Zanzibar government steamer, the *Al-Hathera*, for minesweeping duties), the government had no choice but to turn increasingly to dhows. Dhows were kept so busy that demand exceeded their capacity to carry, and dhows from Arabia sailed south to take advantage of the employment bonanza brought on by the war. Wartime food regulations and shortages also created a black market, and many dhows illegally shipped Mozambican sugar to Arabia. Clove-exporting firms bought new dhows to cope with the demand, encouraged by the belief that these traditional sailing vessels were less likely to attract the attention of enemy submarines. By 1944 nearly a quarter of Zanzibar's exports were being carried by dhow, representing over half a million pounds-worth of trade.

Mauritius became an island in uniform as over 5,000 men were dispatched to the Middle East as members of the British Army's Royal Pioneer Corps, over 1,000 Mauritian women served in the same theater as part of the Auxiliary Territorial Service, and 2,500 men were recruited into the Mauritius Defence Force (a Home Guard formation). The locally raised professional military force, known as the Mauritius Territorial Force, expanded until it comprised two battalions. Renamed the Mauritius Regiment in 1943, the 1st Battalion was sent overseas to form part of the garrison around the naval base at Diego Suarez in Madagascar, and for much of the war, a King's African Rifles battalion garrisoned Mauritius for fear of an enemy raid. An air raid precaution organization and military ambulance service were established, the Fire Service was overhauled, and air raid shelters were prepared. When Japan entered the war and Singapore was lost, a Japanese attack or invasion of Mauritius became a realistic prospect.[80] Flying-boat bases were developed and an aerodrome constructed, and the Admiralty maintained fuel and ammunition stockpiles here. There was also a Coastal Defence Force patrolling the gaps in the reef surrounding Mauritius in thirty-foot motor vessels. Over 8,000 men were conscripted into the Civilian Labour Corps as the colonial government took the necessary powers to control the allocation of labor for war purposes. Mauritian forces were also used to garrison the island's Indian Ocean dependencies, guarding, for example, the cable and wireless station on Rodrigues, and providing forces to defend the naval base on Diego Garcia. New communication links were created by conflict. Never having been visited by an aircraft in 1939, by 1942 Mauritius boasted numerous RAF and Fleet Air Arm facilities, including a Royal Naval Air Station, and by 1944 a regular air service linked it with Madagascar and South Africa. The island was also part of the navy's wireless network across the Indian Ocean. Considerable defensive work was required to prepare the island to withstand an enemy attack, should one be mounted, including the installation of antiaircraft guns, torpedo booms in the main ports, and minefields in the approaches.

As well as acting as a base for military operations in the region, notably the naval and air operations to sink German supply ships and submarines, Mauritius was also used as a gathering point for warships blockading Vichy territory and attempting to intercept Vichy blockade-runners traveling between Indo-China, Madagascar, and Europe. Operation Kedgeree in August 1941 and Operation Bellringer in October 1941, for example, were aimed at Vichy convoys and made use of Mauritian facilities. The latter consisted of a convoy from Tamatave, Madagascar, bound for France and escorted by a Vichy sloop. Mauritius was also a base for covert operations against neighboring Vichy territories. SOE broadcast propaganda from a secret wireless station in a sugarcane field, and mounted operations in Madagascar and Réunion. In the case of Réunion, SOE agents were brought from Mauritius, and operations were conducted along with a Free French destroyer to force the island's staunch Vichy governor and his garrison to surrender. To illustrate the significant and often deleterious ramifications of war, we might consider a report from the commanding officer of the Free French destroyer *Leopard*, which had taken part in the "liberation" of Réunion on November 26–27, 1942, alongside British forces: "The population of Reunion are [*sic*] in danger of starvation. No clothing is available in shops and in parts of the island the French White population are practically naked." There was an immediate need for rice, flour, salt, cooking fats, cattle, and clothing.[81]

Given the threat of Japanese attack or invasion, considered real enough in the early months of 1942, SOE organized stay-behind teams in Mauritius intended to harry Japanese occupiers and supply British forces with intelligence, and plans were made for a scorched-earth policy to destroy key infrastructure should the Japanese threaten to overrun the island. A cable and wireless interception facility was established on the island and came to employ over 300 people, providing a valuable addition to the work of the Far East Combined Bureau, the region's main Bletchley Park outstation engaged in the work of intercepting Japanese military and diplomatic codes, and those of the region's Vichy regimes. Initially the work was centered on the cable traffic that passed through Mauritius (neighboring French territory, for example, relied on British cables in the region), though it increasingly came to play a role in intercepting and deciphering French and Japanese diplomatic, commercial and military wireless traffic.

As has been demonstrated, Africa's ports were essential for Allied military operations—for inserting ground forces, patrolling sea-lanes, moving men, and attacking enemy-held ports that threatened those sea-lanes and that might enable the enemy to sustain campaigns on land. They were also necessary to handle the vast amounts of supplies and equipment that waging war across vast distances entailed. But in order to avoid the impression that African ports were chiefly valued for strategic and military reasons related specifically to the war, it is important to emphasize their continued importance in terms of resource extraction. The history of Western engagement with Africa had, of course, been dominated by the harvesting of African resources and their transport to the coast for shipment overseas. This remained the bedrock of the West's relationship with Africa during the Second World War, and indeed was augmented during the course of it. Now, not only did the colonial powers desperately need to sustain their export of valuable African commodities, wartime damage to the system of international trade, and the Allies' loss of key strategic materials to Japanese occupation further east, meant that African resources became even more important. For example, Allied losses in Southeast Asia and the East Indies meant that demand for African products like rubber, tin, sisal, and pyrethrum rocketed, just as the widening extent of the conflict required the unforeseen recruitment of hundreds of thousands of African soldiers.

An illuminating example of the war's affirmation of the importance of links between African resources and the West—and the facilitative role played by African ports in this relationship—is found in the case of Congolese uranium. In order to expedite the export of uranium from the Shinkolobwe mine in Katanga province, soldiers of the US Army's Corps of Engineers arrived to reopen the disused facility. To expedite the export of this precious material, essential for the progress of the Manhattan Project, they developed new aerodromes and built an improved port at Matadi, the main seaport located nearly 100 miles inland from the River Congo's mouth. The large stockpile of uranium already dispatched by sea to New York in September 1940 by the director of the Union Minièr du Haut Katanga was then able to be supplemented by thousands of tons mined here and sold to the US Army.

Today the Second World War has a vestigial presence in Africa for those who care to look. There are manicured war cemeteries, local and national airports that began life as RAF aerodromes, jetties, wharves, and accommodation buildings, and coastal defense emplacements. The wreck of the *Umbria* still lies off Port Sudan and is regularly visited by scuba divers; the shattered frame of 259 Squadron's Catalina "E," which crashed during landing on June 7, 1943, killing all but one member of the crew, is occasionally visible on Lake St. Lucia's mudflats near Mitchell Island. Despite these visible remains, the enormous impact of the war upon Africans, and the importance of African resources and locations to the major belligerent powers, remains underappreciated. There are numerous reasons for this, including a dominant Western narrative of the war that focuses on battles, strategy, and high politics, not the experiences of colonized peoples or the crucial role of non-Western resources, both human and material, in winning the war. It is also because Africanists seldom focus on military and strategic matters, especially at a pan-continental level, and because the war has been peripheral to African national histories, or viewed individually (in separate colony histories), rather than continentally. As Kwei Quartey argues in *Foreign Policy in Focus*, in an article demonstrating how academic research can help shape popular understanding, the war's historiography needs to be widened to give Africans and other people around the world their due.[82] To achieve this, as this chapter has sought to demonstrate, Africa needs to be viewed as a whole and to be assessed in terms of its strategic significance for the Allied war effort.

African ports and islands were important during the Second World War for three key reasons: (1) because powerful nations required the export of Africa's resources for their economic benefit and war-related utility, and needed to deny the same to enemy states; (2) because sea routes around the continent and leading off from the continent needed to be defended using its ports and island bases; and (3) because fighting took place on air, land, and sea in and around Africa, and ports and islands were therefore contested for military and strategic reasons. The chapter has demonstrated the significance of African ports and islands during the Second World War, and the sheer extent of activity that took place in them and around them. In doing so, it contributes to a slowly emerging literature that gives Africa its due prominence in the military and strategic history of the Second World War, and explains the pattern and significance of the operations that took place on African land and in Africa's coastal waters.

Notes

The archival research for this chapter was generously funded by the Defence Studies Department, King's College London, through the author's Personal Research Allowance. Special thanks are due to my colleague, Dr. Andrew Stewart, who with typical generosity allowed me to pillage his work on Kilindini and supplied copies of files drawn from the British National Archives relating to West Africa Command and Freetown from the Churchill Archives Centre, Cambridge, and from the American National Archives and Records Administration (NARA) regarding Freetown (file RG165) and Kilindini (NARA port photographs and diagrams). Also, to Dr. Daniel Owen Spence of the University of the Free State who kindly sent me prepublication PDFs of two chapters from his book *Colonial Naval Culture and British Imperialism, 1922–1967* (Manchester: Manchester University Press, 2015), which details the history of the locally recruited British East and West African naval formations. Thanks are also due to Dr. Jonathan Hill for kindly reading a version of the chapter. The material was presented to a seminar held jointly by the King's College London Defence

Studies Department's Second World War Research Group and the British Empire at War Research Group. This chapter formed the basis of further work on African and Indian Ocean ports and islands published as Ashley Jackson, *Of Islands, Ports, and Sea Lanes: Africa and the Indian Ocean in the Second World War* (Solihull: Helion, 2018).

1. A landmark study comprising numerous chapters examining aspects of Africa's wartime social, economic, industrial, cultural, and political history is Judith Byfield, Carolyn Brown, Timothy Parsons, and Ahmad Sikaingi, eds., *Africa and World War Two* (Cambridge: Cambridge University Press, 2015). Pre-publication manuscript reviewed by the current author on behalf of the publisher. Africa has been well served by single-country studies on the impact of the Second World War, for example, Nancy Lawler, *Soldiers, Airmen, Whisperers, and Spies: The Gold Coast in World War II* (Athens: Ohio University Press, 2002).

2. Islands retain their military and strategic importance in the modern era. Indian Ocean islands were important for British military activity into the 1970s, RAF Gan in the Maldives, and bases on Masirah and Socotra. Even in the twenty-first century, islands remain important for military power projection. For example, the RAF air station on Ascension Island permits British aircraft to stage to the Falkland Islands in the South Atlantic, and is also used by the United States Air Force aircraft traversing the Atlantic from west to east. A new airport is being built on Tristan da Cunha, a dependency of British-ruled St. Helena. Cyprus houses important RAF and intelligence-gathering facilities, Guam in the Mariana Islands is an American air and naval base, and Diego Garcia in the Indian Ocean provides base facilities for British and American forces, including strategic bombers, allowing targets in a wide region, including Central Asia, to be attacked.

3. The role of Africa in the war, and the African islands in the Indian Ocean, is extensively covered in Ashley Jackson, *The British Empire and the Second World War* (London: Continuum, 2006), chap. 9, "Sub-Saharan Africa," 171–268, and chap. 11, "The Islands of the Indian Ocean," 307–49. See also Ashley Jackson, "Africa: The Strategic Continent," in the article "The British Empire/Commonwealth and the Second World War," *The Round Table: The Commonwealth Journal of International Affairs* 100, no. 412 (2011): 70–75. Extensive coverage of the military campaigns in Africa is provided in Richard Osborne, *World War Two in Colonial Africa* (Indianapolis, IN: Riebel-Roque, 2001).

4. The British and Allied command structures of the Second World War have received surprisingly little scholarly attention, and histories of formations such as East Africa Command, Middle East Command, and South East Asia Command are long overdue. For Allied Forces Command North Africa, there is a very helpful contemporary record, the "History of Allied Force Headquarters," published in three parts by the command itself in 1945 and available online, https://archive.org/details/HistoryOfAlliedForceHeadquartersPart3December1943-July1944.

5. This command was formed in September 1942, when the Indian Ocean islands were transferred from India Command and conjoined for command

purposes with Madagascar. Lt.-Gen. Sir William Platt, general officer commanding in chief, East Africa, "Operations of East Africa Command July 12, 1941 to January 8, 1943," *Supplement to The London Gazette,* July 16, 1946. Part 5 titled "Madagascar, Mauritius, Rodriquez, and Seychelles."

6. South African Air Force Museum, https://saafmuseum.org.za/sunderlands-of-lake-umsingazi/. Langebaan lagoon and Saldanha Bay were used by warships and flying-boats. See TNA, ADM 1/15278, Defence of Saldanha Bay against midget submarines and human torpedo attack.

7. See Arthur Marder, *Operation Menace: The Dakar Expedition and the Dudley North Affair* (Oxford: Oxford University Press, 1976).

8. L. C. F. Turner, H. R. Gordon-Cumming, and J. E. Beltzer, *War in the Southern Oceans, 1939–1945* (Cape Town: Oxford University Press, 1961). See also Arthur Banks, *Wings of the Dawning: The Battle for the Indian Ocean, 1939–1945* (Worcestershire, UK: Malvern, 1998).

9. Archie Munro, *The Winston Specials: Troopships via the Cape, 1940–1943* (Liskeard, UK: Maritime Books, 2005), 430.

10. National Archives and Records Administration [hereafter NARA], Washington. RG165, Box 2892, US War Department (Sierra Leone—Regional Files, 1942–44). Intelligence Report of the Navy Department, from US Naval Observer at Freetown, November 9, 1942, "Sierra Leone—Wharves and Jetties of Freetown Harbor."

11. Wartime Freetown has been the subject of several studies. See Andrew Stewart, "The Second World and the 'Quiet Colony' of Sierra Leone," in *An Imperial World at War*, ed. Ashley Jackson, Yasmin Khan, and Gajendra Singh (Farnham, Surrey: Ashgate, 2015); A. M. Howard, "Freetown and World War Two: Strategic Militarization, Accommodation, and Resistance," in *Africa and World War Two*, ed. Carolyn Brown, Judith Byfield, Timothy Parsons, and Ahmad Sikaingi (Cambridge: Cambridge University Press, 2015); A. Ndi, "The Second World War and the Sierra Leone Economy: Labour Employment and Utilization," in *Africa and the Second World War*, ed. David Killingray and Richard Rathbone (Basingstoke: Macmillan, 1986).

12. The following link details the thirty-two convoy routes to and from Freetown and gives their two- or three-letter code names. See http://www.convoyweb.org.uk/os33/freetn_conv.htm.

13. NARA RG165, Box 2892, Intelligence Report of the Navy Department.

14. The National Archive [hereafter TNA], Kew, CAB 121/189, "West Africa Command." Report on "Defence of British Interests in West Africa," Joint Planning Sub-Committee, Chiefs of Staff, June 22, 1940. Annex: Directive to Lt.-Gen. G. J. Giffard.

15. TNA, CAB 121/189, Dominions Office to High Commissioner South Africa, June 2, 1942.

16. NARA RG165, Box 2892, Intelligence Report of the Navy Committee.

17. NARA RG165, Box 2892, Intelligence Report of the Navy Committee. There was also a map of Pepel Island, seven miles off Freetown at the mouth of the Sierra Leone River, from where iron ore was exported.

18. NARA RG165, Box 2892, Intelligence Report of the Navy Committee.

19. NARA RG165, Box 2892, Intelligence Report of the Navy Committee.

20. TNA, West Africa Command, CAB 121/189 Naval Intelligence Division Report 165, April 16, 1942.

21. TNA, West Africa Command, CAB 121/189 Naval Intelligence Division Report 165, April 16, 1942.

22. Churchill Archive Centre, Cambridge, Admiral Willis to 2nd Sea Lord, December 19, 1941.

23. TNA, CO 267/683/17, Report by the Staff Officer (Intelligence), Freetown, on increased lawlessness in Freetown: Molestation and robbery of service personnel by Africans.

24. TNA, CO 267/683/17, Report by the Staff Officer (Intelligence), Freetown, on increased lawlessness in Freetown: Molestation and robbery of service personnel by Africans.

25. See Deborah Wing Ray, "The Takoradi Route: Roosevelt's Prewar Venture beyond the Western Hemisphere," *Journal of American History* 62, no. 2 (1975): 340–58. See also F. Kenneth Hare, "The Takoradi-Khartoum Air Route," *Climatic Change* 1, no. 2 (1977): 157–72, written by Hare in 1943 for official purposes; Erik Benson, "Suspicious Allies: Wartime Aviation Developments and the Anglo-American International Airline Rivalry, 1939–1945," *History and Technology: An International Journal* 17, no. 1 (2000): 21–42; Yomi Akenyeye, "The Air Factor in West Africa's Colonial Defence, 1920–1945: A Neglected Theme," *Itinerario: International Journal on the History of European Expansion and Global Interaction* 25, no. 1 (2001): 9–24; William Stanley, "The Trans-South Atlantic Air Link in World War Two," *GeoJournal* 33, no. 4 (1994): 459–63.

26. TNA, AIR 2/4494, Overseas: Dominions and Colonies: Bathurst, Gambia: Development for use by Beaufort squadron.

27. TNA, AIR 20/5474, Report of RAF Station Bathurst, August 1941.

28. TNA, CO 968/46/1, Proposed American Airbase at Bathurst: Visit to the UK of Captain Roosevelt. See also CO 968/4/8, Bathurst aerodrome and CO 554/127/9, Naval defense of West Africa: Storage of ammunition at Bathurst. See also ADM 1/20706, Admiralty and Air Ministry oil installations Bathurst and AIR 29/449, Air-Sea Rescue Unit, Bathurst.

29. TNA, PREM 3/502/1, US base at Bathurst.

30. TNA, PREM 3/502/1, US base at Bathurst, minute, July 16, 1942.

31. This subject is covered in William Roger Louis's seminal work *Imperialism at Bay: The United States and the Decolonization of the British Empire, 1941–1945* (New York: Oxford University Press, 1978).

32. TNA, CO 968/46/1, US airbase at Bathurst, Air Ministry to Colonial Office, December 30, 1941.

33. TNA, CO 968/46/1, US airbase at Bathurst, Air Ministry to Colonial Office, November 21, 1941.

34. TNA, HS 3/77, Final report Fernando Po and Spanish Guinea. The HS 3 series contains material relating to SOE operations in East and West Africa.

35. This vignette is taken from James Owen, *Commando: Winning World War II Behind Enemy Lines* (London: Abacus, 2013), chap. 5, "Postmaster," 83–98. Fernando Pó files at TNA include: FO 371/26922, Situation in Fernando Pó; HS 3/77, Final Report on Fernando Po and Spanish Guinea; FO 371/26908, Nigerian labor in Fernando Pó; FO 371/39661, Labor conditions and Axis activity; WO 173/1286, Operation P (Scorpion) later Gracechurch attack on Santa Isabel and occupation of island; and HS 3/86, Operation Postmaster removal of Italian merchant ship and two German vessels from harbor and Santa Isabel.

36. This is drawn from Andrew Stewart's chapter in which he employs Eric Jolley, "An Account of the Development of Kilindini at Mombasa in East Africa as a Naval Base for Eastern Fleet," Mombasa, October 8, 1942, 2–29, TNA, ADM1/13010.

37. From Andrew Stewart, based on Admiralty to C-in-C East Indies, March 14, 1942, 1442A; Admiralty to C-in-C East Indies, April 2, 1942, 2016A, TNA, WO106/5213.

38. From Andrew Stewart, based on Admiralty to C-in-C East Indies, March 14, 1942, 1442A; Admiralty to C-in-C East Indies, April 2, 1942, 2016A, TNA, WO106/5213.

39. To view the photograph, see Ashley Jackson, "Of Sea Lanes, Strategy, and Logistics," http://defenceindepth.co/2014/10/09/of-sea-lanes-strategy-and-logistics-africas-ports-and-islands-during-the-second-world-war/.

40. Kilindini photographs from NARA.

41. For extensive research on and photographs showing the defenses and installations built to defend and service Kilindini and Mombasa, see the Web sites of Dr. Richard Walding (Griffith University, Brisbane): "Mombasa Forts: Kilindini and Mombasa Harbours in World War Two," http://indicator-loops.com/mombasa_forts.htm and "Indicator Loops: Royal Navy Harbour Defences, Kilindini Island, Mombasa," http://indicatorloops.com/mombasa.htm.

42. TNA, ADM 1/12977, "Kilindini," meeting, Admiralty, Review of Bases Commitments in West Africa, South Atlantic, and Indian Ocean, March 17, 1943.

43. Hugh Denham, "Bedford-Bletchley-Kilindini-Colombo," in *Codebreakers: The Inside Story of Bletchley Park*, ed. F. H. Hinsley and Alan Stripp (Oxford: Oxford University Press, 1993), 270–72; Michael Smith, *The Emperor's Codes: Bletchley Park and the Breaking of Japan's Secret Ciphers* (London: Bantam, 2000).

44. TNA, CAB 65/18/12, War Cabinet 38 (41) minutes.

45. TNA, ADM 223/516, "Projected Attack on Suez and Port Sudan," CC EI March 31, 1941. For the Suez Canal during the war, see D. A. Farnie, *East and West of Suez: The Suez Canal in History, 1854–1956* (Oxford: Clarendon Press, 1956).

46. TNA, WO 169/915, War diary G Plans GHQ MEF, January 1941.

47. TNA, WO 169/915, War diary G Plans GHQ MEF, January 1941.

48. TNA, ADM 223/681, Operations Composition—attacks on Massawa, Eritrea: Operation Canvas—occupation of Kismayu, Somalia.

49. TNA, ADM 223/681, Operations Composition—attacks on Massawa, Eritrea: Operation Canvas—occupation of Kismayu, Somalia.

50. Edward Ellsberg, *Under the Red Sea Sun* (New York: Dodd, Mead, and Company, 1946).

51. TNA, ADM 1/14232, Capt. E. Ellsberg USNR recommendation for an award. Minutes March 9, 1943.

52. TNA, WO 169/2654, War diary Detachment no. 4 Docks Group Royal Engineers, Massawa.

53. TNA, WO169/2691, British Troops Sudan and Eritrea: Royal Indian Army Service Corps: Port Transit Depot Massawa. See also WO 177/1084, Massawa Military Hospital.

54. TNA, WO 169/4440, Subareas: 95 Subarea Massawa: Field Supply Depot Massawa.

55. TNA, WO 169/4464, Movement and transport Massawa. See also ADM 116/4690, Naval repair base: Massawa: Development and operation.

56. TNA, ADM 116/5802, History of the Naval Store Department 1939–45, Appendix II, Africa Volume I Massawa, Kilindini, Durban, Port Elizabeth, Simonstown.

57. TNA, ADM 1/12205, US Salvage Unit for Massawa.

58. TNA, ADM 1/13253, Eastern and Mediterranean Fleets reserves of ammunition.

59. TNA, WO 169/2970, East Africa: Lines of communication: HQ Subarea Massawa. War diary, November 1941.

60. TNA, ADM 1/13253, Massawa, Eritrea: Development of ammunition depot to serve Eastern and Mediterranean fleets. Minute April 24, 1942.

61. TNA, ADM 1/13253, Massawa, Eritrea: Development of ammunition depot to serve Eastern and Mediterranean fleets, May 15, 1942.

62. TNA, WO 201/310, Port Sudan: Coast and antiaircraft defensive role and layout, November 1939–April 1944. See also WO 201/315, Sudan: Reports on protective works on oil installations at Port Sudan and Massawa and FO 371/24632/430, Admiralty oil fuel depot at Port Sudan.

63. TNA, WO 78/4848, Port Sudan: Plans.

64. To view the image, see note 40.

65. TNA, WO 169/2595, British Troops Sudan and Eritrea Headquarters: Movement Control Port Sudan. War diary of detached movement control group Port Sudan, August 23 to September 23, 1940.

66. TNA, WO 169/4463, Sudan Headquarters: Movement Control Port Sudan. See also WO 169/2616, British Troops Sudan and Eritrea: Line of Communication Port Sudan Area. See also AIR 29/8, RAF Embarkation Office: Port Sudan.

67. TNA, WO 193/520, Port capacity for vehicles at Suez and Port Sudan, May 14, 1941, D of ST to PSTO Egypt.

68. TNA, AIR 29/146, RAF Operations Record Book, RAF Unit Bender Alula.

69. Athalie Ducrotoy, *Air Raid Sirens and Fire Buckets: Wartime Seychelles, 1939–1945* (Kent: Rawlings Publications, 1997). Elizabeth Watkins, *Cypher Officer*

(Brighton: Pen Press, 2008) recounts the experience of working in the Seychelles on intelligence-gathering work.

70. Martin Thomas, *The French Empire at War, 1940–1945* (Manchester: Manchester University Press, 1998), 71.

71. Thomas, *The French Empire at War*, 142.

72. See also Martin Thomas, "Imperial Backwater or Strategic Outpost? The British Takeover of Vichy Madagascar, 1942," *Historical Journal* 39, no. 4 (1996): 1049–74; Tim Benbow, "'Menace' to 'Ironclad': The British Operations against Dakar (1940) and Madagascar (1942)," *Journal of Military History* 75, no. 3 (2011): 769–809.

73. Thomas, *The French Empire*, 143.

74. TNA, ADM 202/425, Operation ROSE Tuléar Madagascar.

75. TNA, WO 169/18297, East Africa: Command areas and subareas: Tuléar Garrison, war diary, 1944.

76. TNA, WO 169/21766, HQ Troops Tuléar.

77. TNA, WO 169/18297, Commanding Officer Troops Tuléar Garrison, Report for September 1944 to HQ Islands Sub Area, East Africa Command. See WO 169/14173, Tuléar independent garrison company for another year's Tuléar war diary.

78. TNA, WO 193/888, Mayotte islands: Pamanzi and Réunion: Telegrams on occupation, organization, and rebuilding on the islands. East Africa: Mayotte Islands, Pamanzi, June 29, 1942–January 26, 1943; from 121 Force (Madagascar invasion force) to War Office, July 5, 1942.

79. Erik Gilbert, *Dhows and the Colonial Economy of Zanzibar, 1860–1970* (Oxford: James Currey, 2004).

80. See Ashley Jackson, *War and Empire in Mauritius and the Indian Ocean* (Basingstoke: Macmillan, 2001); Ashley Jackson, "The Mutiny of the 1st Battalion The Mauritius Regiment, Madagascar, 1943," *Journey of the Society for Army Historical Research* 80, no. 323 (2002): 232–50.

81. TNA, WO 193/888. The operation to topple Réunion was mounted from Mauritius. In May the following year *Leopard* ran aground off the port of Tobruk and became a total loss.

82. Kwei Quartey, "How West Africa Helped Win World War Two," *Foreign Policy in Focus*, June 6, 2012, https://fpif.org/how_west_africa_helped_win_world_war_ii/. Quartey's article draws on the theme of non-European participation in the war, and detail of West Africa's involvement, developed in the current author's work.

7

"Nos lingua, nos kultura, nos identidadi"

Postcolonial Language Planning and Promotion in Cabo Verde and the Cape Verdean Diaspora

Carla D. Martin

This chapter offers a new appraisal of scholarly and popular representations of Cape Verdean language and culture, taking as its subject promotional and planning activities from Cape Verdean independence in 1975 to the present day. I argue that historical derogatory tropes of degeneracy, inferiority, and impurity applied to Creole cultures have hindered efforts toward language parity between Portuguese—the Republic of Cabo Verde's official colonial language—and Cape Verdean Creole (CVC)—the vernacular of the population. The tropes stem from what noted linguist Michel DeGraff has termed Creole exceptionalism, the widespread and often harmful belief that "Creole languages form an exceptional class on phylogenetic and/or typological grounds."[1] Drawing on extensive archival and ethnographic research in West Africa, Europe, and North America, I analyze major scholarly, literary, artistic, and legislative developments of each decade, with an eye toward the contributions of cultural activists working to valorize CVC. Interventions in language and cultural planning have been made on three continents by institutions like the Cape Verdean Ministry of Culture, the Massachusetts Public School System, and the Portuguese Ministry of Education yet remain limited in their efficacy. When these interventions are studied together, it becomes apparent that debates surrounding the promotion of CVC language and culture center on contentious postcolonial political ideologies, complex notions of local versus global identity, and exceptionalist questions of Cabo Verde's "Africanness," "Portugueseness," and "Creoleness," often stalling the reforms of scholars and policy makers and profoundly affecting the life chances of CVC speakers. Throughout, I contend that popular culture, especially literature and music, longtime safe spaces for CVC, have played an integral role in preserving and promoting the language both in Cabo Verde and the diaspora.

The celebration and reclamation of Cape Verdean culture, especially through language, literature, and music, played an essential role in the movement for Cabo Verde's independence from Portugal. As such, authors, lyricists, composers, and performers played an integral part in the promotion of CVC. Following independence, such work multiplied rapidly as a result of government sponsorship, liberation from Portuguese censorship, and the proliferation of educational and printing opportunities. Nonetheless, Manuel Veiga, a leading Cape Verdean linguist and minister of culture from 1999 to 2009, writes: "it must also be recognized that the major fort where CVC resisted the great glottophagic waves were orality and oral traditions."[2] He suggests that in addition to the Battle for National Liberation, the most humble, simple, even illiterate speakers are to be heralded for their roles as architects of CVC and *crioulidade*, or Creole identity. This romantic celebration of the liberation of CVC, born from the mouths of the oppressed masses, is indicative of a revival of "folk" culture that took place over the decades following independence, often as a direct intervention in defining a unique *caboverdianidade*: an autonomous, updated response to the concept of crioulidade widely discussed in the colonial period.

Despite its ties to the liberation struggle, CVC occupies a somewhat unique position in the larger Creole universe as a language that remains vigorously debated and seemingly stalled legislatively. This has its roots in the long denigration of the language. Historically, Portuguese colonial authorities did not explicitly pass laws delegalizing CVC, but they did require that all citizen interaction in official spheres take place in Portuguese. They also legislated against cultural practices deemed "non-European," such as religious and dance ceremonies conducted in CVC.[3] Scholars, too, over several centuries, reified concepts of language hierarchy, collecting problematic empirical and anecdotal evidence to demonstrate what they perceived as the superiority of the Portuguese language. Today, CVC is one of the more developed Creole languages in terms of quantity of academic study and literary production, but it retains a number of critics.[4] For example, George Lang points out that while literary *Crioulo* is more developed in Cabo Verde than other Lusophone colonies such as Guinea-Bissau or São Tomé and Príncipe, there remain serious limitations: "A purist scheme of linguistic decolonization would have called for the replacement of Portuguese by an authentic national idiom like Crioulo, but in Cabo Verde such has not come to pass. Instead, lip service is paid to writing in Crioulo while most print is in Portuguese." He concludes by classifying CVC as a category of Creole in which "a bona fide literary tradition has found footing, if not exactly thrived."[5] While defining what constitutes a thriving literary tradition is complex, the works in CVC from the twenty-first century in particular leave Lang's argument on shaky ground. I argue that CVC has undergone major advances toward more widespread acceptance and impact in official spheres in the past fifteen years, but that the scholarly study of Cape Verdean Creole remains couched in exceptionalist terms.

In fact, it was my initial difficulty in finding accurate, nonstereotyped studies of the language that caused me to undertake the research that makes up the body of this chapter. It is still all too common to find CVC classified as Cape Verdean Creole Portuguese or Cape Verdean Creole dialect, terms that further confuse and misunderstand CVC's origins and linguistic status.[6] This problem of taxonomy remains true for most Creole languages, with the Library of Congress classifying them under a subclass that includes artificial languages like Esperanto. This chapter is a response to the reality of incomplete accounts of CVC scholarship and the historically weighted exceptionalist attitudes that continue to color scholarly approaches to the language.

Late 1970s

Immediately following independence in 1975, the First Republic of Cabo Verde, which remained under the one-party rule of the Partido Africano da Independência de Cabo Verde (the African Party for the Independence of Cape Verde, or PAICV) until 1991, designated CVC an important part of the rebuilding of the country.[7] CVC was formally recognized as the national language, the maternal language of its people, and a fundamental element of its people's identity. The government also declared that it would take steps to create favorable conditions for the valorization of CVC over time.[8] Yet the appropriate executive and financial conditions were never provided. Other causes were deemed more urgent in the reconstruction of Cabo Verde and thus government efforts faltered. In addition, the original prescription for the "valorization of CVC" was so vague that there was little in the way of accountability or evaluation available to those who did take up the language promotion cause.

Regardless, the years immediately following independence proved immensely productive for CVC. A number of important scholarly and pedagogical studies marked the mid- to late 1970s. Many of these took place in the United States and Portugal as the result of increased scholarly interest in Lusophone Africa during the region's revolutionary period and the efforts of descendants of Cape Verdean immigrants in New England to explore their heritage. These contributions, described below, were made in the fields of literary studies, linguistics and anthropology, legislation, education, and orthographic standardization.

The year 1975 witnessed the publication of two works that defined the study of Lusophone African literature. First, Russell Hamilton published his landmark text *Voices from an Empire: A History of Afro-Portuguese Literature*, which devotes four chapters and over 100 pages to a discussion of Cape Verdean literature. To this day, Hamilton's work remains an important reference on the contributions of the educated literary elite in Cabo Verde from the late 1800s to the early 1970s. Though Hamilton focuses on Cape Verdean literature in Portuguese, which constitutes a large percentage of literature written in the country, he pays a good deal of attention to literature in CVC and discusses the debates over crioulidade held in the publication *Claridade*. His was also one of the first publications to include numerous translations of stanzas from CVC poetry.[9] In many ways, it paved the way for subsequent studies of CVC writing, and Hamilton's doctoral students continue to produce important studies of Lusophone African literature.[10] Second, Portuguese literary critic Manuel Ferreira's groundbreaking anthology *No Reino de Caliban* included a number of writers of CVC, including Sérgio Frusoni, Luís Romano, Ovídio Martins, Gabriel Mariano, and Corsino Fortes, further validating the language as a literary one.[11]

Also in 1975, the Brown University–trained anthropologist Deirdre Meintel published an essay entitled "The Creole Dialect of the Island of Brava," which offers basic theorizing on phonological, morphological, and syntactical elements of CVC. She followed this with a sociolinguistic study, in which she argues that CVC is a powerful symbol of Cape Verdean identity.[12] These now canonical works marked a turning point in anglophone studies of Cabo Verde, providing linguistic explanations of CVC and the significance of CVC in social context. Scholarly interest in Cabo Verde and its linguistic heritage was growing in both the United States and Portugal during the 1970s.

It was in the United States that some of the most groundbreaking advances for CVC speakers came in the form of legislation and curriculum development in Massachusetts. In 1971, the state became the first to pass a bilingual education law in recognition of the role that language and culture played in shaping full childhood participation in school. An entire curriculum from kindergarten through grade twelve was translated into CVC so that students could continue their studies in subjects like math and science while also learning English.[13] Implementation was problematic and disorganized, as is often the case when law dictates pedagogy before it is fully developed, and the resulting bilingual education program took a number of years to meet expectations.

However, numerous successes were achieved even with legislative, curricular, training, and financial challenges. CVC became a language of instruction as part of transitional bilingual education programs for Cape Verdean immigrants to Massachusetts in 1973, two years before Cape Verdean independence. The legislation's effects were significant, with thousands of students in multiple communities (especially Boston and Brockton) enrolled in the programs over a period of decades. Georgette Gonsalves, a first-generation Cape Verdean American who became the director of bilingual education for Boston Public Schools, writes: "It was a very exciting time for those of us whose parents had immigrated to the United States in earlier years. Our own language and identity would emerge along with those of other groups who have long lived in the shadow of colonial oppression."[14] This was a major coup for advocates of CVC language use in education. The United States was the first place in the world, including Cabo Verde itself, where students became literate and completed course work in CVC.

This momentum continued and, in 1976, CVC was officially recognized as a modern language by the State of Massachusetts in House Bill No. 2998, "An act directing the commissioner of education to recognize the Cape Verdean language as a living foreign language."[15] This was a leap forward for advocates of the language—especially considering the long history of exceptionalist thinking surrounding it—and was celebrated in both Cabo Verde and Massachusetts. "Massachusetts moved beyond the limits of Cape Verdean political independence," Gonsalves explains, "and became the first place in the world to support the opening of linguistic independence for the Cape Verdean people!"[16] Beyond curriculum development, there were also substantial gains in staffing and the student population served by the program. In the mid-1990s, programs operated in a number of Massachusetts school districts with large numbers of Cape Verdean students, with at least forty CVC-speaking and trained teachers, paraprofessionals, and support staff working in Boston's bilingual program alone.[17]

The Cape Verdean American intellectuals who spearheaded the bilingual education programs met with great resistance from Cape Verdean

Americans, school authorities, and legislators, yet persisted in their quest. They suggest that the programs were possible only because of the civil rights movement and the passage of the Voting Rights Act in 1965, especially with regard to the protection of language minority voting rights. As Lee D. Baker explains in *From Savage to Negro*, it was by simultaneously manipulating existing attitudes and fighting against the idea of racial inferiority that civil rights leaders were finally able to attain education rights for blacks, and it was this same fight that secured educational rights for second-language learners in the United States.[18] Advocates argued that neglecting the education of CVC speakers was akin to treating their language and culture as degenerate and inferior. As a result of these programs, many Cape Verdean Americans quickly rose in educational status.[19]

As explained above, these programs were not free of problems. The professionals staffing them had a variety of different education backgrounds and were often left to fend for themselves, using CVC in the classroom as they felt was best. Moreover, exceptionalist attitudes and the ingrained tropes of historical inferiority helped stoke controversy.[20] While the creation of a bilingual education program in CVC and English was perfectly logical to many people, some were baffled at the use of a supposedly Creole dialect and cited the fact that CVC was not taught in Cabo Verde itself. Rosalie Porter, a former teacher and vehement critic of bilingual education throughout the 1970s, explained:

In Massachusetts, school officials actually created an alphabet so that Kriolu—an obscure spoken-only dialect of Portuguese used in parts of the Cabo Verde Islands—could be written for the first time. Textbooks and a curriculum followed, and now Massachusetts boasts the only schools in the entire world where classes are taught in Kriolu. (The unenlightened schools of the Cabo Verde Islands continue to teach in Portuguese.) Massachusetts even sends home report cards and school bulletins in Kriolu. The parents have no idea whatsoever what this stuff says—none of them can read Kriolu—but their opinion hardly matters, does it? We know better, we're the teachers. . . . I thought that I, like Alice in Wonderland, had fallen down the rabbit hole. Could anyone really believe that this circuitous route through a non-existent island dialect script would lead to faster learning of English and a better ability to learn subject matter taught in English? (Paul Moreno, "She Fights to Reform Bilingual Education in Massachusetts," Massnews [2000], http://www.massnews.com/past_issues/2000/5_May/maybil.htm. Website no longer in use.)

Porter's comments, part of a much larger debate over bilingual education in the United States, reflect the historic misrepresentation of Creole languages as degenerate. Indeed, her claims that the language is an unwritten dialect ignore not just an emerging literary output but a growing scholarship on it, perpetuating the misconception that CVC is an undeveloped, impure language without a history.

An important response to such criticism came in the form of a standardized CVC orthography, or spelling conventions, developed in Cabo Verde during the 1970s. In 1979, a colloquium devoted to CVC was held in the city of Mindelo on the island of São Vicente. The director-general of culture, linguist Dulce Almada Duarte, worked with colleagues to organize the event, sponsored by the Ministry of Education and Culture.[21] The theme was "Problemática do Estudo e da Utilização do Crioulo" (The Problem of the Study and Utilization of Crioulo). Veiga explains:

> If the "*Luta Armada*" ("Armed Resistance") and the resistance of our people, in the face of colonial oppression, was "an act of culture," in the words of A[mílcar] Cabral, it was necessary to make culture an arm of development in post-Independence. And, the maternal language being one of the most effective instruments in the promotion of integrated and harmonious development, the authorities linked to Culture understood that the realization of a colloquium aiming fundamentally for the valorization of our birth language, subjugated and mistreated so many times, was also an "act of culture" and an important step in the path to development. (Manuel Veiga, *Primeiro Colóquio Linguístico Sobre o Crioulo De Cabo Verde* [Mindelo, Cape Verde: Instituto Nacional de Investigação Cultural, 2000], 9.)

At this colloquium, a proposal was made for a standardized orthography for CVC, whose underlying alphabet was commonly referred to as the *alfabeto de chapéu* (the hat alphabet, nicknamed for the circumflex diacritical marks that characterized it).

This orthography became popular among many proponents of CVC and was the basis for much of the writing published during the 1980s. It was also adopted by the Massachusetts Public School system in its massive curriculum translation and development project for bilingual education programs, though many of the problems already described made implementation tricky. It required special computer formatting for diacritics and privileged the CVC dialect of the island of Santiago over others, which alienated some users. The Alfabeto Unificado para a Escrita do Caboverdiano (Unified Alphabet for Cape Verdean Writing), ALUPEC, which represented an updated system that responded to many critiques of "the hat alphabet" by reducing the need for diacritics and focusing on phonetic/phonological orthography, was later adopted for use in the Massachusetts Public Schools. Thus, despite the unique literary and sociolinguistic studies published in the 1970s and the important legal strides made in Massachusetts, implementation of CVC education and literacy pedagogy still faltered.

The 1980s

The 1980s saw a flurry of important scholarly and literary contributions in CVC, many of them directly engaged with defining a burgeoning sense of caboverdianidade, an extension of crioulidade for an independent Cape Verdean population. In 1980, a chair was established to study the structure of CVC at the Escola de Formação de Professores para o Ensino Secundário (School of Teacher Training for Secondary Education) that offered classes employing the newly developed "hat alphabet" orthography.[22] Though the classes ended just two years later, a number of today's most vigilant CVC proponents received their preliminary training in the study of the language through this program.

Also in 1980, to celebrate the fifth anniversary of independence, the Cape Verdean author Oswaldo Osório published the landmark work *Cantigas de trabalho*, a collection of traditional songs from the island of Santiago that included a 33 RPM album. The book begins with a substantial preface by Manuel Veiga introducing the new orthography. Osório then explains in the introduction that his project was multifold, meant for the "recuperation and promotion of cultural patrimony," "cultural resistance and identity," and "cultural rebirth" necessary to overcome Portuguese colonialism and the realities of the present day. He also argues that the work songs presented in the book must be understood as important pieces of history and artistic creation in their sociohistorical context.[23] This work reflects the desire to subvert the legacy of colonial hegemony and reinvent caboverdianidade.[24]

Manuel Veiga pushed CVC promotion even further with his publications in the 1980s. First, he released the first monolingual grammar of CVC, an analytical study of the language's structure entitled *Diskrison strutural di lingua kabuverdianu* in 1982. In this text Veiga argues that dialectal variation among islands is less of an issue than most assumed and that it was entirely possible to create a writing system that was mutually intelligible to all CVC speakers using an orthography based on phonetic/phonological principles. His groundbreaking claim was that the fundamental base of CVC is the same across islands and that interisland linguistic variation is sufficiently superficial so as not to impede mutual intelligibility. Considering the representative variants studied, Veiga writes for the final summary in Portuguese, "[this study] concludes the existence of a *unique National Language*, which, at a superficial level, manifests in different ways, but not important ones, from island to island" (original emphasis).[25] This claim fit within larger discussions in linguistics on the "myth of the standard," or the folk linguistics belief that there exists a standard language from which dialects vary, often in negative ways.[26] His grammatical study is significantly different than its predecessors because it focuses on the structural linguistics of CVC rather than the etymology as its aim was not to show how CVC is derived from Portuguese.[27] In addition, when this work was published, no other Creole language had a grammar published in its own language.

Veiga's second major contribution in the 1980s came in the form of the first monolingual CVC novel, published in 1987. The novel *Odju d'Agu* is a celebration of life on the island of Santiago. George Lang writes of *Odju d'Agu*:

> The most ambitious work in the Crioulo canon and one of few sustained works in creoles world-wide is Manuel Veiga's *Oju d'Agu*, a quintessential *ethnotext*, a term the Martinican Creole writer Raphael Confiant applies to the (first) novel in (French Guyanese) Creole, *Atipa* (1885) by Alfred Parépou (Confiant 1989:207). According to Confiant, the ethnotext is a universal genre found "at the dawn of all [ethnic] literatures." Two more criteria further specify the Creole ethnotext: the text must be written in "basilectal" Creole, that is in a dialect as far as possible from Portuguese (in this case); and oral genres must be blended into the text, not only in order to record and conserve them, but to demonstrate their continuing relevance within literate culture. The *Kauberdianu* in *Oju d'Agu* and the phonetic alphabet in which it is couched are as independent from Portuguese as Veiga could make them, and though the various stories within the plot are contemporary in flavor, they incorporate a panoply of oral modes, such that it readily serves as an encyclopedia of Cape Verdean folk discourse. . . . Like Tomé Varela's heroine Bibiña Kabral, the principal narrator of *Oju d'Agu*, Palu di Jója, is a *griot*, the African tale teller in whom is vested the collective wisdom of his or her society. The African roots of Cape Verdean culture are further underscored by the allegorical exploration of the neighboring continent's past to which the novel turns near its end. Yet *Oju d'Agu* ultimately conveys a more revolutionary message. . . . Whatever final critical reception time holds for his novel, Manuel Veiga has furnished future readers and writers of Crioulo with a model it will not be easy to rival. (George Lang, "Literary Crioulo Since Independence in São Tomé, Guinea-Bissau and Cape Verde," 58.)

Veiga's novel draws on what, to him, are important symbols of caboverdianidade, using the "deepest" or "most African" variant of CVC and championing the African heritage of Cabo Verde.

There were also numerous influential poetic, theatric, and fiction works published in CVC during the 1980s. They proliferated and diversified the existing literature, exemplifying dialects from different islands, and further privileged the historically neglected oral traditions of the majority population. Artur Vieira wrote and produced the play *Galafo* in 1980 in the dialect of the island of Brava. A collection of poetry by Kaká Barboza, entitled *Vinti xintidu letradu na kriolu* and published in 1984, explores many pan-Africanist themes in relation to Cape Verdean culture, utilizing the dialect of the island of Santiago.[28]

Tomé Varela da Silva, an academic employed by the Cape Verdean government to develop oral tradition and linguistic studies, also began publishing prolifically in the 1980s, quickly becoming one of the most important proponents of CVC writing.[29] His work ranges from Afro- and Cabo Verde–centric fiction and poetry to collected oral traditions and biographical portraits of popular singers from the islands of Brava, Fogo, Maio, and Santiago.[30] The works and research were supported by the Cape Verdean Institute for Culture—a government department devoted to the rigorous study and support of Cape Verdean culture—and published by the Instituto Nacional do Livro e do Disco (the National Institute of Book and Record), which subsidized such projects to document and celebrate the work of noteworthy performers. Two are oral histories and biographies of previously unrecognized women performers that document their enormously important places as tradition bearers: Nasia Gomi and Bibinha Kabral, longtime practitioners of the Santiago Island–specific *finason, sanbuna,* and *batuku* musical genres.[31] The books include introductions to the orthography used, biographies and photographs of the performers, and extensive written records of their creative work. The oral stories recorded in *Na bóka noti* were collected through extensive fieldwork and folklore collection, including stories like the popular folktales of *Nho Lobu ku Xibinhu,* stories about a clever wolf, Lobu, and his naughty nephew, Xibinhu, regularly told throughout Cabo Verde.[32] These are still among the most popular CVC language books (each now in its third or fourth volume and at least second edition) sold in Cabo Verde and the diaspora. Silva's contribution to the promotion of CVC and the recording and celebration of expressive oral traditions is immense.

During this time, as before independence, numerous anthologies and literary journals continued to come and go, and they were most often bilingual in Portuguese and CVC.[33] Financial, staffing, and distribution difficulties have long plagued these initiatives and, for this reason, none of these publications has been successfully released regularly in the long term. A number of poets published in CVC as well, such as Corsino Fortes, David Hopffer

Almada, Arménio Vieira, and José Luís Hopffer Almada, further promoting the written use of CVC.[34] These authors did not necessarily publish in a standardized orthography, however, leading to increased confusion over orthographic and literary practice in the language. Regardless, their work led to increased interest and demonstrated *agu na boka* (thirst in the mouth) for the study and promotion of CVC.

In 1989, a forum was held in the capital city of Praia on the subject of "Alfabetização Bilingue" (Bilingual Literacy), which brought together literacy teachers, professors, writers, and linguists to debate the appropriate educational model for CVC literacy and to reevaluate "the hat alphabet" orthography proposed in 1979. It was decided that the orthography would be difficult to accept for sociocultural and practical reasons and a Comissão Consultiva (Advisory Commission) was formed for the purpose of evaluating how it could be improved.[35] Out of this came a number of important suggestions that would be revisited later, but the etymological and phonological debate raged on in the public and academic spheres. Veiga has argued that, despite the publication of many scholarly accounts of CVC in the 1970s and 1980s, the major contributions in the language were in the areas of literary and musical production and creation, where orthographic debate was less significant than the central questions related to identity and culture.[36] This further supports the hypothesis that CVC language, literature, and music must be understood as mutually sustaining and as integral to discussions of caboverdianidade.

The 1990s

The 1990s marked an unprecedented time for writing, scholarly study, political interventions, and nonprofit educational activism for CVC. A number of literary works were published by authors such as Kaká Barboza, Eutrópio Lima da Cruz, Euricles Rodrigues, and Tomé Varela da Silva focusing heavily on CVC poetry, lyrics, and oral tradition, leading to increased popularity of reading in the language.[37] More and more, these publications utilized the newly proposed standard orthography for writing in CVC, ALUPEC. Some authors even included reading and writing guides in their book prefaces in an attempt to make CVC literacy more accessible. At the same time, scholarly linguistic studies of the language were also published with increasing frequency, including some of the foundational texts of contemporary CVC scholarship. These consisted of a Portuguese language grammar of CVC, dictionaries in both Portuguese and French, as well as dissertations focusing on CVC syntax and grammar by Marlyse Baptista, Nicolas Quint, and Manuel Veiga, who would become leaders in the field of Cape Verdean Creole language studies.[38] Cape Verdean linguist Dulce Almada Duarte also published her *Bilinguismo ou diglossia?*, which included a series of essays demonstrating that the majority of the Cape Verdean population existed in a diglossic situation, where one language was marked as high (or formal) and another as low (informal), rather than the bilingual one of linguistic parity historically romanticized by the Portuguese-speaking elite.[39]

Despite its rising scholarly stature, CVC remained a contested topic in official circles. In 1993, the government-funded Department of Linguistics of the National Institute of Culture concluded that the lack of consensus on the "hat alphabet" orthography would be a major impediment to the promotion of CVC and literacy education.[40] A proposal was made to the then minister of culture, Ondina Ferreira, to create a Grupo para a padronização do alfabeto (Group for the Standardization of the Alphabet) consisting of writers, educators, and linguists. This group then presented a 220-page proposal entitled *Proposta de Bases do Alfabeto Unificado para a Escrita do Caboverdiano*, which proposed the updated phonetic/phonological orthography called ALUPEC in 1994.[41] This marked a major turning point in the writing of CVC as the new orthography was significantly more accessible and usable, and enthusiasts quickly adopted it for use throughout Cabo Verde and the diaspora.

In addition to these efforts on scholarly fronts, the Cape Verdean government released a number of important resolutions and pieces of legislation during this decade. Government resolution no. 8/96 of 1996 called for the government to set research goals and determine which next steps would be necessary to make CVC an official national language alongside Portuguese. Following this, Resolution no. 8/98 of 1998 declared: "Cape Verdean Creole will be valorized, progressively as a language of instruction" (my translation). Later in the same year, the Cape Verdean government released a law decree:

> Being that creole is the language of the quotidian in Cabo Verde and an essential element of national identity, the harmonious development of the Country that necessarily includes the development and valorization [of the language] will not be possible without the standardization of the writing of Creole or be it called the Cape Verdean Language. Thus, the standardization of the alphabet constitutes the first step toward the standardization of writing. So, in the use of the faculty conferred by the paragraph a) of article 216 of the Constitution of the Republic, the Government decrees the following:

Article 11: The Unified Alphabet for the Writing of the Cape Verdean language (Creole) is approved experimentally, from here on designated ALUPEC, and the Bases are published in annex to the present document. (Resolution no. 8/98, Boletim Oficial 10 [Praia: Governo de Cabo Verde, 1998].)

These pieces of legislation marked major turning points toward the promotion and officialization of CVC. They formally recognized its importance to Cape Verdean national identity or caboverdianidade and to the continued development of the country, as well as the need for orthographic standardization and education. However, as will be seen below, their effect for the general population of Cabo Verde has remained limited.

Meanwhile, in the diaspora, the Cape Verdean American community of the United States continued with coordinated efforts to promote CVC. In 1996, the Capeverdean Creole Institute (CCI) was founded in Boston, Massachusetts, as a nonprofit organization dedicated to the promotion of the Cape Verdean language. As described in its literature, the CCI "focuses on active support for the recognition of Capeverdean Creole as an official language in the Republic of Cabo Verde, the implementation of a standardized orthography (ALUPEC), and curriculum development in Cape Verdean bilingual programs in the US and abroad."[42] Though CCI's financial difficulties led it to become a mostly defunct organization in the 2010s, its members have proven important and influential throughout Cabo Verde and the diaspora, through their work in research, education, and language-promotion activities.

The 1990s were also a time when CVC took serious abuse from exceptionalist thinkers. Even as linguists came to question the typical Creole paradigms, denigrating attitudes toward Cape Verdean culture and language persisted. The work of one linguist employed by France's Centre National de Recherche Scientifique (National Center for Scientific Research), Nicolas Quint, stands out. Quint writes disparagingly of CVC as a "very young" language of only a few thousand words with limited options to express complex ideas. He specifically laments the "lexical, and even conceptual, poverty" of CVC and the ways the language supposedly constrains speakers, remarking, "Often, one is surprised by the Badiais's [residents of the Cape Verdean island of Santiago] lack of curiosity. Westerners find them stupid or passive. But how can intelligence be stimulated in an environment so cramped and with so little variety?"[43]

DeGraff offers a critique of Quint as a scholar trapped by the tropes associated with Creole exceptionalism. Quint refers to CVC as a mixed and therefore impoverished language. While he apparently tempers his remarks by suggesting that he does not believe Cape Verdeans and their language to be more stupid or less expressive than Europeans and their languages, he explicitly states otherwise. He echoes historical assumptions about Creole societies as impoverished, simplistic groups whose Creole languages are the most degraded and primitive examples of their inferiority. In so doing, Quint shows an attachment to the outdated idea of Creole languages as "black speech"—Cabo Verde's form once being called "Negro Portuguese" and worse—which leads to problematic, racially laden statements about such topics as the "exotic mulatto" women of Cabo Verde.[44] Quint's ethnographic turn shows a faulty understanding of the relationship between language and race. In essence, Quint returns to the central ideas of early "degenerists": he compares Creole languages to European ones, assuming all along that European languages are the civilized and developed yardsticks by which we should measure all other languages and, by extension, cultures. Such an attitude is especially problematic as Quint has never publicly retracted his statements, continues to write and translate CVC works, and is cited widely by fledgling scholars.[45]

Amidst this ongoing scholarly debate, official valorization of CVC fared only marginally better. In July 1999, the PAICV again brought up the issue of officialization of CVC, this time in the process of constitutional revision. The movement for officializing the language was not passed due to insufficient votes in favor from Movimento para Democracia, or the Movement for Democracy, the party that was then in the majority. As a result, the Cape Verdean National Assembly merely sanctioned "the creation of conditions for [CVC's] officialization and parity with the Portuguese language" in the constitutional revision of 1999.[46] Yet again, the government gave lip service to the promotion of CVC without any executive prescription for how this would be carried out. Still, Veiga argues that this was an important step for language planning and that it helped empower advocates to develop concrete initiatives that included stimulating writing, training teachers, creating and equipping teams for the production of pedagogical materials, incentivizing applied investigation, and awarding scholarships in the linguistic domains.[47]

2000–2016

In the past sixteen years, dozens of contributions have been made in and about CVC, ranging from scholarly to artistic to journalistic to educational, both advancing the development of the language in terms of orthography and education, and highlighting the debates that continue to hinder efforts toward parity with Portuguese. In the realm of literature, a number of important publications included CVC.[48] Cape Verdean anthropologist Humberto Lima published *Un bes tinha Nhu Lobu ku Xibinhu*, a collection of traditional stories recorded in CVC from Fogo and Santiago. Tomé Varela da Silva published a large anthology of contemporary literature entitled *Pós-Claridosos*, which included several CVC writers such as Carlos Barbosa, Euricles Rodrigues, David Hopffer Almada, José Luís Hopffer Almada, Artur Vieira, Manuel Veiga, and Tomé Varela. Kaká Barboza continued his contribution to CVC with the publication of a collection of poetry in ALU-PEC entitled *Konfison na Finata*.[49]

Linguistic and sociolinguistic study of CVC, too, has matured in the past decade. In 2000, Manuel Veiga published *Le créole du Cap Vert: étude grammaticale descriptive et contrastive*, an expanded structural grammar of CVC written in French. In 2002, a team of linguists directed by German scholar Jürgen Lang published *Dicionário do crioulo da ilha de Santiago (Cabo Verde)*, an expansive CVC-German-Portuguese dictionary. Harvard-trained Cape Verdean American linguist Marlyse Baptista published a book based on her doctoral dissertation entitled "The Syntax of Capeverdean Creole" in the same year. In 2004, Manuel Veiga published *A construção do bilinguismo*, a series of essays devoted to how bilingualism could be attained in Cabo Verde. Maria de Fátima Fernandes Lopes Sanches, a student trained at Cabo Verde's own Instituto Superior de Educação, published her thesis research in "Atitude de alguns cabo-verdianos perante a sua lingua materna" in 2005, a sociolinguistic study of attitudes toward CVC among native speakers in Cabo Verde. These publications were accompanied by a number of unpublished theses and dissertations dealing in part or whole with CVC language issues.

Pedagogical and reference texts for learning CVC have also been published and popularized in the past fifteen years. Manuel da Luz Gonçalves and Leila Andrade, both prominent Cape Verdean community leaders and educators in the United States, published the first textbook and English-CVC language learning manual, which has since been updated to include CDs for aural practice.[50] Gonçalves's self-published *Cape Verdean Creole-English Dictionary* in 2016, a CVC-English reference with over 40,000 words, also marks a major contribution. Quint's *Parlons capverdien* (2003) and the children's books cited earlier are also a part of this trend. Manuel Veiga published *O caboverdiano em 45 lições*, a grammatical primer on CVC written for those literate in Portuguese. A group of young artists and authors even formed a group to publish comic books devoted to the traditional *Nho Lobu ku Xibinhu* stories mentioned above, geared toward young children and sold at low prices.[51] They have become a popular gift among Cape Verdean youth. These broad language promotion and development contributions, among many others, have further advanced knowledge of CVC in the academy and general public.

Translation work in CVC has significantly progressed since two American members of the organization SIL International: Partners in Language Development were assigned to work in Cabo Verde in the late 1990s. Their initial work in Cabo Verde focused on documentation, statistical analysis of literacy rates, and sociolinguistic attitudes toward the language. However, after several years of working to document the language, they decided to work with members of local churches to develop writing in CVC. In the early 2000s, they began a long-term Bible translation project, enlisting volunteer clergymen from four Christian denominations to work as team translators.[52] Over the next several years this project developed slowly but with the most thorough organization and documentation of the translation and orthographic process to date in CVC. As a result, multiple publications have been released, including the Gospel of Luke and the Acts of the Apostles.[53] The enthusiasm behind this project is immense, both from the team of volunteer translators trained and equipped by the SIL staffers and from the large numbers of Cape Verdean readers who purchase these translations, which regularly sell out. The organization of translators working on this Bible translation have also published several valuable pamphlets devoted to learning to read in CVC (aimed toward native CVC speakers seeking greater literacy) and a teacher's manual.

Also educational in nature is the increased activity around the teaching and learning of CVC at United States universities. Since 2002, numerous classes have sprung up throughout the New England area devoted to the study of CVC. Currently, it is taught at Bristol Community College, University of Massachusetts–Dartmouth, Massasoit Community College, and Harvard University. The course is offered for credit at these universities, and it has formally been recognized by the University of Massachusetts–Dartmouth as a requirement for a major in Cape Verdean studies, where students must study four semesters of the language to complete their course requirements.[54] In all of these venues, CVC is taught using ALUPEC and the grammatical principles that have been semistandardized by its supporters known as the Alupekadoris. The students who choose to study CVC range in background and interest. Many are heritage learners, either descendants of Cape Verdeans who would like to learn the language for the first time or fluent speakers who would like to improve their literacy skills. Others are not of Cape Verdean descent but have an interest in learning the language due to regional, work-related, or other interests, such as health professionals studying CVC to better serve their patients. Though classes are desired at other venues where large numbers of heritage learners reside, there are only three active CVC instructors in the New England area at present, and their time is increasingly limited due to their many teaching commitments. There is no form of CVC instructor training yet available in the United States.

A number of other New England–based universities and libraries have made it a major goal to improve their collections of materials on Cabo Verde and now boast large collections of CVC language materials. These institutions include but are not limited to the public libraries of Boston, Brockton, New Bedford, as well as the university collections of Harvard, Brown, Yale, Boston University, Rhode Island College, and the University of Massachusetts–Dartmouth. It is most often the case that the cause of CVC is taken up at universities and libraries that cater to Cape Verdean communities or that have a history of strong African studies or Lusophone studies programs.

The rising interest in CVC among institutions of higher education could not, however, overcome the long simmering tensions around bilingual education at lower levels. Despite the success of thousands of students and hundreds of teachers since its implementation thirty years before, the first official CVC program faced extinction in 2003. In that year, "Question 2" of the "Unz bill" outlawed virtually all bilingual programs in Massachusetts.[55] Interestingly, of all bilingual programs that persist in the state (due to loopholes in the law and waivers), most are CVC-English programs. However, the vast majority of Cape Verdean students enrolled in these programs are left with virtually no native language support, and most of the specialized staff have been reassigned to positions that do not utilize their language skills. The loss of the Massachusetts program was a blow to advocates of CVC, shifting official promotion of the language permanently to Cabo Verde.

Cape Verdean government intervention in CVC promotion during the 2000s has been significant, though with still little in the way of practical literacy effect for the population. After years of demonstrated success with the orthography in the United States, ALUPEC was finally signed into law in 1998 as the official orthography for CVC in Cabo Verde for a trial period of five years. Its trial period expired in 2003 with little notice, and two years passed before further action was taken. Shortly before its expiration in 2002 at a forum about "Caminhos da valorização da lingua materna" (Paths to the Valorization of the Maternal Language), the then president of the National Assembly, Dr. Aristides Lima, said:

> The political power must urgently do more than it has done until now. It is called to eventually complete this exercise of cultural disalienation. It is called to recognize the language most spoken by the Cape Verdean

community with a status of equal dignity to that of Portuguese. It is called to recognize for each one of us the right to education in the Cape Verdean language at the side of education in Portuguese; to recognize the right of the use of *crioulo* in correspondence and official documents and even the right to an equal presence of *crioulo* in way of social communication from the State. This is not some favor. It is the seed to implement the imperative of the human right to language and to recognize the right of equality of the two languages that characterize our culture. (Manuel Veiga, "O Crioulo De Cabo Verde: Afirmação e Visão Prospectiva," in *Cabo Verde: Origins Da Sua Sociedade e Do Seu Crioulo,* ed. Jürgen Lang [Tübingen, Germany: Narr Francke Attempto Verlag Gmbh + Co. KG, 2006], 33.)

This was one of the most powerful calls for CVC language rights by a Cape Verdean elected official to date.

In 2005, following significant debate between the country's two largest political parties, PAICV and MPD, the Cape Verdean government passed another ambitious resolution for the "valorization of the Cape Verdean language."[56] The resolution includes provisions allowing for the "creation of conditions for the officialization of CVC" and for the promotion of CVC as a language of instruction because all citizens have a right to use their native language in all walks of life. It recognizes ALUPEC as a viable system for writing in CVC while also allowing the usage of alternative writing models "as long as they are presented in a systematized and scientific way." Simply a resolution, this document will remain ineffectual until there is more legislation to provide strategy for or delegate execution of tasks. In 2006, the prime minister of Cabo Verde, José Maria Neves, decorated CCI for its years of service and advocacy for CVC. Ironically, the decoration speech was given in Portuguese due to perception that the formality of the ceremony excluded CVC.[57]

There was, however, one noteworthy victory for linguistic activists. In 2009, ALUPEC was officially recognized by government decree.[58] This decree was first hotly debated in the National Assembly during another constitutional revision, when the language was unable to garner enough votes to be made official, but the evidence surrounding development of the orthography was convincing enough to members of Parliament to make it official. Moreover, the Cape Verdean Institute of Higher Education and University of Cabo Verde now support a department of Estudos Cabo-verdianos e Portugueses (Cape Verdean and Portuguese Studies) in which ALUPEC is taught, along with classes in sociolinguistics, linguistics, and language pedagogy. While the Cape Verdean government is certainly taking decisive steps with these pieces of legislation, CVC remains unofficial, and all legislation regarding such, all schooling, and all communication in official capacities is still required to be conducted in Portuguese. As of yet, there is no movement toward introducing the use of CVC in Cape Verdean primary education beyond occasional pilot programs, though a number of scholars and pedagogues strongly advocate that it be done.[59]

Though legislation has lagged, Cape Verdean popular media has contributed enormously to the valorization of CVC. The Ministério da Agricultura e Pescas (Ministry of Agriculture and Fishing) has a weekly CVC radio program on agriculture called *Nos gentis* (Our People). Rádio de Cabo Verde gives daily news in CVC in addition to its Portuguese language programming; it even invites calls from the diaspora in CVC during weekend programming. PraiaFM, the most popular radio station on the island of Santiago, has even gone so far as to create a Web site, streaming news, and documentary broadcasts in CVC. In addition, virtually all Cape Verdean diaspora radio programs are conducted in the language (except for the occasional program among the diaspora in Portugal), as are the advertisements and the music played on these stations. One prominent figure, the proprietor of a major radio station in Cabo Verde, explained the decision in terms of best serving its audience. He explained, "If we did not broadcast in CVC, the language that is spoken here, the language of almost all of the music that we play, people simply would not listen. And we are working to switch everything to ALUPEC—our website, our advertising copy, etc. It is official and we feel strongly about using it."[60]

The use of CVC on Cape Verdean television has also started to increase, though the majority of programming is still in Portuguese due to dependence on satellite feeds from Brazil, Portugal, and Lusophone Africa. The daily Cape Verdean news programming is announced entirely in Portuguese, but more and more interviews are now conducted in CVC. Televisão de Cabo Verde (Cabo Verde Television), the only Cape Verdean television network, has also sponsored a small number of programs in CVC. One, called *Kultura* (Culture), which concentrated on art and traditional culture, was popular but stopped being recorded due to financial difficulties. Another produced by the Ministry of Health became quite popular. It involves weekly interviews with local doctors and public health officials on questions of importance to the Cape Verdean population. When a dengue fever outbreak occurred in Cabo Verde in 2009, this program provided an essential public health service to the population. Musicians contributed by creating short music videos to air on television and radio in CVC, singing about how to avoid dengue exposure and destroy mosquito breeding grounds. Throughout the summer of 2009, the Ministry of Culture also aired short television spots to teach the Cape Verdean public how to write in ALUPEC, some of which are available on YouTube.[61]

In 2009, ALUPEC was officially recognized by government decree (Decreto-Lei no. 8/2009). This came as the result of a roundtable held in Praia in November 2008, in which practitioners of ALUPEC were brought together to report on their experiences and argue for the utility of the language. This decree was first hotly debated in the National Assembly during another constitutional revision, when the language was unable to garner enough votes to be made official, but the evidence surrounding development of the orthography was convincing enough to members of Parliament to make just the orthography official. Moreover, the Cape Verdean Institute of Higher Education and University of Cabo Verde now support a department of Estudos Cabo-verdianos e Portugueses (Cape Verdean and Portuguese Studies) in which ALUPEC is taught, along with classes in sociolinguistics, linguistics, and language pedagogy.

Another important development of the past decade is the introduction of the Prémio Pedro Cardoso (Pedro Cardoso Prize), named for one of the most ardent but underappreciated supporters of CVC, which awards 3,000 euros each year to the best piece of writing produced in CVC. The prize emerged from discussions at a Capeverdean Creole Institute cultural exchange and festival held in 2008. It sought to both incentivize and reward literary production in CVC, as a number of similar prizes exist for writing in Portuguese and have been won by Cape Verdean authors such as Arménio Vieira and Mário Lúcio. The first Prémio Pedro Cardoso awarded in 2009 went to the Cape Verdean José Luís Tavares, a resident of Portugal, for his CVC fiction work *Tenpu di Dilubri.* The prize marks another step in designating the use of CVC as a literary language deserving of its own awards and noteworthy writers.

Indeed, written work remains perhaps the most active space for debate and discussion of CVC valorization. A number of newspapers such as *A Semana, A Nação,* and *Expresso das Ilhas* regularly include columns, opinion pieces, cartoons, or poems in CVC. For several years, Manuel Veiga has edited irregularly the column "Na lingua di téra" for the newspaper *A Semana,* a CVC-only column devoted to issues of language and culture. Marciano Moreira, the inspector general for the Ministry of Finance and a longtime CVC activist, now has a weekly column in the newspaper *A Nação,* which is distributed in Cabo Verde and New England. Moreira's work is significant, as his is the first consistent column in CVC in Cape Verdean history.

Internet-based journalism and social media have provided CVC with a broader written reach, with Web sites like FORCV.com and caboverdeonline.com (both based in the United States) occasionally publishing articles and poetry in CVC. Web sites and social networking apparatuses have perhaps proven the most democratic space for CVC use yet, with Cape Verdean youth participating primarily in CVC written in an ALUPEC-like manner. Since youth do not receive formal training in ALUPEC, they adopt certain elements of ALUPEC in their writing, using them in nonstandard ways. It is increasingly common to see CVC used on Facebook, Twitter, Instagram, and in text messages, blogs, and wikis. Indeed, many of the youth I have interviewed prize these spaces as ones in which they can express themselves fully in their language of choice.

Debates and Perceptions

A number of important debates and perceptions inform the continued promotion of and challenges to CVC. M. F. Valkhoff, Baptista, Sanches, and Veiga have all taken up these debates and perceptions to some degree in their research and writing.[62] The resulting studies have on most occasions been based on surveys conducted on small populations and have concluded varying degrees of bilingualism, acceptance of possible CVC officialization, and relationship with the Portuguese language in the Cape Verdean context.[63] Since I am primarily interested in qualitative analysis of CVC diglossia, I have focused my energies on ethnography through interviews, participant observation, analysis of published materials, and social engagement over the past decade. Below, I argue that based on this research, we can posit four major debates that present ongoing challenges to CVC promotion. These debates are closely linked with exceptionalist attitudes toward the language as well as national and diasporic discussions on crioulidade and caboverdianidade. These debates will have to be carefully considered by advocates for CVC if they want to create meaningful social change. Dialogue with and education designed for the general public will be paramount to addressing the language question.

The first major debate focuses on variant choice—the particular dialect of CVC that will become the written standard. Quint is not the only present-day thinker to profess racially based attitudes about Cape Verdeans as an extension of knowledge of their language. Many Cape Verdeans themselves adopt these pernicious attitudes. One prominent example is the racialization of the *badiu* group in Cabo Verde. The word *badiu* refers to people from the southernmost islands of Cabo Verde, especially Santiago, who are typically believed by Cape Verdeans to be more "African," as they generally have darker skin and speak a more "African-sounding" dialect of

CVC. *Badiu* comes from the Portuguese *vadio*, which means *vagabond* or *vagrant* and was originally used to refer to Africans who escaped plantation life and ended up in maroon communities. Among linguists, the badiu dialect of CVC has often romantically been referred to as the "purest" or "most African" version of CVC, thus designating it as best for study of the language.[64]

The badiu stigma holds strong in Cape Verdean society today. People are highly resistant to standardization of CVC for a variety of reasons, chief among them the question of whether a standardized orthography and grammar will privilege a badiu or non-badiu ("more African" or "more Portuguese") dialect. One Cape Verdean educator from the island of São Vicente, which is widely considered more "Portuguese," expressed this issue plainly: "If they teach Kriolu, which dialect will they teach? I could not stand to be called a badiu and to be required to learn badiu speech. Look at how light-skinned I am! I am not badiu and will not speak Kriolu like one."[65] This persistent problem of synonymizing *Creole*, *black*, and *degenerate* plays out in real life and in debates around the standardization and officialization of CVC.

Lang explains the other side of the debate over the concept of badiu, which celebrates Cape Verdean liberation and "connotes the deepest strains of Cape Verdean authenticity, and is associated with a reservoir of oral and musical traditions upon which a distinct national culture could be predicated . . . as emblematic victim of the harsh dichotomy upon which Cape Verdean history was founded, the *Badiu* provides a powerful reminder of past oppression and a symbol of collective liberation."[66] In other words, the work of many Cape Verdean writers and thinkers has involved a glorification of the badiu figure as truest to Cape Verdean history and symbolic of freedom from colonial neglect and injustice. This has proven a very important part of the growth of CVC literature over the past several decades and the development of an idea of caboverdianidade in relation to language valorization. However, such celebration of the badiu concept stands at odds with the beliefs of some Cape Verdeans and with island-specific chauvinism.

Related to this debate is the second major debate, which is over the role of government in language promotion and officialization in Cabo Verde. In general, the PAICV political party has been associated with complete support and activism for CVC. Many individuals who play a prominent role in developing CVC are well-known supporters of PAICV, Barboza, Veiga, and Silva, all natives of Santiago Island among them. MPD, the other political party, has often been accused of being against CVC officialization or at least wavering on the issue. However, many of the major pieces of CVC language-planning legislation have also taken place under MPD, as out-lined earlier in this chapter. Thus, both parties must be understood to have undertaken serious work for the promotion of the language.

A common fear about the role of government in CVC officialization was expressed by one Cape Verdean official, who, when I asked him why he was hesitant to adopt CVC as an official language, said, "Kriolu is just a dia-lect of Portuguese. We are speaking a bad Portuguese here and if we teach Kriolu in schools, our students could not learn Portuguese properly."[67] The official continued, "Those who want to impose the use of Kriolu on Cape Verdeans are the real racists. They want us to continue to speak like Africans, when we are not." He was implying that those Cape Verdean offi-cials who advocate most vehemently for the officialization of the language aim to hold Cabo Verde back by imprisoning it with an inferior, impure language.[68] While this undoubtedly stems from exceptionalist attitudes toward CVC, it also reflects the pragmatic notion that Portuguese is a part of Cape Verdean heritage, and an important one for international rela-tions, education, and more.[69]

Others see the government's role in supporting orthography as prob-lematic, characterizing ALUPEC as an unnecessary or incomplete interven-tion into a still developing language. A member of MPD explained that he writes CVC with the Portuguese orthography and does not like ALUPEC as he thinks, "Language has to grow over time. You can't just say, politi-cally, that something has to be one way immediately. The two languages are historically linked; you don't have to separate them. With one law [rati-fying ALUPEC], you can't resolve a problem."[70] A fellow MPD member continued:

> Today, the real problem in Cabo Verde is Portuguese. No one has a prob-lem speaking Kriolu. They can write it if they want to in their own way. Everywhere everyone is speaking Kriolu; if you go to the Ministry of For-eign Affairs, you hear the functionaries speaking only in Kriolu. It's only when they give an interview on television that they speak in Portuguese.
> . . .
> Now the ALUPEC law has come out, but it's still not agreed upon. ALU-PEC is ugly. You see all those words written tightly; strange. I dislike the use of the letter "k" and the fact that "c" has practically disappeared. . . .
> Really, this is all because of PAICV and Manuel Veiga, the Minister of Culture [at the time]. In fact, everyone working on ALUPEC, and there are only three or four of them, they are all from Santiago. If PAICV loses, if these Santiaguense are out of power, this will all just go away.
> Of course, there is great value to writing in Kriolu, because it is our cul-ture, our stories. But this is not how it should be done. (Alberto Duarte interviewed by Carla Martin, Praia, Cabo Verde, October 7, 2009.)

This opinion may be based partially in political affiliation, but it is also likely weighted by island of origin, racial beliefs, education level, and the perceived importance of Portuguese history in Cabo Verde and the Cape Verdean language.

Yet another member of Parliament, this time from PAICV, has been a strong supporter of ALUPEC since nearly its inception. He told me, over the course of several interviews, about his beliefs on the language, and responded to many critiques.

> It is necessary to apply rules to language. "K" exists in every European language, whether they use it or not (Portuguese included!), so why are people so upset about "k"? People don't understand that we need rules. Every language has at one time or another created rules and a code for that language. . . .
>
> The letter "s" in place of "ç" is another big fight—people don't like change. They're used to writing in Portuguese; they want to stay linked to Kriolu's Portuguese origins. We have had only thirty plus years of independence. The values of colonization have stronger footing than the values of nativism at times. . . .
>
> But there are major contradictions in the opinions. For example, everyone operates political campaigns in Kriolu. If not, the people will say: "Look at that man how he is making of himself as if he is a white Portuguese." The contradiction is that these same politicians insist on Portuguese for everything else, excluding the people who got them elected. . . .
>
> Other people reject ALUPEC out of jealousy. Everyone wants to put their name or mark on something, so unless they can say that it was them that made the alphabet for Kriolu, they won't accept anything. . . .
> (Gregório Fontes interviewed by Carla Martin, Praia, Cabo Verde, October 7, 2009.)

Indeed, the partisan nature of CVC debates is such that many argue that it is PAICV and the badiu dialect that are to blame for CVC's lack of officialization. Surely the CVC language contributions of the late 1990s and 2000s have demonstrated that the CVC valorization process is much more diverse both in terms of partisan politics and island variation. Nevertheless, these perceptions remain and must be combated in the future.

Related to the debates on variant choice and government intervention, many CVC speakers I interviewed during this research insist that they would be in favor of officialization of the language were it not for ALUPEC. In other words, for etymological reasons, they very much prefer the Portuguese-derived orthographies of the past. For example, one of the most stubborn and frustrating parts of the debate over the standardization and officialization of CVC comes in the form of the letter *k* and the idea of Portuguese "survivals" in CVC. Innumerous times, I have witnessed debates erupt over the choice of the letter *k* in ALUPEC over the letter *c*. ALUPEC was developed to be a phonetic orthography, therefore eliminating the need for the letter *c* (*k* and *s* suffice for the two sounds represented by *c*). Yet, because much of the vocabulary in CVC is cognate or false cognate with Portuguese, many people believe that *c* should remain and the words should be spelled exactly as they are in Portuguese. This survivalist trope has a powerful grip on Cape Verdean vocabulary as many people believe it is simply archaic Portuguese vocabulary that has survived, though adulterated, in CVC. A prominent Cape Verdean musician once told me, "We have to know where our words come from. They are Portuguese words. Crioulo is Portuguese. 'K' is not Portuguese."[71] Yet this is not so: the "original" words, though similar, are distant by at least half a millennium and have come to take on culturally specific meanings and phonemically different sounds. The quote above also bespeaks two common misconceptions in folk linguistics: that etymology and morphology are one and the same and that language change is either diachronic or synchronic.

Of course, the vast majority who prefer the old-fashioned way of writing CVC are people who speak Portuguese fluently. It has become a common joke among opponents of ALUPEC to ask, "Why is it not spelled 'ALU-PEK?'" In fact, most often, the acronym ALUPEC is written in Portuguese (Alfabeto Unificado para a Escrita do Caboverdiano). The name can be and is sometimes written in CVC, as Alfabetu Unifikadu pa Skrita di Kabuverdianu, but this renders the corresponding acronym of ALUPEK incorrect or rather derivative of the acronym from the Portuguese name. This naming and acronym incongruity reflects ambivalence on the part of ALUPEC's designers and enthusiasts on how best to represent the orthography to an audience whose literacy is relegated primarily to the Portuguese language. It is a problem in the representation of the writing system and must be addressed moving forward.

Many CVC speakers actually prefer the use of *k* as a nod toward Cabo Verde's African roots. Some Cape Verdeans feel that through the use of *k* they join the ranks of other pan-African movements and throw off the European imposition of the letter *c* in the word *Africa*. The *k* symbolizes all "Afrikans" (at least those using a Latin-derived alphabet), dispersed throughout the world by European forces, coming back together again. This is also a debate over a "French"/"Portuguese" versus an "Anglo-Saxon" appearance. Schiefflin and Doucet explain that *k*: "not only represents the danger of U.S. imperialism, but also has even been claimed to represent the threat of communism."[72] In Cabo Verde, such supporters are most commonly associated with PAICV, the party that has the most explicitly socialist leanings. Yet the *k* debates ring eerily similar to discussions of degeneracy and impurity.

Still other advocates claim a sort of middle ground in relation to the writing of CVC, for different reasons. Mário Lúcio, the current minister of culture and a longtime prominent political official, author, and composer-performer, is perhaps the most outspoken proponent of a middle ground. He agrees that CVC needs one standardized method of writing, but disagrees with the way in which ALUPEC has allowed for two variants, Barlavento and Sotavento (mostly Santiago). Simultaneously, he finds it strange that those who are vehemently against ALUPEC have yet to make any other standardized proposal of their own. "It seems to me that they are not just against ALUPEC, if you know what I mean." Ultimately, he argues for a proposal that would meet somewhere between ALUPEC and Portuguese orthography as a compromise given the complex political embattlement that CVC faces: "All of this debate about the alphabet is unfortunate because thirty years for you to battle to standardize your language . . . the language is already old! We did it wrong. We started with the technical and then we went to politics. This is very bad. . . ."[73]

Another important debate over CVC orthography has to do with the written representation of particular dialects. For example, which version of the pronoun *you*—*bu* on some islands or *bezote* on others—should prevail in a "standardized CVC"? This emphasis again represents a reliance on the myth of the standard. Most educators have chosen a compromise, teaching ALUPEC and vocabulary with attention to major dialects from the Barlavento and Sotavento island groups.[74] Yet many Cape Verdeans in Cabo Verde and the diaspora still find this to be an impassible problem.[75] For all of these reasons, in Cabo Verde, a consistently official orthography has yet to settle. ALUPEC remains little understood technically beyond specialists and enthusiasts. The creators of ALUPEC were quickly swept up by immigration, essential government rebuilding projects, family, and more, and these events and activities interrupted doctoral programs and linguistic activism. Also, the Cape Verdean diaspora is so much larger than and so physically distant from Cabo Verde that many of those qualified and powerful enough to ignite and carry out these discussions live outside the country. The Atlantic Ocean lies between them and the officialization of CVC.

One CVC-English bilingual teacher, himself a graduate of the Boston Public Schools bilingual program, told me:

Starting these [bilingual] programs was hard because so many people have the attitude that studying Kabuverdianu is like wasting time. But once we showed them that bilingual education teaches the kids English better, they realized that being bi- or even multi-lingual is a plus. Now, my cousins in Cabo Verde are jealous that I can write them e-mails in Kabuverdianu and they don't feel comfortable doing the same. (Gerson De Pina interviewed by Carla Martin, Boston, Massachusetts, September 16, 2005.)

This individual's experience reflects the remarkable continuum of shifting attitudes toward CVC and the transnational influence of ALUPEC.

Finally, the exceptionalist specter of Portuguese superiority and significance continues to haunt debates over CVC. There are many who simply do not believe that CVC is an appropriate language for education and business. They argue that Portuguese is the far more developed, useful language for the Cape Verdean people. Most often, this reflects a variation on the exceptionalist trope of degeneracy. One Cape Verdean businessman explained his stance on the use of CVC in official capacities: "But we cannot use Kriolu in business. Who will do business with us? Only our cousins in Brockton [Massachusetts]? In Lisbon? We need Portuguese to globalize."[76] Portuguese is certainly extremely helpful for business (English even more so), but the fact remains that even with Portuguese as an official language, the majority of the Cape Verdean population does not speak it fluently. One of the major aims of bilingual education pedagogy is to improve second-language acquisition through mastery of the first language (in this case CVC).[77] Thus, the idea of Portuguese as the only language of import is not compatible with CVC as the mother tongue of the majority Cape Verdean population. Moreover, members of the diaspora, who hold much potential for development and international trade, are even less likely to speak Portuguese. With this in mind, the argument in favor of Portuguese monolingual education and official status is a weak one.

The trope of degeneracy persists even among Cape Verdean Americans who have witnessed the success of bilingual education programs and who do not themselves speak Portuguese. For instance, after learning that CVC was being taught at Harvard University for the first time in the 2005–6 academic year, one group of Cape Verdean American professionals revolted with a flurry of comments: "How can you teach Kriolu at Harvard?" "It is just a dialect of Portuguese!" "Don't they have Portuguese classes?" "You are going to confuse all of those students, and they will speak bad Portuguese."[78] Their outspoken opposition to the program, and the clear message of CVC inferiority that they shared, is evidentiary of this trope of degeneracy.

I witnessed an especially powerful example of CVC's perceived inferiority when a high-ranking official from the Cape Verdean Ministry of Education visited the United States in December 2005. A group of Boston-area scholars who teach CVC were invited to meet with the official to discuss the CVC language activities in the Boston Public Schools. As we stood around prior to the meeting, we chatted comfortably in CVC, the official included. Yet as soon as we sat at the table, the official stated, in Portuguese, "Well, we are seated at the table and, as is our custom, we will now speak in Portuguese."[79] Those Cape Verdean Americans present were dismayed by this statement and their resulting inability to fully participate in the meeting. One colleague explained her frustration: "In the United States, holding a meeting in Portuguese automatically excludes most Cape Verdean Americans, who never learn the language. Not to mention the fact that this meeting is about using Kabuverdianu in education! Is our own language 'unfit' for use in meetings?"[80] After some halting discussion, the point was raised that perhaps speaking in CVC would allow more people to engage in conversation. The official reluctantly agreed, and the meeting continued in CVC. This interaction reflects how CVC remains in a liminal space, seen by many as unfit for "high" culture or official communication.

Changing Attitudes

While debates about CVC rage on in the public sphere, a number of remarkable, measurable differences in attitude have come about in the past fifteen years. Promotion of CVC, especially during the revolutionary and postindependence period, has especially encouraged a linguistic sensibility among Cape Verdean youth and creative practitioners—authors, comic-book artists, composers, lyricists, and performers. This linguistic sensibility has nurtured a new level of written CVC communication online and via mobile technologies.

Attitudes toward and debates over CVC are long-standing and powerfully linked to exceptionalist tropes. The movement for independence from Portugal sets the stage for the celebration and reclaiming of Cape Verdean culture, including CVC and music. In the years following independence, numerous contributions to language promotion were made both in Cabo Verde and the Cape Verdean diaspora, especially in the United States. These promotional contributions were in the realms of scholarly study, pedagogy and curriculum, literature, legislation, popular media, and music. While constitutional officialization of CVC has repeatedly faltered, the development and officialization of ALUPEC mark important steps in the standardization of the language. Literacy in CVC remains limited, though a critical vibrancy is found in the work of largely self-taught younger generations writing the language online. The topics of variant choice, partisan politics, orthography, and Portuguese-CVC diglossia remain contentious and likely will until further public education campaigns address them more clearly.

Substantial work must be done before a successful transition to bilingualism in Cabo Verde can be navigated. Manuel Veiga argues that the greatest battle in the promotion of CVC is against diglossia, which can be fought with the officialization of CVC, the generalization of its teaching, and the construction of a functional bilingualism.[81] Marlyse Baptista, Inês Brito, and Saídu Bangaru elaborate:

> . . . sound language planning should involve the following chronological steps:
> 1. Officialization of the Cape Verdean language by the government (educational institutions need governmental approval and endorsement to implement educational reforms).
> 2. Creation of a script built on consensus and with which most if not all users may identify.
> 3. The running of a pilot project in which a select group of kindergarten children is taught early literacy in Cape Verdean. We could then compare the rate of literacy acquisition in those classrooms with that in classrooms in which Portuguese is the medium of instruction.
> 4. Adequate description and representation of each variety in each cluster (to facilitate the identification of the linguistic features common to each cluster and the recognition of their disparities). This would be based on adequate corpus planning.
> 5. Textbook development in all subject matters and development of other instructional materials.
> 6. Consultation with didacticians about reading materials.
> 7. Adequate training of teachers and curriculum developers.
> 8. Outreach programs to parents and the general population to inform them about the benefits of the additive approach to subject instruction.
>
> These are the necessary steps (but not necessarily in that order) that should be taken BEFORE the Cape Verdean language is introduced as a language of instruction in schools. (Marlyse Baptista, Inês Brito, and Saídu Bangura, "Cape Verdean in Education: A Linguistic and Human Right," in *Creoles in Education: An Appraisal of Current Programs*, ed. Bettina Migge, Isabelle Léglise, and Angela Bartens [Philadelphia: John Benjamins Publishing Company, 2010], 294–95.)

Ultimately, advocates for CVC use agree on one major point: that CVC should be given equal footing with Portuguese. This is more than just a noble cause; it is a matter of linguistic and human rights and is fundamental to social justice in the Cape Verdean context. Contemporary language activists continue to challenge prejudicial notions about CVC and intervene in ongoing discussions about caboverdianidade. Their work over the past several decades has been key to changing minds and moving toward language equality in Cabo Verde.

Notes

1. Michel DeGraff, "Linguists' Most Dangerous Myth: The Fallacy of Creole Exceptionalism," *Language in Society* 34, no. 4 (2005), 533–91.

2. Manuel Veiga, "O Crioulo De Cabo Verde: Afirmação e Visão Prospectiva," in *Cabo Verde: Origins Da Sua Sociedade e Do Seu Crioulo*, ed. Jürgen Lang (Tübingen, Germany: Narr Francke Attempto Verlag Gmbh + Co. KG, 2006), 29–30. All translations are by the author unless otherwise indicated.

3. Manuel Brito-Semedo, *A Construção Da Identidade Nacional: Análise Da Imprensa Entre 1877 e 1975* (Praia, Cape Verde: Instituto da Biblioteca Nacional e do Livro, 2006).

4. See Veiga, "O Crioulo De Cabo Verde."

5. George Lang, "Literary Crioulo Since Independence in São Tomé, Guinea-Bissau and Cape Verde," *Luso-Brazilian Review* 33 no. 2 (1996): 54.

6. For example, John Holm, *An Introduction to Pidgins and Creoles* (Cambridge: Cambridge University Press, 2000).

7. See Veiga, "O Crioulo De Cabo Verde"; Patrick Chabal, ed., *The Postcolonial Literature of Lusophone Africa* (Evanston, IL: Northwestern University Press, 1996).

8. Jorge Miguéis and Maria Manuela Brito, eds., *Cabo Verde: constituição, lei eleitoral e legislação complementar* (Lisbon: MAI/Stapa, 1995).

9. Russell G. Hamilton, *Voices from an Empire: A History of Afro-Portuguese Literature* (Minneapolis: University of Minnesota Press, 1975).

10. For example, Phyllis Peres, *Transculturation and Resistance in Lusophone African Narrative* (Gainesville: University Press of Florida, 1997); Ellen Sapega, *Consensus and Debate in Salazar's Portugal: Visual and Literary Negotiations of the National Text, 1933–1948* (University Park: The Pennsylvania State University Press, 2008).

11. Manuel Ferreira, *No reino de Caliban: antologia panorâmica da poesia africana de expressão portuguesa* (Lisbon: Seara Nova, 1975).

12. Deirdre Meintel, "The Creole Dialect of the Island of Brava," in *Miscelânea Luso-africana: Colectânea De Estudos Coligidos Por M. F.Valkhoff*, ed. M. F. Valkhoff (Lisbon: Junta da Investigações Científicas do Ultramar, 1975): 205–56; Deirdre A. Meintel Machado, "Language and Interethnic Relationships in

a Portuguese Colony," in *Ethnic Encounters: Identities and Contexts,* ed. George L. Hicks and Philip E. Leis (North Scituate, MA: Duxbury Press, 1977): 49–62.

13. It is not the purpose of this chapter to debate the merits of bilingual education. Suffice it to say that most linguists and pedagogues agree that it is an important form of education for second language learners. See James Crawford, *Bilingual Education: History, Politics, Theory, and* Practice (Los Angeles: Bilingual Educational Services, 1999); Jim Cummins, *Language, Power, and Pedagogy: Bilingual Children in the Crossfire* (Toronto: Multilingual Matters, 2000).

14. Georgette E. Gonsalves, "Language Policy and Reform: The Case of Cape Verdean," in *Education Reform and Social Change: Multicultural Voices, Struggles, and Visions,* ed. Catherine E. Walsh (Mahwah, NJ: Lawrence Erlbaum, 1996), 31–36.

15. The act stated: "The commissioner of education is hereby authorized and directed to promulgate rules and regulations which designate the Cape Verdean Crioulo language as a living foreign language" Commonwealth of Massachusetts, House Bill 2998 (Boston: Commonwealth of Massachusetts, 1976).

16. Gonsalves, "Language Policy and Reform," 33.

17. Gonsalves, "Language Policy and Reform," 34.

18. Lee D. Baker, *From Savage to Negro* (Berkeley: University of California Press, 1998).

19. See Gonsalves, "Language Policy and Reform."

20. Gonsalves, "Language Policy and Reform, '34.

21. Duarte provided some of the earliest pre-independence studies on the language.

22. Veiga, "O Crioulo De Cabo Verde."

23. Oswaldo Osório, *Cantigas De Trabalho: Tradições Orais De Cabo Verde* (Praia: Comissão Nacional para as Commemorações do 50 Aniversário da Independência de Cabo Verde, 1980).

24. See Judith Butler, *Gender Trouble: Feminism and the Subversion of Identity* (New York: Routledge, 1990); Judith Butler, *Excitable Speech: A Politics of the Performative* (New York: Routledge, 1997).

25. Manuel Veiga, *Diskrison Strutural Di Lingua Kabuverdianu* (Praia, Cape Verde: Institutu Kabuverdianu di Livru, 1982), 1.

26. See Rosina Lippi-Green, *English with an Accent: Language, Ideology, and Discrimination in the United States* (East Sussex: Psychology Press, 1997); John H. McWhorter, *The Word on the Street: Debunking the Myth of "Pure" Standard English* (Boston: Da Capo Press, 2001).

27. See, for example, Baltasar Lopes da Silva, *O Dialecto Crioulo De Cabo Verde* (Lisbon: Imprensa Nacional-Casa da Moeda, [1957] 1984); Dulce Almada, *Cabo Verde: Contribuição Para o Estudo Do Dialecto Falado No Seu Arquipélago* (Lisbon: Junta de Investigações do Ultramar, Centro Estudos Políticos e Sociais, 1961).

28. Artur Vieira, *Galafo* (Rio de Janeiro: Edition of the author, 1980); Kaká Barboza, *Vinti Sintidu Letradu Na Kriolu* (Praia: Institutu Kauberdianu di Libru, 1984).

29. He served as director of the government-funded Departamento de Tradições Orais (Department of Oral Traditions) during much of the 1980s, worked as president of the Institudo Cabo-verdiano do Livro (the Cape Verdean Book Institute, the major government-funded printing press), and held a number of other important positions in the Cape Verdean Parliament and the international organization UNESCO. Dina Salústio, ed., *Cabo Verde: 30 Anos De Edições 1975–2005* (Praia, Cape Verde: Instituto da Biblioteca Nacional e do Livro, 2005).

30. For fiction and poetry, see Tomé Varela da Silva, *Kumunhon d'África* (Praia, Cape Verde: Instituto Caboverdeano do Livro, 1986); Tomé Varela da Silva, *Kardisantus* (Praia, Cape Verde: Instituto Caboverdeano do Livro, 1987); Tomé Varela da Silva, *Natal y kontus* (Praia, Cape Verde: Instituto Caboverdeano do Livro, 1988).

31. See Tomé Varela da Silva, *Finasons di nha Nasia Gomi* (Praia, Cape Verde: Institutu Kauberdianu di Libru, 1985); Tomé Varela da Silva, *Nha Bibinha Kabral—bida y óbra* (Praia, Cape Verde: Instituto Caboverdeano do Livro, 1988).

32. Tomé Varela da Silva, *Na bóka noti—un libru di storias tradisional* (Praia, Cape Verde: Instituto Caboverdeano do Livro, 1987).

33. A noteworthy example includes the journal *Raízes, Ponto & Virgula*, and *Fragmentos* (*Roots, Period & Comma*, and *Fragments*).

34. Luis Romano, "Cem Anos De Literature Caboverdiana: 1880/1980," (Sinopse) *África* 8 (1985): 25–49; Salústio, *Cabo Verde*.

35. Manuel Veiga, ed., *Proposta De Bases Do Alfabeto Unificado Para a Escrita Do Cabo-verdiano*, Grupo Para a Padronização Do Alfabeto (Praia, Cape Verde: IIPC, 2006).

36. Veiga, "O Crioulo De Cabo Verde," 31.

37. For examples of these works, see Kaká Barboza, *Son di viraSon* (Mindelo: Spleen-Edições, 1996); Eutrópio Lima da Cruz, *Perkurse de sul d'ilha* (Praia, Cape Verde: Instituto Caboverdeano do Livro, 1999); Euricles Rodrigues, *Na kantar di sol* (Praia, Cape Verde: Edition of the author, 1991); and Tomé Varela da Silva, *Nha Gida Mendi: Simenti di onti na txon di manhan* (Praia, Cape Verde: Institutu Kauberdianu di Libru, 1990); Tomé Varela da Silva, *Konparason di konbérsu* (Praia, Cape Verde: Instituto Caboverdeano do Livro, 1997); Tomé Varela da Silva, *Na altar di nha petu* (Mindelo, Cape Verde: AEC Editora, 1997); Tomé Varela da Silva, *Forsa di amor* (Mindelo, Cape Verde: Publicom, 1999).

38. Manuel Veiga, *Introdução à Gramática Do Crioulo* (Cape Verde: Instituto Caboverdeano do Livro, 1995); French scholar Nicolas Quint's *Lésiku badiu-fransés* (Praia, Cape Verde: Gráfica da Praia, 1996); Nicolas Quint, *Diction-naire français-capverdien* (Paris: L'Harmattan, 1997); Nicolas Quint, *Dicionário caboverdiano-português* (Lisbon: Verbalis, 1998); see also Marlyse Baptista, *The Morphosyntax of Verbs in Capeverdean Creole* (PhD diss., Harvard University, 1997); Nicolas Quint, *Le créole de l'île de Santiago (République du Cap-Vert)* (PhD diss., Université Paris III—La Sorbonne Nouvelle, 1998); Manuel Veiga, "Le créole du Cap-Vert : étude grammaticale descriptive et constrastive" (PhD diss., Université d'Aix Marseille, 1998).

39. Dulce Almada Duarte, *Bilinguismo ou diglossia?* (Praia, Cape Verde: Spleen, 1998).

40. Veiga, *Proposta De Bases Do Alfabeto Unificado.*

41. For more information on the practical use of ALUPEC, see Manuel Veiga, *O caboverdiano em 45 lições* (Praia: INIC, 2002).

42. CCI Board, Capeverdean Creole Institute Mission Statement, unpublished document (Boston: 2005).

43. Nicolas Quint, *Les Îles Du Cap-Vert Aujourd'hui: Perdues Dans L'immensité* (Paris: L'Harmattan, 1997), 58–59, 108; Nicolas Quint, "Linguists' Most Dangerous Myth: The Fallacy of Creole Exceptionalism," trans. Michel DeGraff, *Language in Society* 34, no. 4 (2005): 533–91.

44. Quint, "Linguists' Most Dangerous Myth," 134.

45. Quint provided the introduction for a CVC textbook for French speakers aiming to learn CVC and even the translation of a series of French-CVC children's books: Nicolas Quint, *Parlons Capverdien: Langue et Culture*, Collection Parlons (Paris: L'Harmattan, 2003); Aires Semedo, *Le Loup, Le Lièvre Et La Sorcière Tia Ganga—Lobu, Xibinhu Ku Nha Tiâ Gánga*, trans. Nicolas Quint (Paris: L'Harmattan, 2005); Aires Semedo, *Le Cochon Qui Tord La Queue—Gó Ki Pórka Dja Torsi Rábu—Agora é Que a Porca Torce o Rabo*, trans. Nicolas Quint and Fátima Ragageles (Paris: L'Harmattan, 2007). Quint has never publicly retracted his earlier statements, though I have spoken with a scholar (anonymous by request) who said Quint apologized verbally behind closed doors.

46. Geraldo da Cruz Almeida and Solange Lisboa Ramos, eds., *Constituição Da República Cabo-verdiana* (Lisbon: Pedro Ferreira, 2002).

47. Veira, "O Crioulo De Cabo Verde," 34.

48. For example, Salústio, *Cabo Verde*; Tomé Varela da Silva, *Na bóka noti: un libru di stórias tradisional*, (Praia, Capo Verde: Institutu Kauberdianu di Libru, 2005).

49. Humberto Lima, *Un Bes Tinha Nhu Lobu Ku Xibinhu* (Praia, Cape Verde: INIC, 2000); Tomé Varela da Silva, *Pós-Claridosos: Antologia Da Ficção Cabo-verdiana*, vol. 3 (Praia, Cape Verde: AEC Editora, 2002); Kaká Barboza, *Konfison Na Finata* (Praia, Cape Verde: Artiletra, 2003).

50. Manuel Gonçalves and Leila Andrade, *Pa Nu Papia Kriolu* (Boston: M & L Enterprises, 1994).

51. Jailson Alves, Eurico Fernandes, and Mário Tavares, *Lobu Ku Xibinhu*, vol. 1 (Praia, Cape Verde: ImaJEM, 2008).

52. Steve and Trina Graham interviewed by Carla Martin, Praia, Cabo Verde, October 29, 2009.

53. Ana Eunice Araújo et al., eds., *Lúkas: Notísia Sabi Di Jizus* (Praia: Kumison Kabuverdianu pa Traduson di Bíblia, 2004); Asosiason Kabuverdianu pa Traduson di Bíblia, *Bíblia* (Praia, Cape Verde: Tipografia Santos, 2009).

54. Other classes have been offered through the Harvard Extension School, Dorchester Center for Adult Education, and other community-based organizations on and off since the 1970s, though with irregularity.

55. My undergraduate thesis dealt with the debate over bilingual education in the United States, particularly in relation to the experiences of inner-city

Cape Verdean American students. Carla D. Martin, "Forked Tongue Retold: The 'Exorcism' of Bilingual Education in a Cape Verdean-English Literacy Classroom" (unpublished thesis, Harvard University, 1999).

56. Resolution no. 48, Boletim Oficial 46 (Praia: Governo de Cabo Verde, 2005).

57. The prime minister's attitudes toward CVC have changed over the years, partly as a result of his relationship with members of the CCI. On September 24, 2011, he addressed the United Nations in CVC. Following the event, he wrote on his Facebook page: "This afternoon, I made my speech at the UN General Assembly . . . in the Cape Verdean language. For the first time in history this was done, in this great meeting hall of the Heads of State and of Government, a speech in Creole. I was thrilled and proud. For my country, for the Creole of Cabo Verde, part of humanity's heritage, for all Cape Verdean women and men." FORCV, "PM Neves Faz História Com Discurso Em Crioulo Na ONU," 2011, http://alupeckatentadju.blogspot.com/2011/09/pm-neves-discursou-em-kriolu-na-onu.html.

58. Decreto-Lei no. 8, Boletim Oficial 1/11 (Praia: Governo de Cabo Verde, 2009).

59. Marlyse Baptista, Inês Brito, and Saídu Bangura, "Cape Verdean in Education: A Linguistic and Human Right," in *Creoles in Education: An Appraisal of Current Programs*, ed. Bettina Migge, Isabelle Léglise, and Angela Bartens (Philadelphia: John Benjamins Publishing Company, 2010): 273–96.

60. Dário Gil interviewed by Carla Martin, Praia, Cabo Verde, November 12, 2009.

61. For example, Ministeriu di Kultura, Ministeriu Di Kultura YouTube Channel: Prugrama Lé y Skrebi Lingua Kabuverdianu, http://www.youtube.com/user/ministeriudikultura.

62. M. F. Valkhoff, *Miscelânea Luso-africana: Colectânea De Estudos* (Lisbon: Junta de Investigações Científicas do Ultramar, 1975); Marlyse Baptista, "The Morpho-Syntax of Nominal and Verbal Categories in Capeverdean Creole" (unpublished manuscript, Harvard University, 1997); Maria de Fátima Fernandes Lopes Sanches, *Atitude De Alguns Cabo-verdianos Perante a Língua Materna* (Praia: Instituto da Biblioteca Nacional e do Livro, 2005); Veiga, "O Crioulo De Cabo Verde."

63. Valkhoff consulted forty-four informants, Baptista fifty, Sanches one hundred, and Veiga relied primarily on analysis of published materials.

64. For example, Nicolas Quint, *Dictionnaire Français-Cap-verdien* (Paris: L'Harmattan, 1997); Nicolas Quint, *Lésiku badiu-fransés* (Praia, Cape Verde: N.p., 1996).

65. Vasco Brito interviewed by Carla Martin, Mindelo, Cabo Verde, November 11, 2003.

66. Lang, "Literary Crioulo Since Independence," 57.

67. Jorge Morais interviewed by Carla Martin, Praia, Cabo Verde, February 5, 2004.

68. In this case, those members of PAICV who chose to break with custom and, for a long time, the law, to give speeches in the National Assembly in CVC.

69. It also suggests that historical uses of the comparative method in the study of CVC, a technique from linguistics that involves studying the development of two or more languages with common descent from a shared ancestor side by side, have contributed to exceptionalist attitudes. For more on the comparative methods, see Terry Crowley and Claire Bowern, *An Introduction to Historical Linguistics* (Oxford: Oxford University Press, 2010) or Anthony Fox, *Linguistic Reconstruction: An Introduction to Theory and Method* (Oxford: Oxford University Press, 1995).

70. Adalberto Almeida interviewed by Carla Martin, Praia, Cabo Verde, October 7, 2009.

71. Jorge Coelho interviewed by Carla Martin, Paris, France, April 12, 2004.

72. Bambi B. Schieffelin and Rachelle Carlier Doucet, "The 'Real' Haitian Creole: Ideology, Metalinguistics, and Orthographic Choice," *American Ethnologist* 21, no. 1 (1994): 191.

73. Mário Lúcio interviewed by Carla Martin, Praia, Cabo Verde, October 8, 2009.

74. Baptista, Brito, and Bangura, "Cape Verdean in Education."

75. Veiga, *Proposta De Bases Do Alfabeto Unificado.*

76. Joaquim Araújo interviewed by Carla Martin, Praia, Cabo Verde, June 7, 2007.

77. For example, Crawford, *Bilingual Education*; Cummins, *Language, Power, and Pedagogy.*

78. Carla Martin, unpublished fieldnotes, Boston, MA, December 7, 2005.

79. Carla Martin, unpublished fieldnotes, Boston, MA, December 20, 2005.

80. Fátima Montrond interviewed by Carla Martin, Boston, MA, December 21, 2005.

81. Veiga, "O Crioulo De Cabo Verde," 34.

Part 2

Indian Ocean Islands

8

Africa's Indian Ocean Islands, Near and Distant

Edward A. Alpers

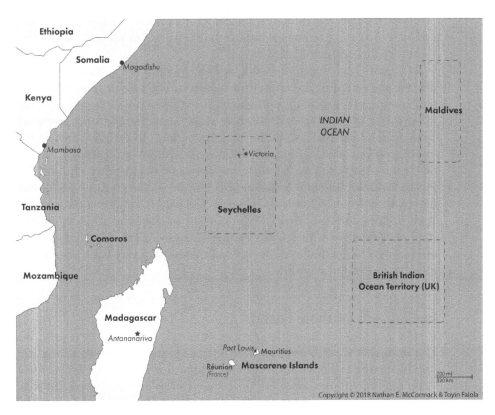

8.1: The Indian Ocean

The eastern littoral of the African continent is dotted with numerous inhabited islands ranging from the distant and near continental in size, like Madagascar, to the small and barely offshore, like Kilwa Kisiwani. Each of these islands, from the Dahlak Archipelago off Eritrea in the Red Sea to the Mascarene Islands of the southwest Indian Ocean, has its own set of historical connections to continental Africa, while all share certain maritime characteristics unique to islands. No less important are Africa's historical relationships with other, more distant Indian Ocean islands including the peopling of Madagascar from Indonesia, the forced migration of Africans to Sri Lanka, Sumatra, and Java, the deployment of African troops from Mozambique in East Timor, and the important trade in cowries from the Maldive Islands and Zanzibar to West Africa. In this chapter I will survey all of these linkages from the beginning of the Current Era to the present with an eye towards integrating Africa's Indian Ocean islands into the broader sweep of African history.[1] In the process of this overview I will also propose that the tripartite grouping of Africa's Indian Ocean islands that I adopt below can help us to understand the relationship of these insular societies with continental Africa.

In view of the enormous geographical range of my survey and the uneven placement of the numerous islands to which I will refer, I think it makes sense to organize my text spatially in terms of proximity to continental Africa. In my conclusion I will try to make a case for how such grouping can be useful for African studies more generally. Accordingly, in the following sections of my chapter I will discuss inshore and offshore islands first, then—for want of a better term—foreland islands next, and, finally, those islands located much farther afield in the Indian Ocean, which I will designate as distant-water islands, a term I borrow from those scholars who study distant-water fisheries. Of course, none of these categories represent rigid classifications with respect to their African orientation; rather, they are simply a hermeneutic device to make sense of a very large number of discrete geographical bodies.

Inshore and Offshore Islands

The inshore and offshore islands of Indian Ocean Africa have a long history of serving as both frontiers of settlement for coastal inhabitants and stepping stones to the continent for Indian Ocean travelers and traders. As African peoples migrated out to the shores of the continent, they learned to take advantage of the protein-rich resources of oceanic waters and to combine these with the specific agricultural or pastoral economies with which they were already familiar. Dugout canoes were adequate transportation for immediate offshore fishing activities and enabled early pioneers to establish fishing camps on these small islands. Over time, some of these camps probably evolved into permanent settlements of fishers and farmers. For sailors approaching the African littoral from across the Indian Ocean, these same islands were regarded as safe landings from which to pursue trading opportunities with mainland peoples. Over time, as extended visits determined by the seasonal monsoon winds created longer-term relationships between non-Africans and Africans who resided along the Indian Ocean littoral and on its offshore islands, mixed communities such as the Swahili-speaking people took shape.[2]

Located at the northwest arm of the Indian Ocean World, the Red Sea offers some interesting variations to this broad portrait because the monsoon regime is restricted to its southern end and because of the prevailing northerly winds that blow down its length. Another factor of its geography is the narrowness of this body of water. Historically, the two most notable island towns off the Red Sea coast are Suakin and Massawa. The foundation of Suakin dates back at least to the tenth-century BCE Egyptian voyages to the Land of Punt and possibly even earlier. Over three millennia, under its own governance and different imperial overlords, it continued to serve as an important emporium for commercial exchange between Egypt and the Indian Ocean, as well as between Sudanic Africa and Arabia. Following the rise of Islam and its expansion into northeast Africa and across to western Africa, it also became the principal port of embarkation across the Red Sea to Jeddah for Africans making pilgrimage to Mecca and Madina (*hajj*).[3] In the absence of serious archaeological research, it appears that Suakin's origins were determined by ancient Egyptian interests rather than as a settlement by Beja or proto-Beja from eastern Sudan. Nevertheless, its island location bears witness to its attractiveness as a well-defended port of trade and its eventual occupation by different imperial powers over many centuries.

Although the origins of Massawa are certainly less ancient than those of Suakin, they are scarcely less obscure. Located off the coast of Eritrea, Massawa offered a deep-water port and safety from mainland attacks that sometimes affected the mainland port of Hergigo, the successor to Axumite Adulis and, later, Zula. Like Suakin, from the sixteenth century on, its history was intimately linked to the Ottoman Empire and Arabia.[4] It is noteworthy that under colonial rule, British for Suakin and Italian for Massawa, both of these island towns were connected by a causeway to the mainland, thereby integrating them more completely with the continental mass from which they were naturally separated.

Stretching from just beyond Massawa out into the southern end of the
Red Sea, the Dahlak Archipelago occupies a quite different place in its relationship to Africa. For one thing, unlike most offshore islands that are continental fragments, the Dahlaks were "formed by coral reefs that emerged
from movements caused by the separation of Arabic clod from the African
one."[5] Although only a few of the 209 islands in the archipelago are populated today, it was a well-known source of pearls from Roman times, when
the islands were controlled by the kingdom of Axum. Pre-Islamic remains
have been identified on the largest island in the group at Dahlak Kebir.
With the decline of the Axumite kingdom from the late sixth century CE,
the islands emerged as an ideal base for pirates to harass commercial shipping plying the southern waters of the Red Sea. In 702 pirate activity caused
Arabs to occupy the Dahlaks and to seize control of the islands, making
them an important stepping stone from Arabia for Islam.[6] During the heyday of the Fatimid Caliphate (909–1171) its independent rulers sustained
a fleet to protect the ships of the dominant Karimi merchants as they traveled between 'Aydhab and Suakin from local pirates, especially those based
around the Dahlak Islands.[7] Over the course of the next two centuries
Dahlak, presumably referring to the largest island of Dahlak Kebir, was the
site of a major emporium for the India trade and its rulers even minted
their own silver coins. It also served as a customhouse for the rulers of this
island-state.[8] Together with Suakin and Massawa, Dahlak was conquered by
Ozdemir Pasha in 1556–57 and thus became integrated into the new Ottoman province of Habesh.[9] Ottoman suzerainty thereby broke the Dahlaks'
role as an independent player in the southern reaches of the Red Sea and
linked the islands permanently to Eritrea. The existence of several Muslim
saints' tombs on Dahlak Kebir and on Shaykh Sa'īd or Green Island near
Massawa serve as reminders of the central role played by these offshore
islands in the expansion of Islam across the Red Sea to northeast Africa.[10]
In the modern period the Dahlaks once served as a Soviet naval base and
are now being developed with financing from Qatar as an ecotourism site;
there is also a Dahlak Marine National Park.[11]

Moving out through the Bab el Mandeb into the Gulf of Aden and
around Ras Hafun down the coast of eastern Africa, the African littoral
is notable for its absence of significant offshore islands until one reaches
the northern limits of the Swahili coast and the Bajuni Islands.[12] These
coral islands extend for some 155 miles south from Kismayu to northern
Kenya.[13] They are divided into a northern group (from Kismayu down to
Buri Kavo) and a southern group in Kenya (from Kiungamwini to Kiwa-
yuu Island). The islands were once home to the Bajuni people, who speak
a dialect of Swahili. The Bajuni, who never numbered more than a few

thousand individuals, were primarily known as fishers who maintained farms on the mainland or traded their fish for grain with the Somali mainlanders with whom they maintained a fraught relationship. Although only the larger islands were inhabited, fishermen annually spent several weeks at temporary fishing camps on uninhabited islands, where they also dried fish for trading along the coast. The Bajuni were also skilled boatwrights who specialized in production of the *mtepe*, a rectangular rigged medium-sized ship that was characteristically Swahili. Bajuni history is closely associated with the elusive mainland site of Shungwaya, often regarded as the original homeland for Swahili speakers. However one regards this powerful myth, the Bajuni probably came to occupy the islands that bear their name no earlier than the fourteenth century. Like claims to "Shirazi" origins among elite Swahili clans, among the Bajuni, certain clans claim southern Arabian origins, yet these are certainly later accretions to the original Bantu-speaking families who crossed from mainland Africa to these islands. Finally, in common with many of the principal towns of the Swahili coast and as reflected in numerous ruins of large pillar tombs and mosques, the heyday for the Bajunis were the centuries from about 1400 to 1800. On several occasions Bajuni fighters participated as Portuguese allies against different centers of Swahili opposition to the Portuguese; they even joined the Portuguese in their final, futile defense of Mombasa against the Omani Arabs in 1728–29.[14] During the colonial and early postcolonial periods many Bajuni migrated south and settled along the Kenya coast, but since the collapse of the Siad Barre regime in 1991 they have been almost completely pushed out of their eponymous island home by Somali refugees from the chaos in Somalia itself.

Evidence for the islands of the Swahili coast is much richer and better known than that for either the Dahlak or Bajuni islands. *The Periplus Maris Erythraei* leaves no doubt that many of the islands of this coastline were already occupied and that their inhabitants practiced a maritime economy.[15] Indeed, there is evidence of two phases of a Later Stone Age occupation site on Zanzibar that has been dated to the centuries before the Current Era.[16] Archaeological data from the tiny inshore islands of Kwale and Koma, lying south of Dar es Salaam and only 2.5 and 6 miles away from the continental landmass, as well as from the farther offshore Mafia Islands, located east of the Rufiji River delta, suggest their occupation by around the third century CE.[17] Literary and archaeological evidence for the coast before the rise of Islam demonstrate that these settlements were already connected to the wider world of the western Indian Ocean. Reflecting both an Anglo-centric bias and the operation of the seasonal monsoon winds, however, the Swahili coast is popularly understood to extend from northern Kenya down to the mouth of the Rovuma River and Cape Delgado, marking the mainland boundary with Tanzania. In reality, the Swahili coast extends beyond Cape Delgado as far south as the mouth of the Lurio River in northern Mozambique and includes the numerous Quirimba Islands.[18] Indeed, during the early Islamic period Swahili outlier communities were established at Sofala and on the Bazaruto Islands of southern Mozambique, while later settlements were founded on Mozambique and Angoche islands. Historical linguistic evidence indicates that Swahili expanded from its northern Kenya origins south along the coast, eventually reaching out to the Comoro Islands, where the different island dialects of Comorian evolved from the eighth century on.[19] This southward expansion is paralleled in the archaeological record for the Early Iron Age. Both of these movements indicate strongly that expansion was accomplished by coastal seafaring, which clearly involved regular island-hopping.[20] What is evident from research published thus far in the twenty-first century is that by exploiting the economic resources of the littoral and occupying its numerous inshore and offshore islands, the Swahili developed into a maritime society that came to differentiate them from Bantu-speaking peoples of the coastal hinterland.[21]

The more familiar story of the Swahili focuses on the role played by their place within the international trading networks of the western Indian Ocean, including a succession of Swahili city-states that controlled commercial exchanges on the African side of these networks.[22] No less featured in the literature is the parallel process of Islamization of Swahili society.[23] Certainly, the role of insular Swahili settlements constitutes an important feature in the history of eastern Africa, nurturing a maritime way of life for their inhabitants and a safe haven for Indian Ocean merchants and sailors to conduct business and wait out the seasonal monsoon. Over time their progeny came to claim both African and Indian Ocean roots, sometimes Arab, sometimes Persian, and sometimes Indian. Whether one examines barely offshore islands like those of the Lamu Archipelago, Mombasa, Kilwa Kisiwani ("on the island"), Mozambique Island, Angoche Island, or Sofala, or those located farther offshore such as Pemba, Zanzibar, or the Mafia group, the imprint of both sets of cultural inputs remains strong. What is most interesting today, however, is how the rich tradition of archaeological research on the Swahili islands has evolved over time from a focus on monumental buildings and an emphasis on Middle Eastern influences on island society to the African contribution to Swahili society and, most recently in research published in the twenty-first century, to the ways in which island settlement itself has shaped the life of the Swahili inhabitants.

Although islands continued to occupy a central place in the history of the Swahili coast to about 1900, even before the modern colonial conquests of this period, changes in Africa's international trading relations began to render some of these islands less economically and politically important. When the Portuguese entered Indian Ocean waters at the very end of the fifteenth century and began to build their short-lived thalassocracy in the early sixteenth century, they forcibly restructured the political order of Swahili islands. To the south of Cape Delgado they occupied Sofala and made Mozambique Island their seat of power; to the north they sacked Kilwa, subdued their rivals in the Lamu Archipelago, and made Mombasa their coastal stronghold at the end of the sixteenth century. When local opposition and Omani imperial expansion removed the Portuguese presence from north of Cape Delgado at the end of the seventeenth century, Mombasa continued as the dominant power along that stretch of the coast. Dynastic change in Oman during the eighteenth century enabled the Mazru'i leaders of Mombasa to declare independence from Oman, but in the first three decades of the nineteenth century Bu Sa'idi Zanzibar emerged as the center of coastal East Africa and Mombasa lost its independence, though not its economic role for the growing ivory trade of the Kenyan interior. From the late sixteenth century on, these political rivalries effected a different transformation on Pemba so that it first became primarily a breadbasket for Mombasa and then, following the 1872 hurricane that devastated clove plantations in Zanzibar, the major producer of cloves for Bu Sa'idi Zanzibar.[24] The explosion of demand for bonded labor that accompanied the economic growth of Zanzibar in the nineteenth century also reduced Kilwa Kisiwani to a backwater, as the previously obscure mainland village of Kivinje to its immediate north became the mainland terminus for the slave trade from east-central Africa and became known as Kilwa Kivinje.[25]

The imposition of colonial rule shifted the focus of economic activity from coastal to continental Africa. The building of the Uganda Railway linked Mombasa to Lake Nyanza and into Uganda, but although Mombasa was the first capital of British East Africa, the railhead at Nairobi replaced it as the capital of Kenya Colony in 1907. Subsequently, although Mombasa remained the principal port for Kenya, the coastal strip of what became Kenya Colony soon was alienated from the center of white settler activity in highland Kenya. The towns of the Lamu Archipelago faded into an economic backwater and Mombasa finally lost its islandness when in 1931 it was joined to the mainland by the old Nyali Bridge. In addition, until Imperial Germany lost its East African colony at the end of the First World War, British Zanzibar was separated from its former outposts on the Mrima coast. Following the Great War, German East Africa became Tanganyika Territory under British Mandate of the League of Nations, but Zanzibar remained separately administered as an Arab-dominated protectorate.

Building on a Bu Sa'idi tradition of tolerating Islamic plurality, Zanzibar Town became an important center for the diffusion of Islam to mainland Africa. When Sufism became a renewed spiritual force in the late nineteenth century and early decades of the colonial period, Zanzibar became the hub for the spread of the Qadiriyya *tariqa* to Bagamoyo and the Kilwa coast, and from these nodes both down to the Mozambique coast and far upcountry.[26]

With the exception of Mombasa, which still retains its prominence as a modern port, the modern economies of the other islands of the Swahili coast are dependent on tourism. Blessed with sandy beaches, numerous species of marine life that make scuba diving a major attraction, and an exotic history that is characterized by the hundreds of stone buildings that date to the heyday of Swahili civilization, the coastal islands of East Africa have become a major destination for European tourists. The designation of many historic ruins on the islands as UNESCO World Heritage Sites from Lamu Town to Mozambique Island has undoubtedly contributed to their attraction for international visitors. As for the islands that make up Zanzibar, although union with Tanganyika in 1964 created the United Republic of Tanzania, it still vigorously maintains its island identity as a semiautonomous region.[27]

In 1902 Portugal decided to hitch its economic future to the booming mineral revolution of South Africa and moved its East African capital south to Lourenço Marques (now Maputo), abandoning Mozambique Island to become another sleepy island backwater. The island finally lost its functions as a major port to the deep-water port at Nacala, and as an administrative center in northern Mozambique when Nampula superseded it in the late colonial period. The island was finally connected to the mainland by a bridge in the 1960s. Beyond the farthest extent of the modern Swahili world, and despite lacking the historic monuments of the Swahili coast, the Bazaruto Islands and Inhaca Island off the coast of southern Mozambique are also important tourist destinations.[28] In addition, the existence of numerous endangered species of marine life, such as various species of marine turtles and dugong, as well as coral reefs, has stimulated several experiments in international and community-based conservation projects in the offshore islands of Tanzania and Mozambique in the twenty-first century. Prominent among these are the Mafia Islands Marine Park, government and NGO collaborations in the Quirimba and Bazaruto islands, and the declaration of the Primeiras e Segundas Islands off Angoche as an

"Environmental Protection Area." Covering more than 3,860 square miles, this is the largest marine preserve in all of Africa.[29]

Over the course of perhaps 2,000 years, the inshore and offshore islands of eastern Africa have evolved from a frontier for pioneering mainlanders paddling dugout canoes to exploit the resources of its rich coastal waters, to safe landings for equally adventurous Indian Ocean seafarers, to fortified bases for competing imperial powers, to colonial backwaters, to safe havens from mainland violence, and finally to international tourist destinations and marine conservation projects. Each of these phases in the history of these islands has been a direct consequence of their geographical and environmental qualities as islands.

Foreland Islands

I have adopted this category, inspired as it is by the seminal work of Michael Pearson on the Indian Ocean,[30] to incorporate those islands that are both located farther out in the Indian Ocean than the much more numerous inshore and offshore islands, and whose inhabitants reflect historically different linguistic traditions from those of the immediate littoral of eastern Africa. In the far north lies Socotra Island, the largest island of a small archipelago of four islands that is now a province of the Republic of Yemen.[31] Although Socotra lies 150 miles east of the Horn of Africa and 236 miles south of Arabia, its geological origins link it to southern Yemen and Oman.[32] It has also historically been more closely connected to south Arabia and the wider Indian Ocean than to northeastern Africa. Its first inhabitants came from the Hadramawt, while modern Socotri is a South Arabian language. Still, there is also evidence that other early settlers arrived from both India and Africa. Certainly, there is an undeniable Somali component to the modern population of Socotra, some of whom are probably the descendants of enslaved forebears. Historically the island was occupied and claimed by different Indian Ocean players, but for much of its history its isolation enabled it to exist as a semi-independent entity. It also has a long history as a haven for different piratical groups. In the first decade of the twenty-first century, Socotra was utilized by Somali pirates during their forays out into the Indian Ocean.

Even though the Comoros are usually associated with discussions of Swahili civilization and its inhabitants are linguistically closely related to (though distinct from) the Swahili language, I include the four volcanic Comoro Islands—Ngazidja, Nzwani, Mwali, and Mayotte (Maore)—in this category. In making this distinction I wish to emphasize the unique character of the Comoros, which notwithstanding their unquestionable links to the Swahili world, were even more intimately connected to Mozambique and Madagascar. In fact, an interesting feature of the place of the Comoros as East African islands is that—reflecting the operation of the seasonal monsoon winds—whereas their original orientation was with the Swahili coast to the north of Cape Delgado, most of their linkages were across the Mozambique Channel to the south of that promontory.

In the first millennium the critical location of the Comoros provided a series of island stepping stones for the maritime expansion of the Swahili-Sabaki languages from Africa and for early Islamic settlement right across to northwest Madagascar, which dates to c. 800–1100 CE.[33] In the nineteenth century this sort of oceanic adventuring and population movement was reversed, moving outward from Madagascar to the Comoros. The first phase was characterized by the era of Malagasy maritime slave raids on the Comoros from about 1785 to 1820.[34] A decade after the end of these raids, political competition in western Madagascar precipitated the occupation of Mwali, the smallest of the islands, in the 1830s by the Malagasy chief Ramanetaka and the creation of a Malagasy ruling dynasty until French occupation in 1886. In a related series of events, the 1830s also witnessed the movement of Malagasy speakers from Madagascar to Mayotte, where they are now scattered in villages across the island.[35]

During the turbulent nineteenth century, the Comoros became more intimately linked to the Mozambique coast through the slave trade. On the one hand, slaving resulted in the forced presence of significant communities of Makhuwa speakers and their descendants on all of the Comoro Islands; on the other hand it intensified family ties between certain Comorian elites and those in coastal Mozambique communities like Moma, Quitangonha, Sanculo, and Angoche.[36] Political instability from the 1880s into the early colonial period on Ngazidja, the largest of the Comoros that was also closest to the East African coast, precipitated the migration of a significant Comorian community to Zanzibar Town, where they became an important element in the civil and religious administration of the Bu Sa'idi sultanate.[37] In addition, another feature of these linkages was the way in which they nurtured Islamic networks around the Mozambique Channel. Most notably, Ngazidja emerged as the center for dissemination of the Shadhiliyya *tariqa* to both Mozambique Island and Kilwa.[38] Finally, in the 1980s, during the Mozambique civil war (1977–92), South Africa was reported to have shipped military supplies to Renamo through the Comoros.[39]

If my inclusion of the Comoro Islands in this group of foreland islands is surprising, no one is likely to dispute that—because of both its distance from continental Africa and its massive size—Madagascar counts for something greater than an offshore island. Separated from India about eighty-eight million years ago, Madagascar is the fourth largest island in the world and in many respects constitutes a world unto itself. Like Socotra, its unique flora and fauna are emblematic of its long island isolation. Its mixed Indonesian and African cultural heritage connects it to both Southeast Asia and East Africa; its common Malagasy language (albeit with numerous dialectical differences) points to its origins in the Austronesian language family. But aside from long-standing scholarly disputes about the chronology of the peopling of Madagascar and the cultural composition of its inhabitants, the fact remains that from at least the sixteenth century Madagascar sustained a variety of economic connections with Africa.[40] For the Portuguese at Mozambique Island, western Madagascar was an important source of food, mainly beef and rice, especially when Luso-Makhuwa relations were tense and rendered access to provisions from the Mozambique mainland difficult. Evidence for this trade in foodstuffs is especially clear for the nineteenth century, but certainly predates that period.[41]

The other major connection between Madagascar and continental Africa was the slave trade. From the establishment of a Dutch colony at Cape Town in 1652, Madagascar served as a source of enslaved labor for that important colonial port. Indeed, James Armstrong and Nigel Worden propose that Malagasy captives constituted about 25 percent of the bonded labor force at the Dutch Cape.[42] During the same era, Arab and Swahili traders engaged in a significant export trade in enslaved labor from northwest Madagascar to the Lamu Archipelago. Most of these captives were subsequently shipped on to Arabia, but many remained on the Kenya coast.[43] In the late eighteenth century, maritime raiders from eastern Madagascar began to plunder the Comoro Islands in search of booty and captives; from 1800 to 1820 they extended their raiding to the African coast, ranging from the Lurio River in the south to the Mafia Islands in the north.[44] Although direct Malagasy attacks on the African mainland came to an end, slave trading between Mozambique and Madagascar did not. This traffic was overwhelmingly in the hands of local Swahili, Arab, and Indian traders. Its sources extended from the Quirimba Islands and small mainland ports south to just north of the Zambesi estuary. From mid-century the center of the slave trade was Angoche, whose ruling class had intimate family and commercial links to the Comoros and northwest Madagascar. In 1877 the queen of the Imerina Kingdom of Madagascar declared an end to the enslavement of so-called Masombika, but in view of the continuing export of captives from the Mozambique coast, it is safe to assume that some of these individuals continued to slip into Madagascar. Indeed, until slavery as an institution was ended by French colonial decree in 1896, it seems evident that the 1877 emancipation had only a limited impact on the continued smuggling of captives across the Mozambique Channel. We can only guess at the magnitude of this trade, but evidence of its significance is testified to by the creation of sizable Makoa communities in western Madagascar whose descendants are still not fully integrated into Malagasy society and culture.[45]

As is well known, facing to the east, away from continental Africa, Madagascar was also a major source of provisions and forced labor to the Mascarene Islands. The Mascarenes were uninhabited until first the Dutch colonized Mauritius from 1638 to 1710. During this period, they introduced a few hundred Malagasy slaves, most of whom soon marooned. Following the colonization by the French of Île Bourbon (Réunion) in 1665 and Île de France (Mauritius) from 1715, the Mascarenes were developed as colonial plantation economies during the course of the eighteenth century. The first French settlers brought with them a handful of West African slaves, but as both colonies slowly grew, they looked to Madagascar and to East Africa to supply bonded labor. The French colonists imported slaves from Zanzibar, Kilwa, Ibo, and Mozambique Island, where they became most deeply engaged with successive Portuguese colonial administrations.[46] As with the example of Masombika and Makoa on Madagascar, East African ethnonyms became a part of the slave system of categorizing labor on both Réunion and Mauritius.[47] When slavery ended on Mauritius in 1835, about 80 percent of the population was of either African or Malagasy origin or ancestry. In the aftermath of abolition, there was still an insatiable demand for labor to work in the island's booming sugar industry. Importation of indentured Indian labor was the answer, and the waves of Indian immigration that entered the island over the next four decades transformed the demography of Mauritius so that by the 1870s, some two-thirds of the population was of Indian origin.[48]

Notwithstanding the Afro-Asian composition of Madagascar and the fact that its people do not speak an African language, or the reality that the population of Mauritius is still overwhelmingly of Indian descent, both independent nations are today included among the modern states of Africa. Although linkages between Réunion and Mauritius continue to reflect their shared French colonial heritage, like Mayotte in the Comoros, Réunion is still French and, accordingly, not considered to be an African island in the political or economic sense. Yet the people of both Mayotte and Réunion are without question linked culturally to Africa and, especially, to Madagascar.

The last of these foreland islands is the Seychelles Archipelago, which lies well to the north of the Mascarenes and about 995 miles east of the Kenya coast. The Seychelles consists of 155 small islands—some of which are granitic and others coral—that remained uninhabited, despite occasional landings, until occupied by the French from Mauritius in 1770.[49] The main islands were initially developed as coconut plantations with African labor provided by the slave trade.[50] Like Mauritius, these islands became British territories during the Napoleonic Wars and were administered from Mauritius until 1903. The African cultural imprint remains a powerful source of identity for the creolized Seychellois population.[51] Although air travel makes reaching the Seychelles directly from Europe and the Middle East possible, the Seychelles Tourism Board still presents itself as an African destination and maintains close links with its African national counterparts.[52]

Socotra and the complex of African islands in the southwest Indian Ocean stand apart from the inshore and offshore islands of the continent by virtue of both their greater distance from that landmass and, consequently, the greater significance of their islandness. To be sure, they are by no means divorced from Africa, but their greater isolation emphasizes their island histories and their positionality in the Indian Ocean. Size is not the issue here since Madagascar constitutes a small continent unto itself, but insularity is a factor of greater significance in this grouping than it is for the inshore and offshore islands of eastern Africa.

Distant-Water Islands

The category of distant-water islands is designed to serve as a catchall for those islands that are (1) clearly not African and (2) are located at some greater distance from Africa than are its inshore, offshore, and foreland islands. The earliest island connection across the Indian Ocean to Africa dates to the Austronesian settlement of Madagascar. This is a subject that has a large and much contested historiography, but the basic elements as they relate to this chapter are that, beginning in the early centuries of the Current Era and continuing over a period of about 1,000 years, different waves of oceanic migrants from what is today Indonesia settled Madagascar.[53] The introduction to Africa of specific food crops and animals from Southeast Asia, such as bananas, water yams, taro, and chickens, suggests that Austronesians may have touched upon the African coastline as well, but to date there is no archaeological evidence to verify such interactions.

Later African connections with the Indonesian Archipelago were few and far between. From the beginning of their South African colony, the Dutch imported slave labor from insular Southeast Asia and from the late seventeenth century they sent political prisoners from their Indonesian base at Batavia (modern Jakarta) to the Cape Colony, where they are sometimes referred to as Cape Malays.[54] Moving in the other direction, the British sent shipments of captive labor from East Africa and Madagascar to their coastal settlements at Benkulen in Sumatra and Banten in Java.[55] In the nineteenth century the Dutch recruited West African soldiers from the Dutch Gold Coast (modern Ghana) to serve in the Royal Netherlands East India Army. Known as Zwarte Hollanders, more than 3,000 West African men were recruited as soldiers for Dutch Indonesia between 1831 and 1872, when Great Britain took possession of the Gold Coast. Most of these soldiers were recruited in Kumasi, although many had origins in what is today Burkina Faso. Although recruitment ended in 1872 and the last West African serving in the Dutch colonial army retired in 1915, the children that these West African soldiers fathered with Indonesian women remained in Indonesia until the end of Dutch colonial rule following the Second World War, after which most resettled in the Netherlands.[56] In a similar example of using African soldiers to police a global colonial empire, in 1910–12 Portugal employed African troops from Mozambique to suppress armed resistance to colonial rule in East Timor.[57] During its liberation struggle against Indonesia, the Revolutionary Front for an Independent East Timor received important diplomatic support from both Mozambique and Angola. Today the Democratic Republic of Timor-Leste maintains postcolonial links with the former Portuguese colonies in Africa through its membership in the Community of Portuguese Language and Culture.

The African diaspora in the Indian Ocean witnessed the forced movement of captive Africans primarily to peninsular Arabia and South Asia, as well as to the foreland islands. During both the Portuguese and Dutch periods of colonial occupation of the island of Ceylon (today's nation of Sri Lanka), however, small numbers of enslaved Africans were transported to that island. Because their numbers were limited and their communities scattered around the periphery of the island, the existence of an African presence in Sri Lanka is often denied or simply not recognized. Nevertheless, there are definite African elements in the musical genre known as *kafferingha baila* that is still practiced by some of the so-called Burgher communities of Sri Lanka.[58]

A quite different distant-water island connection involves the trade in cowry shells (*Cypraea moneta*) from the Maldive Islands, located off the southwest coast of India, to West Africa. The Maldives number almost 1,200 low-lying islands situated in twenty-six atolls protected by coral reefs. About 200 of these islands are inhabited. Not surprisingly, Maldivians were notable seafarers. Cowry shells are mentioned in several medieval sources as being traded from the Maldives. In their oceanic travels Maldivian sailors often used cowries as ballast; eventually they traded cowries to Africa. Cowries were used as a form of money in eastern Africa, but more importantly as early as the eleventh century they made their way to the Mediterranean and then across the Sahara to West Africa.[59] However, the heyday of the trade in cowries from the Maldives came with the rise of the transatlantic slave trade. As carefully researched by Jan Hogendorn and Marion Johnson, cowry shells from the Maldives became the most widely used money in West Africa from the seventeenth century right through into the early colonial period, when they were largely replaced by European coinage.[60] Notwithstanding European seaborne power in the early modern Indian Ocean, the sultan of the Maldives was able to retain control of the trade in Maldivian hands. Accordingly, cowries were mostly shipped from the Maldives to Ceylon and Bengal, from where the Dutch and English, respectively, shipped them to their West African ports. Maldivian *monetas* dominated the West African market because of their small size, their durability, and the fact that they retained their exceptional whiteness. Hogendorn and Johnson estimate that the volume of cowries traded to West Africa in the eighteenth century, at the height of the transatlantic slave trade, exceeded ten billion shells.

A larger variety of cowry shell (*Cypraea annulus*) thrives in the offshore waters of East Africa. In the eighteenth century these cowries were traded from the Quirimba Islands and Sofala not only to Surat and Bengal, but also to West Africa.[61] In the middle of the nineteenth century cowries were still reckoned to be an important article of export trade from the Portuguese customhouse at Ibo.[62] While the Portuguese were maintaining the export of cowries, however, the same business experienced a short-lived boom at Zanzibar; between 1850 and 1878 the German firm of O'Swald & Co. shipped some 27,000 tons of cowries to West Africa.[63] In the end, the export of huge numbers of the slightly blue *annulus* shells from Zanzibar precipitated a disastrous devaluation of cowries in West Africa from the 1850s. Just as Maldive cowry-shell money persisted into the early colonial era in West Africa, *moneta* continued to be used as money in remote regions of eastern Africa until about 1921, when colonial coinage replaced them.[64]

By and large, when we think about Africa's islands, we mostly ignore those islands that are not in any usual geopolitical sense African. Yet as I hope this last section of my chapter demonstrates, the distant-water islands of the Indian Ocean are in a variety of ways linked historically to Africa. By including them in this survey I seek to remind ourselves of their place in the history of Africa's Indian Ocean islands.

Why Islands Matter

As several more detailed chapters in this volume make clear, I have only scratched the surface of a great many topics that link the islands of the Indian Ocean with continental Africa. What I hope to have demonstrated, however, is that islands have played a variety of critical roles in the history of Africa. Whether we regard them as frontiers of settlement for pioneering African populations; as safe havens for outsiders to obtain a perch on this vast continental land mass; as centers for imperial domination; as economic and religious hubs for connections to the world beyond Africa and for the penetration of the continent; or, lastly, as newly emerging sites of international tourism and environmental protection, Africa's Indian Ocean offshore islands have occupied important and evolving places over time. Regarding those that I am calling foreland islands, if their connection to the continent has not always been as intimate, they have played an especially important role in the scattering of forced African migrants through the slave trade. Finally, the distant-water islands that lie well beyond Africa show how varied and fascinating are the connections between these far-flung Indian Ocean islands and Africa.

At a more comprehensive level, Africa's Indian Ocean islands historically provided critical integration nodes that linked Africa to wider regional and international networks. As frontier societies, they also served as laboratories for the integration of diverse populations of Africans and non-Africans from across the Indian Ocean World.[65] The dynamic construction of island populations over time, as well as their commercial and cultural connections to both the African continent and the non-African societies with which they interacted also provide valuable comparative examples of how similar processes of interaction occurred on the continent itself. As such, islands can be seen as belonging very much within the broader context of, rather than peripheral to, African studies. Taken together, then, understanding the historical significance of Africa's Indian Ocean islands, both near and far, adds an important dimension to the rich history of Africa itself.

Notes

1. Since other contributors to this volume discuss in greater detail different aspects of the history of some of these islands, I will try not to duplicate their contributions, although there will surely be some overlap. For a quite different attempt to write about Africa's Indian Ocean islands, see Edward A. Alpers, "Indian Ocean Africa: The Island Factor," in *East Africa and the Indian Ocean* (Princeton: Markus Wiener, 2009), 39–54, which was originally published in 2000. For a recent strategic analysis of the African islands of the southwest Indian Ocean, see Tor Sellström, *Africa in the Indian Ocean: Islands in Ebb and Flow* (Leiden, Netherlands: Brill, 2015).

2. Edward A. Alpers, *The Indian Ocean in World History* (New York: Oxford University Press, 2014), 11, 49–50.

3. Abdel Rahim Salim, "Suakin: On Reviving an Ancient Red Sea Port City," *TDSR* 8, no. 2 (1997): 63–74, http://iaste.berkeley.edu/pdfs/08.2f-Spr97salim-sml.pdf. It is worth noting as well that Suakin Island is only one among an archipelago of small islands off the coast of Sudan. See G. R. Tibbetts, *Arab Navigation in the Indian Ocean before the Coming of the Portuguese* (London: The Royal Asiatic Society of Great Britain and Ireland, 1971), 416–17.

4. Jonathan Miran, *Red Sea Citizens: Cosmopolitan Society and Cultural Change in Massawa* (Bloomington: Indiana University Press, 2009), 2–3, 36–42.

5. "Dahlak, the Origin of the Islands," Dahlak—The Islands, http://www.dahlak.eu/the_islands.html.

6. Stuart Munro-Hay, "The Foreign Trade of the Aksumite Port of Adulis," *Azania: Archaeological Research in Africa* 17, no. 1 (1982): 107–25; Timothy Insoll, "Dahlak Kebir, Eritrea. From Aksumite to Ottoman," *Adumatu* 3 (2001): 39–50; Timothy Insoll, *The Archaeology of Islam in Sub-Saharan Africa* (Cambridge: Cambridge University Press, 2003), 49–58.

7. S. Y. Labib, "Kārimī," in *Encyclopedia of Islam*, 2nd ed., ed. P. Bearman et al. (Leiden, Netherlands: Brill, 2010), Brill Online.

8. Roxani Eleni Margariti, *Aden & the Indian Ocean Trade* (Chapel Hill: University of North Carolina Press, 2007), 123, 165–68.

9. Giancarlo Casale, *The Ottoman Age of Exploration* (New York: Oxford University Press, 2010), 108.

10. Insoll, "Dahlak Kebir," 43; Miran, *Red Sea Citizens*, 189–90.

11. "Qatar's US$115 Million Dahlak Island Project," *TesfaNews*, June 28, 2013, http://www.tesfanews.net/qatars-us115-million-dahlak-island-project/.

12. My primary source for this account of the Bajuni Islands is Derek Nurse, "Bajuni Database," http://www.ucs.mun.ca/~dnurse/bajuni_db.html.

13. Although today Kismayu is a mainland town, Kismayu Island may have been the original Bajuni settlement and, like Suakin and Massawa, "was only attached to the mainland in the 1960s." Nurse, "Bajuni Database," 9.

14. Justus Strandes, *The Portuguese Period in East Africa,* trans. Jean Wallwork, ed. J. S. Kirkman (Nairobi: East African Literature Bureau, 1961), 202, 218, 246, 256.

15. Lionel Casson, *The Periplus Maris Erythraei: Text with Introduction, Translation, and Commentary* (Princeton, NJ: Princeton University Press, 1989), §16.

16. Ceri Shipton et al., "Reinvestigation of Kuumbi Cave, Zanzibar, Reveals Later Stone Age Coastal Habitation, Early Holocene Abandonment and Iron Age Reoccupation," *Azania* 51, no. 2 (2016): 197–233; Felix A. Chami, "Chicken Bones from a Neolithic Limestone Cave, Zanzibar: Contact between East Africa and Asia," in *People, Contacts and the Environment in the African Past,* ed. F. Chami, G. Pwiti, and C. Radimilahy (Dar es Salaam: Dar es Salaam University Press, 2001), 84–97.

17. F. A. Chami, "The Early Iron Age on Mafia Island and Its Relationship with the Mainland," *Azania* 34, no. 1 (1999): 1–10.

18. Mark Horton and John Middleton, *The Swahili* (Oxford: Blackwell, 2000), 5; Ricardo Teixeira Duarte, *Northern Mozambique in the Swahili World: An Archaeological Approach,* Studies in African Archaeology 4 (Uppsala: Uppsala University, Department of Archaeology, 1993).

19. Derek Nurse and Thomas J. Hinnesbusch, *Swahili and Sabaki* (Berkeley: University of California Press, 1993).

20. Horton and Middleton, *The Swahili,* 39–46; see also Adria LaViolette and Jeffrey Fleischer, "The Urban History of a Rural Place: Swahili Archaeology on Pemba Island, Tanzania, 700–1500 AD," *International Journal of African Historical Studies* 42, no. 3 (2009): 433–55.

21. See, e.g., Colin Breen and Paul J. Lane, "Archaeological Approaches to East Africa's Changing Seascapes," *World Archaeology* 35, no. 3 (2003): 469–89; Annalisa C. Christie, "Overview of Work Conducted in the Mafia Archipelago 2008–2010," *Nyame Akuma* 79 (2013): 30–44; Annalisa C. Christie, "Exploring the Social Context of Maritime Exploitation in Tanzania between the 14th–18th c. AD: Recent Research from the Mafia Archipelago," in *Prehistoric Marine Resource Use in the Indo-Pacific Regions,* ed. R. Ono, A. E. Morrison, and D. J. Addison, Terra Australis 39 (N.p.: ANU E-Press, 2013), 97–122; Alison Crowther et al., "Coastal Subsistence, Maritime Trade, and the Colonization of Small Offshore Islands in Eastern African Prehistory," *The Journal of Island and Coastal Archaeology* 11, no. 2 (2016): 211–37.

22. Chapurukha M. Kusimba, *The Rise and Fall of Swahili States* (Walnut Creek: Altamira Press, 1999).

23. Randall L. Pouwels, *Horn and Crescent: Cultural Change and Traditional Islam on the East African Coast, 800–1900* (Cambridge: Cambridge University Press, 1987); Randall L. Pouwels, "Eastern Africa and the Indian Ocean to 1800: Reviewing Relations in Historical Perspective," *International Journal of African Historical Studies* 35, no. 2–3 (2002): 385–425.

24. Abdul Sheriff, *Slaves, Spices & Ivory in Zanzibar: Integration of an East African Commercial Empire into the World Economy, 1770–1873* (London: James Currey, 1987), 27, 54, 57, 64.

25. Edward A. Alpers, *Ivory and Slaves in East Central Africa* (London: Heinemann Educational Books, 1975), 234–38.

26. See B. G. Martin, *Muslim Brotherhoods in Nineteenth Century Africa* (Cambridge: Cambridge University Press, 1976), 152–76; August Nimtz, *Islam and Politics in East Africa: The Sufi Orders in Tanzania* (Minneapolis: University of Minnesota Press, 1980); Felicitas Becker, *Becoming Muslim in Mainland Tanzania, 1890–2000* (Oxford: Oxford University Press for the British Academy, 2008), 78–79, 181—186; Edward A. Alpers, "East Central Africa," in *The History of Islam in Africa*, ed. Nehemia Levtzion and Randall L. Pouwels (Athens: Ohio University Press, 2000), 311–12; Liazzat Bonate, "Islam in Northern Mozambique: A Historical Overview," *History Compass*, 8, no. 7 (2010): 583–84.

27. See, e.g., Ray Naluyaga, "CCM Opposes Zanzibar's Push for Greater Autonomy," *The East African*, August 24, 2013, http://www.theeastafrican.co.ke/news/CCM+opposes+Zanzibars+push+for+greater+autonomy+/-/2558/1966148/-/c0hnwez/-/index.html.

28. Although the Bazaruto Islands were connected to the Swahili world before the sixteenth century, the Gaza Nguni invasion of southern Mozambique in the nineteenth century caused the ancestors of their modern populations of Tsonga speakers to flee to these offshore islands, overwhelming the original inhabitants. See Malyn Newitt, *A History of Mozambique* (Bloomington: Indiana University Press, 1995), 256–62; B. I. Everett, R. P. van der Elst, and M. H. Schleyer, eds., *A Natural History of the Bazaruto Archipelago, Mozambique*, Oceanic Research Institute Special Publication No. 8 (Marine Parade, South Africa: South African Association for Marine Biological Research, 2008), 32.

29. Jennifer Lee Johnson, Julia Wondolleck, and Steven Yaffee, "The Mafia Island Marine Park," Marine Ecosystem-Based Management in Practice, http://webservices.itcs.umich.edu/drupal/mebm/?q=node/58; for Mozambique, see Edward A. Alpers, "Maritime Mozambique," *Tsingy: Revue du CRESOI Centre d'Histoire de l'Université de La Réunion, Études des Sociétés de l'océan Indien* 18, Dossier Le Mozambique (2015): 15–34.

30. Michael Pearson, *Port Cities and Intruders: The Swahili Coast, India, and Portugal in the Early Modern Era* (Baltimore and London: Johns Hopkins University Press, 1998), 67; Michael Pearson, *The Indian Ocean* (London: Routledge, 2003), 31.

31. See Jean-Louis Guébourg, *Socotra, une île hors du temps* (Bordeaux: Centre de recherches sur les espaces tropicaux [CRET] de l'Université Michel de Montaigne-Bordeaux 3, 1998).

32. Jan Batelka, "Socotra Archipelago—a Lifeboat in the Sea of Changes: Advancement in Socotran Insect Biodiversity Survey," *Acta Entomologica Musei Nationalis Pragae* 52, supplementum 2 (2012): 5, www.aemnp.eu/PDF/52_s2/52_S2_1.pdf.

33. Pierre Vérin, "Histoire ancienne du Nord-Ouest de Madagascar," *Taloha* 5, Numéro spécial (1972); Henry Wright, "Early Seafarers of the Comoro Islands: The Dembeni Phase of the IX–Xth Centuries," *Azania* 19 (1984): 13–59; Philippe Beaujard, "East Africa, the Comoros Islands and Madagascar

before the Sixteenth Century: On a Neglected Part of the World System," *Azania* 42, no. 1 (2007): 15–35.

34. See Jean Martin, *Comores: quatre îles entre pirates et planteurs*, vol. 1 (Paris: L'Harmattan, 1983), 81–110; Alpers, *East Africa and the Indian Ocean*, 131–46.

35. See Martin, *Comores*, 1:124–36, 1:263–316, 2:33–42, 2:136–43; Marie-Françoise Rombi, "Les langues de Mayotte," in *Les langues de France*, ed. Bernard Cerquiglini (Paris: Presse Universitaire de France, 2003), 305–18.

36. Alpers, *East Africa and the Indian Ocean*, 147–66.

37. Anne K. Bang, *Sufis and Scholars of the Sea: Family Networks in East Africa, 1860–1925* (London: RoutledgeCurzon, 2003), 54.

38. Bang, *Sufis and Scholars of the Sea*; Alpers, *East Africa and the Indian Ocean*, 159–64; Bonate, "Islam in Northern Mozambique," 583.

39. William Finnegan, *A Complicated War: The Harrowing of Mozambique* (Berkeley: University of California Press, 1992), 33–34; Alex Vines, *Renamo: Terrorism in Mozambique* (Bloomington: Indiana University Press, 1991), 67–68; Pierre Verin, *Les Comores* (Paris: Karthala, 1994), 214–16.

40. For different summaries of this scholarship, see Gwyn Campbell, "The Debate over Malagasy Origins," *ZIFF Journal* 2 (2005): 5–14; Solofo Randrianja and Stephen Ellis, *Madagascar: A Short History* (Chicago: University of Chicago Press, 2009), 17–43. For a more recent intervention, see Karl Alexander Adelaar, "Austronesians in Madagascar: A Critical Assessment of the Works of Paul Ottino and Philippe Beaujard," in *Early Exchange between Africa and the Wider Indian Ocean World*, ed. Gwyn Campbell (New York: Palgrave Macmillan, 2016), 77–112.

41. Alpers, *East Africa and the Indian Ocean*, 28–29, 174–75.

42. Piet Westra and James Armstrong, eds., *Slave Trade with Madagascar: The Journals of the Cape Slaver Leijdsman, 1715 / Slawe-Handel Met Madagaskar: Die Joernale van die Kaapse Slaweskip Leidsman, 1715* (Cape Town: Africana Publishers, 2006); James Armstrong and Nigel Worden, "The Slaves, 1652–1834," in *The Shaping of South African Society, 1652–1840*, 2nd ed., ed. Richard Elphick and Hermann Giliomee (Cape Town: Miller, 1989), 109–83.

43. Thomas Vernet, "Slave Trade and Slavery on the Swahili Coast, 1500–1750," in *Slavery, Islam and Diaspora*, ed. Behnaz A. Mirzai, Ismael Musah Montana, and Paul E. Lovejoy (Trenton, NJ: Africa World Press, 2009), 37–76.

44. Alpers, *East Africa and the Indian Ocean*, 131–46.

45. See Gwyn Campbell, "Madagascar and Mozambique in the Slave Trade of the Western Indian Ocean, 1800–1861," *Slavery and Abolition* 9, no. 3 (1988): 166–93; Gwyn Campbell, "The East African Slave Trade, 1861–1895: The 'Southern' Complex," *International Journal of African Historical Studies* 22, no. 1 (1989): 1–27; Edward A. Alpers, "The African Diaspora in the Indian Ocean: A Comparative Perspective," in *The African Diaspora in the Indian Ocean*, ed. Shihan de Silva Jayasuriya and Richard Pankhurst (Trenton, NJ: Africa World Press, 2003), 35–36; Klara Boyer-Rossol, "Les Makoa en pays sakalava: Une ancestralité entre deux rives, Ouest de Madagascar, XIXe–XXe siècles,"

in *Les traites et les esclavages. Perspectives historiques et contemporaines*, ed. M. Cottias, E. Cunin, A. de Almeida Mendes (Paris: Karthala, 2010), 189–99; also Klara Boyer-Rossol, "Entre les deux rives du canal du Mozambique: histoire et mémoires des Makoa de l'Ouest de Madagascar, XIXe–XXe siècles" (unpublished PhD diss., Université Paris-Diderot, 2015).

46. See Edward A. Alpers, "The French Slave Trade in East Africa (1721–1810)," *Cahiers d'Études Africaines* 10, no. 37 (1970): 80–124; José Capela and Eduardo Medeiros, "La traite au départ du Mozambique vers les îles françaises de l'Océan Indien—1720–1904," in *Slavery in South West Indian Ocean*, ed. U. Bissoondoyal and S. B. C. Servansing (Moka, Mauritius: Mahatma Gandhi Institute, 1989), 247–309.

47. Edward A. Alpers, "Becoming 'Mozambique': Diaspora and Identity in Mauritius," in *History, Memory and Identity*, ed. Vijayalakshmi Teelock and Edward A. Alpers (Port Louis: Nelson Mandela Centre for African Culture, 2001), 117–55; Edward A. Alpers, "When Diasporas Meet: The Musical Legacies of Slavery and Indentured Labor in the Mascarene Islands," in "When Diasporas Meet: The Musical Legacies of Slavery and Indentured Labor in the Mascarene Islands," unpublished conference paper.

48. Richard B. Allen, *Slaves, Freedmen, and Indentured Laborers in Colonial Mauritius* (Cambridge: Cambridge University Press, 1999); H. Ly Tio Fane Pineo, *Lured Away: The Life History of Indian Cane Workers in Mauritius* (Moka: Mahatma Gandhi Institute, 1984); Marina Carter, *Servants, Sirdars and Settlers: Indians in Mauritius, 1834–1873* (Delhi: Oxford University Press, 1995); Marina Carter and James Ng Foong Kwong, *Forging the Rainbow: Labour Immigrants in British Mauritius* (Mauritius: Alfran, 1997).

49. Deryck Scarr, *Seychelles Since 1770: History of a Slave and Post-Slavery Society* (Trenton, NJ: Africa World Press, 1999).

50. Moses D. E. Nwulia, *The History of Slavery in Mauritius and the Seychelles, 1810–1875* (Rutherford: Farleigh Dickenson University Press, 1981).

51. For a valuable consideration of islandness and creolization, see Robin Cohen and Olivia Sheringham, "The Salience of Islands in the Articulation of Creolization and Diaspora," *Diaspora* 17, no. 1 (2008): 6–17.

52. Alain St. Ange, "Growing Sustainable Tourism: The Seychelles Approach," http://www.iipt.org/IIPT%20Book/articles/Alain%20St.%20Ange.Seychelles.pdf.

53. See note 40 above; also Philippe Beaujard, *Les Mondes de l'Océan Indien*, 2 vols. (Paris: Armand Colin, 2012), 2:347–69. For an important new contributions to this debate, see Murray P. Cox, Michael G. Nelson, Meryanne K. Tumonggor, François-X. Ricaut, and Herawat Sudoyo, "A Small Island Cohort of Island Southeast Asian Women Founded Madagascar," *Proceedings of the Royal Society B*, published online March 21, 2012, doi: 10.1098/rspb.2012.0012; Atholl Anderson, Aaron Camens, Geoffrey Clark, and Simon Haberle, "Investigating Premodern Colonization of the Indian Ocean: The Remote Islands Enigma," in *Connecting Continents: Archaeology and History in the Indian Ocean World*, ed. Krish Seetah (Athens: Ohio University Press, 2018), 30–67.

54. Armstrong and Worden, "The Slaves"; Kerry Ward, *Networks of Empire: Forced Migration in the Dutch East India Company* (New York: Cambridge University Press, 2009).

55. Richard B. Allen, "Satisfying the 'Want for Labouring People': European Slave Trading in the Indian Ocean, 1500–1850," *Journal of World History*, 21, no. 1 (2010): 45–73; for the wider picture, see Richard B. Allen, *European Slave Trading in the Indian Ocean, 1500–1800* (Athens: Ohio University Press, 2014).

56. Ineke van Kessel, "The Black Dutchmen. African Soldiers in the Netherlands East Indies," in *Merchants, Missionaries & Migrants: 300 Years of Dutch-Ghanaian Relations*, ed. W. M. J. van Kessel (Amsterdam: KIT Publishers, 2002), 133–34; Ineke van Kessel, "West African Soldiers in the Dutch East Indies: From *Donkos* to Black Dutchmen," *Transactions of the Historical Society of Ghana*, new series, 9 (2005): 41–60; Ineke van Kessel, "Labour Migration from the Gold Coast to Dutch East Indies: Recruiting African Troops for the Dutch Colonial Army in the Age of Indentured Labour," in *Fractures and Reconnections: Civic Action and Redefinition of African Economic and Political Spaces: Studies in Honour of Piet J. J. Konings*, ed. Jan Abbink (Hamburg: Lit Verlag, 2012), 61–85.

57. Constancio Pinto and Matthew Jardine, *Inside the East Timor Resistance* (Toronto: Lorimer, 1997), 6. See also João Paulo Borges Coelho, "African Troops in the Portuguese Colonial Army, 1961–1974: Angola, Guinea-Bissau and Mozambique," *Portuguese Studies Review* 10, no. 1 (2002): 131–34.

58. Edward A. Alpers, "The African Diaspora in the Northwestern Indian Ocean: Reconsideration of an Old Problem, New Directions for Research," *Comparative Studies of South Asia, Africa & the Middle East* 17, no. 2 (1997): 75–76; there are a number of videos of *kafferingha baila* performances available on YouTube.

59. Andrew Forbes and Fawzi Ali, "The Maldive Islands and Their Historical Links with the Coast of Eastern Africa," *Kenya Past and Present* 11 (1981): 15–20.

60. Jan Hogendorn and Marion Johnson, *The Shell Money of the Slave Trade* (Cambridge: Cambridge University Press, 1986).

61. António Alberto de Andrade, *Relações de Moçambique Setecentista* (Lisboa: Agência Geral do Ultramar, 1955), 150, 214, 216, 352, 377.

62. Jeronymo Romero, *Supplemento á Memoria Descriptiva e Estatistica do Districto de Cabo Delgado com um Noticia ácerca do Establecimento da Colonia de Pemba* (Lisboa: Typographia Universal, 1860), 130.

63. Sheriff, *Slaves, Spices & Ivory*, 99, 134.

64. Forbes and Ali, "The Maldive Islands."

65. See Burkhard Schnepel and Edward A. Alpers, eds., *Connectivity in Motion: Island Hubs in the Indian Ocean World* (New York: Palgrave Macmillan, 2018) for a wider comparative perspective.

9

Monsoon Metropolis

Migration, Mobility, and Mediation in the Western Indian Ocean

William Bissell

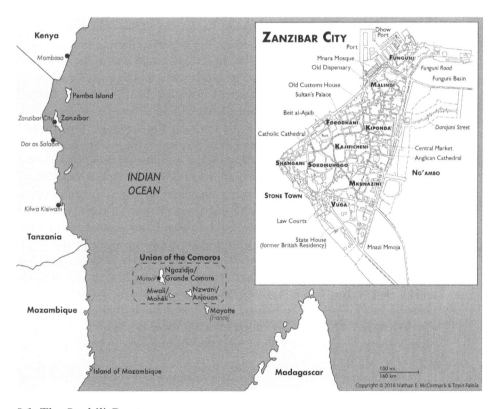

9.1: The Swahili Coast

The documentary *As Old as My Tongue* (2009) opens with a shot of a *jahazi* (dhow) floating at sea, its sails billowing in the Indian Ocean breeze, and then cuts to the image of an early modern map, tracking the long ocean journey following the monsoon winds from India and Arabia all along the African coast down to Zanzibar.[1] Against this visual backdrop, the voice one hears is that of Bi Kidude, the irrepressible diva of Zanzibari *taarab* and *unyago* music, who then appears on screen, shown with her band at sea on the deck of the dhow, preparing to launch into a performance.[2] Bi Kidude is wearing her trademark kerchief, her face lined with experience, wise and wry and fierce—an altogether formidable presence. Often described as a legend, certainly Kidude's early life was shrouded in mystery. Her birthdate unknown, she was a poor rural coconut harvester's daughter who grew up rough, sang and traveled mostly in obscurity, and rose to fame only in the last decades of her life. She defied conventions of gender and social norms, smoking, drinking, and living as she pleased, driven by the power of that uncompromising voice.

In the documentary, she describes the origins of her music, sometime perhaps in the 1920s as a youth, when she began to hang out at the port during monsoon season, drawn by the transoceanic traffic there, where no "good girl" was ever supposed to go. "I was a hooligan, a beach hooligan" (*mhuni wa pwani*), she laughed, dressing like a sailor in ragged clothes and barefoot, transgressing Zanzibari notions of respectable or moral behavior in multiple ways. In the city, she said, the news would spread that the Arab *jahazis* had arrived, the ones with wealth, beautifully appointed, with rugs and everything inside, just like a "ship" (*meli*). And when these dhow crews from ports all over the Indian Ocean would land in Zanzibar, they would gather along the shore to entertain themselves, and there Bi Kidude first heard the pulsating rhythms of their *madumbak* drums. Like her legendary mentor, Siti bint Saadi, Bi Kidude learned over time how to appropriate these Arab musical forms brought by the monsoon and to remake them in creative ways for African audiences, taking her songs on the road, making them speak to new audiences across Tanganyika, and eventually finding her way back to the coast, where her music played a crucial role in the ritual lives of women, initiating young girls into marriage. "I have always called myself a *mwizi wa Taarab*, or a Taarab thief because no one ever taught me," said Bi Kidude, "I stole it by listening to the Arabs and Siti."[3]

In the outlines of this tale, we can locate many of the crucial features of urban life and island experience in the western Indian Ocean, Zanzibar in particular. Erik Gilbert has written of the "familiar louche quality" of Indian Ocean ports from Mukalla to Aden, Mombasa and Zanzibar, linked by cosmopolitan and hybrid populations, shared Indo-Arab-African architectural forms, cultural practices, and exchanged goods.[4] Connected by the monsoon winds, these cities have long served as meeting grounds, markets, and sites of mediation, where the shoreline in particular constituted an especially liminal zone of intersection and exchange. In the mid-1870s, one European observer described the Zanzibar beach at low tide as the "native Bois de Boulogne, the place of assignation and the ballroom," where Zanzibaris of the popular classes would gather under the moon, "summoned by the irresistible music of the tom-tom and fife."[5] As this suggests, the shore has long served as a shifting space for cultural exchanges and encounters that could not occur in the more settled spheres of terra firma. Shaped by broader Indian Ocean processes, the beach is a meeting ground, "a double-edged space, in-between; an exit space that is also an entry space; a space where edginess rules."[6]

Along these lines, Pamila Gupta has recently highlighted "the interstitiality of island-ness in the Indian Ocean,"[7] and in considering the example of Bi Kidude this insight seems critical on multiple levels: interstitial in the sense of the in-between spaces where land and sea meet, where lines of identity and belonging get crossed, where cultural practices, performances, and possibilities are exchanged and altered, and novelty bumps up against the ordinary and everyday. "Urban islands" conjures up images of isolated spheres and sharply distinct zones, but as Bi Kidude's life suggests, Indian Ocean cities and islands compel us to think about more fluid and contested sets of connections and circulations. Zanzibar city has long been marked by its distinctive island identity, and this chapter will explore the myriad ways that islandness has played a central role in shaping urban lives and possibilities—environmentally, socially, culturally, and economically. Urban theorists have long reminded us that cities must be situated within a wider set of sociocultural, spatial, and environmental relations. Yet what different stakes are involved in exploring urban intersections when we approach and analyze the city not from a territorial perspective but across a more fluid milieu, infused and informed by currents across the sea?

Monsoon Materialities

Writing from the vantage point of postcolonial independence, inscribing a moment when the 1964 revolution in Zanzibar had abruptly reoriented the islands toward a pan-Africanist and socialist future, the novelist Abdulrazak

Gurnah reflected on the eclipse of the monsoon trade, eloquently capturing its impact even in the wake of its disappearance. When the annual
dhow traffic across the Indian Ocean came to a close, he observed,

> the last months of the year would no longer see crowds of sailing ships
> lying plank to plank in the harbour, the sea between them glistening with
> slicks of their waste, or the streets thronged with Somalis or Suri Arabs or
> Sindhis, buying and selling and breaking into incomprehensible fights,
> and at night camping in the open spaces, singing cheerful songs and
> brewing tea, or stretched out on the ground in their grimy rags, shouting
> raucous ribaldries at each other. In the first year or two after that, the
> streets and the open spaces were silent with their absences in those late
> months of the year, especially when we felt the lack of the things they
> used to bring with them, ghee and gum, cloths and crudely hammered
> trinkets, livestock and salted fish, dates, tobacco, perfume, rosewater,
> incense, and handfuls of all manner of wondrous things. (Abdulrazak
> Gurnah, *By the Sea* [New York: The Free Press, 2001], 16.)

Gurnah grew up in the Malindi quarter in Zanzibar city, where many
gained a living from the sea, right next to Funguni, where the vast majority of dhow crews resided when they came to Zanzibar, and he knew the
scene well. Like other Zanzibaris who came of age in this maritime milieu,
he was keenly aware of how urban life and sociability were shaped by periodic inflows of novel people, cultural forms, and goods from across the
sea. Indeed, it is no accident that it was precisely there that Bi Kidude
came down to the Arab ships to hang out with the sailors and listen to
their music. This fluid Indian Ocean milieu certainly took on historically
specific forms in the twentieth century, but it was also fed by much longer-
term material and environmental currents.

Michael Pearson has analyzed what he calls the "monsoon regime," the
system or enduring structure of weather patterns, periodicity, and wind
flows variously designated as *mawsim* in Arabic or *msimu* in Kiswahili.[8] These
terms cover alternating currents of monsoon winds and seasons, shifting
direction annually between northeast flows from November to March and
southwest from roughly April to August.[9] Once the cyclical code of the
monsoon was cracked, beginning perhaps as early as the seventh century
BCE, regular seasonal patterns of seaborne movement along the Indian
Ocean rim became possible. The emergence of this long-distance oceanic
trade "undergirded the Indian Ocean as an interregional arena of economy and culture."[10] While the Swahili coast may have been situated at the
edge of this environmental and ecological system, it was deeply marked by
its long-term impact.

At the broadest level the long-distance trade was made possible by differing ecological zones and the divergent products that could be regularly exchanged between them: fish and *boriti* (mangrove poles), dates, spices, and slaves. Along these trade routes, cultural ideas, relations of exchange, and modes of sociability also circulated, creating durable patterns of interaction over time. While facilitating movement across the Indian Ocean in one sense, the monsoon system also punctuated or hindered it with significant pauses that had real social consequences, "requiring dhows to spend a long time between the monsoons in their ports of destination" while waiting for the winds to shift.[11] Interactions between seafaring outsiders and locals were also greatly facilitated by the spread of Islam as a shared ethical, social, and ideological horizon, fostering the growth of an ecumene as well as the sense of cosmopolitan participation in a much wider community. In this respect, we can understand the emergence of Swahili society as a distinctive island and coastal formation, a liminal zone where land and sea meet and a range of African groups intersected with diverse peoples drawn from around the Indian Ocean rim, fashioning a distinctive sociocultural world over time.

The emergence of what John Middleton has called a mercantile "middleman society" occurred in the absence of a single state or overarching political control. Indeed, the Swahili coast was constituted as a network of "complexly organized congeries of communities" where city-states rose and fell based on their capacity to assimilate, absorb, and incorporate outsiders, translating trading relations into the enduring idioms of kinship, blood, and reciprocity.[12] Michael Pearson has emphasized the littoral as a frontier zone, highlighting its permeability, and we can certainly see how a certain fluidity and flexibility has long characterized the adaptive qualities of Swahili cultural worlds, especially on the islands.[13] For well over a millennium prior to 1964, writes G. Thomas Burgess,

> Zanzibar figured as a small part of a vast Indian Ocean world of trade, monsoons, and Islam that had fostered a nearly uninterrupted flow of goods and people. This world was multi-cultural and multi-lingual; it produced a number of diasporas and a patchwork of ethnic enclaves in islands and port cities along its ocean rim. Along the coast of East Africa, Arab and Persian merchants and settlers gradually assimilated into local Swahili-speaking society, which though predominately African in ancestry, was unique from societies of the interior due to its reception of people, ideas, and commodities from overseas. If anything was distinct about Swahili coastal towns, it was their cosmopolitanism. (G. Thomas Burgess, "Memories, Myths, and Meanings of the Zanzibari Revolution," in *War and Peace in Africa*, ed. Toyin Falola and Raphael Chijioke Njoku [Durham, NC: Carolina Academic Press, 2010], 431.)

Imperial Currents, Island Colonialism

Until the early nineteenth century, Zanzibar was simply one node in a network of Swahili city-states on the edge of the western Indian Ocean trading system. It was by no means the most prominent or important, but that status was soon to change, as Zanzibar was transformed into the center of an expansive Omani Empire that was gradually overtaken and subsumed within the British imperium. The formation of a new and dynamic urban center in Zanzibar was intricately connected to its island location in an Indian Ocean world that was being increasingly incorporated within global economic and political circuits through this dual colonial impact.

Zanzibar was located on the southern edge of the monsoon system where dhows could reasonably expect to make the outward and return journeys within a year. While the Omanis faced ongoing military resistance in more established sites such as Mombasa, the local dynasty in Zanzibar proved susceptible to accommodation. Omani interest in Zanzibar came as the Busaidi dynasty consolidated its power in Oman itself, turning away from the desert interior and expanding its transoceanic links. Britain was increasingly asserting itself as a maritime power in the Indian Ocean, cultivating local allies and seeking to consolidate its hold over trade routes to India. In this effort, Oman occupied a strategic location, and the Busaidis allied themselves with the British, controlling the emergent shipping industry out of Muscat, cultivating Indian merchant capital as a source of finance, and consolidating their power all along the East African coast.

The growing Omani presence in East Africa was sparked by economic expansion, changing patterns of trade, and the political shift of the Omani capital to Zanzibar in the 1830s. Arab traders had long held a monopoly on the Indian Ocean slave trade but were facing growing resistance. The Omani expansion across the Indian Ocean was facilitated by their alliance with the British, but this increasingly unequal partnership came with ever greater costs. The Napoleonic Wars had disrupted Zanzibar's slave trade with the French islands, and British victories did not bode well for the reopening of these markets. Moreover, beginning with the Moresby Treaty of 1822, the British sought to impose increasing restrictions on the trade to the Gulf, cutting into the revenue of Omani merchants as well as diminishing state receipts at Zanzibar.[14] Seeking to adapt to these new conditions, Omani merchants in Zanzibar drew upon their wider circulations in the Indian Ocean world, including local knowledge gained from other islands. In particular, they benefited from their experience in the French sphere, where slave labor had long been deployed to cultivate valuable tropical commodities for export. With the example of the Mascarenes in mind, merchants in Zanzibar recognized that while slaves could no longer readily be transported across the Indian Ocean, the products of their labor faced no such restrictions. And an ideal product lay close at hand—cloves, the seedlings of which had been introduced to Zanzibar in the early nineteenth century by an Omani merchant with an enthusiasm for all things French, who had previously lived in the Seychelles, Île de France, and Île Bourbon.

With the opening of the plantation sector came increasing numbers of colonial settlers, land alienation, and flows of unfree labor drawn from a wide array of mainland African societies. In 1819 there were only about 1,000 Omanis living in Zanzibar, but by 1840 there were as many as 5,000. A mania for investment in cloves was well under way, marked by what Sheriff calls a "feverish expansion."[15] From a transshipment site of the slave trade across the Indian Ocean, Zanzibar was rapidly being transformed into a plantation society fueled by slave labor and the export of island spices and ivory. In the first half of the nineteenth century, plantation wealth fueled the growth of urban Zanzibar as profits from the agricultural sector were increasingly invested by the elite in urban properties. Once a small fishing settlement and trading town, Zanzibar city was being transformed into the capital of East Africa. Omanis sunk their wealth into substantial multistoried dwellings along the seafront and into Shangani, following the tradition of aspiring patricians all along the Swahili coast who sought to mark their newfound status by building in stone. Much of the iconic architecture of what later became known as "Stone Town" was also intrinsically linked to its island origins as stone structures were built out of coral rag limestone and held up by mangrove poles or *boriti*, a long-term staple for export to the Gulf, undergirding commonalities in architectural styles around the Indian Ocean rim.

The plantation sector was socially critical, shaping Zanzibar as a slave society, displacing indigenes, alienating land, and giving elite Omani landowners precedence in terms of status displays, political prominence, and the wealth necessary to underwrite stone mansions and large households in the expanding urban center. But the clove sector had already peaked by the 1840s, and agriculture was plagued by volatility and increasing levels of debt. The second half of the nineteenth century was marked by the rising economic role of trade and transshipment, with Zanzibar playing a classic entrepôt role. Indian merchant capital had long been crucial to the Busaidi sultanate, and its role only increased as Zanzibar became an expansive center of mercantile capitalism linking the African mainland to the United States, Europe, the Gulf, India, and China. Zanzibar continued to be linked to the long-distance

Indian Ocean trade following the monsoon circuit, but was transformed into the political and economic heart of the system. All foreign traders, beginning with American ships out of Salem, were forbidden from dealing directly with ports along the African mainland; merchants had to come through Zanzibar at a time when the island had a very favorable balance of trade with an array of US and European partners, driven by demand for ivory and spices to supply a rising bourgeoisie. As a result, urban growth was increasingly fueled by the rising trade in commodities originating on the African mainland, and this sector was dominated by Indians, driving smaller Arab and Swahili traders out of their formerly preeminent positions.

Between 1820 and 1870, the South Asian population of the islands grew fifteenfold. In the 1840s, Browne noted that the southern section of the city was already inhabited by "wealthy Banyan, Hindoo, and Muscat merchants" who had "acquired splendid fortunes in the ivory and gum-copal trade, and in commercial transactions with agents in the East Indies."[16] An urban quarter, or *mtaa*, of the city was already called "Hindostan," occupied by "industrious Hindoo merchants. . . . They have numerous shops, with goods and wares exposed for sale, such as Persian rugs, Madras cloths, combs, beads, queensware, spoons, knives, coffee, spices, and every thing required by the mass of the citizens. The Banyans occupy separate streets, and are large dealers in gum copal, ivory teeth, honey, sugar, and other articles of commerce."[17]

By 1860, the town's population had grown to include about 60,000 inhabitants. On top of this total, as British consul Rigby noted, "during the north-east monsoon there are probably from thirty to forty thousand strangers added to the permanent population. During the last few years, the population of the town has been rapidly increasing, and entire new quarters have been built."[18] South Asian migration was increasing year by year, he noted, and "the bazaars are extensive, and well supplied with articles of foreign manufacture. Nearly all the shopkeepers and artisans are natives of India."[19] Twenty years later, John Robb wrote of the continuing "steady" increase of Indian settlers to urban Zanzibar, attributing this to "increased facilities of communication and extended knowledge of the place and its promises of lucrative trade" in Western India.[20]

Hindus tended to cluster in the central area behind the fort, market, and Customs House, while Khojas settled in the *mitaa* (quarters) behind the royal residences from Kiponda to Malindi, stretching back to the tidal creek. Over time this area was built up into an extended commercial bazaar, with narrow streets and shopfront dwellings leading to Darajani and across the creek into Ng'ambo, where poorer Khoja, Bohoras, and Sunni Muslims took up residence in the latter nineteenth century. As this suggests, beyond a tiny merchant elite, the South Asian population was diverse in status and wealth, with the majority living in modest circumstances as humble shopkeepers, artisans, craftspeople, cooks, and petty traders. In general, as the western triangular peninsula was built up, with a greater proportion of stone structures, the city was also built out as slaves, clients, and poorer immigrants flocked to Ng'ambo, living in popular quarters across the creek.

One thing all observers agreed upon: the growing urban population of Zanzibar was "very mixed."[21] Elite Omanis "with a taste for foreign luxuries such as handsome furniture and dress, costly mirrors, china etc."[22] mingled with Arabs from the Hadhramaut, the coast, and Indian Ocean islands, working as porters, sailors, or in the caravan trade. In the sultan's retinue were Baluchi mercenaries, Abyssinians, and Persians; Khojas and Hindus formed the majority of South Asian urbanites, but there were significant groups of Bohora, Parsis, and Goan Christians. Given the long history of exchange and intermarriage along the coast, distinguishing between long-resident Arabs, Shirazi, and Swahili was always a challenge for outsiders, who fell back on the stereotyped images of "half-caste," "mulatto," or inter-mixed races. Sufficient numbers of Malagasy resided in Ng'ambo to have an entire quarter named after them, and a large Comorian population also resided there. Long-term coastal or free Africans were joined by a large and growing number of slaves drawn from a wide array of African societies in the mainland interior. In addition, there were also indigenous inhabitants of the islands, most of whom were eventually relegated to less fertile lands in the north or west of the islands, including Wahadimu, Watumbatu, and Wapemba.

Subsuming the Sultanate

Following the shift of the Omani capital to Zanzibar under Sultan Seyyid Said, the islands rapidly became central nodes in an expansive and far-flung empire, its fortunes linked to wider globalizing processes. In the late 1830s, a visiting American missionary noted that the sultan was a "powerful prince, possessing a more efficient force than all the native princes combined, from the Cape of Good Hope to Japan." His power was not based on just the projection of military force or possession of territory, however, but the capacity to project power as needed while managing commercial, social, and political relations with clients on a vast scale:

The sultan is a powerful prince, possessing a more efficient naval force than all the native princes combined, from the Cape of Good Hope to Japan. His resources are more than adequate to his wants: they are derived from commerce, he owning himself a great number of merchant vessels; from duties on foreign merchandize, and from tribute money and presents received from various princes, all of which produce a large sum. . . . His possessions in Africa stretch from Cape Delgado (latitude 10 south) to Cape Guardafui (latitude 12 north); and from Cape Aden in Arabia to Rusel Hand; and thence they extend along the northern coast of Arabia (or the coast of Aman) to the entrance to the Persian Gulf. He claims also the sea coast and islands within the Persian Gulf, including the Bahrein islands and the pearl fishery contiguous to them, with the northern part of the gulf as far as Scindy. It is true that only a small portion of this immense territory is garrisoned by his troops; but all is tributary to him. His vessels trade not only with the countries named, but also with Guzzerat, Surat, Demaun, Bombay, Bay of Bengal, Ceylon, Sumatra, Java, the Mauritius, Comoro islands, Madagascar, and the Portuguese possessions in East Africa. (Mr. Burgess, "Eastern Africa: Letters from Mr. Burgess, Dated Sept. 11th, 1839," *Boston Missionary Herald* 86 [1840], 121.)

Using Zanzibar as an island base, the sultanate unified its position all along the *mrima* coast that stretched from modern Kenya into Tanganyika, maintaining a monopoly over outside access to resources and raw materials on the continent, while cultivating political clients and allies deep into the African interior. In this sense, the islands grew to transnational prominence in the nineteenth century as a dynamic and growing point of convergence linking Africa, the Arab world, Asia, Europe, and the United States.

Over the longer term, several developments threatened this far-flung, diffuse, and emergent empire. First, there were increasing British restrictions on the slave trade that cut into a key source of the sultan's revenues while undermining his authority in Zanzibar itself. Succession disputes offered Britain further opportunities to intervene, even as successive sultans depended more and more on British power to maintain their hold on the throne. Greater dependence and debt were met with increasing levels of challenge from European powers, as the scramble for Africa intensified. The territorial limits of the sultan's dominions on the mainland had never been precisely defined, much less defended in terms of active military occupation or sovereign possession. As German adventurers laid claim to mainland territory formerly held by the sultan, Britain refused initially to intervene, using European competitors as a way to exert greater power over an increasingly weakened sultan. Even then, British authorities negotiated with the Germans only when their own colonial hegemony seemed potentially at risk in the region; if unchecked, the rising German presence threatened British access to the headwaters of the Nile while weakening their hold over the western Indian Ocean. In the end, the "rights" to one set of islands would be swapped in exchange for another. Britain agreed to cede Heligoland in the North Sea to Germany if Germany in exchange would recognize a British protectorate in Zanzibar. This negotiation between imperial rivals led to the Anglo-German Agreement of 1890, and the sultan had little choice but to accept the "protection" of his powerful backers in exchange for being allowed to maintain at least a nominal hold on the throne.

Britain backed into the establishment of a protectorate in Zanzibar, largely driven by considerations in Europe, the Indian Ocean, and the continent itself. While proponents of formal colonial control touted the strategic and economic value of these East African islands, these promises were highly speculative at best. At the time, there was no clear idea what the establishment of a protectorate might actually entail, and British officials struggled to establish the bare rudiments of colonial administration while trying to find sufficient resources to pay for colonial occupation. Soon after he arrived to take over the protectorate, the new consul general, Gerald Portal, announced his intentions to "establish this place as not only a mere port of transshipment but also a great market."[23] A month later, he vowed that Zanzibar could be transformed into a "port of great value," becoming the "East African Hong Kong."[24] The early decades of colonial rule would be haunted by efforts to reformulate the economy on a more productive basis, generating sufficient revenues for reinvestment and growth. However, the imposition of British colonialism had itself created a series of contradictions that continued to severely hamper these intentions and render their efforts fruitless.

"Now is the critical time for Zanzibar," Portal wrote soon after his arrival. "Now & the next few months are to decide whether Zanzi. is to be a valuable possession—the most thriving commercial center of East Africa—or whether it is to be only a small Arab clove-growing island."[25] Most of the island's revenues were dependent on Arab landowners and the plantation sector. Having justified their tightening of control over the sultanate by placing greater restrictions on the slave trade, the British regime found itself compelled to move to abolish slavery on the islands itself, threatening already restive elite Arab interests and compromising the primary source of labor on which clove production depended. Moreover, the sector was burdened insofar as Arab landowners were already heavily indebted to Indian merchant capital in the city. At the time, Portal hoped to move toward the declaration of Zanzibar as a free port, but his goal of reinvigorating the

transshipment trade and reviving Zanzibar as a central market for imports
and exports had already been sharply compromised—by the British themselves. The island, after all, had become a central entrepôt and emporium
only insofar as it was the principal gateway to gain access to resources and
goods obtained from the African interior. But the declaration of British
rule over Zanzibar entailed abruptly cutting the island off from its interior possessions, while firmly establishing German competition on the
mainland and leading to the growth of rival ports in Dar es Salaam and
Mombasa. The isolation of the islands was rendered complete when British
officials forced the sultan to sell his final holdings on the *mrima* coast to the
Germans and then appropriated the funds to pay off speculative metropolitan investors in the failed Imperial British East African Company. This
stripped the sultanate of further assets while guaranteeing that for decades
to come, Zanzibar would remain just a series of clove-growing islands, just
as Portal once feared.

Insular/Cosmopolitan: Contested Island Identities

"In Zanzibar town all the known races of the world meet and mingle,
Esquimaux and Australian aborigines perhaps excepted," observed an
Anglican missionary.[26] Subsequent European visitors concurred, sounding
quite similar themes: "The old city of Zanzibar remains what it was, and
rejoices in such a mass of picturesque humanity as is surely to be seen in
no other African city. . . . It is thoroughly cosmopolitan, though not in
the European sense."[27] These colonial descriptions were invariably framed
from a particular positioning, with an isolated European outsider standing
back and separating himself from the urban swirl, seeking to find a privileged vantage point and visual perspective on the heterogeneous crowds
passing by. "It is quite instructive to stay for a time at some busy spot in
the city and watch the varied crowd go by," as a British resident enthused.
"There are few places of the same size where one can study the races of
mankind with greater facility and ease. . . . [Here] the spectator will be able
to rub shoulders with some of the wilder and less-known people of Africa
and of Asia."[28] References to Zanzibar as "cosmopolitan" often went hand
in hand with comparisons to other "Oriental" or "Eastern" cities, as a later
British resident, Claud Hollis, revealed:

> The islands are set like emeralds in the Azanian sea. . . . In the capital
> there is an Eastern atmosphere and glamour not possessed by any other
> town in East Africa. . . . The population numbers over 200,000. . . . Forty
> thousand of these people live in the capital, and the streets are rendered

very picaresque during the northeast monsoon, or, as it is called locally, the dhow season—that is to say, at the present time of the year—by the arrival of many hundreds of wild-looking men from Arabia, the Persian Gulf, and Somaliland, whose ancestors helped to make its history. (Claud Hollis, "Zanzibar: Present Conditions and Interests," *Journal of the African Society* 28, no. 111 [1929]: 218.)

As this suggests, during the colonial period the monsoon system continued to bring dhows, sailors, and goods to urban Zanzibar and then back again across the Indian Ocean with the seasonal winds. As Gilbert notes, dhows carried large crews comparative to their size in order to handle the "unwieldy spars of their lateen rigged sails" and many extra sailors tagged along to engage in trade on their own account or to see the wider world.[29] During the dhow season, Zanzibar, like other ports around the Indian Ocean rim, would fill up with heterogeneous dhow crews who crowded into the city, living with and interacting with locals for extended periods, waiting for the winds to turn. The dhows conveyed a "very large floating population"; in 1945–46, for example, more than 300 foreign dhows came to Zanzibar, carrying more than 6,000 sailors.[30] Three years later, almost 9,700 arrived in dhows—6,600 crew and more than 3,000 passengers—and at least half found living space in the city with locals in Malindi and Funguni.[31] Sheriff highlights the "social impact of this substantial movement of people to and fro, year in and year out" that the monsoon circuit made possible, emphasizing the "intermingling and integration" between sailors and locals.[32] Indeed, interviewing old *nahodhas* (captains) in the dhow port of Sur, Sheriff references their nostalgic memories of Zanzibar as "the island of dreams."[33]

Nonetheless, for all the references to cosmopolitanism in Zanzibar or gestures toward cultural, religious, and social unities across the Indian Ocean world, we should not overlook enduring distinctions and differences. If seas link or join sociocultural milieus across great distances—serving as "a medium of transport, of exchange, and of intercourse"[34]—then islands can also serve to separate and differentiate. The long-term circulation of goods and people through ports along the Indian Ocean rim did not create a seamless and shared universe. As Edward Simpson and Kai Kresse remind us, the extensive history of trade and migration across the Indian Ocean has not eradicated difference but instead has shaped societies "where differences are recognized and individuals are, to a greater or lesser extent, equipped with the skill to navigate through such differences. If it makes sense to speak generally of 'Indian Ocean cosmopolitanism,' it is in this sense of social contestation based on a struggle with history that is not so much shared as held in common."[35]

Inhabiting islands can be a precarious business; where, how, and on what grounds one might obtain a sure foothold—culturally, socially, politically—is often up for grabs. Social contestation has certainly been no stranger to Zanzibari shores. Indeed, it is the very fabric out of which the islands' history was formed. As Gilbert reminds us, only a very small percentage of Zanzibar's nineteenth-century population was indigenous in the strict sense.[36] The vast majority of Zanzibaris were immigrants, either by compulsion or choice, drawn to the isles from Africa or across the Indian Ocean world at various historical moments. In a dynamic and expanding social world where virtually everyone came from somewhere else and many were on the move, questions of who truly belonged in the islands and on what grounds became especially acute. Struggles over identity, belonging, and status were all the more intense in sociocultural contexts marked by fluid boundaries, competing colonial regimes, the violence of slavery, and the uneven expansion of global capitalism.

The impact of dual colonialism on the islands—initially Omani, then British—opened up new conjunctures for cosmopolitan intersections but also utterly altered the sociopolitical and economic landscape in which these encounters could occur. No question, the Swahili coast had long been structured by hierarchies and signs of sociocultural distinction: between patrician and plebian, freeborn and slave, men and women, locals and outsiders, long-established kin groups and recent arrivals. But these older lines of distinction took on new shape and salience in a colonial context structured by a newly assertive Omani elite, an expansive state, land alienation, the marginalization of indigenes, and the large-scale importation and enslavement of Africans from the mainland interior.

Over the long durée, Swahili society all along the coast and islands was shaped by its interstitial positioning both spatially and socially, distinguished by its marked differences from inland African societies as well as more recent arrivals from across the Indian Ocean. There was a long-established tradition of coastal exceptionalism, honed in practice and embodied in social performance. These distinctions operated all the more powerfully in social worlds that looked outward to lands across the Indian Ocean as the loci of prestigious origins (Shirazi identity, for example, or *sharif* descent) and the source of Islamic revelation, learning, and sites of sacred pilgrimage. In the context of the Omani conquest, the rise of the Busaidi dynasty, and the formation of slave society, local notions about the cultural and civilizational superiority of the coast assumed rather different forms in nineteenth-century Zanzibar. In local terms, to be "civilized" was to possess *ustaarabu*—that is, to manifest all the comportment, characteristics, and cultural capital expected of an "Arab" (*mwarabu*, pl., *waarabu*).

In this sense, *wastaarabu* or *waungwana* (the civilized or free-born) were contrasted with *washenzi* (savages or barbarians) who lacked the cultural sophistication, refinement, or knowledge that a "proper" Zanzibari should wield. With the growth of the caravan trade and plantation slavery in Zanzibar, *washenzi* came to be associated especially with cultural others in the African interior—newly arrived captives, unfamiliar with Swahili custom, non-Islamic, unacculturated, "raw" or "savage." In Zanzibari society the most trusted slaves were *wazalia*—those born on the island, fluent in Kiswahili and practicing Muslims, long-serving, proven, and fully integrated within local kin and social networks. Even the rawest slave brought to the island could eventually hope to become Swahili or even Arab over time by accepting Islam, adopting local ways, becoming fluent in Kiswahili, gaining greater autonomy, and dressing and acting "appropriately" in line with coastal cultural expectations.[37]

It is important to note, however, that while cultural markers of identity in Zanzibar were fluid, they were never equally open and up for grabs; indeed, by the later nineteenth century, the entire cultural terrain was configured in a way that distinctly privileged wealthy, elite, male, and Arab interests. Relations of superiority and domination, patron and client, master and slave, insider and outsider were pervasive throughout Zanzibari society, structuring the terms of negotiating and navigating sociocultural life. Ideally, these social relations would be worked out within a moral economy of reciprocal duties and obligations—unequal, absolutely, but governed by social expectations of respect (*heshima*), rights, and due regard. In practice, however, struggles to define social terms of engagement could often be conducted with far greater harshness and hardness, etching lines of stark inequality and essentialized notions of difference.

This is especially true in a colonial context such as Zanzibar, where Arabocentric discourses often emphasized the cultural uniqueness of Arab identity; where Omani elites sought to assert their alleged superiority; and where civilizational difference was deployed to argue which groups were best and who truly belonged. This coastal emphasis on distinction was reinforced by a rigid and racist British colonial ideology that sought to protect elite Arab interests, maintain the Busaidi sultanate at least as a ceremonial front, and treat Arabs as an established and rightful aristocracy in order to protect social stability. By contrast, during the colonial period Indians were depicted as intrusive capitalists, merchants, and traders, and often designated as interlopers or outsiders. "Africans" occupied the bottom of the social hierarchy, regarded as sources of manual labor in agriculture, porterage, and petty trades. Hence, within colonial Zanzibar, cosmopolitan encounters, exchanges across lines of cultural difference, and social unities across the Indian Ocean rim were often powerfully undercut by alternative logics and crosscurrents based on exclusion, ineradicable difference, and the denigration of cultural groups cast as uncivilized and dangerous outsiders/others.

In colonial Zanzibar, markers of cultural difference, identity, and social status were always contested in daily practice, very much struggled over and subject to debate. This is precisely what makes Bi Kidude's example—as with Siti before her[38]—so deeply resonant: a young girl of African descent, poor, rural, and of humble origin, mingling on the margins between sea and shore with Arab sailors, listening to and learning their music. Over time, she appropriated—stole, as she insisted—Arab rhythms and musical forms, mastering this music from across the Indian Ocean and remaking it in distinctively coastal African terms that proved deeply relevant to a mass Swahili audience. From the streets, she rose to become at the end of her life the very embodiment of Zanzibari cultural tradition, challenging elite and Arab ideas about cultural value, performance, and propriety: a *taarab* thief indeed, turning the masters' tools to other ends right under their very noses. Bi Kidude's success is all the more striking precisely because of her exceptional capacity to cross over barriers and boundaries. Kidude was uncompromising, forceful, charismatic, and richly talented, but even so, the outcome of her trajectory was never predetermined, but sustained instead by her willingness to breach convention, stay close to her roots, and chart her own course over the long haul.

Following the Second World War, in the years leading up to independence, locally known as *zama za siasa*, or the time of politics, the discursive terrain of Zanzibari identity and belonging had become especially charged, as everyday life was intensely politicized and racialized.[39] The political calendar of Zanzibar was punctuated by a series of bitterly fought electoral exercises that set an ostensibly nonracialist (but Arab-identified) coalition, the Zanzibar Nationalist Party and the Zanzibar and Pemba People's Party (ZNP/ZPPP), against an "African" racial nationalist party, the Afro-Shirazi Party (ASP). Political, economic, and social differences were increasingly interpreted in racialized terms as essentialized differences between "African" and "Arab" infused the terrain of everyday social life and practice. As Jonathon Glassman argues, while the ZNP/ZPPP coalition regularly claimed to be nonracialist, in reality much of their rhetoric and policy were premised on coastal exceptionalism, extremist Arabocentric rhetoric, and antimainlander bias (including campaigns of squatter evictions) that singled out "Africans" as criminals, savages, or aliens.[40] Alternatively, propagandists within the ASP were responsible for some of the most extreme racial demagoguery, cultivating racial nativism and threatening "Arabs" with expulsion or extermination.

In this intensely divided climate, adherence to a political ideology and membership in a moral community was cemented by extremist rhetoric within an in-group portraying others as posing imminent risks. Increasingly, political ideologues cast opposing groups in dehumanizing terms, portraying them as racialized enemies whose "inherently" violent tendencies and savage instincts could only be forestalled by immediate—even pre-emptive—action. When others responded to this threatening rhetoric with equal if not greater vehemence, matters could quickly spiral out of control, sparking violent responses and the imperative of retribution. In this climate, "rumors were notable for their ability to render ideology or fantasy in the form of remembered experience, which in turn could prompt individuals to take up arms or act in other ways that gave such fantasies material form."[41] In this sense, Glassman examines how a "war of words" pitting Africans, especially those from the mainland, against "Arabs" could all too quickly escalate into racialized dehumanization and spasms of violence, most notably in the pogrom of June 1961 and culminating in the mass killings and social trauma that occurred in the immediate wake of the Zanzibar revolution in January 1964.

Race and Revolution: Reorienting the Islands away from the Indian Ocean

The history of the islands has been characterized by recurrent tensions: between the continent and the Indian Ocean, land and sea, African and Arab, cosmopolitanism and insularity, popular practice and elite aspirations. In these shifting dialectics of openness and exclusion, shaped by alternating or oscillating currents, the revolution marked a dramatic point of departure—imprisoning or expelling Zanzibaris of Arab or Indian descent, closing the islands off from the Indian Ocean trade, ending capitalism, and reorienting the islands to a pan-African and socialist future tied to the continent.

In the short term, the revolutionary uprising quickly overthrew the sultanate and brought the political rule of the newly installed ZNP/ZPPP coalition government to an abrupt end, but the revolution was hardly led by a coherent and disciplined political vanguard, and the initial violence of the revolt quickly spiraled out of control, with house-to-house sweeps, thefts, targeted reprisals, rapes, beatings, and revenge killings. Conservative estimates range anywhere from 3,000 to 12,000 dead;[42] Arab landed estates and properties were seized; there were mass detentions of perceived opponents of the revolution; and many Indian businesses were subsequently nationalized or shut down. As a result, many Zanzibaris of Arab and Indian descent fled the islands, seeking asylum on the mainland or returning across the Indian Ocean to "homes" they had never known. Official accounts of the revolution, produced by Afro-Shirazi proponents, cast the uprising as an African liberation movement that rose up to end colonial domination and Arab feudal oppression. But if the revolution ostensibly claimed to oppose racial exclusion and overcome colonial divisions, it ironically tended to reinscribe, reinforce, and reiterate precisely these divides. In the wake of revolutionary violence aimed at Arabs and Indians, efforts to nationalize the economy, to Africanize the civil service and city, to seize landowners' estates and redistribute land could all be reinterpreted in racialized terms as an uprising of Africans seeking to turn the tables on Zanzibaris who had lorded it over them, seeking revenge against Arab and Indian "outsiders" or "others." These depictions were neatly reversed by exiled opponents of the revolution, who in turn described the uprising as a civil war, mainland invasion, or even ethnic cleansing.

Beliefs that Zanzibar was turning away from the Indian Ocean world and choosing an African future were only reinforced in April 1964, when the first presidents of the mainland and islands, Julius Nyerere and Abeid Karume, summarily announced a political union. Tanganyika and Zanzibar joined together to create the new Republic of Tanzania. In mid-1965, the Zanzibar government moved to outlaw the Indian Ocean monsoon trade, banning any port calls by dhows that had put in at Arabian ports during the previous year. In the ensuing decades, Gilbert explains:

> Zanzibar was a different and poorer place for the loss of her regional trade connections. The loss of income from the seasonal influx of sailors hurt everyone from the big merchants who sold hardware and naval stores to street vendors who sold tea and *mandazis*. Related industries, such as mangrove cutting and the transshipment of dhow cargoes like salt and dried fish to the mainland collapsed. . . . The texture of daily life for rich and poor changed. Dried shark, what Burton called the "goût" of Zanzibar, was a staple of the poor; it has virtually disappeared from the local diet. Ghee from Socotra and Somalia was also enjoyed across class lines, it too has disappeared. Dates, carpets, brass work and other commodities that enjoyed a slightly more elite market also disappeared. People also ceased to move back and forth between Arabia and Zanzibar. . . . Under the Revolutionary Government, Zanzibar became increasingly isolated from the regional economy, and in time, from the global economy as well. As the western Indian Ocean reoriented itself towards

an economy based on Gulf oil and Indian manufactured goods, Zanzibar remained cut off from those changes. (Erik Gilbert, *Dhows and the Colonial Economy of Zanzibar, 1860–1970* [Oxford: James Currey, 2004], 159–60.)

This is precisely the cultural moment that Gurnah described earlier when the monsoon trade came to an end in the 1960s, upending the seasonal rhythms of the city, the movement of goods in and out with the dhows, and the raucous sociability (and music!) brought by thousands of sailors drawn from across the Indian Ocean.

During the 1960s and 1970s, Zanzibar became a far more insular and isolated space, even as its island identity and independence were subsumed by mainland forces. State security penetrated everyday life as authoritarian rule held sway, zealously seeking to police the boundaries of the body politic, controlling who and what could enter or leave. East German and Chinese advisers arrived with plans for mass public housing and socialist "new towns." The government established links with Third World and Africanist liberation movements and pursued Africanization in terms of land redistribution, urban housing, economic life, and state bureaucracies. Maritime links, trade, and cultural connections across the Indian Ocean were sharply curtailed during the revolutionary period as political leaders in Zanzibar sought to relocate the islands within alternative circuits, asserting the primacy of socialist connections, pan-Africanism, nonaligned solidarities, and anticolonial or liberation struggles on the continent.

Reconfiguring Indian Ocean Circuits and Connections

The isolation wrought by the revolution, political repression, restrictions on travel and trade, as well as the loss of sovereignty were resented by many urban Zanzibaris, and widespread economic decline, rationing, and urban collapse were experienced by all. With few other options available, the Revolutionary Government made overtures to external advisers, NGOs, and eventually the West. By the mid-1980s, as African states were forced to accept structural adjustment across the continent, the Zanzibar regime began to reverse course on policies of closure and control, opening the islands to external capital, welcoming back exiles from the Gulf and India, promoting mass tourism, and pursuing neoliberal policies—privatizing the economy and opening up the state to multiparty politics.

Zanzibar's reinsertion within wider circuits of capital, commodities, migration, and mediation hinged precisely on its Indian Ocean location, images of cultural fusion, invocations of shared "heritage," and its "unique" island identity. In the late 1970s and early 1980s, the Revolutionary Government initially sought assistance from Chinese and Western urban planners as a means of reversing widespread urban deterioration, housing shortages, and economic decline.[43] Despite their ideological differences, these outside groups of consultants concurred in asserting that the older section of the city, associated with colonial elites and the predominance of Arabs, Indians, and Europeans in the urban sphere, should be restored and preserved as a cultural asset. "The Stone Town itself is a unique tourist attraction," an early team of United Nations consultants stated, "an Arab casbah with a colorful past that is reflected in the varied historic buildings, the narrow bazaar streets, and the elaborately carved wooden doorways. The very name of Zanzibar evokes images of an exotic life in one of the major spice islands of the world."[44] If properly burnished and branded, they believed, the colonial core of the city could regenerate Zanzibar's economy, allowing the islands to compete with the Seychelles and other island destinations for the mass European and American tourist markets.

As tourism rapidly took off as a major source of hard currency, landmark structures were emptied of residents and remade in the city, even as many buildings were converted to hotels, high-end shops, cafés, or clubs. Outside the city, resort development proliferated all along the northern and eastern coasts, transforming once quiet fishing villages and rural communities. In 2000 the Stone Town of Zanzibar was inscribed on UNESCO's World Heritage List, depicted as an "outstanding manifestation of cultural fusion and harmonization." This colonial section of the city, dating mostly from the second half of the nineteenth century and later, was described as a material reflection of the "long-term interchange of human values"; the site allegedly "gives an authentic impression of the living Swahili culture."[45] In this sense, "ancient" or "old" Indian Ocean connections were being resurrected or reinvented even as the city was being opened up to novel uses, investments, and crowds of outsiders. Elite Arab, South Asian, or colonial European influences were highlighted, while African contributions to the city were minimized or ignored. Exotic imagery of sultans and harems, intrepid explorers and intrigues were repackaged to reposition Zanzibar in the global marketplace, providing compelling cultural scripts as to why tourists should visit the isles rather than go to Mauritius, Réunion, or the Seychelles.[46] At the same time the Zanzibari government favored the luxury market, emphasizing high-end resorts, honeymoon packages, spas, and all the exclusive exotica of an island paradise getaway drawing on the "sun, sea, and sex" tourism trade. As with other Indian Ocean islands, Zanzibari entrepreneurs and external investors have drawn upon "island imaginaries" to position the isles in a highly competitive global market-place, invoking "the style and grace of colonial living, the sexuality and conviviality of 'natives,' the opportunity to occupy Edenic enclavic para-dises, and the chance to experience colonial life."[47] Material displacement and dislocation has accompanied this privatized reimagining of the city as poorer and working-class Zanzibaris, without access to external capital or family connections, have increasingly been priced out of the city, strug-gling to keep pace with the spiraling costs of housing, education, health care, and even basic foodstuffs. In seeking work, many face competition for low-paying service jobs from mainland Tanzanians or Kenyans in a highly unequal economy driven by powerful outsiders whose sources of wealth seem elusive or mysterious—exiles, expatriates, or tourists who effortlessly seem to come and go.

Capitalizing on the history and heritage of the city has brought ques-tions of identity and belonging back to the fore in ways that intersect with cultural developments and political life. As the islands have been resitu-ated within global circuits of capital, commodities, and consumption, cul-tural production has also played a key role, again based on the reassertion of long-term connections with the wider Indian Ocean World or pan-Afri-can continental links. In remaking the islands as distinctive sites of culture and seeking to locate them on a global map of places to be, Zanzibari art-ists, cultural activists, and entrepreneurs have led the way. Diverse groups and forces have fed these processes, but the Tamasha la Nchi za Jahazi (Festival of the Dhow Countries), also known as the Zanzibar International Film Festival (ZIFF), certainly has played a key role, linking cultural per-formance with economic development while creating an enduring founda-tion for new connections between the islands and the world beyond.

Since the late 1990s, Zanzibar has been host to a series of wide-ranging cultural festivals, drawing audiences, performers, journalists, and locals to the isles. Each year these festivals highlight different themes, showcasing film, dance, music, and cultural debates from around the Indian Ocean, East Africa, and elsewhere on the continent, including the diaspora. Diverse motivations are at play: to raise the visibility of local culture, to stimulate indigenous cultural industries, to support economic development and tourism, to present alternative voices and resist Euro-American notions of globalization, and to restore Zanzibar's historic cultural significance. To this end, ZIFF proponents have worked to resituate Zanzibar regionally and within a wider transnational Indian Ocean milieu, branding it as the age-old center of "dhow countries" (*nchi za jahazi*), the "dhow region," or "dhow culture." In the process, ZIFF has spawned related efforts, such as the Dhow Countries Music Academy, while the Sauti za Busara (Voices of

Wisdom) music festival has sought to place the islands at the heart of the continent moving to a pan-African beat (and, in her final years, featuring acclaimed performances from Bi Kidude as a Zanzibari roots icon).

Over the years, ZIFF has frequently highlighted strikingly similar themes of connection and continuity across the Indian Ocean basin: the festival is rooted in images and ideas of crosscultural dialogue, communication, and exchange.[48] These visions posit Zanzibar as the core of a unified dhow sphere stretching across the Indian Ocean, where disparate worlds have been allegedly knit together into a cohesive fabric by the incessant movement of ships back and forth across the seas over the centuries. ZIFF commemorates these oceanic continuities while seeking to recreate them for a new age: bringing performers and films to Zanzibar from around the Indian Ocean basin, while showcasing Zanzibari culture in an island setting intended to draw a global audience. These idioms, of course, have a specific history and cultural context, invoking a return to forms of cosmopolitanism that the revolution is often depicted as bringing to an end. Such images are framed by certain ideological aims and seek to respond to wider sociopolitical and economic currents. They have also proved particularly resonant for educated and more elite Zanzibaris of an older generation, intellectuals, activists, and artists, those who were educated or lived abroad, and others who looked back to an allegedly more tolerant, pluralistic, and cosmopolitan island world before the revolution.

For ZIFF and Busara these cultural engagements have very practical motivations: providing jobs and training for youth; stimulating the growth of culture industries; asserting the value of culture and arts for economic development; and connecting local, regional, and global circuits. In staging the festivals, two other currents seem especially prominent. The first is an emphasis on speaking back to or resisting the hegemony of Western-dominated models of globalization by foregrounding alternative African voices, south-south intersections, and cultural exchanges between Africa, South Asia, and the Arab world. Second, and related to this, have been efforts to showcase ideals of cultural reciprocity and engagement that do not hinge on violence, domination, or capitalist expropriation. Last, and most important in the wake of the 1998 bombings in East Africa, 9/11, and the wars that ensued in Afghanistan and Iraq, were efforts to explore representations of Islam beyond reductionist Western stereotypes founded in religious extremism, intolerance, or fundamentalist terror.

These new modes of cultural connection have hardly gone unchallenged. Invocations of "dhow culture" have little resonance in the popular imagination among ordinary Zanzibaris; many associate the festivals with foreigners, lament the influence of globalized popular culture on youth, or feel dispossessed by tourism, accusing the state of cashing in while not providing development in the common interest. And the opening of the islands to mass tourism, rising from fewer than 10,000 visitors in the mid-1980s to almost 200,000 annually by 2015, has been accompanied by powerful countercurrents. Wealthier exiled Zanzibaris of Arab or Indian descent or their children have returned from the Gulf, India, Europe, or Canada to invest or reclaim property, together with a sizable number of expatriates. Relations have been renewed with the Gulf states, and the Zanzibar government's attempt to join the Organization of Islamic Cooperation in the late 1980s sparked a constitutional controversy that has continued to the present. Coastal exceptionalism has deep roots in the isles as we've seen, and Zanzibari nationalists have long objected to the union with the mainland imposed by Karume and Nyerere a few short months after the revolutionary takeover. The creation of Tanzania in April 1964 is typically represented as an antidemocratic moment that compromised the sovereignty and cultural uniqueness of the islands, subsuming a formerly independent state within a political union with the mainland over which it had formerly ruled. The perceived loss of self-determination and autonomy was only intensified after the consolidation of mainland and island parties into a single ruling party in 1977, and the belief that Zanzibar was being increasingly reduced from a partner into a mere regional player ruled by mainland interests.

Of course, these political tensions were only sharpened when they took on older racial and religious overtones, setting mainlanders against islanders, Africans against Arabs, and Christians against Muslims. These debates about the islands' place in the Tanzanian polity, greater self-determination or subjugation, and the nature of Zanzibari identity itself have played out in the context of the contested reemergence of multi-party politics. Between 1995 and 2010, there were a series of bitterly contested elections in Zanzibar between the Revolutionary Party (CCM) and the Civic United Front (CUF), resulting in civil strife, allegations of fraud, corruption, violent confrontations, and state repression. The opposition party, CUF, was frequently linked in political discourse to Arab interests, outsiders, and the ancien regime, represented as a threat that would ally itself with the Gulf, reverse the revolution, and bring back elements of the old order. Opposition leaders, in turn, portrayed the ruling party as representing the continued dominance of African mainlanders, against increased local autonomy for the islands, and indifferent or opposed to Islamic interests. Even after the formation of a government of national unity in 2010, joining CUF and CCM, these struggles continued in altered form as debates over the union and a proposed new constitution divided

Zanzibaris (and Tanzanians) into different camps, with incommensurate views about the islands, their identity, and their proper sociopolitical place in the global order of things. These island debates and disputes are only the latest incarnation of far older (and ongoing) processes. The history of the islands has always been caught up in an oscillation between openness and exclusion, synthesis and sovereignty, fluidity and fixity. In this sense, sociocultural processes seem to echo geographical and environmental positionings. Islands, after all, can be understood as essential points of arrival or departure, set off or apart from the surrounding seas, or they can be conceptualized in less determinate ways, fluidly linked in relation with wider systems, networks, and processes. As one astute ethnographer of cultural collisions has noted, "the action most worth watching is not at the center of things, but where the edges meet. I like shorelines, weather fronts, international borders. There are interesting frictions and incongruities in these places."[49] Islands are similar sites, caught betwixt and between, where struggles over identity and history and future direction become all the more acute. Whether Zanzibar remains a part of Tanzania, or becomes something else—a regional Swahili center, a pan-African cultural mecca, or a transnational gateway to the Indian Ocean world— remains very much to be determined. But the islands and its people have developed over millennia through diverse historical moments of encounter and engagement with global forces and forms, whether Indian Ocean trade, the spread of Islam, slavery, colonialism, capitalism, the Cold War, circulations of popular culture, or mass tourism. As elsewhere in Africa, the Swahili world has shown itself to be particularly adept at the arts of extraversion, accommodating, absorbing, and appropriating outside influences as sources of "local" cultural invention and ingenuity.[50] Island cultures in Zanzibar have emerged out of this long conversation between competing forms of cosmopolitanism, pointing often in divergent directions, at the junctures where sea and sand ebb and flow.

Notes

1. Andy Jones, *As Old as My Tongue: The Myth and Life of Bi Kidude* (London: ScreenStation Productions, 2009), film.

2. *Taarab* is a sophisticated genre of orchestral music popular in East Africa and elsewhere, drawing on African, Arab, and South Asian influences. It is very much a trans–Indian Ocean genre, involving competitive performance styles and elaborate Kiswahili poetic forms. Women play key roles as singers, performers, and audiences. Taarab performances are central to the celebration of Swahili weddings, while *unyago* is a woman-centered genre of ritual, dance, and

musical performance celebrating the coming of age of young girls, instructing them about sexuality and married life.

3. Ally Saleh, Fiona McGain, Kawthar Buwayhid, and Javed Jafferji, *Bi Kidude: Tales of a Living Legend* (Zanzibar: Gallery Publications, 2008).

4. Erik Gilbert, *Dhows and the Colonial Economy of Zanzibar, 1860–1970* (Oxford: James Currey, 2004), xii.

5. James Christie, *Cholera Epidemics in East Africa* (London: Macmillan, 1876), 275.

6. Greg Dening, *Beach Crossings: Voyaging Across Times, Cultures, and Self* (Philadelphia: University of Pennsylvania Press, 2004), 16.

7. Pamila Gupta, "Island-ness in the Indian Ocean," in *Eyes Across the Water: Navigating the Indian Ocean*, ed. Pamila Gupta, Isabel Hofmeyr, and Michael Pearson (Pretoria: Unisa Press, 2010), 276.

8. Michael Pearson, *The Indian Ocean* (London: Routledge, 2003).

9. Abdul Sheriff, *Slaves, Spices, and Ivory in Zanzibar* (London: James Currey, 1987), 10–11.

10. Sugata Bose, *A Hundred Horizons: The Indian Ocean in the Age of Global Empire* (Cambridge, MA: Harvard University Press, 2006), 10.

11. Abdul Sheriff, "People on the Move," *ZIFF Journal* 1 (2004): 27.

12. John Middleton, *The World of the Swahili* (New Haven, CT: Yale University Press, 1992), 20.

13. Michael Pearson, "Littoral Society: The Concept and the Problems," *Journal of World History* 17, no. 4 (2006): 356.

14. Sheriff, *Slaves, Spices, and Ivory in Zanzibar*, 48.

15. Sheriff, *Slaves, Spices, and Ivory in Zanzibar*, 51.

16. James Ross Browne, *Etchings of a Whaling Cruise, with Notes of a Sojourn on the Island of Zanzibar* (New York: Harper and Brothers, 1846), 331.

17. Browne, *Etchings of a Whaling Cruise*, 361.

18. C. P. Rigby, "Report on the Zanzibar Dominions," in *General Rigby, Zanzibar, and the Slave Trade*, ed. Mrs. Charles E. B. Russell (London: Allen and Unwin, [1860] 1932), 329.

19. Rigby, "Report on the Zanzibar Dominions," 337.

20. John Robb, *Medico-topographical Report on Zanzibar* (Calcutta: Office of the Superintendent of Government Printing, 1879), 7.

21. Rigby, "Report on the Zanzibar Dominions," 329; Robb, *Medico-topographical Report*, 7; Christie, *Cholera Epidemics*, 333.

22. Rigby, "Report on the Zanzibar Dominions," 332.

23. Gerald Portal to Lord Salisbury, October 23, 1891, Mss.Afr.s.105, Rhodes House Library, Oxford, United Kingdom [hereafter RHL].

24. Portal to Sir H. Percy Anderson, November 2, 1891, Mss.Afr.s.105, RHL.

25. Portal to Sir H. Percy Anderson, November 19, 1891, Mss.Afr.s.105, RHL.

26. Rev. Walter K. Firminger, "The Protectorate of Zanzibar," in *British Africa*, 2nd ed., *The British Empire Series*, vol. 2 (London: Kegan Paul, Trench, Trubner, & Co., 1901), 272.

27. Percy Evans Lewin, "Zanzibar: The Island of Cloves," *The Queen: The Lady's Newspaper,* September 19, 1908, 530.

28. Maj. Francis Barrow Pearce, *Zanzibar: The Island Metropolis of Eastern Africa* (London: T. Fisher Unwin, 1920), 199.

29. Erik Gilbert, "Coastal East Africa and the Western Indian Ocean," *The History Teacher* 36, no. 1 (2002): 17.

30. Sheriff, "People on the Move," 28.

31. Senior Commissioner Pakenham to Chief Secretary, July 17, 1948, AB 39/234, Zanzibar National Archives, Zanzibar, Tanzania.

32. Sheriff, "People on the Move," 28.

33. Sheriff, "People on the Move," 30.

34. Abdul Sheriff, *Dhow Cultures of the Indian Ocean: Cosmopolitanism, Commerce, and Islam* (London: Hurst & Co, 2010), 17.

35. Edward Simpson and Kai Kresse, "Introduction: Cosmopolitanism Contested: Anthropology and History in the Western Indian Ocean," in *Struggling with History: Islam and Cosmopolitanism in the Western Indian Ocean,* ed. Edward Simpson and Kai Kresse (New York: Columbia University Press, 2008), 15.

36. Gilbert, *Dhows and the Colonial Economy of Zanzibar,* 16.

37. William Cunningham Bissell, *Urban Design, Chaos, and Colonial Power in Zanzibar* (Bloomington: Indiana University Press, 2011), 44–45.

38. Laura J. Fair, *Pastimes and Politics: Culture, Community, and Identity in Post-Abolition Urban Zanzibar, 1890–1945* (Athens: Ohio University Press, 2001).

39. Michael Lofchie, *Background to Revolution* (Princeton, NJ: Princeton University Press, 1965).

40. Jonathon Glassman, *War of Words, War of Stones* (Bloomington: Indiana University Press, 2011).

41. Glassman, *War of Words,* 264.

42. Anthony Clayton, *The Zanzibar Revolution and Its Aftermath* (London: C. Hurst, 1981), 81.

43. William Cunningham Bissell, "Casting a Long Shadow: Colonial Categories, Cultural Identities, and Cosmopolitan Spaces in Globalizing Africa," *African Identities* 5, no. 2 (2007): 181–97.

44. Royce LaNier et al., *The Stone Town of Zanzibar: A Strategy for Integrated Development* (Zanzibar: Ministry of Lands, Housing, and Construction/UN HABITAT, 1983), 10.

45. UNESCO World Heritage List, http://whc.unesco.org/en/list/173/documents.

46. William Cunningham Bissell, "Engaging Colonial Nostalgia," *Cultural Anthropology* 20, no. 2 (2005): 215–48.

47. Uma Kothari and Rorden Wilkinson, "Colonial Imaginaries and Postcolonial Transformations: Exiles, Bases, Beaches," *Third World Quarterly* 31, no. 8 (2010): 1408.

48. William Cunningham Bissell, "From Dhow Culture to the Diaspora: ZIFF, Film, and the Framing of Transnational Imaginaries in the Western Indian Ocean," *Social Dynamics* 38, no. 3 (2012): 479–98.

49. Anne Fadiman, *The Spirit Catches You and You Fall Down* (New York: Farrar, Straus and Giroux, 1997).

50. On extraversion, see Jean-Francois Bayart, *The State in Africa* (London: Longman, 1993); Karin Barber, "Views of the Field: Introduction," in *Readings in African Popular Culture* (Bloomington: Indiana University Press, 1997), 1–12.

10

The Mascarenes, Indian Ocean Africa, and Global Labor Migration during the Eighteenth and Nineteenth Centuries

Richard B. Allen

The Mascarene Islands of Mauritius and Réunion have long languished on the periphery of African studies. Surveys of African history pay little or no attention to the islands or the Mauritian dependencies of Rodrigues and, until they became a separate British Crown colony in 1903, the Seychelles. This indifference stems partly from the islands' geographical isolation hundreds of miles east of the African mainland and Madagascar. The islands' shallow historiographical footprint also reflects the fact that Mauritius and Réunion were not occupied permanently by humans until 1638 and 1663, respectively, while Rodrigues remained uninhabited until 1756 and the Seychelles were not colonized until 1770. The continuing reluctance of many Africanists to look beyond the beaches at Mogadishu, Mombasa, and Mozambique as they reconstruct eastern and southern Africa's history has likewise helped to ensure that the islands continue to be ignored. So has the fact that coming to terms with Mascarene history entails exploring complex patterns of social, economic, cultural, and political interaction between Indians, Southeast Asians, and Chinese as well as Africans, Malagasies, and Europeans. The failure of Mauritian, Réunionnais, and Seychellois historians to situate local developments in regional, global, or comparative contexts further reinforces the perception that the islands played little or no role in African history during the eighteenth and nineteenth centuries.[1]

Similar attitudes plague studies of labor migration in the European colonial world. The pervasive Atlantic-centrism in modern slavery studies continues to hobble our understanding of European slave trading[2] and often obscures the fact that millions of enslaved Africans reached parts of the world other than the Americas between the sixteenth and mid-nineteenth centuries.[3] Studies of transoceanic slave trading in the Indian Ocean are, in turn, afflicted by a high degree of Africa-centrism and a tendency to focus on the northwestern Indian Ocean to the exclusion of other parts of this oceanic world.[4] This practice of privileging certain geographic regions over others is matched by a propensity to draw a sharp dividing line between the pre- and postemancipation eras in the colonial world and an attendant proclivity to view the free and forced migrant labor trades that flourished before and after the abolition of slavery in the British Empire in 1834 as separate and distinct phenomena unto themselves.[5] Studies of the slaves, convicts, and indentured laborers who reached the Mascarenes between the late seventeenth and early twentieth centuries attest as much.[6]

Arguments that East Africa and the western Indian Ocean need to be viewed as a unified region,[7] work published in 2004 and 2009 on labor migration in the Indian Ocean and in the emerging field of global labor history,[8] astute observations about the limitations of oceanic world-based approaches to labor migration,[9] and new perspectives on the multidimensionality of British imperial networks[10] indicate that this preoccupation with the particular in migrant labor studies is no longer sustainable. Scholarship published in 2014 on European slave trading in the Indian Ocean confirms as much, revealing as it does that Europeans traded slaves on a truly global scale and that the free and forced labor trades associated with European colonialism became increasingly intertwined during the late eighteenth and early nineteenth centuries.[11] In so doing, this scholarship highlights the connections between Indian Ocean Africa and the Mascarenes during the eighteenth and nineteenth centuries and the islands' role in the labor trades that figured prominently in eastern and southern Africa's increasing integration into the capitalist world economy that took ever more definitive form during this era. Last, but far from least, this scholarship reminds us that these free and forced labor diasporas were central to the development of the multicultural societies that became a hallmark of social, economic, cultural, and political life in many parts of the Indian Ocean colonial world.

Trading Slaves

Slaves first reached the Mascarenes in 1642 during the Dutch East India Company's (Vereenigde Oostindische Compagnie, or VOC) initial attempt (1638–58) to colonize Mauritius.[12] The number who did so during this and a second VOC attempt at colonization (1664–1710) is unknown, but was undoubtedly small. Six Mauritian-based expeditions obtained 502 slaves at Madagascar between 1642 and 1647, many of whom were subsequently forwarded to the VOC's administrative center at Batavia (Jakarta) in Java.[13] The legal status of the Malagasy laborers who reached the Île de Bourbon (Réunion) between its colonization by the French in 1663 and the late 1680s is uncertain, but slavery was a de facto reality on the island by 1687.[14] While the total number of slaves who reached Réunion during the late seventeenth and early eighteenth century is unknown, colonial censuses reveal that the island housed 58 slaves in 1674, 113 in 1690, 384 in 1709, 633 in 1714, and 1,776 in 1725, and that a substantial majority of these individuals were of Malagasy origin.[15]

Slaves reached Mauritius again shortly after the island was colonized in December 1721 under the auspices of the French Compagnie des Indes. At least 23 slave cargoes of Indian, Malagasy, Mozambican, and West African origin arrived on the island, now called the Île de France, between 1722 and 1735.[16] Compagnie ships also landed no fewer than 21 cargoes of Malagasy, Mozambican, and West African slaves on the Île Bourbon between 1729 and 1735.[17] These and subsequent imports increased the size of the Mascarene slave population from 1,800 in 1725 to 7,221 in 1735, and then to 22,599 by 1757–58.

The Compagnie's bankruptcy in 1765, the advent of royal rule in 1767, and the issuance of a decree in 1769 that opened the Îles de France et de Bourbon to free trade by all Frenchmen had a significant impact on regional slaving interests as the agreement that Jean-Vincent Morice, a Mauritian-based merchant, negotiated with the sultan of Kilwa in 1776 illustrates. In their accord, the sultan promised to supply Morice with 1,000 slaves each year and to bar other Europeans from trading for slaves in his territories.[18] The extension of free trade privileges to Americans in 1784 and then to all foreign nationals in 1787 turned the islands into a major regional commercial entrepôt that attracted shipping, including slave traders, from throughout the Indian Ocean and as far away as northern Europe and the United States.[19] These decrees, together with high mortality and low birth rates among the islands' slaves and the demand for laborers to produce the foodstuffs and maritime stores needed by the increasing numbers of French and other European ships operating in the Indian Ocean,

Table 10.1. Estimated slave exports to the Mascarenes, 1670–1848

Place of origin	1670–1769	1770–1810	1811–48	Total exports
Madagascar	35,314–37,931	46,203–53,427	43,808–51,365	125,325–142,723
Eastern Africa[a]	10,677–11,468	99,614–115,189	75,767–88,835	186,058–215,492
India	4,994–5,723	14,755–18,200	—	19,749–23,923
West Africa	1,184–1,363	—	—	1,184–1,363
Southeast Asia	—	—	3,804–4,759	3,804–4,759
Total	52,169–56,485	160,572–186,816	123,379–144,959	336,120–388,260

Source: Richard B. Allen, "The Mascarene Slave-Trade and Labour Migration in the Indian Ocean during the Eighteenth and Nineteenth Centuries," in *The Structure of Slavery in Indian Ocean Africa and Asia*, ed. Gwyn Campbell (London: Frank Cass, 2004), 41.

[a] Mozambique and the Swahili Coast.

spurred the importation of ever larger numbers of slaves between the early 1770s and the islands' conquest by the British in 1810. An inventory of 721 known, probable, possible, and unsuccessful slaving voyages to Madagascar, Mozambique, the Swahili Coast, and India between 1770 and 1809 attests to the intensity of the Mascarene trade; the inventory also highlights the Seychelles' role as a "refreshment" station for slavers bound for Mauritius and Réunion from the Mozambican and Swahili coasts.[20] Colonial censuses confirm the scale of this traffic, revealing that the Mascarenes housed 71,197 enslaved men, women, and children by 1787–88, a figure that climbed to almost 133,000 in 1807–8. These censuses and available information on slave mortality suggest that 52,200 to 56,500 slaves were exported to the Mascarenes between 1670 and 1769, mostly after 1721, and that such exports totaled 160,600 to 186,800 between 1770 and 1810 (table 10.1).

Mascarene slaves came from a global catchment area that stretched from Senegambia eastward to Madagascar, Mozambique, and the Swahili Coast and thence to India, Southeast Asia, and even China. Early nineteenth-century observers noted the presence of "blacks of every ethnicity" on Mauritius: Anjouanais from the Comoros; Abyssinians from the Horn of Africa; Bambaras, Guineans, and Wolofs from West Africa; Bengalis, Malabars, and Talingas (Telegus) from India; and "Malays" and Timorese from Southeast Asia.[21] Detailed slave registers compiled following Mauritius's formal inclusion in the British Empire in 1814 reveal that slaves from Madagascar, Mozambique, and the Swahili coast, the most important sources of Mascarene bondmen and -women, came from a large number of ethnocultural populations. The first such register, compiled in 1817, records that the island's Malagasy slaves included individuals identified as Ambanivolo, Andrantsay, Antaisaka, Antalaotra, Antanosy, Antatsimo, Betanimena, Maninga [*sic*], Marvace [*sic*], Merina (Amboalambo, Hova), and Sakalava.[22] Other sources report Antateime [*sic*] and Betsileo among the island's Malagasy bondmen and women.[23] Slaves of "Mozambican"[24] origin likewise came from diverse ethnocultural populations, some of which were located as far away as modern Malawi and eastern Zambia. The 1817 register includes references to individuals identified as Bisa, Ekoti, Kamanga, Lolo (Lomwe), Makonde, Makua, Maravi, Mrima, Mujao (probably Yao), Ngindo, Nyambane, Nyamwezi, Sagara, and Sena, as well as other groups whose modern identity remains uncertain. Besides Malays and Timorese, the 1817 register and other sources also record the presence of men, women, and children from Bali, Java, Makassar, Nias, and Sumatra on the island, as well as individuals identified as Chinese.[25]

In addition to importing large numbers of slaves, the islands also functioned as a center from which colonial and metropolitan French merchants mounted slaving expeditions destined for the Americas, the Cape of Good Hope, and India. At least 115 such voyages occurred between 1718 and 1809, the overwhelming majority of which took place between 1770 and 1809.[26] Ninety-four of these voyages entailed the shipment of slaves, mostly acquired in Mozambique (Ibo, Inhambane, Mozambique Island, Quelimane, Quirimba) or along the Swahili Coast (Kilwa and Zanzibar in particular) to French colonies in the Caribbean, especially Saint Domingue.[27] Mascarene-based voyages also carried slaves to Spanish possessions along South America's Río de la Plata during the late 1790s and early 1800s.[28]

The British conquest of the Mascarenes in 1810 inaugurated an era during which the islands became the center of a notorious illegal slave trade, the impact of which reverberated throughout the western Indian Ocean into the 1830s and 1840s, if not beyond. On February 15, 1811, British governor Robert Farquhar, concerned about alleviating the economic distress caused by the Royal Navy's blockade of the islands prior to their capture and placating the restive white population in his charge, asked the secretary of state for the colonies in London to exempt Mauritius and Réunion from the 1807 parliamentary ban on British subjects engaging in the slave trade, a request that was promptly denied.[29] Later that same year, Farquhar advised London that "every precaution" was being taken to prevent the illicit importation of slaves into the islands and that these measures had resulted in ships being seized and sent to the Vice-Admiralty court at Cape Town for adjudication.[30] Such endeavors failed, however, to dissuade those willing and able to satisfy the local demand for chattel labor, and early in 1812, Farquhar reported the existence of a "suspected unlawful commerce in slaves"[31] in the islands. The traffic to which he referred soon became a source of considerable frustration for British and French authorities and a wellspring of friction between not only these officials and the islands' white residents, but also, after the Treaty of Paris in 1814, returned Réunion to French control, between Britain and France.

British officials never doubted that large numbers of slaves reached Mauritius and Réunion between 1811 and 1814. In November 1813, Réunion's lieutenant governor, Lt.-Col. Henry S. Keating, reported that he had "Strong reasons to believe that Slaves arc continually landed, at the different parts of this Island, and vessels are employed exclusively for that Illicit traffic."[32] The following January he asserted that 9,000 to 10,000 slaves had been landed on the island since 1811.[33] Colonial authorities appreciated that this clandestine traffic was driven by a strong local demand for chattel labor and the proximity of well-established markets in Madagascar and along the eastern African coast capable of satisfying that demand. In December 1819, acting Mauritian governor Maj.-Gen. Ralph Darling noted the vigor with which the illegal trade was conducted and the avidity with which colonists purchased newly landed slaves.[34] Darling's assertions are substantiated by the fact that colonial and Vice-Admiralty courts at Mauritius condemned 48 captured slave ships and 4,612 "Liberated Africans" between 1811 and 1825, mostly between 1815 and 1819.[35] Hubert Gerbeau's identification of 212 to 216 slave cargoes either destined for or reaching Réunion on at least 89 vessels between 1818, when France formally abolished its slave trade, and the early 1830s further attests to the intensity of this illicit traffic in chattel labor.[36]

While contemporary observers agreed that large numbers of slaves reached the Mascarenes after 1811, it is difficult to determine how many did so with any precision. Farquhar reportedly estimated that at least 30,000 slaves were landed on Mauritius between 1811 and early 1821.[37] Other contemporary observers also subscribed to this figure, while still others put the number of Mauritian imports at 50,000 or more.[38] Even those unwilling to estimate how many slaves had been introduced into the colony acknowledged that large numbers were involved. In 1826, Royal Navy Capt. Fairfax Moresby, who had captured two notorious slavers in 1821 and negotiated the 1822 treaty ending European slave exports from the sultan of Oman's possessions along the Swahili coast, characterized the illegal Mauritian trade as "vast."[39] The Commission of Eastern Enquiry, appointed in 1826 to investigate various matters in the colony, including allegations that local officials had countenanced, if not actually facilitated, the illegal trade, concluded that "considerable numbers" of slaves had reached the colony before 1818.[40] Réunionnais authorities likewise appreciated that large numbers of slaves reached that island after 1818. Available evidence suggests that some 52,550 slaves landed in Mauritius and the Seychelles between 1811 and circa 1827, and that approximately 55,000 slaves reached the Île Bourbon illicitly between 1811 and circa 1833.[41] These figures and information about slave mortality rates en route to the islands indicate that the 1810s, 1820s, and early 1830s witnessed the exportation of 119,500 to 144,000 or more African and Malagasy men, women, and children to the islands. Not infrequently, the Amirantes and the Seychelles served as transshipment points for illicit cargoes bound for Mauritius and Réunion.[42]

The evidentiary and other problems facing those who study slave trading in the Indian Ocean make assessing the Mascarene trade's impact a difficult exercise.[43] The number of slave exports to the islands between the late seventeenth and mid-nineteenth centuries (336,000 to 388,000) clearly pales in comparison to the more than 9.4 million exports from West and West Central Africa to the Americas during the same period. To assess the Mascarene trade's historical significance only in such terms, however, is to ignore the regional and other contexts within which this activity occurred. We may note, for instance, that the Mascarene trade consumed 69 to 75 percent of an estimated minimum of 450,000 to 565,000 slaves traded by Europeans within the Indian Ocean basin between 1500 and 1850, and accounted for approximately 20 percent of the total volume of the French slave trade between 1670 and 1848.[44]

More than forty years ago, Edward Alpers argued that the Mascarene demand for chattel labor was the major driving force behind the dramatic expansion of the Malagasy and East African slave trades during the late eighteenth century.[45] While Thomas Vernet's work points to the existence of a larger, more extensive slave trading system along the eastern African coast than previously believed before French and Omani slavers began to make demands on this system during the mid-eighteenth century,[46] there can be little doubt that the Mascarene trade played a significant role in expanding trans-oceanic exports from eastern Africa, especially during the late eighteenth and early nineteenth centuries. The Mascarenes consumed more than one-half of all European slave exports from eastern Africa between 1670 and the early 1830s (table 10.2). Overall, Europeans accounted for 37.2 to 52.0 percent of an estimated 637,000 to 833,000 transoccanic exports from eastern Africa during the eighteenth century and 58.4 to 66.3 percent of an estimated 810,000 to 1 million such exports between 1801 and 1873.[47]

Table 10.2. European slave exports from eastern Africa and Madagascar, 1670–1833

| Period | To Americas | | To Mascarenes | | |
	Known	Estimated	Estimated	Total exports	% TEM[a]
1670–1769	23,491	42,041	45,991–49,399	69,482–90,440	66.2–54.6
1770–1810	89,203	101,120	145,614–168,189	234,817–269,309	62.0–62.5
1811–33	180,498	204,214	119,575–140,200	300,073–344,414	39.8–40.7
Total/ Average	293,192	346,375	311,180–357,788	604,372–704,163	51.5–50.8

Sources: Allen, "The Mascarene Slave-Trade," 41; *Voyages: The Trans-Atlantic Slave Trade Database*, http://www.slavevoyages.org.

[a] Total exports to the Mascarenes.

The Mascarene trade's impact on social, economic, and political life in Indian Ocean Africa is apparent in other ways. Gwyn Campbell and Pier Larson have discussed the important role that slave trading, and the Mascarene trade in particular, played in the rise of the Merina kingdom in highland Madagascar during the late eighteenth and early nineteenth centuries, Anglo- and Franco-Merina relations, and sociopolitical developments on the Grande Île during the nineteenth century.[48] The Mascarene trade is also central to understanding a hitherto ignored diaspora of Malagasy-speaking peoples that may have entailed the largest movement of an African people in the Indian Ocean basin.[49] Attempts to suppress the illicit slave trade figured prominently in Omani sultan Seyyid Said's decision to develop the clove industry on Zanzibar and Pemba, an industry that, because it soon consumed hundreds of thousands of African slaves, encouraged ever greater British involvement along the East African coast during the mid- and late nineteenth century.[50]

The Mascarene trade's economic impact is difficult to assess with any precision, but the trade clearly funneled substantial quantities of specie in the form of piastres or Spanish dollars ($) into regional commercial networks and local governmental coffers.[51] Available information on slave prices, projected slave exports to the islands, and an 1820 report that 35 percent of the purchase price of Malagasy slaves had to be paid in coin[52] afford an opportunity to estimate the trade's overall value and impact on regional mercantile liquidity. Reports on the average cost of slaves on the Swahili Coast in 1776 ($25)[53] and Madagascar in 1769 ($27 to $34)[54] suggest that Malagasy, Mozambican, and East African dealers realized $3,645,000 to $5,733,000 between 1770 and 1810 from the sale of slaves destined for the Mascarenes, of which at least $1,276,000 to $2,007,000 may have been paid in coin. Projections based on the purchase price ($18 to $28) of slaves at Zanzibar in 1821[55] suggest that the illegal trade to the islands generated another $2,152,000 to $3,926,000 in sales between 1811 and the early 1830s, of which at least $753,500 to $1,374,000 was paid in specie. These estimates are broadly in line with Pedro Machado's research on Gujarati merchants' activities in Mozambique. More specifically, Machado argues that French slavers paid as much as $1.5 million in coin to Portuguese and Gujarati merchants in Mozambique during the 1790s, silver that contributed to Gujarati bankers' ability to discount the bills of exchange that were crucial to facilitating commercial activity in the region, and that perhaps as much as $2.9 million in specie circulated in the region from 1811 to 1831.[56]

The Mascarene trade's economic impact can also be discerned in other less readily quantifiable ways. The islands relied heavily on imported foodstuffs throughout the eighteenth and nineteenth centuries.[57] While Mozambique and the Swahili Coast occasionally supplied provisions and other merchandise to the Île de France,[58] Madagascar remained a crucial source of rice, livestock, and other foodstuffs such as salt meat.[59] Historians have long appreciated that the Malagasy rice, beef, and slave trades were closely interconnected.[60] The scale of this commerce is indicated by the fact that at least 570 ships are known to have reached Mauritius from the Grande Île between 1773 and 1809, with 30 to 46 such arrivals in some years.[61] A survey of 145 declarations made by captains arriving at Port Louis from Madagascar between May 1802 and February 1809 graphically illustrates the extent to which these trades were intertwined; just four of the cargoes in question apparently consisted only of slaves.[62] What we know about individual cargoes shed additional light on this activity. The 900-ton *L'Eléphant*, for example, loaded 200 slaves and 343 cattle when it visited the Malagasy coast in 1782.[63] Twenty years later, *Le Reparateur* carried 150 cattle, 4 sheep, 5 goats, 400 fowls, 20,000 pounds of rice, 60 barrels of salted meat, and 11 slaves when it sailed from Fort Dauphin.[64] This commerce continued unabated during the 1810s and 1820s. The Commission of Eastern Enquiry noted that a fleet of 55 Mauritian-based luggers and schooners engaged in this coastal trade and that many of these vessels, especially those used to transport bullocks, were "fitted out in a manner that renders it difficult to distinguish them from those equipped for the slave trade."[65] Other indications of the islands' economic ties with eastern Africa during the late eighteenth and early nineteenth centuries include

Mascarene-based merchants investing, at least occasionally, in Portuguese slaving ventures,[66] Mauritian colonists and Portuguese merchants jointly purchasing slave ships,[67] and a Mozambican-based Gujarati merchant's purchase of a well-known Portuguese slaver in late 1805 or early 1806, and then, in partnership with Portuguese merchants, of two other slave ships at Port Louis in 1806 and 1807.[68]

A New System of Slavery?

The illegal Mascarene trade's demise during the late 1820s and early 1830s and the abolition of slavery in the British and French empires in 1834 and 1848, respectively, inaugurated a new era in migrant labor history marked by the movement of more than 2.2 million indentured African, Chinese, Indian, Javanese, Melanesian, and other non-European laborers throughout and beyond the colonial world between the 1830s and the 1920s. The origins of this labor diaspora date to the first decade of the nineteenth century when Chinese laborers were recruited to work on Trinidad and the British East India Company's colony of St. Helena in the South Atlantic.[69] The first significant use of such contractual labor, however, occurred in the Mascarenes, where the rapid expansion of the Mauritian and Réunionnais sugar industries after the mid-1820s generated a demand for field hands that local slave populations could not meet. The late-1820s witnessed the recruitment and transportation of some 3,100 Indian workers to Réunion from the former French slave trading enclaves of Pondichéry (Puduch-cheri), Karaikal, and Yanam in southern India, and 1,500 Chinese and Indian laborers recruited in Calcutta, Madras, Penang, and Singapore to Mauritius.[70] These undertakings failed, however, partly because of worker resistance to poor living and working conditions, and it was not until 1834–35 that large-scale indentured immigration to Mauritius began in earnest. More than 25,000 indentured Indians arrived in Mauritius between 1834 and 1838 where they labored alongside the colony's newly emancipated slaves, transformed into "apprentices" when slavery was abolished on the island on February 1, 1835, in local cane fields.

Mauritius has long been regarded as the crucial test case for the use of indentured labor in the postemancipation colonial plantation world,[71] and the island's importance in this global labor diaspora is underscored by the fact that more indentured workers (452,602), mostly from India but also from China, the Comoros, Madagascar, Mozambique, Southeast Asia, and Yemen, reached its shores than any other European colony. The success of the Mauritian experiment with indentured labor led to the introduction of hundreds of thousands of such workers throughout and beyond the colonial plantation world before this system came to an end during the 1920s. No fewer than 366,400 of these laborers, mostly from India but also from Africa and China, reached other British and French colonies in the western Indian Ocean between c. 1850 and 1920, including Kenya (39,437), Natal (152,184), Réunion (111,120), and the Transvaal (63,695).[72]

This postemancipation labor system is frequently characterized as "a new system of slavery."[73] While the extent to which it was or was not such a system remains a subject of debate,[74] a defining feature of indentured labor studies has been the tendency to examine the indentured experience in various European colonies in isolation from one another and from the slave regimes that preceded them.[75] As noted earlier, this historiographical preoccupation with the particular is no longer tenable. Not only were European slave trading, abolitionism, and the origins of the indentured labor trades inextricably intertwined, but the recruitment of indentured Indians cannot be disassociated from indigenous slave systems in the subcontinent.[76] Structural connections between slavery and indenture are also a hallmark of the *engagé* system that entailed securing 50,000 ostensibly liberated slaves and "free" contractual laborers along the East African coast and in Madagascar to work in Réunion and on the French-controlled islands of Mayotte in the Comoros and Nosy-Bé off Madagascar's northwest coast during the second half of the nineteenth century.[77]

Studies of indentured labor in Mauritius, Réunion, South Africa, and British East Africa rarely attempt to situate this activity in broader regional or comparative contexts. A review of published scholarship leaves little doubt, however, that the complex economic and other ties created between the Mascarenes and Indian Ocean Africa during the mid-eighteenth and early nineteenth centuries remained intact, albeit differentially so, following the Mascarene slave trade's demise. The Natal sugar industry's early development, for instance, depended on canes and skilled workers imported from Mauritius, while the indentured laborers recruited to work on the colony's sugar estates and construct its railroads included Indians from Mauritius.[78] Not only were Natal's colonists keenly aware of developments in Mauritius when they campaigned for the right to import Indian labor, but the official responsible for establishing the colony's recruitment system in India visited Mauritius en route to the subcontinent, where he toured several sugar estates and collected information about how Indian immigrants were treated.[79] That Mauritius continued to maintain economic and other ties with southern and eastern Africa during the second half of the nineteenth century is attested to in other ways. Aboobaker Amod, the first Indian merchant to reach Natal (1875), came from Mauritius, while other Indian merchants who established themselves in Natal and elsewhere in South Africa during the latter part of the nineteenth century also had and maintained Mauritian connections.[80] The island likewise played a significant role in the movement of Chinese traders, craftsmen, and workers throughout the western Indian Ocean during the late nineteenth century. Between 1888 and 1898, some 2,000 Chinese proceeded from Port Louis to South Africa, while the 1880s and 1890s witnessed other Chinese leaving Mauritius for the Comoros, Madagascar, Réunion, and the Seychelles.[81]

Concluding Thoughts on Mauritius and the Indian Ocean World

As others have noted, the social, economic, cultural, and political connections between islands in the western Indian Ocean and continental Africa have been and continue to be complex and multifaceted.[82] Studies such as Gabriel Rantoandro's work on the free Malagasy immigrants who facilitated the beef, rice, and slave trades between the Grande Île and the Mascarenes,[83] Nigel Worden's thoughtful comparison of slavery and its aftermath in the Cape Colony and Mauritius,[84] Pier Larson's meticulous reconstruction of the life histories of individuals such as Ratsitatanina and Aristide Corroller,[85] and research on the Mauritian and Réunionnais slave trades attest that relations between the Mascarenes and eastern and southern Africa have been equally complex and multifaceted.

Despite such studies, the extent, dynamics, and impact of the multidirectional ties between the Mascarenes and Indian Ocean Africa still remain poorly understood. Scholarship on British imperial careering during the long nineteenth century underscores the need to explore these relationships and their regional and pan-regional consequences with greater diligence.[86] Sir G. Lowry Cole, for example, moved directly from his governorship of Mauritius (1823–28) to that of the Cape Colony (1828–33), a transfer that invariably raises questions about the extent to which his experience in Mauritius influenced his tenure at the Cape. Sir Arthur Hamilton Gordon's career later in the century raises similar questions on a broader imperial scale; Gordon served as governor of Trinidad (1866–70), which housed a large indentured Indian population, before occupying Government House in Port Louis (1871–74) from whence he moved on to govern Fiji (1875–80), where he oversaw the initial introduction of indentured Indian laborers, before continuing to New Zealand (1880–82) and finally to Ceylon (1883–90), a colony that also depended heavily on

Indian migrant labor. The need to examine comparable connections in the French colonial empire is illustrated by Karin Speedy's work on the role that Réunionnais whites and "coolies" played in the development of New Caledonia's plantation sector during the 1860s and 1870s, and the island's involvement in establishing the so-called "blackbird" trade in Melanesian laborers to Queensland during the second half of the nineteenth century.[87]

Recent scholarship on the intraregional commercial networks created by Indian Muslim merchants in southeastern Africa, the role that South African and Australian Muslim communities played in constructing an international Muslim public opinion at the beginning of the twentieth century, and the ways in which knowledge of the Mauritian experiment with indentured Indian labor influenced the debate over using such laborers in New South Wales likewise highlight that coming to terms with these multi-dimensional, transoceanic relationships bears directly on our understanding of eastern and southern African and Indian Ocean history.[88] These studies raise important questions not only about how concepts of "cosmopolitanism" may deepen our understanding of connections between eastern and southern Africa and the wider western Indian Ocean World, but also about the need to apply such concepts outside the East African-Indian nexus that dominates discussions about Indian Ocean cosmopolitanism.[89] Ramachandra Guha's 2014 study of Mahatma Gandhi's tenure in South Africa does likewise. Guha notes that officials in the Transvaal held up Mauritius as a dramatic example of what might happen if "Asiatic" immigration to the province was not controlled, and that Thambi Naidoo, one of Gandhi's staunchest supporters and the activist leader of South Africa's Tamil community, and Haji Ojer Ally, who accompanied Gandhi on his trip to London in 1906, were both Mauritian-born.[90] Gandhi's 1901 visit to Mauritius and his subsequent dispatch of Manilal Doctor to the colony six years later is, in turn, widely regarded as inaugurating the process that led ultimately to Mauritian independence in 1968.[91]

Equally important is the need to assess how these transoceanic networks influenced social, economic, cultural, and political developments in the Mascarenes themselves. Historians of Mauritius and Réunion have paid little attention to the ways in which regional trade and migrant labor networks shaped the islands' society, economic, and culture beyond describing the slave and indentured labor trades' demographic impact. However, a careful reading of published scholarship on the Mauritian decolonization process, the structure and functioning of Mauritian democracy, how immigrant communities have become integrated into Mauritian society, and the role that ethnicity and ethnic identity play in local politics, creolization processes, and nation-building points to the need to delve more deeply into the ways in which these transoceanic connections have shaped and continue to influence Mauritian, Réunionnais, and Seychellois life.[92]

The necessity of doing so is perhaps best illustrated by the modern sociopolitical phenomenon known as *le malaise créole* in which Mauritians of African and Malagasy ancestry attribute their current marginal status in the country's social and economic life to their ancestors having reached the island as slaves rather than "free" immigrant laborers.[93] This *malaise* played a major role in the Mauritian government's decision in 2008 to establish a Truth and Justice Commission (TJC) to investigate the legacy of slavery and indentured labor.[94] In its findings and recommendations, the TJC argued that fostering greater social and economic justice and equity required greater public knowledge and understanding of the Mauritian past in all of its complexity, an argument that included an implicit acknowledgment of the need to situate the Mauritian past in broader contexts.[95] Changing Mauritian attitudes about cultural heritage attest to a growing awareness of these contexts,[96] a development that underscores the need for those interested in memory and identity to transcend their preoccupation with slavery and slave trading[97] and pay due attention to the ways in which peoples, such as those who inhabit Indian Ocean Africa and the western Indian Ocean, seek to understand their rich historical experience in all of its complexity.

Notes

Abbreviations: CO—Colonial Office records, National Archives of the United Kingdom (NAUK), Kew; MNA—Mauritius National Archives; PP—British Parliament Sessional Papers; T—Treasury records, NAUK.

1. For example, Auguste Toussaint, *Histoire des îles Mascareignes* (Paris: Éditions Berger-Levrault, 1972); André Scherer, *Histoire de La Réunion* (Paris: Presses Universitaires de France, 1974); P. J. Moree, *A Concise History of Dutch Mauritius, 1598–1710: A Fruitful and Healthy Land* (London: Kegan Paul International, 1998); Deryck Scarr, *Seychelles Since 1770: History of a Slave and Post-Slavery Society* (London: Hurst & Company, 2000); Amédée Nagapen, *Histoire de la colonie: Isle de France—Île Maurice, 1721–1968* (Rose Hill, Mauritius: Éditions de l'Océan Indien, 2010).

2. Hubert Gerbeau, "The Slave Trade in the Indian Ocean: Problems Facing the Historian and Research to be Undertaken," in *The African Slave Trade from the Fifteenth to the Nineteenth Century* (Paris: UNESCO, 1979), 184–207; Edward A. Alpers, "The African Diaspora in the Northwestern Indian Ocean: Reconsideration of an Old Problem, New Directions for Research," *Comparative Studies of South Asia, Africa and the Middle East* 17, no. 2 (1997): 62–81.

3. Patrick Manning's *The African Diaspora: A History Through Culture* (New York: Columbia University Press, 2009) reflects the Atlantic-centrism in African diaspora studies. On the number of African slaves shipped across the Red Sea and Indian Ocean, see Paul E. Lovejoy, *Transformations in Slavery: A History of Slavery in Africa*, 3rd ed. (Cambridge: Cambridge University Press, 2012), passim. On the significance of the African diaspora in the Indian Ocean, see Pier Larson, "African Diasporas and the Atlantic," in *The Atlantic in Global History, 1500–2000*, ed. Jorge Cañizares-Esguerra and Erik R. Seeman (Upper Saddle River, NJ: Pearson Education, 2007), 129–47. On the African diaspora in the Indian Ocean, see Joseph E. Harris, *The African Presence in Asia* (Evanston, IL: Northwestern University Press, 1971); Shihan de Silva Jayasuriya and Richard Pankhurst, eds., *The African Diaspora in the Indian Ocean* (Trenton, NJ: Africa World Press, 2003). For a critique of the dominant Afro-Atlantic model in African diaspora studies, see Paul Tiyambe Zeleza, "African Diasporas: Toward a Global History," *African Studies Review* 53, no. 1 (2010): 1–19.

4. Markus Vink, "'The World's Oldest Trade.' Dutch Slavery and Slave Trade in the Indian Ocean in the Seventeenth Century," *Journal of World History* 14, no. 2 (2003): 131–77.

5. Richard B. Allen, "Slaves, Convicts, Abolitionism and the Global Origins of the Post-Emancipation Labor System," *Slavery and Abolition* 35, no. 2 (2014): 328–48.

6. J.-M. Filliot, *La traite des esclaves vers les Mascareignes au XVIIIe siècle* (Paris: ORSTROM, 1974); Moses D. E. Nwulia, *The History of Slavery in Mauritius and the Seychelles, 1810–1875* (Rutherford, NJ: Farleigh Dickinson University Press, 1981); J. V. Payet, *Histoire de l'esclavage à l'Ile Bourbon* (Paris: Éditions L'Harmattan, 1990); Karl Noël, *L'esclavage à l'Isle de France* (Paris: Éditions Two Cities, 1991); Sudel Fuma, *L'esclavagisme à La Réunion, 1794–1848* (Paris: L'Harmattan, 1992); Marina Carter, *Servants, Sirdars and Settlers: Indians in Mauritius, 1834–1874* (Delhi: Oxford University Press, 1995); Anthony J. Barker, *Slavery and Antislavery in Mauritius, 1810–33: The Conflict between Economic Expansion and Humanitarian Reform under British Rule* (London: Macmillan Press Ltd., 1996); Deryck Scarr, *Slaving and Slavery in the Indian Ocean* (London: Macmillan Press Ltd., 1998); Vijaya Teelock, *Bitter Sugar: Sugar and Slavery in 19th Century Mauritius* (Moka, Mauritius: Mahatma Gandhi Institute Press, 1998); Clare Anderson, *Convicts in the Indian Ocean: Transportation from South Asia to Mauritius, 1815–33* (Basingstoke, UK: Macmillan, 2000); Hubert Gerbeau, "L'esclavage et son ombre: L'île Bourbon au XIXe et XXe siècles" (Thèse pour le doctorat d'État, Université de Provence [Aix-Marseille I], 2005); Megan Vaughan, *Creating the Creole Island: Slavery in Eighteenth-Century Mauritius* (Durham, NC: Duke University Press, 2005); Prosper Ève, *Le corps des esclaves de l'île Bourbon* (Paris: Presses de l'Université Paris-Sorbonne, 2013).

7. For example, Edward A. Alpers, "The Islands of Indian Ocean Africa," *Emergences: The Journal of Media and Composite Cultures* 10, no. 2 (2000): 373–86; Erik Gilbert, "Coastal East Africa and the Western Indian Ocean: Long-Distance

Trade, Empire, Migration, and Regional Unity, 1750–1970," *History Teacher* 36, no. 1 (2002): 7–34.

8. Clare Anderson, "Convicts and Coolies: Rethinking Indentured Labour in the Nineteenth Century," *Slavery and Abolition* 30, no. 1 (2009): 93–109; Jan Lucassen, "A Multinational and Its Labor Force: The Dutch East India Company, 1595–1793," *International Labor and Working-Class History* 66 (2004): 12–39.

9. Peter A. Coclanis, "Atlantic World or Atlantic/World?," *William and Mary Quarterly*, 3rd ser., 63, no. 4 (2006): 725–42; Peter A. Coclanis, "Beyond Atlantic History," in *Atlantic History: A Critical Appraisal*, ed. Jack P. Greene and Philip D. Morgan (Oxford: Oxford University Press, 2009), 337–56; Jennifer L. Gaynor, "Ages of Sail, Ocean Basins, and Southeast Asia," *Journal of World History* 24, no. 2 (2013): 309–33.

10. For example, Durba Ghosh and Dane Kennedy, "Introduction," in *Decentring Empire: Britain, India and the Transcolonial World*, ed. Durba Ghosh and Dane Kennedy (New Delhi: Orient Longman, 2006), 1–15.

11. Richard B. Allen, *European Slave Trading in the Indian Ocean* (Athens: Ohio University Press, 2014), 3.

12. Claude Allibert, "Les hollandaise et Madagascar," in *Cultures of Madagascar: Ebb and Flow of Influences/Civilisations de Madagascar: Flux et reflux des influences*, ed. Sandra Evers and Marc Spindler (Leiden, Netherlands: International Institute for Asian Studies, 1995), 91–93; Moree, *A Concise History*, 31.

13. Moree, *A Concise History*, 31–32, 36; Piet Westra and James C. Armstrong, *Slave Trade with Madagascar: The Journals of the Cape Slaver* Leijdsman, *1715/ Slawe-Handel met Madagaskar: Die Joernale van die Kaapse slaweship* Leijdsman, *1715* (Cape Town: African Publishers, 2006), 11.

14. Jean-Marie Desport, *De la servitude à la liberté: Bourbon des origines à 1848* ([Réunion]: Comité de la Culture, de l'Éducation et de l'Environment, 1989), 8; Hai Quang Ho, *Contribution à l'histoire économique de l'île de la Réunion (1642– 1848)* (Paris: L'Harmattan, 1998), 53.

15. Payet, *Histoire de l'esclavage*, 17. Of the island's 6,570 slaves in 1735, 57.1 percent were Malagasy compared to 10.7 percent of African origin and 7.2 percent of Indian origin. The remaining 22.3 percent were identified as Creole, i.e., locally born.

16. Robert Chaudenson, "À propos de la genèse du créole mauricien: Le peuplement de l'Île de France de 1721 à 1735," *Études créoles* 1 (1979): 43–57.

17. Jean Mettas, *Répertoire des expéditions négrières françaises au XVIIIe siècle*, vol. 2, *Ports Autres que Nantes*, ed. Serge et Michèle Daget (Paris: Société Française d'Histoire d'Outre-Mer, 1984), 223–24; Ève, *Le corps esclaves de l'île Bourbon*, 45, 60–63.

18. G. S. P. Freeman-Grenville, *The French at Kilwa Island* (Oxford: Clarendon Press, 1965), 10–24; Edward A. Alpers, *Ivory and Slaves in East Central Africa* (Berkeley: University of California Press, 1975), 150–51; Auguste Toussaint, *Le mirage des îles: Le négoçe française aux Mascareignes au XVIIIe siècle* (Aix-en-Provence: Edisud, 1977), 20ff.

19. Allen, *European Slave Trading*, 73. Slave cargoes reached the islands on "Arab" (probably Omani), American, Portuguese, and Spanish as well as French ships.

20. Allen, *European Slave Trading*, 68, 80. On the Seychelles as a refreshment station, see also Peter A. Nicholls, "'The Door to the Coast of Africa': The Seychelles in the Mascarene Slave Trade, 1770–1830" (PhD diss., University of Kent, 2018), esp. 103–7.

21. Raymond Decary, *Les voyages du chirurgien Avine à l'île de France et dans la mer des Indes au début du XIXe siècle* (Paris: G. Durassié & Cie, 1961), 17; M. J. Milbert, *Voyage pittoresque à l'Ile de France, au Cap de Bonne-Espérance et à l'Ile de Ténériffe*, vol. 1 (Paris: A. Nepveu, 1812), 257. The descriptor "Malay" could refer to slaves from the Indonesian archipelago as well as Malaya.

22. T 71/566, Registry of Personal Slaves, 1817; T 71/571, Registry of Plantation Slaves, 1817.

23. Baron d'Unienville, *Statistiques de l'île Maurice et ses dépendances suivie d'une notice historique sur cette colonie et d'un essai sur l'île de Madagascar*, 2nd ed., vol. 1 ([Île] Maurice: Typographie The Merchants and Planters Gazette, 1885–86), 257.

24. The descriptor *Mozambique* referred to slaves exported from the Swahili coast as well as Mozambique.

25. Marina Carter, "A Servile Minority in a Sugar Island: Malay and Chinese Slaves in Mauritius," in *Le monde créole: Peuplement, sociétés et condition humaine XVIIe–XXe siècles*, ed. Jacques Weber (Paris: Les Indes Savantes, 2005), 259–60.

26. Allen, *European Slave Trading*, 68–69.

27. Other Mascarene-based slaving ventures carried slaves from India, Madagascar, and West Central Africa (Angola, Cabinda, Malimbe) to the Americas. Allen, *European Slave Trading*, 69.

28. Jerry W. Cooney, "Silver, Slaves and Food: The Río de la Plata and the Indian Ocean, 1796–1806," *Tijdschrift voor zeegeschiedenis* 5, no. 1 (1986): 36–37, 41; Jean-Pierre Tardieu, *La traite des noirs entre l'océan Indien et Montevideo (Uruguay) fin du XVIIIe siècle et début du XIXe* (Paris: L'Harmattan, 2010); Alex Borucki, "The Slave Trade to the Río de la Plata, 1777–1812: Trans-Imperial Networks and Atlantic Warfare," *Colonial Latin American Review* 20, no. 1 (2011): 94–95.

29. PP 1826 XXVII [295], 6–7, R. T. Farquhar to Earl of Liverpool, February 15, 1811, and Earl of Liverpool to R. T. Farquhar, May 2, 1811.

30. CO 167/7, Despatch, R. T. Farquhar to Earl of Liverpool, October 26, 1811.

31. PP 1826 XXVII [295], 10, R. T. Farquhar to Earl of Liverpool, February 1, 1812.

32. CO 167/23, B, No. 4, Lt.-Col. Henry S. Keating to Capt. Molloy, November 23, 1813.

33. CO 167/23, C, No. 67, Lt.-Col. Henry S. Keating to Capt. Molloy, January 8, 1814, and E, No. 66, Lt.-Col. Henry S. Keating to R. T. Farquhar, January 8, 1814.

34. PP 1826 XXVII [352], 122, Maj.-Gen. Darling to Henry Goulburn, December 17, 1819.

35. CO 167/141, Return No. 19, Return of the Number of Prize Negroes Apprenticed in the Colony of Mauritius from the Year 1813 to 1827 inclusive. On prize Negroes in Mauritius, see also M. Carter, V. Govinden, and S. Peerthum, *The Last Slaves: Liberated Africans in 19th Century Mauritius* (Port Louis: Centre for Research on Indian Ocean Societies, 2003).

36. Gerbeau, "L'esclavage et son ombre," 1311–12. Serge Daget reports that ninety-four ships participated in the Réunionnais trade between 1815 and 1831. Serge Daget, "Révolution ajournée: Bourbon et la traite illégale française, 1815–1832," in *Révolution française et océan Indien: Prémices, paroxysmes, héritages et déviances,* ed. Claude Wanquet and Benoît Jullien (Paris: Éditions L'Harmattan, 1996), 336.

37. Nwulia, *The History of Slavery,* 46. Nwulia does not cite this estimate's provenance.

38. CO 172/38, Three Years Administration of the Isle de France (otherwise called Mauritius) . . . , 344; Sadasivam Reddi, "Aspects of Slavery during the British Administration," in *Slavery in South West Indian Ocean,* ed. U. Bissoondoyal and S. B. C. Servansing, (Moka, Mauritius: Mahatma Gandhi Institute Press, 1989), 108; Hubert Gerbeau, "Quelques aspects de la traite illégale des esclaves à l'Ile Bourbon au XIXe siècle," in *Mouvements de populations dans l'océan Indien* (Paris: Librairie Honoré Champion, 1979), 292.

39. PP 1826—27 VI [90], 67, Capt. Fairfax Moresby, R.N., before the Select Committee on the Mauritius Slave Trade, May 22, 1826.

40. PP 1829 XXV [292], Report of the Commissioners of Inquiry Upon the Slave Trade at Mauritius [hereafter Slave Trade Report], 27.

41. Richard B. Allen, "Licentious and Unbridled Proceedings: The Illegal Slave Trade to Mauritius and the Seychelles during the Early Nineteenth Century," *Journal of African History* 42, no. 1 (2001): 100; Gerbeau, "L'esclavage et son ombre," 1330.

42. Allen, *European Slave Trading,* 153, 158. For a fuller discussion of the Seychelles' role in the illegal Mascarene trade, see Nicholls, "'The Door to the Coast of Africa,'" 108–67.

43. Gerbeau, "The Slave Trade in the Indian Ocean."

44. Allen, *European Slave Trading,* 19, 23. The Mascarenes accounted for 23.2 to 26.0 percent of all French slave trading from 1770 to 1810, and 39.0 to 42.8 percent of all such activity between 1811 and 1848.

45. Edward A. Alpers, "The French Slave Trade in East Africa (1721–1810)," *Cahiers d'études africaines* 10, no. 37 (1970): 80–2.

46. Thomas Vernet, "Slave Trade and Slavery on the Swahili Coast, 1500–1750," in *Slavery, Islam and Diaspora,* ed. Behnaz Mirzai, Ismael Musah Montana, and Paul E. Lovejoy (Trenton, NJ: Africa World Press, 2009), 37–76.

47. Allen, *European Slave Trading,* 24. These figures include exports by Arab, Muslim, and Swahili merchants to the Middle East and South Asia.

48. Pier M. Larson, *History and Memory in the Age of Enslavement: Becoming Merina in Highland Madagascar, 1770–1822* (Portsmouth, NH: Heinemann, 2000); Gwyn Campbell, *An Economic History of Imperial Madagascar, 1795–1895: The Rise and Fall of an Island Empire* (Cambridge: Cambridge University Press, 2005).

49. Pier M. Larson, "Enslaved Malagasy and 'Le Travail de la parole' in the Pre-Revolutionary Mascarenes," *Journal of African History* 47, no. 3 (2007): 457–79.

50. Abdul Sheriff, *Slaves, Spices and Ivory in Zanzibar* (London: James Currey, 1987), 50; Richard B. Allen, "Suppressing a Nefarious Traffic: Britain and the Abolition of Slave Trading in India and the Western Indian Ocean, 1770–1830," *William and Mary Quarterly*, 3rd ser., 66, no. 4 (2009): 873–94.

51. By most accounts, the capitation tax on slaves exported from Tamatave added almost $33,000 (£6,600) to Merina royal coffers in 1821. Ludvig Munthe, Charles Ravoajanahary, and Simon Ayache, "Radama I et les anglais: Les négociations de 1817 d'après les sources malgaches ('Sorabe' inédits)," *Omaly sy anio* 3–4 (1976): 55; Gwyn Campbell, "Madagascar and the Slave Trade, 1810–1895," *Journal of African History* 22, no. 2 (1981): 208; Gwyn Campbell, "The Adoption of Autarky in Imperial Madagascar, 1820–1835," *Journal of African History* 28, no. 3 (1987): 400. However, others put this figure at $40,000 (£8,000) a year (Scarr, *Slaving and Slavery*, 132). The 1822 Moresby Treaty, which banned European slave exports from the sultan of Oman's possession along the Swahili coast, reportedly cost the sultan 40,000–50,000 Maria Theresa dollars (approximately £8,400–£10,500) each year (Sheriff, *Slaves, Spices*, 50).

52. CO 167/49, Enclosure No. 32, Deposition of Guillaume Bonne . . . , enclosed in Despatch No. 9, Maj.-Gen. R. W. Darling to Earl Bathurst, February 26, 1820.

53. Robert Ross, "The Dutch on the Swahili Coast, 1776–1778: Two Slaving Journals, Part I," *International Journal of African Historical Studies* 19, no. 2 (1986): 334–35.

54. Allen, *European Slave Trading*, Appendix D.

55. CO 167/92, Compte courant de la deuxième traite de noirs du brick le succès a zanzibard, côte oriental D'affrique [7 mars 1821]; Commencé le present bouillard de traite à zanzibard le 9 Février 1821. Prie possetion de la maison du Gouverneur le 9 Février 1821 à raison de Commancé la traite le 10 Février.

56. Pedro Machado, *Ocean of Trade: South Asian Merchants, Africa and the Indian Ocean, c. 1750–1850* (Cambridge: Cambridge University Press, 2014), 241.

57. Auguste Toussaint, "Le trafic commerciale entre les Mascareignes et Madagascar, de 1773 à 1810," *Annales de l'Université de Madagascar*, Série lettres et sciences humaines 6 (1967): 35–89; Madeleine Ly-Tio-Fane, "Problèmes d'approvisionnement de l'Ile de France au temps de l'Intendant Poivre," *Proceedings of the Royal Society of Arts and Sciences of Mauritius* 3 (1968): 101–15. On the need to investigate the regional traffic in foodstuffs, see Edward A. Alpers,

"The Western Indian Ocean as a Regional Food Network in the Nineteenth Century," in *East Africa and the Indian Ocean*, by Edward A. Alpers (Princeton, NJ: Markus Weiner, 2009), 23–38.

58. For example, MNA: F 4/886, 26 nivôse An IX; GB 26/715, April 28, 1806; GB 26/973, December 29, 1807.

59. On Madagascar's role in supplying the provisions needed to maintain European trading networks within and beyond the Indian Ocean, see Jane Hooper, *Feeding Globalization: Madagascar and the Provisioning Trade, 1600–1800* (Athens: Ohio University Press, 2017).

60. Jean Valette, "Le commerce de Madagascar vers les Mascareignes au XVIIIe siècle," *La revue de Madagascar* 33 (1966): 35–52.

61. Auguste Toussaint, *La route des îles: Contribution à l'histoire maritime des Mascareignes* (Paris: SEVPEN, 1967), 193–238. Unfortunately, comparable data do not exist for Réunion.

62. MNA: F 4, Municipalité du Port Nord-Ouest, Registre pour l'enregistrement des déclarations d'arrivées de capitaines de navires et des cautionnements, 7 juillet 1794–20 septembre 1803; GB 26, Bureau Central de Police, Registre pour servir à l'enregistrement des déclarations d'arrivées de capitaines, 7 vendémiaire XII (30 septembre 1803)–15 octobre 1810, 10 janvier 1811–19 avril 1815.

63. MNA: OB 21/73, September 16, 1782.

64. MNA: F 4/1156, 23 messidor An X.

65. Slave Trade Report, 32. According to Charles Dorval, a notorious slave trader, twelve such vessels participated in the illegal slave trade. CO 415/10/A.298, French Vessels engaged in the Slave Trade as stated by Mr. Dorval (1826).

66. MNA: NA 18/7C/60, February 7, 1772.

67. MNA: NA 32/6/1, October 16, 1788.

68. Machado, *Ocean of Trade*, 208, 233–35.

69. Allen, "Slaves, Convicts," 332–33.

70. Huguette Ly-Tio-Fane Pineo, *Lured Away: The Life History of Indian Cane Workers in Mauritius* (Moka, Mauritius: Mahatma Gandhi Press, 1984), 14–17; Huguette Ly-Tio-Fane Pineo, *Chinese Diaspora in the Western Indian Ocean* (Rose Hill, Mauritius: Éditions de l'Océan Indien/Mission Catholique Chinoise, 1985), 268–69; David Northrup, *Indentured Labor in the Age of Empire* (Cambridge: Cambridge University Press, 1995), 60; Marina Carter and James Ng Fong Kwong, *Forging the Rainbow: Labour Immigrants in British Mauritius* (Mauritius: Alfran Co. Ltd., 1997), 4–5; Jacques Weber, "L'émigration indienne à La Réunion: 'Contraire à la morale' ou 'utile à l'humanité'? (1829–1860)," in *Esclavage et abolitions dans l'océan Indien, 1723–1860*, ed. Edmond Maestri (Paris: L'Harmattan, 2002), 309–10; Satyendra Peerthum, "'A Cheap Reservoir of Mankind for Labour': The Genesis of the Indentured Labour System in Mauritius, 1826–1843," in *Angajé: Explorations into the History, Society and Culture of Indentured Immigrants and Their Descendants in Mauritius*, vol. 1, *Early Years*, ed. Vijayalakshmi Teelock, Anwar Janoo, Geoffrey Summers, Marc Serge Rivière,

and Sooryakanti Nirsimloo-Gayan (Port Louis, Mauritius: Aapravasi Ghat Trust Fund, 2012), 158–59.

71. I. M. Cumpston, *Indians Overseas in British Territories, 1834–1854* (London: Oxford University Press, 1953), 85.

72. Northrup, *Indentured Labor*, 159–60.

73. Those who subscribe to this notion follow Hugh Tinker, *A New System of Slavery: A New System of Slavery: The Export of Indian Labour Overseas, 1830–1920* (London: Oxford University Press, 1974; 2nd ed., London: Hansib, 1993).

74. For arguments that this characterization is at least something of a misnomer, see Bridgette Brereton, "The Other Crossing: Asian Migrants in the Caribbean. A Review Essay," *Journal of Caribbean History* 28, no. 1 (1994): 99–122; Carter, *Servants, Sirdars*, 1–6; Northrup, *Indentured Labor*, 154.

75. Richard B. Allen, "Re-conceptualizing the 'New System of Slavery,'" *Man in India* 92, no. 2 (2012): 225–45.

76. Benedicte Hjejle, "Slavery and Agricultural Bondage in South India in the Nineteenth Century," *Scandinavian Economic History Review* 15, nos. 1–2 (1967): 71–126.

77. Prominent studies include: François Renault, *Libération d'esclaves et nouvelle servitude: Les rachats de captives africains pour le compte des colonies françaises après l'abolition de l'esclavage* (Paris: Les Nouvelles Éditions Africaines, 1976); Sudel Fuma, "La traite des esclaves dans le bassin du sud-ouest de l'océan Indien et la France après 1848," in *La route des esclaves: Système servile et traite dans l'est malgache*, ed. Ignace Rakoto (Paris: L'Harmattan, 2000), 247–61; Jehanne-Emmanuelle Monnier, *Esclaves de la canne à sucre: Engagés et planteurs à Nossi-Bé, Madagascar, 1850–1880* (Paris: L'Harmattan, 2006).

78. Surendra Bhana and Joy B. Brain, *Setting Down Roots: Indian Migrants in South Africa, 1860–1911* (Johannesburg: Witwatersrand University Press, 1990), 21, 25.

79. Thomas R. Metcalf, "'Hard Hands and South Healthy Bodies': Recruiting 'Coolies' for Natal, 1860–1911," *Journal of Imperial and Commonwealth History* 30, no. 3 (2002): 1, 3. On the competition between Natal and Mauritius for agricultural laborers and markets, see Peter Richardson, "The Natal Sugar Industry in the Nineteenth Century," in *Crisis and Change in the International Sugar Economy*, ed. Bill Albert and Adrian Graves (Norwich, UK: ISC Press, 1984), 238.

80. Bhana and Brain, *Setting Down Roots*, 66, 79, 105, 108, 111, 168, 177; Goolam Vahed and Surendra Bhana, *Crossing Space and Time in the Indian Ocean: Early Indian Traders in Natal, A Biographical Study* (Pretoria: Unisa Press, 2010), 19–23. See also Vishnu Padayachee and Robert Morrell, "Indian Merchants and Dukawallahs in the Natal Economy, c. 1875–1914," *Journal of Southern African Studies* 17, no. 1 (1991): 71–102; Goolam Vahed, "Passengers, Partnerships, and Promissory Notes: Gujarati Traders in Colonial Natal, 1870–1920," *International Journal of African Historical Studies* 38, no. 3 (2005): 449–79, esp. 450–54.

81. Ly-Tio-Fane Pineo, *Chinese Diaspora*, passim.

82. Edward A. Alpers, "A Complex Relationship: Mozambique and the Comoro Islands in the 19th and 20th Centuries," *Cahiers d'études africaines* 41, no. 161 (2001): 73–95.

83. Gabriel Rantoandro, "Contribution à l'étude d'un groupe social peu connu du XIXe siècle: Les maromita," *Omaly sy anio* 16 (1982): 41–60.

84. Nigel Worden, "Diverging Histories: Slavery and Its Aftermath in the Cape Colony and Mauritius," *South African Historical Journal* 27 (1992): 3–25.

85. Pier M. Larson, "The Vernacular Life of the Street: Ratsitatanina and Indian Ocean Créolité," *Slavery and Abolition* 29, no. 3 (2008): 327–59; Pier M. Larson, "Fragments of an Indian Ocean Life: Artistide Corroller Between Islands and Empire," *Journal of Social History* 45, no. 2 (2011): 366–89; Pier M. Larson, "La rue coloniale: Ratsitatanina et la créolité dans l'océan Indien," in *Traites et esclavages en Afrique orientale et dans l'océan Indien*, ed. Henri Médard, Marie-Laure Derat, Thomas Vernet, and Marie Pierre Ballarin (Paris: Karthala, 2013), 441–60.

86. David Lambert and Alan Lester, eds., *Colonial Lives Across the British Empire: Imperial Careering in the Long Nineteenth Century* (Cambridge: Cambridge University Press, 2006).

87. See Karin Speedy, *Colons, créoles et coolies: L'immigration réunionnaise en Nouvelle-Calédonie (XIXe siècle) et le tayo de Saint-Louis* (Paris: L'Harmattan, 2007); Karin Speedy, "Who Were the Réunion 'Coolies' of 19th-Century New Caledonia?" *Journal of Pacific History* 44, no. 2 (2009): 123–40; Karin Speedy, "From the Indian Ocean to the Pacific: *Affranchis* and *Petits-Blancs* in New Caledonia," *PORTAL Journal of Multidisciplinary International Studies* 9, no. 1 (2012); Karin Speedy, "The *Sutton* Case: The First Franco-Australian Foray into Blackbirding," *Journal of Pacific History* 50, no. 3 (2015): 344–64.

88. See, respectively: Eric Germain, "Southern Hemispheric Diasporic Communities in the Building of an International Muslim Public Opinion at the Turn of the Twentieth Century," *Comparative Studies of South Asia, Africa and the Middle East* 27, no. 1 (2007): 126–38; Takashi Oishi, "Indian Muslim Merchants in Mozambique and South Africa: Intra-Regional Networks in Strategic Association with State Institutions, 1870s–1930s," *Journal of the Economic and Social History of the Orient* 50, nos. 2–3 (2007): 287–324; Rose Cullen, "Empire, Indian Indentured Labour and the Colony: The Debate over 'Coolie' Labour in New South Wales, 1836–1838," *History Australia* 9, no. 1 (2012): 84–109.

89. For example, John C. Hawley, ed., *India in Africa, Africa in India: Indian Ocean Cosmopolitanisms* (Bloomington: Indiana University Press, 2008); Edward Simpson and Kai Kresse, eds., *Struggling with History: Islam and Cosmopolitanism in the Western Indian Ocean* (New York: Columbia University Press, 2008).

90. Ramachandra Guha, *Gandhi before India* (New York: Alfred A. Knopf, 2014), 191, 205, 208, 212.

91. Adele Smith Simmons, *Modern Mauritius: The Politics of Decolonization* (Bloomington: Indiana University Press, 1982), 46–47; Larry W. Bowman, *Mauritius: Democracy and Development in the Indian Ocean* (Boulder, CO: Westview Press, 1991), 29; Vijayalakshmi Teelock, *Mauritian History: From Its Beginnings*

to Modern Times, rev. ed. (Moka, Mauritius: Mahatma Gandhi Institute, 2009), 351–54.

92. See Simmons, *Modern Mauritius;* Bowman, *Mauritius;* Thomas Hylland Eriksen, *Common Denominators: Ethnicity, Nation-Building and Compromise in Mauritius* (Oxford: Berg, 1998); Amenah Jahangeer-Chojoo, *La rose et le henné: Une étude des musulmans de Maurice* (Moka, Mauritius: Mahatma Gandhi Institute Press, 2004); Patrick Eisenlohr, *Little India: Diaspora, Time, and Ethnolinguistic Belonging in Hindu Mauritius* (Berkeley: University of California Press, 2006); Huguette Ly-Tio-Fane Pineo and Edouard Lim Fat, *From Alien to Citizen: The Integration of the Chinese in Mauritius* (Rose Hill, Mauritius: Éditions de l'Océan Indien, 2008).

93. Rosabelle Boswell, *Le malaise créole: Ethnic Identity in Mauritius* (New York: Berghahn Books, 2006).

94. The TJC was inspired by South Africa's post-apartheid Truth and Reconciliation Commission (TRC). The TJC's second chairman, Dr. Alex Boraine, was a major architect of the TRC and served as its deputy chairman (1996–98).

95. Truth and Justice Commission, *Report of the Truth and Justice Commission,* vol. 1 (Port Louis, Mauritius: Government Printing Office, November 2011), 391–454.

96. For example, Corinne Forest, "Aapravasi Ghat World Heritage Site: A Change in the Perception of Heritage in Mauritius," in *Angajé,* vol. 3, *Post-Indenture Mauritius,* ed. Vijayalakshmi Teelock et al. (Port Louis, Mauritius: Aapravasi Ghat Trust Fund, 2013), 193–208; Diego Calaon and Corrine Forest, "Archaeology and the Process of Heritage Construction in Mauritius," in *Connecting Continents: Archaeology and History in the Indian Ocean World,* ed. Krish Seetah (Athens: Ohio University Press, 2018), 253–90.

97. For example, Douglas Hamilton, Kate Hodgson, and Joel Quirk, eds., *Slavery, Memory and Identity: National Representations and Global Legacies* (London: Pickering & Chatto, 2012).

11

The Island as Nexus

Zanzibar in the Nineteenth Century

Jeremy Prestholdt

In April 1840 a 300-ton merchant vessel from the small African island of Zanzibar arrived in New York City. The sultan of Zanzibar and Oman, Sayyid Saʿīd bin Sultān Āl Busaʿīdī, had dispatched the ship to the United States on an extraordinary mission. Part of Zanzibar's ambitious effort to pioneer more favorable trade relations with overseas partners, the *Sultana* would be the first ship representing either an African or Arabian state to visit the United States. The voyage of the *Sultana* captured, in microcosm, East Africa's extraversion in the nineteenth century as well as the rapidly changing social circumstances of the region's great entrepôt.

The *Sultana*'s crew represented Zanzibar's increasing sociocultural diversity and rigid social hierarchy. Onboard were East African domestic slaves and many South Asian sailors. The chief officers, Muhammad Juma and Muhammad Abdullah, were Swahili and Persian, respectively. The head of the mission was the secretary to the sultan, Ahmad bin Naʾaman. Ahmad bin Naʾaman's career was emblematic of Zanzibar's elite at mid-century. Born in Bahrain, Ahmad bin Naʾaman studied at an English school in Bombay, took up residence in Zanzibar, made the hajj, and in the service of the sultan traveled to London in 1834.[1]

The *Sultana* carried gifts to the American president, Martin Van Buren, but diplomacy was not the primary object of its mission. The *Sultana* sailed to the commercial heart of the Western Hemisphere to conduct business. It delivered to New York the most valued products of the western Indian Ocean region, including dates, ivory, Persian rugs, 11.5 tons of coffee, and the first major shipment of cloves from Zanzibar Island.[2] The ship's return cargo included almost 90,000 yards of American manufactured cloth (*merekani* in Swahili) and luxury fabrics, as well as thousands of pieces of china, red and white beads, gold leaf, muskets, music boxes, and soap—a product commonly used to wash imported cloth.[3] Such items were typical of Zanzibar's import trade at mid-century, which reflected the consumer tastes of a cross-section of East Africans. China, gold leaf, and broadcloth were used for ornamental and adornment purposes in Zanzibar, while beads and *merekani* found a large market on the African mainland. Ahmad bin Na'aman was also commissioned to procure luxury items for many of Zanzibar's wealthiest residents, objects such as chandeliers, glass plates, watches, lamps, and mirrors.[4] Most of the goods the *Sultana* brought back to Zanzibar, like the majority of East Africa's imports, were objects destined for the social realm of display and public communication.

The *Sultana*'s voyage to New York was one of many trading missions launched from Zanzibar in the nineteenth century. Such missions included direct trade with India, China, the Ottoman Empire, Mauritius, France, Germany, and Britain.[5] In the first decades of the century, Americans and western Europeans dominated the trade with the North Atlantic. Sayyid Sa'īd and his successors did not change this. Yet, the *Sultana*'s inversion of East Africa's commercial relationship with Atlantic states demonstrated the significant investments Zanzibari elites were prepared to make in order to procure those items in demand in eastern Africa and the wider Indian Ocean region.[6]

More precisely, the *Sultana*'s sojourn to New York as well as the other voyages it made to Bombay, London, Hamburg, and Marseilles, were evidence of the extraversion of the East African coast and attempts by Zanzibaris to exert greater control over the trade that delivered incredible wealth to the island. At the same time, the *Sultana*'s crew and the consumer goods procured in New York reflected the cultural politics of the burgeoning metropolis of Zanzibar. The people and objects on board the *Sultana* offer a snapshot of how the rapidly expanding economy of nineteenth-century East Africa facilitated new social engagements in its island metropolis, including diverse forms of consumption and subjection.

Between the 1830s and the early twentieth century the island of Zanzibar (Unguja) was the primary node of linkage among eastern African, Indian Ocean, and Atlantic basin economic systems. More precisely, the seat of the sultanate of Zanzibar and Oman was a *nexus*, a critical point of economic and social interrelation that reflected diverse interests and broadcasted shifting sociocultural trends. Few ports in the world have commanded a relationship with such a vast hinterland as Zanzibar in the nineteenth century. The island capital acted as an interface between the greater eastern African region—stretching from Lake Malawi to the Congo and southern Somalia—and ports as distant as Boston, Cape Town, and Canton. Zanzibar City thus became a metropolis in the latter nineteenth century, one that embodied the dividends and tensions of eastern Africa's economic growth.[7]

This chapter examines the articulation of African socioeconomic trends with broader global currents as evident in Zanzibar between the 1830s and the 1880s. In this era, which represented the height of Zanzibar's influence, the city's polyglot residents, slave and free, attempted to capture wealth from global exchanges and translate it into social position, among other things. To illuminate this confluence of economic and social interests, I focus on the metabolic processes of the nexus, or how Zanzibaris converted imported people and things into the productive instruments of labor and local social relations.[8] One of the most revealing dimensions of the Zanzibar nexus was the island's indulgent, competitive, and often oppressive consumer culture. Zanzibar's rapidly evolving consumer culture evidenced the deployment of global symbols in the service of local image-making practices. By focusing on how demands for commodities and labor shaped an important node of global interface during a period of hastening global integration, we can better appreciate the particular socioeconomic logics of the nexus.

To sharpen the analytical focus further, I will concentrate on urban Zanzibar and its two most important categories of imports: apparel and enslaved people. Apparel—clothing, jewelry, and other accoutrements—and slaves encapsulated Zanzibar's transoceanic and transcontinental relationships. In nineteenth-century Zanzibar, clothing was almost exclusively imported from other world regions, including western India, China, southern Arabia, western Europe, and North America. In contrast, most slaves, who often represented the greatest financial investments of Zanzibaris, were brought to the island from societies adjacent to eastern Africa's caravan roads, an area that stretched from southern Ethiopia to the Lakes Region, eastern Congo, the northern shores of Lake Malawi. However, a small number of slaves were brought to Zanzibar from as far afield as Madagascar, India, and southeastern Europe. Zanzibari slave owners often purchased slaves for their productive value, yet enslaved people, like consumer objects, were also valued for their ability to represent wealth, power, and prestige.[9] Many urban slave owners purchased slaves for the symbolic social capital they could provide and so assessed them much as they did inanimate objects. Indeed, the process of objectifying and commodifying people evidenced the lack of a neat conceptual boundary between "humanness" and "thingness" in the minds of slave owners.

In the first half of this chapter I explore the uses of imported objects in Zanzibar City, with an emphasis on apparel. The demographic diversity of Zanzibar and the end of historic sumptuary codes led to a common interest in consumer goods as means both to claim and represent social position. Greater wealth encouraged the consumption of a widening array of goods, including East Asian silks, South Asian cotton goods, southern Arabian turbans, western European jackets, and American shoes. Each evidenced Zanzibar's position between African and overseas markets, as well as the emerging island aesthetic. In the second half of the chapter I focus on how urban Zanzibaris perceived slaves as social investments and thus often deployed them in ways akin to objects of display. Yet, unlike objects, enslaved people attempted to negotiate their relationship with their owners and, in some cases, claim a higher position within Zanzibar's oppressive social hierarchy. Though many slave owners imagined their captives to be akin to objects, enslaved people developed strategies for projecting desirable self-images within spaces of subjection, strategies that often emphasized materiality alongside piety and clientage. More precisely, Zanzibar's hierarchical concepts of ownership and power encouraged enslaved people to seek greater autonomy through acquiring signs of ability such as fine clothes and dependents. In the city of Zanzibar an evolving social hierarchy encouraged those both at the top and bottom toward similar aspirations for respect through the ownership of foreign objects of prestige as well as the control of people.

Global Exchange, Consumer Culture, and Zanzibar Island

Consumer desire is situated at the intersection of culture and economy. It reflects and reinforces changing social norms. It also translates these norms into the precise language of commerce. Thus, reflection on the rationales for and consequences of consumption practices can provide a window on shifting social relationships as well as processes of global economic relation.[10] An approach to global engagements that considers the cultural logics of demand alongside the circumstances of commercial exchange can offer fresh perspectives on how Africa's articulation with the global economy was affected by cumulative endogenous and exogenous forces.[11]

Overseas interests in East African products and East Africa's diversifying consumer tastes fashioned Zanzibar's economy. Over the course of the nineteenth century, the consumption of imported goods increased tenfold across the region. Maxims such as, "it is always far more easy to dispose of a cargo at Zanzibar than to procure one" pepper the correspondences of European and American residents of the city.[12] Zanzibaris of all socio-economic backgrounds were concerned with the acquisition of imported consumer goods either for personal use or trade to the African mainland. Zanzibaris came to rely on imported fashions as means of communication in the public realm. As the East Africa region became more completely integrated into expanding global markets, Zanzibaris purchased imported consumer goods in volumes that surpassed previous eras. In addition to the major open-air markets in Zanzibar, all of the city's major thorough-fares were lined with retail shops.[13] Zanzibar was eastern Africa's premier marketplace.

In the early nineteenth century, the East African savannah was one of the few world regions where large numbers of elephants remained. More-over, East Africa's elephants had tusks of soft ivory, the variety coveted by manufacturers of jewelry and other ivory products. The region also pro-duced rubber as well as high-grade copal used for varnish by the furniture industry.[14] With the establishment of plantations on the coast, as well as on Zanzibar and Pemba islands, sesame, sugar, grains, and cloves were pro-duced in unprecedented volume. At mid-century, East Africa was also one of the few remaining slave-exporting regions in the world.[15] Since Indian, European, and American manufacturers were mechanizing production and overseas firms in Zanzibar were competing with each other for African consumers, the average price of imported consumer goods on the island fell during the second half of the century. At the same time, the price for ivory and other East African exports increased. These convergent price curves offered consumers increasing purchasing power and brought Zanzi-bari merchants great wealth.[16]

In the nineteenth century Zanzibar experienced great political changes as well. Omani influence at the coast had been significant since the end of the seventeenth century, but Omani commercial interests, largely financed by Indian capital, expanded in the early 1800s. To better exploit economic opportunities in eastern Africa, the Busaʿīdī sultan Sayyid Saʿīd shifted Oman's capital from Muscat to Zanzibar, a well-positioned island only twenty-five miles from the mainland caravan terminus at Bagamoyo. Additionally, Sayyid Saʿīd extended his rule over much of the coast to Somalia. Unlike the Portuguese Estado da India, which had once domi-nated the coast, the sultan made Zanzibar a free port and encouraged significant foreign investment. In the early decades of the nineteenth century, Zanzibar-based commercial firms, most of which were subsidiar-ies of Indian financial houses, began offering generous lines of credit.

This credit fueled trading ventures to the interior, increased agricultural production for export, and brought more cash into circulation within coastal cities. Simultaneously, enterprising traders from mainland societies expanded routes to the coast and pioneered new roads. For instance, Stephen Rockel has shown how Nyamwezi merchants in central Tanzania augmented an older trade in salt and iron across central Tanzania with direct links to port towns. There they bartered for imported consumer goods, which they transferred to interior societies.[17]

The East African region lacked navigable rivers to connect the coast and the interior, but caravans such as those led by Nyamwezi merchants facilitated vast networks of exchange. Roads reached from coastal towns such as Kilwa Kivinje, Bagamoyo, and Mombasa to Lake Malawi, the eastern forest belt, and the kingdom of Buganda on the shores of Lake Victoria. Caravans with porters numbering into the thousands became mobile markets trading imported cloth, beads, and brass wire for export commodities, provisions, and slaves. As a result, the Indian, British, and American cloth brought to Zanzibar reached markets more than a thousand miles inland.

As the nineteenth century progressed, Zanzibari merchants forged links with ever more distant partners. At the beginning of the century foreign vessels trading in Zanzibar typically hailed from other East African ports, southern Arabia, or western India. By the end of the 1820s, ships flying American, French, and British flags also frequented Zanzibar. Within a few decades, vessels from most world regions were visiting the port city. In the mid-1860s not only were South Asian, Yemeni, Omani, Comorian, Somali, American, French, Portuguese, and Hanseatic vessels visiting Zanzibar but so too were Egyptian, Turkish, Danish, Sardinian, Hanoverian, Prussian, Italian, Spanish, and even Argentine merchant ships. Eager to increase revenues and maintain Zanzibar's position as the regional entrepôt, Sayyid Saʿīd and his successors severely restricted foreign access to other regional markets. Overseas trade was thus channeled through the sultan's customhouse.

Throughout the century, cloth constituted the largest category of imported trade goods by volume at Zanzibar. Western Indian cottons, notably the indigo cloth known as *kaniki*, had dominated the region for centuries.[18] But in the 1840s and 1850s unbleached American cloth (*merekani*) found a market across East Africa that soon rivaled the kaniki. Merekani also became an important means of tribute in the caravan trade, or gifts in recognition of a ruler's authority. In many East African societies merekani acted as a common component of bride wealth. As a testament to the interpenetration of use- and exchange-values in East Africa, merekani even became one of the region's few currencies. The dramatic increase in demand for American cloth evidenced the changing tastes of East Africans.[19] Yet, tastes changed so rapidly that foreign merchants could not always cater to new trends. To address changing consumer demand and add value to imports, artisans in coastal cities and inland trade centers frequently altered imported textiles. Based on information provided by caravan leaders and porters, they added colors and patterns and wove borders onto imported cloth.[20]

By the time the *Sultana* sailed for New York, Zanzibar was a crucial link in the regional distribution of imported apparel. It was also becoming a center of remanufacture that responded to and influenced regional consumer demands. For example, in the 1850s Zanzibaris found a market in Nyamwezi (northwestern Tanzania) for the *kitambi banyani*, a white Indian-made cloth, which artisans in Zanzibar stamped with a narrow red border. Similarly, Zanzibaris gave Surati white cotton loincloths broad border stripes of indigo, red, and yellow, which increased their marketability among diverse consumers in the interior. An even more remarkable example of how Zanzibaris remade imported consumer goods was the *leso*, a popular item of Muslim women's fashion at the coast. The leso was a remanufactured cloth made from colorful men's handkerchiefs that were exported from Manchester to Bombay and then imported at Zanzibar. In Zanzibar, the handkerchiefs were stitched together to form large wrappers that gave a stunning play of pattern and color. The style quickly traveled west from Mombasa along the caravan routes, finding eager buyers in non-Muslim societies. Recognizing the market for leso, western Indian manufacturers began printing cloths with the distinct, multiple handkerchief pattern. By the twentieth century the leso was so ubiquitous across the northern East Africa region that it was the most commonly used term for many varieties of bright, printed cloth. By refashioning imports and manufacturing for market niches, Zanzibar's artisans responded quickly to shifts in consumer demand and translated imported goods into objects of local desire.[21]

The rapid acceleration of interconnectivity fueled by trade, forced migration, travel, and a polyglot population encouraged a dynamic, Creole consumer culture in Zanzibar.[22] Wealth, poverty, master-slave relationships, ethnicity, and gender divisions functioned as social barriers, but Zanzibaris of all backgrounds found themselves within two common matrices of interaction: language or the use of Swahili as a lingua franca, and consumer culture or an emphasis on imported objects to communicate social distinction. Swahili was Zanzibar's language of choice, but how it was used was of little concern to the city's immigrant residents.[23] Consumer culture, on the other hand, became a finely calibrated means of identity negotiation in a changing urban environment. Consumer goods such as clothing, jewelry, and household wares proved critical dialogic devices. In the ephemeral social milieu of nineteenth-century Zanzibar, the island's consumer culture offered a concrete set of social references for aspiration, respect, honor, and even freedom.

Clothing Zanzibar

The sweeping changes of nineteenth-century East Africa were perhaps nowhere more evident than in Zanzibar City, where new status codes encouraged a culture of conspicuous consumption. First, Sultan Sayyid Sa'īd dismantled the sumptuary regulations that once reserved many symbols of status for the political elite. The new sultan was a transplant from Muscat who represented his authority through the delegitimization of an older political system dominated by the hereditary ruler of Zanzibar, the Mwinyi Mkuu. Sayyid Sa'īd had little interest in maintaining the symbolic import of the Mwinyi Mkuu's drums, carved chairs, and other regalia. After relegating the old political elite to the periphery of the Busā'īdī commercial capital, the new sultan was faced with the project of establishing symbols of his authority. In response, Sayyid Sa'īd embraced new consumer technologies that drew deeply on contemporaneous global material culture.

In the 1840s and 1850s Sayyid Sa'īd concentrated on a variety of objects to demonstrate his authority. In addition to decorating his palaces with clocks, mirrors, and a variety of imported furniture, he purchased an 1,100-ton frigate—nearly four times the size of the *Sultana*—manufactured at Bombay and christened it *King of the World* (*Shah Allum*). Liberalizing much of Zanzibar's trade, concentrating on foreign objects to represent the sultanate, and sending ships such as the *Sultana* to America, Europe, and South Asia to procure such items, the new sultan began to release consumer goods from most of their earlier sumptuary restrictions.

Sayyid Sa'īd liberalized status codes and so encouraged a culture of consumption more indulgent and ostentatious than that of either pre-Busa'īdī Swahili city-states or Oman.[24] A second way in which structural shifts of nineteenth-century East Africa were evident in Zanzibar City was the heightened importance of consumer goods for negotiating social relations. This stemmed both from the liberalization of consumer culture in Zanzibar and the city's demographic diversity, what one British resident typified as "a mingling together of so many tribes and races."[25] By mid-century, at least half of all urban Zanzibaris had been brought to the city as slaves, mostly from East Africa. Zanzibar's free population included local Swahili as well as residents who hailed from places as distant as Muscat,

Bombay, Unyanyembe, Moroni, and Mogadishu. Most new Zanzibaris were vying for social position and inclusion, and, in this regard, consumer goods offered the most tactile mode of social communication. The diversity of imports combined with the possibility for some to accumulate modest, even significant, fortunes meant that forms of status representation were constantly in flux.

Jonathon Glassman's analysis of the urban Mrima (northern coast of Tanzania) has demonstrated how nineteenth-century parvenus destabilized structures of authority in novel ways by enhancing their prestige through access to imported goods.[26] Imported goods offered new paths to respectability that could be unfettered from prerequisite genealogies or long histories of residence in the coastal region. A similar pattern emerged in Zanzibar. Due to the rapid expansion of Zanzibar's economy in the early nineteenth century, its dominance by immigrant Busaʿīdīs, and its demographic diversity, "patina"—a mode of social relation anchored to notions of historical distinction that dominated in Swahili cities—was in many ways replaced by "fashion"—a mode of social relation unbound from formal sumptuary regulations.[27] Any Zanzibari could wear any cloth, own any piece of porcelain, or buy any clock, though price and availability restricted certain items to relatively small groups.[28] By destabilizing conventional political and social relationships, the Busaʿīdī state weakened the law of patina and ushered in an era of unrestrained consumption in which an increasing volume and diversity of consumer goods encouraged myriad forms of status-driven expression.

Conspicuous consumption became a hallmark of the new Zanzibar. Indeed, the most valuable consumer goods, such as expensive cloth, clocks, and foodstuffs imported from India and Europe, found their largest regional market in Zanzibar City. Social signs rendered through consumer objects were incessantly negotiated in the public realm, often in relation to their increasing abundance. The movement of population, free-floating cultural materials of distant origin, and the possibility for many to accumulate modest, even very significant fortunes meant that forms of status presentation in the material realm were diverse. Even a person of relatively meager means could travel abroad, trade, or otherwise accumulate signs of distinction. The majority of Zanzibaris, including those forcefully taken from their home societies, engaged in this consumer culture and ascribed to its material norms as a means of demonstrating integration into Zanzibari society. Consumer goods offered a key means of staking out an identity, of making a new life at the coast.[29]

Zanzibaris selectively adapted conglomerations of clothes and other accoutrements culled from global currents to develop a particular sociocultural code. This code not only reflected trans–Indian Ocean trends from Bombay and Muscat, but it also made these relevant to the Zanzibari social environment. Yet, throughout the latter nineteenth century the Zanzibari culture of fashion was to a significant degree informally shaped by the tastes of the Arab elite. More precisely, Busaʿīdī patricians and other wealthy Zanzibaris affected a marked cultural hegemony, particularly in regard to taste and respectability. Zanzibar's elite developed a mode of distinction, following Pierre Bourdieu, contingent on significant wealth and social distance.[30]

For most Zanzibaris, imported cloth was the primary means to represent one's place in this new consumer regime. Unlike in many interior societies where clothes made from local plant fibers and skins were frequently worn, virtually everyone in Zanzibar, free and enslaved, wore cloth imported from India, the United States, or elsewhere. For Zanzibar's plebian majority, aspiration to the fashions of the elite led to the rapid appropriation of goods that had once been the preserve of a small few. One such item was the *kizibao*, or embroidered waistcoat made from European broadcloth, popular among parvenus in the early nineteenth century. By the mid-nineteenth century, the kizibao was one of the greatest investments for men of lesser means, including ex-slaves. It became so popular in Zanzibar City that the style spread to trade fairs in the interior, confirming Zanzibar's cultural influence in the wider region. For women, the *ukaya* (muslin head covering), *kisutu* (English square cloth dyed in Bombay), and leso similarly were signs of Zanzibari consumer culture. Regardless of their means, both men and women sought items of apparel that reflected status and adherence to the Islamic material norms of urban Zanzibar. I will return to this point in the final section.

The most remarkable example of the use of consumer goods to claim social inclusion was the umbrella. In Swahili societies umbrellas had long been symbols of the state as well as male patrician identity. In early nineteenth-century Zanzibar, however, umbrellas of British, Indian, Chinese, and American manufacture became common accoutrements of South Asian businessmen and wealthy Arab women. The umbrella, Richard Burton noted in the late 1850s, "shows dignity."[31] By the 1870s umbrellas had become fashionable among even those of meager means. Marginal groups in Zanzibar, including slaves, defied conventions by carrying umbrellas. As a result, umbrellas were invested with new meanings. No longer symbols of patrician status, they became associated with a broader Zanzibari aesthetic. Imported umbrellas came to be seen as a common symbol of Zanzibari cosmopolitanism. In appropriating the status symbols of the elite, Zanzibaris of lower social status democratized the use of a consumer object and transformed it into something more than an elite accessory.[32] The material strategies of Zanzibar's plebian majority thus entailed a double motion: claims to social citizenship in Zanzibar and assertions of difference from those of lesser social status, including slaves and outsiders.

The ascent of fashion in nineteenth-century Zanzibar pressured elites to seek out new symbols of distinction. As freed slaves and the wider plebeian population claimed forms of culturedness that mirrored those of the wealthy, elites pursued new strategies for material differentiation. Wealthy Zanzibaris searched for objects that could simultaneously magnify social distance from their poorer neighbors and support claims of ability and authority. Elites also attempted to distinguish themselves from their social peers. These converging interests frequently led to an increase in personal debt as well as more ludicrous extremes. For instance, since the amount of jewelry a husband could buy for his wife was a public measure of ability, some wealthy Zanzibari men purchased a painful profusion of necklaces, armbands, bracelets, and earrings for their wives.[33] Wealthy Zanzibaris also invested in expensive carriages even though the island boasted few roads to accommodate them.

Modes of claiming distinction were usually concentrated on clothes and interior decor. For instance, wealthy Zanzibaris invested large sums in silk and silk-cotton clothing. They filled their homes with china, imported curios, and mirrors, which visually magnified their possessions. Perhaps the most iconic objects of elite consumption were American and European wall clocks. Few regulated their day by clocks since prayer times struck a common rhythm of life. Yet, clocks were exceedingly rare beyond coastal towns and their machinations pleased local audiences. Thus, they became indispensable objects of display for elites and synonymous with urban culture.

The greatest example of the use of consumer goods to represent personal ability and authority was Sultan Barghash bin Sa'īd's (Sayyid Sa'īd's son) Beit al Ajaib, or House of Wonders. Constructed at Zanzibar's seafront as the most prominent structure in the city, the House of Wonders was one of the largest buildings in East Africa on its completion in 1883. Beit al Ajaib served largely symbolic purposes, evidenced by its narrow rooms and vast central auditorium. Indicative of the wider culture of nineteenth-century Zanzibar, the building evidenced the creolization of globally circulating symbols. Inspired by British Indian architecture, the House of Wonders had wide four-sided verandahs, French doors accented by low-hanging lamps, richly worked wooden overhangs, and immense Indian-designed carved doors. Barghash also laid the floor of Beit al Ajaib with a French black-and-white marble and filled the building with large European chandeliers. In front of the House of Wonders Barghash built a high tower in which he installed East Africa's largest clocks.[34]

The contents of the House of Wonders were carefully selected to impress both visitors and residents. An opulent reception room boasted Persian carpets, red velvet and gilt wood furniture, music boxes, timepieces, barometers, thermometers, anemometers, telescopes, and opera glasses. The Beit al Ajaib also housed swords, spears, rifles, pistols, portraits of famous personalities, and photographs of important cultural sites around the world. Barghash visited London's Hall of the Great Exhibition (Crystal Palace) in 1875, and it is likely that his visit provided the inspiration for the House of Wonders. Like the Crystal Palace, the House of Wonders was ornamented with objects of manufacture representing cutting-edge scientific technologies, including tools used for measurement and magnification.[35] The House of Wonders was in many ways a museum of the contemporary world. In the imposing structure Barghash demonstrated to his subjects that he had the power to possess rare objects collected across the globe.

In the 1880s Sultan Barghash would see Zanzibar's influence in the region dwindle and his mainland possessions fall into the hands of European powers. By the end of the decade much of East Africa was under European colonial rule. The colonial epoch ushered in alternative hierarchies, belief systems, and concepts of global relation, all of which gave rise to new consumer demands in eastern Africa. Yet, in Zanzibar many earlier fashions persisted. At the turn of the century, the abolition of slavery offered new economic and social possibilities to a substantial sector of the population. As in earlier decades, clothing was a primary means of representing freed slaves' integration into Zanzibari society.[36]

Social Distinction and the Enslaved

At the height of the nineteenth-century economic boom, enslaved people were the most valued commodity in the city of Zanzibar. Slavery, much like the island's consumer culture, was a common facet of life. Scholars of East Africa have produced incisive analyses of the many forms that slavery took in Zanzibar and across the region. This literature has shed light on the productive capacity of slaves, their social interests and relationships with their masters, hierarchies within slave communities, international efforts to end the regional slave trade, and the socioeconomic process of emancipation. Some analysts have suggested that slave owners did not only emphasize the economic use value—that is, the material productive capacity—of their slaves. Most masters also desired slaves for their social use value: their ability to augment retinues and lineages.[37] In a general sense, slave owners often purchased slaves to reflect and enhance individual prestige, or their "wealth in people."[38] Therefore, the material and symbolic use values of enslaved people were not mutually exclusive.

Extending the insights of earlier analyses, I suggest that some slave owners in Zanzibar City purchased enslaved people for largely social symbolic purposes.[39] They believed that slaves, like consumer objects, could enhance one's public persona and so build prestige. By interpreting slaves in similar terms as inanimate consumer goods, Zanzibari slave owners regularly converted their captives into symbols whose perceived value had little to do with their strength, fertility, or skills. Those who served primarily symbolic purposes made up a minority of domestic slaves, but reflection on such symbolic subjection can offer insight into the social imagination of Zanzibaris in the nineteenth century.

In the second half of the century the increasing demand for and affordability of slaves from the African mainland radically altered rural and urban life in Zanzibar. Slaves often represented a household's greatest investment, and by the 1860s the majority of Zanzibar's population was either enslaved or recently freed. Most Zanzibaris were therefore of immediate mainland extraction. Out of a sample of over 3,000 slaves emancipated in 1860, 93 percent had been imported to the island, an average that was surely higher in the burgeoning plantation sector.[40] Therefore, most of Zanzibar's enslaved population had not been born into slavery (*wazalia*) but rather experienced capture, pawnage, sale, and resale. It was a population that had not only been subjugated but also socially remade. Slave trading and slave marketing were processes of desocialization and commodification that created the conditions by which a slave purchaser could approach the enslaved in much the same way as he would a consumer object: with the desire to employ the purchase to further his own social interests. These were processes, in short, of negating individual self-definition—the creation of a person ostensibly without self-interests, a "nonperson."[41] In slave-owning ideologies, so closely were the symbolic uses of slaves and consumer goods aligned that Zanzibaris differentiated between slaves and objects with the simple distinction of those "things" that could speak, or slaves, versus those that could not, or inanimate objects.[42]

In the city of Zanzibar "raw" slaves were often desired for their perceived blankness onto which owners might project images of themselves through naming, dressing, and ornamenting. Slaves were evaluated in relation to the possibilities of what a prospective owner could say of him- or herself through the enslaved person. More precisely, the value of domestic slaves often lay, in part, in their capacity not only to perform an owner's will but also to draw attention to and accumulate social capital for him or her. For slave owners who did not depend on their slaves' physical labor, factors related to appearance counted more than artisanal skills.[43] Zanzibaris perceived slaves from beyond East Africa, and lighter-skinned slaves in particular, as conferring greater prestige on their owners. Thus, Zanzibar's elite was willing to invest vast sums in Ethiopian, southeastern European, and South Asian slaves, women in particular. Physically attractive slaves, particularly those women sought as concubines (*suria*), commanded the highest prices. Interest in Ethiopian, Georgian, Indian, or Congolese concubines as objects of personal prestige and sexual labor was therefore bound to a culturally relative aesthetic and changing social valuation.[44]

The slave's journey to Zanzibar usually entailed violent separation from kin, multiple sales, and circuitous travel. Slave narratives provide ample evidence of harrowing sojourns.[45] The narrative of a slave named Bahr Zain, who was purchased by Muhammad Wazir, a Zanzibari of Gujarati descent, offers a case in point. When Bahr-Zain testified in British Consular Court, she claimed to have been taken while still young from "Amhara" (northwestern Ethiopia). She was first sold to a merchant from Al Hudaydah on the Red Sea coast of Yemen and brought to Zanzibar by a Shihri (Yemeni) man. She was then sold three more times before ending up in the hands of a Persian, who again sold her. Her new owner also resold her, and at some point she was sold to a resident of Chole, where she was purchased by Muhammad Wazir and brought back to Zanzibar.[46] In nine years Bahr-Zain had traveled thousands of miles across the Red Sea and Indian Ocean basins, lived in several towns, and been the property of eight owners.

Such narratives reveal the circuitous journeys of the enslaved and so challenge a foundational myth of slavery in Zanzibar: that enslavement was a direct transaction between a male family member and a slave trader. The myth held that slaves had been justly exchanged and entrusted to traders by their family members, or those who had the right to sell them. This reflected the slave owner's paternalistic self-image since the sale of the slave could be seen as constituting a direct transferal of rights over the person from biological father to "adopted" father. The myth also maintained that the enslaved had no great value to their families, which made the further suggestion that they were better off in Zanzibar than in their home societies seem tenable. In the myth of exchange, slavery could be imagined as a form of redemption that validated both the slave buyers' devaluation of his or her purchase and the forced social dependency of the enslaved.[47]

A complementary myth of rebirth infantilized the enslaved and justified the parameters of their objectification. For Zanzibari slave owners, purchase was often perceived to be a quasi-humanitarian act of taking responsibility for a forfeited and neglected person. Slaves could indeed speak, but slave owners likened them to small children without the capacity to define themselves beyond the will of fictive parents.[48] Ideologically, slaves were often incorporated into households as neither junior kin nor simple laborers but rather as perpetual dependents whose lives would be entirely directed by those who facilitated their rebirth. The "social death" of slavery was therefore part of a process of repression and denial of the slaves' self-identity initiated by the slave trade and followed by forms of "social rebirth" in Zanzibar.[49] Social death and rebirth were both integral to slavery's suppression of personhood.

Zanzibaris placed a premium on honor (*heshima*). In the middle of the nineteenth century heshima was to a great degree determined by free birth, ancestry, influence, and wealth. The concept of wealth included financial assets as well as social capital, or the dependency of children, slaves, and spouses.[50] Even in the high-revenue plantation sector of the late 1880s, where the economic utility of human labor was greater than slaves' symbolic use-value, the sheer number of slaves in one's position was perceived as an indication of distinction and heshima. In his seminal study of plantation slavery in Zanzibar, Frederick Cooper argued that, regardless of the returns of the clove industry, "the slaves' . . . presence conveyed prestige." The British consul at Zanzibar in the early 1840s was more emphatic. Consul Hamerton explained that a "man's respectability and wealth . . . is always estimated by the number of slaves he is said to possess."[51]

Urban slave owners depended on the symbolic value of slaves to a greater degree than did their counterparts in the countryside. Urban slave owners tasked their slaves with myriad labors, from cooking and conducting business to construction and child rearing.[52] Yet, in an era of increased consumption and public display, urban slaves played other roles as well. Salme binti Sa'īd, the daughter of Sultan Sayyid Sa'īd and one of the few elite women to record her experiences, wrote that possessing large numbers of slaves was an indispensible symbol of social standing in Zanzibar.[53] Poorer urban slave owners, such as ex-slaves, Hadrami, and Comorian immigrants, tended to depend more on their slaves economically than did their wealthy counterparts. These urban masters often hired their slaves out as day laborers, or *vibarua*. Nevertheless, many observers were quick to point out that while poor people dreamed of the wealth a slave might produce, the image of oneself as possessor, and the social capital accrued from the investment in a slave, was often more desirable than any financial reward.[54]

Zanzibaris often yearned for the social position afforded by the ownership of another person. According to many observers of nineteenth-century

Zanzibar, when a slave was freed his or her first great investment was often in a slave.[55] For instance, when Bahr-Zain (see above) married her master and thus gained her freedom, she used her bridewealth to buy two of her own slaves.[56] In the 1840s Consul Hamerton claimed that when a freed slave saved up enough money to buy his own slave, he "lounge[d] about from place to place with a sword under his arms, calling himself an Arab."[57] Hamerton's image is laden with common stereotypes of Zanzibari men as idle and undirected, but the larger point is important: the acquisition of a slave by an ex-slave could facilitate an opportunity for social advancement. Another Western resident of Zanzibar wrote that since "work is the badge of the slave," freed slaves endeavored to purchase their own slaves to not only provide financial support but also to create for themselves a new mode of sociality. Buying a slave was a means to represent oneself as something better than work, to change one's social "badge."[58] Indeed, even for some of the poorest in Zanzibar, the ideal of slave ownership was not to put their slaves out to work but rather to keep them in the house. Slaves spoke of investing windfalls of cash in their own domestic slave whom they would keep at home, if possible.[59]

Regardless of the social position of Zanzibari slave owners, all engaged in projects of remaking slaves to serve their interests. Almost immediately after arriving in the city, enslaved people were subjected to corporeal refashioning. Slaves often arrived malnourished and sick, and thus slave dealers attempted to force them to look beautiful, healthy, in a word, desirable. Since a slave purchaser sought potential in the market, slave dealers worked to evidence the representational uses to which their charges could be put by remaking them for display. The slave market was in this way a horrible masquerade in which, for instance, newly arrived women were forced to wear a profusion of gold, beads, expensive clothes, flowers, and elaborate hairstyles.[60] Similarly, their bodies were smeared with coconut oil and their eyes were highlighted with kohl. In the market, the recent arrival was stripped of her identity and given raiment that sparked the imagination, interest, and desire of potential buyers. In their forced reclothing, slaves were imagined as new things, objects that could speak but were desired only for their ability to satisfy their owners' demands and enhance their owner's self-image.[61]

The market was a compulsory performance that muted the individual voice of the slave. After purchase, this performance continued. Masters usually gave their slaves new names and clothing. Relatively poor urbanites reclothed their purchases with about two yards of merekani cloth, which would be replaced periodically.[62] At the other end of the social spectrum, when a new female slave was brought into the sultan's residence, she was given relatively opulent attire, but she was allowed only three days to lay aside all of her former clothes and redress in the clothes assigned her.[63] Regardless of where a slave was to live, both renaming and reclothing were acts of a new owner's domination. They evidenced the ability and desire to deny the enslaved person's history and publicly constitute them anew.

Perhaps the most extreme example of slave owners' efforts to project their self-image through the bodies of their slaves was *wapambe* (sing. *mpambe*). Wapambe, literally "those who are decorated," were specially dressed and ornamented female slaves who were meant to signify the wealth and ability of their owners. Since apparel mediated the relationship of the body to the self and the public sphere, redressing by an owner was an unambiguous scene of domination. Charles Devereux, a visitor to Zanzibar who served in the British antislave trade squadron, wrote of the arrival of a wealthy Zanzibari's *mpambe* at the British consulate. Her adornments were so profuse that they seemed to symbolically negate the wearer. Devereux specifically noted the name of the mpambe's owner (who was not present), but of the enslaved girl he wrote only "On her neck was a heavy silver chain, of tasteful workmanship, to which were attached sundry articles, the use of which I could not guess. A lighter chain, to which other nick'nacks were attached, also decorated her throat. On each of her arms she had heavy armlets, from the wrist to the elbow; and on her legs, heavier anklets reached from the ankle half-way up to the knee, where the gold was met by a red silk wrapper."[64]

Eunuchs were similarly adorned. They often gained more autonomy than wapambe, but they received elaborate costumes akin to "decorated" women. Zanzibari owners of eunuchs frequently purchased for them turbans, embroidered jackets, fine *kanzus* (long white shirt), and expensive armory, including swords and pistols.[65] Eunuchs and other high-priced slaves from southeastern Europe or Ethiopia were frequently stationed at the doors and entranceways of the houses of elites. Sayyida Shewâne, whom Sayyida Salme writes of in her memoirs, used her slaves to reflect her importance in similarly overt ways. According to Salme, Shewâne sought out the most handsome slaves and weighted them with expensive weaponry and jewelry. The large retinue of bedecked slaves then accompanied her when she appeared in public.[66]

Slave owners' projections of the vacant, voiceless slaves were always only fictions. Despite the efforts of slave owners to craft images of themselves through their human property, slaves did not imagine themselves as vessels for the desires of others. Slaves had their own interests, even if their social strategies depended on the patronage of their owners or former owners. The words and actions of slaves reveal a host of quotidian efforts to distinguish themselves from objects and to remake themselves within the parameters of Zanzibar's social strictures. One of the most visible ways slaves sought to reclaim suppressed personhood was by taking command over objects, by making social claims through consumer goods.

Consumption, Slavery, and Self-Definition

The concept of freedom carried multiple meanings in nineteenth-century Africa. In many societies leaving one's master and self-sufficiency were not ideal social conditions. As Suzanne Miers and Igor Kopytoff have suggested, slaves often perceived total autonomy as impractical and instead desired social belonging in their new societies, commonly through patron-client relationships and enduring social ties with their former master.[67] Yet, as Jonathon Glassman has demonstrated, slaves and freed people in coastal East Africa did not always desire simple social inclusion; they often flatly rejected certain forms of belonging. Rather, slaves in Zanzibar and elsewhere along the urban coast frequently sought to define the terms of their belonging and exercise choice in the kinds of relationships, including those of clientage, to which they would be a part.[68] Regardless of their relationship to their owners or former owners, what most slaves and ex-slaves in Zanzibar seemed to desire was something similar to the interests of others: the ability to define their place in the social order. They sought opportunities to represent their own political and social interests, sometimes in contradiction and sometimes in accordance with the interests of their owners or former owners. The desire for self-definition was a direct response to the processes of subjection, and for newly freed people, it usually took the form of renaming and reclothing. In choosing new names and purchasing new clothes, ex-slaves appropriated symbols that signified citizenship in free society.

Slaves, freed people, and other Zanzibaris of mainland birth put a high premium on material consumption. Violently uprooted from their homes and harboring little hope of a return, most slaves and freed slaves desired security and social inclusion in coastal society. More precisely, the radical social displacement affected by the slave trade created a fissure with their homes and encouraged slaves to stake out a social place in Zanzibar.[69] Since slave owners attempted to remake slaves by giving them clothes after purchase, one of the primary aspirations of the enslaved was to lay claim to a new social position by reclothing themselves in "respectable" dress. Symbols of coastal culture received particular emphasis in such efforts to gain respectability.[70] The trials of British Indian subjects suspected of holding slaves in Zanzibar offer a rare window on this phenomenon. During the proceedings, slaves were often called on to testify against their owners. When asked of her plans after manumission, Suedi, a seventeen-year-old enslaved girl in Zanzibar City, replied that she would work in order to be able to obtain "good food and clothing."[71] Indeed, freed slaves often spent relatively large sums on clothing to signal their social distance from slavery.[72]

Fashion could be both a useful and oppressive tool. For those who commanded only minimal resources, the system of fashion could foreclose social aspiration. Since Zanzibaris placed a premium on the symbolic qualities of clothing, the inability to purchase certain kinds of dress consigned the poor to the margins. Nevertheless, Zanzibar's consumer culture proved a critical tool for efforts to claim distinction and respect. For slaves and poor freedmen of mainland birth, the primary symbols of transcending slavery were items of Swahili adornment associated with Muslim modesty: fezzes, canes, and the kanzu. Thus, American and Indian cloth, when fashioned into a kanzu, became a vehicle for the relocation and grounding of identity. For women, the *ukaya* head covering, which was similarly associated with Muslim social norms, became an essential symbol of integration. Jewelry was also so important to freedwomen's appearance that, according to Salme binti Sa'īd, even beggars were "decked out" in various ornaments.[73]

The consumption of Swahili clothes at once symbolized integration into a stratum of Zanzibari society and announced distinction from slavery. Slaves or ex-slaves seeking to remake themselves thus adopted and then manipulated the material codes of Zanzibar society for their own social ends.[74] In a very similar way to fashion among the wealthy, this dual movement of claiming similarity to some and simultaneous difference from others typified the fashion strategies of poorer Zanzibaris. Swahili clothing and jewelry signified a cultural elsewhere distinct from interior societies and a social position distinct from slavery. These material goods offered the possibility of new personas, of corporate as well as individual prestige within the social grammars of Zanzibar City.

The strategies of slaves and ex-slaves for self-making hinged on the twin abilities of self-definition and self-direction. In most instances of manumission, freed slaves maintained a client relationship with their former owners, even if they lived apart from them. Yet, self-definition could result in the choice to stay with a former master after manumission. In cases of total dependency, freed slaves had no alternative. For example, Kaiser Koor, a ten-year-old dancing girl born in Kachchh, India, remained with her former owner, likely because she had no other means of support.[75] Some ex-slaves, however, chose to remain in their former master's home despite their ability to leave. In such cases, one's position may not have been significantly altered by legal manumission, but the ability to define oneself was. When a thirty-year-old Yao woman (whose name is unreadable in the surviving records) was emancipated in 1873, she told a court in Zanzibar that she had lived with her owner for twenty-three years of her own will and that she would make up her mind as to where she went "as she pleas[ed]."[76] While we cannot know why she remained with her former owner, the woman's statement suggests she now thought of herself as something different from her owner's projection. In choosing to stay with her former owner she, at least in part, defined herself.

The social conditioning process of slavery created fetters more difficult to loosen than the shackles that initially bound the enslaved. This was the trauma of social death and rebirth. It was a form of subjection through which slaves would be forced to negotiate a new life in Zanzibar, regardless of their skills or the status of their master. "Freedom" (*uhuru*) was thus more than a legal state. It was reinscription: self-fashioning within the hierarchical strictures of Zanzibar, which could include buying particular types of clothes and even purchasing a slave. Uhuru, in short, was the creation of a more desirable social space within the strictures of coastal social hierarchy.[77] Rather than challenging the consumer culture of nineteenth-century Zanzibar, the self-making projects of the city's plebian majority fully engaged it. Through their consumer choices Zanzibari slaves and ex-slaves accessed networks of global exchange even while they participated in relationships contingent on extreme inequality.

Conclusion: The Island in the World

This chapter has sought to understand Zanzibar as a nexus—a point of social and economic interaction that reflected complex interests and broadcasted shifting cultural trends—through the consumer practices that emerged in the nineteenth century. Imported goods and enslaved people evidenced the economic ties that bound Zanzibar to numerous transoceanic and transcontinental networks; but they did far more. As Zanzibar's polyglot residents attempted to pool and display wealth gained from global exchanges, imported goods and slaves became critical social levers. Zanzibaris defined and challenged intimate as well as impersonal relationships using the material goods available in the city. At Zanzibar's apogee, its urban residents depended on imported objects and the mass commodification of people to build a prestige economy that translated transoceanic cultural trends for a wider audience while at the same time addressing changing local social circumstances.

In representing aspirations publicly, new consumer goods were tools in the constitution of personhood and strategies of distinction across Zanzibar's social spectrum. Slave owners often used enslaved people to similar ends, but through myriad quotidian choices urban slaves challenged the representational power of their owners. Slaves redressed and renamed themselves, gained economic autonomy from their owners, and even purchased their own slaves. These strategies represented a means of claiming a social identity that was distinct from that forced on them by their masters, yet largely consonant with the island's social norms.

Zanzibar's consumer culture was an engagement with global cultural flows and a deployment of imported symbols in the service of local image-making practices. In tracing the biographies of people and consumer goods through Zanzibar, we can discern ways in which their intersection encouraged social bonds and tensions within circumscribed island space. Through the lens of imported goods and enslaved people we can also appreciated the hierarchies that islanders built and challenged. At the interface of eastern African, Indian Ocean, and Atlantic systems, Zanzibar's social universe integrated vast global space and encouraged extreme forms of oppression. The nexus of Zanzibar was in this way both mirror and interpretation of world historical change in the nineteenth century, an era of interdependence as well as increasing inequality.

Notes

1. "Arrival of an Arabian Ship—Trade between the United States and Muscat," *New York Morning Herald*, May 5, 1840; "Long Island Railroad Company," *New York Spectator*, May 28, 1840; H. Eilts, "Ahmad bin Na'aman's Mission to the United States in 1840, The Voyage of Al-Sultanah to New York City," *Essex Institute Historical Collections* 98 (1962): 218–77. Ahmad bin Na'aman would later become the chief secretary, interpreter, and army paymaster under Sultan Sayyid Said's son, Sultan Majid bin Said. US Consulate, Zanzibar, Reel 2, vol. 4–5, Speer, "Report on Zanzibar, 1862."

2. A. Jiddawi, "Extracts from an Arab Account Book, 1840–1854," *Tanganyika Notes and Records* 31 (1951): 27.

3. Jiddawi, "Extracts from an Arab Account Book," 29; "Trade with Muscat," *New York Morning Herald*, August 10, 1840.

4. "Marine List, Port of New York: Memoranda," *New York Spectator*, August 10, 1840; Eilts, "Ahmad bin Na'aman's Mission," 252; Jiddawi, "Extracts from an Arab Account Book," 29; letter from William H. Feely, March 14, 1845, Richard P. Waters Papers, Peabody Essex Museum Archives, Salem, MA [hereafter PE], MH-14.

5. Eilts, "Ahmad bin Na'aman's Mission," 272. In the years immediately following the *Sultana*'s voyage, Sayyid Sa'īd would sent several vessels to London and Marseilles, one with a cargo totaling 100,000 $MT, or about twice that of the average cargo leaving Zanzibar on a European vessel. Charles Ward to James Buchanan, March 13, 1847, United States Consulate, Zanzibar [hereafter USCZ], Reel 1, vols. 1–3. American and European merchants, however, were concerned about the sultan's mercantile pursuits, particularly his direct trade with the United States and Europe since he imported all goods duty-free. F. R. Peters and J. Pollock to Sultan Sayyid Said, February 20, 1847, Zanzibar National Archives [hereafter ZNA], AA1/3; Hamerton to [obscure], January 3, 1847, ZNA AA1/3.

6. In the year and a half before the *Sultana*'s sojourn to New York, thirty-two American vessels had visited Zanzibar. "The Muscat Ship Sultani," *Portsmouth Journal of Literature and Politics,* May 16, 1840.

7. Norman Bennett, *A History of the Arab State of Zanzibar* (London: Methuen, 1978); Abdul Sheriff, *Slaves, Spices, and Ivory in Zanzibar* (London: Heinemann, 1990); Erik Gilbert, "Zanzibar: Imperialism, Proto-Globalization, and a Nineteenth Century Indian Ocean Boom Town," in *Globalization and the City: Two Connected Phenomena in Past and Present,* ed. Andreas Exenberger, Philipp Strobl, Günter Bischof, and James Mokhiber (Innsbruck: Innsbruck University Press, 2013), 123–39.

8. My reference to metabolism is inspired by and expands J. R. McNeill's insight into urban processes of taking in water, foodstuff, fuel, and so forth and creating waste. J. R. McNeill, *Something New under the Sun: An Environmental History of the Twentieth Century World* (New York: W. W. Norton & Co., 2000).

9. For a concise reflection on the blurred distinction between economic and uneconomic uses of slaves, see Gwyn Campbell, "Slavery and Other Forms of Unfree Labor in the Indian Ocean World," in *The Structure of Slavery in Indian Ocean Africa and Asia,* ed. Gwyn Campbell (London: Frank Cass, 2004), xix–xx.

10. Arjun Appadurai, ed., *The Social Life of Things: Commodities in Cultural Perspective* (Cambridge: Cambridge University Press, 1986). On the mediation of African social relations through the market, see, for example, Jonathon Glassman, *Feasts and Riot: Revelry, Rebellion, and Popular Consciousness on the Swahili Coast, 1856–1888* (Portsmouth, NH: Heinemann, 1995); Joseph Miller, *Way of Death: Merchant Capitalism and the Angolan Slave Trade, 1730–1830* (Madison: University of Wisconsin Press, 1988).

11. I develop this point in greater detail in Jeremy Prestholdt, *Domesticating the World: African Consumerism and the Genealogies of Globalization* (Berkeley: University of California Press, 2008).

12. Christopher P. Rigby to Wood, May 1, 1860, India Office Library, British Library [hereafter IOL] L/P&S/9/37; Richard F. Burton, *Zanzibar: City, Island, and Coast,* vol. 1 (London: Tinsley Brothers, 1872), 320.

13. James Christie, *Cholera Epidemics in East Africa: An Account of the Several Diffusions of the Disease in That Country from 1821 till 1872, with an Outline of the*

Geography, Ethnology, and Trade Connections of the Regions Through Which the Epidemics Passed (London: Macmillan, 1876), 356.

14. On ivory and copal, see N. Thomas Håkansson, "The Human Ecology of World Systems in East Africa: The Impact of the Ivory Trade," *Human Ecology* 32, no. 5 (2004): 561–91; Thaddeus Sunseri, "The Political Ecology of the Copal Trade in the Tanzanian Coastal Hinterland, c.1820–1905," *The Journal of African History* 48, no. 2 (2007): 201–20.

15. Frederick Cooper, *Plantation Slavery on the East Coast of Africa* (New Haven: Yale University Press, 1972); Sheriff, *Slaves, Spices, and Ivory.* The export slave trade did not, however, play as important a role in East Africa's economy as it had in Atlantic Africa.

16. Sheriff, *Slaves, Spices, and Ivory*; Jeremy Prestholdt, "On the Global Repercussions of East African Consumerism," *American Historical Review* 109, no. 3 (2004): 755–81.

17. Stephen Rockel, *Carriers of Culture: Labor on the Road in Nineteenth-Century East Africa* (Portsmouth, NH: Heinemann, 2006).

18. Pedro Machado, "Cloths of a New Fashion: Networks of Exchange, African Consumerism and Cloth Zones of Contact in India and the Indian Ocean in the Eighteenth and Nineteenth Centuries," in *How India Clothed the World: The World of South Asian Textiles, 1500–1850*, ed. Tirthankar Roy, Om Prakash, Kaoru Sugihara, and Giorgio Riello (Leiden, Netherlands: Brill, 2009), 53–84.

19. Merekani was so popular that both British and Indian manufacturers counterfeited the textile, a process that included stamping the fabric with fraudulent American marks. W. S. W. Ruschenberger, *A Voyage Round the World; Including an Embassy to Muscat and Siam, in 1835, 1836, and 1837* (Philadelphia: Carey, Lea & Blanchard, 1839), 47.

20. Prestholdt, "On the Global Repercussions."

21. Prestholdt, *Domesticating the World*; Mackenzie Moon Ryan, "A Decade of Design: The Global Invention of the Kanga, 1876–1886," Textile History 48, no. 1 (2017): 101–32.

22. On the concept of creolization in an Indian Ocean context, see, for instance, Françoise Vergès and Carpanin Marimoutou, "Moorings: Indian Ocean Creolisations," trans. Stephen Muecke and Françoise Vergès, *Portal* 9, no. 1 (2012): 1–39.

23. On the use of Swahili in Zanzibar, see Edward Steere, *A Handbook of the Swahili Language, as Spoken at Zanzibar* (1870; repr., London: Society for Promoting Christian Knowledge, 1894); C. Sacleux, *Dictionnaire Swahili-Français* (Paris: Institut d'ethnologie, 1939).

24. Sayyid Sa'īd's daughter, Sayyida Salme, offered many examples of this new opulence and its divergence from Muscat's social norms in her autobiography, Emily Ruete [Sayyida Salme], *Memoirs of an Arabian Princess*, reprinted in *An Arabian Princess Between Two Worlds: Memoirs, Letters Home, Sequels to the Memoirs, Syrian Customs and Usages*, ed. E. Van Donzel (New York: E. J. Brill, 1993).

25. G. Ward, ed., *Letters of Bishop Tozer and His Sister Together with Some Other Records of the Universities' Mission from 1863–1873* (London: Office of the Universities' Mission to Central Africa, 1902), 92.

26. Glassman, *Feasts and Riot*, 47, 53. Glassman argued that the ever-wider distribution of prestige goods gave relatively poor people an opportunity to "contest the precise meanings of what had once been exclusive markers of status and political power" (37).

27. Grant McCracken theorizes this distinction between systems of fashion and patina in *Culture and Consumption* (Bloomington: Indiana University Press, 1988), 16.

28. For analogies elsewhere on the continent, see, for instance, Phyllis M. Martin, *The External Trade of the Loango Coast, 1576–1870* (Oxford: Oxford University Press, 1972); Phyllis Martin, *Leisure and Society in Colonial Brazzaville* (Cambridge: Cambridge University Press, 1995); Jeremy Rich, *A Workman is Worthy of His Meat: Food and Colonialism in the Gabon Estuary* (Lincoln: University of Nebraska Press, 2009).

29. Laura Fair offered particularly rich accounts of changes in fashion among nonelites in *Pastimes and Politics in Zanzibar: Culture, Community and Identity in Post-Abolition Urban Zanzibar* (Athens, OH: Heinemann, 2001); Laura Fair, "Remaking Fashion in the Paris of the Indian Ocean: Dress, Performance, and the Cultural Construction of a Cosmopolitan Zanzibari Identity," in *Fashioning Africa: Power and the Politics of Dress*, ed. Jean Allman (Bloomington: Indiana University Press, 2004), 13–30.

30. On the intersection of taste, class, and hegemony, see Pierre Bourdieu, *Distinction: A Social Critique of the Judgment of Taste* (New York: Routledge, 1984). For a nuanced discussion of the relationship between elite and non-elite fashions in Zanzibar, see Laura Fair, "Veiling, Fashion, and Social Mobility: A Century of Change in Zanzibar," in *Veiling in Africa*, ed. Elisha P. Renne (Bloomington: Indiana University Press, 2013), 15–33.

31. Richard Burton, *The Lake Regions of Central Africa*, vol. 1 (London: Longman, 1860), 34.

32. Jeremy Prestholdt, "Mirroring Modernity: On Consumerism in Nineteenth Century Zanzibar," *Trans/forming Cultures* 4, no. 2 (2009): 165–204; Sarah Fee, "Hostage to Cloth: European Explorers in East Africa, 1850–1890," *Textiles and Politics: Textile Society of America 13th Biennial Symposium Proceedings*, Washington, DC, September 18–22, 2012.

33. Elizabeth and Henry Jacob, *A Quaker Family in India and Zanzibar, 1863–1865*, ed. Y. Bird (York, UK: Ebor Press, 2000), 164–65.

34. On the uses of clocks and the symbolism of the Beit al Ajaib, see, Prestholdt, *Domesticating the World*.

35. "The Sultan of Zanzibar," *New York Times*, July 17, 1875.

36. Laura Fair has demonstrated that the long and colorful Indian printed cloth known as *khanga* came to be a primary sign of ex-slave and other plebian women's adherence to postabolition social norms in Zanzibar. Fair, "Remaking Fashion in the Paris of the Indian Ocean." See also Ryan, "A Decade of Design."

37. In East Africa slavery was a form of subjection fixed not only by law but also, as many scholars have shown, by social dependency. Jonathon Glassman,

"The Bondsman's New Clothes: The Contradictory Consciousness of Slave Resistance on the Swahili Coast," *Journal of African History* 32, no. 2 (1991): 277–312; Elizabeth McMahon, *Slavery and Emancipation in Islamic East Africa: From Honor to Respectability* (New York: Cambridge University Press, 2013); Abdulaziz Lodhi, *The Institution of Slavery in Zanzibar and Pemba* (Uppsala: Scandinavian Institute of African Studies, 1973). For a closer analysis of the experiences of rural slaves on Zanzibar and Pemba Islands, see Cooper, *Plantation Slavery* and McMahon, *Slavery and Emancipation*.

38. Jane Guyer, "Wealth in People, Wealth in Things," *Journal of African History* 36, no. 1 (1995): 83–88.

39. For analogies to this practice in the Atlantic and Mediterranean, see Monica Miller, *Slaves to Fashion: Black Dandyism and the Styling of Black Diasporic Identity* (Durham, NC: Duke University Press, 2009); S. Marmon, "Domestic Slavery in the Mamluk Empire: A Preliminary Sketch," in *Slavery in the Islamic Middle East*, ed. S. Marmon (Princeton, NJ: Markus Weiner, 1999); M. Ennaji, *Serving the Master: Slavery and Society in Nineteenth Century Morocco* (New York: St. Martin's Press, 1998).

40. "List of Slaves Unlawfully Held in Slavery by British Indian Subjects at Zanzibar and Its Dependencies, Who Have Been Emancipated at the Consulate [1860]," ZNA A12/3. Of the 259 additional slaves emancipated by the British consul between 1863 and 1874, only three were born in Zanzibar. "Return of Slaves Emancipated by Lieut. Col. Playfair, from the Date of His Assuming Charge of British Consulate Zanzibar [n.d.]," ZNA A12/3. See also James Christie, "Slavery in Zanzibar as It Is," in *The East African Slave Trade*, ed. Edward Steere (London: Harrison, 1871); Sheriff, *Slaves, Spices, and Ivory*, 230.

41. Igor Kopytoff and Suzanne Miers, "African 'Slavery' as an Institution of Marginality," in *Slavery in Africa: Historical and Anthropological Approaches*, ed. Suzanne Miers and Igor Kopytoff (Madison: University of Wisconsin Press, 1977), 3–81.

42. Edward Steere, *Swahili Tales, as Told by the Natives of Zanzibar* (London: Bell and Daldy, 1870), 497. The place of the enslaved in regimes of consumption is conspicuously absent in studies of both consumption and slavery. Nevertheless, two decades ago, Jane Guyer argued for a rethinking of the boundaries between personhood and "thingness." Guyer, "Wealth in People, Wealth in Things." See also Rey Chow, "Where Have All the Natives Gone?," in *Displacements: Cultural Identities in Question*, ed. A. Bammer (Bloomington: Indiana University Press, 1994), 125–51.

43. R. Thornton, "Notes Towards a Theory of Objects and Persons," *African Anthropology* 4, no. 1 (1997): 41.

44. Abdul Sheriff, "Suria: Concubine or Secondary Slave Wife? The Case of Zanzibar in the Nineteenth Century," in *Sex, Power, and Slavery*, ed. Gwyn Campbell and Elizabeth Elbourne (Athens: Ohio University Press, 2014), 66–80. On the trade in Indian girls from Bombay to Zanzibar, see Lt. Kemball, "Papers Relative to the Measures Adopted by the British Government for Effecting the Suppression of the Slave Trade in the Persian Gulf," *Selections from the Records of*

the Bombay Government, No. 24, New Series (Bombay: Bombay Education Society's Press, 1856), 650.

45. See, for instance, Marcia Wright, *Strategies of Slaves and Women in East Central Africa* (Bloomington: University of Indiana Press, 1989); Elisabeth McMahon, "Trafficking and Reenslavement: The Social Vulnerability of Women and Children in Nineteenth-Century East Africa," in *Trafficking in Slavery's Wake: Law and the Experience of Women and Children,* ed. Benjamin A. Lawrance and Richard L. Roberts (Athens: Ohio University Press, 2012), 29–44; McMahon, *Slavery and Empancipation,* chap. 2; W. J. Rampley, *Matthew Wellington: Sole Surviving Link with Dr. Livingstone* (London: Society for Promoting Christian Knowledge [c. 1930]); Edward A. Alpers, "The Story of Swema: Female Vulnerability in Nineteenth-Century East Africa," in *Women and Slavery in Africa,* ed. Claire Robertson and Martin Klein (Madison: University of Wisconsin Press, 1983), 185–219; Edward A. Alpers, "Representations of Children in the East African Slave Trade," *Slavery & Abolition* 30, no. 1 (2009): 27–40; Rebecca Wakefield, *Memoirs of Mrs. Rebecca Wakefield, Wife of the Rev. T. Wakefield,* ed. R. Brewin (London: Hamilton, Adams, 1879), 203.

46. Consul Rigby, Consular Court, Zanzibar, ZNA A3/11. In many British consular court cases, slaves were asked to testify. In the Kadhi's court, a slave was allowed to testify against another slave, but not against his master. Speer, "Report on Zanzibar, 1862," USCZ, reel 2, vols. 4–5.

47. Speer, "Report on Zanzibar, 1862," USCZ, reel 4–5.

48. This notion of slaves as childlike subordinates was common in many African societies. See, for example, Suzanne Miers and Igor Kopytoff, eds., *Slavery in Africa: Historical and Anthropological Approaches* (Madison: University of Wisconsin Press, 1977); Fred Morton, "Small Change: Children in the Nineteenth Century East African Slave Trade," in *Children in Slavery Through the Ages,* ed. Gwyn Campbell, Suzanne Miers, and Joseph C. Miller (Athens: Ohio University Press, 2009), 55–70.

49. Orlando Patterson, *Slavery and Social Death: A Comparative Study* (Cambridge, MA: Harvard University Press, 1982). On social death as part of a longer process, see Frederick Cooper, "The Problem of Slavery in African Studies," *Journal of African History* 20, no. 1 (1979): 103–25.

50. For a nuanced discussion of the changing meaning of *heshima* in the late nineteenth and early twentieth centuries see McMahon, *Slavery and Emancipation.*

51. Cooper, *Plantation Slavery,* 78. Consul Hamerton to Secret Department, January 2, 1842, IOL L/P&S/9/12. Christie similarly wrote that for Arabs in Zanzibar, wealth was "indicated by the number of his domestic slaves." Christie, *Cholera Epidemics,* 328. See also M. Catherine Newbury, "Colonialism, Ethnicity, and Rural Political Protest: Rwanda and Zanzibar in Comparative Perspective," *Comparative Politics* 15, no. 3 (1983): 253–80. As evidence of the kind of social capital slave owners commanded, Jonathon Glassman has shown that a slave owner's prestige and wealth could be further enhanced when slaves achieved renown in the caravan trade or dance societies. Glassman, *Feasts and Riot,* 80,

90; Margaret Strobel, *Muslim Women in Mombasa, 1890–1975* (New Haven, CT: Yale University Press, 1979), 49–50; Claire Robertson and Martin Klein, eds., *Women and Slavery in Africa* (Madison: University of Wisconsin Press, 1983).

52. Katrin Bromber, "Mjakazi, Mpambe, Mjoli, Suria: Female Slaves in Swahili Sources," in *Women and Slavery: Africa, the Indian Ocean World, and the Medieval North Atlantic*, vol. 1, ed. Gwyn Campbell, Suzanne Miers, and Joseph C. Miller (Athens: Ohio University Press, 2007), 111–27; Sheriff, "Suria."

53. Ruete, *Memoirs of an Arabian Princess*, 150.

54. Hamerton to Secret Department, January 2, 1842; Christie, *Cholera Epidemics*, 382; "The Story of Rashid bin Hassani of the Bisa tribe, Northern Rhodesia," recorded by W. F. Baldock, in *Ten Africans*, ed. Margery F. Perham (London: Faber and Faber, 1936), 81–120.

55. Joseph Osgood, *Notes of Travel* (Salem: George Creamer, 1854), 50–51; Capt. Philip Colomb, *Slave-Catching in the Indian Ocean: A Record of Naval Experiences* (1873; repr. London: Dawsons of Pall Mall, 1968), 371.

56. Consular Court, Zanzibar, September 21, 1863, ZNA A3/11; Proceedings of the Criminal Court of Zanzibar for 1867/1868 ZNA AA7/1.

57. Hamerton to Secret Department, January 2, 1842; Christie, *Cholera Epidemics*, 328.

58. Charles New, *Life, Wanderings, and Labours in Eastern Africa* (1873; repr., London: Frank Cass, 1971), 64.

59. *Correspondence Respecting Sir Bartle Frere's Mission to the East Coast of Africa 1872–73*, LXI, C. 867 (1873), 49.

60. J. Holman, *Travels in Madras, Ceylon, Mauritius, Cormoro Islands, Calcutta, Etc.* (London: Routledge, 1840), 50. See also New, *Life, Wanderings, and Labours*, 29–30. This strategy of subjection and presentation for sale was common in many other slave societies. See, for example, Saidiya Hartman's *Scenes of Subjection* (Oxford: Oxford University Press, 1997) and Walter Johnson's study of the US slave market, *Soul by Soul: Life in the Antebellum Slave Market* (Cambridge, MA: Harvard University Press, 1999), chap. 4–5. To mark individuals as slaves, traders also shaved patterns in the hair. "Translations of two papers found . . . dated 20 Rabia il Akher 1282 [12 September 1865], Zanzibar," ZNA AA3/25.

61. Joseph Osgood, *Notes of Travel* (Salem, MA: George Creamer, 1854), 50.

62. Hamerton to Secret Department, Zanzibar, January 2, 1842; Speer, "Report on Zanzibar, 1862," USCZ, reel 2, vol. 4–5. For a further discussion of *wapambe*, see Glassman, *Feasts and Riot*, 130, 132–33.

63. Ruete, *Memoirs*, 157.

64. Devereux, *A Cruise in the "Gorgon*,*"* 414.

65. Ruschenberger, *A Voyage*, 49.

66. Ruete, *Memoirs*, 251–52.

67. Miers and Kopytoff, *Slavery in Africa*; Wright, *Strategies of Slaves and Women*.

68. Glassman, *Feasts and Riot*; Frederick Cooper, Thomas Holt, and Rebecca Scott, "Introduction," in *Beyond Slavery: Explorations of Race, Labor, and Citizenship*

in Postemancipation Societies, ed. Frederick Cooper, Thomas Holt, and Rebecca Scott (Chapel Hill: University of North Carolina Press, 2000), 5.

69. Slaves often maintained that return to their home societies was impossible. See, for instance, George L. Sullivan, *Dhow Chasing in Zanzibar Waters on the Eastern Coast of Africa* (London: S. Low, Marsten, Low & Searle, 1873), 186.

70. Fair, *Pastimes and Politics*; Fair, 'Remaking Fashion," 13–30.

71. "Depositions of Various Male and Female African Slaves Found in Possession of Kanoo Munjee a Banian, British Subject, Residing at Zanzibar," February 5, 1860, ZNA AA3/11.

72. For the role of actual and metaphorical clothing in the discourses of slavery, see Glassman, "The Bondsman's New Clothes," 277–83; Fair, *Pastimes and Politics.* On the idea of consumption as constituting of "social citizenship," see Don Slater, *Consumer Culture and Modernity* (Cambridge, MA: Blackwell, 1997), 4–5.

73. Ruete, *Memoirs,* 157.

74. Fair, *Pastimes and Politics,* chap. 2.

75. Fair, *Pastimes and Politics,* chap. 2.

76. "Return of Slaves emancipated by Lieut. Col. Playfair, from the Date of His Assuming Charge of British Consulate Zanzibar [n.d.]," ZNA A12/3.

77. Jonathon Glassman has suggested that on the nineteenth-century East African coast, slavery and freedom (*uhuru*) were not necessarily discrete categories. "Uhuru was not a status one was born with," Glassman asserted, "but was rather a condition bestowed on a slave, by the master or some other powerful patron." Thus, when one "was granted uhuru, one exchanged bonds with the master for a new type of bond with one's benefactor." Glassman, *Feasts and Riot,* 113; Glassman, "The Bondsman's New Clothes."

12

Slavery and Postslavery in Madagascar

An Overview

Denis Regnier and Dominique Somda

As Igor Kopytoff has well shown, historians were the first to document the specificities of African and Asian systems of slavery in the mid-twentieth century.[1] Anthropologists at that time were reluctant to tackle this subject since they were preoccupied with rehabilitating the much-maligned reputation of the people they studied. As their unease with the topic faded away, a number of pioneering studies appeared that confronted slavery.[2] Their authors were primarily concerned with the question of a universal definition of slavery, that is, one that would be applicable to non-Western societies, as well as with the local definitions of slave status and the reconstruction of past indigenous systems of slavery; they also discussed issues such as the Marxian approach to slavery as a mode of production and the cultural variations in systems of slavery. In the mid-1990s, however, the research agenda on slavery was significantly impacted and reshaped by a major UNESCO project, launched in 1994 and called the Slave Route, which supported the worldwide organization of academic conferences and exhibitions on slavery and the slave trade, and the publication of books on the subject.[3] The interests of anthropologists and historians shifted during this period from questions of slavery as an aspect of indigenous social organization and a mode of production to questions about the cultural implications of enslavement and the trade, especially in the construction of social memory and identity. Indeed, during this period ethnographies and historical accounts dealing with slavery increasingly focused on its remembrance.[4]

These global trends have also been followed in Malagasy and Indian Ocean scholarship. In Madagascar, two major conferences were organized as a direct consequence of the UNESCO project: the first, held in Antananarivo in 1996, commemorated the 100th anniversary of the colonial abolition and was mostly concerned with documenting past slavery and its legacy in the present; the second, held in Toamasina in 1999, addressed the topic of slavery and the slave trade on the East Coast.[5] During these meetings it became apparent that the scientific study of slavery and postslavery raised specific concerns in Madagascar because of the concomitance of the colonial conquest (1895) and the abolition (1896), which means that both events are often closely associated, not least because Malagasy slavery provided a convenient moral justification for the French takeover.[6]

In 2004, Sudel Fuma, then holder of a UNESCO chair at the Université de La Réunion, launched a regional project called "La route de l'esclave et de l'engagé dans l'océan Indien," which focused on collecting oral memories.[7] Another important aim of the project was to foster the development of a "roots and heritage" tourism around significant sites of memory in the islands of the southwestern Indian Ocean. Many African countries, on both western and eastern coasts, have tried to develop the potential for tourism of slave trade's sites, the most famous case being probably that of the island of Gorée in Senegal.[8] Yet despite the geographic proximity of Réunion and Mauritius, which are home to a large number of slave descendants tracing their origins to Madagascar, the efforts deployed by the UNESCO project—especially in the south-east of Madagascar, near Tôlañaro (Fort-Dauphin)—have not yet materialized in noticeable slavery-related touristic developments. Although this question would require further investigation, we believe that the relative failure of these attempts at establishing memorial sites in Madagascar is linked to the widespread silence on slavery, a topic to which we will return.

Our main goal in this chapter is to place postslavery issues in Madagascar into an historical and comparative framework. We do so by first highlighting the particular significance of slavery and the slave trade in the history of Madagascar, especially during the late eighteenth and nineteenth centuries, and the importance of the distinction between the two abolitions of 1877 and 1896. We then draw from a number of ethnographic studies to frame comparative questions on Malagasy postslavery, in particular questions about the condition of slave descendants and the persistence of their discrimination in present-day Madagascar. The overview we provide does not aim to be exhaustive; rather, we seek to identify a set of questions that are core issues in the study of Malagasy postslavery, and to indicate questions that remain controversial, unanswered, or understudied.

Slavery, Slave Trading, and the Two Abolitions

Slaves have been traded in the maritime networks of the western Indian Ocean for at least 2,000 years.[9] In Madagascar, the existence of slavery may date back to the first Southeast Asian settlements, which probably occurred between the fourth and sixth centuries.[10] Scholars seeking to reconstruct the early occupation of the island find it plausible that slaves were among the Southeast Asian settlers since ship crews from Indonesia were probably comprised of people with different social statuses and may have included slaves who were left behind in the semipermanent settlements of this remote colony.[11] If not earlier, slaves probably comprised an important part of the population of Madagascar as early as the tenth century. By that date, two main commercial systems existed in the western Indian Ocean. One was in the hands of Muslim merchants from the Persian Gulf, southern Arabia, and the Swahili coast who traded along the shores of East Africa and in the northern Indian Ocean, and the other was in the hands of the Southeast Asians, who sailed to the Comoros and Madagascar. It is likely that slaves circulated in both systems since during this period Muslim merchants sent East African slaves to southern Arabia and the Gulf, while the Southeast Asians probably used slave labor in the iron industry of their settlements.[12]

The arrival of Portuguese vessels in the Indian Ocean in 1488 marked the beginning of a new era of slave trading, one that would supersede in intensity and extension the ancient Indian Ocean trade.[13] As far as Madagascar is concerned, one of the most important events in this era of European slave trading is the transformation that occurred in the second half of the eighteenth century, when a new regional network started to export slaves from Madagascar to the Mascarene Islands. According to Pier Larson, between 1770 and 1820 highland Madagascar supplied about 70,000 slaves to the French colonies of Île de France (Mauritius) and Île Bourbon (Réunion). Even though the average population loss to export slavery may seem rather low compared with that of other African countries in the Atlantic, this export slave trade provoked nonetheless "profound, economic, and cultural dislocations that flowed from practices of enslavement and highland Madagascar's links to a global economy of mercantile capitalism."[14]

The demand from the Mascarene Islands also affected the coasts, not only the west coast ruled by Sakalava kings (allied with Muslim merchants), which dominated the slave trade in the late seventeenth and early eighteenth centuries,[15] but also the east coast ports that had provided slaves for the Mascarenes long before the Merina expansion in the second half of the eighteenth century. In the southeast, around Fort-Dauphin, Frenchmen established slave trading posts before being forced out by the Merina army in 1825.[16] The north and northeast coast remained nonetheless the most active competitors of Merina slave suppliers. Between 1785 and 1820, Sakalava and Betsimisaraka launched slaving raids in northern Madagascar, the Comoros, and the coast of Mozambique.[17]

In 1820, a treaty signed between the British and the Merina king Radama I made the export slave trade illegal.[18] This led to the development of an illegal trade network through which slaves continued to be shipped from East Africa.[19] A number of these slaves were disembarked on the western coast of Madagascar, from where they were further shipped to the Mascarenes.[20] Following the abolition of slavery in Mauritius (1835) and Réunion (1848), slaves were replaced in these islands' plantations by indentured laborers from the northwest of Madagascar.[21] On the island, internal slavery grew in significance, especially in the highlands, as Merina rulers launched wars to expand or defend their kingdom. During these wars, Merina soldiers brought captives back to Imerina, which they could no longer send to the Mascarenes. At the same time, the importation of African slaves continued and peaked in the second half of the nineteenth century due to an increased demand for labor in Imerina because free men were mobilized in the wars.[22] Throughout the nineteenth century, slavery continued to play an important role in Madagascar, especially for the economic development of the Merina kingdom, and a market for slaves continued to flourish until the abolition of slavery in 1896.[23]

In most Malagasy societies a number of servile statuses existed, which intersected with strikingly different living conditions. In most Malagasy kingdoms, royal servants and slaves existed alongside commoners' slaves, although in most cases the latter seem to have been the privilege of only the wealthy. Interestingly, a few kingdoms seem to have not allowed slavery.[24] The different servile statuses defined unequal rights to marriage, property, inheritance, etc. The condition of slaves seems to have varied greatly; while some slaves and servants have been known to achieve fame, glory, and wealth, for most of them the terms of endearment and kinship used by their masters only masked the harsh conditions and abject poverty they endured. It must be noted that European observers often stressed the "mild" character of slavery in Madagascar as they compared it with the other forms of slavery they were familiar with, namely, Ancient (that is, Greek and Roman) and plantation slavery in the New World.[25] Their judgment, however, was never corroborated by former slaves' narratives. To the contrary, contemporary anthropological accounts often insist on the abjection, humiliation, and terror inherent in slavery.[26]

The differences between categories of slaves were reflected in rich terminologies.[27] In Imerina, for example, commoners' slaves were called *andevo* and distinguished from the royal slaves called *Tandapa mainty* (Tsiarondahy) and from the royal servants (Manisotra, Manendy, Antehiroka).[28] In Anôsy, where only members of the royal family were allowed to own slaves (*ondevo*) and to have servants, the servile population, called *tandonaky*, was divided into three categories: royal slaves (*tôva*) and royal servants (*mpitako* and *tsariky*).[29] Everywhere in Madagascar such past distinctions are being forgotten and increasingly replaced by a single category that refers to all slave descendants, for example "blacks" (*mainty*) in Imerina and "unclean people" (*olo tsy madio*) among the Betsileo. These categories have their binary counterparts—that is, "whites" (*fotsy*) and "clean people" (*olo madio*)—which are used to refer to all nonslave descendants.[30]

In continuity with Radama's decision, under external pressure, to abolish the export slave trade, two abolitions of slavery took place by the end of the nineteenth century. The Merina queen, Ranavalona II, decided the first abolition in 1877. It was a partial emancipation insofar as it concerned exclusively the Masombika, also called Makoa, a category that comprised all the slaves who had been imported from East Africa and their descendants. The queen gave them land and the status of free subjects in the Merina kingdom.[31] The French colonial government decided the second abolition: a decree freed all the slaves without exception in 1896. These two abolitions were very different with respect to why and how they freed the slaves. They also had very different consequences. In our view, it is important to keep these differences in mind in order to understand the historical trajectories of former slaves and the current conditions of slave descendants in Madagascar.

Another important point to keep in mind is the specificity of the Malagasy islanders' attitudes toward slavery and slave descendants, in comparison with those present on the African continent. Although a number of similarities and regularities exist, such as the tendency to avoid marrying slave descendants or to silence personal histories of slavery, there are also specific features that, to our knowledge, are hardly found in continental Africa. This seems to be the case of the view, widespread in the island but seemingly absent on the continent, that slaves and their descendants are deeply polluted and polluting persons, a point to which we will return. It has been suggested that such a way of conceptualizing slavery might be a legacy of the Southeast Asian settlers of Madagascar, who had come from Indianized regions of insular Southeast Asia and had presumably brought with them a strong sensitivity to the ritual pollution caused by enslavement. True or not, this hypothesis points to the fact that Madagascar is an Afro-Asian island with a complex history of cultural influences. When dealing with slavery and postslavery issues we therefore need to take into account the full range of possible influences, and compare the Malagasy views with those found in both continental Africa and insular Southeast Asia.

Comparing the Trajectories of Former Slaves and Their Descendants

In this article we are not primarily concerned with the history of Malagasy slavery but with postslavery issues: our focus is on the legacies of slavery and abolition in contemporary Madagascar. These legacies must be understood in the light of the transformation, outlined earlier, that took place in the late eighteenth and early nineteenth centuries. The commoditization of slaves, the increase of the number of slaves in the Malagasy population (especially in the highlands), the perpetual risk of enslavement, and the role played by slavery in the political history of the nineteenth century have been accompanied, almost paradoxically, by an apparent effacement of explicit memories relating to these traumatic histories, as if it were a case of collective amnesia. Yet these "painful memories" are present, albeit "somewhat veiled and indirect,"[32] both among free and slave descendants, and are often implicit in ritual symbolism as well as in historical narratives.[33]

It is interesting to note on that matter, compared to other countries with a comparable traumatic history of slavery and in spite of a steady scholarly interest, academic conferences on slavery took place only very late on the island as a consequence of the UNESCO project mentioned earlier.[34] It is also noteworthy that according to some who attended these first meetings, they were emotionally charged events: even though they were scholars, many Malagasy found it difficult to talk about these issues. If anything, these academic meetings showed clearly that slavery was still a very sensitive topic more than a century after abolition.

It is no surprise that the legacies of slavery and abolition have been investigated first and foremost in Imerina, despite the fact that slavery was also extremely important in other regions, most notably in the development of the Sakalava kingdom on the western coast and the Betsimisaraka kingdom in the east.[35] An obvious reason for this concentration of academic attention is that Imerina, as explained earlier, once heavily relied on slaves for its economy and consequently it had the largest number of slaves in its population on the eve of abolition.[36] In comparison to what has been done for the Merina case, the study of postslavery in the rest of Madagascar has remained largely overlooked. Yet ethnographic accounts indicate that in all the other Malagasy societies the condition of slave descendants would also be worthy of close attention, irrespective of whether these societies are small-scale and never developed into large kingdoms like those of the Merina and the Sakalava.[37] Even among the Malagasy societies that are reputedly the most "egalitarian," such as the foraging Vezo and Mikea in western Madagascar, issues of slave ancestry are far from benign since people usually avoid marrying those they identify as slave descendants.[38] Yet in these groups such issues have never been investigated.

It is striking that, until the late 1990s to the 2000s, the andevo (that is, the "slaves," a term that also refers to slave descendants) in Madagascar have often been studied only in passing. Few anthropologists have sought to put themselves in their shoes and see society from their perspective. Many of them have described the condition of the andevo from the point of view of free descendants, indicating what they lacked or how they differed from free descendants—as if they were a residual category—instead of focusing on their specific historical experience and its consequences. These implicit biases are still present in much of the anthropological scholarship on Madagascar. While a focus on what slaves lacked during the preabolition era is certainly justified, it seems to us that anthropologists' tendency to approach present-day slave descendants with the same conceptual grid (as "people who lack X," where X can be land, tombs, history, ancestors, ancestral blessings, and so on) has somewhat hindered the detailed and intimate study of how slave descendants experience their condition in the various societies of the island. The fact that free-descent informants often express prejudice inherited from the past—for example, when they say that "andevo have no tombs" or "andevo have no ancestors"—is no excuse for confusing these views with the actual condition of those who are called andevo.

In Maurice Bloch's seminal study *Placing the Dead*, little is said about slave descendants even though, as Bloch commented, "if the difference between *andriana* [nobles] and *hova* [commoners] was never great [in traditional Merina society], the difference between these two groups and the *andevo* (slaves) was fundamental."[39] This quasi-absence of slave descendants in the monograph that arguably set a standard for modern anthropological work on Madagascar is particularly striking because Bloch made clear at the same time that slave descendants formed a very large part of the Merina population.[40] We write with the privilege of hindsight, of course, but some of Bloch's early reviewers noticed the paradox and exhorted the author to focus on slave descendants in the future.[41] A few years later,

Bloch addressed the issue in two essays. In the first, he compared the social implications of freedom for the slaves who were held by the Merina and for those who were held by the Zafimaniry.[42] The second essay made use of the same comparative material, but framed the question somewhat differently in terms of modes of production and ideology.[43] Much later Bloch returned to the topic of slavery in yet another essay on slave descendants in Antananarivo's slums who are possessed by royal spirits. In this last essay he argued that the crucial problem of slaves (and former slaves) was "the interruption in blessing" that occurred during enslavement: "When people are taken as slaves, their ties to their ancestors are broken, because they no longer receive blessing from their ancestors at the various familial rituals."[44]

According to Bloch, the position of slaves in traditional Merina society was that of junior members of families who could never become full members of society because they had no ancestral territory and their children were condemned to the same fate: slaves "were outside the social system in its ideological representation."[45] After abolition, ex-slaves had mainly three options: (1) to return back to the areas from which they had been taken (if this was possible); (2) to stay in the villages where they were slaves and to keep working on their former masters' estates (often on a share-cropping contract); or (3) to find empty land where they could start a new life by building terraces and cultivating rice. While the consequences of the first option are difficult to evaluate, the most important consequence of the second option was the continuation of a type of obligation between former masters and former slaves in ancient Merina villages. The slave descendants played the role of caretakers for the free descendants' land and tombs (known as *valala miandry fasana*, "the grasshoppers who guard the tombs"), and sometimes provided servants, often children, for their houses in Antananarivo or elsewhere. This was because, as documented by Bloch, many free-descent Merina left peasantry to take up opportunities in education, administration, or business, and kept their ancestral land only for ideological reasons. Even though they accepted this situation of dependency, the descendants of slaves resented it bitterly.

Those among the freed slaves who chose the third option and went to new empty lands found themselves in the company of the free Merina who could not live on their ancestral land because of the growing population and resulting land shortage. Although they started off on an equal footing, ex-slaves and free Merina usually lived in separate villages. What happened was that, because of their endogamous marriage rules, the free Merina were at first less able to form local kinship networks than the former slaves, who could marry whomever they wanted, provided it was not close kin. So while the free Merina remained somewhat isolated in the new lands, former slaves were able to organize agricultural and political coop-eration more easily. This advantage turned to a disadvantage because the free-descent Merina, through their endogamous marriages, kept kinship links with administrators, teachers, or businessmen who lived in town, and through these links they had access to new sources of power and wealth, whereas slave-descent rural peasants did not. It is interesting to note here that Bloch's views on Merina slave descendants have been recently challenged by David Graeber, who argued that the slave descendants he observed in the region of Arivonimamo (west of Antananarivo) were actu-ally more successful than the free descendants because they had managed to buy land compared to those free descendants who did not care much about keeping it, precisely because they lived in the capital.[46]

According to Bloch, the slaves held by the Zafimaniry had, unlike Merina slaves, access to land. But the Zafimaniry are shifting cultivators and free Zafimaniry tended to give their slaves the already semiexhausted lands. Since they had land, however, most of them stayed in their villages after being freed. Later the ex-slave villages were the first to turn to rice irrigation and they benefited most from education through Catholicism, from the trade of wood carvings, and from tourism. Consequently, pres-ent-day Zafimaniry slave descendants are generally better off than the free descendants. Since the ex-slaves have no positive marriage rules, they can marry outside Zafimaniry country and therefore have kinship links out-side the rather cramped territory where the free descendants must marry. Bloch concludes that, unlike in the Merina case, slave descendants among the Zafimaniry have been more successful than the free descendants. The comparative framework in terms of socioeconomic success proposed by Bloch seems to us extremely useful for the study of postslavery in Mad-agascar, and much remains to be done to have a better idea of whether former slaves and their descendants have managed to achieve equality in economic terms. Yet this perspective is clearly not sufficient because the economic success of slave descendants has not necessarily been accompa-nied by equality in terms of social status: prejudice against slave descen-dants remains deep in some regions of the island, where even wealthy slave descendants can still be viewed as subalterns.

A prime example of this situation is found among the southern Bets-ileo, where slave descendants are commonly called "unclean" or "dirty" people.[47] These derogatory labels still stick to groups of slave descendants who have otherwise achieved some kind of economic and political equality, for example, because their ancestors were among the first settlers and thus among the founding fathers of a local community.[48] Yet this achievement remains ambiguous and fragile since in spite of their efforts, slave descendants have not managed to shed the inferior status that was once ascribed to them: commoner descendants continue to view them as unclean and strictly refuse to marry them.

In Anôsy, slave descendants endure a fate that is in many ways similar and yet different.[49] As in southern Betsileo, they are also described as dirty people and cannot marry commoner descendants. They live in separate neighborhoods. Their economic and political empowerment, while not completely inaccessible, remains difficult. Former slaves, after abolition, often stayed on their former masters' estates, which were in most cases royal residences. Their continuing presence in these places, more than any known genealogy or history, is an indication of their slave ancestry. Such an ascription of slave status on the basis of geographic cues feeds widespread suspicion. This suspicion extends to the descendants of commoners who choose to reside, for various reasons, in the incriminated areas. Yet a reputation of slave descent brings the most definitive shame, even though the economic and political aspects of slavery and slave origins are commonly deemphasized. Instead, the Tanôsy insist on the moral and ritual devaluation of slaves and their descendants. Thus, they are generally oblivious of the complex circumstances of past enslavement. However, they often justify enslavement by saying that the slaves became slaves because in the past they behaved sinfully. Their alleged wrongdoing included bestiality and gluttony, especially at funerals. The various roles and categories that slaves and servants had in the past are similarly overlooked by the Tanôsy, yet they are often able to recall a single servile duty that epitomize the abject condition of slaves and their degraded status: slaves were forced to clean royal corpses and some slaves used to be slaughtered to lie under their masters in their graves. Today, members of the royal family continue to summon slave descendants when their highest-ranking relatives die. The ritual cleansing of corpses is viewed as a polluting act—among commoners, it falls to the less honorable kinsmen—and the slave descendants' impurity is explicitly connected to this function. Tanôsy slave descendants are still considered as slaves because slavery is believed to be an ingrained, transmissible moral defect rather than a legal status that can be abolished.

In an attempt to compare the situation of slave descendants across different societies of the island, Margaret Brown stressed the relative ease with which slave ancestry is acknowledged in an ethnically mixed (Makoa/Betsimisaraka) community of the Masoala peninsula northeast of Madagascar.[50] Such ease surprised Brown because much Malagasy scholarship had shown that slave ancestry is not easily acknowledged and that the topic is difficult to discuss openly. Eva Keller's 2008 observations also confirm

Brown's: she stresses that in Masoala slave descent has become "invisible" and slave descendants engage "in the same daily activities and the same ritual practices as those of free descent."[51] But what factors, asked Brown, would explain the social acceptability of slave ancestry in some Malagasy societies and its concurrent stigmatization in others? She argued that the common ideology of ancestral power, according to which people's lives depend heavily on their ancestors' power, and the fact that slaves had been wrenched from their own ancestors, is not sufficient to explain why stigmatization occurs because the slave descendants she observed shared the same reverence for the ancestors as other Malagasy and yet readily discussed slave ancestry and intermarried with people of free descent. Brown suggested that acceptability and stigmatization vary according to three factors: (1) social structure (absence or presence of rank; nature of the kinship system; marriage rules); (2) resource availability; (3) historical patterns of migration and ethnic mixing.

On the whole, we agree with Brown's suggestion that these three factors are crucial to account for the different levels of acceptability and stigmatization of slave descent found in the various societies of Madagascar. Yet we also think that she missed a highly important point. As her own example in Masoala shows, acceptability and stigmatization also depend on whether people perceive slave identity as being internal or external to their own group. In Masoala, the Betsimisaraka consider that the Makoa are another ethnic group (*foko*) that had client relationships with them in the past. By comparison, in other Malagasy contexts where discrimination against slave descendants is strong, such as among the Betsileo or the Tanôsy, slave descendants are usually considered to be internal: they are perceived as people who have fallen down from a higher status within the Betsileo or the Tanôsy groups. We would therefore suggest that one of the main reasons for the acceptability of slave status in Masoala is the fact that the Betsimisaraka tend to view the Makoa as a different ethnic group rather than as subalterns among the Betsimisaraka. In our opinion, it is precisely this kind of ethnicization of Makoa identity, partly encouraged by their liberation by the Merina queen in 1877 and by the memorial practices of the Makoa themselves, that renders intermarriage possible and makes public acknowledgment of slave ancestry unproblematic.[52] It is important to note, in that regard, that the Makoa remember their own history as a forced displacement from continental Africa rather than as a downfall that would have occurred within Madagascar. They also try to keep their own specific cultural identity. Consequently, despite facing problems of social integration,[53] they do not necessarily feel ashamed and obliged to keep silent about their history, unlike what happens in the case of slave descendants who are perceived (and perceive themselves) as internal, that is, as slave descendants who have Malagasy (and not African) origins.

Accounting for the Discrimination and Its Regional Variation

Indeed, it does seem that the strongest discriminatory practices against slave descendants mostly take place in situations where *andevo* (slaves) are perceived as internal in the sense outlined earlier. The distinction between these two ways of conceptualizing "slaves" (internally and externally) in Madagascar seems to us more relevant than, say, making a distinction between coastal and highland Malagasy with respect to the level of stigmatization of slave descent. At first sight there seems to be a correlation, insofar as people in the highlands are perhaps more likely to view slave descendants as internal while on the coast they are more likely to view them as external, that is, as people whose ancestors have been forcefully brought from continental Africa to Madagascar. However, things are not that simple. In Antananarivo and Imerina, for example, where the issue of slave descent is increasingly racialized, the *mainty* (blacks) are seen as both internal (as a group that has been integrated into the Merina ranking system after the royal abolition of 1877) and external (as people with African origins).[54]

In some contexts, former slaves and their descendants have sometimes continued to dwell, after abolition, in the southwestern parts of villages as prescribed by the astrological system that is used in many Malagasy societies and attributes the southwest direction to those of slave status.[55] When they did so, they often accepted sharecropping arrangements with their former masters and until today those who chose this option have remained stuck in relations of dependency.[56] Yet after the 1896 abolition many freed slaves chose to leave their former masters and looked for new land to cultivate for their own benefit. In these endeavors, they sometimes joined groups of landless free descendants and together they founded new villages where the old spatial distinctions were not relevant anymore.[57] Consequently, distinctions between slave and free village parts are still visible today but this is only true of the ancient villages that were founded before 1896. In towns, the old spatial distinctions have become increasingly difficult to read because of the changes brought about by rapid demographic expansion and urban migration. In Malagasy popular imagination, however, some neighborhoods of the capital Antananarivo are still strongly associated with slave descent because many slaves lived in these areas in preabolition times.[58] The extent to which this popular perception still corresponds to a sociological reality remains an open question.

Another question that would require further investigation is whether access to land has ever posed a serious problem to the estimated 500,000 slaves who were freed in 1896. As James Sibree, a fine observer of nineteenth-century Madagascar, noted in 1870, "the country is so sparsely populated that the land is, comparatively [compared to Europe], of little value, so that almost everyone possesses some piece of ground which he can cultivate; even the slaves have their rice-patch. There is very little of that abject grinding poverty so common in the crowded populations of European cities. Except in the near vicinity of Malagasy towns, a good deal of the land appears open to anyone living in the neighborhood to cultivate and enclose at pleasure, so that no one need want at least the bare necessaries of life."[59] Sibree's account thus suggests that access to land may not have been an issue for freed slaves after 1896. Provided they moved away from the towns and started cultivating free land in less populated areas, they were probably able to do so with little obstacles.[60] Another account, however, goes against this idea and characterizes slave descendants in the southern Betsileo highlands as people who are inherently landless because their slave ancestors did not have the right to possess land and their descendants did not manage to have access to land after abolition.[61] As a result of this landlessness, the argument goes on, slave descendants in the Betsileo southern highlands do not have ancestral tombs, so "they are defined as people without history, without ancestors and without descent groups."[62] This account attracted criticism for overgeneralizing a very local situation and for overinterpreting the data.[63] A particularly salient issue here is that of ancestral tombs, which are of utmost importance in Madagascar since they are central markers of group identity and are built on one's *tanindrazana* (ancestral land).[64]

Slave descendants' tombs are particularly important for the study of postslavery issues in Madagascar because their existence shows that most slave descendants have managed to reancestralize themselves, meaning that they have built tombs that now contain several generations of dead/ancestors (*razana*). Although their genealogies remain shallow, they can fully engage in ritual activity directed at these ancestors. Unlike land, the issue of tombs must have been a difficult one for freed slaves upon abolition because during enslavement, their dead were not buried in kin-based collective tombs so that after abolition, freed slaves were hardly able to take out their dead and place them in the new tombs they built on the lands they started to cultivate.[65] Over the last century the dead/ancestors have nonetheless accumulated in the tombs of former slaves and their descendants, so that they have been increasingly able to normalize tomb-centered ritual activity and to become proud of their tombs, which are sometimes more lavish and better maintained than those of noble descendants.[66]

To account for the persistence of the discrimination against slave descendants, the argument has been put forward that in some Malagasy contexts, free descendants essentialize the andevo.[67] Essentialization here refers to psychological essentialism, a way of thinking that has been well studied by cognitive and social psychologists. Among the southern Betsileo, commoner descendants seem to regard slave descendants as people who have an unclean essence. They view the uncleanliness of slave descendants as impossible to cleanse and as necessarily transmitted from parents to children. Such an essentialist construal, however, does not seem to be a relic of precolonial ways of thinking about slaves. It is more likely an unexpected but wide-ranging outcome of the 1896 colonial abolition of slavery. The circumstances of abolition made it impossible for freed slaves to be ritually cleansed as it was the custom among the southern Betsileo, and therefore commoners systematically avoided marrying former slaves. This avoidance in turn reinforced their prejudice against them. The circular process of marriage avoidance and prejudice reinforcement must have been going on since the aftermath of slavery and played a leading role in the essentialization of slave descendants.

In Madagascar the legacy of slavery has rarely brought the slave descendants together in defense of their rights. Notable exceptions originated from Antananarivo. Jean-Roland Randriamaro has described the emergence of social movements and political parties that made a significant impact on national politics from the late 1940s to the mid-1970s.[68] The Parti des Déshérités de Madagascar (PADESM, Party of the Disinherited of Madagascar),[69] which rallied slave descendants against their former masters, was founded in June 1946. Ambitiously aimed at serving the disenfranchised population of the nation, it claimed to unite the *mainty*, a heterogeneous category lumping together—mostly in Antananarivo and Imerina—slave descendants, descendants of royal slaves and servants, and *Côtiers* (a category regrouping people who moved from various coastal areas). The PADESM's first national secretary was a slave descendant. A major anticolonial uprising took place between March 1947 and December 1948, and their political opponents steadily accused the PADESM of collaborationism. It was suspected of being manipulated by the French colonial rule to counter the rise of the nationalist Mouvement Démocratique de la Rénovation Malgache (MDRM). Another movement, the MFM,[70] was created in 1972. It recruited the ZOAM (or ZWAM),[71] the underprivileged, undereducated, and "transgressive" youth inhabiting

Antananarivo's impoverished neighborhoods, although the leadership and core of the party was comprised of students and teachers. The ZOAM played a critical role in the unfolding events. That year, the political unrest brought to power forces overtly hostile to the traditional hierarchy. The appointment of radical and social reformist colonel Ratsimandrava was a response to the mainty youth's demands. Ratsimandrava, however, was assassinated only six days after his ascent to power. PADESM and MFM disappeared during the second republic. After Ratsiraka's takeover and the formation of the Democratic Republic of Madagascar in 1976, the ZOAM became de facto a government institution. During the second republic, the mainty youth of Antananarivo were described as a manipulable and suggestible mass rather than a militant and empowered force.[72] Jennifer Jackson describes this as a case of "reification of class categories."[73] She also observes that in developing the *zomaka* argot, which became a "covert instrument of political struggle" and an "object symbolic of an ideology of class struggle," the ZOAM normalized the mainty as a category of speakers. The political crisis of 2002, she explains, contributed to the reinvigoration of this argot and it has not only become a slang spoken by urban speakers across class lines but it was also "reengaged in the genres of political cartoons and mass media arts as a mode of political allegiance in identity resistance to politics."[74]

Yet the limited presence of parties and social movements protesting against stigmatization and marginalization, and committed to the empowerment of slave descendants in contemporary Malagasy politics, sharply contrasts with the increasing politicization of slaves and slave descendants in West African contexts.[75] In Madagascar, where the majority of slave descendants are still trying to achieve a more equal status through reancestralization and intermarriages with free descendants, such mobilizations are not observed. It might not come as a surprise that one of the latest incarnations of a political and cultural affirmation by slave descendants is found among the Makoa youth participating in the budding Malagasy hip-hop movement modeled after the American gangsta rap.[76] The lyrics of the Makoa emcees celebrate their African origins through favorable stylistic and thematic associations with a globalized, thriving blackness.

On the contrary, where slave descendants continue to reside among the descendants of those who once enslaved their ancestors, slavery has remained a difficult subject matter to discuss both publicly and privately. The reserve regarding slavery is often justified by two opposite arguments: slavery is either no longer relevant or too serious an issue to be evoked at all. Claims of equality (achieved or yet to come) hide the persistence of the stigma, but secrecy does not eliminate prejudice.

In 2012 Luke Freeman analyzed the silence on slavery observed among Betsileo free and slave descendants. He notes that "the effect of this silence is cumulative: the more the stigma of slavery is avoided, the more 'unspeakable' it becomes."[77] It is indeed difficult to fight what cannot be named. The use of euphemisms to allude to former servile status is widespread in Madagascar. These euphemisms generate ambiguities. Those used in rituals, for example, can become opaque to a number of people, both among free and slave descendants.[78] In Anôsy, royal slaves and slave descendants are frequently described as *panopo* (servants), a term also used for commoners, that is, people who were subjected only to the authority of the kings.[79] Slave descendants are also known as *olo ratsy* (bad people) and *olo tambany* (people of the bottom), but these terms carry little specificity and may also describe people who are marginalized because of their indigence. Finally, as in other regions of Madagascar, kinship terms are commonly used in Anôsy to address and refer to slave descendants. Noble descendants address them contemptuously as *zanak'ampela* (children of the women, that is, uterine parents). These equivocal designations entwine the identities of commoners and slave descendants, and such entwinement often prevents any definitive, unanimous identification of the latter. Doubts are further augmented by the Tanôsy restriction of open communication about historical knowledge beyond one's own descent group. This contrasts with other Malagasy contexts, for example, the southern Betsileo, where genealogical speeches are publicly given at funerals and serve as a means of keeping a social memory of origins.[80]

Implications of Postslavery Studies

In this chapter we have attempted to give a broad overview of slavery and postslavery issues in Madagascar. We hope to have shown that despite an increasing amount of studies, many of these issues require further investigation and discussion. We believe that this scholarship is extremely important in the case of Madagascar because oversimplifications about slave descendants and the ensuing prejudice are widespread in the island and beyond. A particularly telling but highly regrettable example of such oversimplifications can be found in a 2012 report on contemporary forms of slavery in Madagascar written for the United Nations. In its short section on the island's history of slavery, one can read, for example, that "The nobles and commoners [among the Merina] are generally light-skinned, whereas those in the latter two castes [that is, the mainty and the andevo] are dark-skinned," that "The Andevo live in slums located in the low villages, below the villages on the hill where the nobles and commoners settled," and that "most Andevo and Mosambika are illiterate."[81]

Oversimplifications of this kind are not just benign misrepresentations. They can provide "official" justifications for stigmatizing people on the basis of racial traits, places of residence, or illiteracy. Scholars should avoid relaying such simplistic statements and strive to make clear instead that popular perceptions of slave descendants' identity have been historically constructed and therefore do not reflect the present situation. As we have explained, ideas of slave descendants as "ancestorless people," for example, no longer correspond to a lived reality because, as far as we know, slave descendants now have tombs and dead/ancestors in these tombs.

The study of postslavery appears to be a particularly complex and sometimes slippery area of inquiry within Malagasy studies. Therefore, an extremely careful attention should be paid to local contexts in order to understand the full picture and avoid privileging one perspective—for example, the Merina case—over others. The construal of slave descendants among the Merina, the Betsileo, the Zafimaniry, the Betsimisaraka, and the Tanôsy—to go back to the few examples we have given here—is far from identical because it is the outcome of different local (although inter-related) histories. In urban, multiethnic, and more politically conscious Antananarivo, as in the Malagasy diaspora and the media, the representation of slave descendants is also different. To make sense of these differences we have tried to provide some analytical tools. We have highlighted in particular three processes that account for the ways slave descendants are viewed in different Malagasy contexts. While the Makoa, who were freed in 1877 by the Merina queen, seem always to be ethnicized as a slave descent group with external origins, southern Betsileo and Tanôsy slave descendants tend to be essentialized as people whose origins are Malagasy and whose servile history is therefore internal. In Antananarivo, one of the most salient aspects of the problem is an increasing racialization—arguably a specific case of essentialization—of the differences between slaves and nonslaves. We do not claim, however, that the processes of ethnicization, essentialization, and racialization we have highlighted are sufficient to define how slave descendants are perceived across the Malagasy social spectrum. Sociocultural phenomena such as the discrimination against slave descendants in Madagascar need sophisticated and empirically grounded accounts rather than simplistic generalizations. We have only begun to scratch the surface.

Notes

1. Igor Kopytoff, "Slavery," *Annual Review of Anthropology* 11 (1982): 207–30.
2. See in particular Suzanne Miers and Igor Kopytoff, eds., *Slavery in Africa: Historical and Anthropological Perspectives* (Madison: University of Wisconsin Press, 1977); James Watson, ed., *Asian and African Systems of Slavery* (Berkeley: University of California Press, 1980); Anthony Reid, ed., *Slavery, Bondage and Dependency in Southeast Asia* (St. Lucia: University of Queensland Press, 1982); Claude Meillassoux, *The Anthropology of Slavery: The Womb of Iron and Gold* (Chicago: University of Chicago Press, 1992).
3. On the goals and achievements of the Slave Route project, see UNESCO, *The Slave Route: 1994–2014: The Road Travelled* (Paris: UNESCO, 2014).
4. See, for example, Rosalind Shaw, *Memories of the Slave Trade: Ritual and the Historical Imagination in Sierra Leone* (Chicago: University of Chicago Press, 2002); Anne C. Bailey, *African Voices of the Atlantic Slave Trade: Beyond the Silence and the Shame* (Boston, MA: Beacon Press, 2005); Ana L. Araujo, *Public Memory of Slavery: Victims and Perpetrators in the South Atlantic* (Amherst, MA: Cambria Press, 2010); Alice Bellagamba, Sandra E. Greene, and Martin A. Klein, eds., *African Voices on Slavery and the Slave Trade*, vol. 1, *The Sources* (Cambridge: Cambridge University Press, 2013).
5. These conferences resulted in the publication of two books: Ignace Rakoto, ed., *L'esclavage à Madagascar: Aspects historiques et résurgences contemporaines* (Antananarivo: Institut de Civilisations—Musée d'Art et Archéologie, 1997); Ignace Rakoto and Eugène Mangalaza, eds., *La route des esclaves: Système servile et traite d'esclaves dans l'est malgache* (Paris: L'Harmattan, 2000).
6. Jean-Pierre Domenichini and Bakoly Domenichini-Ramiaramanana, "L' 'esclavage' dans la société malgache," in *Formes extrêmes de dépendance. Contributions à l'étude de l'esclavage en Asie du sud-est*, ed. Georges Condominas (Paris: École des Hautes Études en Sciences Sociales, 1998), 399–410; Gabriel Rantoandro, "L'esclavage comme enjeu de la mémoire à Madagascar," in *Le Monde créole. Peuplement, sociétés et condition Humaine XVIIe–XXe siècles. Mélanges offerts à Hubert Gerbeau*, ed. Jacques Weber (Paris: Les Indes savantes), 369–83.
7. Sudel Fuma, ed., *Mémoire orale et esclavage dans les îles du sud-ouest de l'océan Indien: Silences, oublis, reconnaissance* (Saint-Denis: Université de la Réunion, 2004).
8. Other renowned sites include Elmina Castle in Ghana, Ouidah in Benin, and Stone Town (Zanzibar) in Tanzania.
9. On these networks, see Philippe Beaujard, "L'Afrique de l'Est, les Comores et Madagascar dans le système-monde avant le XVIe siècle," in *Madagascar et l'Afrique. Entre identité insulaire et appartenances historiques*, ed. Didier Nativel and Faranirina V. Rajaonah (Paris: Karthala, 2007).
10. On early human settlements in Madagascar, see Robert E. Dewar and Alison F. Richard, "Madagascar: A History of Arrivals, What Happened, and Will Happen Next," *Annual Review of Anthropology* 41 (2012): 495–517. The questions surrounding the first arrival of populations from Southeast Asia in

Madagascar are still debated. On recent archaeological discoveries suggesting that hunter-gatherers from East Africa already occupied the island by 2000 BC, see Robert E. Dewar, Chantal Radimilahy, Henry T. Wright, Zenobia Jacobs, Gwendolyn O. Kelly, and Francesco Berna, "Stone Tools and Foraging in Northern Madagascar Challenge Holocene Extinction Models," *Proceedings of the National Academy of Sciences* 110, no. 31 (2013): 12583–88. The first Southeast Asian settlers probably reached Madagascar during the first millennium AD, but the exact date is controversial. In any case, most scholars agree that Southeast Asians had established permanent settlements by the ninth century at the latest. See Solofo Randrianja and Stephen Ellis, *Madagascar: A Short History* (London: Hurst & Company, 2009), 17–43; Alexander Adelaar, "Towards an Integrated Theory about the Indonesian Migrations to Madagascar," in *Ancient Human Migrations: A Multidisciplinary Approach*, ed. Peter N. Peregrine, Ilia Peiros, and Marcus Feldman (Salt Lake City: University of Utah Press, 2009), 149–72.

11. See Alexander Adelaar, "Borneo as a Cross-roads for Comparative Austronesian Linguistics," in *The Austronesians: Historical and Comparative Perspectives*, ed. Peter Bellwood, James Fox, and Darrell Tryon (Canberra: Australian National University Press, 1995), 83–88.

12. Claude Allibert, "Migration austronésienne et mise en place de la civilisation malgache. Lectures croisées: linguistique, archéologie, génétique, anthropologie culturelle," *Diogène* 218, no. 2 (2007): 6–17.

13. On European slave trading, see Richard B. Allen, *European Slave Trading in the Indian Ocean, 1500–1850* (Athens: Ohio University Press, 2014).

14. Pier Larson, "A Census of Slaves Exported from Central Madagascar to the Mascarenes between 1775 and 1820," in *L'esclavage à Madagascar. Aspects historiques et résurgences contemporaines*, ed. Ignace Rakoto (Antananarivo: Institut de Civilisations—Musée d'Art et d'Archéologie, 1997), 121–45. On Madagascar and the slave trade, see also Jean-Marie Filliot, *La traite des esclaves vers les Mascareignes au XVIIIe siècle* (Paris: Office de la recherche scientifique et technique outre-mer, 1974); Gilbert Ratsivalaka, "La traite européenne des esclaves en Imerina au début du XIXe siècle," *Tantara* 7–8 (1979): 113–35; James C. Armstrong (1984), "Madagascar and the Slave Trade in the Seventeenth Century," *Omaly Sy Anio* 17–20 (1983–84): 211–33; Gwyn Campbell, "Madagascar and the Slave Trade, 1810–1895," *Journal of African History* 22, no. 2 (1981): 203–27; R. J. Barendse, "Slaving on the Malagasy Coast, 1640–1700," in *Cultures of Madagascar: Ebb and Flow of Influences*, ed. Sandra Evers and Marc Spindler (Leiden: International Institute for Asian Studies, 1995), 137–55; Gwyn Campbell, *An Economic History of Imperial Madagascar, 1750–1895: The Rise and Fall of an Island Empire* (New York: Cambridge University Press, 2005), 213–42.

15. Gwyn Campbell, "The Structure of the Trade in Madagascar 1750–1810," *The International Journal of African Historical Studies* 26, no. 1 (1993): 132.

16. Dominique Somda, "Et le réel serait passé. Le secret de l'esclavage et l'imagination de la société (Anôsy, sud de Madagascar)" (PhD diss., Université de Paris Ouest Nanterre La Défense, 2009), 28.

17. Pierre Vérin, "Histoire ancienne du nord-est de Madagascar," *Taloha* 5 (1972): 155–58; Edward Alpers, "Madagascar and Mozambique in the Nineteenth Century: The Era of Sakalava Raids (1800–1820)," *Omaly sy anio* 5–6 (1977): 37–40; Campbell, "The Structure of the Trade," 140. On the connections between the Sakalava and the Betsimisaraka in the context of the slave trade, see Stephen Ellis, "Tom and Toakafo: The Betsimisaraka Kingdom and State Formation in Madagascar, 1715–1750," *Journal of African History* 48, no. 3 (2007): 439–55.

18. Radama I's 1817 discourse proclaiming the abolition of the slave trade can be found in James Sibree, *Madagascar and Its People* (London: The Religious Tract Society, 1870), 558–59.

19. Randrianja and Ellis, *Madagascar*, 125.

20. Gwyn Campbell, "The East African Slave Trade, 1861–1895: The Southern Complex," *The International Journal of African Historical Studies* 22, no. 1 (1989): 25.

21. Campbell, "Madagascar and the Slave Trade," 212.

22. Campbell, "The East African Slave Trade," 7.

23. There is some disagreement among scholars on the importance of slavery in the expansion of the Merina kingdom. Some suggest that its economy relied essentially on slave labor, while others argue that slavery played a significant role only in its early economic development, and that at a later stage the Merina kingdom relied more on corvée labor (*fanompoana*) than on slavery. See Campbell, *An Economic History*, 113–22.

24. The Sahafatra kings and the Antankarana rulers, for example, did not own slaves or use servants. See Oliver Woolley, *The Earth Shakers of Madagascar: An Anthropological Study of Authority, Fertility and Creation* (London: Continuum, 2002), 250; Laurent Berger, "Les raisins de la colère des ancêtres Zafinifotsy (Ankaraña, Madagascar): L'anthropologie au défi de la mondialisation" (PhD diss., École des Hautes Études en Sciences Sociales, 2006), 577.

25. For European accounts on Malagasy slavery in the late nineteenth century, see, for example, Sibree, *Madagascar and Its People*; C. André, ed., *De l'esclavage à Madagascar* (Paris: Arthur Rousseau, 1899); Jean-Baptiste Piolet, *Madagascar et les Hova: Description, organisation, histoire* (Paris: Delagrave, 1895), 99–102; William Cousins, "The Abolition of Slavery in Madagascar, with Some Remarks on Malagasy Slavery Generally," *Antananarivo Annual and Madagascar Magazine* 5, no. 21 (1896): 446–50; Joseph Sewell, *Remarks on Slavery in Madagascar* (London: Elliot Stock, 1876).

26. David Graeber, "Painful Memories," *Journal of Religion in Africa* 27, no. 4 (1997): 374–400; Somda, "Et le reel serait passé."

27. Louis Molet, "Le vocabulaire concernant l'esclavage dans l'ancien Madagascar," in *Perspectives nouvelles sur le passé de l'Afrique noire et de Madagascar* (Paris: Publications de la Sorbonne, 1974), 45–65.

28. Gustave Julien, *Institutions sociales et politiques de Madagascar* (Paris: Guilmoto, 1908), 177.

29. Somda, "Et le réel serait passé," 272–75.

30. Janine Ramamonjisoa, "'Blancs et noirs,' les dimensions de l'inégalité sociale. Documents socio-linguistiques," *Cahiers des Sciences Sociales* 1 (1984): 39–77; Denis Regnier, "Clean People, Unclean People: The Essentialisation of 'Slaves' among the Southern Betsileo of Madagascar," *Social Anthropology* 23, no. 2 (2015): 152–68.

31. See Georges-Sully Chapus, trans., "Lettre du Rev. J. Richardson au sujet de la libération des Mozambiques," *Bulletin de l'Académie Malgache* 18 (1935): 79–83. Jean-Pierre Domenichini and Bakoly Ramiaramanana, "1877: une abolition de l'esclavage?," in *L'esclavage à Madagascar. Aspects historiques et résurgences contemporaines*, ed. Ignace Rakoto (Antananarivo: Institut de Civilisations— Musée d'Art et d'Archéologie, 1997), 233–45.

32. Graeber, "Painful Memories," 375.

33. Pier Larson, "Reconsidering Trauma, Identity, and the African Diaspora: Enslavement and Historical Memory in Nineteenth-Century Highland Madagascar," *The William and Mary Quarterly* 56, no. 2 (1999): 339.

34. For comments on these conferences, see Hubert Gerbeau, "L'esclavage dans les sociétés du sud-ouest de l'océan indien à partir des années 1960. Permanences, rémanences, resurgences," *Revue des Mascareignes* 4 (2002): 179–96; Rantoandro, "L'esclavage comme enjeu."

35. On slavery and its legacy in Imerina, see, among others, Ramamonjisoa, "Blancs et noirs"; Lolona Razafindralambo, "La notion d'esclave en Imerina (Madagascar): Ancienne servitude et aspects actuels de la dependence" (PhD diss., Université de Paris Ouest Nanterre La Défense, 2003); Lolona Razafindralambo, "Inégalité, exclusion, représentation sur les hautes terres centrales de Madagascar," *Cahiers d'Études Africaines* 3, nos. 179–80 (2005): 879–904; David Graeber, *Lost People: Magic and the Legacy of Slavery in Madagascar* (Bloomington: Indiana University Press, 2007); Lolona Razafindralambo, "Esclavage et inégalités: Entre constructions sociales et differences 'naturelles,'" in *Esclavage et libération à Madagascar*, ed. Ignace Rakoto and Sylvain Urfer (Paris: Karthala, 2014), 95–106. On the importance of slavery for the Sakalava kingdoms, see in particular Gillian Feeley-Harnik, "The King's Men in Madagascar: Slavery, Citizenship, and Sakalava Monarchy," *Africa* 52 (1982): 31–50; Sophie Goedefroit, *A l'ouest de Madagascar. Les Sakalava du Menabe* (Paris: Karthala, 1998); Michael Lambek, "Revolted but Not Revolting: Reflections on the Sakalava Division of Labour and Forms of Subjectivation," *Slavery and Abolition* 25, no. 2 (2004): 108–19.

36. Estimates vary between 50 percent (Bloch) and about half of this figure (Campbell). See Maurice Bloch, *Placing the Dead: Tombs, Ancestral Villages, and Kinship Organization in Madagascar* (London: Seminar Press, 1971), 35; Gwyn Campbell, *An Economic History of Imperial Madagascar: The Rise and Fall, 1750–1895* (New York: Cambridge University Press, 2005), 159.

37. The forest-dwelling Tanala and Zafimaniry are good examples. On slavery among the Tanala, see Philippe Beaujard, "Esclavage et groupes sociaux en pays Tanala," in *Formes extrêmes de dépendance. Contributions à l'étude de l'esclavage en Asie du sud-est*, ed. Georges Condominas (Paris: École des Hautes Études en

Sciences Sociales, 1998), 203–15. On slavery among the Zafimaniry, see Maurice Bloch, "The Social Implications of Freedom for Merina and Zafimaniry Slaves," in *Madagascar in History: Essays from the 1970's*, ed. Raymond Kent (Albany, CA: The Foundation for Malagasy Studies, 1979), 269–97; Maurice Bloch, "Modes of Production and Slavery in Madagascar: Two Case Studies," in *Asian and African Systems of Slavery*, ed. James Watson (Oxford: Blackwell, 1980), 100–134.

38. Rita Astuti and Bram Tucker, personal communications.

39. Bloch, *Placing the Dead*, 71.

40. Bloch, *Placing the Dead*, 4.

41. Razafintsalama, "Maurice Bloch. The Significance of Tombs and Ancestral Villages for Merina Social Organization," *Archipel* 1, no. 1 (1971): 225; Louis Molet, "Maurice Bloch. Placing the Dead," *L'Homme* 12, no. 3 (1972): 149.

42. Bloch, "The Social Implications."

43. Bloch, "Modes of Production."

44. Maurice Bloch, "The Slaves, the King, and Mary in the Slums of Antananarivo," in *Shamanism, History, and the State*, ed. Nicholas Thomas and Caroline Humphrey (Ann Arbor: University of Michigan Press, 1994), 135.

45. Bloch, "The Social Implications," 276.

46. See Graeber, *Lost People*.

47. See Sandra Evers, *Constructing History, Culture and Inequality: The Betsileo in the Extreme Southern Highlands of Madagascar* (Leiden: Brill, 2002); Denis Regnier, "Clean People, Unclean People."

48. Denis Regnier, "Pourquoi ne pas les épouser? L'évitement du mariage avec les descendants d'esclaves dans le Sud Betsileo (Madagascar)," *Études Rurales* 194 (2014): 103–22.

49. See Somda, "Et le réel serait passé."

50. Margaret Brown, "Reclaiming Lost Ancestors and Acknowledging Slave Descent: Insights from Madagascar," *Comparative Studies in Society and History* 46, no. 3 (2004): 616–45.

51. Eva Keller, "The Banana Plant and the Moon: Conservation and the Malagasy Ethos of Life in Masoala, Madagascar," *American Ethnologist* 35, no. 4 (2008): 660.

52. On the Makoa, see Maurice Scrive and Noël Gueunier, "'Histoire du peuple': Souvenirs sur l'esclavage des Makoa du Nord de Madagascar," *Études Océan Indien* 15 (1992): 177–97; Gabriel Rantoandro, "Makoa et Masombika à Madagascar au XIXe siècle. Introduction à leur histoire," in *Madagascar et l'Afrique: Entre identités insulaires et appartenances historiques*, ed. Didier Nativel and Faranirina V. Rajaonah (Paris: Karthala, 2007), 137–61; Klara Boyer-Rossol, "De Morima à Morondava. Contribution à l'étude des Makoa de l'Ouest de Madagascar au XIXe siècle," in *Madagascar et l'Afrique. Entre identité insulaire et appartenances historiques*, ed. Didier Nativel and Faranirina V. Rajaonah (Paris: Karthala, 2007), 183–217; Klara Boyer-Rossol, "Les Makoa en pays sakalava: Une ancestralité entre deux rives, Ouest de Madagascar, XIXe–XXe siècles," in

Les traites et les esclavages: Perspectives historiques et contemporaines, ed. Myriam Cottias, Élisabeth Cunin, and António de Almeida Mendes (Paris: Karthala, 2010), 189–99; Klara Boyer-Rossol, "Makua Life Histories: Testimonies on Slavery and the Slave Trade in the 19th Century in Madagascar," in *African Voices on Slavery and the Slave Trade,* vol. 1, *The Sources,* ed. Alice Bellagamba, Sandra E. Greene, and Martin A. Klein (New York: Cambridge University Press, 2013), 466–80. For an extensive account on the Makoa, see Klara Boyer-Rossol, "Entre les deux rives du Canal du Mozambique: Histoire et mémoires des Makoa de l'Ouest de Madagascar (XIXe–XXe siècles)" (PhD diss., Université Paris Diderot, 2015).

53. On the difficult social integration of the Makoa in the Antsihanaka region and near the capital Antananarivo, see Malanjaona Rakotomalala and Célestin Razafimbelo, "Le problème d'intégration sociale chez les Makoa de l'Antsihanaka," *Omaly Sy Anio* 21–22 (1985): 93–113; Michel Razafiarivony, "Les descendants des anciens esclaves importés d'Afrique à Madagascar: Tradition et réalité," *Journal of Asian and African Studies* 70 (2005): 63–80.

54. Razafiarivony, "Les descendants des anciens esclaves." The distinction of internal/external that we propose here relies on people's perception of slave descendants *today*: are they Malagasy or do they have foreign (that is, African) origins? These perceptions may of course be far from accurate from an historical point of view. The distinction internal/external is not exactly equivalent to the distinction insider/outsider, which is mainly used to talk about migration and precedence in Madagascar.

55. Jean-Claude Hébert, "La cosmologie malgache, suivie de l'énumération des points cardinaux et l'importance du nord-est," *Taloha* 1 (1965): 84–149.

56. For examples among the Betsileo, see Conrad Kottak, *The Past in the Present: History, Ecology, and Cultural Variation in Highland Madagascar* (Ann Arbor: University of Michigan Press, 1980); Luke Freeman, "Speech, Silence, and Slave Descent in Highland Madagascar," *Journal of the Royal Anthropological Institute* 19, no. 3 (2012): 600–617.

57. Regnier, "Pourquoi ne pas les épouser."

58. Catherine Guérin-Fournet, *Vivre à Tananarive: Géographie du changement dans la capitale malgache* (Paris: Karthala, 2007), 37–38, 367–90.

59. Sibree, *Madagascar and Its People,* 223.

60. For an historical example among the southern Betsileo, see Regnier, "Pourquoi ne pas les épouser," 119.

61. Evers, *Constructing History;* see also Sandra Evers, "Expropriated from the Hereafter: The Fate of the Landless in the Southern Highlands of Madagascar," *Journal of Peasant Studies* 33, no. 3 (2006): 413–44.

62. Evers, "Expropriated from the Hereafter," 430.

63. Denis Regnier, "Why Not Marry Them? History, Essentialism and the Condition of Slave Descendants among the Southern Betsileo" (PhD Diss., London School of Economics, 2012)] 211–17; Regnier, "Pourquoi ne pas les épouser," 107–10.

64. On the importance of tombs and burials in Madagascar, see in particular Bloch, *Placing the Dead;* Mike Parker Pearson and Denis Regnier, "Collective

and Single Burial in Madagascar," in *Gathered in Death: Archaeological and Ethnological Perspectives on Collective Burial and Social Organisation*, ed. Aurore Schmitt, Sylviane Déderix, and Isabelle Crevecoeur (Louvain-La-Neuve: Presses universitaires de Louvain, 2018), 41–62.

65. On the necessity to move ancestors to a new tomb when founding an "ancestral land," see Denis Regnier, "La fondation d'une nouvelle terre ancestrale dans le Sud Betsileo (Madagascar): Dilemme, transformation, rupture," in *(Re)Fonder. Modalités du commencement dans le temps et l'espace*, ed. Philippe Gervais-Lambony, Frédéric Hurlet, and Isabelle Rivoal (Paris: de Boccard, 2017), 121–28.

66. Graeber, *Lost People*.

67. Regnier, "Clean People, Unclean People."

68. Jean-Roland Randriamaro, *PADESM et luttes politiques à Madagascar: De la Deuxième Guerre mondiale à la naissance du PSD* (Paris: Karthala, 1997); Jean-Roland Randriamaro, "L'émergence politique des Mainty et des Andevo au XXe siècle," in *L'esclavage à Madagascar. Aspects historiques et résurgences contemporaines*, ed. Ignace Rakoto (Antananarivo: Institut de Civilisations—Musée d'Art et d'Archéologie, 1997), 357–81.

69. The Malagasy name of the PADESM, Fikambanan'ny Mainty sy ny karazany, signals explicity that it is a party of "blacks" (mainty), that is, of people considered to be of slave descent.

70. In Malagasy: Mpitolona ho amin'ny Fanjakana'ny Madinika. In French: Militants pour le Pouvoir Prolétarien.

71. This slang term is often presented as an acronym. Jean-Roland Randriamaro reports two definitions: ZWAM, for Zatovo Western Amerikana Malagasy (Western American-Malagasy Youth), a nod to the popularity of Western movies among Malagasy youth. The second is ZOAM, for Zatovo ory asa Malagasy (Unemployed Malagasy Youth). See Randriamaro, "L'émergence politique," 364. For Jennifer Jackson, their name is even more explicit: they are the Zatovo Western Andevo I' Madagascar (The Western Slaves of Madagascar). She argues that ZOAM is actually ZOAM's politicized reincarnation. See Jennifer Jackson, *Political Oratory and Cartooning: An Ethnography of Democratic Process in Madagascar* (Oxford: Wiley-Blackwell, 2013), 47–48. See also Marco Gardini, "L'activisme politique des descendants d'esclaves à Antananarivo: Les heritages de Zoam," *Politique Africaine* 140, no. 4 (2015): 23–40.

72. See, for instance, Ramamonjisoa "Blancs et noirs," 41.

73. Jackson, *Political Oratory*, 52.

74. Jackson, *Political Oratory*, 53.

75. See, for instance, Eric Hahonou, "Culture politique, esclavage et décentralisation: La demande politique des descendants d'esclaves au Benin et au Niger," *Politique Africaine* 11 (2008): 169–86; Ould Ahmed Salem, "Bare-foot Activists: Transformations in the Haratine Movement in Mauritania," in *Movers and Shakers: Social Movements in Africa*, ed. Stephen Ellis and Ineke van Kessel (Leiden, Netherlands: Brill, 2009), 156–77; Olivier Leservoisier, "Nous voulons notre part! Les ambivalences du mouvement d'émancipation des Saalfaalbe

Hormankoobe de Djeol (Mauritanie)," *Cahiers d'Études Africaines* 179–80 (2005): 987–1014.

76. Klara Boyer-Rossol, "From the Great Island to the African Continent through the Western World, Itineraries of a 'Return to the Origins' through Hip-hop Music in Madagascar (2000–2011)," in *Marronnage and Arts: Revolts in Bodies and Voices,* ed. S. Meylon-Reinette (Cambridge: Cambridge Scholars Publishing, 2012), 161–77.

77. Freeman, "Speech, Silence, and Slave Descent," 600–617.

78. Denis Regnier, "Les esclaves morts et leur invocation dans les rituels du Sud Betsileo," *Études Océan Indien* 51–52 (2014): 253–76.

79. Somda, "Et le reel serait passé."

80. Regnier, "Pourquoi ne pas les épouser," 114–15.

81. UN Human Rights Council, "Report of the Special Rapporteur on Contemporary Forms of Slavery, Including Its Causes and Consequences. Addendum. Mission to Madagascar (December 10 to 19, 2012)," July 24, 2013, 4.

13

The Comoros

Strategies of Islandness in the Indian Ocean

Iain Walker

The Comoros and Islandness

In the first issue of the *Island Studies Journal*, in a discussion of the possibility of developing a coherent theory of island studies, Pete Hay cites Jean-Didier Hache, who asks, in a somewhat doubtful take on island studies, "whether islands have anything in common besides their watery surroundings."[1] Slightly curiously, Hay did not develop this line of thinking in that particular article, but instead went on to express similar doubts about some of the currents in nissology[2] at the time, concluding with a plea for a phenomenological approach to island studies. This seemed an eminently logical response to the enormous differences in sizes, populations, economies, political systems, cultures, in general, the astonishing diversity of islands that risked rendering an "island studies" paradigm somewhat hollow: what can usefully be said about Manhattan, Iceland, and Bermuda that constitutes them as members of a group that has commonalities and that is qualitatively different from another group that includes places such as São Paolo, Kamchatka, and Gibraltar? There seems to be very little that islands have in common that "mainlands" (and here too, there are problems of definition: are large islands such as Great Britain "mainlands" to their smaller companions?) do not share; and as if this were not enough, the extension—and metaphorization—of the concept of island to desert oases, cities, villages in the rainforest, seemed to render impossible any coherent and cohesive theoretical approach to island studies.[3]

Various attempts have been made to resolve the dilemma by stressing the power relations pertaining between islands and mainlands, by inscribing analyses within the context of postcolonial studies, or by emphasizing the shore and the bounded character of islands (thus differentiating them from oases, for example). These approaches have had some success in analytical terms, but still have not coalesced as "island studies" in any satisfactory fashion.[4] For example, many islands have indeed been colonized and dominated, but so, too, have they themselves colonized and dominated, for example, British islanders on the African or Asian mainland, or Japan in Korea. What seems more useful is to return (perhaps obviously) to, firstly, thinking more specifically about how islandness itself shapes islands—and I use the term *islandness*, which refers to a way of being in the world, rather than *insularity*, since this latter, in its social rather than its geographical sense, is as much a feature of isolated mainland communities as of islands[5] and, secondly, how *locally specific features* of islandness are important in defining islands and framing their relationships with the world.

Specificity and locality are key to any analysis of islands and islandness since islands are islands by virtue of a geographical feature that only has local implications: they are separated *from their neighbors* by water. They may be separated by water from people and places further away, but this is not relevant, nor, indeed, is it a defining feature. Both Great Britain and France are separated from North America by water, but this does not make France an island, nor is Great Britain an island by virtue of the water between it and North America, but rather by virtue of the water that separates it from France: were Great Britain not separated from France by water, no amount of Atlantic Ocean would make it an island.[6] This may sound obvious, but it leads us to an acknowledgment that Britain's power relations with its colonies had little to do with Britain's insular identity: the fact that Britain was an island was largely irrelevant to its relationship with Kenya, for example, but if Britain may not have been peripheral to its colonies in Africa, there is a persuasive argument for suggesting that it is peripheral to the European mainland. Similarly, to turn to the case in hand, I will argue that what is relevant to the Comoros, and to Comorians, is *local* islandness, and consequently *local* peripheralization: peripheralization not to Europe or Asia, but peripheralization within the western Indian Ocean, to the African coast, and to Madagascar. And thus, even though the Comoros have not been particularly peripheral to Europe or Asia, this local peripheralization has been instrumental in shaping relationships with Europeans and Asians.

The second aspect of Comorian islandness concerns the sea itself. In 2013, Hay returned to the theme of islands and their watery surroundings, this time observing what should have been evident from the start but seems to have been lost in the struggle to find commonalities, that all islands are different, but also recognizing that it is the sea that is the defining and the differentiating feature of islands.[7] In the Comoros, it is important to emphasize the role of the sea, this very significant physical feature, in creating a social isolation that subsequently shaped perspectives upon the world. My point of departure here is therefore that it is the specificity of Comorian relationships with the sea and people who arrive from (beyond) it that have shaped Comorian culture, the economy, and social practice generally in ways that are uniquely Comorian—uniquely Comorian responses to islandness. This is not to suggest that other islands are not shaped by the sea since they almost certainly are, nor even that they are not shaped by the sea in the same way since some, too, almost certainly are, but to allow for the possibility of a variety of relationships with the sea and those who come from it. Comorian relationships with the sea are highly ambivalent, the sea is a hostile place, populated by djinns, and those who venture onto it do so at their own risk: only fishermen, a social class with low status, readily venture onto the sea, and their low status is a direct reflection of the fact that they do so.[8] This is all the more peculiar given that Comorians depend on external trade for their well-being: like many islanders, many of their needs are imported. However, with a few exceptions, Comorians have not traded themselves, traveling to the East African coast or to Madagascar, but rather they have relied on others coming to them. This fact requires a particular strategy of engagement with the Other, the offlander (if I may coin an expression for those who are not islanders), and this strategy of engagement has been a constant throughout the history of Comorian interaction with visitors.

In what follows I explore the strategies of interaction that Comorians have developed over the centuries, and I suggest that contemporary Comorian relationships with the world continue to be framed by historical patterns of engagement that have evolved in the context of local islandness. Godfrey Baldacchino asks, "how do islanders 'make sense' and derive meaning out of being at the receiving end of a powerful cultural, financial and technological regime [. . .] that they cannot control?"[9] His answer, that "islanders" exercise 'agency-in-context,' compliance rather than commitment,"[10] is not entirely satisfactory since the reality in the Comorian case is more nuanced: compliance is transformed into commitment, but in a process in which Comorians remain firmly in control, or, perhaps more significantly, in which they believe they remain in control. Nevertheless, they are well aware that in some respects they are relatively powerless. Outsiders have choices and need to be persuaded to come to the islands—in the context of local peripheralization, to come to Ndzuani rather than go to Kilwa—and so Comorians are, initially at least, required to manage relationships within parameters established by the center. In a more Foucauldian sense, the power relations between islanders and offlanders are more processual than might appear at first glance. Islanders are not entirely impotent; they can, in certain fields and at certain times, wield power over outsiders. Comorian responses to their islandness are aimed at exercising agency and rejecting powerlessness and peripherality, either separately or where they coincide.

For analytical purposes, I have characterized Comorian interactions with the world through four phases of alignment: with the Portuguese, the English, the French, and the Arabs. These phases are not arbitrary constructs, but at the same time they did not (and do not) operate to the exclusion of other relationships. There have been other phases, both concurrent and overlapping, and not all islands maintained the same relationships at the same time. Nevertheless, the importance of relationships with external partners has induced Comorians to privilege certain groups of outsiders over others, indeed, seizing with enthusiasm attributes and characteristics of their partners and often rejecting alternative propositions that might appear to be more appealing but which risk perturbing the existing relationships upon which they depend—the proverbial bird in the hand. I am not proposing a functionalist or materialist interpretation of the Comorian worldview, but I do suggest that economic considerations have been fundamental in shaping it, even if these economic considerations later cede place to more symbolic ones and even if they are based on a certain worldview, an apprehension of the world. Thus, regardless of how important these relationships may be to Comorians, basic social structures and cultural practices are preserved (even if flexibly) through time.

The Portuguese: Developing a Strategy

Reconstructions of Comorian history prior to the arrival of European navigators in the region are either largely speculative, based on (sometimes dubious) interpretations of scattered phrases or even isolated words in classical texts, or are based on a hitherto small handful of archaeological findings. It is clear, however, that upon the arrival of the Portuguese in the Indian Ocean at the beginning of the sixteenth century, the islands were deeply embedded in a trading network that extended from southeast Africa and Madagascar through an arc to northern Australia that took in much of the Indian Ocean littoral (and hinterlands) and at its extremities reached into both the western Pacific and the Mediterranean. It has long been a truism that on rounding the Cape of Good Hope, the Portuguese found themselves struggling to participate in markets that had no need of them and to which they had little to offer. The Comorian islands were incorporated into these networks, although, like other small islands with few commodities for sale, effort was required to maintain their relationships. Although details are sparse, it seems that by the fifteenth century the islands were reasonably prosperous places. Ibn Majid[11] suggested that traders could profitably visit the Comoros (of which Ngazidja was the most famous island), as did his student Sulayman,[12] while da Gama's second fleet were told at Mozambique "that these islands produce much meat, much ginger and sugar cane, that they have very good waters and that it is a fertile land."[13] In 1506 Pero Ferreira Fogaça, the captain of Kilwa, reported that "it is [in the Comoros] that Kilwa and Mombasa supply themselves, and all the other islands in the region, and who find themselves stones,"[14] and slaves were apparently a mainstay of the economy, Comorians acting as middlemen, relieving Arab and Turkish traders from having to negotiate the perils of the mainland: traders came to the islands from as far away as the Red Sea and Socotra to purchase slaves.[15]

Although the Portuguese probably realized fairly swiftly that obtaining adequate provisions on the mainland might prove difficult, we have evidence that initial Comorian contacts with the Portuguese were hesitant; this seems logical given the present hypothesis: Comorians would have been well incorporated into regional trading networks and given their interests vested within these networks, it would be unlikely that they should endanger their relationships by choosing to engage with people who at best were unwanted newcomers and at worst had attacked Comorian allies on the coast, for the Comorians would have heard of the Portuguese sack of Mombasa in 1500 and the exaction of tribute from Kilwa in 1502. Thus, when in early April 1503 Vasco da Gama's second fleet was becalmed for a full ten days well within sight of the islands, apparently the islanders made no attempt to approach the ships.[16] The latter were probably somewhat apprehensive about dealing with the newcomers: whether or not they made efforts to encourage them to land is uncertain, but they certainly did not send out any boats, thus appearing to confirm a lack of enthusiasm about the prospect of contact. They would have had little idea of how to deal with these people as they had no blueprint, as it were, for interacting; perhaps they were not sufficiently like the passing mariners to be able to entice them ashore. Nevertheless, ten days is a long time to do nothing, even if it was Id.

Fairly rapidly, however, the prospect of Portuguese supremacy and their desire for foodstuffs seem to have persuaded Comorians that trade was probably in their interests. As noted earlier, Fogaça, the captain of

Kilwa, had recognized the possibility of supplies being obtained from the Comoros, islands both far more fertile (with their volcanic soils) than the African mainland and safer from the depredations of hostile locals. To the Portuguese and the Swahili of the coast, the islands were certainly more accessible than the rather desolate scrubland occupied by non-Muslims in the Mozambique hinterland. In 1506 he twice mentioned the Comoros in letters to the king, in August reporting that they produced large quantities of rice, millet, cattle, goats, chickens, fruit, sugar, ginger, and (again) "stones which are worth much; because they are rare,"[17] and in December suggesting that the Portuguese supply themselves in the Comoros: "Gonçalo Vaaz . . . was to go and discover the islands of Comoro for there is much to discover there . . . in the islands of Comoro, Sire, there are enough supplies to provide for a great number of people."[18] Eric Axelson confirms that there was a shortage of foodstuffs in Kilwa as in Mozambique, stating that supplies "had to be sought from far-lying islands such as Pemba and the Comoros."[19]

There are regrettably few Portuguese texts upon which to draw: unlike their European successors, the French, the Dutch, and the British, the Portuguese rarely left narrative accounts. There is evidence, however, and as Fogaça's enthusiasm might suggest, of a Portuguese presence in the islands. There are references to the Comoros throughout the century during which the Portuguese were effectively the only Europeans present in the ocean. Some are sparse, brief mentions from passing ships, while others are more sustained: in 1521 Sebastião de Sousa wrote to the king to say that trade could be developed with the Comoros;[20] in 1547 Alvaro Barradas visited the islands;[21] and in the 1550s Balthazar Lobo de Sousa was sufficiently well acquainted (or had access to a source sufficiently well acquainted) with the islands to provide quite a lengthy description, largely accurate, that was reproduced in Diego de Couto's *Decadas De Asia*. Lobo de Sousa notes that "a few years ago an honorable nobleman petitioned King Sebastian to grant him a license to conquer [the Comoros]," but this does not seem to have been followed up.[22] Nevertheless, the islands were certainly valued by the Portuguese: "so greatly convenient are these islands to Mozambique, and to the Portuguese who live there, for the supply of provisions, for the surrounding country is most poor and sterile."[23]

If written references to the islands' contact with the Portuguese are sparse,[24] the circumstantial evidence for trade between the two groups is strong. Although not necessarily indicative of direct contact, within a hundred years of the Portuguese arrival, papaya and pineapple were growing in the Comoros; more conclusive, the fact that when other ships began arriving in the archipelago at the very end of the sixteenth century, they found that Portuguese was the language of communication on all the islands, indicate of sustained and widespread contact, and something of a contrast to the situation in Madagascar. Thus, in 1602 the Dutch admiral George Spilberg found that the king of Mwali spoke "tolerably good Portuguese."[25] François Martin arrived in Mwali later the same year to find a rather cosmopolitan place where "many spoke Portuguese,"[26] while François Pyrard (who accompanied Martin and likewise observed the cosmopolitan character of the population) noted that the Wamwali[27] were "very good friends" of the Portuguese.[28] Indeed, upon learning that Pyrard and his companions were French, the Wamwali asked if they, too, were friends of the Portuguese. When Pyrard replied in the affirmative, he was told that he should have gone to Mozambique and done his business there. Do we deduce from this that the Wamwali were suspicious of the French and had no desire to risk their relationship with the Portuguese by trading with a possible enemy? Clearly their relationship with the Portuguese was important, for Pyrard also relates not only that the Portuguese came to the Comoros but that the Comorians would fill their dhows with foodstuffs and take them to Mozambique, where they would barter their cargoes for cotton cloth, gold, and ivory. Further evidence of the Portuguese presence in the region is provided by John Fryer,[29] who suggests that the substantial ruins he saw in Mutsamudu on Ndzuani in 1673 were the remains of a Portuguese factory, and Spilberg who, while at Mayotte, saw a dhow in which Portuguese mestizos were transporting a cargo of slaves to Madagascar:[30] clearly the locally born Portuguese population were as much at home in the region as the Arabs, Turks, and Persians and it is certainly possible—indeed likely—that Portuguese mestizos from Mozambique settled in the Comoros, converting to Islam, marrying local women, and serving as traders, interpreters, and middlemen.

Finally, the length and the significance of the relationship is reflected in the importance of the Portuguese in Comorian culture. The Portuguese have literally become mythical in the islands. The chronicle of Said Hussein[31] states that the first humans to come to the island of Ngazidja were Portuguese and the Bandamadji chronicle,[32] although not according the Portuguese first-settler status, does have them arriving before the Arabs; the Portuguese are also cited as among the first or early settlers in the Mdjongwe myth[33] and in the manuscript of Omar Aboubakari.[34] Given the importance of Arab culture in the Comoros, the temporal priority of the Portuguese is an astounding reversal of social precedence.

This mythologization of the Portuguese is pervasive in the islands. Oral tradition often attributes external non-Arab influences to the Portuguese and both structures and cultural features that are of uncertain provenance are attributed to them. Thus there is, according to tradition, a ruined Portuguese trading post at Ikoni on Ngazidja; Wangazidja tell of villages (on the other side of the island) inhabited by blonde-haired, blue-eyed descendants of Portuguese navigators, this despite the fact that the Portuguese are not stereotypically blonde-haired and blue-eyed; and mysterious tombs in the north and east of the island are Portuguese, and although this may well be so, this claim is inscribed within a wider attribution of all things non-Muslim but foreign to the Portuguese. Inyehele, a fifteenth-century king of Hamahame, on the island's northeast coast, was said to be the issue of the rape of his mother by a Portuguese sailor even though the date of his death (1470) renders this impossible. The high status accorded to the Portuguese is indicative of the importance of the Portuguese to Comorians, and the relationships that they maintained with the latter. Crucial economically, the relationships were underpinned by according the Portuguese a social place in Comorian historical narratives that could, retroactively, validate the economic aspects of those relationships.

The English: Preaching to the Converted

In the early seventeenth century the status of the Portuguese in the Indian Ocean changed somewhat rapidly. Both the English and the Dutch formed officially sanctioned trading companies (the English East India Company in 1600, the Dutch Vereenigde Oostindische Compagnie in 1602) and sent a rapid succession of fleets into the ocean where they encountered and fairly swiftly challenged Portuguese dominance.[35] If early Dutch and English navigators report (as noted earlier) strong pro-Portuguese sentiments in the islands, allegiances shifted surprisingly rapidly as the growing presence of representatives of other European powers led to challenges to the Portuguese presence and to Portuguese superiority. So, if in 1602 Pyrard was told to go and do business in Mozambique, by 1613 the Wamwali seemed to have changed their minds, not only denying that they traded with them, but telling the East India Company captain Walter Payton (in Portuguese, of course) that had the English been Portuguese, "they would have put us all every man to the sword."[36] Shortly thereafter the English were victorious in a battle against a 1,500-ton Portuguese carrack that was run aground on Ngazidja and burned, clearly demonstrating to the Comorian bystanders where their better interests would lie.[37]

One Comorian concern would undoubtedly have been to maintain their customary trading relationships with their kin and coreligionists of the East African coast. The Portuguese seem not to have disrupted these links, but seem rather to have inserted themselves into them. Payton, who returned to Mwali in 1615, records the Comorian role in local trading networks: "They have traffique on the Coast of Melinde, Magadoxo, Mombassa, Arabia and Saint Laurence: they carrie Slaves taken in warres, which they sell for nine or ten Rials of eight, and are sold againe in Portugall for one hundred. At Momboza and Magadoxo I understood of great Trade for Elephants Teeth and Drugges."[38] Sir Thomas Roe, who also stopped at Mwali on his way to the court of the Great Mogul, noted that the locals traded to Mozambique in forty-ton junks, and met a slaver from Lamu taking his cargo to Madagascar.[39] Like the Portuguese before them, the English did not attempt to disrupt these relationships, and were accepted as trading partners.

Nevertheless, although Comorians were anxious to preserve their economic interests, they maintained newcomers at arm's length where local culture and social practices were concerned. Economic proximity was acceptable and welcome; social proximity and undesirable cultural influences were to be avoided, and so Roe, again, notes that while happy to do business, a priest on Mwali "cryed out if we came neere them or their Church, they would kill us."[40] This protection of local culture was also generally enforced regarding women (foreigners were rarely allowed to see them) and on occasion contact generally: at least one group of visitors, intending to visit the main town on Mwali, were turned back on a pathway across the island by hostile villagers who appeared to be unwilling to let them visit parts of the island away from the customary anchorages.[41]

By the end of the seventeenth century the English had decided upon Ndzuani (which they called Johanna) as their preferred port of call in the archipelago, largely due to its safer anchorage: "[Mwali is] the better island of the two, though not so big, nor quite so mountainous; it being more plentifully, as 'tis said, stored with provisions; but not furnished with so safe an harbor for ships as Johanna."[42] More generally, the islands were, for the English, the first reliable port of call after St. Helena on the route to India for, like the Portuguese before them, the English were wary of the mainland; Ndzuani provided a safe anchorage, a reliable source of provisions, and a welcoming population. The islands, and Johanna in particular, were chosen as a reliable port of call for English fleets in the region. By the 1630s, instructions to commanders to call at the Comoros were able to refer simply to "the islands," apparently without ambiguity.[43] By mid-century, so frequent was the passage of English ships in the Comoros that vessels arriving to find no other ships there found this noteworthy.[44]

If the English preferred the Comoros, the sentiment was reciprocal: the English rapidly assumed the status of favorites in the eyes of "Johannamen."[45] Fryer, who visited in 1673, observes how the Wandzuani "are courteous to strangers, but above all to the English."[46] An affinity with the English, as much for their omnipresence as for any particular qualities they might have displayed, led to various offers of land to the newcomers, including "a piece of ground [which] was probably given by the Sultan of Johanna to Captain Christopher Brown when the latter called at the island in the summer of 1626."[47] Brown's Garden, as it came to be known, would be the preferred place of refreshment for English ships for the next two centuries or more. This affinity was also manifested in offers of the island itself. In 1663, the king of Ndzuani wrote to Charles II, offering him his island, although this letter apparently never reached its addressee. The offer (this time of both Ndzuani and Mwali) was renewed by his son and successor, Mynea Shaw, in another letter, taken to London by his brother Abdalla Shaw in 1676. Although the East India Company felt obliged to decline the offer, they did accept the gift of Brown's Garden, formally presented to them during this visit by Abdalla Shaw.[48]

It is not clear what prompted these offers: unlike later offers, which were indeed the product of specific political threats, in the latter part of the seventeenth century there does not seem to have been any particular event that would have menaced Ndzuani.[49] It is possible then that it was inscribed within a general strategy of attracting the English to the island since it was becoming increasingly obvious that they were the group of foreigners most likely to be economically beneficial and who, equally, it would likely have been prudent not to upset. The English were visibly able to exercise their influence over the Portuguese, if only indirectly, as in refusing to side with the Portuguese in a dispute between the latter and the king of Ndzuani in 1662,[50] and perhaps also attracted sympathy during events such as the sinking of the *Herbert*, which was attacked by a numerically superior fleet of French ships as it lay at anchor off Ndzuani in 1690.[51] The English were not only evidently superior to their European competitors (morally, perhaps, if not always victorious militarily), but they appeared to side with Ndzuani in local conflicts, occasionally supporting them in their squabbles with Mwali, either by supplying them with weapons or by transporting Ndzuani troops to Mwali and actively intervening by their sides. This enthusiasm for the English on Ndzuani is well documented; of the other islands we have less information, although given episodes such as the role of the *Scarborough* and the *Severn* in a Ndzuani invasion of Mwali, one might imagine that the English were less favorably viewed there.[52]

Although a command of English would clearly be beneficial to those Wandzuani who wished to do business with the English, the ubiquity of the language on the island suggests that there is something else at work. John Ovington notes that the king's brother spoke English.[53] John Pike, visiting in 1704, commented on the number of Wandzuani who spoke English.[54] And by the end of the century, a visitor could report that "most of the people speak a little English,"[55] which, if true, is quite extraordinary for an island whose inhabitants (unlike later colonized peoples) were under no obligation to do so. Indeed, the evidence is that Wandzuani were not only amicable toward the English, they were attempting to become English: in order to be like the English, so they said, they chose themselves a queen—remarkably swiftly, given that Pike visited in June 1704, barely two years after the accession of Queen Anne to the throne[56]—and by the mid-eighteenth century, these affinities were being expressed explicitly: "Englishman come, alla one brother come," according to the Swede Olof Torén, who visited in 1750.[57] Henry Rooke renders it as "Joanna-man and English-man all brothers,"[58] while Ovington states that it is "a common proverb now among them, *Johanna-man, English-man, all one.*"[59] Shortly thereafter visitors began to report that Wandzuani had also assumed English names: Lord Sidmouth, Admiral Lord Rodney, and Commodore Blankett were just some of the characters familiar to visitors in the late eighteenth and early nineteenth centuries.[60]

Reasons for this affinity for the English—by now the only Europeans regularly visiting the island—were not hard to find. One visitor observed that the local economy was scarcely thriving: "a trifling trade with the neighbouring islands, the continent and the gulphs, in cocoa-nuts, cowries, honey and a few coarse cloths brought them sometimes by small vessels from India."[61] While this observation may not have been particularly well informed—trade with the African coast and the Arabian peninsula in a number of commodities, including slaves, was reasonably well developed—passing ships were a particularly welcome supplement to other sources of revenue: this same source estimated that gifts to the king and purchases from his estates "produce him from each ship five or six hundred dollars."[62] William Milburn provides a helpful list of the payments that should be made to some of these individuals. Thus the "Prince of Wales" (who was, perhaps obviously, the king's son) expected $15 and, "independent of the above . . . asks for, and expects a barrel of gunpowder."[63] Trying to convince the English that they were of their ilk is an understandable strategy: it was aimed, with some success, at establishing a sense of responsibility toward the Wandzuani on the part of the English.

By the early nineteenth century, Johanna would have been as familiar to the English as the English were to the Wandzuani. The island was a regular port of call on the passage to India and a number of civil servants described the island in their memoirs or journals. The English were clearly to be cultivated and encouraged, and, by the same token, their adversaries discouraged. Ovington notes that neither the French nor any other nation were as welcome as the English. We must also remember that, as with the Portuguese, there were English who settled, some voluntarily, others less so, victims of shipwrecks or delinquents thrown off their ships. They would certainly have taken local wives, but also contributed to the dissemination of a knowledge of things English, including the language.[64] Ndzuani was indeed a cosmopolitan place.

The French: Hobson's Choice

By the end of the eighteenth century, not only were the English the preferred trading partners but there was very little competition. The Dutch had long forsaken the Comoros for the Cape of Good Hope, while the French had Île de France (Mauritius). Following the loss of Mauritius to the British in 1814, however, France began to seek other ports of call in the region and returned to Ndzuani. As the prime minister of Ndzuani, who went by the name of Bombay Jack, explained, French interests in the island were to be discouraged at all costs:

> Long, long time since—(early in 1800)—Frenchmen came here—like Joanna very much; ask no questions, come on shore, build huts, buy food, and then begin plant *cotton*. I no like this. Frenchmen very civil, but very sly; when cotton grow and money come, they take Joanna, and we go into the sea: no, no, that not do—Bombay Jack too cunning. Cotton planted—cotton coming up well. One dark night, when Frenchmen all sleep, we go *very quiet*, boil water, and pour it *very quiet* over all cotton plants. Next morning Frenchmen wake—cotton plants all dead; they come to me; I tell 'Cotton always do so—a little time good—good, and then all die one night.' Very well. Frenchmen next day pack up, go on board little ship and go away. Good bye, good bye. (Cited in Mrs. Erskine Norton, "A Visit to Joanna," *The Dublin Penny Journal* 2, no. 78 [1833]: 206.)

Although this episode occurred at what would appear to have been the high point of English-Comorian relations, it also presaged the end. The increased French presence in the region and Comorian participation in the slave trade worked together to marginalize the English even as the latter opened a consulate on Ndzuani.[65] France occupied Mayotte in 1841 (formalized in 1843) and began to register local shipping under the French flag. Due to the lack of an antislavery treaty between Britain and France, French-flagged vessels based in Mayotte (or, indeed, elsewhere) were immune from British inspection. The slave trade had long been the lynchpin of the Comorian economy and became proportionally increasingly important following the opening of the Suez Canal in 1869, when the few remaining ships that had not forsaken Ndzuani for Mauritius finally ceased to call at the island, effectively putting an end to Ndzuani's role as a supply point on the route to India. French "support" for Comorian slave traders (as it was perceived by Comorians) led to the rapid development of rival factions: Mayotte was already French; on Ngazidja the kingdoms (or sultanates), always in conflict, formed pro- and anti-French blocs, or perhaps more accurately pro-French and pro-Zanzibari alliances, the latter implying an often uneasy relationship with the British, which finally led to the cession of the island by the slave-trading sultan Said Ali ibn Said Omar of Bambao. Said Ali's father, Said Omar, was a francophile member of the Ndzuani royal family who had effectively been exiled to Mayotte by the sultan of Ndzuani and who received significant support from France in its attempt to win the archipelago over from the British.[66]

Signs that the end of the Comorians' special relationship with the British were nigh began with the closure of the consulate in 1865. Many Comorians saw British antislavery patrols as contrary to their interests, although some, such as Sultan Abdullah of Ndzuani, signed antislavery treaties with the British with (apparently) no intention of respecting their terms; when the British finally relinquished the Comoros to the French sphere of influence in 1885, this was simply a recognition of a fait accompli, putting an end to a relationship that had lasted for 250 years. France established protectorates over the three remaining islands the following year and despite some appeals to Britain and Zanzibar, the islands were to remain firmly within the French colonial system until the late twentieth century.

Comorian affection for the French developed slowly. Although French connivance (perhaps not explicit) in Comorian slave-trading in the latter part of the nineteenth century was of some importance to the local economy, by the end of the century France had enforced the abolition of slavery and, further, were apparently unconcerned about Comorian economic interests. Much of the agricultural land on all four islands was appropriated by French colonial plantations companies, who drove the local populations off the land and then employed them at derisory wages. Forced to pay taxes, the latter had little choice but to engage in wage labor. Perhaps unsurprisingly, it was Comorians outside the archipelago who embraced their new French identity—the community in Zanzibar fairly rapidly realized that French status had positive repercussions on their position in the British protectorate.[67] Within the islands, however, it was not until mid-century that pro-French sentiment and a sense of French identity became widespread, largely as a result of French efforts to win Comorians over in their struggle against the spread of pan-Arabism and growing nationalist sentiment that had been felt in the Comoros during and immediately following the Second World War.[68] The new status of the island as an autonomous territory—it had hitherto been administered as a province of Madagascar—with attendant responsibilities toward and expectations of the French state provided the impetus for the development of a sense of French identity in the islands. A materialist argument, perhaps, but once there was an economic advantage to being French, then Comorians appeared to be more prepared to do so.

French economic and social investment in the islands, although never substantial, nevertheless grew significantly between 1945 and the 1970s. Infrastructure projects saw the construction or upgrade of roads, schools, airfields, hospitals, and ports, and the islands sent representatives to the Assemblée Nationale in Paris; islanders enjoyed full rights to French citizenship and the freedom of movement that this status accorded them. In the early part of this period, this was of minor concern, but in the 1970s and 1980s, and particularly following independence and as the islands were more closely integrated into world systems, the attractions of the metropole for the education and employment opportunities it offered were evident. During the 1980s Comorian dependence on France, either directly through subsidies and aid programs, or indirectly through France's proxy, the mercenary Bob Denard and his associates, was so complete that no attempt was made either to develop other relationships or to criticize French policy.[69] The economic importance of France was explicitly recognized: in an echo of Bombay Jack's encounter with the French cotton planter, a former American diplomat, when asked why the United States had closed their embassy in the country, explained that every time they wanted to set up a program, the Comorian government had effectively replied, "Can we just check it's ok with the French first?"

Comorian economic dependence upon France was, as one might expect, accompanied by claims to French identity. During the interwar period, when French neglect of the islands reached its zenith, Comorian expressions of social identity remained orientated toward Zanzibar and the Islamic world. Following the war, as France began to invest in the islands, Comorians developed expressions of French identity, and the mythology of colonial schoolchildren obediently reciting "*nos ancêtres les Gaulois*" was transformed into a very real identification with France. These identifications were reflected both in daily practice and in ritual events. Comorians increasingly adopted French dress: by the end of the 1980s, the *kandu* and *kofia* of the men, and the women's *shiromani* were giving way to bareheaded men and women wearing, respectively, shirts and trousers, and dresses, the latter sometimes somewhat revealing.

Expressions of affinity with France included a mastery of the French language, which, while not ubiquitous, was nevertheless (and remains) widespread, analogous, undoubtedly, to the enthusiasm for the use of English in the eighteenth century; and France was long the ideal destination for emigrants, very much to the exclusion of other countries, either in Europe or elsewhere in the region. This enthusiasm for all things French is explicitly recognized by Comorians. As I have noted elsewhere,[70] declarations that "we are more French than the French" are commonplace and this pro-French sentiment was most visibly (and slightly alarmingly) demonstrated by the declaration by secessionist leaders of Ndzuani in the late 1990s that they wished to be recolonized by France. This desire was expressed symbolically in several ways. In particular, the French franc was in common circulation on the island,[71] and the French flag was flown prominently at a number of locations.

While it is expected that a former colony be orientated toward its former colonial power, the extent to which France filled the Comorian imagination in the late twentieth century is indicative of something deeper, akin to the eighteenth-century Comorian enthusiasm for all things English. If it is understandable that the political system be based on the French system, the appropriation of French culture in ritual contexts is more significant. The meals served at wedding feasts are now four courses—a starter, a main dish, salad, and dessert. While the main dish remains quintessentially Comorian (rice and boiled meat), the other courses are very much French in inspiration. Similarly, the internal layout of contemporary houses, the celebration of birthdays, the adoption of Western (qua French) dress in ritual contexts (wedding dresses and lounge suits), all are indicative of a particular form of sociocultural assimilation of things French. That many are associated with European practice more generally does not remove the "Frenchness" of these practices since France is often a synecdoche for Europe generally.[72]

This lack of differentiation does not detract from the symbolism of France: unlike the seventeenth and eighteenth centuries, when ships of several nations visited the islands, for much of the twentieth century, contact with other European nations was minimal. Although there was a regular air service between Moroni and Zanzibar for much of the late twentieth century, contact with both British and Portuguese East Africa was both discouraged and difficult; likewise, diplomatic representation of Western powers in the independent Comorian state was generally limited to France, Belgium, and South Africa (the latter a trade mission). It was difficult for most Comorians to oppose France with another European society simply because there were none with which to compare.

The Arabs: A Return to Roots?

In the 1990s French policy toward Africa in general and the Comoros in particular underwent a realignment. International condemnation of France's role in Rwanda in 1994 and the death of Jacques Foccart in 1997 were accompanied by a growing realization that French neocolonial policies in Africa were no longer in France's best interests.[73] A the same time, France imposed visa requirements upon Comorians without French citizenship who wished to travel to Mayotte, part of a policy aimed at a full political incorporation of Mayotte into the French republic,[74] while visas to mainland France itself, for employment or for education, were becoming increasingly difficult to obtain. Aid programs, formerly operated by the French government, were henceforth largely to be subcontracted to NGOs and the overall budget reduced, while French budgetary support for the Comorian government itself was also cut. From an economic point of view, therefore, France was increasingly reluctant to provide. Comorians would need to look elsewhere.

In 1977 Comorian president Ali Soilihi had applied to join the Arab League. This move, probably doomed to fail given the Soilihi regime's attacks on certain aspects of religious practice in the Comoros, was undoubtedly economic in character. The unilateral declaration of independence of the Comorian State in 1975 prompted the complete withdrawal of French aid; this was followed by the forced repatriation of some 17,000 refugees from Madagascar and a volcanic eruption in the south of Ngazidja, forcing the evacuation of an entire village. The state coffers were empty and, with the exception of China, the revolutionary regime had few friends and less money. The Arab League had the latter, and perhaps could be persuaded to join the ranks of the former. Unfortunately, the application was turned down.

In 1993, under President Said Mohamed Djohar, an Arabophile descendant of the Prophet (and, perhaps ironically, a half-brother of Ali Soilihi), the country lodged another application. This time, according to one of those responsible for receiving the Arab League delegation that visited the islands to discuss the request, more care was taken:

> Djohar told me to assemble the Arab community of Ngazidja, he said it was our last chance to join the Arab League, so let's change our policy. "I'm asking you to receive the delegation at the airport, dressed as Arabs." So 24 of us went to the airport dressed in *thobe* and *keffiyeh*, and we met the delegation, we spoke Arabic to them. The delegation were here for the weekend, there were twelve of them. Djohar asked the local families to receive them in their homes, so they came to my house, we cooked Arab food, *shurba*, *mutabbaq* and *harira*, for them on Thursday. On Friday after prayers they went to the Wadaane's house and they washed their hands with a jug, Arab style, and ate pilau, and after the meals they took the delegation to meet the women. The last meal was with the Saggafs at Mitsamihuli, there they ate sitting on the floor. Before they left they said, "Say no more, there's no need for further investigation" and signed the agreement. (An account of the episode by one of the members of the reception party.)

And, indeed, shortly thereafter Comorians were "certified as Arabs" and admitted to the Arab League.

Over the two decades since the Comoros were granted membership of the Arab League it has become clear that this was a strategy that has borne fruit. Although France remains engaged, the reduced possibilities for travel to France has seen students applying for scholarships to institutions in Arab League member states such as Morocco, Sudan, Kuwait, and Saudi Arabia and returning not only with stronger Islamic affiliations—which causes some disquiet in the country—but with a familiarity with the Arab world that provides not only a basis for further contacts but a template for practice. Similarly, economic opportunities in the islands, increasing shunned by French investors due to political instability and lack of opportunities, are taken up by Arabs, individuals and companies, from the UAE, Syria, Kuwait, and, in the early twenty-first century, Qatar.

Financial and budgetary support is also increasingly being provided by the Arab League, and particularly the Gulf states. Several years ago, the road networks of Ngazidja had fallen into such a state of disrepair that travel not only around the island but in the "streets" of the capital was an undertaking fraught with hazards. A gift of tarmac from Libya quickly solved the worst of the problems. The emir of Sharjah, upon discovering kin in the Comoros, undertook to finance the new Friday mosque in Moroni as well as establishing a technical school and a *waqf* (charitable trust) for the Comoros in Sharjah. More significantly, the Arab League, fellow Muslims,[75] have an interest in the well-being of one of their own and are prepared not only to invest, but to assist. This in not an entirely altruistic affair: as one Comorian diplomat admitted, there is risk that the failings of one of their members bring shame upon the entire Arab League and that for the sake of their own honor, the Islamic states, outwith the framework of the Arab League, have an interest in maintaining a semblance of normality in the Comoros. This at least partially explains gifts such as the 540 million Comorian francs[76] in budgetary assistance given by Qatar in early 2010.

Comorian perspectives upon the Arab world are, predictably, shifting to take account of the economic benefits of "being Arab"; Arabs are once again being presented positively, viewed in a favorable light, particularly when set next to other Comorian partners who, if unnamed, are often implicitly criticized: "The destabilisations of the Comoros have never been committed by the Arab states. We have four heads of state who have been assassinated and the relationships with the Arab League have never been involved. You will never find an Arab state in any way involved in these destabilising attempts. The Arab partners have worked to preserve stability in the archipelago, as seen in Sudan's presence during the liberation of the island of Ndzuani [in 2008]"[77]

In certain respects, this is nothing new: despite historical enthusiasm for the Portuguese, English, and French, Comorian-Arab relationships have always been valued and Arab practices have long been incorporated into Comorian ones. Indeed, the self-identification of Comorians as Arabs is one of the foundations of Comorian culture since to deny Arab origins (or to fail to claim them, which is much the same thing) is to accept mainland African ancestry: pagans and slaves. However, the Arab world was not incorporated into Comorian social discourse or cultural practice in the postwar period in the specifically mimetic way that the French were, nor had Arabs been specifically compared to other partners in a discourse of preference that is characteristic of the processes I have been discussing here.[78] It is only since the late 1990s that a transition toward an Arab-orientated praxis seems to have occurred within the context of general French disengagement but prompted specifically both by the "pull" of Arab League membership and the "push" of the imposition of visa requirements for travelers to Mayotte, the so-called "Balladur visa."

Islander Identities

I have previously analyzed the maintenance of barriers between acceptable, even welcome external influences and core sociocultural practice as integral to Comorian strategies of belonging and interaction in wider contexts.[79] The high degree of dependence upon outsiders and the accompanying hazards of both physical and sociocultural proximity required the establishment of mechanisms by Comorians to manage these relationships: to encourage proximity while preventing what would have been perceived as negative social influences. "Imitation" of others—manifested in claims to Portuguese origins and, as we have seen, "English," "French," or "Arab" behavior—encouraged proximity, but the fact that these forms of behavior were indeed imitative of their partners allowed a distance to be maintained. Imitations were almost caricatures, designed to fool nobody, wherein precisely lay the success of the strategy: flattered and amused by clumsy attempts at imitation, the English continued to visit. Had the imitations been more successful, it is likely that the English might have felt threatened rather than charmed.

In the preceding discussion I have sketched out some of the strategies that Comorians have engaged in in order to manage their relationships with outsiders. These modes of representation have several elements to them. Discursive representations of quite complex relationships and processes are not only revealing about Comorian attitudes toward outsiders but perhaps more importantly retroactively accord Comorians agency that they may not otherwise have had in those relationships. As Wamwali become aware that the English are more likely to offer them economic advantages, they assert hostility toward the Portuguese. The French, not particularly well disposed toward the Johannaman's greatest allies, the English, are unwanted and so they must be dispensed with. Arabs are the new potential providers, and so it is loudly declaimed for all to hear that, unlike others, they have never interfered in the Comoros. However, in all three cases, the declaration is subsequent to changes in relationships between the groups concerned: Wamwali assert hostility toward the Portuguese once they become aware that the Portuguese no longer exercise supremacy among the Europeans in the Indian Ocean. However, making these assertions allows Wamwali to claim ownership of the processes underlying them and thus appear to exercise control over their own destiny.

Secondly, these declarations are claims to identity. Bombay Jack, in relating his story to Mrs. Erskine Norton, is reinforcing a commonality of sentiment between the two: the English would certainly have done likewise and the Comorians really are English: they have the same attitudes toward the same Other. Moreover, as if proof of their common identity, Bombay Jack told Mrs. Erskine this story over a glass of wine in her cabin: one can imagine the party chuckling over how they had duped the French. Indeed, Mrs. Norton seems to have been thoroughly taken in: "Their veneration

for the English is so great," she writes, "that I am sure with a little management, we might effect any change we judged proper,"[80] including,
no doubt, planting cotton. Mrs. Norton was thoroughly amused by her
sojourn on Ndzuani, but bearing in mind that during the twenty years that
had elapsed since the alleged event, Bombay Jack must have told his story
countless times over a glass of wine in an English traveler's cabin, one sus-
pects that the last laugh was on him. The English kept coming, despite
finding Comorians amusing, ridiculous, or both; and despite some English
claims to the contrary, it is unlikely that Comorians ever thought they were
truly English. Comorian claims to identity were part of a process of asserting common interests, a strategy that was hardly unique to the Comoros.

What has all this to do with islandness? On the face of it, Comorians had
no need to engage in any particular strategy in order to attract offlanders.
Islands, for the European navigators, were relatively easily accessible: an
English ship had nothing but St. Helena between the Downs and Johanna,
a voyage of some 10,000 miles; a journey by land of similar length in the
seventeenth century would have been arduous and fraught with perils.
However, for local neighbors, access is somewhat more complicated. An
inhabitant of the mainland might have a variety of ways of traveling from
one place to another—by foot, on the back of an animal, by canoe, stop-
ping here and there on the way to take refreshment or shelter from the
rains; but prior to the advent of air travel in the twentieth century, an East
African attempting to reach the Comoros could do so only by boat, with
the attendant insecurity and costs.

Somewhat paradoxically, therefore, an island is easy to reach from afar
but comparatively difficult to reach from nearby. Neighbors were therefore
less likely than more distant people to engage with the Comoros; given the
difficulty of attracting neighbors (who were more likely to deal with their
own neighbors), Comorians could at least compete on an equal footing
with those from afar. But, for the Europeans, and all other things being
equal, the choice was almost arbitrary: to call at Ndzuani or Malindi made
little difference to them.[81] Active engagement was required and the stakes
were higher since mainlanders could trade with neighbors, Comorians had
none.

Indeed, it is the fact that the Comoros are not particularly isolated that
bestows the characteristic of islandness upon them: this is the "apparent contradiction between 'openness and closure'" referred to by Baldacchino.[82] Islands are not particularly difficult to get to: it just requires
that first step and vice versa, of course. A further feature that I suggest
shapes Comorians'—and undoubtedly other islanders' perspectives on
the world—is the horizon: for islanders, the rest of the world is visibly

absent from the horizon. This observation is important since it is likely to induce a sense of unease among people who are wary of the sea as it disempowers: Comorians had no knowledge, no way of predicting, and no way of inquiring when the next ship would arrive. While this is equally true of mainlanders in a port, the difference is that mainlanders are not isolated, surrounded by sea, and are not as dependent upon those arriving, unheralded, from the sea, for their well-being, even their very existence. Finally, although there have been historical shifts in the character of peripheralization largely due to the shift from sea to air travel, I suggest that the same strategies are being engaged today despite the different modes of communication for in several important ways, air travel is similar to sea travel: the lack of control over arrivals, the unpredictability of visits, the limited points of access, perhaps even a fear of the air analogous to the fear of the sea. Comorians' social practice and strategies of engagement have been developed over many centuries of interactions through maritime links and remain resistant to the development of air travel.

Notes

1. Jean-Didier Hache, "Toward a Political Approach to the Island Question," in *Competing Strategies of Socio-Economic Development for Small Islands*, ed. Godfrey Baldacchino and Rob Greenwood (Charlottetown: Institute of Island Studies, University of Prince Edward Island, 1998), cited in Pete Hay, "A Phenomenology of Islands," *Island Studies Journal* 1, no. 1 (2006): 20; compare with Godfrey Baldacchino, "Editorial: Islands: Objects of Representation," *Geografiska Annaler: Series B, Human Geography* 87, no. 4 (2005): 247–51.

2. "The Study of Islands on Their Own Terms," Grant McCall, "Nissology: A Proposal for Consideration," *Journal of the Pacific Society* 63–64 (1994): 106.

3. Just as an example, Phillip Vannini's somewhat romanticized vision of island life could equally well apply to, say, the western New South Wales town of White Cliffs, more than 310 miles from the sea. That said, Australia is an island, too. Phillip Vannini and Jonathan Taggart, "Doing Islandness: A Nonrepresentational Approach to an Island's Sense of Place," *Cultural Geographies* 20, no. 2 (2013): 225–42.

4. For an overview, see Lisa Fletcher, "'. . . Some Distance to Go': A Critical Survey of Island Studies," *New Literature Review* 47–48 (2011): 17–34.

5. Thomas Hylland Eriksen, "A Future-Oriented, Non-ethnic Nationalism? Mauritius as an Exemplary Case," *Ethnos* 3–4 (1993): 197–221; Stewart Williams, "On Islands, Insularity, and Opium Poppies: Australia's Secret Pharmacy," *Environment and Planning D: Society and Space* 28, no. 2 (2010): 290–310; Francois Taglioni, "Insularity, Political Status and Small Insular Spaces," *Shima:*

The International Journal of Research into Island Cultures 5, no. 2 (2011): 45–67; and not all islands are "insular."

6. Note that the water between Britain and Ireland is not a defining feature either: the landmass would still be an island if the two islands were joined. In the first instance, islands are defined by their relationships to continents and not to other islands.

7. There is a small subset of islands in lakes and rivers, few of which have significant populations. There are some exceptions, such as the island of Montreal and Île Jésus, both in Quebec, with populations of 1.9 million and 400,000 respectively, and a number of African lacustrine islands, such as Idjwi (Lake Kivu) and Ukerewe (Lake Victoria), both with populations in excess of 100,000, but none of these are more than a couple of miles from the "mainland."

8. Iain Walker and Moussa Said Ahmed, "Two Fisherman's Songs from Ngazidja, Comoro Islands," *Wasafiri* 26, no. 2 (2011): 59–62. In this respect, it would be difficult to argue that all islands are alike: Polynesians are not, to the best of my knowledge, afraid of the sea.

9. Godfrey Baldaccino, "Studying Islands: On Whose Terms? Some Epistemological and Methodological Challenges to the Pursuit of Island Studies," *Island Studies Journal* 3, no. 1 (2008): 40.

10. Baldaccino, "Studying Islands," 41.

11. Ahmad ibn Mājid al-Sa'dī, *As-Sufaliyya: "The Poem of Sofala." Arabic Navigation Along the East African Coast in the 15th Century,* trans. Ibrahim Khouri (Coimbra: Junta de Investigações Científicas do Ultramar, 1983).

12. Sulayman ibn Ahmad al Mahri, "al 'Umda al Mahariyya fi dabt al 'Ulum al Bahariyya," in *Arab Nautical Sciences: Navigational Texts and Their Analysis,* part 1, vol. 1, ed. Ibrahim Khuri (Damascus: Arab Academy of Damascus, 1970).

13. Paul Teyssier and Paul Valentin, *Voyages de Vasco da Gama: relations des expéditions de 1497–1499 & 1502–1503: récits & témoignages* (Paris: Éditions Chandeigne: Librairie Portugaise de Paris, 1995), 274.

14. Eric Axelson, *South-East Africa, 1488–1530* (London: Longmans, Green and Co., 1940), 243. The stones were possibly basalt for construction purposes since coral was presumably available on the mainland. The English would also have had recourse to these stones in the late seventeenth century for repairs at Fort St. George in Madras.

15. Claude Allibert and Said Korchid, "Une description turque de l'Océan Indien au XVIè siècle. L'Océan Indien Occidental dans le kitab-I Bahrije de Piri Re'is (1521)," *Etudes Océan Indien* 10 (1988): 9–51.

16. The Portuguese stated that the islanders (possibly of Ndzuani) lit fires in an attempt to attract their attention, but this is only supposition—the islanders could certainly have approached the ships in canoes had they so desired—and the fires may have been lit simply as part of the celebrations of Id al Fitr. The Portuguese, for their part, did not land since their ships were full of plunder from India and they had no desire to risk losing their cargo to hostile islanders. Jean Philibert Berjeau, ed., *Calcoen, a Dutch Narrative of the Second Voyage of*

Vasco da Gama to Calicut, Printed at Antwerp Circa 1504 (London: Basil Montagu Pickering, 1874).

17. Axelson, *South-East Africa*, 240–43.

18. Letter from Pero Ferreira Fogaça, captain of Kilwa, to the King. Kilwa, December 22, 1506, in *Documents on the Portuguese in Mozambique and Central Africa*, vol. 1, ed. A. da Sylva Rego, T. W. Baxter, and E. E. Burke (Lisboa Centro de Estudos Históricos Ultramarinos, 1962), 759–61; See also Axelson, *South-East Africa*, 240–43.

19. Axelson, *South-East Africa*, 90.

20. Letter of September 17, 1521, summary in Axelson, *South-East Africa*, 263, but otherwise unpublished.

21. Barradas was apparently wrecked there, but managed to save his cargo. Gaspar Correa, *Lendas da India*, vol. 4, part 2 (Lisbon: Typographia Da Academia Real Das Sciencias, 1866), 598.

22. Diego de Couto, *Da Asia de Diogo de Couto* (Lisbon: Na Regia Officina Typografica, 1782), VII, iv, 5:318.

23. François Pyrard, *Voyage de François Pyrard de Laval contenant sa navigation aux Indes Orientales, Maldives, Moluques, Bresil; les divers accidens, adventures et dangers qui lui sont arrivez en ce voyage* (Paris: Samuel Thiboust, 1619), 49.

24. Many of the letters summarized in *Alguns documentos* and in *Documents on the Portuguese* no longer appear to exist, possibly lost in the Lisbon earthquake and fire of 1755.

25. René Augustin Constantin de Renneville, *Recueil des voyages qui ont servi à l'établissement et aux progrès de la Compagnie des Indes orientales, formée dans les Provinces unies des Païs-bas*, vol. 4 (Rouen: Pierre Caillous, 1725), 44.

26. François Martin, *Description du premier voyage faict aux Indes Orientales par les François en l'an 1603* (Paris: Laurens Sonnius, 1604), 23.

27. I use here Comorian linguistic conventions for naming islanders, prefixing the name of the island with *m-* (singular) or *wa-* (plural).

28. Pyrard, *Voyage de François Pyrard*, 47.

29. John Fryer, *A New Account of East-India and Persia, in Eight Letters Being Nine Years Travels Begun 1672 and Finished 1681* (London: Printed by R. R. for Ri. Chiswell, 1698).

30. Fryer, *A New Account of East-India and Persia.*

31. Sultan Chouzour, "Histoire et sociologie de Ngazidja. Le manuscrit de Saïd Hussein," *Etudes Océan Indien* 1 (1982): 16–53.

32. Moussa Said Ahmed, *Guerriers, Princes et Poètes aux Comores dans la Littérature Orale* (Paris: L'Harmattan, 2000).

33. Widespread, e.g., Mariama Ali Mkufundi, "L'origine des gens aux Comores et la coutume de Manyahuli," *Etudes Océan Indien* 1 (1982): 149–51.

34. Guy Cidey (Fou'ndi Kana-Hazi), *Histoire des Iles: Ha'ngazidja, Hi'ndzou'ani, Maïote et Mwali* (St. Denis: Editions Djahazi, 1997); Gernot Rotter, *Muslimische Inseln vor Ostafrika. Eine Arabische Komoren-Chronik des 19. Jahrhunderts* (Beirut: Franz Steiner Verlag, 1976).

35. The French were slightly slower to appear, although a number of ships appeared under the aegis of a succession of short-lived trading companies prior to the establishment of the Compagnie française pour le commerce des Indes orientales in 1664. Note that Portuguese relationships with others in the Indian Ocean was affected by the Iberian union of crowns between 1580 and 1640, which included negative effects on the historical alliance with England and a subordination of Portuguese colonial interests to those of the Spanish.

36. Samuel Purchas, ed., *Purchas his Pilgrimes*, vol. 2 (London: Printed by William Stansby for H. Fetherstone, 1625), 489.

37. William Foster, ed., *Letters Received by the East India Company from Its Servants in the East: Transcribed from the 'Original Correspondence' Series of the India Office Records Vol V. 1617 (January to June)* (London: Sampson Low, Marston, 1901), 142–48.

38. Purchas, *Purchas his Pilgrimes*, 529.

39. Purchas, *Purchas his Pilgrimes*, 536–38.

40. Purchas, *Purchas his Pilgrimes*, 537.

41. Robert Challes, *Journal du voyage des Indes Orientales: à Monsieur Pierre Raymond, conseiller secrétaire du Roi, receveur général des finances du Bourbonnais; Relation de ce qui est arrivé dans le royaume de Siam en 1688* (Genève: Droz, 1998), 123–24.

42. Fryer, *A New Account of East-India and Persia*, 15–16; compare with William Foster, *The English Factories in India 1624–1629. A Calendar of Documents in the India Office, etc.* (Oxford: Clarendon Press, 1909), 356.

43. William Foster, *The English Factories in India 1630–1633. A Calendar of Documents in the India Office, etc.* (Oxford: Clarendon Press, 1910), passim.

44. For example, Foster, *The English Factories in India 1624–1629*, 263, 265.

45. Although perhaps not exclusively: the Dutch seem to have been welcome at Mayotte for much of the seventeenth century, until such time as the colony at the Cape of Good Hope, founded in 1652, replaced the Comoros as a Dutch supply point on the route east.

46. Fryer, *A New Account of East-India and Persia*, 19.

47. William Foster, *The English Factories in India 1637–1641. A Calendar of Documents in the India Office, etc.* (Oxford: Clarendon Press, 1912), 170. This would appear to be the first mention of Brown's Garden, which lay about a mile west of Mutsamudu where the village of Paje is today.

48. Streynsham Master, *The Diaries of Streynsham Master 1675–1680 and Other Contemporary Papers Relating Thereto*, ed. Sir Richard Carnac Temple, vol. 1 (London: J. Murray, 1911), 235. See India Office records E/3/88, *East India Company, Original Correspondence. Letter Book 5, 1672–1678*; see also reference (presumably) to this offer in John Ovington, *A Voyage to Suratt, in the Year, 1689, Giving a Large Account of That City, and Its Inhabitants, and of the English Factory There* (London: Printed for Jacob Tonson, 1696), 110.

49. It is possible that the offers were prompted by growing pirate activity in the region, although the worst excesses of the pirates did not occur until the end of the seventeenth century. In the late eighteenth and early nineteenth

centuries, raids by Malagasy slavers led the rulers to offer to place the islands under British protection on several occasions: in 1796, in 1800, and a third time in 1803, this latter being an offer of all four islands. See India Office Records, H/473 *Wellesley Papers No. 17 1799–1800,* "Letter from King Abdulla of Johanna to Duncan 18th July 1800, Offering the Island to the Company," India Office Records, H/511 *Home Miscellaneous Series, Letters, 1807–1813.* "Memorandum Relative to the Offer of King Baba to Cede the Island of Johanna to the Company 16th Aug 1796 to 25th Feb 1807."

50. William Foster, *The English Factories in India 1661–1664. A Calendar of Documents in the India Office, etc* (Oxford: Clarendon Press, 1923), 130,

51. See Robert Challe, *Journal du voyage des Indes Orientales: à Monsieur Pierre Raymond, conseiller secrétaire du Roi, receveur premier des finances du Bourbonnais; Relation de ce qui est premie dans le royaume de Siam en 1688* (Geneva: Librairie Droz S.A., 1998); Ovington, *A Voyage to Suratt.*

52. Anne Molet-Sauvaget, *Documents anciens sur les iles Comores (1591–1810)* (Paris: Centre d'études et de recherches sur l'Ocean Indien occidental, INALCO. Travaux et documents no. 28, 1994).

53. Ovington, *A Voyage to Suratt,* 111.

54. Molet-Sauvaget, *Documents anciens sur les iles Comores (1591–1810).*

55. Henry Rooke, *Travels to the Coast of Arabia Felix and from Thence by the Red Sea and Egypt to Europe, Containing a Short Account of an Expedition Undertaken against the Cape of Good Hope. In a Series of Letters* (London: Printed for R. Blamire, 1783), 26; it might be prudent to read this as "most of the people he met."

56. Molet-Sauvaget, *Documents anciens sur les iles Comores (1591–1810),* 67.

57. Olof Torée, *Voyage de Mons. Olof Torée aumonier de la Compagnie suedoise des Indes Orientales, fait à Surate, à la Chine &c. depuis le premier Avril 1750. jusqu'au 26. Juin 1752* (Milan: Chez les Freres Reycends, 1771), 12.

58. Rooke, *Travels to the Coast of Arabia Felix,* 26.

59. Ovington, *A Voyage to Suratt,* 118.

60. As cited in almost every account by visitors. See, for example, William Jones, "Remarks on the Island of Hinzouan, or Johanna," *Asiatic Researches* 2 (1807): 77–107; Anon., *A Letter from a Gentleman on Board an Indiaman to His Friend in London, Giving an Account of the Island of Joanna in the Year 1784* (London: John Stockdale, 1789); see also Jeremy Prestholdt, "Similitude and Empire: On Comorian Strategies of Englishness," *Journal of World History* 18, no. 2 (2007): 113–38, for a lengthy and illuminating discussion of Ndzuani and the English.

61. Anon., *A Letter from a Gentleman on Board,* 17–18.

62. Anon., *A Letter from a Gentleman on Board,* 12.

63. William Milburn, *Oriental Commerce: Containing a Geographical Description of the Principal Places in the East Indies, China, and Japan, with Their Produce, Manufactures, and Trade* (London: Black, Parry, and Co, 1813), 77.

64. See William Foster, *The English Factories in India 1642–1645. A Calendar of Documents in The India Office, etc.* (Oxford: Clarendon Press, 1913); see also

John-Henry Grose, *A Voyage to the East-Indies, with Observations on Various Parts There* (London: Printed for S. Hooper and A. Morley, 1757), 38.

65. The British consulate on Ndzuani was opened in November 1848. The first consul, Josiah Napier, died and was replaced by William Sunley in 1852. See Gary Clendennen and Peter Nottingham, *William Sunley and David Livingstone: A Tale of Two Consuls* (Madison: African Studies Program, University of Wisconsin, 2000); Zanzibar Archives Series AA1/5, *Correspondence Outgoing from Johanna Consulate. 1848–1866*.

66. This period of Comorian history has received significant attention and it is not my intention to repeat it here. See Malyn Newitt, *The Comoro Islands: Struggle against Dependency in the Indian Ocean* (Boulder: Westview Press, 1984); Jean Martin, *Comores: quatre îles entre pirates et planteurs* (Paris: L'Harmattan, 1983).

67. Iain Walker, "Identity and Citizenship among the Comorians of Zanzibar, 1886–1963," in *The Indian Ocean: Oceanic Connections & Creation of New Societies*, ed. Abdul Sheriff and Engseng Ho (London: Hurst & Co., 2014).

68. See, for example, reports and correspondence from the period in CAOM GGM/6(8)D32, Gouvernement Général de Madagascar, fonds local, Politique et administration generale, *Madagascar. Affaires comoriennes. 1937–1948*.

69. The egregious exception to this was the repeated UN General Assembly resolutions on Mayotte between independence and 1994. France remained in occupation of Mayotte following the Comorian declaration of independence and the island remains a French possession. See Wilfrid Bertile, *Mayotte à l'heure de la départementalisation* (Paris: Harmattan, 2012) for a recent overview of the political history of Mayotte.

70. See Iain Walker, "Mimetic Structuration, or, Easy Steps to Building an Acceptable Identity," *History and Anthropology* 16, no. 2 (2005): 187–210; Iain Walker, *Becoming the Other, Being Oneself: Constructing Identities in a Connected World* (Newcastle: Cambridge Scholars Publishing, 2010).

71. Admittedly partly as a result of an embargo placed on the island by the federal authorities in Moroni, which, among other things, prevented supplies of banknotes from reaching Ndzuani.

72. Speaking once of a friend with a Comorian, I pointed out, in response to a comment about the French, that Luca was in fact from Italy. "Yes," came the reply, "he's a Frenchman from Italy."

73. Perhaps cynically, I am hesitant to suggest that France realized they were no longer acceptable, but this is possible.

74. Now achieved, with the departmentalization of Mayotte in 2011: for the purposes of our discussion, we now leave Mayotte behind.

75. All the Arab League states have Muslim majorities and although the organization has no official religion, it is clear that Islam is a principle that does much to foster a sense of cohesion within the organization.

76. Slightly more than €1 million.

77. Mouslimou Ben Moussa, former Comorian ambassador to Saudi Arabia, interviewed in *Al Watwan*, September 24, 2013, 4.

78. Although an argument may be made for this having been done in the interwar period of French neglect. Note that European visitors' travel narratives often referred to the presence of Arabs in the Comoros, either residents or traders, but only in passing and it is difficult to piece together much beyond an awareness that the Europeans were very much peripheral to daily life in the islands.

79. Walker, *Becoming the Other, Being Oneself.*

80. Norton, "A Visit to Joanna," 207.

81. This is not entirely true since, as already observed, the Portuguese found the Mozambique hinterland far less prosperous and more hostile an environment in which to trade than the Comoros. However, the choice could as easily have been a more prosperous site on the mainland.

82. Godfrey Baldacchino, "The Coming of Age of Island Studies," *Tijdschrift voor Economische en Sociale Geografie* 95, no. 3 (2004): 274; compare with Thomas Hylland Eriksen, "In Which Sense Do Cultural Islands Exist?," *Social Anthropology* 1, no. 1b (1993): 133–47.

14

Gendered Pioneers from Mayotte

An Ethnographic Perspective on Travel and Transformation in the Western Indian Ocean

Michael Lambek

Islands of a certain size impose constraints but also opportunities on their inhabitants. Marginal to large landmasses and to the states and empires that occupy them, they can sometimes evade the full effects of colonialism or manipulate them to their own advantage, maintaining a sense of community, autonomy, and difference. In some circumstances, like Hong Kong, they may become wealthy hubs of commerce, while in others, like Antigua, they subside in impoverishment. In the former case they may attract population, while in the latter they are characterized by emigration. These are ideal types. In this chapter I chart the actual experience of residents of Mayotte, a former French colony and an island that has managed to move between these extremes.

When I first conducted fieldwork in Mayotte (Maore) in 1975, the population was around 45,000 in an area some 145 square miles. By 2001 the population had nearly tripled, and according to the 2012 census, it reached 212,645 inhabitants. In this chapter, I focus on the dynamics of expansion, not only population growth within Mayotte, but the sense of the borders of citizenship extending widely beyond its literal shores. My account is ethnographic and also historical, that is, it gives an ethnographic account of a specific period of history, roughly from 1975 to 2002 when I completed the first draft.

According to long-standing cartographic and geographic convention, the territories of islands cannot expand and contract the way those on large landmasses do. Yet the reach of states extends beyond individual landmasses, reconfiguring places and the distances between them. Over the years of my study, the distance between Mayotte and other places has both stretched and shrunk in various ways. Many of the people counted in the 2001 census of Mayotte resided at least part-time in Réunion, 1,056 miles distant and accessible by direct flight. Politically, Mayotte detached itself in 1976 from the Comoro Islands (as they became liberated from France as an independent republic). Mayotte was then demarcated by the French state as a *collectivité territoriale*, changing status in June 2001 to *collectivité départmentale*, and in March 2011 a full *département d'outre mer*.[1] Whatever else these statuses mean, they have enabled people to readily acquire the papers to move freely between Mayotte and Réunion (a département d'outre mer of long standing) and even to metropolitan France (almost 5,600 miles distant) and within the EU, and to enjoy rights of citizenship in these places. By contrast, the nearest island in the Comoro Archipelago is only about 43 miles distant, but it has become another country.

In this chapter I examine aspects of this new intranational mobility. My attention is largely restricted to people originating in the pair of neighboring villages of Kibushy speakers I have studied since 1975 and which I refer to as Lombeni. This chapter utilizes data collected on short visits to both Mayotte and Réunion in the summers of 2000 and 2001, as well as during a number of earlier stays in Mayotte and Mahajanga, Madagascar. At the time, Mayotte was in the process of what the French government referred to as an *évolution statuaire* (statutory evolution), subject to evaluation but likely en route to full integration in the French state (as in fact happened). Political boundaries and identities really did change. Travel between Mayotte, Réunion, and metropolitan France became "intranational" rather than international, and migrants from Mayotte formed "internal" diasporas in Réunion and the metropole. Conversely, travel to the other islands in the Comoro archipelago itself became more difficult, while travel from them to Mayotte became highly desirable. However, the focus of this chapter is not on the flooding of Mayotte by people from the other Comoro Islands seeking entry to fortress Europe via the gateway that Mayotte has become.

People traveled off Mayotte for a number of reasons, including pilgrimage, education, pleasure, and trade. Most saliently, because of the novelty, numbers involved, distance, and duration, people migrated to Réunion, and increasingly to metropolitan France, in search of economic opportunity. Those who did so were frequently originally among the poorer members of the community. They hoped to find work, but they went, in the first instance, because of the greater social benefits available. Until Mayotte achieved full departmental status, its citizens had rights to greater benefits from the state if they resided in Réunion or metropolitan France than in Mayotte itself. Benefits included higher allowances for children, unmarried mothers, seniors, and the unemployed, and for housing. During this period, virtually all people from Mayotte (Maorais) living in Réunion or France said they planned to return permanently to Mayotte. Mayotte, they said, was where they felt "really at home" (*teña an nakahy*).

Three Takes on Change

When I returned to Mayotte in 2000 after five years' absence, people had three things they wanted to tell me. One was a narrative of prosperity and growth. This was especially evident in the young people who had achieved the educational qualifications to gain jobs in the white-collar sector or in skilled trades as drivers, electricians, etc. Their wealth, prospects, and outlook were particularly displayed at weddings, celebrated by means of elaborate *dîners-dansants* at which, as one participant admitted, they "played at" (or "practiced") being European (*vazaha*). The "suitcase" (*valise*) that new husbands brought their wives and that once contained clothing and jewelry had expanded to include refrigerators, freezers, television sets, VCRs, and the occasional washing machine, all paraded on the back of a truck. But the positive narrative was also evident in the voices of older and poorer people.

When Dady Aïsha, one of the oldest women of Lombeni, looked down from her house on the hillside, she expressed satisfaction at the changes in her view. "The community is clear now," she said, "with no more dirty palm thatch." The houses of raffia poles and wattle and daub that had once stood in a clearing in the secondary forest had been replaced by structures of cement and brick with metal roofs and their number had doubled. The forest had retreated and the village trees—coconut, kapok, and fruit—had fallen in storms or were cut down on French government orders. Bulldozers cut steps for new houses into the hills, exposing gashes of red earth. The village, which had been reached in 1975 only by canoe or steep forest paths, now had paved roads traversed by school buses, taxis, and the cars of a large number of daily commuters.

Dady Aïsha was emphatic that the present was better than the past, and indeed everyone spoke approvingly about the changed appearance of the village. Those who had traveled appreciated the even larger and "cleaner" communities in Réunion. From her balcony above St. Dénis, Dady Moussy, another older woman from Mayotte, spoke in terms similar to those of Dady Aïsha about the very different (and spectacular) view there. She waxed eloquent, not over the dramatic steep green and flower-covered hillsides, nor the blue expanse of ocean, but over the urban growth, the conquest of the countryside by the city, and the increase in population it represented.

In Mayotte, the appearance of "modernity" and the expansion of houses and people was mirrored by a retreat of the spirits that once lurked on the outskirts of the villages. It was the bush spirits, not humans, who disliked the smell of gasoline or were disturbed by the noise of machines and who moved deeper into the forest. In other words, spirits migrated in the opposite direction from humans. It was not that people have stopped believing in spirits, but rather that the conditions for encountering or knowing spirits of this kind contracted.[2] In sum, people approved of the outward changes and the new opportunities. Lingering doubts or anxieties at cultural loss were displaced elsewhere.

The second thing people had to tell me, in some contradiction to the first, was a narrative of impoverishment, commoditization, and the final collapse of the agricultural economy. Dry rice cultivation, once the basis of subsistence, had been abandoned over a decade earlier due to declining yields, changes in the allocation of labor, and the availability of relatively cheap (though less tasty) imports. Ylang-ylang and vanilla, cash crops that during the 1970s had created a mini-boom and comprised a substantial form of wealth for enterprising villagers, no longer had a significant market and had been largely uprooted (following earlier histories of sugarcane, copra, and sisal). In 2000, banana plants were suffering from disease or lack of water and a high rate of theft; tomato, and chili pepper no longer flourished without fertilizer, pesticides, or irrigation; and even manioc was less productive. "Farming," concluded my mentor, Tumbu Vita, "can no longer support people."

Not only did people purchase much of their food, they struggled with a host of new or growing expenses: water, electricity, and phone bills, schoolbooks, clothing, and packed lunches for their children. Many adults suffered in demeaning, low-paying jobs or unemployment, and there was a pervasive sadness among those who no longer had the means to do decent work.

Tumbu Vita, who generally shared Dady Aïsha's appreciation of the present, summed it up: "What was better about the past was food. Everyone could eat. Now it is difficult—everyone needs money. From the moment children first open their eyes they need money. Our country is now fixed up [*taninay voadzary*]. We have cars and electricity. Houses are better, there are refrigerators, and so on. But *we have become poor*. There are lots of nice objects but now one cannot eat without money." He describes a shift from primarily subsistence and cash crop cultivation to wage labor, unemployment, and welfare.

The third thing people talked about, and again in some contradiction to the first, was that the village was "empty." A large number of those born and raised there, people with rights of residence and owners or builders of village houses, were absent. For the most part, they had not moved to Mamoudzou, the urban core of Mayotte, where, during earlier decades, a number of enterprising people had lived. That kind of residential dislocation for work had been partly replaced by daily commuting.

"Everyone is in Réunion [Laruñó] or France [Farantsa]," people said. Indeed, almost every family had kin in those places and many of those who had not yet gone were thinking about it. Although some young people had left to pursue their studies, often on government scholarships, the main reason people gave for migration was not the first narrative of expansive modernity but the second one of impoverishment, namely, that they could no longer survive on Mayotte. The majority of those who make the trip were people without work. In the face of the demise of both subsistence and cash crop production, they were former cultivators or the offspring of cultivators who had not been able to complete French schooling or acquire employment as skilled labor.

Although life in Réunion was more expensive and more commoditized than in Mayotte, state benefits were higher and enabled both social reproduction and some savings. Frequently women went first, started collecting unemployment and child benefits, and then sent their husbands money for a ticket. Their partners followed and collected unemployment as well. Because Islamic marriages were not recognized by the state and because the women went ahead, some households were also able to take advantage of allowances offered to single mothers.

Empty, Growing Villages

How to account for the "emptiness" yet expansion of the villages? There were two factors. First, social reproduction has always been marked by the building of houses for young women on their first marriage, and the goal of married couples has been both to provide such houses for their daughters and, more recently, to build better houses for themselves. Paradoxically, housing is one of the things that fuels migration; people emigrate in order to acquire the means to build houses at home in Mayotte. Houses were often under construction or even completed in the village while their owners continued to live in Réunion.

The move to Réunion, everyone said, was temporary. As soon as the level of benefits was raised in Mayotte and equalized with the rest of France, people would move back. The migrants were biding their time. There was great hope, unrealized, that the equalization of benefits would be an outcome of the change in political status arranged in 2000. The migrants were also ensuring their children acquired skills that would prove income generating upon their return. Young people took courses and did apprenticeships in Réunion and France as plumbers, electricians, bakers, auto mechanics, gendarmes, and so forth.

Second, most houses were in fact occupied, but the owners had been temporarily replaced by Anjouanais. These were economic refugees who had crossed from Anjouan at some considerable risk to themselves in small boats during the night. Prior to 1976 Anjouan and Mayotte formed part of a single country and people could move easily between the neighboring islands. But the same political transformation that enabled people with identity papers issued by Mayotte to travel freely to Réunion prevented people from Anjouan (Ndzwani), Grande Comore (Ngazidja), and Moheli (Mwali) from migrating to Mayotte. Without papers, they were somewhat dependent on local villagers, who hired them for odd jobs, cattle guarding, and, of course, house construction. Salaries were neither regulated nor taxed, and the village employers, who were poor themselves, uneasily recognized the exploitation. If discovered by the police, migrants were sent back to Anjouan.

Unlike the majority of economic migrants from Mayotte to Réunion, the Anjouanais were not already married, or at least did not travel with their families. Indeed, they sought to legitimate their new residence by means of kinship and affinity. Some linked up with kin who were the descendants of earlier generations of migrants. Many engaged in marriage (that is, in the first instance, Islamic unions, not registered by the state) with citizens. Young women became the second (or more) polygynous wives of established villagers or the first wives of those too poor to purchase a sufficiently large "suitcase," while male migrants often found divorced or widowed local women. This gave them a foothold in the community and a source of livelihood, but still left them outside state law and benefits.

The picture is one of successive displacements: as people from Mayotte moved to Réunion and France, Comorians moved to Mayotte. However, the two movements are not equivalent. The first is legal and the second informal. In the first, the migrants both received state benefits and expect them as their right, while in the second the migrants did not receive most benefits and were much more vulnerable. Moreover, while the Maorais in Réunion expected to return home and invested in that return, I suspect most Anjouanais had fewer such hopes or were less likely to realize them; their return home was through force. Anjouanais migrants established new roots through marriage and kinship in Mayotte in a manner that most Mahorais have not done in Réunion. Thus, the number of actual inhabitants of the village had not declined while the number of those with claims to or interest in residence had grown.

If there were fewer spirits to fear at night on the path, villagers said it was people who had become dangerous. Some attributed the rise in theft to Anjouanais immigrants, but there was also a general worry that children were no longer under parental control and had become delinquent (*voyous*; note the French word). Instead of working in the fields as they once did, youth were said to hang around the village and smoke marijuana (*bangy*). Surprisingly to me, increased parental control was one reason people gave for moving to Réunion or France.

A Brief Historical Perspective

Mayotte is a small island and was once relatively insignificant in regional exchanges. In precolonial times Anjouanais sailors were more likely than Maorais to join European sailing vessels en route to India; Grande Comorians were more likely to travel to East Africa. It was Grande Comorians who had a significant impact on East African Islam in the nineteenth century and their numbers were always much larger than those of the Maorais. At the end of the eighteenth century Mayotte was the victim of annual raids from Madagascar, while after French appropriation in 1841 it had a plantation economy firmly under the yoke of Réunionais planters. It was Mayotte's relative insignificance and powerlessness relative to the other islands in the archipelago that influenced the majority of its population to vote in the referenda of 1974 and in higher numbers in 1976 to stick with France rather than join the Comoros, which declared independence in 1975. Mayotte had more Malagasy speakers than the other islands and in the 1970s it already included large settlements of Grande Comorians as well as some Anjouanais. There was a somewhat cosmopolitan feel to the place, a term that seems more accurate than *polyethnic*.

In the 1970s people said, "How can we become independent? We have no manufacturing, we don't even produce our own soap." They remembered the Second World War and the year people had to wear sacks because the importation of clothing had stopped. Now there is a soap factory, but Mayotte is much more dependent on imports than before. In 1975 it produced the majority of its basic foodstuffs; in 2001 virtually all food was imported, and largely by monopoly holders. A South African woman owned the supermarket, meat-packing plant, soap and plastic factories. She controlled the import of beef and chicken and was setting up a chicken plant. The protein staple throughout the island was her frozen chicken wings (*mabawa*), selling wholesale for 13 ff per two pounds and at 15 ff per two pounds from the freezers of the village shopkeepers. Local fish was more expensive: 18–20 ff per two pounds fresh on the beach or 23–25 ff from the freezer. Fifty-five-pound sacks of rice cost 100 ff in town and 105 in the village shops. Coca-Cola was delivered weekly from the local bottling plant and had a high turnover in village shops.

The market that five years earlier had been full of Malagasy fruit, vegetables, and meat was empty of these products as the result of a government ban consequent to a cholera epidemic in Madagascar that was long over. The ban helped the South African importers, limited access to fresh produce, and significantly reduced the means of many petty traders in and from Madagascar.

Mayotte can no longer be considered an economic periphery in any simple sense. It is a periphery as far as access to the means of production or being remote from centers of decision making are concerned. But it is not peripheral with respect to what one might call the means of consumption. It is a part of France and the EU. The currency was the franc in this period and shortly after changed to the euro. The sources of loans, grants, and subventions are those available in Europe. The economy is entirely artificial, dependent on French government subsidies, jobs, and benefits, as well as import controls. Claude Allibert's depiction of Mayotte as a *plaque tournante* (nerve centre) of the Indian Ocean has now become apposite. Mayotte is an economic magnet for Comorians and Malagasy and sends a good deal of money to the Sakalava temple in Mahajanga. The number of French sojourners has increased enormously—and many original inhabitants have by now spent a good deal of time in France and elsewhere. Having completed a full French education, young people are "hybrid" relative to their parents' generation and cosmopolitan with respect to a broader "culturescape." Geographic mobility is by now a taken-for-granted feature of life.

Population expansion is connected to a decline in infant mortality that preceded any demographic transition in birth rates by more than a generation. But it is also connected to the changing political topography of the region and interisland movement. During the 1970s and into the 1980s, the people of Mayotte were inhibited from out-migration to a degree they had not been previously subject. When Mayotte refused to join the emergent independent Comoran republic, interisland travel was severely curtailed. Many in the preceding generations had gone to Madagascar, but in the mid-1970s travel to Madagascar became both difficult because of the absence of regular transport, and unappealing for political and economic reasons. Indeed, 1976 saw a reverse migration from Mahajanga after the massacres of Comorians there.

Since the 1990s the population has been greatly enhanced by increased migration to Mayotte on the part of both Malagasy and Comorians. Some draw on preexisting kin ties in order to establish a basis for acquiring French papers. The vast majority are from Ndzwani (Anjouan) and are without papers. They have an incentive to have children as this gives them rights to stay.

This is not the place to write about the huge influx of informal migrants or the measures taken against them. Instead, I single out three points from this brief overview. First, the relative immobility of the population that characterized my ethnographic experience in 1975–76 was a product of that time and not of long-standing. Over the *long durée*, population movement has been much more typical of the region.

Second, it is evident that population movement responds and is sensitive to microfluctuations in political and economic constraints and incentives. The world expands or contracts according to the means of transportation available and the perceived balance of opportunities at either end of the routes.

Third, the status of migrants is established by means of successive regimes of law and citizenship and such laws, more than anything else, configure the colonial and postcolonial patterns of migration and trade.

Gendered Pioneers

In 1975 I lived for the first six weeks in town in a relatively elite household of women whose polygynous husbands traveled between the islands. Some of those women had traveled too, but the picture was one of matrilocal households with mobile men. By contrast, in 2001 village women were more mobile than men. Postmarital residence was still largely and ideally uxorilocal. (To be more precise, the household cycle was patri-uxorilocal with successful men or married couples gathering their married offspring, especially their daughters, around them, within the same village and supplying them each with a house on marriage.) But women traveled in order to establish and support their households and to help build houses for their daughters.

The first person to leave the village of Lombeni for Réunion was Nafouanty, a newly married woman who, in fact, was taken there by her husband, a goldsmith from a larger village that had been opened to new opportunities earlier on. He went originally in 1982 in order to look after a brother who remained hospitalized after an automobile accident and brought his wife the following year. Nafouanty and her husband divorced, but both remained in St. Dénis. Their daughters have grown up there and speak Creole more easily than Kibushy. When I met the girls in St. Dénis in 2000, they were watching *ER* in French in their sitting room.

The second person to arrive was probably Sakina. When her husband was killed by a drunk driver in 1984, she went to Réunion at Nafouanty's suggestion because of the benefits she could acquire there as a widowed mother of three children. Sakina was not one to sit back. She saved her monthly benefits until she had enough for trade goods and airfare and began the first of what were many trips as a long-distance trader. By 2001 she had not only moved goods between Réunion and Mayotte but had collected merchandise in East Africa, Mauritius, France, Dubai, and even farther afield. In addition, she sponsored and supported a number of relatives from Lombeni in Réunion.

As a young girl in 1975, Sandaty used to stop and stare at me as the lone white foreigner in the village. In 1980 I helped celebrate her wedding. A decade later her husband was stricken by a blinding headache and airlifted to hospital in Réunion, where he died within a few days. With the help of relatives living there, he was buried in the Muslim cemetery in St. Dénis. Sandaty did not relocate, but she used the modest monthly payments that were by then available to widows of government employees with young children in Mayotte to start a shop and she, too, began to travel in search of merchandise.

When Sandaty first told me about having visited Mumbai and Bangkok, I simply didn't believe her. In fact, by 2001 she had been to Bangkok four times on wholesale shopping expeditions organized by an entrepreneur. Groups of local women traveled by air, stayed a couple of weeks in Dubai and other destinations, worked through translators, and shipped their merchandise home by container. A trip to Thailand cost Sandaty 7,000 ff. She imported children's clothing, planning the arrival for the end of Ramadan, when everyone purchases gifts for their children. She left her own children with kin while she traveled. Sandaty's brother also owned a shop and she introduced the pattern of transnational shopping to her sister-in-law. Although people on Mayotte have long referred to themselves as "the poor" (*maskin*), a result of Sandaty's travels in Asia was to put this into perspective.

Sandaty never moved to Réunion, but she sponsored a school vacation for her grown son in 2000 that coincided with my own visit. We went together to the grave of his father (who had been my friend) and visited a good many other villagers who had relocated to communities in Réunion. He carried a bag full of traditional women's wrappers printed with political slogans from the recent referendum in Mayotte that he was selling in Réunion on his mother's behalf and in order to subsidize his trip. He sold the four pieces necessary for a full garment (*complet*) for 100 ff. They cost 80 ff in Mayotte where, in fact, just three pieces (thus 60 ff) suffice for a complet. One of the designs was a *cameo* portrait of Bwenzena, a woman leader of the pro-French political movement.

Of course, not all village entrepreneurs are women. Noman, a former cultivator some five years my senior, became a successful contractor, bidding for government contracts and building houses and drainage ditches. He managed some ten employees, including younger kin and Anjouanais. By 2001 Noman had been to Mecca, sent two daughters and three sons to metropolitan France to study and his wife subsequently to visit them, and had himself traveled to Kenya, Mauritius, Réunion, and Dubai for merchandise for a village shop he had established. Noman also studied both Islam (*'ilim fakihy*) and cosmology (*'ilim dunia*) and has a cabinet full of books in Arabic to prove it. He rotated as deliverer of the Friday sermon for some five years, but stopped because he "had too much on my mind." Noman showed me a home video his wife brought back from France. One son, married to a Grand Comorienne from Mayotte whom he met in France, lived in a high-rise in Toulouse; the other siblings lived together in a high-rise in Lyon.

A La Réunion

Sakina (mentioned earlier) raised her children in Réunion. One daughter, whom I met when she visited Lombeni for a family wedding, barely spoke Kibushy. A son had taken up with a Réunionaise of South Asian descent and had a child. Sakina never stuck to a nuclear family model. Among the people she helped bring to Réunion were her mother, Moussy, then in her seventies, and her younger brother Abdoul.

Moussy had been coming to Réunion for about ten years, but made regular trips back to Mayotte. She was a bit defensive about her lifestyle since her husband remained in Mayotte. She said she wouldn't travel without his acquiescence, but was happy to have some autonomy. Moussy explained that she could not survive on the pension her husband received in Mayotte. She sent him a portion of her monthly benefits and also helped the offspring of a deceased son. She concluded, "I worry about them a lot and that is really why I come to Réunion. I have become a person of two places."

Having tried a number of living arrangements, Moussy looked after her daughter's subsidized apartment in St. Dénis during Sakina's frequent absences. It was in a nice building, with several large rooms, but on the outskirts of town. Sakina bought her mother a monthly pass on public transportation. Moussy said the only thing that held her back was fear of voyous; some Maorais, whose ethnicity is visible from their clothing, were the victims of taunts and threats by xenophobic youth. Moussy helped care for various grandchildren and other younger kin who stayed in town or passed through. She also worked informally as a healer, dispensing herbal medicine she brought from Mayotte or grew in Réunion. In addition to trips to Mayotte, Moussy saved enough to go on the hajj, costing around 12,000 ff, with assistance from kin. She was accompanied by her brother and his wife and by Sandaty.

While some migrants found employment in the formal sector in Réunion and others worked in the informal economy (in both cases, most frequently in the building trades and therefore mostly men), their main source of support was state benefits. These were of varying amounts for unemployment, old age, single mothers, dependent children, and housing. To receive monthly payments, one registered at the social security office and collected at a different spot. Some people collected monthly all year long, asking relatives to go in their place on months when they were back in Mayotte. Other people, making shorter trips or single sojourns in Réunion, just collected for the months they were present. During her frequent stays in Mayotte, Moussy left an identity card with her brother, who picked up her stipends on her behalf. Once she was cut off for two months, but was reinstated following a complaint by Sakina. Mahorais became skilled at dealing with the bureaucracy, learning how to combine ostensible submissiveness and courtesy with strategy and persistence.

Several women from Lombeni visited Réunion in order to help daughters or daughters-in-law following childbirth. They stayed a few weeks or months and would begin collecting benefits. Their daughters and sons made return visits to Mayotte in order to have their sons circumcised, to attend weddings and mortuary rituals, or just to be "on vacation" (*en vacances*). But if women's kin obligations induced travel, they also constrained it. Several women said they could not leave Mayotte so long as their aged parents were alive there. Those who relocated felt guilty or had sisters who remained behind to look after the parents. Moussy said that she couldn't have come to Réunion without married daughters to look after her husband in Mayotte, but many younger women felt less concern about leaving husbands. Zalia's husband worked in Mayotte, but he drank and didn't look after her well financially. So she traveled to Réunion for a few months at a time and collected sufficient benefits to cover her airfare and needs upon her return. By contrast, when Daoulaty arrived in Réunion to get away from her mother-in-law, she was soon followed by her husband and, a few months after that, by the mother-in-law herself, who quickly made up with her.

Hadia, a young woman with two small children, said she came to Réunion because she had no work at home. Her husband had work, but there was a new sense in her historical cohort that both members of a couple should be receiving a wage. In Réunion she had no wage employment either as most women from Mayotte did not. However, social security was considered equivalent to a wage both for its economic consequences and for its contribution to personal dignity. It was largely women who received benefits, or who received larger amounts, handled most of the household money, and managed the savings. In both Réunion and Mayotte, where the equivalent benefits were smaller, certain sums were paid by the state directly to women.

Married couples generally maintained separate bank accounts and had an understanding as to which spouse was responsible for what. Usually, in Réunion as in Mayotte, the husband provided the subsistence needs for the household and could do what he liked with the remainder of his salary, while the wife accumulated and managed the savings and could spend on extras for herself and the household. Unlike the case in Mayotte, in Réunion women did not own houses; couples shared responsibility for finding a residence and, I think, for paying rent. Savings from both parties were directed in large part into the houses the couple was building for themselves (the wife) and for their daughters back in Mayotte. Visits to Mayotte during the dry season entailed working on or monitoring house construction in the village.

Some men used portions of their income to maintain polygynous unions. These could be transnational. I knew one man who boasted of having wives in Mayotte, Réunion, and Madagascar; he would alternate a few months with each of them. For people making a little money, Madagascar was a good place to invest as life was cheaper there. In addition to men who took wives or girlfriends, an increasing number of people, mostly women, went to Madagascar to hold their spirit-possession ceremonies. People also contributed money toward the annual collective ceremonies and renovation projects for the ancestral spirits there.

Receiving social benefits from the state was understood neither as shameful nor as charity, but rather as a right. People argued that France was responsible for Mayotte and that if there were no jobs available, people still had the right to basic income. In this they were perfectly in accord with modern political philosophy and indeed with the French government's institution of the RMI, the Revenu Minimum d'Insertion, social welfare for the unemployed. With the exception of things like trips to Mecca, and the occasional polygynist, migrants lived frugally but decently. They bought nice furnishings, which they planned to take back with them to Mayotte. They ate a staple of rice served with chicken legs purchased frozen in bulk, supplemented with frozen beef or fish, and sought the best bargains. At 20 ff per two pounds, fish was cheaper than in Mayotte and the rice (at 200 ff for 110 pounds of broken jasmine grains) was better quality. Chicken legs (350 ff for a twenty-two-pound carton) were a kind of index of the standard of living in Réunion; they replaced the frozen wings that had become the protein staple in Mayotte.

France

Sakina's youngest brother, Abdoul, was sent to Réunion by his older siblings at the age of ten in 1987. Because he was too old for the state school, they placed him in a Catholic one and paid the fees. He left school in 1996, a year before the *bac*, and participated in what was then obligatory military service for a year.[3] Happily for him, this included a stage in France studying telecommunications and computing, which he supplemented with training as a sound technician. He then acquired a series of excellent jobs in Mayotte, beginning with the phone company and later with the government. In 2001 Abdoul's monthly salary was 5,600 ff per month. He was building a six-room house for himself and his family and planning to rent out the three-room one he currently occupied, a strategy he estimated to be the best investment. Housing construction costs were indexed according to income; for him, three rooms cost between 30,000 and 40,000 ff to build, payable in monthly installments. He drove a new Peugeot that cost 80,000 ff (much more than in the metropole, he pointed out) and was paying back the bank loan at 2,000 ff per month. Abdoul owed his success not only to his own talents and enterprise but also to his sister Sakina's original move to Réunion and to her support as well as that of other siblings.

It was not only men who were so upwardly mobile. One of Moussy's granddaughters completed a higher degree in Réunion and was returning to Mayotte to teach special education. She married a cousin and fellow villager who had also entered the white-collar class. Another granddaughter passed her bac in Mayotte and was awarded a scholarship direct to France.

She received 10,000 ff every three months (a high amount, her mother thought, because her father was deceased). While I was visiting the mother, who had struggled for years to support her children, she opened a money order from her daughter for 500 ff. This young woman (the daughter) had become engaged before she left. As the fiancé was himself about to leave for France, the mother held the contractual part of the wedding (*kufungia*) so that the couple could start living together on his arrival. She expected a letter once the marriage was consummated, with some sign of blood. The celebration of the virgin marriage (*harussy*) was postponed until their return. The ideal of the virgin bride was still in place while the decoupling of the stages of marriage had become common.

Other women were not virgins when they left for France and went in order to marry, not study. One uneducated young woman, Amina, had a child out of wedlock in Mayotte. She responded to a marriage request from a stranger in the metropole and set off to join him. Before Amina left, she built herself a small house with the money earned from doing the work given to the unemployed. (This minimally paid labor, known as *chomage*, included sweeping public buildings, collecting trash, and tidying the beach; it was given in periods of rotation to all who sought it.) Once Amina arrived in Marseille and found the husband satisfactory, she sent for her child. She also sent money to her mother. Amina's mother was hoping to visit her in France once she was freed from the obligations of caring for her own young children and aging parents. She said her husband could fend for himself or take up with an Anjouanais woman during her absence. In the meantime, Amina had returned to visit the village. People said, "She left with nothing, but now she has become a somebody [*ulun'belu*]."

Not all mail-order brides have such positive experiences. Sandia, too, had a child in Mayotte and then went off to marry a man in France whose picture she had been sent. She didn't like him, separated, and eventually found a man from Mayotte in Lyon with whom she had two more children. People said she wouldn't return to Mayotte until she had the money to put up a house. Sandia's case is interesting because she is the product of several generations of interisland migration. Her father's father came to Mayotte from the inter-island of Mwali and married the daughter of indentured laborers originally from East Africa. Sandia's father, Bako, left home as a young adult and settled in Antsiranana (Diego Suarez), Madagascar, where he sold bananas in the market. Diego had a thriving community of Mahorais who maintained a mosque and numerous rituals. Bako sent home money to purchase land, but never returned himself. He was once ready to do so, but his savings were stolen and he stayed on to rebuild his fortune. Bako's mother traveled to Madagascar and collected his elder daughter to raise in Mayotte. Many years later, after Bako's death, this woman went to collect her younger sister, Sandia, when Sandia was in early adolescence. So Sandia herself had lived in three very different settings.

A woman in her fifties on a visit in Mayotte said she had originally gone to France to follow her children. She married an Algerian in Marseille. "I need some way to keep warm when it's too cold and cool when it's too hot, don't I?" she said. Her husband spoke better French than she did and cooked his own food. He did not seem to have much say about her visiting home.

The husbands of these women were described as *Africains*; in most cases it was unclear to me whether they came from North or West Africa. They sought brides with citizenship papers in order to legitimate their own residence; Mayotte proved to be an ideal source. Although the men were culturally different and spoke different languages from their wives, they, too, were Muslim.

Several women spoke to me of migrating with their children in order to acquire welfare benefits and a good education. One woman said that instead of Réunion, she hoped to "jump ahead" to France. A woman visiting for her father's memorial (*mandeving*) lived in Marseille with her Grand Comoran husband and six children. She said her children studied better there, with less distraction and wandering about. The goal of providing children with a better education was commonly expressed by women and men.

More than one woman, who considered herself the underappreciated wife in a polygynous marriage, said she was saving to take the youngest children to go live in France. One woman, who spoke no French, declared herself unafraid. She would join one of the village women already in France. She had no plans to remarry and said her husband could follow if and when he wished.

Occasionally the gender positions were reversed. One man disappeared from the village, writing after a few months to ask his children and wife to join him in Marseille. The wife sent the younger children, but declared she had too many interests in Mayotte to go herself. Another man whose older sons were in France, one studying and the other in the army, planned to send their sisters to join them so that they might earn money to contribute to the houses he was building them in Mayotte.

Réunion Again

People left Mayotte with the intention of returning, and there was a fair amount of visiting between migrants and their families despite the cost. Those traveling between Mayotte, Réunion, and France without benefit of state subsidy acquired tickets by participating in a rotating savings circle (*shikawa*) of about ten people, selling a cow, or receiving a loan from those who had gone ahead, in a form of chain migration. Women in Lombeni participated in shikawa that demanded contributions of 200–500 ff per month; in Réunion such contributions were 1,000–1,500 ff.

If the movement is comparable to the urban migration characteristic of much of the African continent and the world in general over the last few decades, it has a specific twist in small places like Mayotte, where the move is off-island. However, there was a kind of paradox since most migrants from Lombeni to Réunion lived not in St. Dénis, but in smaller towns. The largest congregation was located in St. André (San'tan'dré), in the cane-growing northeast, where certain patterns of life back home could be reproduced. Some residents of St. André were able to cultivate manioc and fruit and they engaged in regular interhousehold visiting. Migrants in other locations could find themselves more isolated from fellow Maorais. There was a trade-off: the best government-subsidized housing—in modern high-rises—was often the most isolating. Television and the telephone took on a centrality they lacked back home.

Claude Dernane, the director of the Maison de Mayotte à la Réunion at the time, estimated that 95 percent of Mahorais families on Réunion didn't work (officially) and were on government assistance (RMI). He added that approximately 90 percent lived in unsanitary housing and that 80 percent of the children had trouble following school programs.

While some migrants did complain of poor housing, in general they saw things differently. One woman with many children who had lived in St. André since 1999 was able to pay 1,000 ff from her benefits into a monthly savings association in addition to rent. Her husband worked in the informal sector and they were able to do some small-scale subsistence cultivation. "So," she concluded, "you can see that we have enough to live on." Other than being bothered by expressions of anti-Comorian prejudice on the part of some citizens, she was satisfied. She said, "The money is what 'makes us drunk on' [*mankamamo*; that is, crazy about] Réunion."

Moussy's brother, who is considerably younger than Moussy, preceded her to Réunion. Led by his wife in 1991, he worked in the official sector as a carpenter and then a mason. The couple provided their several children with a solid education in both the French and Islamic school systems. Construction work declined with the importation of prefabricated building parts and the work became increasingly deskilled. The brother then took odd jobs, engaged in various kinds of nonmonetary exchanges (for example, giving his mechanic a therapeutic massage), and, along with his wife, drew on social assistance. His family's monthly rent in a large, airy—indeed beautiful—apartment on a hillside adjacent to the most luxurious hotel in the city was around 4,000 ff, but after subsidies, their cost was only 1,700 ff. The housing assistance was calibrated to his employment record and number of children, but the quality of the flat was also a matter of luck and time. It took several years for the family to find such a good apartment.

The quality and cost of housing inhabited by Maorais is quite variable, from the spectacular to the "unsanitary" bidonvilles. Another family paid 3,500 ff for a shabby private house in a poor location in St. Paul while awaiting government housing. They left a quarter of St. Dénis because of ethnic harassment and were hoping for a location near a mosque. The husband earned some 6,000 ff per month officially in construction and hence was ineligible for free health care. His wife received an RMI of 1,500. Her husband supplied the family's protein (*shireo*) and also gave her 1,000 ff per month. He used a portion of his salary for building houses in Mayotte for daughters from a previous marriage.

Migrants compared the quality of life in both places. Réunion was described as "cleaner" than Mayotte. But a young man who spent seven years in Réunion and felt it had more opportunity for advancement nevertheless returned home because, he explained, there was more "breathing space" (*nafass*) in Mayotte. He illustrated this by saying that when he was ill, he could spend weeks recuperating at his mother's. The point, I think, is that there was a wider field of less commoditized relations in Mayotte.

The Ends of Migration

No one in Mayotte was afraid to travel; everyone was eager to see new places. The gendered patterns of movement exhibited the demands placed on women but also their ambition, initiative, and autonomy. People traveled for many reasons. One was to receive maximal benefits, which, as French state policy would have it, enabled people to achieve a minimally acceptable standard of living, especially when it was accompanied by various kinds of informal work and exchange. In some instances, migration was the price paid for personal and social dignity. For most people, the terms and recognition of this dignity were established back home.

There was a difference perhaps between the people who traveled in order to further "traditional" social ends back home—acquiring the means to hold weddings or build houses—and those who traveled on new agendas of education for its own sake, and so forth. But the difference should not be exaggerated and most people's projects combined both. One man explained that he migrated to Réunion "like everyone" in order to educate his children. Unlike Mayotte, he said, in Réunion parents received help with school supplies. "In Mayotte the rich get richer and the poor fall further behind, so we leave."

The situation began to look different the longer people stayed away and especially for the next generation. This was evident with respect to language; those educated in Réunion spoke Creole, a language that was unknown in Mayotte (since the time of the planters) and, as people eventually noticed, useless for mobility in metropolitan France.

While some people who returned to Mayotte described life in Réunion as boring and said they had lived in front of the television, migrants did engage in a number of activities. There was informal work of various kinds, and many people studied at French or Muslim institutions. An Islamic teacher from the Grande Comore offered widely attended classes in St. Dénis. Cassettes of sermons were circulated. The range of musical and dance forms of Islamic piety that were engaged in so intensely in Mayotte were also practiced in Réunion. One young woman concluded that, for migrants, Réunion "has become Mayotte" (*Eto izeo fa Maore*).

Throughout this period of geographic mobility, dual residence on the part of many, and extensive travel on the part of a significant minority, and despite the reproduction of Mahorais life in Réunion and in various communities in the metropole, eyes were kept steadily on the horizon of economic and social success back in Mayotte.

Notes

This chapter is a slightly revised version of Chapter 10 of *Island in the Stream: An Ethnographic History of Mayotte* (Toronto, 2018) and reprinted with permission of the University of Toronto Press.

1. These are all French administrative terms and they refer to progressive incorporation into the French state, which is composed of ninety-six departments in metropolitan France and five overseas departments.

2. Compare with Alan Howard, "Speak of the Devils: Discourse and Belief in Spirits on Rotuma," in *Spirits in Culture, History, and Mind*, ed. Jeannette Mageo and Alan Howard (New York: Routledge, 1996), 121–45.

3. The *baccalauréat* is the French diploma necessary for pursuing university studies.

Contributors

RICHARD B. ALLEN is a professor of history at Framingham State University. He is a noted expert on the slave trade in the Indian Ocean, receiving among other honors a National Endowment for the Humanities Award to study the subject. He has been widely published in both journals and edited collections and his recent monographs include *European Slave Trading in the Indian Ocean, 1500–1850* and *Slaves, Freedmen and Indentured Laborers in Colonial Mauritius.*

EDWARD A. ALPERS is a research professor (emeritus) of history at the University of California, Los Angeles. Alpers has previously taught at the University of Dar es Salaam in Tanzania and has spent a Fulbright year at the Somali National University in Mogadishu. His research interests include the African diaspora in the Indian Ocean and Lusophone Africa. He is a pioneering scholar of the Indian Ocean world and his extensive list of publications includes *The Indian Ocean in World History; East Africa and the Indian Ocean;* and *Ivory and Slaves in East Central Africa,* along with numerous articles in scholarly journals and edited collections.

WILLIAM BISSELL is a professor of anthropology at Lafayette College. His interests include colonialism, power, and inequality in Africa as well as cities, cultural production, African film, and media. His first book, *Urban Design, Chaos, and Colonial Power in Zanzibar,* explored the British Empire's chaotic and often unsuccessful urban planning schemes in colonial Zanzibar and was a finalist for the Herskovits Award. He has published articles in edited volumes and journals including *African Arts, Development,* and the *Journal of Urban History.* He is also the editor (with Marie-Aude Fouéré) of *Social Memory, Silenced Voices, and Political Struggle: Remembering the Revolution in Zanzibar* (2018).

TOYIN FALOLA is the Jacob and Frances Sanger Mossiker Chair in the Humanities at the University of Texas at Austin. He is a fellow of the Historical Society of Nigeria and of the Nigerian Academy of Letters. Falola is author and editor of more than one hundred books on topics ranging from the Atlantic World to the African diaspora, though he is best know for his work on the cultural, religious, and intellectual history of Nigeria. His individual monographs include *The African Diaspora: Slavery, Modernity, and Globalization* (University of Rochester Press, 2014); *Colonialism and Violence in Nigeria;* the memoir *A Mouth Sweeter Than Salt;* and *Nationalism and African Intellectuals* (University of Rochester Press, 2004).

JOSHUA BERNARD FORREST is a professor of history and political science at La Roche College. The recipient of two Fulbright Fellowships, he studies the relationship between ethnicity, subnationalism, and politics in Sub-Saharan Africa. He has previously published in journals and collected volumes and his individual monographs include *Subnationalism in Africa; Lineages of State Fragility: Rural Civil Society in Guinea-Bissau;* and *Namibia's Post-Apartheid Regional Institutions* (University of Rochester Press, 1998).

ASHLEY JACKSON is a professor of imperial and military history at King's College London and a visiting fellow at Kellogg College Oxford. At the time of writing he has published fourteen books on aspects of British imperial history with a concentration on the empire during the Second World War, including *The British Empire and the Second World War; Persian Gulf Command: Iran and Iraq during the Second World War,* and *Of Islands, Ports, and Sea Lanes: Africa and the Indian Ocean in the Second World War.*

MICHAEL LAMBEK is a professor of anthropology and Canada Research Chair at the University of Toronto Scarborough. He conducts long-term ethnographic fieldwork in the Indian Ocean islands of Mayotte and Madagascar. He has written on spirit possession, Islam, the anthropology of knowledge, therapeutic practice, memory, historicity, and ethical life, among other topics. His books include *The Weight of the Past: Living with History in Majunga, Madagascar* (2002); *The Ethical Condition* (2015); and *Island in the Stream: An Ethnographic History of Mayotte* (2018), from which the present chapter is drawn.

CARLA D. MARTIN is the founder and executive director of the Fine Cacao and Chocolate Institute (FCCI) and a lecturer in the Department of African and African American Studies at Harvard University. She is a social anthropologist with interdisciplinary interests that include history, agronomy, ethnomusicology, and linguistics. She has researched the longstanding problem of language inequality in Cape Verde and its large diaspora and how scholars and creative artists have both perpetuated and challenged this inequality. Her writing has appeared in *Transition Magazine; Social Dynamics; The Root;* and edited volumes among other venues. Her current research focuses on the politics of fine cacao and chocolate in global perspective.

ENRIQUE N. OKENVE is a lecturer in the Department of History and Archaeology at the University of the West Indies at Mona (Jamaica). His research focuses on the social and cultural transformations that central African societies experienced as result of European colonization. He is currently working on a book manuscript that addresses the development of Fang tradition as the conceptual instrument that aided local communities to retain power vis-à-vis the Spanish colonial state. He has recently published an article on the transformation of genealogical memory among Fang-speaking peoples in mainland EG (2018, *Ayer*). He has also published papers on the role of race in the development of the Spanish discourse of domination (2016, *Afro-Hispanic Review*) as well as the connection between territoriality, ethnicity, and nationalism in colonial EG (2014, *International Journal of African Historical Studies*). His published work also includes an examination of contemporary political conditions in EG (2009, *Afro-Hispanic Review*).

R. JOSEPH PARROTT is an assistant professor of history at the Ohio State University. An historian of international, transnational, and American history, he is currently revising a manuscript that cuts across diplomatic, activist, and sociopolitical history to explore Portuguese decolonization in Africa as a noteworthy component in transforming western engagement with the global south. His work has been published in *Race & Class* and *Modern American History*.

JEREMY PRESTHOLDT is a professor of history at the University of California, San Diego. He specializes in African, Indian Ocean, and global history with emphases on consumer culture and politics. His first book, *Domesticating the World: African Consumerism and the Genealogies of Globalization*, addressed East African demands for imported goods and how these shaped global exchanges in the second half of the nineteenth century. His most recent book, *Icons of Dissent: The Global Resonance of Che, Marley, Tupac, and Bin Laden*, explores popular attraction to four global icons as a way of tracing the development of shared global imagery and charting the commodification of political sentiment since the 1960s.

DANIELLE PORTER SANCHEZ is an assistant professor of history and Africana studies at Muhlenberg College. She is a cultural and urban historian of modern Africa, with particular interests in urban history, expressive culture, and resistance in Cabo Verde and Congo-Brazzaville.

GERMÁN SANTANA PÉREZ is a professor of modern history at the Universidad de Las Palmas de Gran Canaria. His scholarly interests include the history of the Canaries and Africa as well as the comparative history of Atlantic islands stretching from Africa to the Caribbean. His publications include *Historia de Canarias; La Puerta Afortunada;* and *El Comercio Interinsular de Lanzarote, 1635–1665.*

DENIS REGNIER is a lecturer with the Équipe d'Accueil Sociétés Traditionnelles et Contemporaines en Océanie (EASTCO), Université de la Polynésie française. Previously a postdoctoral researcher at the Fonds de la Recherche Scientifique (F.R.S.–FNRS), he was trained in anthropology and researches the condition of slave descendants in the southern highlands of Madagascar. His articles have appeared in numerous journals including *Social Anthropology* and *Pacific Studies.* Dr. Regnier's ongoing work in Madagascar focuses on slavery, essentialism, marriage, kinship, ritual, funerary practices, naming, and healing.

GERHARD SEIBERT is a professor of anthropology at Universidade da Integração Internacional da Lusofonia Afro-Brasileira (UNILAB), Brazil. His research focuses on lusophone African countries, and he has published widely on issues concerning São Tomé and Príncipe, Cabo Verde, Mozambique, and Brazil-Africa relations. His first monograph, *Comrades, Clients, and Cousins: Colonialism, Socialism, and Democratization in São Tomé and Príncipe,* is widely considered the definitive volume on the recent history of the African archipelago. Before joining UNILAB, Seibert spent a number of years as researcher at the Instituto de Investigação Científica Tropical (IICT) in Lisbon and the Centro de Estudos Africanos—Instituto Universitário de Lisboa (CEA-IUL). He is coeditor of the book *Brazil–Africa Relations: Historical Dimensions and Contemporary Engagements, From the 1960s to the Present,* published by James Currey in 2019.

DOMINIQUE SOMDA is currently on the faculty of the International Honors Program, School for International Training. Trained as a sociocultural anthropologist, she has been a visiting professor at the University of Pennsylvania and at Reed College and held postdoctoral positions at the Fondation Maisons des Sciences de l'Homme in Paris and at the London School of Economics. Her work explores how inequality—or conversely, egalitarianism—emerges through everyday practices, a thematic interest that has led her to engage with the anthropology of democracy, Christianity, and feminist and postcolonial studies. Her regional focus is Madagascar.

MICHAEL UGARTE is a professor emeritus of Spanish at the University of Missouri. He studies eighteenth-, nineteenth-, and twentieth-century Spanish literature and has published extensively in modern peninsular Spanish literature as well as cultural studies and postcolonial literature. He is the author of five books, including *Africans in Europe: The Culture of Exile and Emigration from Equatorial Guinea to Spain* and *Madrid 1900: The Capital as Cradle of Culture.*

IAIN WALKER is research officer at Martin Luther University and research associate at the Max Planck Institute for Social Anthropology, both in Halle, Germany. He studies identity and ethnicity in the Indian Ocean, along with issues of migration, globalization, and notions of home and belonging, as well as age systems. His articles and chapters have concentrated on culture, ethnicity, and identity on the Comoros Islands, but he has also published on broad regional and diaspora topics. He was for many years a research officer with the Centre on Migration, Policy and Society (COMPAS), University of Oxford.

Index

abolition, 51, 80, 148, 256, 295, 303–4, 328, 346–58, 382
Abyssinians, 275, 297
acculturation, 21, 24–25, 81, 132, 134, 143
Aden, 175, 186, 188, 190, 192, 221, 269
Africa, extraversion in, 290, 317–18
Africa, scramble for, 276
African nationalism, 26–27, 201, 257
African Party for the Independence of Guinea and Cabo Verde (PAIGC), 2–3
Afro-Shirazi Party (ASP), 282, 284
agronomy/agronomic, 107, 113, 116, 118
Alawite Kingdom, 50
Ally, Aji Ojer, 306
Alpers, Edward, 8, 12, 30, 245
Amod, Aboobaker, 304
ancestors, 24, 263n28, 279, 307, 351–53, 355–57, 359, 361, 368n65
ancestral tombs, 357
Andalusians, 357
Andevo, 349, 351, 356, 358, 361
Anglo-German Agreement of 1890, 277
Angoche, 250, 252, 254–55
Angola, 17, 22, 45–46, 70–71, 77, 80–81, 258, 266n57
Angolares, 71, 73, 77–78
Annobón, 50, 129–30, 149n2, 151n17, 154n68, 158–60, 162–65, 168n15

Anôsy, 349, 354, 360, 363
Antananarivo, 346, 352, 356, 358–59, 361, 367n53
Arab elites, 277, 281, 286, 326
Arab landowners, 277, 284
Arabia, 8, 15–16, 197–98, 247–48, 253, 255, 258, 268, 276, 279, 319, 322, 347, 378, 386
Arabocentric discourses, 281, 282
architecture, 26, 273, 327
Arguín, 31, 43
As Old as My Tongue, 268
Atlantic World, 5–11, 28, 47, 51
autonomy, 30, 71, 96, 105, 110, 118–19, 142–44, 146–47, 281, 289, 320, 333–34, 337, 397, 407, 414; of Canhabac, 105, 110, 118–19; political, 71, 96, 147; of women, 30
Axum, 247–48
Azores, 6, 49, 183

Bab el Madeb, 186
Bajuni Islands, 248–49, 261n12
Baluchis, 275
bananas, 40, 52, 55–56, 179, 257, 411
Bantu-speakers, 8, 99, 249, 250
Barcelona, 54–55, 162
Barreto, Honorio, 104, 111
Bata, 57, 127, 139, 155n75, 152
Batavia, 258, 296
Bazaruto Islands, 250, 252, 263n28
Betsileo, 298, 349, 353–55, 357–58, 360–61
Betsimisaraka, 350, 354–55, 361
Bi Kidude, 27, 30, 268–70, 282, 288

Bioko, 5–6, 13, 17, 27, 29, 125–49, 149n1, 151n17, 155n79, 158–60, 162–63, 165, 182

Bioko-Rio Muni differences, 141, 143, 145, 155n75

Bohora, 275

Bourbon, Île de, 51, 256, 273, 296, 300, 347

Brazil, 16–17, 19, 46, 51, 63n32, 68, 71, 73–75, 91, 180–81, 226, 420

Britain, 16, 49, 51, 65n58, 119, 170, 174–76, 180–81, 186–88, 195, 258, 272, 276–77, 299, 318, 370–71, 382, 391n6

British protectorate, in Zanzibar, 277, 383, 394n49

Bubi acculturation, 140, 141, 143

Bubi cocoa agriculture, 137, 138; cooperatives, 142, 143

Bubi demographic crisis, 135, 136

Bubi exclusión, 128, 129, 130, 147, 148, 149

Bubi land access, 139, 140, 143

Bubi nationalism, 127, 128, 144, 148; identity, 148, 149n1; Unión Bubi, 127, 128, 146

Bubi population size, 135, 136, 150n5, 152nn40–41

Bubi precolonial trade, 131, 132, 136

Bubi settlement of Bioko, 129, 130, 131, 150n12

Bubi uprising, 138

Bubi-Fang relations, 127, 145–46, 155n75

Bubi-Krio (Fernandinos) relations, 132, 133, 138, 153n56

Bubi-Kru relations, 134, 135, 151n28

Busaidi(s), 272–73, 280–81

Cabo Verde, 2–4, 6, 13–14, 16–17, 21, 23, 25–27, 29, 35n36–37, 44–49, 56, 58–59, 77, 80–81, 208–17, 219–37

Cabral, Amilcar, 2, 3, 18, 27, 214

Cádiz, 40, 45, 51

Campbell, Gwen, 301

Canaries, 5–6, 15, 17, 21, 28, 39–60

canoes, 96, 98–103, 106, 115–16, 118, 165–66, 183, 247, 253, 383, 391n16, 399

Cape Aguer, 41–43

Cape Blanco, 43, 53

Cape Bojador, 41, 43, 45

Cape Colony, 258, 305

Cape Delgado, 250–51, 254, 276

Cape Juby, 53, 56

Cape Nun, 53

Cape Town, 11, 172, 175–76, 255, 298, 319

Capuchin missionaries, 52

Carlos I, 42

Casa Africa, 59

Casa de Contratación, 45

Castile, 41–42, 48, 61n14

Castilian, 39–42, 45–46

cattle, 43, 46, 48, 98–100, 109, 113, 302, 375, 402

center-periphery discussion, 129, 148, 149

cereal, 48, 49, 50, 55

ceremonies, 114, 210, 409

Ceylon, 173, 175, 184–85, 189, 193–94, 258–59, 276, 305

Chama cha Mapinduzi (CCM), 289, 263n27

China, 8, 16, 23, 58, 81, 180, 194, 198, 273, 275, 297, 303–4, 318–19, 385

Chinese, 88, 285–86, 294, 298, 303, 305, 326

city-states, 250, 271–72, 324

Civic United Front, 289

Clarence (Santa Isabel, Malabo), 129, 131–34, 151n28; foundation, 131, 132

cocoa, 29, 54, 68–69, 75–84, 91–92, 93n31, 125, 129–30, 132, 134–46, 148, 155n72, 380

cocoa agriculture, 136, 137, 138, 139, 140, 155n71

coffee, 19–20, 22, 54, 68, 75–77, 84, 91, 109, 135, 136, 274, 317

Cold War, 290

Cole, Sir G. Lowry, 305

colonial taxes, 111, 118

commercialism, 119

Commission of Eastern Enquiry, 302

commodities, 10, 30, 59, 200, 271–72, 274, 284–85, 287, 319, 322, 374, 380

commoners, 348–49, 351, 354, 358, 360–61

Comoro Islands, 192, 197, 250, 253–55, 276, 398

Comoros, 8–9, 13, 15–16, 18, 22, 25–26, 30, 171–72, 192, 253–56, 298, 303–5, 347–48, 371–89, 403

Compagnie des Indes, 296

consumer culture, 319–20, 323–26, 328, 335–37

contraband, 45, 47

contract labor, 69, 77–78, 80, 91

contract worker, 77–81

corvée (prestación personal), 138, 140, 153n44, 153n53

cosmopolitanism, 4, 9, 14, 22, 27, 35n45, 271, 279, 283, 288, 290, 306, 326

cowry shells, 258–59

Creole, 9, 14–15, 17, 21–25, 28–29, 35n37, 70–71, 75–78, 80–81, 90, 208–11, 213, 216, 219–22, 227, 229, 323, 406, 415; Creole Institute (CCI), 220, 225, 227,

241n57; creolization, 13–14, 129, 21, 133, 265n51, 306, 327, 339n22; population, 17, 77–78; society, 25, 70–71

Cuba, 17, 50, 54, 81, 135, 158, 159, 167

Cubillo, Antonio, 57

cultural identity, 26, 71, 143, 355

Dahlak Archipelago, 246, 248–49

Dakar, 53, 56–57, 176

Dar es Salaam, 249, 278

Darajani, 274

Darling, Maj. Gen. Ralph, 299

decentralization, 9, 98, 102, 103–5, 113

Dhow(s), 8, 197–78, 268, 270–71, 279, 284–85, 287–88, 376; Dhow Countries Music Academy, 287; Dhow culture, 287–88

Doctor, Manilal, 306

Dutch, 9, 19, 43, 47–48, 50, 63n75, 70, 74, 131, 256, 258–59, 375–77, 381; colonial rule, 255, 258; Dutch East India Company, 196

East Timor, 246, 258

education, 2, 80, 98, 118, 141–43, 155n75, 208, 212–15, 218–21, 223–26, 228, 230–31, 234–36, 287, 353, 385, 398–99, 404, 412–14

Egypt, 162, 174–76, 180, 187, 189, 247, 322

elders, 105–7, 114, 117, 119

Elmina, 45, 362n8

emigration from islands, 398

England, 45, 47, 49, 51, 63n32, 65, 119, 160, 393n35

epidemic outbreaks, 129, 135–36, 404

Equatorial Guinea, 5, 29, 50, 52–55, 57–58, 85, 125, 127,

129, 144–49, 150nn5–6, 160,
162–65; autonomous status,
144; constitution, 146, 147;
decolonization of, 127, 143,
144, 145, 146, 147, 155n81;
ethnic composition, 150n6;
independence, 145, 146, 147;
nationalism, 143, 144, 146;
provincial status, 144, 148, 150n5
Eritrea, 173, 186, 191, 246–48
essentialization, 358, 361
ethnicization, 356, 361
European contacts, 130; Portuguese
contact, 130, 131, 151n17;
Spanish contact, 150n2, 151n17;
Spanish occupation, 149n2;
treaties, 125, 149n2, 151n17
European Union, 39, 58, 60
Exclusive Economic Zone (EEZ),
90

Fang, 27, 127–29, 138–40, 146, 149–
50, 156n87, 160–62, 419; Fang in
Bioko, 127
farming, 98, 106, 108, 113, 115–18,
136, 138–39, 400
Farquhar, Robert, 298–99
Fernando Pó, 54–55, 75, 78, 125,
135, 137, 141, 143–44, 149n2,
150n5, 151n28, 152n31, 172,
177, 182–83. *See also* Bioko
Fiji, 305
fishing, 53, 115, 226; Society of
Canarian African Fishing, 53
forestry, 118
forests, 19, 71, 75, 98, 106, 111, 118,
167, 322, 365n37, 370, 399–400
Forros, 70, 75–78, 81
Fort Dauphin, 302, 346, 348
Funguni, 270, 279

Gambia, 58, 64n45, 170, 172,
180–82

Gandhi, Mahatma, 306
gender, 14, 105, 107, 119, 268,
323, 412, 414; balance, 98, 118;
relations, 107; spaces, 118
genealogies, 325, 357
Gerbeau, Hubert, 299
German(s), 52, 55–56, 80, 137, 153,
171, 176–77, 182–83, 188, 198,
205n35, 251–52, 259, 277–78,
285, 318
Glassman, Jonathon, 129, 282–83,
325, 334, 340n26, 342n51,
344n77
global economy, 20, 285, 320,
347
globalization, 29, 147, 161, 287
Gordon, Sir Arthur Hamilton, 305
governance, 8, 10, 12, 15, 17, 22,
104–5, 113, 118, 247
Gran Canaria, 44, 46, 52, 55–57, 59,
61n14, 64n43
Great Britain, 49, 51, 65n58, 119,
258, 370–71
Guha, Ramachandra, 306
Guha, Ranajit, 163–64
Gujarati merchants, 302–3. *See also*
merchants, Indian
Gulf of Aden, 248
Gulf of Guinea, 6, 54, 71, 75, 91,
125, 131–32, 136–37, 140–42,
145, 148, 149n2, 158, 160, 172,
174, 182–83
Gurnah, Abdulrazak, 270, 285

Hadramawt, 253
harems, 286
Havana, 51, 64n43
Heligoland, 173, 277
Hergigo, 247
heritage, 2, 3, 211, 216, 223–24,
230, 241n57, 255–56, 286–87,
307, 346
Hinduism, 23–24, 274–75

Ibo, 256, 259, 298
Ile de France, 256, 273, 296, 302, 347, 381
Imerina, 255, 348–50, 356, 365n35, 255
immigrants, 24, 26, 54, 131, 197, 211–12, 275, 280, 304–7, 323, 325, 331, 403
immigration, 27, 233, 256, 303, 306
Imperial British East African Company, 278
imperialism, 6, 20, 27, 29, 51–53, 57, 232
indentured labor, 9, 22–23, 256, 295, 303–7, 348, 411
Indian Ocean connections, 30, 287
Indian Ocean rim, 270–71, 273, 279, 282
Indian Ocean world, 9, 20, 30, 48, 247, 261, 271–72, 279–80, 284, 287, 290, 305–6
Indonesia, 8, 246, 255, 257–58, 310n21, 347, 363n10
Inhaca Island, 252
Islam, 8–9, 13, 15, 21, 23, 59, 247–50, 252, 254, 271, 280–81, 288–90, 238, 376, 383, 387, 395n75, 401–3, 407, 413, 415; Afro-Islam, 9; Islamization, 250; Organization of Islamic Cooperation, 26, 289
island identities, 21, 24–25, 27, 278
ivory, 8, 15, 46, 251, 273–74, 317, 321, 376

Jahazi, 268, 287. *See also* Dhow(s)
Jeddah, 247
Joint Development Zone (JDZ), 85–91

Karume, Abeid, 284, 289
Keating, Lt. Col. Henry S., 299

Kenya, 8, 174–75, 185, 248–51, 255, 257, 276, 287, 304, 371, 407
Khojas, 274–75
Kilwa Kisiwani, 8, 22, 246, 250–52, 254, 256, 296–97, 373–75
Kismayu, 185, 187, 248, 261n13
Krio (Fernandinos), 129, 130; British influence, 133, 134, 152n31; cocoa agriculture, 136, 153n56; creolization, 129, 133, 134; settlement in Bioko, 129, 132

La Palma, 40, 45, 47, 61n14
labor conditions, 138, 139, 155n79
Lamu Archipelago, 250–51, 255
Larson, Pier, 301, 305, 347
Liberia, 45, 54, 138–40, 151n28, 179–80
Lisbon, 16, 45, 62n26, 72, 108, 111, 234
London, 49, 57, 60, 174, 181, 201, 298, 306, 317–18, 328, 338n5, 379
Luanda, 46, 57, 71

Madagascar, 4, 8, 10, 13–15, 17–18, 21, 23–25, 27, 30, 56, 171–72, 175–76, 192–95, 197–99, 246, 254–58, 276, 296–97, 299, 301–5, 320, 346–61, 371–73, 376, 378, 383, 385, 398, 403–5, 409, 411
Machado, Pedro, 302
Madrid, 46, 57, 59–60, 65n58, 137
Mãe Júlia, 109–10
Mahgreb, 42
Mainty, 349, 356, 358–59, 361, 368n69
Makhuwa, 254–55
Makoa, 256, 349, 345, 355, 359, 361, 367n53

Malagasy, 4, 17, 24–25, 28, 195, 254–56, 275, 296, 298, 300–302, 305, 307, 346, 348, 350–51, 355–61, 403–5; culture, 4, 256; language, 254–55, 403; nationalism, 195; polities, 17

malaise créole, 307

Maldives, 202n2, 259

Malindi, 270, 274, 279, 389

mangrove poles (boriti), 271, 273

mangrove swamps, 114, 183

maroons, 71, 73

Mascarene islands, 30, 246, 256, 294, 347. *See also* Mauritius; Réunion

Masoala, 354–55

Masombika, 255–56, 349

Massawa, 171–72, 184, 186–90, 24748, 261n13

Mauritius, 3, 8, 13, 16–17, 19, 21–26, 30, 48, 51, 171–73, 175, 192, 194, 198–200, 256–57, 276, 286, 294, 296–300, 302–6, 318, 346–48, 381–82, 406–7

Mayotte, 17–18, 26–27, 30, 197, 254, 256, 304, 376, 382, 385, 387, 195n69, 397–415

memory, 307, 345–46, 360

merchants, 13, 40, 43, 45, 74, 83, 96, 100–101, 173, 176, 182, 186, 197, 274–76, 296, 317, 322–23, 347; American, 187; Arab, 272–73, 338n5; British, 45, 49; in the Canaries, 40, 43; Castilian, 45; French, 104, 298; Indian, 250, 272, 274, 277, 281, 302, 304–6; Italian, 183, 189, 205n35; Omani, 20, 272–73; Portuguese, 302–3; Zanzibari, 321–22

migrant labor, 133, 137, 138, 142, 153n49, 295, 303, 306–7; Fang migrant workers, 138, 139, 154n60; Kru migrant workers, 134, 135, 151n28; Liberian migrant workers, 138, 139, 140; Nigerian migrant workers, 129, 143

migration, 3, 7–11, 14, 19, 22, 27, 30, 59, 80, 116, 130, 246, 150n12, 254, 257, 279, 285, 295, 323, 355–56, 367n54, 401, 404–5, 411, 413, 414; forced, 246, 323; labor, 30, 295; of South Asians, 275, 279; of youth, 116

Mikea, 351

Mindelo, 56, 214

missionary influence, 129, 138, 140

modernization, 115–16

Mombasa, 8–9, 12, 15–16, 22, 174–75, 184–85, 197, 249–52, 269, 272, 278, 294, 322–23, 374

monetarization, 98, 113, 116–18

monsoon, 9, 16, 21, 30, 247, 250, 268, 270–72, 274, 279, 284–85; trade, 16, 21, 270, 284–85; winds, 8, 13, 247, 249, 254, 268–70

moral economy, 281

Moresby, Capt. Fairfax, 299

Moresby Treaty, 272, 312n51

Morice, Jean-Vincent, 296

Mozambique, 9, 16–17, 77, 174, 246, 250, 252, 254–55, 258, 295, 297–98, 302–3, 348, 374–78; Mozambique Channel, 174, 192, 194–95, 197, 254, 256; Mozambique hinterland, 375, 396n81; Mozambique Island, 8–9, 250–52, 254–56

msimu, 271

Mukalla, 269

Muscat, 272, 274, 321, 324, 326, 339n24

Muslims, 9, 21, 24, 26, 42, 248, 275, 281, 289, 306, 323, 335, 386, 395n75, 406, 412, 415; merchants, 21, 306, 347

Naidoo, Thambi, 306
Napoleonic Wars, 257, 272
Natal, 17, 176, 304–5
natural resources, 88, 115, 160
New Caledonia, 306
New Zealand, 305
Ng'ambo, 275
Nile, 277
9/11, 288
nobles, 351, 360–61
Nyerere, Julius, 284, 189

oil, 20, 29, 55, 68–69, 84–92, 147,
    162, 164, 167, 179, 185, 285, 332
olonho, 106–10, 114
Omani, 9, 20, 22, 106, 175, 249,
    251, 253, 272–73, 275, 280–81,
    299–301, 312n51, 317–18, 321–
    24; empire, 272; merchants, 20,
    272–73
oquinca, 106–7, 114
Organization of African Unity
    (OAU), 57
Organization of Islamic
    Cooperation, 289

palm oil, 52, 107, 109, 113, 131–32,
    136
Pan-Africanism, 285
Paris, 19, 53, 56, 85, 125, 137, 194,
    383
Parsis, 275
Parti des Déshérités de Madagascar
    (PADESM), 358–59
peanuts, 98, 100, 109–10
Pemba, 20, 197, 250–51, 282, 300,
    321, 375
Persian Gulf, 174, 192, 276, 279,
    347
Persian(s), 250–51, 271, 275–76,
    318, 330, 376
plantation, 17–22, 25–26, 35n36,
    49, 54, 69, 71–73, 75–82, 84, 91,

109–10, 135, 138–40, 160, 182,
    228–29, 251, 257, 273, 277, 281,
    303–6, 321, 329, 331, 348, 382;
    agriculture, 6, 10, 17–20, 22,
    130, 136, 139–40; cocoa, 54, 75,
    77, 79, 91, 125, 130, 132, 134,
    136–37, 139; economy, 68–69,
    75, 81–84, 91, 134, 403; islands,
    13–14, 16–19, 22–24; owners, 71,
    81, 109, 118, 130, 132, 134, 137,
    139; society, 35n36, 273
pontas, 108
ponteiros, 113
Portal, Gerald, 277–78
Portugal, 3, 15, 17, 41–43, 50–51,
    69, 74, 77, 79, 125, 131, 149n2,
    160, 183, 209, 211–12, 226–27,
    235, 252, 258, 378
Portuguese: colonialists, 17, 78,
    81, 93n31, 111, 209, 215, 256,
    393n35; merchants, 44, 46, 101,
    202; soldiers, 111–12
postslavery, 346, 350–51, 353, 357,
    360–61
Praia, 14, 47, 56, 218, 226–27, 230–31
privatization, 84
Product Sharing Contract (PSC),
    88, 90

Quirimba Islands, 255, 259

racialization, 228, 361
Radama I, 348
Ranavalona II, 349
Rantoandro, Gabriel, 305
Ras Hafun, 248
Reconquista, 42
Red Sea, 174, 177, 186–87, 189–90,
    192, 246–48, 330, 374
Réunion, 16–19, 21–23, 26, 30, 48,
    172, 175, 192–93, 199, 256, 286,
    294, 296–300, 303–7, 346–48,
    398–99, 401–3, 405–10, 412–15

Ribeira Grande, 47, 100, 101, 108, 120n4
rice, 55, 109, 113, 197, 199, 255, 302, 305, 384, 404, 410; farming, 98–99, 107, 109–10, 113–17, 352–53, 357, 375, 400
Río de la Plata, 298
Rodrigues, 175, 192, 198, 294

Saint Domingue, 298
Sakalava, 298, 347, 350–51, 404
Salem, 274
São Tomé, 6, 13, 15–20, 22–23, 25, 27–28, 45, 68–91, 130–31, 136, 139, 210; São Tomé and Príncipe, 20, 28, 68–69, 75–77, 81, 84–88, 90–91, 130–31, 139, 210; São Tomé and Príncipe refugees, 131, 151n15
Sauti za Busara, 187
Sayyid Sa'īd bin Sultān Āl Busa'īdī, 318, 321–22, 324, 327, 331, 338n5
seafaring, 96, 105, 118, 250, 271
Senegambia, 297
serviçais, 77–78, 80
Seychelles, 9, 13, 17, 19, 21, 22, 171–73, 175, 192–93, 257, 273, 286, 294, 297, 300, 305
Seyyid Said, Sultan, 301
Shangani, 273
shellfish, 107
Shirazi, 249, 275, 280, 282, 284
shore, 12, 30, 100, 109, 130–31, 147, 173, 175–76, 178, 185, 192, 246, 268–80, 282, 302, 319, 322, 347, 371, 397
shoreline, 5, 109–10, 113–15, 185, 269, 290
Siti bint Saadi, 268
slavery, 7, 13, 23–25, 30, 45, 69, 75, 78, 80, 109, 119, 164, 256, 280–81, 290, 296, 304–5,

307 328–31, 335–36, 345–54, 358–61; abolition of, 51, 77, 256, 177, 295, 303, 328, 348, 358, 382; slave capturing, 118; slave descendants, 346, 349–61, 387n54; slave revolt, 28, 74; slave trade, 8, 15–16, 48, 50, 65, 70–71, 75, 100–101, 103, 110, 131, 139, 251, 254–55, 257, 259–60, 272–73, 276–77, 298–302, 304–5, 131n65, 328, 331, 334, 339n15, 345–49, 382
socialism, 81–82, 233, 269, 283, 285
Socotra, 202n2, 253, 255, 257, 284, 374
Sofala, 250–51, 259
South Africa, 252, 17, 48, 56–57, 170, 174–76, 179–80, 191, 193–94, 198, 252, 254, 258, 304–6, 385, 404. *See also* Cape Colony; Natal; Transvaal
Southeast Asia, 23, 189, 194, 200, 255, 257–58, 294, 297, 303, 347, 349–50, 362–63
Speedy, Karin, 306
spices, 271, 273–74
spiritual, 96, 106–7, 113–14, 117–18, 25
spiritual ceremonies, 114, 117
Sri Lanka, 246, 258
stigmatization, 355–56, 359
Stone Town (Zanzibar), 273, 286, 362n8
structural adjustment, 82, 285
Suakin, 191, 247–48, 261n13
Sufism, 9, 252; Qadiriyya, 252; Shadhiliyya, 255
sugar, 6, 18–20, 40, 42–44, 46, 68–69, 71–72, 75–76, 80, 92, 198–99, 256, 274, 303–4, 321, 375; sugar mills, 73–75; sugar production, 17–19, 29, 68, 70, 72–74, 91, 256, 303–4, 321;

sugarcane, 44, 69, 71, 199, 374–75

Sultana (ship), 317–18, 323–24, 338nn5–6

sultanate, of Zanzibar, 254, 273, 276–78, 281, 283, 318, 324

Sur, 179

Swahili, 8–9, 15, 22, 247, 249–52, 254–55, 263n20, 275, 280–82, 290, 317, 323, 325, 375; city-states, 250, 272, 324; coast, 8–9, 13, 16, 18, 21–22, 24, 30, 184, 249–52, 254, 271, 273, 280, 297–302, 310n24, 312n51, 347; culture, 21–22, 250, 253, 271, 281, 286, 290n2, 335; identity, 21, 33n21; society, 250, 271, 280, 326; traders, 8, 255, 274

taarab, 30, 268, 282, 290n2

Tanganyika, 175, 197, 252, 268, 276, 284

Tanôsy, 354–55, 360–61

Tanzania, 8, 18, 26–27, 250, 252, 284, 287, 289, 290, 322, 323, 325

taxes, 40, 47, 49, 73, 111, 113, 116, 118, 382

Tenerife, 40, 42, 44, 46, 50–52, 56, 61n13, 62n25, 63n32, 64n45, 65n58

tourism, 20–21, 28, 52, 248, 252, 257, 260, 285–87, 289–90, 346, 353

trading farms, 108, 110

transshipment, 186, 273, 277–78, 284, 300

Transvaal, 304, 306

Trinidad, 76, 303, 305

Truth and Justice Commission (TJC), 307, 316n94

UNESCO, 239n29, 345–46, 350; World Heritage List, 252, 286

United Nations, 57–58, 146, 241n57, 286, 360

United States, 14, 29, 51, 65n58, 164, 174, 181, 202, 211–13, 220, 222–24, 228, 235, 240n55, 273, 276, 296, 317, 326, 338n5, 383

unyago, 30, 268, 290n2

urban planning, 417

ustaarabu, 280

Vernet, Thomas, 300

Vezo, 351

wars, 96, 113, 257, 272, 287, 345

wars of pacification, 111

wars of resistance, 96, 345

washenzi, 281

wazalia, 281, 329

Worden, Nigel, 11, 255, 305

World War II, 29, 80, 91, 143, 170–74, 189, 200–201, 258, 282, 383, 403

Yemen, 23, 253, 303, 322, 330

youth, 113–18, 222, 228, 235, 268, 288, 358–59, 403, 408

Zafimaniry, 365n37

Zanzibar, 3–4, 8–10, 12–16, 18, 20–23, 25–27, 30, 35n36, 129, 179, 185, 197–98, 246, 249–42, 256, 259, 268–90, 298, 301–2, 317–37, 382–83, 385; authoritarian rule in, 285; colonial descriptions of, 278, 286; cultural fusion in, 13, 25, 275, 278–82; elections in, 289–90; festivals in, 287–88; nationalists, 289; revolution of 1964, 169–71, 283; Zanzibar city, 269–70, 273, 319–20, 324–26, 329, 335; Zanzibar Town, 9, 252, 254, 278

Zanzibar and Pemba People's Party (ZPPP), 282–83

Zanzibar International Film Festival/Tamasha la Nchi za Jahazi, 287–88

Zanzibar Nationalist Party (ZNP), 282–83

Zatovo ory asa Malagasy (ZOAM), 358–59, 368n71

Printed and bound by CPI Group (UK) Ltd, Croydon, CR0 4YY

24/04/2025

14661355-0001